THREE ROADS
TO GETTYSBURG

Also by Tim McGrath

James Monroe: A Life

*Give Me a Fast Ship: The Continental Navy
and America's Revolution at Sea*

John Barry: An American Hero in the Age of Sail

THREE ROADS

— TO —

GETTYSBURG

MEADE, LEE, LINCOLN, AND
THE BATTLE THAT CHANGED THE WAR,
THE SPEECH THAT CHANGED THE NATION

TIM McGRATH

CALIBER

DUTTON CALIBER
An imprint of Penguin Random House LLC
1745 Broadway, New York, NY 10019
penguinrandomhouse.com

Copyright © 2025 by Tim McGrath
Penguin Random House values and supports copyright. Copyright fuels creativity,
encourages diverse voices, promotes free speech, and creates a vibrant culture. Thank you
for buying an authorized edition of this book and for complying with copyright laws by not
reproducing, scanning, or distributing any part of it in any form without permission. You
are supporting writers and allowing Penguin Random House to continue to publish books
for every reader. Please note that no part of this book may be used or reproduced in any
manner for the purpose of training artificial intelligence technologies or systems.

DUTTON and the D colophon are registered trademarks
of Penguin Random House LLC.

Maps courtesy of Ted McGrath

Book design by Laura K. Corless

LIBRARY OF CONGRESS CATALOGING-IN-PUBLICATION DATA
has been applied for.

ISBN 9780593184394 (hardcover)
ISBN 9780593184417 (ebook)

Printed in the United States of America
2nd Printing

The authorized representative in the EU for product safety and compliance is
Penguin Random House Ireland, Morrison Chambers, 32 Nassau Street,
Dublin D02 YH68, Ireland, https://eu-contact.penguin.ie.

—CONTENTS—

For Cyd—Our North Star

Gettysburg, October 7, 1972

— FOREWORD —

One day in May 1863, Elizabeth Young Curtis reached for the family Bible, nestled on a bookcase inside her modest Philadelphia home.

The book was massive and ornate. It once belonged to her mother's parents, David and Elizabeth McFetridge, but the Bible was simply embossed *Fetridge*, as it had been published by John E. Potter's company in the 1850s, when a *Mc* or an *O* before the name could have made trouble in the City of Brotherly Love. The Know-Nothing Party held influence there by both votes and weapons. Many a factory, shop, or workhouse bore the sign "NINA," the acronym for "No Irish Need Apply."[1]

Elizabeth took the Bible down, set it on the desk in the small drawing room, and began leafing through the elaborately designed text and detailed illustrations until she arrived at the "Family Records" section dividing the Old and New Testaments.

Her beautiful handwriting already graced the page marked "Weddings," where, on December 23, 1845, she had recorded her marriage to her husband, Richard. On the next page, "Births," Elizabeth had lovingly entered the birth dates of their six children, the oldest now almost fully grown. Dipping her pen in an inkwell as black as the newly purchased widow's weeds she was wearing, she wrote "Richard J. Curtis, Killed at the Battle of Chancellorsville, May 3rd, 1863" on the page titled "Deaths."

Then, through tears, the Widow Curtis composed a poem:

Dearest Husband, thou hath left us: Here the loss we deeply feel,
But to God who hath bereft us: He can all our sorrows heal.

Little thought we when we parted, That we'd never meet again,
But thou has left us broken hearted, And our tears are all in vain.
To him the trumpet's piercing breath, Now sounds to arms in vain,
He is quartered in the arms of death, He'll never march again.
This cruel war has struck the blow, That robbed me of my dear.
But now to war he'll go no more. His loss we feel severe.
Cease, cruel War, oh, cease this strife, And view the work that thou hast
    done,
Thou has left six children fatherless, And a loving wife to mourn.

At the outset of the war, Richard had enlisted as a private with the 26th Pennsylvania Volunteer Infantry Regiment. Since 1862, its soldiers had seen more than their share of action: the Seven Days' Battles during the Peninsula Campaign, Second Bull Run, and at Fredericksburg, where Richard was promoted to corporal. In late April 1863, the Army of the Potomac, under Major General Joseph Hooker, had moved once again against General Robert E. Lee's Army of Northern Virginia. May 3 was the third day of the Battle of Chancellorsville. It was Richard's last day; unbeknownst to Elizabeth, she had gone from being "Mrs. Curtis" to "the Widow Curtis."[2]

Her grief was also mixed with financial terror. While Congress had passed what was considered to be a generous pension plan in 1862, including funds for widows and orphans, the process of applying for and receiving payments was notoriously slow. By January 1, 1863, nearly 11,000 applications had been filed; fewer than seven hundred had been approved. How was Elizabeth to keep a roof over her head, and feed six children?[3]

Her poem was accurate: it was a cruel war, indeed.

Days earlier, in Washington, D.C., President Abraham Lincoln had been sitting, fidgeting, and pacing the floor of the U.S. Army's telegraph office ensconced in an old library next to the War Department. For the past two years it had served as his second home. Day and night, he loomed over the operators' desks, anxiously anticipating word from the numerous battlefronts within and along the boundaries of the Confederate States of America. Over time, messages of victory in the west from General Ulysses S. Grant and Admiral David Farragut were mixed with the growing list of the Army of the Potomac's defeats at the hands of the Army of Northern Virginia. As May began, the fretful president had heard nothing yet from Joseph Hooker, the fifth general to lead the Union's major army.[4]

Upon assuming command, Hooker had raised expectations among his generals and men, bragging that his impending victory could result in his becoming a dictator. Lincoln, upon learning this, wired Hooker that he would risk a dictatorship if the general gave Lincoln the victory over Lee that the nation craved. On May 4, days before Elizabeth Curtis learned of Richard's death, a courier brought the news Lincoln had both awaited and silently dreaded. The Battle of Chancellorsville was over, a total disaster for Hooker and his army.[5]

This latest embarrassment and tragedy overwhelmed the president. "My God!" Lincoln cried at the news. "What will the country say! What will the country say!"[6]

Newspapers and politicians wasted no time blaming Lincoln as much as—if not more than—Hooker for this latest debacle. In Northern cities, hamlets, and farms, thousands of mothers and fathers scanning the casualty lists printed in newspapers found that they had lost sons; wives and lovers discovered their beloved lay dead in Virginia; children were tearfully told their brothers or fathers were never coming home.

By June, Lincoln began receiving reports that Lee was certain to invade the North again. This time, unlike his first foray in 1862, he would have a sizable army, its morale never higher, while the Army of the Potomac must once again hope for a savior who might—*might*—defeat Lee, already becoming more legend than man. The question—*What will the country say?*—soon became secondary to another: *What will Lincoln do?*[7]

Chancellorsville was the North's latest setback and Lee's tactical masterpiece. In three days, with 51,000 men, Lee had thoroughly outthought and outfought "Fighting Joe" Hooker and his force of 120,000. Confederate casualties were high—13,000—but the Union forces had lost 17,000. In the year since Lee had assumed command, he had bested no less than four opponents whose better-armed, better-clothed, and better-fed army lacked only one thing to succeed: better leadership.[8]

But Lee was a realist as well as a strategist, and he knew the math. The enemy, whom Lee diplomatically referred to as "those people," could absorb the high losses at Chancellorsville far better than the South. The Confederate states did not possess sufficient numbers to replace the killed, wounded, and captured as easily as the United States could. Lee had lost 25 percent of his men. One was irreplaceable: the indomitable General Thomas J. "Stonewall" Jackson, shot accidentally by his own soldiers. The grieving Lee had called Jackson "my right arm." Lee was well aware that he could win battle after battle and the South could still lose this war.[9]

In addition to dwindling numbers of boys still at home, the South was slowly strangling economically due to the successful blockade of its coastline and the loss of New Orleans in 1862—a major international port and a linchpin of the Confederate economy. President Jefferson Davis craved recognition of the Confederacy by Great Britain and other European nations, but these potential allies sat on their diplomatic and economic hands, waiting to see if the South could win its independence from the North before risking a backlash from the British Empire's working classes regarding slavery.[10]

Now, with Grant besieging Vicksburg, the last Confederate stronghold on the Mississippi River, President Davis was under pressure to send Lee and a large detachment of his army to save Vicksburg from capture. But Lee adamantly believed the only chance to save the Confederacy was to march north and defeat the Army of the Potomac on its own ground. Victory there might lead to the capture of Washington, recognition of the Confederacy by Great Britain and France, and a successful end to the war.[11]

In the waning daylight of June 27, 1863, James Hardie, a mutton-chopped, middle-aged lieutenant colonel, left his War Department office, just a block from the White House, and strode purposefully through the bustling city's cauldron of civilians and military personnel. A veteran of the Mexican War and Indian campaigns in the Pacific Northwest, Hardie was no stranger to the rigors of army life. During the current conflict, he had seen battle on numerous occasions and had commanded above the rank he was currently saddled with. Yet now, in the third summer of the war, Hardie was leaving Washington under the cover of darkness not to meet his own fresh battlefield glory but to deliver a message. Tucked carefully into his coat pocket was a handwritten letter from the president of the United States.[12]

Washington, D.C., was a war zone waiting for the war to show up. Its arsenal was the largest yet seen in the Western Hemisphere. Cannons were everywhere: at street corners and in straight rows at the arsenal; it took nine teams of oxen to pull a twenty-five-ton Rodman gun down Pennsylvania Avenue, its massive weight cracking the pavement, before being shipped to the battlefronts. Teamsters prodding the oxen with bullwhips passed cattle herds grazing on what would later become the Washington Mall. Troops drilled everywhere, often beneath the still-unfinished Capitol Dome; they practiced their marksmanship on Mason's Island, across from Georgetown; they marched past the U.S. Christian Commission building, where veterans crippled in battle milled with volunteers, clergy, and poor white and Black Americans, all watching the untested warriors prepare for their turn to face the horrors of war. While Lincoln's Emancipation Proclamation officially freed the enslaved living in the Confederacy on January 1, 1863, Congress had abolished slavery in the district in 1862. The nation's capital was overcrowded; epidemics of smallpox and typhoid leapt from the city slums to the better neighborhoods. One fatality from typhoid was the president's own son, his beloved Willie.[13]

In the evening the only citizens on the streets were carousers on leave, a few prostitutes, and homeless African Americans and poor whites seeking a doorway or alley to get some sleep in. Once at the train station, Hardie instructed an engineer and a fireman to take him directly to Frederick, Maryland. To go as fast as possible—Baltimore & Ohio trains sometimes reached speeds of more than twenty-five miles an hour—the engineer and the fireman unhooked any unneeded cars from the train that would slow them down. Once Hardie boarded, the train chugged out of the fortified city, rolling northwest. There was a half-moon that night, but little could be seen in the dark, and Hardie was too preoccupied to notice any scenery. A few hours later the locomotive's wheels and brakes screeched and steam hissed from its sides as the engineer brought it to a halt.

Hardie's orders forbade him from getting a night's rest: the president's note had to be delivered at once. Despite the late hour, Hardie managed to rent a horse and buggy from a livery stable and headed for the encampment of the Army of the Potomac's 5th Corps, a few miles away. At about 3 a.m., Hardie came face-to-face with the man his commander in chief had sent him to find.

Rousing a general—particularly one whose nickname, "Old Snapping Turtle," was well-earned—was not an enviable task for a subordinate, even for Hardie, who was also the general's friend. Reaching into his coat pocket, he handed George Gordon Meade his dispatch. To the colonel's bemusement, Meade, surprised at the sight of an officer sent all the way from the capital in the middle of the night, assumed he was being arrested for insubordination or, at the very least, being relieved of duty, having tangled days earlier with "Fighting Joe." The two generals were poles apart regarding their duty, their approach to command, even their politics, Hooker being an unabashed Radical Republican, while Meade was a Northern Democrat.[14]

Assuming the worst, Meade declared that his "conscience was clear, and void of offense towards any man." Hardie, informing him he was neither arrested nor relieved, urged Meade to read the dispatch.[15]

Donning his spectacles and holding a lantern in one hand, Meade read the message:

General Order No. 194
War Department
June 27, 1863

By direction of the President, Major General Joseph Hooker is relieved of command of the Army of the Potomac, and Major General George G. Meade is appointed to the command of that army. By Order of the Secretary of War.

Hardie then informed the stunned Meade of what he already knew: elements of Robert E. Lee's Army of Northern Virginia were now in south-central Pennsylvania, sure to march east toward Philadelphia, Baltimore, or even Washington itself once Lee's entire force was reunited. Meade was acutely aware of the gravity of the president's dispatch. The humiliation at Chancellorsville was less than two months old, and rumors had been circulating among officers and soldiers alike that Hooker would be replaced—but by whom? Counting George McClellan twice, the Union's major armies in Virginia had endured six commanders in less than two years, each general's career smothered under the weight of the army's failures and Lee's relentless aggression. And now the tainted crown was being forced onto Meade's head. The paper he held in the lantern light might as well have been his own death warrant. Hardie waited for his friend's reply.

Meade's answer stunned Hardie. He refused the promotion. John Reynolds, commander of 1st Corps, was senior to Meade and, he believed, more deserving. Reynolds was beloved by the men and, Meade knew, more popular with the officers than Meade could ever be. Reynolds was the logical choice. Meade informed Hardie he would telegraph the War Department immediately to request that his orders be rescinded.[16]

Despite his surprise at the orders, Meade had sensed they were coming, having included his apprehensions of the possibility in letters to his wife, Margaretta (called Margaret by Meade). "You know how reluctant we both have been to see me placed in this position," he'd confided. The Army of the Potomac's previous commanders all had different approaches in everything from organization to battlefield tactics, and each of them had been found wanting. *Let this cup pass from me . . .* and give it to Reynolds.

It was only when Hardie insisted that this was not an offer but a presidential order that Meade reluctantly acquiesced. "I've been tried and condemned without a hearing," he groused to Hardie, "and I suppose I shall have to go to the execution."[17]

Meade's dismay at being ordered to take command was almost immediately replaced by his innate sense of duty and his talents for organization and leadership. His aides, their tent next to Meade's and already unhappily awakened by Meade and Hardie's conversation, were summoned to transcribe dispatches to Lincoln and Henry Halleck, general in chief of the armies of the United States, accepting the command, and to the army's other generals, his peers only minutes earlier, now his subordinates.[18]

As soon as he could spare a few minutes, Meade composed another message himself, to Margaret. "I had nothing to do but accept," he told her, "and exert my utmost abilities to command success. This, so help me God, I will do." Fully aware that Lee was determined to fight the next battle in Pennsylvania, Meade asked Margaret to "pray earnestly, pray for the success of my country (for it is my success besides)."[19]

Northern citizens were unaware of Lincoln's appointment of Meade, but they were acutely aware that Lee and the Army of Northern Virginia were loose and fearfully anticipated where he might strike. In choosing Meade, Lincoln had appointed a Pennsylvania general to defend his state and the Union's cause against Lee, who was hoping to win (or at least end) the war and gain independence for the Confederacy.

Lee and Meade did not know where their armies would clash. Ironically, neither of them was close enough to his advance forces to choose the battlefield.

By happenstance, it would be at the crossroads town of Gettysburg.

SON OF THE PRAIRIE

Abraham Lincoln his hand and pen he will be
Good but god knows When[1]

—ABRAHAM LINCOLN,
from the early 1820s

O ne wonders if Abraham Lincoln would have written so modestly about his upbringing and surroundings had he known he would become one of history's immortals. Many figures, including those higher born or with much smaller accomplishments, have stretched, exaggerated, or outright lied about their biographies with barely a pang of guilt, including more than a few American presidents.

But the sixteenth president was made of sterner stuff. Did he prevaricate, befog, or withhold elements of the truth during his career? Yes. But he was almost ensorcelled by the truth. Lying was an anomaly to Lincoln; when the press and public bestowed the nickname "Honest Abe" on him, it did not spring from sarcasm.

Throughout his life he remained understated about his genealogy. "I know so little of our family history," he commented to distant relative, Solomon Lincoln, in 1848, although he did know the basics:

I was born Feb:12th. 1809 in Hardin county, Kentucky. My father's name is Thomas; my grandfather's name was Abraham,—the same of my own. My grandfather went to Rockingham county in Virginia, to Kentucky,

about the year 1782; and, two years afterwards. Was killed by the indi-
ans. We have a vague tradition, that my great-grand father went from
Pennsylvania to Virginia, and that he was a quaker. Further back than
this, I have never heard any thing.[2]

Lincoln would have happily provided Solomon with more information, but "owing to my father being left an orphan at the age of six
years, in poverty, in a new country, he became a wholly uneducated
man." Lincoln meant no pique with his father; that was just his reason
for the lack of further detail.[3]

Thomas witnessed his father Abraham's murder by a Native American raiding party while building his new home. His mother, Bathsheba
Lincoln, then took her children with her family to central Kentucky.
From his teens, Thomas worked at any job that helped put coins or food
on the table—as a day laborer, soldier, surveyor, and prison guard. He
had a knack for carpentry. He was tall for the times, five foot, ten inches,
big-boned and barrel-chested. Regarded as someone one would want
on their side in a fight, Thomas neither looked for trouble nor walked
away from it. He made his reputation as "a peaceable man." In a photograph of him in later years he wears a perceptible frown while his clear
eyes stare straight at the cameraman. Age has taken some of his dark
hair and softened what was once a firm jawline. Surely, Tom Lincoln
was someone to reckon with.[4]

By 1806, Thomas was the owner of a two-hundred-plus-acre farm
in Hardin County when two local merchants contracted him to build,
man, and take a flatboat laden with their goods down the Mississippi to
New Orleans. It was tedious and sometimes dangerous work, as flatboats manned by amateurs often sank.[5]

He returned in May, having bought himself a fine beaver hat and a
pair of silk suspenders. Among his other purchases were ample supplies
of linens, silk, scarlet cloth, buttons, and bolts of cloth. Not all of this
finery was for his mother and sister. Tom, now twenty-eight, was in
love.[6]

Nancy Hanks had been a small child when her grandparents, Joseph and Ann Hanks, took her from Virginia to Kentucky. Likely illegitimate, she was living with neighbors of Thomas Lincoln when they met. They were married at a simple ceremony on June 12, 1806. Thomas soon took her to Elizabethtown, where he had built a small home; his carpentry skills kept him steadily employed. The following February, they had their first child, Sarah, whom they called Sally.[7]

Two years later, the young family was living in Sinking Spring, where Tom had bought 348 acres of farmland. They were cooped up in a sixteen-by-eighteen-foot log cabin when the fourth member of the family, christened Abraham, was born on February 12.[8]

The Lincolns spent just two years in Elizabethtown; fallow farmland and the question of Thomas's ownership saw to that. He took his family northeast to Knob Creek, where he found more productive acreage, built another log cabin, and soon found demand for his carpentry skills. Knob Creek, with its picturesque hills, lay a few miles from the Cumberland Trail, which ran from Louisville to Nashville, Tennessee. Here, Sally and little Abe attended "ABC schools" in cabins similar to their home. In 1812 another baby, christened Thomas, was born, but he died days afterward.[9]

Thomas Lincoln's growing status—he was among the top taxpayers in Hardin County—soon brought him into conflict with veterans from an earlier war. Many Continental Army officers from the Revolutionary War had been awarded thousands of acres on the frontier for their services, and disputes frequently arose when they learned that settlers like Tom Lincoln were living on acreage they had legally bought from agents that was not theirs to sell. Lincoln was one of ten farmers who were evicted and was forced to leave the state. Years later, Abe mentioned another reason for the family's departure: "This removal was partly on account of slavery."[10]

Abe's parents belonged to a Baptist church that was stridently against slavery. Although being antislavery did not carry much risk in Hardin County, where over 40 percent of the population were enslaved persons, their free or cheap labor cut into Tom's getting work more than once.

Between Thomas's land title difficulty and the growing competition of cheap labor, leaving Kentucky looked to be an astute move. In the fall of 1816, Thomas packed up his family and crossed the Ohio River, bound for Indiana. Once there, he chose a plot of promising farmland on Pigeon Creek, in Spencer County.[11]

Abe called the land "unbroken forest," endless underbrush "with many bears and other wild animals still in the woods." By the time he was seven Abe, already tall for his age, was given an axe and shown how to use it. It was the start of endless days of hard work and blisters for the next sixteen years: the axe was like an extension of his arm, "less, of course, in plowing and harvesting seasons." Working alongside his father, the Lincolns soon had an eighteen-by-twenty-foot log cabin for their new home.[12]

He was also expected to hunt game. One day a flock of wild turkeys approached the Lincoln cabin, and Abe grabbed his father's rifle and shot one. Killing the bird immediately filled him with a sense of guilt that lasted a lifetime. In 1860, he would publicly attest he "has never since pulled a trigger on any larger game."[13]

In 1818, Nancy Hanks Lincoln contracted the "milk sickness," a disease from the tainted milk of cattle that ate the poisonous white snakeroot plant. Humans suffered tremors, severe abdominal pain, and constant vomiting. It was an agonizing death for Abe and Sarah to witness. Nancy's kindnesses to them, her own work ethic, and her devotion never left Abe. "All that I am, or ever hope to be," he later declared, "I owe to my angel mother."[14]

Another crisis for Nancy's children came the following year, one not as heartbreaking as her death, but no less challenging. With their cousin Dennis Hanks left with Abe and Sally for company, Thomas returned to Kentucky in search of a new wife. He was gone for weeks, leaving the three to fend for themselves. Abe later recollected how "the panther's scream, filled night with fear" while "bears preyed on the swine."[15] Thomas not only returned with a wife but an entire family. The new Mrs. Lincoln was the former Sarah Bush Johnston, a Kentucky widow. With Sarah's two daughters and son, the small cabin now sheltered eight; it would remain their home for twelve years.[16]

Thomas Lincoln believed in diligent work and did not drink alcohol, traits he passed on to his son. He also was quite the storyteller and loved a good joke. But there was also a streak of depression inside him. "Everything I ever teched either died, got killed, or was lost," Thomas once bitterly remarked. His sense of humor and dark spells became ingrained in his son.[17]

Abe and Sally continued their education at various ABC schools, but Abe's schooling was often interrupted by chores at home and his father's growing habit of "hiring out" his son. It was a normal practice along the frontier, and as Abe grew, he became a steady source of income for his father. Being big for his age, he worked on farms, ran errands, did basic carpentry, butchered hogs, and even served some time operating a ferryboat.[18]

Abe also split rails, a task that required as much strength and endurance as skill. He would place or roll a tree trunk across two logs, looking for a side with no knots. Maul in hand, he then put an iron wedge in the center, tapped it into the log until firmly in place, then drove it deep enough to make a substantial crack in the log. He followed this with wedges several feet on either side of the first, driving them through the timber until it split in half. He repeated the process on both halves, giving his boss (or father) four equal rails. Then it was on to another trunk, and another, and another. Rail splitting could be as dangerous as it was tedious. "One day, while I was sharpening a wedge on a log, the ax glanced and nearly took my thumb off," Abe later recalled, showing his listener the scar.[19]

Work took precedence over schooling. In his adult years he concluded that "the aggregate of his schooling did not amount to one year." Instead, he began educating himself at home, reading anything and everything he could get his hands on, from the Bible to poetry, from Parson Weems's *The Life of Washington* to *Robinson Crusoe*. Abe later admitted that "my father had suffered greatly for the want of education," and legend has it that Thomas frowned on Abe's getting one, but his stepmother insisted otherwise. "Mr. Lincoln never made Abe quit reading to do anything if he could avoid it," she later recalled.[20]

Sarah devotedly stepped into Nancy's role as Abe's mother, and he lovingly responded. "Abe never gave me a curious word or look," and he would do anything she asked of him. He in turn called her "his best Friend." As Abe grew through his boyhood, teenage years, and into adulthood, her encouragement was a constant in his life. Under Sarah's watch, he and Sally developed close relationships with Sarah's children. In 1826, Sally married Aaron Grigsby; she died two years later in childbirth (the baby was stillborn), plunging Abe into a deep, angry sadness, believing that Grigsby and his family's delay in not riding for a doctor caused her death.[21]

By this time Abe was at or near his full height of six feet four, rail-thin yet muscular. There was no fat on the bone. Having seen (and enjoyed) those times when he witnessed Tom hold court at stores, picnics, or town gatherings, Abe had already begun acquiring his own reputation for spinning a good yarn or telling the funniest of jokes. Well-versed in the Bible, he never officially joined his parents' church. Like Thomas, however, he had proven his fighting skills more than once, although he shared his father's wish to avoid fights and stop others. During one fight involving, ironically, the Grigsby brothers, Lincoln declared himself "the big buck of the lick." When it was over, no one was inclined to take him on.[22]

In the spring of 1828, nineteen-year-old Abraham Lincoln and a friend, Allen Gentry, boarded a flatboat at Gentry's Landing on the Ohio River near Rockport, Indiana, to begin the long journey down the Ohio and Mississippi Rivers to New Orleans.[23]

Gentry's father, James, was Pigeon Creek's most successful citizen, with a 1,000-acre farm, a busy store, and the landing bearing his name on the Ohio River. He had the flatboat loaded with a hefty supply of agricultural goods to sell in the Crescent City. Allen had made the voyage before, but this was Abe's first trip away from home. Although a newcomer to this journey, Abe was an easy choice for the Gentrys. Lean, muscular, and intimidating, Abe would make the perfect "bow-hand—working the foremost oars," as his cousin recalled decades later. The boys would be paid $8 a month.[24]

Abe and Allen built the craft, likely with help from Abe's father, who no doubt gave them advice on navigating their way downriver. Once they arrived at their destination, they were to get the best price possible for the elder Gentry's goods, break up the flatboat and sell the lumber, and book passage back on a steamboat—a comfortable reward for their efforts.[25]

Boatbuilding is not work for amateurs. A poorly made flatboat would not get five miles down the river. It took seasoned hands to build and caulk; a properly constructed boat could take up to 2,000 boat pins to hold it together. Abe and Allen's oblong-shaped boat was forty feet long with a fifteen-foot beam. It was tedious and sometimes dangerous work, as flatboats manned by amateurs often sank.[26]

Springtime brought flood tides from melting snow, quickening the river's flow and giving even veteran keelboat men challenges aplenty, as a former Mississippi pilot named Samuel Clemens knew all too well:

> It is a remarkable river in this: that instead of widening toward its mouth, it grows narrower; grows narrower and deeper. From the junction of the Ohio to a point half way down to the sea, the width averages a mile in high water: thence to the sea the width steadily diminishes, until, at the "Passes," above the mouth, it is but little over half a mile. At the junction of the Ohio the Mississippi's depth is eighty-seven feet; the depth increases gradually, reaching one hundred and twenty-nine just above the mouth.[27]

For weeks, the two youths made their way down the Mississippi, their small, clumsy craft part of the traffic heading up- and downriver. There were small pirogues, canoes favored by trappers; keelboats manned by men who poled their boats steadily downriver; barges, usually carrying at least a mast and jib and square sail, taking advantage of any wind; and the newcomers to the Mississippi: steamboats, their churning paddle wheel propelling them up- or downstream with ease, especially compared to the boys' ungainly craft.[28]

Instead of a rudder, most flatboats were steered by a sweep: a long oar that further calloused Abe's already roughened hands and put his biceps to good use. The boys learned to handle the Mississippi's endless S curves, especially from Missouri southward. The spring floods uprooted old trees, sending them into the river, where they became snags or battering rams. Sandbars caught many a flatboat, and high water could suddenly create whirlpools spinning between the eddies close to shore and the river's current. At sundown, Abe and Allen either ran their boat onto the riverbank for a full night's rest or waved a lantern in the darkness to let other traveling watercraft see them.[29]

They may also have joined a convoy of other flatboats drifting down-river, "for mutual convenience" as much as for protection from river pirates. It also sped up the trip: one flatboat man recalled how the convoy "lashed together side by side, thus also facilitating our progress by obtaining a greater scope of the current." Approaching Chickasaw Bluffs, just above Memphis, they encountered two of the most danger-ous hazards on the river: the "Devil's Raceground," where the powerful current exhausted the strongest of rivermen keeping their sweeps (and their flatboats) steady, followed a couple miles later by the "Devil's El-bow, a precarious bend in the Mississippi where the wreckage of un-lucky flatboats drifted along the shores."[30]

Days later, they drifted past the busy port of Vicksburg, perched high on a bluff rising majestically above the riverbank. But the boys dared not spend too much time taking in the view. The Grand Gulf awaited them, where the river quickly narrows and the current acceler-ated between two eddies. One steersman declared that "skill and dex-terity are necessary to keep a boat" in the current and keep the flatboat from "being sucked into one or the other eddy." Abe and Allen earned their wages that day.[31]

Near the end of their journey, they began stopping at towns along the "Sugar Coast," near Baton Rouge. One night, as Lincoln later wrote,

> [we] were attacked by seven negroes with intent to kill and rob [us]. [We] were hurt some in the melee, but succeeding in driving the negroes from the boat, and then "cut cable"—"weighed anchor" and left.[32]

Lincoln never put in writing how he and Allen fended off their at-tackers. Whether they fought better or were able to scare the men off with their guns, we will never know. Soon afterward, Abe and Allen reached New Orleans. Although they had heard descriptions of the city, it was something else to see it for themselves. Their flatboat was one of over a hundred tied up along the levee.[33]

By 1828, New Orleans was renowned for its international aura and allure. Gaudy mansions encircled the outskirts of town while business headquarters, hotels, eating establishments and taverns wore glorious shades of the brightest hues. The wharves and streets were a veritable Babel of English, French, Spanish, German, and the patois of the native Creoles. The streets hummed with activity. Top-hatted merchants and lawyers bound for banks and the courthouse brushed past European and Caribbean sailors. Carriage drivers wended their way past street vendors hawking baked goods or linens and satins. The wives of the wealthy gentry, wearing the latest fashions from Paris, avoided contact with the Native Americans, Blacks, and islanders as best they could. At sunset, New Orleans became a bacchanalia, its citizenry joined by sailors, rivermen, and other visitors as hotel owners, tavern keepers, gambling house managers, and brothel *mesdames* happily took their money. In New Orleans, every night was New Year's Eve.[34]

An earlier visitor to New Orleans noted that "only a few of the streets are paved"; their cleaning done "by slaves chained together, with hardly any clothes on their backs, sent for the purpose, at the discretion of their masters, as a punishment for some delinquency.[35] Abe also saw advertisements and broadsides for auctions of the enslaved.

The city's white population numbered about 25 percent, and there was also a sizable number of mixed-race peoples. While free Blacks were somewhat safe on the streets of New Orleans, their numbers did not compare to the thousands of enslaved Blacks in and around the city who worked on the docks, in the warehouses, and in other local businesses.

The enslaved arrived at the auction houses in "Droves": chained two by two, they silently waited their turn to mount the auction block. Abe had walked among enslaved persons all his life, but the selling of so many and their expressions—some defiant, some sullen, many downcast, more fearful—shook him hard. It left an indelible mark on him for the rest of his life. His parents' church, and their own beliefs, had made an impression on his thinking, and he had doubtless seen auctions in his childhood. But here, in this city like no other, the contrast cut fast and cut deep.[36]

Their work finished, Abe and Allen booked homeward passage on a steamship. For Abe, the journey to New Orleans was a rite of passage. He had never been so long away from home, left to his own wits and judgment. The teenager who pushed his flatboat away from the Rockport shoreline was not the same Abe who several weeks later strode down the steamboat gangplank at the Rockport dock. He was, at the very least, on his way to becoming his own man.[37]

In 1829, another outbreak of milk sickness struck Pigeon Creek. Thomas, having read about the promise of available land in the state of Illinois, sold his livestock and farm, squared accounts, bought three wagons, hitched them to oxen and horses, and with his family and various in-laws—thirteen in all—headed for the Sangamon River and a new homestead in Macon County, Illinois, in March 1830, one month after Abe's twenty-first birthday.[38]

Illinois was unsettled country. "Chicago was only a frontier fort and trading post," one historian noted decades later. Now, nearly two hundred miles south, Abe helped his father in clearing their new acreage: cutting down trees, clearing brush, splitting rails for fences before building a cabin and barn. With his cousin John Hanks, Abe was hired out that summer to other farms.

A chilling rain fell steadily on December 20; it turned to snow on Christmas Eve. It was the first of sixty days of storms, a "benumbing horror" of snow and sleet falling from the skies like a celestial avalanche. Crops were destroyed, livestock froze to death en masse, and settlers put their lives at risk each time they ventured outside for firewood or to bring in snow to melt for drinking water. The snow reached four to six feet in some areas, the drifts often twice as high.[39]

Venturing out one day to split rails for Macon County sheriff William Warnick, Lincoln fell through the ice covering the Sangamon River. He arrived at Warnick's cabin with frostbitten feet, forcing him to remain there for three weeks before he could walk back home. Although unable to work, Abe was able to read, and he pored over War-nick's copies of the new state's statutes, opening the possibility of a career in law.[40]

His zeal for bettering himself now took on a sense of urgency and brought out his father's consternation. Whether Thomas expected Abe to grow out of his love of reading (and learning) as he entered adult-hood, we do not know. His son was a frontier abnormality, a tough young man unafraid of frontier labor and, on the surface, well suited to the frontier lifestyle. But he wanted more. He wanted to *be* more.

As the harsh winter thawed, Abe; his cousin John Hanks; and his stepbrother, John Johnston, were hired by an aspiring merchant, Den-ton Offutt, to take a flatboat from Beardstown, Illinois, to New Orleans. Offutt offered them $12 per month each, telling them to meet him in Calhoun, the county seat of Sangamon County named for South Caro-lina politician John C. Calhoun. Offutt would have a flatboat waiting for them. Around this time, Tom Lincoln was preparing to move his brood yet again, this time to Coles County, fifty miles southeast.[41]

Abe and the two Johns found Offutt in Calhoun but no flatboat. It fell to the three to build one, eighteen by eighty feet, substantially big-ger than Abe's first craft. On a visit to the Sangamon waterfront, the county assessor was struck by Abe's incongruous appearance, his "boots off, hat, coat and vest off. Pants rolled up to his knees and shirt wet with sweat and combing his fuzzie hair with his fingers as he pounded away on the boat."[42]

Offutt joined them on the trip, his cargo including barrels of salted pork and three dozen hogs. The live cargo gave the four men a couple of character-building tasks. The first was getting the swine aboard. Of-futt suggested sewing their eyes closed, which, while giving the hogs great pain, only increased their determination to stay put. Instead, Abe resorted to the obvious, hog-tying them and bringing them on board by the tried-and-true method.[43]

The second incident occurred when they rounded the Sangamon's curve at the budding settlement called New Salem, where the flatboat got stuck on a milldam that tipped it a third of the way into the river. The boat began filling with water as the barrels slid downward, and the frightened hogs did their best to make their slippery way aft. New Salem townsfolk rushed to the riverbank, reveling in the unexpected entertainment.

Abe came up with a solution. After unloading the live and the dead pork ashore, he borrowed an auger and drilled a hole in the tipped end, letting the water run out. With a mallet he plugged the hole with a dowel, then led the men in dropping the flatboat off the dam and reloaded the cargo. Offutt, as impressed by Abe's quick thinking as was the crowd, offered Abe the twin positions of manager and clerk for his new store at $15 a month. Abe accepted.[44]

After returning from New Orleans, Abe spent July at the new family farm, informing his father that he had a job and was going to make his own way. On the surface, Offutt was merely offering an unproven man employment in a rustic, unproven settlement. He did not know that he was giving Abe the chance to become Abraham Lincoln.[45]

New Salem in 1831 was small in population but large in optimism. It was more crossroads hamlet than village, with a hundred citizens living in log cabins on a bluff above the Sangamon River. The smith, cooper, and miller depended on the patronage of settlers living outside New Salem who lacked such essentials. Lincoln arrived before Offutt's supplies did and "made a crop of corn" working for a local farmer. Upon his arrival, Offutt and Lincoln set up shop. The store was under immediate pressure to succeed; to finance his venture, Offutt had borrowed money from a local politician at 60 percent interest.[46]

Lincoln was a relative newcomer in New Salem when he encountered the Clary's Grove Boys, the toughest gang in the area. Led by Jack Armstrong, they were known for the occasional neighborly good deed, coupled with a well-earned reputation for practical jokes, hard drinking, and fighting. They were also handy on election days when a candidate's success might depend on their influence on timid voters. Offutt, always looking for a way to make money, began boasting that his clerk could whip Armstrong—and bet $10 Lincoln could do it. Armstrong readily accepted the challenge.[47]

The two already knew each other. Lincoln had supported Armstrong in his successful campaign for constable (small wonder the Clary's Grove Boys spent little if any time in jail). Armstrong easily defeated his opponent, the merchant John Rutledge. On the day of the match, out-of-towners and New Salem citizens jostled each other for the best view of the scrap held on the small front yard of Offutt's store. As onlookers downed whiskey and made their side bets, rules were negotiated: Armstrong was happy for a no-holds-barred rumble, but Lincoln insisted on a clean match. Armstrong agreed.[48]

An acquaintance described Armstrong as "a regular bully . . . very stout, and tricky in wrestling." But having agreed to fair play, the taller and equally strong Lincoln had the upper hand until a desperate Armstrong broke the rules and threw Lincoln, who angrily got back on his feet just as the crowd, their wagers in the balance, took sides at the top of their lungs. It fell to Rutledge to wade into the middle of the near riot to break it up. Both sides claimed victory, but the match was a draw.[49]

Instead of festering animosity, the two rivals became good friends, and Lincoln was considered an unofficial member of the gang. With this fight, Lincoln won over both elements of New Salem society and made a strong political ally in the bargain.

His hard-fought bout with Armstrong did not interfere with his reputation as a voracious reader and budding debater. Methodist preacher Peter Cartwright, "the Lord's Breaking Plow," was a successful state legislator in between his successful camp meetings and baptismal marathons. With his odd combination of abolitionism while being a rabid Jackson Democrat, Cartwright was used to holding sway over his listeners with his mix of Jacksonian politics and warnings of hellfire to evildoers. Cartwright was soon interrupted by Lincoln, who had grown tired of Cartwright's pompous pontificating. The well-dressed preacher-politician sneered at this gawky, poorly dressed upstart clerk, and the two took to debating. To the crowd's surprise, Lincoln more than held his own: one observer remembered how Lincoln "quite beat him in the argument."

The more casual observer also could not help noticing Lincoln's love affair with books. One visitor to town found himself having to share a bed with Lincoln. Suspicious at first, the man saw Lincoln stretched out on the grass, engrossed in his reading, and fears of being pickpocketed or worse subsided. "A man who reads a book as hard as that fellow seems to," he reasoned, "has got too much to think of besides my watch or my small change."[50]

Offutt's general store failed. Next, Lincoln partnered with one William Berry, who succeeded in drinking away both their investment and scant profits. When Berry died, Lincoln was stuck with the debt. State law only required him to repay half, but Lincoln saw himself responsible for the full amount. Although it took him thirteen years to pay off what he sardonically called his "national debt," his steadfast honesty earned him a lifelong nickname: "Honest Abe."[51]

Another stepping stone in Lincoln's rise in New Salem prominence came in 1832. The Sauk and Meskwaki Native Americans (also called Sac and Fox) crossed the Mississippi from Iowa in hopes of reclaiming land in Illinois lost in the 1804 Treaty of St. Louis. Fifteen hundred warriors, women, and children were led by Ma-ka-tai-me-she-kia-kiak, called Black Hawk by the whites in an effort to find both food and allies in regaining at least some of the tribal lands. Panic among the white settlers compelled Governor John Reynolds to call for volunteers to drive Black Hawk back to Iowa, or worse.[52]

No less than sixty-eight men from New Salem volunteered to serve as a company in the 4th Regiment of Mounted Volunteers. They overwhelmingly chose Lincoln as their captain. For the next two months the regiment drilled and marched under command of General Samuel Whiteside, an old Indian fighter of the War of 1812. Lincoln's company saw no fighting during the conflict, save for their captain: two wrestling matches pitting Lincoln against other regiments' officers over choice campsites, as if the contestants were medieval kings' champions fighting to the death over a contested city. Lincoln won one.[53]

While Lincoln and his men missed combat, they did witness the grisly consequences of the war and the brutality of both sides. It fell to his company to bury the mutilated corpses of other Illinois militia after the Battle of Stillman's Run, the men scalped, beheaded, and castrated.

Later the company came across the remains of two white women, the older one scalped, the younger one's abdomen ripped apart, her unborn baby hanging from a tree. The barbarities unsettled them all, but when a Native American entered their encampment acting as a courier with a safe conduct pass from Secretary of War Lewis Cass, and Lincoln's men wanted to kill him outright, he objected, declaring he would fight any man who challenged his authority. No one did.[54]

Having already won the New Salem volunteers over with his amiable toughness, Lincoln also made an impression on the other enlisted men. To a man, they all liked Lincoln. Major John T. Stuart admired the captain's "good natured" approach to leadership. Stuart also mentioned accompanying Lincoln and a General Henry "to the hoar houses" of Galena; in light of Lincoln's saintly status, Stuart made sure to add that they went "purely for fun—devilment—nothing else."[55]

The Black Hawk War ended quickly. By summer's end, most of Black Hawk's people had been slaughtered; the chief was captured and sent east to see the might of the U.S. government before being returned to Iowa, his spirit irreparably broken. Lincoln returned to New Salem, proud of his captaincy yet looking on that summer with a humorous aside or two. Years later he would recall his "good many struggles with the mosquetoes" while fondly declaring he had "not since had any success in life which gave him the most satisfaction."[56]

Lincoln's lack of combat experience did not lessen his reputation when he returned to New Salem. It did encourage him to improve his lot in life. He continued attending the local debating society's meetings, honing his skills in argument and seasoning them with his disarming humor. His incessant reading, already a habit, now included Shakespeare, Burns, and other poets, reciting them with an innate ability to be engaging without appearing pretentious. He began to study grammar, aided by several of New Salem's better-educated residents, including Mentor Graham. "If you ever expect to go before the public in any capacity I think it the best thing you can do," Graham advised. In 1833, Lincoln was appointed postmaster, allowing him to read everything from the *Sangamo Journal* to the acts of Congress before delivering them to their subscribers.[57]

Before departing for the war, Lincoln had felt confident enough to announce his candidacy for the state legislature. He was twenty-three and self-educated but saw politics as his best way to get ahead. Most of all, he wanted to *matter*, not just to be somebody but somebody with a purpose in life. A short speech given at a small hamlet near Springfield is a template for the thousands of speeches he would make—sincerity without cloying, humility without fawning, humor that made a point:

> *Fellow citizens, I presume you all know who I am—I am humble Abraham Lincoln. I have been solicited by many friends to become a candidate for the legislature. My politics are short and sweet, like the old woman's dance. I am in favor of a National Bank, I am in favor of the internal improvement systems, and a high protective tariff. These are my sentiments and political principles. If elected I shall be thankful; and if not it will be all the same.*[58]

One month after his twenty-third birthday, the young candidate issued a "Communication to the People of Sangamo County," which went into detail about the contents of the above remarks. While the building of a future railroad was sound in thought, it was foolhardy in expense; instead, he advocated improving the Sangamon River by straightening its winding curves, thereby widening it for larger boats, making it better suited to the settlement's commerce. He called public education "the most important subject we as a people can be engaged in."[59]

Finally, he declared the reason for his candidacy. "I have no other [ambition] so great as that of being truly esteemed of my fellow men, by rendering myself worthy of their esteem." His idol, Henry Clay, could not have said it better. Three decades later, as president, Lincoln would sign two bills: the Morrill Land Grant College Act, providing land (often former Native American lands sold to the government) to build agriculture colleges, and the Pacific Railway Act, promoting the construction of the transcontinental railroads—both climaxing Lincoln's lifelong advocacies for internal improvements and education.[60]

No fewer than twelve candidates were vying for the four General Assembly seats allotted to Sangamon County. Among Lincoln's opponents was Peter Cartwright, the Jacksonian minister he had tangled with earlier. On August 4, the entire slate of candidates appeared in Springfield. News had just reached the frontier communities that President Andrew Jackson had vetoed the renewal of the National Bank's charter, an act hailed by Democrats, while Clay's National Republicans (soon to be called Whigs), including Lincoln, believed the bank a foundation of sound economic policy.

Few had read the details of Jackson's veto statement, and when Lincoln asked the usually loquacious Cartwright if the veto was correct, the preacher avoided answering. Lincoln, the novice among the slate, gave a cutting response, comparing Cartwright's dodge to the hunter who fired at a four-legged creature without being sure if it was a deer or calf. The man's summation was Lincoln's punch line: "I shot so as to hit it if it was a deer and miss it if it was a calf." A howling laughter emanated from the crowd, perhaps the first time that one of Lincoln's perfect anecdotes sold his point of view far better than his argument.[61]

On election day, Cartwright was among the winners. Lincoln won an overwhelming vote in New Salem, but his newcomer status hurt him elsewhere, and he finished eighth. He took his licking in stride. Two years later he added the job of county surveyor to his postmaster duties, studying into the night to learn the intricacies of the craft. Using his travels to acquaint himself with potential voters—particularly influential Clay supporters—he never missed a chance to tell a joke or story and slip his political aspirations into the conversation. When he ran as a Whig in 1834, he finished second in total votes, winning a seat in the State Assembly. At twenty-five, Abe Lincoln was a politician.[62]

A stagecoach carried New Salem's new representative the hundred miles to Vandalia, then the state capital of Illinois. Vandalia was visually a larger version of New Salem: approximately one hundred buildings, mostly log cabins. A shabby brick structure served as the capitol, with the House of Representatives holding session on the first floor while the

Senate convened on the second. Once there, Lincoln reconnected with John T. Stuart, whom he had met during the Black Hawk War. Most of the politicians boarded at the Vandalia Inn, which had a large dining room and thirteen guest rooms. Lincoln and Stuart roomed together, the six-foot-four-inch newcomer coming up with novel ways of sharing a bed that was always too short. Vandalia was also home of the state supreme court and the federal district court. When both the legislature and courts were in session, the population swelled, and Vandalia became the social center of the Midwest, with nightly parties and dances.[63]

Lincoln had a lot of catching up to do to justify his $3-a-day salary. Being newly elected, he adopted the tried-and-true approach of listening more than speechifying. Vandalia was yet another step in his education and maturation. He duly attended the sessions, serving on several committees, but spent most of his time learning the official and unofficial "rules" of governance, not only from fellow legislators but also from the lobbyists and officials who frequented the capitol and taverns. Lincoln was often at the courthouse, listening attentively to veteran attorneys making their arguments, some relying on cogent reason, others on emotive theatrics, and some occasionally using both.[64]

He was also rubbing shoulders with the powerful men of the state. While there were some as rawboned as he, most of the politicians—and certainly the lawyers and judges—were better educated, better dressed, and better mannered than he was, and financially immeasurably better off. Among Lincoln's new acquaintances was another up-and-comer in politics, a twenty-one-year-old Easterner who had left New York to make his name in the West. He had recently been admitted to the bar, and elected State Attorney for Illinois's First District. His name was Stephen A. Douglas.[65]

During this legislative session, Stuart saw Lincoln's potential and suggested he study law. Lincoln needed no prodding. Stuart, a seasoned attorney, lent his lawbooks to his roommate. Over the next two years, Lincoln devoured the collection, including *Blackstone's Commentaries*, often walking the twenty miles from New Salem to Stuart's law office in Springfield to borrow them. Nothing deterred him from his reading, not even the ribbing he received from the Clary's Grove Boys, who could not fathom why such a skilled laborer wanted a desk job. Towns-folk found him so distracted that the once affable postmaster would fail to return a greeting. Henry E. Dummer, then Stuart's law partner, initially thought Lincoln "the most uncouth looking young man I ever saw"; by the end of Lincoln's studies, Dummer called his newly acquired knowledge "Strong and acute." Lincoln "surprised us more and more at every visit," Dummer added. Lincoln was admitted to the bar on September 9, 1836.[66]

On the legislative side, Lincoln did address his responsibilities to his constituents. His first proposed bill, cosponsored with Stuart, said that any "horse, mare, or colt" showing up on another's property "shall be vested in the taker up." He also sponsored bills restricting the jurisdiction of justices of the peace and authorizing a toll bridge in Sangamon County.

In the course of time, especially after being admitted to the bar, Lincoln developed his political gifts and legislative skills, applying them to his marrow-deep belief in the Clay/Whig policies of education, internal improvements, a national bank, and tariff protection. But the main focus of his early elective years was the improvement of central Illinois. Foremost on his list was relocating the capital from Vandalia to Springfield. By 1836, despite his youth and relative inexperience, he became the leader of the "Long Nine," a group of Sangamon County Whigs, most over six feet in height.[67]

His first significant political triumph came in the 1836–37 session, when the legislature ran near amok with spending bills originating from lawmakers determined to have a say in the capital's relocation. No less than seven sites (including Vandalia) were under consideration. Understanding that if Springfield were chosen, it would get its necessary infrastructural improvements as a matter of course, Lincoln abandoned his conservative fiscal beliefs. If another city or county needed canals, roads, or other construction projects, Lincoln let their representatives know nine votes could be had for the asking in return for their support regarding Springfield. In contemporary vernacular, the "Rail Splitter" was now a "log roller."[68]

This spending spree surged through the Panic of 1837, busting the state debt to unthought-of amounts. It also resulted in accusations of corruption against the Long Nine in general, and one of them in particular. At one contentious session, General William L. D. Ewing, former governor, House Speaker, and staunch Democrat, addressed the Whigs regarding Lincoln's machinations. "Have you no other champion," he shouted, pointing at Lincoln, "than this coarse and vulgar fellow," adding he could not "condescend to break a lance with your low and obscure colleague." Lincoln vindictively responded in kind until his allies thought "he was digging his own grave": Ewing had proven even after the slightest of insults his consummate skills as a duelist. Lincoln was unafraid. Friends of both potential combatants convinced both men to reject the code duello.[69]

When the debates ended, Lincoln and the Long Nine won every vote on the capital question. He defended his questionable tactics in the *Sangamo Journal*, arguing that Illinois's "great population" being in the north, "a more central location was desired." Springfield would become, and still is, the capital of Illinois.[70]

When Abe Lincoln arrived in New Salem in 1832, he took up lodging at James Rutledge's tavern. Rutledge, impressed with young Abe's politeness and sincerity, introduced him to his family, including his daughter, Ann. Four years younger than Abe, with auburn hair and blue eyes, Ann was described by another boarder as "very handsome and attractive, as well as industrious and sweet spirited." Her teacher, Mentor Graham, called her a "tolerably good Schollar," both "Amiable" and "Kind."[71]

Abe's relationship with Ann Rutledge is clouded in legend. Contradictory recollections question whether theirs was a love affair or something less. It is safe to say that Abe was smitten, but there are two opinions as to where Ann's feelings lay.

Ann had her share of New Salem suitors and settled on John McNeil, a New York–born New Salem resident. Unlike Lincoln's mercantile ventures, McNeil's store was successful enough to allow him to purchase a great deal of property. By 1832, he and Ann were engaged.

Shortly afterward, McNeil confessed to Ann that his real name was McNamar; he had changed it when he came west to eliminate any contact with his poorer family in New York. His fortune made, he pledged to marry Ann upon his return from New York, where he would travel to provide for his parents. Ann agreed.[72]

At first McNamar sent letters to Ann (often delivered by postmaster Lincoln), but as time passed the correspondence slowed to a trickle and stopped altogether. The wagging tongues of New Salem took note. Here was this charming young lady, beloved in New Salem, now abandoned by a scalawag who had lived among them under an assumed name. Was any part of his story true?[73]

It was at this point when Abe began courting Ann, balancing his campaign for her hand with his surveying, mail deliveries, and constant self-imposed studies. After Lincoln's death, his law partner, William Herndon, began requesting narratives about Lincoln from every conceivable source and amassed plenty from the New Salem residents still living. Their recollections are colorful, vivid, poignant, and often conflicting, especially concerning Abe and Ann. At a quilting bee, one woman recalled how Abe "sat beside her and whispered words of love in her ear," Ann becoming so "worked up" that she "made long irregular stitches." By 1835, according to some of her family sources and friends, they were either engaged or planning to be after Abe was admitted to the bar. As for Ann's betrothal to McNamar, her brother Robert attested he had "no doubt but Ann had fully determined to break the engagement."[74]

In the spring of 1835, an unrelenting, disastrous rain besieged Illinois for weeks. Soon parts of New Salem were a foot deep in water. Mud caked the sidewalks and roads; soaked grounds bred insects that feasted off the drenched residents of the mid-state counties; the waste of outhouses defiled the muddy streets. That summer, malaria and typhoid ran rampant through New Salem. Lincoln joined those others healthy enough to nurse their neighbors or join the burial details digging mass graves. When a tornado tore through New Salem, it seemed as if the God of the Plagues of Egypt had settled among them.[75]

In August, Ann was stricken; New Salem residents differed as to whether it was consumption, malaria, or typhoid. According to the family, Abe spent some time alone with Ann. "How sad his face was when he came out of the room," a niece of Ann's later recollected. Ann Rutledge died on August 25.[76]

At first, Abe stoically bore his grief until another long spate of rain returned. Elizabeth Abell, in whose house Lincoln was staying during Ann's illness, told Herndon she had never "seen a man mourn a companion more than he did for her." During another stormy day Lincoln told Abell that "he could not bear the idea of it raining on her grave." Friends feared for his sanity. He began muttering the verses to the poem "Mortality" aloud to himself:

> *The maid on <u>whose</u> cheek, on <u>whose</u> brow, in <u>whose</u> eye,*
> *Shone <u>beauty</u> and pleasure,—her <u>triumphs</u> are by;*
> *And the <u>memory</u> of <u>those</u> that <u>beloved</u> her and praised*
> *Are <u>alike</u> from the <u>minds</u> of the <u>living</u> erased.*[77]

It took months for Lincoln, with the help of many friends, to pull himself together. Some believed Lincoln's breakdown was exclusively because of Ann's death; others considered it a factor, but not the only one. Mentor Graham believed that Lincoln's exhaustive studying, along with Ann's death, caused his "partial and momentary derangement."[78]

Whether Abe and Ann had marriage in their future may never be known. Some of Herndon's subjects, including most of Ann's relations, insisted that was their future; other New Salem residents and descendants were equally adamant that Ann remained faithful to McNamar and would have married him.[79]

Ironically, weeks after Ann's death, John McNamar returned to New Salem, his wagon weighed down with new furniture, fully intending to live up to his pledge. According to one of Herndon's interviews, McNamar was so distraught, he left the unloaded furniture outside, to be ruined by another day of rain. During his return, "I saw and conversed with Mr. Lincoln," McNamar told Herndon, adding, "I thought he had lost some of his former vivacity." That he had.[80]

For months, Elizabeth Abell and Abe's other friends watched him work through his grief over Ann's death. But by 1836 she believed the time was right to set Lincoln on the bridal path, certain she had the right woman for him: Elizabeth's sister, Mary Owens.[81]

Lincoln had met Mary before in 1833, and found her "intelligent and agreeable." Other residents went further. The black-haired, dark-eyed girl was remembered as "a fine looking woman" with "beautiful and even teeth." One man compared her to a heroine out of a romance novel. "No woman that I have seen has a finer face," Lincoln admitted. Her excellent education was obvious in her speech and correspondence. She was also rich: the Owens family owned a sizable plantation in Kentucky, with enough enslaved persons that her father hired them out.[82]

Accordingly, Elizabeth continually mentioned Mary in her conversations with Lincoln until he seemed to surrender to her plot. Recollecting his meeting with Mary three years earlier, he "saw no good objection to plodding life through hand in hand with her," hardly an enthusiastic rejoinder from someone looking forward to attending a ceremony that climaxes with the phrase "'til death do us part." Elizabeth sent for Mary anyway.[83]

Three years had passed since Miss Owens's last visit, but the village's surviving citizens were still enthralled with her. Not so her mail-order husband-to-be. Lincoln's reaction was a combination of cold feet and an acid tongue honed on the political stump but rarely directed at a woman. "She did not look as my imagination had pictured her" is the kindest comment he made. "I knew she was over-size," he pointedly confided to a friend's wife, "but she now appeared a fair match for Falstaff." In a further bit of tavern boy's insult, Lincoln said Mary reminded him of his stepmother, Sarah, "not from withered features, for her skin was too full of fat," but "from her want of teeth." Regarding appearance, the homely Lincoln might have looked in a mirror.[84]

Still, Lincoln felt honor bound. "What can I do?" He had promised this marriage to Mary's sister. Having "made a point of honor and conscience in all things, to stick to my word," "Honest Abe" was stuck. Abe and Mary's time together was soon anything but engaging. He tried to imagine her as handsome while recognizing that her innate intelligence complemented his own intellectual appetite. Meanwhile, Mary endured his demonstrated lack of manners with her and other women: his not helping her horse ford a stream while riding nor assisting a mother carry her child up a hill cooled her interest in marriage. Lincoln soon left for Vandalia for the legislative session.[85]

Absence did not make either heart grow fonder. Their correspondence was civil but rarely romantic (Lincoln signed off as "Your friend"). When Lincoln finally proposed—by letter—he spoke of Mary leaving her family estate in Kentucky for Springfield ("rather a dull business"), and openly declared, "You would have to be poor without the means of hiding your poverty," and pointedly asked, "Do you believe you could bear that patiently?"[86]

It became obvious that Mary could not and would not. She "thought Mr. Lincoln was deficient in those little links which make up the great chain of woman's happiness." It was Mary who broke up the relationship. In a rambling letter to Eliza Caldwell Browning, wife of Lincoln's close friend Orville, he ruefully confessed that "I was really a little in love with her" after all. As for marriage? "I can never be satisfied with any one who would be block-head enough to have me."[87]

Mary Owens married Jesse Vineyard, her sister's brother-in-law, in 1841. They moved to Missouri, where the slaveholding Vineyard became an ardent proslavery activist. As Mary later put it, she and Abe "differed as widely as the South is from the North."[88]

Miss Owens's decision proved correct. During their haphazard courtship, Lincoln had begun publicly questioning the legality of slavery and judging it immoral. In 1837, after the Illinois General Assembly received several memorials from states as far north as Connecticut and as far south as Mississippi "relative to the existence of domestic slavery," a select committee of both houses deplored "the unfortunate condition of our fellow men" now under bondage in the United States and the District of Columbia. The committee used harsher language in condemning abolition societies, concluding that "the arm of the General Government has no power to strike their fetters from them." The General Assembly ordered copies of the resolution sent to the states that had sent theirs.[89]

Not every representative agreed with the majority. Lincoln and Dan Stone, a Whig lawyer from Springfield, made their dissent public. While the two attorneys agreed that Congress "has no power, under the constitution, to interfere with the institution of slavery in the United States," it did have that power "to abolish slavery in the District of Columbia," adding "that power ought not to be exercised unless at the request of the people of said District."[90]

The following year Lincoln went a step further. In a speech to the Young Men's Lyceum of Springfield, an emerging civic hub of the town, Lincoln spoke at length on the sanctity of the law in a time of "increasing disregard for law in our country," citing mob lynchings and murders across the states, using as an example the hanging of "negroes suspected of conspiring to raise an insurrection" in Mississippi, where such hangings were perfectly legal. "Dead men were seen literally dangling from the boughs of trees upon every road side," he declared. In a sense, considering the times, Mary Owens was right: Lincoln was becoming a true Northerner.[91]

Lincoln had already moved to Springfield when he warned Mary Owens of its dullness. Although it was named the new capital in 1837, it would not be official until 1839. As with most frontier settlements, the beauty or ugliness lay in the eye of the beholder. One visitor described how "small clusters of infant trees . . . rise like bowers of romance to hedge on the village with beauty." Others were less infatuated. "Heat operating on the privies, sink holes, stables, and other receptacles of filth, causes them to send up an abundance of pestilential effluvia," one resident complained.[92]

The *Sangamo Journal* reported "an epidemic of mad dogs," and an ordinance warned that anyone disturbing Springfield inhabitants with pranks ranging from "noisemaking revelry . . . ringing bells, hallooing or shouting" to "setting fire to tar barrels in the night" would be "fined at the sum of five dollars."[93]

In Springfield, Lincoln struck up a friendship with Ninian Wirt Edwards, son of a former Illinois governor. Two months younger than Lincoln, Edwards had already served as state attorney general and had been recently elected to the Illinois House. He had married John Stuart's cousin, Elizabeth Todd of Kentucky. Their home, perched atop "Aristocracy Hill," soon became the center of Springfield's social affairs. One relative later recalled their house "brilliantly illuminated by firelight, astral lamps and candles," while another visitor waxed eloquent over "the sumptuous, yet not extravagant, arrangements of Mrs. Edwardses' supper table." Regular attendees of the Edwardses' soirees called themselves "the coterie"; uninvited residents called them the "Edwards clique."[94]

In 1839, Elizabeth's younger sister, Mary, came for an extended visit. Their father, Robert Smith Todd, had served under General William Henry Harrison during the War of 1812 and fought at the Battle of the Thames, where the great Native American Confederacy leader Tecumseh was killed. Todd went on to successful careers in law, banking, business, and politics and served as both state representative and senator. The Todd home in Lexington was a handsome house where Mary and her five siblings were raised. Mary was six when her mother, Eliza, died in childbirth; her father then married Elizabeth Humphreys and they had nine children together.[95]

Mary's idyllic childhood ended with her father's remarriage. Betsy Humphreys Todd was the epitome of the evil stepmother. The children she brought forth from this marriage were *the* children; Mary and her siblings were inferiors. Todd's business and political duties kept him absent for weeks; brother George would sue Betsy "for malignant and continued attempts" to "poison the mind of his father towards him." Mary would later recall her childhood as "desolate."[96]

But even as a child, Mary was resilient. The Reverend John Ward's school for girls in Lexington became her first sanctuary. When dispatched at fourteen to Madame Mentelle's boarding school, she flourished, mastering French (the only language spoken at the school), poetry, and the social arts. One classmate called her "a merry, companionable girl . . . She was really the life of the school."[97]

When at home, Todd's guests included many fellow Whig politicians, including Henry Clay and his cousin, the abolitionist Cassius Marcellus Clay. Mary grew so entranced by their after-dinner discussions that her sisters called her a "violent little Whig." By age twenty-one, she had developed a bubbly and vivacious personality, every inch of her small frame a lady, yet totally unafraid to dominate the conversation with recitations of poetry or political opinions, be it in a parlor or at the dinner table.[98]

Two issues were interwoven in the Todd family. Robert Todd was a slaveholder; from childhood Mary was accustomed to several enslaved persons tending to the Todd family's needs. As she grew older, Mary, like her siblings, became "antislavers" while Betsy's children supported the "peculiar institution." Four of Mary's half brothers and three brothers-in-law would fight for the Confederacy; four were killed.[99]

The other matter was familial. Mental illness ran deep in the Todd family. They had intermarried over the years, including her maternal grandparents and her own parents. One brother, Levi, would be divorced for "a confirmed habit of drunkenness" and "cruel and inhuman manner," while another, George, earned a reputation during the Civil War for "fits of madness," taking them out on Union prisoners while serving as a field surgeon.[100]

Lincoln was thirty-one years old when he met Mary at one of the Edwardses' parties. They made a decidedly odd couple: at five feet two inches, Mary possessed a buxom torso, frequently wearing dresses that showed off her shoulders. Brown hair, stylishly done, framed a round face that contained a small nose, small mouth, and blue eyes that missed nothing. Lincoln seemed twice her size, his perennially gaunt frame an even sharper contrast next to Mary's plumpness. Her ease at social patter also clashed with Lincoln's awkwardness with the ladies. She loved dancing; Lincoln avoided it at all costs. Mary's expression instantly told what she was thinking; Lincoln forever tried to mask his feelings behind an amiable bemusement.[101]

Still, the two struck up a relationship based on what they *had* in common. Mary was the third young woman in Lincoln's life who was intelligent. In Mary he found another lover of poetry, particularly that of Robert Burns. Add to that the fact that Mary was not only a "violent Whig" but someone who had spent hours sitting alongside his hero, Henry Clay—once telling Lincoln of riding her new pony to Clay's home as a child—and a relationship was kindled.[102]

Lincoln found himself charmed by Mary's wit and her passion for and grasp of politics and "drawn by some superior power" to her company. Mary observed that Lincoln "was a rising man," a fact that piqued her interest in him as a potential husband. Throughout 1840 their courtship was interrupted by Lincoln's circuit riding and legislative sessions.[103]

At first both Ninian and Elizabeth Edwards seemed happy with their unintended matchmaking, but they soon thought otherwise. Elizabeth sternly counseled her sister that both her own and Lincoln's "natures, mind—Education—raising &c" guaranteed they "could not live happy as husband & wife." Besides, Mary had other willing suitors, including Stephen Douglas, now Lincoln's perennial political opponent on all issues.[104]

Lincoln, too, began having doubts. In the fall of 1840, Ninian Edwards's cousin Matilda visited Springfield. "A lovelier girl I never saw," Mary believed. Lincoln's friend and circuit roommate, Joshua Speed, became totally infatuated. Matilda's blond hair reminded him of sunbeams, her blue eyes beguiling, her "form as perfect as that of the Venus de Médicis." Speed was not the only captivated man in Springfield. His friend Lincoln apparently was as well. Elizabeth came to believe that Lincoln "hated Mary and loved Miss Edwards."[105]

On New Year's Day 1841, Lincoln informed Speed that he wanted to be released from his engagement to Mary. Speed's narrative regarding this episode is the closest to the truth we have: his friend was "very unhappy about his engagement . . . Not being entirely satisfied that his heart was going with his hand."[106] Whether Lincoln became exasperated with Mary's flirtations or had misgivings (as Elizabeth Edwards put it) about "his ability and Capacity to please and support a wife," or if he truly was in love with Matilda Edwards remains unresolved to most Lincoln scholars. Whether, perhaps, Matilda Edwards rekindled the ghost of Ann Rutledge, while Mary took on another ghost of betrothals past—Mary Owens—we have no way of knowing.[107]

For the next year Lincoln went on a bender of depression. "Lincoln went crazy," Speed believed, and he "had to remove razors from his room." He became an absentee representative at House sessions, "reduced and emaciated in appearance," according to his friend James Conkling. Lincoln confessed to John Stuart, "I am now the most miserable man living." For a man who had walked with sadness all his life, this bout grew so serious that Lincoln sought medical help. Desperate after a "Most discreditable exhibition of myself," he turned to Dr. Anson G. Henry, a fellow legislator, for advice and got it. "Dr. Henry," he told Stuart, "is necessary for my existence."[108]

Although his friends worried that Lincoln might turn to suicide, he did make clear to Speed that that was not an option. He was "more than willing to die" but for one true thing. In Lincoln's mind, "he had done nothing to make any human being remember that he had lived."[109]

During this time, Mary entertained other suitors but would not commit herself so long as there seemed to be a chance of Lincoln's return. She had already dismissed Douglas, declaring, "I love him not." For a while during Lincoln's melancholia, she considered another Democrat, Lyman Trumbull, whom she believed to be "talented and agreeable." But, as with her other pursuers, Lyman was not Abe.[110]

Over the course of 1841, Lincoln worked his way out of his depression. With the help of his friends, particularly Speed, Lincoln returned to the road he had set for himself. With Stuart gearing up for a run for Congress, Lincoln went into a law partnership with Stephen T. Logan, a sickly-looking, uncouth attorney with a remarkable talent for swaying juries (and, like Stuart, a cousin of Mary Todd). Lincoln returned to riding the Eighth Judicial Circuit, taking up cases large and small as before. He returned to his duties in the Assembly but declined to run for reelection that fall. In letters written to Speed, then in Kentucky, Lincoln declared, "I have been quite clear of hypo since you left," referring to his depression, and that he had found at least one hopeful answer: "Avoid being *idle*." And in a postscript to one letter he added, "I have been quite a man since you left."[111]

In the fall of 1842, Lincoln walked up the hill to the Edwards home to call on Mary. On November 4, in the presence of a few relatives and friends, they were married in the Edwardses' parlor. Lincoln presented Mary with a wedding band inscribed "Love is Eternal." The newlyweds possessed widely different personalities and character traits that guaranteed clashes over the next twenty-three years. But they did have one thing in common: a perpetual, adaptable toughness. It would see them through disappointments, upheavals at home and in the country, the deaths of two sons, and, later, the deaths of hundreds of thousands of other American sons.[112]

The marriage also fulfilled Mary Todd's singular ambition. In her lifetime, as in earlier generations like Abigail Adams's, there was no room on the political stage for a woman—even one as intellectually bright and politically vocal as Mary—a fact that made marriage for her as much an act of aspiration as of love. "She was an Extremely Ambitious woman," her sister later asserted, "& often Contended she was destined to be the wife of some future President."[113]

Nine months after their marriage, Mary gave birth to the first of four sons, Robert Todd. Freed from his electoral responsibilities, Lincoln had the time to expand his law practice, which meant extensive absences from Mary and the baby in the spring and fall. His cases during his circuit-riding years ranged from property claims, debts, assault and battery, and, on several occasions, murder. He excelled at jury trials, using everything from his height to his seemingly offhand gestures. Always a master of timing, he knew when to make a humorous aside and when to take the jury on a more dramatic journey. On the chessboard of a trial, Lincoln often ceded the "pawns" of a case to his opponent without losing any point that would prevent him from earning the verdict. "Any man who took Lincoln for a simple-minded man," one fellow country lawyer observed, "would wind up with his back in a ditch."[114]

His departure from the state legislature did not mean Lincoln had abandoned his (and Mary's) collective ambitions. In 1843, after two terms, John Stuart was retiring from Congress. "Your county and mine are almost sure to be placed in the same congressional district," Lincoln wrote Alden Hall, Tazewell County's state representative, adding, "I would like to be it's [sic] Representative." To Richard S. Thomas, another ardent Whig, he was equally clear, in folksier fashion: "Now if you should hear any one say that Lincoln don't want to go to Congress . . . [t]he truth is, I would like to very much." His candidacy was short-lived. There were other Whigs, senior in service, blocking the way. At a regional Whig convention that spring, Lincoln lost out to his good friend Edward D. Baker, who in turn lost out to veteran politician John J. Hardin at the state convention.[115]

Hardin won the election that fall but could only serve one term. Before the convention ended, Lincoln urged the party to adopt the Democrats' practice of open nominating conventions and urged the Whigs to adopt a rotating system of Whig candidates for the Seventh Congressional District. This would prevent intraparty bickering over candidates, he asserted, and ensure more Whig victories. After all, he stated, "a house divided against itself cannot stand." The motions passed, making it apparent that Hardin would be succeeded by Baker, followed by Lincoln. It was the first time he used the "house divided" analogy. It would not be the last.[116]

In 1844, the Lincolns purchased the only home they would ever own. Situated on Eighth and Jackson Streets in Springfield, the one-and-a-half-story structure was a stone's throw from Lincoln's law office. A second son, Eddie, named after Baker, arrived in 1846. By this time Mary Lincoln had accustomed herself to a level of domesticity the daughter of a rich slaveholder would have once thought unthinkable. While her sister Elizabeth lived up the hill in the lap of luxury, Mary was now cooking, cleaning, making do on Lincoln's often skimpy earnings—in addition to chopping wood, drawing well water, and being the sole parent to her boys when Lincoln was away. Somehow, Lincoln was able to afford a maid for Mary to assist with the children, but it still fell to her to run the household, often without her husband.[117]

That same year Lincoln parted ways with Logan to set up his own firm, choosing young William "Billy" Herndon, then clerking in the Lincoln-Logan office, as his junior partner. Herndon was intelligent, high-strung, and prone to bouts of drinking. But he also respected Lincoln without idolizing him and was a fierce opponent of slavery. The two men moved into an office at the run-down Tinsley Building, where their mutual lack of neatness resulted in rising piles of depositions, deeds, and bills, often topped by a note of Lincoln's: *When you can't find it anywhere else, look in this.*[118]

Lincoln anticipated the nomination for the Seventh Congressional District seat in 1846, but an unforeseen development threatened his ascent. Hardin wanted the seat back, and, confident that most Whigs would support him, he expected Lincoln to step aside. Instead, Hardin was completely outmaneuvered. Lincoln corralled supporters, asking them to ward off any challenges Hardin might make, clandestine or otherwise. "The Beardstown paper is in the hands of my friends. The editor is a Whig, and he personally dislikes Hardin," he penned to one, listing all his likely supporters and assuring that "I shall go it thoroughly, and to the bottom." To another Whig on the fence, Lincoln's argument was concise: "Turn about is fair play." To potential supporters, Lincoln pointedly called Hardin "talented, energetic, usually generous and magnanimous." Hardin withdrew his candidacy.[119]

Lincoln's Democratic challenger was his old foe, Peter Cartwright, still a fire-eater on the stump. Cartwright, his love of God and ardor for Jesus Christ well-known to all, sought to defeat Lincoln with the Almighty's assistance, accusing Lincoln of being an atheist—an "infidel." In a state full of churchgoers, this was a damning allegation, and Lincoln knew it; this was no time for him to publicly grapple with his lack of churchgoing, let alone his doubts about God. It called for an irrefutable response, and Lincoln wrote a handbill denying "Charges of Infidelity" at his own expense. "That I am not a member of any Christian Church, is true; but I have never denied the truth of the Scriptures," he attested, "and I have never spoken with intentional disrespect of religion in general."[120]

After a well-laid-out defense of his defense of religion, Lincoln ended with a coup de grâce:

I do not think I could myself, be brought to support a man for office, whom I knew to be an open enemy of, and scoffer at, religion. Leaving the higher matter of eternal consequences, between himself and his Maker, I still do not think any man has the right thus to insult the feelings, and injure the morals, of the community in which he may live. If, then, I was guilty of such conduct, I should blame no man who should condemn me for it; but I do blame those, whoever they may be, who falsely put up such a charge in circulation against me.[121]

The election was held in August. Lincoln won in a walk, 6,340 votes to Cartwright's 4,829.[122]

The Lincolns began the daunting task of relocating to Washington. It meant trusting Billy Herndon to keep the practice afloat, getting their sons packed, and traveling eight hundred miles from Springfield to the nation's capital. Lincoln grew a tad uncertain of his mission. "Being elected to Congress, though I am very grateful to our friends, has not pleased me as much as I expected," he wrote to Speed in October.[123]

In Congress there were two prevalent issues facing the new representative. The spread of slavery was one. The new war with Mexico was the other.

TWO

SON OF THE SOUTH

In June 1825, Robert E. Lee left Alexandria, Virginia, for the United States Military Academy at West Point. His journey marked the first time he had been away from family and any distance outside Virginia. After a series of coach rides that got him to New York City, he boarded a steamer that took Lee and other young men like him up the Hudson River.

"The banks of the Hudson are quite beautiful and here and there are very well cultivated," another traveler recollected; farther upriver "there is a fine view of the high Catskill Mountains." At West Point, the steamer docked at a wooden quay with a guardhouse. After brief questioning by the sentry, the boys climbed the steep path to the academy entrance.

Robert passed the oral entrance exam with ease. He was five feet, ten inches tall but carried himself with a natural dignity that made him look taller. He possessed his late father's good looks and charm. Henry Lee III gave Robert a public life that was hard to live up to—and a private life even harder to live down.[1]

Other members of the extended Lee family served the patriot cause during the American Revolution as politicians and diplomats willingly risking "their lives, their fortunes, and their sacred honor," as their colleague Thomas Jefferson put it. But the Lee whose star shone brightest during the Revolution was Robert's father.[2]

Henry Lee III was a Princeton College graduate, studying law, when the war broke out. An excellent horseman, he was made a captain of dragoons. Like many American officers, he lacked actual military training. But he was handsome, courageous, and daring to the point of recklessness. Once, after he and ten troopers were ambushed by a seemingly overwhelming number of British cavalry while patrolling the outskirts of Valley Forge at daybreak, Henry Lee III found his inner Henry V and inspired his men to fight with him. "Baffled by the bravery of my men," the enemy withdrew, he reported to General George Washington, and the legend of "Light Horse Harry" was born.[3]

Washington offered the young cavalryman an aide-de-camp position with his staff, but Lee declined, as he was "wedded to my sword." He was promoted to major and given command of a mixed corps of cavalry and infantry soon called "Lee's Legion." For the rest of the war, from New Jersey to the Carolinas to Yorktown, Lee burnished his legend. His service to General Nathanael Greene during the Carolina campaign prompted Greene to later call Lee "one of the first Officers in the world."[4]

He also acquired a reputation for cruelty. When a captured deserter was brought before Lee, he issued an order that the man's head be cut off and mounted as a warning.[5] Washington was horrified. "Your proposal which respects cutting off [deserters'] heads and sending them to the Light Troops had better be omitted," he warned Lee, as it would cause more resentment than fear. Lee's self-importance and disregard of others brought another reproach from Washington. "You will not forget that you owe me a horse," he chided Lee, adding, "It is necessary to remind a man of his debt lest he should forget his creditor." Light Horse Harry was becoming a lovable thug.

Dissatisfied over his rank, Lee resigned his commission and embarked on another campaign, the winning of a wife. He had set his cap for his cousin "the divine Matilda" Lee, heir to Stratford Hall, a magnificent,

sprawling estate with its own wharf on the Potomac River in Westmoreland County. They were married at Matilda's home in 1782. Among the
guests was a beaming Washington.

Lee's rise in politics was as meteoric as his military career. He replaced another young veteran, James Monroe, as a delegate to Congress. A devout Federalist, he joined James Madison's bloc in support
of the Constitution at the Virginia ratification convention. After a brief
stint in the Virginia House of Delegates, Lee was elected governor of
Virginia in 1791.[6]

By the end of the 1790s, Lee was considered an aristocratic scalawag. Land speculation by retired army officers and congressmen was
rampant, and Lee fell prey to schemes he was certain would bring quick
wealth. When a sizable investment on a land deal with Robert Morris,
the financial wizard of the Revolution, came crashing down, Lee blamed
"the failures of Morris." Eventually, relatives and acquaintances tired
of Lee's lathering optimism over his latest get-rich-quick schemes, yet
nothing seemed beneath him. On one occasion he borrowed a horse
from a neighbor who had the mount saddled and brought to Stratford
by one of his enslaved men. Weeks later the slave returned. Limping
from his journey, he told his owner that Lee had sold the loaned horse.
When asked why he didn't come back sooner, the man replied that Lee
"sold me too."[7]

Before Matilda died in 1790 from complications of childbirth, she
wisely left Stratford to her children. By then it had lost much of its august luster. Furniture, housewares, and other valuables were sold to pay
debts. When a commission in the French army was offered in 1793, Lee
declined, having found another opportunity: marriage to Anne Hill
Carter, whose father, Charles, was considered the richest man in Virginia, owning thousands of acres and hundreds of enslaved persons.
Carter reluctantly consented, well aware of Lee's financial pratfalls and
his penchant for besmirching his own honor. The ceremony took place
at Shirley, the family plantation on the James River. The newlyweds
returned to the governor's house in Richmond.[8]

With each demand from a creditor, Ann Carter Lee's husband lost
his allure. When the Whiskey Rebellion broke out, arch-Federalist Lee

led the Virginia militia into Pennsylvania, hoping to win back President Washington's favor. All it did was increase public hostility toward Lee's political bent, resulting in his losing the governorship. The family repaired to Stratford, which by this time had reached a melancholy low.[9]

Washington finally had his fill with his disgraced protégé in 1795 when Lee bought Washington's shares of the aptly titled Dismal Swamp Company for $20,000. Lee promised to repay Washington in three annual installments. Instead, Lee tried to palm off his debt by returning some of the shares. "It was not agreeable to me to be paid in that way (because it was the money I wanted)," an angry Washington wrote. Lee's final payback came in words, not cash. After the president's death, Lee immortally eulogized him as "first in war, first in peace, and first in the hearts of his countrymen.[10]

As the 1800s began there was no letup on the demands for Lee to pay his debts. Repairing to Stratford only gave the Lees a roof over their head. Harry and Ann had children of their own: a daughter, Anne Kinloch, and two sons she named after her relations—Charles Carter Lee arrived in 1798, Sydney Smith Lee in 1802. In the family tradition, all of them were born at Stratford Hall. In the spring of 1806, Ann learned she was pregnant again. With no servants and only her stipend to pay expenses, Stratford had become dank and depressing, and the ceaseless physical work and unending terror of her financial straits took their toll on Ann's health. It is no wonder she considered herself "an invalid."[11]

She moved back to Shirley, but as her time drew closer, she wanted to return to Stratford and have the baby there. "I trust, Mr. Lee, you will certainly bring a conveyance for me," she wrote Harry, adding, "Do not disappoint me." He did not. Ann returned to Stratford in a carriage (borrowed, of course) in November, and on January 19, 1807, Robert Edward Lee was born, named after another of Ann's brothers.[12]

One year later, Henry IV came of age and became master of Stratford, now having shrunk in size to 236 acres. In 1809, the law finally caught up with Light Horse Harry. He was first sent to the Westmoreland County jail and then transferred to Fredericksburg's. He was released in 1810. Throughout his imprisonment, Lee toiled away at an autobiography of his war exploits. Upon his release, Ann made it clear that the family would not remain at Stratford, its ghostly appearance almost too reflective of her husband's fading honor. Bowing to her wishes, Lee moved the family to Alexandria, taking with them the half dozen enslaved persons they still owned. During their years in Alexandria, the Lees lived in two modest but comfortable homes, again supported by Ann's allowance and other assistance from her extended family.[13]

As a little boy, Robert was aware of his father's legendary deeds during the Revolution, if not of Harry's financial misadventures. But he must have noticed the respectful greetings that sometimes came his father's way on Alexandria's streets. Now in his fifties, Lee was still fairly handsome, but a portrait shows a fuller face and an extra chin, his eyes staring out warily, as if even the artist was owed money. He was cocksure that his published memoirs would restore his fortune. They did not.

In 1812, Lee seemed to have reached rock bottom. When a friend in Baltimore was being harassed by pro-war mobs over his Federalist newspaper's anti-war editorials, Lee was one of fifty staunch Federalists who rushed north to his defense, as much for the adventure as for a chance to stand up for his principles, confident he could defend the newspaper building against any mob.

He was wrong. On the night of July 27, local militia broke up a battle between the paper's supporters and a mob, sending the Federalists to jail. The following day, rioters stormed the jail and dragged the Federalists into the street, where they were brutally beaten. Lee was stabbed repeatedly with penknives while hot candle grease was poured into his eyes; he was left for dead in the street.[14]

Lee returned home bandaged and disfigured, described in the press as "black as a negro," his health and looks forever ruined. Creditors showed no pity. With nothing left for him but a life of embarrassment, Lee abandoned his family and headed to the Caribbean, where for the next six years he wandered from port to port, writing home occasionally promising to return, encouraging his sons to study "Alexander, Caesar, and Hannibal." Gravely ill, he sailed for home in March 1818, only getting as far as Cumberland Island, Georgia, and cared for by Louisa

Catherine Greene, the late general's daughter. Lee died on March 25, having not seen his wife or Robert for six years.[15]

Years later, Robert recalled his father's "letters of love and wisdom" to his brothers. Light Horse Harry's encouragements would inspire Robert his entire life; his example of financial mismanagement would haunt him.[16]

By 1818, Ann Carter Lee excelled at making do with little money. She diligently did her best to personify and instill habits of hard work, honesty, and frugality in her children, urging them to "practice self-denial and self-control." She added a healthy dose of faith in God: in Ann's eyes, Jesus Christ was "the only rock of your salvation." In her youngest son she found a more-than-willing disciple.

By this time, eleven-year-old Robert knew all too well that his father's wartime and political triumphs were inextricably intertwined with his utter lack of financial self-control. In the six years of his father's self-imposed exile, Lee had watched his mother add a father's responsibilities to her own. But by 1820 Ann's health was spent, and with his brothers Carter at Harvard (spending money like his father) and Smith a midshipman in the navy, Robert became master of the house.[17]

He assumed his mother's household tasks, juggling his school hours at his aunt's plantation, Eastern View, with his new duties. Through his teens, he considered himself Ann's "outdoor agent & confidential messenger," taking her for carriage rides when she felt well enough. Each week the boy was seen at the Alexandria markets, a basket on his arm, having added shopping to his chores, done without complaint. He was fond of activity, even running with the dogs during a fox hunt. He possessed a pleasant gentility; keeping his disappointments and frustrations to himself was soon a habit. The fact that he had inherited his father's temper made this even more remarkable.[18]

The total few enslaved persons owned by Harry and Ann were often hired out as another source of income. But any money coming in left Ann's hands as quickly as she grasped it. That year she acquired another expense, one she would willingly finance: it was time to attend to

Robert's formal education. After all, an unlettered man to her was "an awkward figure in every situation," especially for a Lee or Carter.[19]

Ann enrolled Robert in the Alexandria Academy, under the tutelage of William B. Leary, who assigned Euclid and the classics to his students, particularly the military writings of Tacitus, Cicero, and Caesar. Robert studied under Leary until the latter was arrested for debt in 1823. Robert, recalling his father, never cast any aspersions Leary's way. Decades later, when Lee was president of Washington College, he thanked Leary "for the affectionate fidelity which characterized your teaching and conduct toward me."[20]

Now sixteen, Robert was handsome, athletic, and already an expert horseman. Leary's arrest might have presented a problem for Robert in furthering his education, but he had a solution that was not only his personal choice but a financially necessary one: West Point.[21]

That Light Horse Harry's youngest son would choose a military career was no surprise to anyone, yet it was not welcome news to Harry's widow. But seeing his desire to live up to his father's example in uniform (and live down his example out of it), Ann went to work on getting Robert what he wanted. In February 1824, Robert crossed the Potomac to meet John C. Calhoun, President Monroe's secretary of war. Robert listened intently as Calhoun told him to apply in writing, including a list of the subjects he had studied. Lee did; his detailed summation of his studies was followed by letters from Virginia congressmen, Lee's brother Carter and half brother Harry, and climaxed by an endorsement from retired general and presidential candidate Andrew Jackson.[22]

Robert's first military offensive proved a delayed victory. He was accepted but, due to the high number of Virginia applicants, would not be admitted until 1825. Among other future brothers-in-arms was Joseph E. Johnston, whose father had served under Light Horse Harry during the Revolution. Instead of resting on future laurels, Robert took advantage of the new academy for boys just established in the house next door by a Quaker, James Hallowell, who marveled at how Robert could complete his assignments while being primary caretaker to his mother.[23]

Robert's departure for West Point put a period on his years in Alexandria and signified the end of his boyhood. It also ended them for his mother. "How can I live without Robert?" she asked her cousin, Sally Lee. "He is both son and daughter to me." Ann's health worsened steadily; unable to manage without Robert, she moved to Georgetown, where Carter had embarked on a law career with little success. "If he makes any money," she complained to Smith, "he must be laying it up, for we see little at home." For Ann, some things never changed.[24]

Robert was among the forty-six in their class who finished their four years at the academy. Many would later serve on one side or the other in the Civil War. But for the next four years they were cadets, subject to the hazing of upperclassmen and the imperious rebukes of their instructors. Everything from fistfights to fiction seemed to be forbidden at West Point.[25]

The academy was entering its ninth year under the direction of Colonel Sylvanus Thayer. With his serious countenance, grayish hair, and piercing eyes, Thayer looked every inch the combination of military officer and academic taskmaster. He revolutionized West Point, establishing an honor system, a severe disciplinary code, constant examinations, and a curriculum that ranged from mastering French (the language of the best military works) to mathematics, the sciences, and topography. Under Thayer's command, West Point became the best engineering school in the Western Hemisphere. In Robert Lee, Thayer had the perfect student.[26]

And Cadet Lee *was* perfect. In the coming four years, he did not receive a single demerit. Only one other cadet in academy history shares that distinction, and that was Charles Mason, a classmate of Robert's. When not in class, they drilled, and drilled, and drilled again. Their uniforms consisted of a gray coat with three rows of gold buttons trimmed with black braid, leather shoulder straps, and gray trousers in the winter (white in summer). Their headwear was a leather shako.[27]

Academy regulations dictated that Robert spend his first two years at West Point before applying for a furlough. His excellent grades and faultless behavior guaranteed his application was approved. On June 30,

1827, he boarded a ship bound for New York, and from there took a series of coach rides to Washington and his brother Carter's home on O Street. There occurred a joyous, likely tearful reunion between Ann and her son, no longer the teenager, handsomer than ever in his uniform. Robert looked good in gray.[28]

For the next two months, Robert resumed being his mother's coachman, caregiver, and confidant, taking her to visit family and friends in northern Virginia, where he made an impression as much by his looks and demeanor as by his devotion to Ann. One young girl remarked on how "his beauty and fine manners [were] constantly commented on." Robert and Ann's summer tour of friends and family included visits to Arlington, the mansion overlooking the Potomac, home to George Washington Parke Custis, Martha Washington's grandson.[29]

In 1802, at twenty-one, Wash had inherited a fortune in money, thousands of acres of land, and over one hundred enslaved persons, a considerable number of whom he put to work building the mansion he would call Arlington. Two years later he married sixteen-year-old Mary "Molly" Lee Fitzhugh, whose father was the original owner of one of the Alexandria houses where Ann Lee raised Robert.[30]

Wash and Molly proved that opposites attract. The beautiful Molly was a pious Episcopalian who would cofound a women's group opposed to slavery; like Custis, she supported the American Colonization Society, an organization of white Northerners and Southerners—many of the latter slaveholders—dedicated to the repatriation of free Blacks and the emancipated enslaved to Africa. Molly's paunchy, balding husband, on the other hand, was a dilettante who took turns at farming, sheep breeding, painting, and politics—losing interest once they, or he, proved unsuccessful.[31]

Conversely, he remained fixated on completing Arlington, commissioning architect George Hadfield to design the first grand Grecian-themed domicile in America. The outside structure took Custis's enslaved persons and contracted artisans sixteen years to complete (it would be another forty years before the interior was deemed acceptable). Once completed, it was compared to the "Temple of Theseus." Arlington, with its two-story Greek portico, still looms over the landscape—just what Custis intended. The magnificent Doric columns appeared to be marble but were wooden, covered by cement and painted; the stone walls are actually stucco.[32]

A distant cousin of Robert's, Mary Anna Randolph Custis, was the only one of the Custis offspring to live beyond early childhood. She was precocious and well-read, spoke both Greek and Latin, and was artistically talented; some of her landscapes still grace Arlington's walls. She was also a bit spoiled and temperamental. Small, slender, and long-necked, Mary more resembled her father than her mother, her brown eyes set far apart from a narrow nose, her jawline firm, with a small mouth. Mary's personal servant, Maria Carter Syphax, was her half sister: daughter of her father and an enslaved woman, Arianna Carter. We do not know if Mary was aware that Maria was related.[33]

Robert and Mary had known each other since childhood, planting trees together at Arlington. No one knows when they grew fond of each other, but Robert's courtship was evident to all during his 1827 furlough. Mary did have her share of suitors, including Smith Lee (and perhaps Carter Lee as well). For all his charm and manners, Robert was still the serious cadet, poring over his studies while in Virginia, prompting Mary to comment that "all the beaux have absconded except that all-admiring & admired one Mr. Lee. He is so much occupied in the duties of his profession that he has but little time for the frivolous affairs of the heart."[34]

Robert returned to West Point in the fall. He did not catch Mason in class rank, but his diligent study habits helped him master engineering, artillery, and tactics. Even his free hours were spent in a book, reading everything from Machiavelli to Rousseau, sharpening both the mechanical and the artistic sides of his brain. Few if any academy graduates have gotten more from their years at West Point than Robert E. Lee. His fellow cadets had begun calling him the "Marble Model" for everything from his strong build and graceful comportment to his unfailingly good manners. Joe Johnston recalled that Lee was

full of sympathy and kindness, genial and fond of gay conversation and even of fun, while his correctness of demeanor and attention to duties,

personal and official, and a dignity as much a part of himself as the ele-
gance of his person, gave him a superiority that everyone acknowledged
in his heart.[35]

Another brief furlough in the summer of 1828 brought Robert back to Georgetown, where he found his mother's health worsening and Mary Custis still available. He finished his final exams in June 1829 with an astounding 1,966½ points out of 2,000, still behind Charles Mason with 1,995½. (Two years later, Mason resigned his commission and embarked on a career in law, business, and politics.)[36]

Upon graduation, Robert Edward Lee was commissioned brevet second lieutenant in the Engineer Corps. The "Marble Model" was on the long road to becoming the "Marble Man."[37]

Once again Robert had a few weeks' leave to visit home. By now his mother was back at another Lee plantation, Ravensworth, under the Fitzhugh family's watchful care. "I never calculate on living longer than from one season to another," Ann had told Smith Lee. She died on July 26. Her will left most of her personal effects to her daughters, along with $10,000 each from her trust fund. The rest of her unspecified estate was divided between her three sons.[38]

Amid the sorrow, Robert provided a bit of whimsy to his siblings. His "confused sentences" and other mumblings were at first taken as out of character for the most organized and self-controlled family member, but Robert's sister Mildred soon discerned his mutterings were not over Ann. Her brother's rambling, to himself and anyone in the room, was over Mary Custis. Mildred coyly let her know that Robert was, indeed, smitten. That August, Lee was assigned to Cockspur Island in the Savannah River. A new fort, named after Revolutionary War hero Casimir Pulaski, was under construction. Lee's commanding officer would be Major Samuel Babcock.[39]

Where Sylvanus Thayer had immediately grasped in 1817 that the cadets under his watch would become the engineers responsible for surveying, designing, constructing, and at times jury-rigging the forts

President Monroe had in mind, Major Samuel Babcock, West Point '08, did not. The one salvation Lee found in Savannah was his West Point friend Jack MacKay and family. MacKay's fortuitous first assignment was at nearby Oglethorpe Barracks, an easy stretch of the legs for MacKay to visit his Savannah home, where his four rollicking sisters happily held court, enthralling Savannah society. Lee delighted in their company, filling his letters to Mary with their antics at dances and parties, carefully adding (in hopes of curbing any jealousy from Mary) that, although he might have been given "a sugar plum!!!—or a mint drop!!!" there was not one kiss to be had from any of them.[40]

In the summer of 1830, Babcock's failing health won him a long furlough and put a stop to Robert's assignment as well. He arrived in Virginia with two goals in mind: winning Mary Custis was one; winning over her father was the other.[41]

Robert's brother Carter had moved to New York, so Lee stayed at Ravensworth and other Lee and Carter homes. A pall hung over Ravensworth: William Henry Fitzhugh had died, possibly accidentally poisoned just before Robert's return. Mary, laid low at her uncle's passing, turned to her faith for comfort. Always religious, she now became an avatar of evangelism. Robert, on his visits that summer, maintained his calm pleasantness, but beneath the surface he was unnerved at the change in Mary. While his mother had instilled in him an abiding but quiet faith, Mary's zealotry was foreign to him.[42]

But Mary's religious fervor was no obstacle to Robert's mission. He already knew that Mary was the love of his life and that her mother was receptive to his courtship. He included Molly in conversations, and if she entered the parlor just as Robert began reading Shakespeare or Goethe with Mary—well, that was fine with him. He had also been at Arlington enough times to show Mary's father that, while he was no rich scion of Virginia, he was also no Light Horse Harry.

During one of Robert's long parlor readings of a Sir Walter Scott adventure, Molly suggested that Mary take Robert into the dining room for a piece of cake, where Mary got a marriage proposal. Both Molly and Mary happily announced the news in letters sent throughout Virginia. Mr. Custis was not so glad. "The Father has not yet made up his mind, though it is supposed [he] will not object," Robert told Carter. He returned to Cockspur in November, certain of Mary's love, Molly's blessing, and Custis's wariness.[43]

Lee's return to duty coincided with a new commanding officer. Lieutenant Joseph K. F. Mansfield saw the error in Babcock's plans but believed a more experienced engineer was needed. Captain Richard Delafield's later arrival would give Robert the task of serving two masters. He spent Christmas in Savannah with the MacKays, making sure to tell Mary, "I followed your wishes exactly & went to Church." With unending harsh winds and cold temperatures not seen in years, there was little work done on Fort Pulaski.[44]

A visitor from his childhood added to Lee's responsibilities. While in Baltimore before heading to Cockspur, Robert had found Nat, the family's old, enslaved coachman, "in such low health that I determined to bring him out here . . . He is very weak & feeble & his cough still continues bad." Nat arrived at Christmas. Robert arranged for a physician and nurse to check on him in Savannah and visited him when in town; Mrs. MacKay also looked in. Robert was confident that Nat would recover, but he died in March. "So he too is gone," Robert lamented.[45]

Lee had hoped to "gain exceedingly" from Delafield, "a gentleman & a scientific & practical Engineer." But he now found himself condescendingly treated like a novice apprentice. When Mary hinted in a letter that Robert was "lazy," he got testy. "Did you ever build a Fort Miss Molly?" he pointedly asked. He was taken aback by Mary's increased preachiness, along with a copy of the New Testament she insisted he read. Although she pledged not to "weary" him about religion, she did. Robert informed Mary that "you may send me as many 'written sermons' as you chose," but he was not as engaged in his faith as much as she was in hers, being "the same sinful Robert Lee."[46]

Orders transferring him to Fortress Monroe in Virginia moved him closer to his betrothed but also increased his anxiety. "I cannot wait any longer," he declared. "I will ask the General for a Furlough & if he will not grant it I will take it . . . And He & his Uncle Sam may go to France For what I care." Lee's marble veneer had cracked, temporarily.[47]

By springtime, Custis accepted the inevitable: the name "Lee" would be added to his Washington/Custis/Randolph/Fitzhugh lineage. His doubts about Robert's family history did not prevent him from being fond of his daughter's choice, but Custis also had fretted over whether Mary could adjust to the social and financial challenges of being an officer's wife after a lifetime of advantages. In an honest moment, Custis might have realized that Robert's noble qualities were second nature and not an act. Or perhaps it occurred to Custis that he might—*might*—make a Custis out of Lee yet, something his daughter would not have minded at all.[48]

Giving his daughter away gave Custis pause; giving her a grand wedding was a loving task, especially since Custis was cash poor as usual. Still, rooms were repainted, the finest food and drink procured, and invitations sent to the finest Virginia families. The smallness of Arlington's interior was logistically tested: three guests were assigned to each available bed. On June 30, Robert and his best man, his brother Smith, looked resplendent in their respective army and navy uniforms, while Mary and her six bridesmaids-in-waiting wore colorful gowns.[49]

The only thing Custis could not provide Mary was sunshine. Torrential rain soaked the arriving guests. Virginia Theological Seminary's first professor, Dr. Reuel Keith, arrived so drenched his clothing required changing before officiating. His jury-rigged togs, appropriated from Custis's armoire, threatened the solemnity of the occasion: Keith was tall, Custis short. Keith sought to redirect stares at his ludicrous appearance with Calvinist-like "remarks" that Robert compared to "my Death warrant" while Mary's hands perceptibly shook. From that point onward, however, it was "a happy day" forever in Robert's mind.[50]

Unseen (or disregarded) foibles in a spouse during courtship are often not as forgivable after the vows. The Lees had a pleasant honeymoon, mostly spent at Ravensworth and Arlington, before Robert reported to Fort Monroe, where Mary compared their two-room apartment to "a piece of chalk," then summoned her mother, she being a more organized housekeeper. Fortunately, Mrs. Custis assured Lee that she had no thought whatsoever of visiting. Mary then suggested Robert's sister Anne come instead. The only third party to arrive was Mary's enslaved attendant, Cassie. Soon the personality differences between the couple became evident to Robert: he was obsessively punctual, fastidious, and personable. Mary was none of these. In one instance, when her hair became hopelessly entangled, she merely cut it all off.[51]

Workwise, Robert was far happier at Fort Monroe than at Cockspur. He was assigned completion of "Castle Calhoun" on Rip Raps, a man-made shoal opposite Fort Monroe in Hampton Roads named after the loose stone used to build breakwaters and other water supports. He reported to Captain Andrew Talcott, who graduated second in Thayer's first graduating class at West Point (1818). Robert described Talcott as "a man of a first rate mind, of great acquirement, & gentlemanly feeling." The two became lifelong friends.[52]

For the first time in his career, Lee was in total control of a project. Fort Calhoun would be his responsibility for the next three years. Its great challenge mirrored Fort Pulaski's: building a massive construction atop a treacherous foundation. Unimpeded by a difficult boss, Lee went happily to work. Nothing, including freezing, inclement weather, supply shortages, and even a cholera outbreak, dimmed Lee's drive to move construction forward. He also put both his education and growing expertise toward any challenges. When sand seeped through piping and water began accumulating at the base of the structure, Lee used pressurized brick to keep the sand out. His resourcefulness was noticed by both Thayer and Talcott.[53]

There was one delay—a work shortage—that Lee could not correct. He and Mary had been at Hampton Roads just a few weeks when word reached Fortress Monroe that an enslaved preacher, Nat Turner, had led a rebellion of seventy slaves in Southampton County, fifty miles southwest. Turner saw a solar eclipse in February as a sign of retribution coming; a second eclipse in August signified the time had come. His permitted travels to preach at other plantations allowed him to spread his gospel. For two days, Turner and his enslaved followers, armed with the tools their masters had given them for their daily tasks—hammers, shovels, pitchforks, and the occasional axe—killed dozens of white men, women, and children before local militias caught up with them. Those rebels who were not killed outright were either hanged or sold to plantations out of state.[54]

Immediately, the garrison at Fort Monroe was put on alert, but the insurrection was crushed before their assistance was required. Lee tried to alleviate the worries of his friends and family, particularly Mrs. Custis. As the "profoundly concerned" husband of her daughter, he informed his mother-in-law of those enslaved Blacks "defending their masters" as opposed to Turner's rebels. Lee's opinion of slavery did not differ much from that of his father-in-law. Speaking at an American Colonization Society meeting, Custis advocated "the removal of free persons of colour," as that "interferes, in no way whatever, with the rights of property."[55]

In December 1831, Lee was granted a few weeks' leave for the Christmas season and took Mary back to Arlington. She had already made it clear to him that life at Fort Monroe was no life at all. For starters, there was no chaplain, and the officers' parties were boring, their wives equally so. She found their social events "rather stupid," confessing to her mother that her ennui "is my fault." After all, "there are not many persons here very interesting." When it came time to leave Arlington after the New Year, Lee returned alone.[56]

In June, Mary returned to Fort Monroe with four enslaved persons, her mother, and another boarder on the way: Mary was pregnant. She gave birth to a son, George Washington Custis Lee, on September 16. "I have an heir," Lee rejoiced to Carter, "large fat & hearty." Mary was not as happy. Lee hoped to be the father that he never had but was soon a father in absentia. Once they were well enough to travel, Mary, little Custis, Mrs. Custis, and the four enslaved attendants departed for Arlington, returning Lee to an imposed bachelorhood.[57]

It was the start of a pattern in the Lees' marriage Mary readily accepted. Both she and her mother sought to convince both their husbands that it would benefit Robert to "withdraw . . . from his present profession and yield to him the management of affairs" at Arlington, but neither husband would have it. Lax as Custis was in his stewardship of Arlington, he was not about to turn it over to Light Horse Harry's son—not yet. Calling Custis "the Major"—his honorary title in the Virginia Militia—Lee acerbically commented to his brother Carter how Custis "is busy farming. His corn field is not yet enclosed or ploughed." The letter was written in May. Lee judged Custis as Light Horse Harry, minus his father's military accomplishments and courage.[58]

Mary would forever prefer being at Arlington, with or without her husband. Doctors discovered Mary suffered from "Rheumatoid diathesis," which they treated with everything from long bed rest and heat to bleeding her with leeches. In fourteen years she would give birth to seven children, each pregnancy more difficult than the last. By the 1850s, her susceptibility to any illness and her worsening arthritis would relegate her to an invalid's existence. Mary would accompany Robert, with children and enslaved assistants in tow, on several of his assignments, but Arlington was always a captivating siren calling her home.[59]

Lee viewed—and would always view—this balancing act of marriage and duty with mixed emotions. On a surveying mission to Michigan in 1835, he received a letter from Mary. Their first daughter had just been born, and Mary's recovery was so slow that she insisted Robert obtain leave and head home. Most of Lee's letters to her began with "My Dear Mary" or "Molly." Not this one. "Why do you urge my *immediate* return, & tempt one in the strongest manner, to endeavour to get excused from the performance of a duty, imposed on me by my Profession, for the pure gratification of my private feelings?" It was not so much a question as a rebuke.[60]

Lee remained optimistic that Mary's trips to the mineral springs of western Virginia would be "endeavoring to strengthen the body" but became convinced that "her nervous system is much shattered. She has an almost horror of crowded places, an indisposition to make the least effort, and yet a restless anxiety which renders her unhappy and dissatisfied." That said, he found it much easier to enjoy army social life without Mary than with her. Once, when Mary and her mother left for another extended stay in Arlington, Lee confided to Talcott, "I am as happy as a clam in high water."[61]

He also honed his talents as a flirt. There is no record anywhere that Lee was ever unfaithful to Mary, but he was unquestionably fond of female company. From his earlier letters to Mary from Cockspur, Lee regaled both wife and friends with his platonic dalliances. Among these friendships was Talcott's wife, Harriet, whom he called *our beautiful Talcott*," particularly to her husband. He freely admitted to Jack MacKay that his austere bearing weakened at the sight of beautiful women. "The Daughters of Eve," he wrote, "are formed in the very poetry of nature," and he "open[ed] to them, like the flower to the sun."[62]

As at Cockspur, Lee's efforts building Fort Calhoun broke down. By 1834, constant infighting between the engineers stationed at Fort Monroe and the artillery officers climaxed when the War Department dismissed all the engineers at Old Point save Lee. He was soon rescued by the head of engineers, General Charles Gratiot, who saw promise in Lee and made him his assistant. Hoping to find a home for his family in Washington, Lee could only find a room in Mrs. Ulrich's boardinghouse. Lee would be commuting from Arlington, much to Mary's delight if not his.[63]

The St. Louis–born Gratiot was one of the first cadets at West Point. Lee looked forward to being in the nation's capital and the hub of activity, and Gratiot soon put him in charge during Gratiot's inspection travels. But Lee found reports, budgets, and correspondence beyond tedious. While he was an ardent advocate for the engineering corps— and the corps budget—to senators and congressmen, he was an engineer, not a clerk or politician. He told Gratiot that "the duties of the office . . . had no charms for me" and requested a field assignment.[64]

Lee got what he asked for. Talcott had been ordered to lead an expedition to conduct a survey of the Ohio-Michigan border, a bone of such fierce contention that both states' governors had thought nothing of sending out their militias to harass prior surveyors lest they rule the wrong way. For five months the two officers and friends put up with "the badness of the Roads & the darkness of the night" until returning to Virginia in October. Back in Arlington, Mary fell ill again. Her recovery took months; meanwhile, he returned to his desk job in Washington. By springtime, Mary had the mumps but was improving.[65]

By June 1836, Mary's chronic health issues were not the only difficulty Lee faced. Grateful as he was to Gratiot, he abhorred his assignment. Talcott's decision to leave the army added to his frustrations. After congratulating his friend on his decision, Lee shared his frustrations with Talcott: "I am looking and hoping," Lee confided, "for some good opportunity to bid an affectionate farewell to my dear Uncle Sam."[66]

Again Gratiot provided an opportunity. The city of St. Louis was rising in importance, while the Mississippi River was falling along the town's riverbanks, threatening its commercial survival. Congress allocated funds for the mammoth task of correcting the course of the country's primary business route out west, and Gratiot believed his thirty-year-old assistant was the engineer for the job. It meant an indefinite absence from his Mary and his three children (their third, William Henry Fitzhugh, called "Rooney," was born May 31).[67]

Lee accepted. While he was sincerely sorry to leave his family, he certainly would not miss Washington—or Arlington, for that matter. Once more, he shared his true feelings with Talcott in a tongue-in-cheek missive that Mary certainly did not read prior to posting. "I shall leave my family in care of my *eldest son*"—the five-year-old Custis—"who will take them over the mountains somewhere this summer," adding that Custis's grandmother would be the official escort to the mineral springs. Lee left his brood and in-laws in June. "They wanted a skillful engineer," Lee wrote lightheartedly to Jack MacKay, "and sent me."[68]

"The first time I ever saw St. Louis, I could have bought it for six million dollars, and it was the mistake of my life that I did not do it," Mark Twain whimsically commented in 1883. His professional recollection of the Mississippi from his decades-earlier river pilot days is worth noting, regarding

one of the Mississippi's oddest peculiarities,—that of shortening its length
from time to time. If you will throw a long, pliant apple-paring over your
shoulder, it will pretty fairly shape itself into an average section of the
Mississippi River; that is, the nine or ten hundred miles stretching from
Cairo, Illinois, southward to New Orleans, the same being wonderfully
crooked, with a brief straight bit here and there at wide intervals. The two-
hundred-mile stretch from Cairo northward to St. Louis is by no means so
crooked, that being a rocky country which the river cannot cut much.[69]

Twain's comments about the Mississippi are more picturesque than
the engineering and survey reports Lee read about his forthcoming assignment. The burgeoning city of St. Louis sat below the confluence of
the Missouri and Mississippi Rivers, with the latter its city limit to the
east. There, two islands—actually large sandbars—were the immediate
problem. The island upstream, called Bloody Island (being a haven for
dueling), sat almost dead center in the Mississippi, its current overrun-
ning it, sending silt, sand, and debris south to Duncan's Island, which
engorged itself on the deposits. Topographically speaking, the St. Louis
riverfront was being marooned.[70]

Robert Fulton's creation of the steamboat was never better received
than on the Mississippi. For twenty-five years, merchants, farmers,
trappers, and travelers took advantage of the new craft. With the combination of British engine design and Nicholas Roosevelt's paddle
wheel, the steamboat's superlative storing space for goods and food-
stuffs far surpassed those of flatboats, keelboats, and barges. As their
design improved, they became floating hotels, with unheard-of creature
comforts for their passengers. Over two hundred steamboats plied the
"Father of Waters" by 1837, but with nature taking the river away from
St. Louis, the city's hope of being the dominant port on the Mississippi
was imperiled.[71]

In accepting his assignment, Lee was replacing a Missouri hero,
Henry Miller Shreve, a legendary steamboat pioneer and captain. He
was the first to skipper a steamboat from Pittsburgh to New Orleans,
carrying munitions for General Andrew Jackson's defense of New

Orleans against the British. While not a trained engineer, Shreve had correctly determined that St. Louis's island woes were not the source of the problem. That lay 170 miles north: the Des Moines Rapids and, farther upstream, the Rock River Rapids, not far from Moline, Illinois.[72]

Lee's assistant was Montgomery C. Meigs, fresh from West Point, the ink on his brevet second lieutenant's commission barely dry. He thought Lee "a man of kind and amiable character," with dark, deep-set eyes; a full beard would cloak his pleasant grin later in life. Meigs saw how Lee's "noble and commanding presence" was "admired by all women and respected by all men." He would be Meigs's role model until 1861.[73]

The two men set out on a circuitous route, from Washington to Philadelphia, to purchase surveying equipment, and from there to Pittsburgh and passage by steamboat to Louisville, where they met with Shreve, who helped Lee obtain three barges and the *Pearl*, a small steamboat Shreve had just constructed. He also assisted Lee in finding rivermen tough enough for the task that lay ahead. Lee and Meigs went on, accompanying two ladies downriver to Jefferson Barracks in Lemay, taking pains to assure Mary they were "of *proper* behavior."

Lee found his lodgings in St. Louis—from the overcrowded dinner table to the "dark, *dirty* room" he and Meigs shared—"intolerable." For Lee, the accommodations reflected St. Louis in general, calling the frontier city the "dirtiest place I was ever in." Nor had he experienced such heat and humidity, even in Georgia. "It is *astonishingly* hot here, Thermometer 97° in the House," he informed Mary. There was a drought; Lee described the Missouri dust as an "impalpable powder" permeating everything and "ankle deep" in the streets. It was two weeks before his watercraft arrived—a portent of things to come (or not come) for Lieutenant Lee's first leadership assignment. He immediately had them refitted; he wanted to see the rapids before the river dropped below a navigable level.[74]

Once aboard, with his small fleet heading upriver, Lee's optimism returned. When he first arrived, he had found "the Scenery of the Mississippi" to be "monotonous and uninteresting." Now, on his northward passage, he waxed eloquent. "This is a beautiful country, and must one day be a great one," he wrote Jack MacKay. Once at the rapids, "I dug down 3½ feet into the Soil," he informed Carter. "You could cultivate [it] with your feet." He grew fonder of those he encountered, particularly the "wimming," as the Midwesterners pronounced "women." For Lee, they "alone show the only true heroism that is here exhibited."[75]

Time was of the essence: the river was less than two feet above its usual lowest level. Lee and his crew saw the Des Moines Rapids first. These ran for eleven miles, mostly a consistent set of rock ledges with negligible interruption. To the north, Lee and company saw that the Rock River Rapids ran four miles longer and posed a greater problem. They ran in a series of barriers called "chains" separated by stretches of calm waters and pools before the next set roiled the river. The descent of the Mississippi through both sets was over twenty-two feet.

St. Louis's mayor, John Fletcher Darby, took an immediate liking to Lee. Ten years after Lee's death, Darby described Lee as Americans have known him for generations:

> He worked most indefatigably, in that quiet unobtrusive manner and with the modesty characteristic of the man. He went in person with the hands every morning about sunrise, and worked day by day in the hot, broiling sun . . . He shared the hard task and common fare and rations furnished to the common laborers . . . but never on any occasion becoming too familiar with the men . . . winning and commanding the esteem, regard, and respect of every one under him. He also slept in the cabin of the steamboat, moored to the banks near their works.[76]

Foul weather and the channel's intricate windings thwarted a thorough survey of the challenging torrents, but Lee found his task a fulfilling one. Once his surveys were completed, he returned to St. Louis to tackle Duncan's and Bloody Islands. After comparing Shreve's suggestions with his own surveys of the islands, Lee made his report to Gratiot and Congress.[77]

His plan was deceptively simple: to use what nature provided to solve the problem wherever possible. Instead of setting up dams and dikes to block the current, he proposed placing them along the flow line, thereby redirecting the current without blocking it. That way, the Mississippi's flow would remove the sandbars and silt from Duncan's Island and, eventually, the island itself.

Lee was even more practical regarding the rapids. Shreve believed that over 1 million cubic yards of rock and boulder clay deposits needed to be blasted to create a man-made channel. Instead, Lee proposed blasting less than 100,000 yards of rock in the existing channel and reshaping the abrupt turns through the Rock River Rapids, placing buoys to allow a safer passage. With winter setting in, Lee and Meigs returned east in time for Christmas.[78]

Lee returned to St. Louis in May 1838 without Meigs but with his growing family and one enslaved girl named Kitty. The trip was interrupted by a spate of illnesses among the children and steamboat delays down the Ohio. Mary's homesickness for Arlington was further exacerbated when they learned that the house Lee believed he had rented was occupied and the steamboat carrying recently acquired furniture had blown up. The Lees were rescued by Governor William Clark (of Lewis and Clark), who put them up in his downtown home. It was not long before Mary complained that young Custis failed "to sit down to his lessons," while Rooney was "an unsettled brat." Mary would be exiled in St. Louis for over a year.[79]

Earlier, Lee had sent his detailed estimate of the costs for his Mississippi projects: $502,841. Congress, reeling from the Panic of '37, gave him $50,000. With Meigs unavailable, Lee's assistant was Lieutenant Horace Bliss. As if lack of proper funds were not obstacle enough, the weather wreaked havoc on Lee's schedule. He spent less than three weeks blasting the Des Moines Rapids and no time at all at Rock River Rapids. He also redrew his proposed dam at Bloody Island, succeeding in completing that, at least. But these were small successes compared to the grandeur of his original plans; even Gratiot's promoting Lee to captain did little to improve his mood.[80]

To make matters worse, the Mississippi froze over surprisingly early. Mary was pregnant again, making an overland journey impossible. The family's first Christmas away from Arlington was interrupted by unforeseen tidings for Lee: Gratiot had been found guilty of fraud. "News of his *death*," Lee confided to Talcott, "would have been less painful to bear." Completing his assignment seemed doomed. When an impoverished Congress gutted his next expenditure to $20,000, Lee informed Bliss, "We shall be obliged to hang up our fiddle." Once the Mississippi thawed, he took his family back to Arlington.[81]

And yet he still looked for a way to finish his undertaking. When orders arrived to return to St. Louis, Lee immediately obeyed, days before his new daughter, Annie, was born. Upon his arrival he discovered that his Bloody Island dam had worked until it was perforated by ice floes. The shortage of funds allowed Lee to repair what had been broken but do little else. The current mayor, Dr. William Carr Lane, offered tepid support, but John Fletcher Darby helped Lee raise funds from prominent citizens. Their support helped Mayor Lane approve $15,000 to augment Lee's federal allotment.[82]

Buoyed by Darby's victory, Lee wasted no time heading to the Des Moines Rapids, where his crew blasted and removed 2,000 tons of stone, creating a four-mile channel that proved his solution correct. Meanwhile, his repaired dam downriver was making Duncan's Island disappear. "There is now 15 feet of water where it was formerly dry," Lee reported. Despite weather, politicians, and lack of money, Lee's plans were succeeding.

In fact, Lee had done his job *too* well, as far as a coterie of Illinois speculators was concerned. Having scooped up land on their side of the Mississippi and hoping the pre-Lee river's conditions would make them rich, they obtained an injunction from an Illinois judge ordering Lee to cease work immediately. After some perfunctory work on the rapids, and making his official report and inventory, Lee began the long trek back to Virginia.[83]

He anticipated a joyful family reunion when he arrived at Arlington at the end of 1839, but he found it mixed with sad news from relations elsewhere. He was barely unpacked when a letter from his sister Anne arrived, informing him that her little son Robert, named for Lee, had been "run over by a loaded dray and had his head entirely *crushed* by the wheel." Anne never recovered from the loss. Another letter arrived, written by his half brother Harry's widow, Anne McCarty Lee, now destitute and begging for financial rescue. Lee, barely making his own ends meet, could only offer her $180. She died in Paris in the summer of 1840.[84]

With no further funding from Congress available, Lee went back to St. Louis to close shop. Boats, equipment, and Lee's furniture were all sold. Frustrated at not completing his assignment after three years of battling the forces of nature, Gratiot's fall from grace, and the prolonged absences from his family, Lee took solace in what he had accomplished with a shoestring budget and little manpower. Years later, Darby wrote that by his "rich gift of genius and scientific knowledge Lieut. Lee brought the Father of Waters under control," making "a deep and secure harbor . . . for the people of this city."[85]

Historians have long noted that Lincoln's two passages down the Mississippi changed him. Lee, on the other hand, changed the Mississippi.[86]

Lee had met Gratiot's successor, General Joseph Gilbert Totten, while on leave from St. Louis. The Connecticut-born chief engineer had entered West Point's first class at the ripe old age of fourteen. He viewed engineering as a science, forever researching and looking to improve ordnance as well as everything from a fort's casemates to its ramparts. Now in his fifties, Totten's blond hair had grayed; a photograph of him reveals a broad face, large nose, and a professorial expression befitting a man whose idea of relaxation was serving as a regent at the Smithsonian Institute and the American Philosophical Society and as harbor commissioner of New York.[87]

Totten and Lee took an immediate liking to each other. He had already offered Lee an instructor's position at West Point that Lee quickly dismissed, "the *art*" of teaching being something "I have never found that I possessed." Totten made Lee chief engineer at Fort Hamilton in Brooklyn at the Narrows, the strait between Brooklyn and Staten Island that connects the Upper and Lower New York Bay. Work on the fort and three nearby sites—Fort Lafayette, Battery Hudson, and Battery Morton—would be Lee's principal assignment until 1846.[88]

Once again, he was heading to his post alone. Another child, Eleanor Agnes, was born that winter. He arrived at the fort in April 1841. His task, while a major renovation project, seemed light compared to changing the course of the Mississippi, but still daunting: rebuilding walls and casemates and increasing the fort's firepower. The garrison consisted of one artillery unit and a white cow belonging to the garrison. Lee looked for accommodations large enough for his family and at least two enslaved servants, finding an affordable but rat-infested house and stable that also required repairs and a coat of whitewash. After buying a bedstead, chairs, a pitcher, and a basin, he summoned Mary and the children, filling his letter with niceties about New York. "The Sea breezes are very cool and refreshing," he wrote, "& the view is extensive . . . You can get everything you desire in New York."[89]

Mary, still weakened from childbirth and her chronic health issues, spent most of the summer indoors. Lee had purchased a carriage for rides to the fort or along the Brooklyn waterfront. To his relief, the children loved New York. Crossing from Fort Hamilton to Staten Island, Lee rescued a dog from drowning and brought her home, to his children's delight. He named her "Dart." Lee found his work time consuming and boring, but delighted in his children's company, as his son, Robert Jr., later attested:

> He was always bright and gay with us little folk, romping, playing, and joking with us . . . I have seen him join my elder brothers and their friends when they would try their powers at a high jump put up in our yard. Our greatest treat was to get into his bed in the morning and lie close to him, listening while he talked to us in his bright, entertaining way . . . Although he was so joyous and familiar with us, he was very firm on all proper occasions . . . I always knew that it was impossible to disobey my father.[90]

Not so, young Robert confessed, with Mary: "My mother I could sometimes circumvent, and at times took liberties with her orders . . ."

His father had feared this even to the point of asking his mother-in-law to warn Mary of her laxity, asking Mrs. Custis "to *make* her do what is right." But Mary Lee's permissiveness seemed intermingled with her infirmities: when Annie accidentally poked her eye with a pair of scissors, and when Rooney lost the tips of two fingers playing with a straw cutter in the stable, it was the father, not the mother, who sat up nights with them.[91]

In February 1846, the last of the Lee children, Mildred, was born. By this time Lee had all but finished his work at the Narrows, having built (and after a hurricane rebuilt) walls, casements, and quarters. He also endured assignments in Washington, assisting Totten with clerical duties despite his "horror at the sight of pen, ink, and paper," and more seriously considered resigning his commission. The army had lost its allure for Captain Lee.[92]

Then came Mexico.

THREE

SON OF THE NORTH

In 1831, two years after Robert E. Lee graduated from the United States Military Academy, fifteen-year-old George Gordon Meade came to West Point. Having failed in his first attempt to enter the academy, he was accepted as a cadet for the class of 1835.[1]

But where Lee sought a military career, Meade was there by circumstance, not choice. There was no tuition at the academy, which was exactly what his widowed mother could afford. Payment for West Point consisted of four years of education and training, followed by a minimum of one full year of military service. Nor was George born in the United States. His birth took place in Cádiz, Spain, on New Year's Eve, 1815, in the midst of a military, geopolitical, and family maelstrom.[2]

He was the son of Richard Worsam Meade, a brilliant businessman with a well-deserved reputation for getting his way. His relentless drive was understandable. Richard's grandfather, Robert, had emigrated from Ireland and established a mercantile firm in Philadelphia. Richard's father, George, took the firm to new heights of success in the pre-Revolution years. The firm survived the tumultuous years of the American Revolution, but by 1801 George Meade was bankrupt, another victim of the land speculation craze of the post-Revolutionary years that punished more often than rewarded the pursuit of western lands.[3]

Not so his son Richard, who bypassed land grabs for the tried-and-true mercantile path to wealth since colonial days. Well educated, he began his career as a supercargo for his father's merchantmen on their voyages to the Caribbean, where his accounting talents were welded to an innate and astute business sense. In 1796 he sailed to Santo Domingo to make his own fortune amid the Haitian Revolution. Four years later he returned to Philadelphia. He was just twenty-two, and already rich.

Richard purchased a handsome brick house on stylish High Street (now Market) and married Margaret Coates Butler, daughter of a New Jersey merchant. The artist Gilbert Stuart captured her winning countenance: brown hair and eyes, with a calm but somewhat sad expression above a firm jawline, looking as if she awaited bad news. The surviving portrait of Richard, seated at a desk whose drawer handles are carved lions' heads, shows a tall, impeccably dressed, short-haired man turning toward the painter; his expression a tug-of-war between serenity and unbridled ambition.[4]

As he climbed the social ladder, Richard Meade ran roughshod over everyone during a business deal, regardless of their title or standing. In 1803 he sailed to Spain and established a trading house in Cádiz, the bustling southwestern port in Andalusia. Two years later, he sent for Margaret and their two little daughters. Over the next eighteen years, eight more children would be added to the family.[5]

Despite a British naval blockade during the Napoleonic Wars, Cádiz remained a vital hub of the merchant trade between Spain and her Western Hemisphere colonies. Richard soon became the agent for the U.S. Navy, adding to his influence with both the Spanish government and President Thomas Jefferson's back home. The Meades hosted lavish dinners at their ostentatious hacienda, where Richard amassed a stunning collection of artwork, including paintings by Titian, Rubens, Van Dyck, and Goya. Praise and envy by American visitors over Meade's massive library reached Jefferson, himself renowned for his vast collection of books.[6]

But his library was not the only thing Jefferson was hearing about Richard Meade. When his campaign to replace Joseph Yznardi as U.S. consul failed, Meade accused Yznardi of misconduct in office. Fed up with Meade's "lying, malicious, and impudent conduct," Jefferson retained Yznardi. It was the beginning of Meade's fall from grace.[7]

In 1810, Meade sent Margaret and their six children back to Philadelphia just before a French army besieged Cádiz. Meade's support of Spain's resistance was invaluable, his fleet of merchantmen providing 250,000 barrels of flour that kept Cádiz's citizens and garrison from starving. The siege was lifted after the Duke of Wellington's victory at Salamanca in July 1812. For his contributions to Spain's defense, Meade was offered and gracefully declined full citizenship. The reestablished Cortes of Cádiz, a liberal government with probusiness leanings, supported Meade and other merchants. Margaret returned to Cádiz with their six children. By 1814, two more had arrived.

Postwar Spain proved anything but stable. Factional unrest permeated the country, while in Latin America wars for independence spread throughout the Spanish colonies. Meade was aware of the political and civil upheaval swirling around him, but the Spanish owed him the bulk of his fortune, having loaned the government hundreds of thousands of dollars to support Cádiz and resistance to the French siege. Meade's investigation into the matter convinced him that Spain's treasurer general, Don Victor Soret, was making personal use of the funds Meade had lent to the government. He publicly accused Soret of misprision of Meade's huge loan. In the dead of night, Soret sent a detachment of guards to Meade's house and threw the American in jail for three months.[8]

When the Supreme Council of War deigned to release Richard, it also found him guilty of libel, fining him 2,000 ducats. Meade paid the fine, continued to seek restitution, and returned to his business dealings. Family matters gave Richard and Margaret some respite in early January 1816 when a coterie of Americans and Spaniards, dressed in their best finery, crowded the altar of Nuestra Señora del Rosario in Cádiz to witness the christening of the ninth Meade child. Richard's financial and political escapades had not dimmed the luster of his prominence, nor compelled Cádiz society to decline a Meade invitation.[9]

But Meade's days of influence were numbered. The Cortes had lost power, and a dispute over finances with the British minister, Henry

Wellesley, 1st Baron Cowley, did not go well. "These people," Meade bitterly complained to his partner, James Leander Cathcart, "are as obstinate as they are ignorant." In May 1816, Meade was once again seized in his home and brought to the Castillo de Santa Catalina, an old, crumbling fortress then used as a prison. This time Meade was confined in a dungeon for eighteen months. In 1817, Margaret and the children returned to Philadelphia.[10]

With no one of influence helping him in Spain, Meade looked homeward, appealing to his contacts in the federal government for help. One acquaintance, Congressman John Sergeant of Philadelphia, took up Meade's cause, and soon others followed; even Abigail Adams intervened. When a letter from Margaret arrived at the White House, President James Monroe had his secretary of state, John Quincy Adams, demand Meade's release. It was ignored.[11]

The deus ex machina that set Meade's release in motion stemmed from Monroe's and Adams's efforts to purchase Florida from Spain while support for Meade's release grew in Congress. Led by Speaker of the House Henry Clay (whose flock of Merino sheep had arrived in a Meade ship), Congress passed a resolution calling Meade's imprisonment "cruel and unjustifiable" and urging Monroe "to afford Mr. Meade" the government's "aid and protection." He was released in June 1818.[12]

Richard did not immediately book passage home to see his family. Instead, he went to Madrid, as doggedly determined as ever to win back the fortune he had lent the Spanish. He won a settlement for his loans during the Peninsular War, expenses as an agent for other claimants, and a settlement for his wrongful imprisonment. The settlement totaled $491,153.62. In Washington, Margaret presented a detailed record of her husband's claim, certain that Congress would finally pay Meade his due.[13]

Now came the American government's turn in denying Meade. As part of the Adams-Onís Treaty to acquire Florida, the United States assumed the Spanish government's debts from American claims, including Meade's. It allocated $5 million for all claims. Meade's claim came to 9.8 percent of the allocated funds. Instead, Congress called

Margaret's letter "somewhat argumentative" and sought any ploy to prevent Richard Meade from collecting anything. How, each official wondered, could they give one man nearly 10 percent of the total budget for claims, depriving so many other "less fortunate" citizens with claims totaling much less? Well into the 1820s, Congress and the Monroe administration picked apart both Richard's financial claim and the veracity behind it.[14]

Upon arriving from Spain, Meade went from office to office, congressman to senator, cabinet member to president. Any veneer of politeness or courtesy soon evaporated. Adams accused him of "malice and treachery," lost any interest in getting Meade so much as a pittance, and made his opinion known to Congress. The Court of Claims viewed Meade's claim as "a mixed character" of bills, losses, depreciation, and interest. Meade's huge sum, the Court of Claims determined, "is *not* the debt" the United States "had agreed to assume."[15]

Meade did not concede defeat. He appealed to Clay, Daniel Webster, and other renowned lawyers in Congress as much for their legal expertise as their political support, delivering a petition signed by over a thousand citizens supporting his financial crusade. Meade's appeals ended when Adams assumed the presidency in 1825. Descendants would appeal to each Congress for the next thirty years, to no avail. Only in his forties, the strain of his financial miseries and years in prison began taking a toll on his health.[16]

In between battles with his government and efforts to reestablish himself as a businessman to be reckoned with, Meade found little time to spend with his brood of children. (One, named Catherine, died in infancy.) His oldest daughter, Henrietta, married U.S. Navy captain Alexander James Dallas, son of James Madison's treasury secretary. Meade's oldest son, Richard, entered the Naval Academy. Meade's second son, George, was attending a well-regarded Philadelphia elementary school during the years his father was battling Congress.[17]

George's fellow pupils came from Philadelphia's upper class. He preferred school to a home dominated by his mother and six sisters, with a brother far too old to be much of a playmate. Years after his death, George's son described him as "an amiable boy, full of life, but rather disposed to avoid the rough-and-tumble frolics of youths of his age; quick at his lessons, and popular with both teachers and scholars." In 1826, when Richard moved the family to a modest home in George-town, near Washington, D.C., to continue pursuing his claims, George was sent to the American Classical and Military Lyceum, a boarding school in Mount Airy near Philadelphia.[18]

The lyceum was a multistoried, broad expanse of a building, dwarfed on one side by a copse of tall weeping willows. One of its founders, Augustus L. Roumfort, an early graduate of West Point, viewed the ly-ceum as a preparatory school for the academy, teaching his boys En-glish, French, Latin, Greek, arithmetic, and algebra. His board of directors included Revolutionary War general Thomas Cadwalader, Congressman Charles Jared Ingersoll, financier Nicholas Biddle, and Richard Worsam Meade. Years after Meade's death, his son, George Jr., described his father's reminiscences of daily life at the lyceum:

> The boys [were] instructed in the manual of arms and company drill, and at certain times they performed sentry duty. An "officer of the day" was regularly appointed, whose duty it was to report any breach of discipline, and the report was read aloud after breakfast to the assembled cadets. It was sought to instill a high sense of honor into the performance of their duties.[19]

Young George excelled at mathematics and was popular with teach-ers and schoolmates alike, several of whom became lifelong friends. Richard, his accessible funds diminishing as quickly as his health, in-formed Margaret that George's "mathematical head fitted" the boy for West Point. He was twelve years old in June 1828 when his mother summoned him to Georgetown; his father was dying. George did not arrive in time to see him. Richard Worsam Meade died on June 25, two days after his fiftieth birthday. Margaret and her children accompanied Richard's coffin to Philadelphia, where he was buried in the family crypt at St. Mary's Roman Catholic Church.[20]

After the services, George returned to the lyceum to finish the school year. He did not return in the fall. George's education at the lyceum was a luxury Margaret, now a widow, could not afford. Richard had willed his vast art collection and property to her, but she was not about to liquidate anything yet. The estate was valued at nearly $70,000, a pittance compared to his once formidable wealth. As Margaret took up Richard's case against Congress, she put the family on a taut budget.[21]

Margaret enrolled George at a small school in Washington under the tutelage of twenty-year-old Salmon P. Chase, whose own father had died when Chase was a child. Tuition ran between four and twelve dollars. Chase was studying law under William Wirt, James Monroe's attorney general, and he had been a teenage teacher while attending Dartmouth. Despite Chase's shy awkwardness, he proved an insightful teacher. Months later, Chase's acceptance to the bar put an end to his academic career. Margaret then sent George to attend the Mount Hope Institution in Baltimore in December 1829.[22]

The curriculum at Mount Hope was intense, as Meade's son recalled:

During a year he read, in Latin, Caesar's Commentaries and six of the orations of Cicero; in French, Telemaque and Charles XII of Sweden; in mathematics, Colburn's Arithmetic and Algebra, Walker's Geometry, Playfair's Euclid, and trigonometry in Gummies' Surveying; Goodrich's History of the United States, Hart's Geography, and the greater part of Comstock's Chemistry and Natural Philosophy; which was doing well for a lad of fifteen. The principal of the school pronounced him a boy of decided parts, of uncommon quickness of perception and readiness in acquiring knowledge; studious withal, and exceptionally correct in his deportment . . . [H]e left with the respect of the teachers and the affection of his school-mates.[23]

His year at Mount Hope also provided a change of course from his lyceum years. George no longer saw himself bound for the military. Instead, the pursuit of law—and, later, politics—became his ambition.[24]

By 1830, Margaret's older children were settled. Richard was embarking on a naval career and Charlotte had married U.S. Army captain James Duncan Graham, West Point '17, already a successful topographical engineer. Elizabeth Meade had married Alfred Ingraham, a Philadelphia banker. Then, in 1829, Maria del Carmen Meade, just eighteen, married Hartman Bache, great-grandson of Benjamin Franklin and another West Point alumnus (class of '18) with engineering talents. This left Margaret with five children at home ranging in age from eight to twenty-two years old. George, now the third youngest but the oldest boy at home, became Margaret's next mission in whittling down the number at the dinner table.[25]

Neither meanness nor finances led Margaret to move so quickly to get George out of the house; rather, it was to guarantee the best education she could get for him. With his older brother Richard in the navy, Margaret turned to the army. Her late husband had already envisioned that as George's destination, but she needed only to look at the successes of her sons-in-law, as well as her son's aptitude and ambition. Besides, a West Point education was free, paid for by service in the army for one year after graduation. A boy with George's academic achievements could have been an engineer as readily as a barrister.[26]

George was two months past his fourteenth birthday when Margaret sat down at her desk in Georgetown and wrote to John Eaton, Andrew Jackson's secretary of war. "I offer my son, George Meade, as a candidate for the appointment of Cadet in the Military Academy," she opened. After a brief biographical sketch, she added that "his character and qualifications will appear with the enclosed certificate of his Teachers at Germantown."[27]

George was not chosen for the next class, but Margaret was not done with Eaton or West Point. George remained at Mount Hope through 1830, and Margaret again wrote Eaton, adding a letter from Frederick Hall, Mount Hope's founder and headmaster, praising George's "uncommon quickness of perception" and a "general deportment of high commendation"—perfect language to describe a future officer and gentleman. The second attempt was successful. Jackson, whose actions in

Florida had indirectly doomed Richard Meade's recovery of his fortune, now signed his son George's appointment.[28]

Preparations to get George ready for the academy that summer were interrupted by sad news. His oldest sister, Henrietta Dallas, just twenty-nine, died in Pensacola, Florida, in July. The stoic Margaret found getting George packed and sent off to West Point kept her mind occupied.

The boy who wanted to study law would study war, and at the best engineering school in the Western Hemisphere. Years later, during the Mexican-American War, Margaret confessed to George that "I was cruel enough to send you to West Point, an act for which I shall never forgive myself, and never cease to regret." But in 1831 her choice was simple.[29]

West Point had not changed very much structurally in the two years between Robert E. Lee's graduation and George Meade's arrival, but there had been a seismic shift academically. That new force was named Dennis Hart Mahan.

Appropriately, Mahan first arrived at the academy on July 4, 1820, an eighteen-year-old son of Irish immigrants. As a boy, he was constantly drawing, and when he learned that drawing was taught at West Point, he applied for an appointment. Young Mahan became one of the academy's true success stories: "drawing" led to mathematics, and mathematics led to engineering. He proved so gifted in the field that Superintendent Sylvanus Thayer appointed him an instructor in his third year as a cadet. Mahan graduated first in his class in 1824 and remained on the faculty until 1826, when he was granted a leave of absence to study engineering in Europe, including attendance at France's School of Artillery and Engineering at Metz. He returned to West Point in 1830 as a professor of engineering.[30]

No one took to Thayer's synthesis of blackboard and brain more than Mahan, whose chronic nasal issues made him sound as if he were suffering from an eternal cold, pronouncing the two m's in "common" as b's, giving him the nickname among cadets of "Old Cobbon Sense."

A photograph of Mahan in middle age shows a Cassius-like "lean and hungry" head and frame, but nothing "dangerous" about his determined expression.[31]

The efforts of Thayer, Mahan, and other similarly minded officers at West Point not only succeeded in changing the curriculum but also in instilling an esprit de corps interwoven with the cadets' studies. One cadet marveled at how they

> *come together with all the sectional prejudices, habits, and knowledge . . .*
> *Their former habits, manners, and prejudices soon become extinct. They*
> *form a new character, a national character, which is no where else formed*
> *in the country . . . They separate and are scattered to every part of the*
> *country; but their feelings are not separated, and their interests are not*
> *divided, and generally never will be.*[32]

Such was the bond at West Point when George arrived.

The fifteen-year-old Meade, fifth youngest in a class numbering ninety-four, found life at West Point exacting and not entirely to his taste. He made friends easily, including fellow Philadelphian John C. Pemberton. Classmate Herman Haupt described Meade as "dignified, courteous and gentlemanly but rather reserved." While "naturally studious," he exhibited a rebellious streak, particularly regarding conduct. Robert E. Lee's perfect score of zero demerits was safe from Cadet Meade. Neatness and perfect conduct were not his innate characteristics; Meade's jacket was frequently unbuttoned, and his accumulation of 168 demerits would have been unthinkable to a cadet like Lee.

But West Point's habit of weeding out the less interested, capable, or desirable cadets did not include him. Throughout his four years he showed flashes of talent and accomplishment. While his record in conduct, infantry and artillery tactics, and drawing was undistinguished, he scored highly in French, natural and elemental philosophy, and rhetoric and moral philosophy. George's successes in language and reasoning show that his aspirations for the law were well-founded.[33]

West Point did not train lawyers, so George did make the most out of his lot. His proficiency in mathematics had him ranked in the upper third of his class, and with his brothers-in-law as examples, he applied himself diligently to Mahan's courses on civil and military engineering. Mahan was a stern taskmaster, combining the principles of engineering with reason and pragmatism. He stressed "active defense," the practice of protecting troops behind strong entrenchments, the futility of frontal assaults, and developing both a sense of tactical knowledge and good instincts. Such an approach, Mahan lectured, would surely lessen casualties while assuring success. George, unlike some other cadets, never forgot it.[34]

The lessons Mahan learned during his years in Europe were conveyed to his students. Having studied the works and principles of European architects Jean-Baptiste Rondolet and Jean-Nicolas-Louis Durand, Mahan approached architecture as a combination of functional soundness and "cobbon sense"; structural soundness, decades before Louis H. Sullivan's "form follows function" became theory, practice, and cliché. Beneath the veneer of Mahan's lectures on sound military engineering lay his goal: generations of American civil engineers for a growing country.[35]

In Cadet Meade, Mahan had a willing acolyte. Somewhere, sometime, at West Point, Meade saw that his future lay in engineering if not in the military. Instead of studying a case, building an argument, and coming to the courtroom prepared to do battle, Meade learned how to survey the topography, efficiently and thoroughly design what required building, and then build it. By the time he returned to the academy after his second-year furlough, he was determined to finish his schooling, serve his required year in the army, and embark on an engineering career.[36]

On July 1, 1835, Meade graduated nineteenth in a class that now numbered fifty-six. Fellow graduates included Haupt and Montgomery Blair, later Abraham Lincoln's postmaster general (Haupt's brilliance in logistics would greatly benefit Meade twenty-eight years later). George was breveted a second lieutenant. His middling standing in class kept him out of the engineering corps; instead, he was assigned to Company C, 3rd Artillery.

Academy graduates were awarded a three-month furlough before starting their assignments, but Meade had another duty in mind: family lore has it that he accepted a three-month assignment with the Long Island Railroad as an assistant surveyor, as much to repay his mother for his officer's uniform as to make any and all contacts that would enhance a civilian career. Railroads were the future, and if Meade's road in life lay in engineering and not law, he might as well start making his way.[37]

The 3rd Artillery had been ordered to Tampa Bay, but family connections allowed Meade to travel to Florida in grand style. His brother-in-law Captain Alexander Dallas had been appointed commodore of the West Indies squadron. Meade was given permission by the War Office to accompany Dallas aboard the USS *Constellation*, one of the original frigates designed by Joshua Humphreys and launched in 1797, still seaworthy enough to serve as Dallas's flagship. They sailed from Hampton Roads, Virginia, on October 8, 1835.[38]

Storms accompanied the *Constellation* on her southbound voyage, but she escaped the more damaging hurricanes that nearly toppled the Ponce de Leon lighthouse at Key Biscayne. Farther south, at Carysfort, the lightship anchored there was severely damaged. Second Lieutenant Meade's main challenge was battling a roiling stomach and getting his "sea legs." In just a week, the *Constellation* anchored at Trinidad, the first in a series of port visits that involved the firing of salutes, diplomatic rituals, and festive dinners—a much more refined trip than the one Meade's regiment was making.[39]

For the next two months, Dallas continued his roundabout cruise of courtesy calls and parties at ports on the islands and the Spanish Main. But upon docking in Havana in January 1836, grisly news returned the Americans aboard *Constellation* to duty in earnest. In December, Major Francis Langhorne Dade had led two companies of soldiers out of Fort Brooke on Tampa Bay to resupply and reinforce the garrison at Fort King (at present-day Ocala). The detachment included classmates of Meade's, Second Lieutenants Richard Henderson and John Low Keais. On December 28, a large war party of Seminoles massacred the soldiers. Only three survived; Henderson and Keais were among the dead.[40]

While his father's wealth had been stripped away by the time George was still a child, family connections assisted him in getting an appointment to West Point. Now, for the past two months, connections were reunited with privilege, and George Meade got a taste of what life had been like for his parents before he was born. The leisurely sail through the Caribbean, the pomp, parties, fine food and drink, were climaxed by congratulations from dignitaries he did not know for embarking on a military career that had not yet begun. It also kept him from arriving at Fort Brooke with his classmates, now dead in the Florida lowlands. The responsibility of wearing a uniform eventually includes bearing the sorrowful weight of loss—and an often accompanying sense of guilt. Those emotions came for Meade that day in Havana.

Dallas made sail for Key West to get more details. Rumors had reached the island that Fort Brooke was under siege by the Seminoles, so Dallas requisitioned what craft and extra hands he could find to carry a battalion of marines up the Gulf of Mexico and get them and Meade to Fort Brooke. Their arrival on January 22 broke the siege. Soon, other boats from New Orleans arrived, bearing militia, food, and arms, and Dallas bid goodbye to his young brother-in-law and returned to Key West.[41]

The fort's log palisades and blockhouse bore little resemblance to the defenses at West Point or Fort McHenry in Baltimore. Built after the Seminole Treaty of 1823, it was more stockade than fort; sitting alongside the Hillsborough River, it would serve as both western port and headquarters in what would become the Second Seminole War. The barracks and other rooms were spacious enough to provide some degree of air circulation as the often oppressive humidity allowed. When Meade's fellow officers had learned the 3rd Artillery was assigned to Florida, they warned him of the potential health hazards for a Northerner unused to the heat of the Deep South, but what could Meade do? Orders were orders. He soon learned how accurate his friends' predictions were.[42]

Meade was reunited with another Philadelphian, Lieutenant Andrew

Atkinson Humphreys. Five years Meade's senior, they had met at West Point; Humphreys found the new second lieutenant "an intelligent, a polished, and witty young officer."[43]

The Seminole uprising soon spread across Florida—including an attack on the Cape Florida lighthouse in Key Biscayne—prompting President Jackson to send his best general, Winfield Scott, to end the growing conflict. Scott's heroism during the War of 1812 was only eclipsed by Jackson's victory at New Orleans. The two nearly fought a duel after the war and maintained a tenuous truce. Scott would turn fifty in 1836; at six feet, four inches, his legendary girth was already thickening his waistline.[44]

Scott anticipated arriving at Fort Drane, his chosen headquarters in northern Florida, in early February. But he was still in Savannah when his preconceived plan reached the fort. Believing that the bulk of Seminole resistance—some 5,000 warriors, women, and children—was in the swamps of "the Cove" of the Withlacoochee River, Scott's plan called for a three-pronged attack. General Abraham Eustis was to attack from Volusia in the east, General Duncan Clinch from Fort Drane, and a third force led by Colonel William Lindsay from Fort Brooke. Meade and the 3rd Artillery would march out with Lindsay.[45]

Scott did not reach Florida until February 22. His force totaled 5,000 army regulars and militia, with Clinch's force ordered to drive the Seminoles out of the swamps and into the waiting hands of Lindsay in the south and Eustis in the east. Each wing would depart on March 8. Scott was confident of swift and sure success.[46]

But the general's grand design failed. The militiamen promised from South Carolina and Georgia had not arrived, nor had rifles, ammunition, tents, and other required supplies. The offensive was postponed to March 25. Seminoles attacked Eustis's forces before they could start their march. Lacking accurate maps, Clinch's and Lindsay's wings slogged through dense woodland and swamps and encountered token resistance; when they reached the Cove, they found the Seminoles had left. Short of supplies and exhausted, all three wings returned to Fort Brooke.[47]

For Lieutenant Meade, this first campaign was equally disappointing, personally if not professionally. Warnings that the skinny Philadelphian would fare poorly in Florida's climate proved correct. Another Northern officer vividly lamented to his wife of the other enemies the soldiers faced:

> We all suffer here in Florida almost eaten up by fleas, ants, cockroaches and almost all manner of vermin. Even the sand is swarming with fleas, and little flies that bite,—and then for our quarters.[48]

At one point during the march, Meade was ordered to take a detachment of soldiers, marines, and at least one cannon to retrace Dade's route to his massacre. When one marine was noticeably suffering from the heat and march, Meade told him to mount the cannon and rest for a while. When the marine's lieutenant ordered him off, Meade countermanded the order and let him resume his perch on the cannon, the first known instance of Meade's standing his ground and protecting a serviceman. Thirty years later, when Meade was commanding the Army of the Potomac, the now ex-marine sent the major general a short letter thanking him for the kindness he had extended years earlier.[49]

Within days, Meade was laid so low by an attack of fever that he was sent back to Fort Brooke with the other sick soldiers. He was beset by recurring attacks of the "shivers and sweats" over the next couple of weeks. Finally, a surgeon declared him unfit for duty, and Colonel Lindsay gave Meade an assignment that got him out of Florida. A sizable party of peaceful Seminoles (men, women, and children) was being deported to the Indian Territory, the mainly unsettled land west of Arkansas (now Oklahoma). With a small band including another ill officer and a surgeon, Meade was to take the Seminoles by schooner from Tampa to New Orleans, where they would then head up the Mississippi River on flatboats. Being unfamiliar with the Seminole language, Meade would have had to rely on an interpreter to translate orders. The entourage departed in mid-April, reaching Little Rock, Arkansas, on June 1.[50]

Little Rock was Meade's first visit to a town of size in the Deep South. Sitting beside the Arkansas River, Little Rock was looking to discover itself as Americans moved into the state or passed through it. Most of Arkansas's enslaved population worked on farmlands or as domestic servants, but a sizable number worked in the town itself, hired out by their owners as artisans, construction workers, or laborers at the brick factory or the iron foundry, at times hiring themselves out. Some African Americans were even "living out," residing full-time away from their owners' domiciles. Meade was witnessing something uncommon in his antebellum years down south: an enslaved community within the white community allowed to enjoy independent recreation, build and run successful churches, even passively possess a semblance of independence in relationships with white residents, unheard-of in the South.[51]

Meade and his detachment reboarded their flatboats and headed upriver to Fort Smith, wending their way between the Ouachita and Boston Mountains. From there they traveled overland to Fort Coffee and Indian Territory, where Meade turned his charges over to Lieutenant Jefferson Van Horne, another U.S. Military Academy graduate and Pennsylvanian. Despite the challenges of the several-hundred-mile trek, Meade made no references to any incidents in his report.[52]

He was back at Fort Brooke by June 28 when he learned that he had been promoted from brevet second lieutenant to second lieutenant. Instead of risking being felled by fevers a second time, Meade was ordered to Washington and later dispatched to the arsenal at Watertown, Massachusetts, in July. The climate there suited him better, but the assignment held no allure whatsoever. He had believed all along that his year of service was payment enough for his engineering skills. Besides, his brother-in-law Major James Duncan Graham had a job for him that did not require that Meade stay in the army. Second Lieutenant Meade resigned his commission on October 28, 1836, two months before his twenty-first birthday, certain that his military career was over.[53]

There were many others like Meade (and unlike Lee) who resigned to find more lucrative work in the private sector. A shavetail lieutenant like Meade could wait a quarter century for his captaincy, all the while supporting himself and his family on a paltry lieutenant's salary. West Point was well-known for the caliber of its engineering program; between 1835 and 1836, more than one hundred officers resigned their commissions, forcing Congress in 1838 to change the requirement of education and service at the academy from five years to eight. Had Meade tarried, his service would have lasted three more years.[54]

The 1830s marked the beginning of advancements in transportation coinciding with westward expansion. Internal improvements such as roadways and canals had been on the agenda of many a president since Washington, but Congress rarely approved them, unsure of how to reconcile interstate construction of roadways and canals with individual states' sovereignty.

The railroads changed all that. Proven engineering skills in surveying, design, and construction became paramount, and academy-trained engineers were a commodity much in demand. As the boom in rail transportation grew, so did the need for engineers. Other schools used West Point textbooks and enlisted West Point graduates into their faculty. By 1850, Brown University president Francis Wayland acknowledged that no other institution had done more "to build up the system of internal improvements in the United States" than West Point.[55]

Major Graham, chief engineer for the Alabama, Florida and Georgia Rail-Road, offered his brother-in-law a position as assistant surveyor. While the job included a $1,000 salary and expenses, there was a catch: Meade would be returning to Florida. The 210-mile track would connect Pensacola with Columbus, Georgia. Completion of the project was anticipated by 1839. Meade accepted.[56]

The mid-1830s saw an economic boom, with both land speculation and commercial development bursting in Florida. The first "train" in the state originated in Tallahassee, its flatcars carrying cotton bales and passengers on wooden benches pulled by mules until the locomotive arrived. Soon the Alabama, Florida and Georgia Rail-Road had a half-million dollars, enough to purchase fifty miles of track and six locomotives. Meade arrived in Pensacola with his work cut out for him.[57]

But his first civilian job lasted months, not two years. The Panic of 1837 saw to that. Like countless others, the Bank of Pensacola closed, and the new railroad closed with it. Meade's second stay in Florida was shorter than his first. Learning of Meade's availability, Captain William Henry Chase of the topographical bureau of the U.S. Army Corps of Engineers offered him work surveying the Texas-Louisiana border and examining the Sabine River's navigability. He found himself in charge of a small crew, making direct reports to President Martin Van Buren's secretary of war, Joel Poinsett. He completed the assignment in six weeks.[58]

His next job was both longer and fortuitous. For years, travel had been occasionally closed on the lower Mississippi by giant sandbars called "mud blockades." New Orleans officials sought solutions from experts on both sides of the Atlantic; even the renowned British geologist Sir Charles Lyell was stymied by the sheer size of the blockage. In 1837, Congress ordered a complete survey of the Mississippi River Delta to find a solution.[59] Meade applied for a position and was appointed principal assistant engineer and given one of the two work brigades.[60]

The physical task of making soundings, measuring, and monitoring the growth of sandbars and assessing what could be done to improve navigability took six months. Afterward the officers traveled to New York City, where they spent the winter of 1838–39 writing and editing their report while drawing accurate maps and charts. Meade's contributions were deemed sound at the time by Talcott, but it was Humphreys, who would revisit the Mississippi Delta twelve years later, who concluded that Meade's "original experiments" led to substantial improvements in the Mississippi's navigation while increasing commerce. Meade's talents as an engineer were confirmed on the Mississippi by supervisor and coworker alike.[61]

In between his assignments, Meade divided his time between Philadelphia and Washington, where his mother still resided. He soon began traveling in the capital's social circles; being "intelligent, well-educated, vivacious," Meade was "naturally welcomed." Whenever absent from home, he kept in touch with Margaret. When in Washington, "he sat at his mother's right hand," one onlooker later recalled, with "an air of tenderness . . . so blended with indescribable deference and courtesy . . . [H]ad she been a queen-mother," the guest added, "her son could not have shown her more princely respect."[62]

Meade's growing confidence in his skills did not guarantee a timely new assignment. Other West Point graduates with engineering backgrounds were getting steady assignments, not because they were better than him but because they were still in the army. Meade was coming to the bittersweet conclusion that steady work might require reenlisting. By 1839, intermittent assignments were not enough. Meade would need steady work if he wanted to marry a certain congressman's daughter.

Margaretta Sergeant was the oldest of ten children born to John and Margaretta Sergeant. Her father's family had been prominent Philadelphians. After graduating from Princeton in 1795, John studied law under the politically influential Jared Ingersoll and was admitted to the bar in 1799 at the age of nineteen. Over the years he served in the Pennsylvania legislature, in Congress, and as President John Quincy Adams's minister plenipotentiary to Mexico. Sergeant was a staunch abolitionist and firm supporter of the Second National Bank. In 1832, the first year of presidential nominating conventions, the National Republican Party chose Henry Clay as its presidential candidate, with Sergeant winning the vice presidential nomination. They were opposed by the Democratic slate of President Andrew Jackson and Martin Van Buren. Jackson easily won reelection.

Sergeant returned to Congress as a member of the newly formed Whig Party in 1837 and later turned down offers of a cabinet post and a seat on the Supreme Court. Upon his death in 1852, *The American Law Register* "believed that no statesman except John Sergeant, has obtained a position in the halls of Congress by the side of Lowndes, Calhoun, Clay, and Webster, and at the same time retained an acknowledged standing at the head of our profession, unsurpassed by any competitor."[63]

Sergeant made sure young Margaretta (called Margaret by her family) was well educated. She spoke at least three languages and was an accomplished pianist. Now in her twenties, she had years of experience serving as hostess for her father's parties and receptions. A portrait of Margaret in her youth reveals a dark-haired, oval-faced girl wearing a pleasant, confident expression. It is easy to see why Meade would have been attracted to her.[64]

The Meade and Sergeant families had been friends for generations. Sergeant was particular regarding their suitors' backgrounds and standing in society. George was obviously well educated, talented, and of good character. His financial standing, especially during his recent years of sporadic assignments as an ex–army officer, was another matter.

The young ex-officer Margaret Sergeant fell in love with hardly resembled the George Gordon Meade we think of today. The Civil War photographs of a gaunt, middle-aged, balding man wearing an irascible expression are decades removed from a description of Meade in his twenties provided by an in-law:

> He wore his hair down to the nape of his neck, as was the fashion of the day, and for long afterwards . . . a man with long ringlets, looking as to his head like a cavalier of the time of Charles I. He was, in a word, a dandy . . . Without being particularly good-looking in face and figure, he was tall and slender and graceful, with an air of the highest breeding.[65]

Meade's frustrating idleness ended in January 1840 with a return to the Sabine River, accompanying a commission to establish a boundary line between the United States and the Republic of Texas. He was back east that summer and joined the Sergeants on their vacation at Schooley's Mountain, New Jersey, popular for its mineral springs. While there, the topographical bureau selected him to partake in the survey of the oft-disputed northeastern boundary dividing the United States from the British territories of eastern Canada.[66]

Once again, Meade's commanding officer would be his brother-in-law, Major James Graham. This relationship did not hurt Meade's chances for work, nor was it uncommon in government appointments. It is worth noting that neither Graham nor Meade's other brother-in-law, Hartman Bache, gave Meade an assignment purely for family reasons; Meade had already proven his worth to them with results.

That said, the task of surveying the large expanse of northern Maine and points north would take years, not months. Steady work in Maine would keep Meade in the field from spring through autumn but also provide for a husband and wife. When Graham ordered a halt to the surveying for the winter of 1840–41, Meade headed to Washington, hopeful—and nervous—of obtaining Sergeant's blessing to marry Margaret.[67]

He need not have worried. By this time Meade's character and obvious devotion to Margaret had won Sergeant over as well. In November, Sergeant gave Margaret's sister, Sarah, to Virginia congressman Henry Wise in marriage. George and Margaret's wedding was held at the Sergeant home in Philadelphia on New Year's Eve 1840, Meade's twenty-fifth birthday.[68] Later, the *new* Margaret Meade was honored by *the* Margaret Meade with a party in the bride's honor in Georgetown. After a short honeymoon, they returned to Washington, where Meade did clerical work at the newly formed U.S. Army Corps of Topographical Engineers until springtime sent him back to Maine.

The surveying days were long; Meade frequently worked nights until dawn, as he and the team took "Astronomical calculations." The men found themselves up until 5 a.m., sleeping until 11. In a letter to sister-in-law Sarah Wise, Meade described a routine night with more than a little homesickness:

> *We dined about 5 and after dinner I smoked a cigar while Schroeder played upon his guitar some of the airs of Margaret's piano pieces. This of course induced many lively imaginings of scenes of happiness now passed but which I hope soon to enjoy again. As soon as it was dark we commenced looking out for rockets and other signals which are made by the parties in advance placing stations on the line, and had it not proved a cloudy night the affair would have been closed by observing till 2 or 3 o'clock in the morning.*[69]

Meade had a special reason to be melancholy. Margaret was pregnant.

Once again, Graham closed camp in the fall. Upon his return to Washington, Meade was introduced to his son, John Sergeant Meade, born November 4. The joy over his firstborn was soon muted. Congress passed a bill placing limits on the government surveys given to the To-pographical Engineers. Even the influence of his brothers-in-law could not offset the obvious: Meade, as a civilian, could have been out of work indefinitely. There was only one recourse left to him.[70]

Rather than blatantly use his father-in-law's influence in Congress, Meade asked Margaret's brother-in-law, Henry Wise, for assistance. Later, Wise was one of the "Corporal's Guard," a bloc of congressmen who supported Tyler's unpopular policies and presidency. Wise inter-ceded on Meade's behalf, and on May 19, 1842, President John Tyler signed Meade's reappointment to the army as second lieutenant, as-signed to the Topographical Engineers.

Meade's six-year absence meant a significant loss of seniority, but he considered it a small price to pay for full employment. He was back in Maine to finish the boundary survey (the dispute was resolved that summer with the Webster-Ashburton Treaty) and stayed to chart the Aroostook River from its mouth to its source. The assignment lasted through 1843, when Meade got the break of his dreams. He was as-signed to the Topographical Engineers' headquarters in Philadelphia.

He wasted little time getting to Washington, weeks after his second son (named George) was born. The Meades moved to Philadelphia, where they found a house on Fourth Street. Once settled, he walked the few blocks to the topographical office on Seventh and Spruce Streets to report to his commanding officer, his brother-in-law, Major Hartman Bache. Meade was in his hometown, in his own house, assured steady work in a field he enjoyed. Besides, Bache had an intriguing assignment for him.[71]

Ninety miles from Philadelphia, the mouth of Delaware Bay has been its maritime entrance since the city's founding in 1682. Over the next 150 years, coming and going, the river carried merchantmen with holds filled to bursting with goods; packets bearing passengers across the At-lantic; enemy frigates bringing battle or their American counterparts taking it to pirate havens or other countries in wartime; and, until 1780, "blackbirders"—ships carrying captured Africans to be sold into slavery.

The mouth of the Delaware was less than welcoming. Dangerous shoals awaited the ship lacking an experienced pilot who knew where the treacherous waters with intriguing names lay: Inner Fork of Shears, Egg Island Flats, Crow Shoal, and Joe Flogger. Another had the peaceful moniker of Brandywine, twelve miles west of the Delaware's mouth. This shoal was so perilous and deadly that, for decades, a lightship was anchored there, each mast carrying a lamp, casting their illumination across the bay. It was a solution, but not a good one.[72]

By 1840, the Industrial Revolution was well underway. New machines were changing the way textiles were being produced. The use of coke instead of coal lowered the overhead in ironworks. Steam engines were no longer an unheard-of marvel; railroads were just beginning to change transportation on land and beginning to replace canvas at sea. And engineering breakthroughs along the coastlines were accelerating the building of more efficient lighthouses.

The United States had witnessed a boom in the construction of lighthouses in the early 1800s, with more than one hundred constructed in the 1830s. But building more did not mean they were built better. Since 1825, captains and sailors returning from Europe reported at length about the British and French lighthouses they had seen. They marveled at their new system of lights and their efficiency of communication to traveling mariners. Once home, American tars complained to officials and politicians about the woeful inadequacies of the beacons on their home coastlines. European lamps were brighter, the oil of better quality, and the lighthouses sounder in construction and regularly inspected, ensuring the keepers were steadfastly alert while increasing the odds of safe passage in dangerous or unfamiliar waters.[73]

A tug-of-war over improving the safety and effectiveness of American lighthouses pitted mariners, journalists, and merchants against entrenched officials who considered their suggestions and complaints frivolous and unwarranted. But after the 1836 presidential election, Congress ordered eight officers to conduct a thorough investigation. Among them was Hartman Bache, who was unflinching in his opinions.

Not only were many lighthouses and quarters "badly constructed," but the United States was technologically behind Europe, "where the aid of science has been called in to render more perfect the different methods of illumination," something Benjamin Franklin's great-grandson could not ignore.[74]

Five years later, Congress ordered that a new lighthouse be designed and built on Brandywine Shoal. A previous attempt to construct a woodpile lighthouse in 1827 did not last a year due to heavy seas and ice floes. Bache recommended a stone foundation—a veritable artificial island—to support an elliptical-shaped lighthouse. Instead of a stately, cylindrical spire, Bache envisioned a short, chunky-looking structure. He anticipated the cost to be a whopping $124,000. Colonel John James Abert, Bache's commander, disapproved: the project was too expensive.[75]

The solution, both in terms of sound structure and lower costs, came from an engineer in Ireland. Alexander Mitchell was a Belfast Academy engineer with a successful brickwork business. He was also blind. In 1832, seeking a way to build sound lighthouses on shoals and sandbanks, Mitchell came up with the screw pile. His invention worked like a giant corkscrew, going deep into the water's floor, with a long enough flange above the surface to secure the structure. "Mitchell's mooring screw" revolutionized lighthouse construction. At a drastically reduced cost of $40,000, Congress approved giving this newfangled technology a try at Brandywine Shoal. Bache wanted Meade to take on the project.[76]

To reach the shoal, Bache and Meade acquired an old schooner they renamed *Alexander Mitchell*. Their trips downriver were accompanied by a crew of sailors, surveyors, and laborers, as Bache and Meade assessed the six-mile-long shoal, its depth and the shiftiness of the bottom. Back in their cramped office, plans were drawn, redrawn, and drawn again. Bache had already familiarized himself with the current pattern as well as the challenges of ice and nor'easters in winter. The goal was to situate a lighthouse not only where its light would do the most good but where it would survive the swells, storms, and ice floes for decades, not years.[77]

Meade fell in love with the assignment. Drawing on his experience on the Mississippi, he happily took soundings in the bay and filled notebooks with observations on the currents, tides, and changes of season. Here was a meaningful calling that would save ships, the goods in their holds, and, most important, the men aboard them. Meade relished every aspect of the task, from being on the Delaware in all kinds of weather to refining plans. Each day brought the idea of the new lighthouse closer to reality.[78]

Young Richard Meade Bache, Meade's nephew, also worked on the project and saw a side of Meade rarely mentioned in recollections of generals who served with and under him in the Civil War. During one trip back to Philadelphia, young Bache saw a display of Meade's "kindness of heart, and indifference to discomfort" under less-than-pristine circumstances. Meade, Bache, and another passenger were returning aboard a collier, a coal ship, that Bache found to be unbelievably filthy and uncomfortable. "Even the cabin of the vessel was ground-in with such dirt, not by any means impalpable, for it felt gritty," Bache recalled. When dinner was served,

> the chief dish was one of execrably boiled rice, flanked by a small piece of salt-pork, and without a condiment to use by way of disguise for the food. Not a sign, however, did Lieutenant Meade, delicately as he was nurtured, give, that he was not dining sumptuously . . . [H]e ate with avidity the soggy rice and rusty pork before him, and laughed merrily at my discomfiture . . . Here was a man who, at his own table, was ever on the lookout for tidbits to share with an appreciative guest, and now he was eating a mess fit for a savage, and apparently relishing it.

Later that night, Bache saw another glimpse into Meade's personality when one passenger became sick. "It is trying enough to be ill anywhere, and to nurse anywhere," Bache recalled, "but to be ill or to nurse in the cabin of a collier, illuminated by a single miserable candle, is wretchedness itself." But Meade immediately began nursing the man through his intestinal challenges.[79]

Delaware Bay's proximity to family also did wonders for Meade. His home became well-known for "occasions when music was the attraction of the evening, and the concerted pieces of his musical wife, on the piano, led by the first violinist of Philadelphia society . . . brought responsive silence for the enjoyment of the time." At parties Meade was "an excellent *raconteur*," one guest recalled, with the "rare inestimable gift, of ignoring the irrelevant, of treating his subject with sprightliness . . ."[80]

By the summer of 1845, the plans for Brandywine Shoal were nearing completion and Meade anticipated the beginning of construction on the first American lighthouse of its kind. Summoned to Major Bache's office on August 12, Meade expected a report on the status of supplies, or some wrinkle in the plans to be resolved.

It was, indeed, some wrinkle. Bache had new orders for Meade from Washington. There was another boundary dispute—not with Great Britain and Canada but with Mexico. Congress and President James Knox Polk were looking to annex Texas. And annexation meant war.[81]

— FOUR —

MEXICO AND WASHINGTON

In the 1840s, a bitterly divided Congress could not seem to resolve a crisis at their southern border along the Rio Grande.

Freed from the Panic of 1837, Americans in the 1840s experienced a rebirth of nationalism. Americans looked westward to lands yet unsettled by whites, populated by Native Americans and Mexicans. A fur trader, Zenas Leonard, predicted that "these hills and valleys will be greeted with the enlivening sound of the workman's hammer and the merry whistle of the ploughboy." It was Americans' "manifest destiny" for the country to stretch itself from the Atlantic to the Pacific Ocean. Annexing Texas was just the beginning. And in James Knox Polk, the proponents of Manifest Destiny had a like-minded president.[1]

The very word "annexation" divided the country between proslavery Southerners and antislavery Northerners, the latter including John Quincy Adams, now a Massachusetts congressman and the strongest voice in the House against both annexation and slavery. Like many Americans, Adams believed the two were inextricably and immorally entangled. Since the arrival in Texas of Stephen Austin's American colonists in 1824, slaveholding "Texicans" had shown their disdain for the Mexican antislavery policies. Many an enslaved person escaped bondage in Texas by crossing the Rio Grande for Mexico and freedom.[2]

The Mexican government's reaction to news of Texas's annexation was predictable. Its president, José Joaquín de Herrera, ordered an army raised to move on Texas. Instead, its commander, General Mariano Paredes y Arrillaga, immediately led his troops into Mexico City and named himself president. Polk's diplomatic overtures and offers to purchase Texas, the territory called New Mexico, and upper California were summarily rebuffed. Paredes intended to march to Corpus Christi and attack General Zachary Taylor's forces there. Polk's secretary of war, William Learned Marcy, ordered Taylor "to advance and occupy, with the troops under your command, positions on or near the east bank of the Rio del Norte"—the Rio Grande.[3]

In the late morning of May 8, 1846, Taylor sat astride his horse, Old Whitey, as the sun beat down on his dust-covered 2,200 soldiers and officers. They were on the second day of their march from Taylor's supply base, Point Isabel, to the unfinished American fort on the Rio Grande across from the Mexican city of Matamoros. Taylor had halted his troops for good reason: just ahead, at an area where groves of trees grew among the high chapparal, the road was blocked by a Mexican army of 4,000. The place was called Palo Alto; among Taylor's aides was Lieutenant George Meade.[4]

In September 1845, after a series of trains, stagecoaches, and boats (missing one thanks to an overlong visit to his sister Elizabeth Ingraham in Louisville), Meade reached General Zachary Taylor's Army of Occupation encampment in Corpus Christi, Texas. Founded three hundred years earlier by Spanish explorers, Corpus Christi was considered a trading post but was actually a smuggler's paradise. Taylor's troops camped outside Corpus Christi in endless row after row of tents stretching down the beach.[5]

Sixty years old, Taylor had fought in every war from 1812 to the Seminole Wars. Grayish-white hair and sideburns framed a weathered face with gray eyes, a thick nose, and lines etched by endless days spent overseeing work on his plantation. His stocky frame was supported by short, stout legs. His troops called him "Old Zach." The press would soon give him another nickname: "Old Rough and Ready."[6]

Meade found Taylor "a plain, sensible old gentleman, who laughs very much . . . and thinks there is not the remotest probability of there being any war." The camp rumor, Meade told Margaret, was that Taylor "is a staunch Whig, and opposed in *toto* to the Texas annexation, and therefore does not enter heart and soul into his present duties." Taylor assigned Meade to his staff, joining senior engineer Captain Thomas Jefferson Cram and Lieutenant Thomas J. Wood, fresh from West Point.[7]

Taylor's army was unique in American history: all 3,554 soldiers and officers were regulars. More than 40 percent of them were foreign born, mostly Irish and German. Those not American citizens were more likely to desert if the mood or conditions suited them, but most weathered the winter on the Nueces River with little complaint. Taylor was also blessed with a fine roster of junior officers, many of whom would, like Meade, distinguish themselves in Mexico: Braxton Bragg, Ulysses S. Grant, John Sedgwick, Ephraim Kirby Smith, and George Sykes among them. Meade and the others were anxious for action.[8]

After a winter of inactivity, the dispatch that Taylor, Meade, and the rest of the army had anxiously awaited arrived. On March 8, after days of rain and wind, the town's saloonkeepers and prostitutes sadly watched as Taylor's army began departing Corpus Christi for the north bank of the Rio Grande, where they would construct a fort across from the Mexican town of Matamoros. Meade joined the advance guard, consisting of Colonel David E. Twiggs's 2nd Dragoons, its officers' plain shell jackets smartly bordered with gold trim, the cavalrymen's hats fitted with a bright orange band. They were followed by Major Samuel Ringgold's light artillery, his brass guns glistening in the sunlight. Twiggs's force made an impression on those Mexicans scouting the Army of Occupation for the Mexican government. Meade was responsible for plotting the line of march.[9]

Located on the banks of the Rio Grande, Matamoros was an array of solid stone and adobe structures neatly planned for defense against Comanche raids. With a population of 16,000, it was the largest city in northern Mexico. Construction soon began on "Fort Texas": a rudimentary star-shaped earthworks. Sweating under the Mexican sun, American soldiers looked up from their labor to see scores of Matamoros's young ladies bathing themselves on the south bank of the river while Mexican soldiers toiled day and night, erecting ramparts and placing batteries along the city walls. Their commander was the flamboyant Cuban-born general Pedro de Ampudia.[10]

Ampudia sent a message to Taylor, giving him twenty-four hours to return to the east bank of the Nueces River. Otherwise, "arms, and arms alone, must decide the question" of which country rightfully owned Texas. Taylor refused. If Ampudia wanted to start a war, Taylor was fine with that. Ampudia's threat was followed by a series of deadly Mexican provocations. Taylor's quartermaster, Colonel Trueman Cross, was murdered; Meade recounted how Ampudia was observed wearing Cross's watch. A patrol sent to find Cross was ambushed. Meade believed these killings instilled "a burning desire to avenge." Newspapers back home used Cross's murder to fan pro-war sentiment.[11]

Mexican forces soon had a new commander, redheaded, freckled, and ambitious General Mariano Arista, relegating the resentful Ampudia to second-in-command. Arista's infantry and cavalry brought the total force in Matamoros to roughly 5,000. When Taylor learned that Arista had dispatched 1,600 cavalrymen under General Anastasio Torrejón to cross the Rio Grande miles above Fort Texas, he sent a detachment of cavalry under Captain Seth B. Thornton to reconnoiter. Thornton rode into an ambush, resulting in eleven of his men killed and six wounded. The rest were brought to Matamoros. "I had the pleasure of being the first to start the war," Arista boasted, while Taylor plainly reported that "hostilities may now be considered as commenced." He dispatched letters to the governors of Texas and Louisiana, asking for volunteers.[12]

Torrejón's dragoons then rode toward Point Isabel, ambushing a company of recently arrived Texas Rangers. Once news of the incident reached Point Isabel, Ranger captain Samuel Hamilton Walker galloped to Fort Texas to inform Taylor. Sensing Arista was up to something, Taylor had Walker reconnoiter. After sighting a brigade and batteries crossing the river, Walker raced back to Taylor with the news.[13]

In fact, Arista had crossed the Rio Grande with a large force days earlier, shielded by Torrejón's cavalry. Once united, this force would cut

Taylor off from Point Isabel and his supplies. Taylor ordered 2,200 troops assembled for a forced march to Point Isabel, leaving five hundred men of the 7th Infantry under Major Jacob Brown's command to defend the fort against the Mexican troops remaining in Matamoros. Taylor departed on May 1 and reached the port before Arista's forces could cut him off. Meade went with Taylor.[14]

Meade was supervising the refortifying of Point Isabel on May 3 when the distant rumble of cannons gave the Americans pause: Fort Texas was being bombarded. Taylor, not wanting to leave until Point Isabel was properly protected, sent Walker riding to the fort with one simple order: Defend it to the last man. Listening to the dull echoes of the guns weighed on Taylor's men. Some were frustrated at not hastening back to join their comrades; others knew the time for their entering the fight would come soon enough. One, "a young second-lieutenant who had never heard a hostile gun before," kept his initial thoughts to himself. "I felt sorry I had ever enlisted," Ulysses S. Grant would recall decades later.[15, 16]

On May 7, Taylor led his men out of Point Isabel, informing his troops that if they encountered Arista on their march, they would fight, and that "their main dependence must be in the bayonet." Encumbered by two hundred supply wagons, the Americans made only seven miles that day, with Taylor's cavalry keeping a weather eye for Torrejón's dragoons. That night Meade took time to write to Margaret, "We were all obliged to leave our baggage in the fort, and in my trunk I left your miniature," then added some prebattle humor: "I very much fear some impudent shell has ere blown you up, and you will have been in action before myself." The next day was Palo Alto.[17]

Through his looking glass, Meade saw the Mexican line stretching over a mile, anchored on their right at a wooded hill, with cavalry just behind them. To their left, Torrejón's lancers waited at the edge of a stretch of marshland. Taylor's army was less than a mile from Arista's line when he ordered a halt. After placing his guns and dragoons, Taylor gave another order: not to fix bayonets but to fill canteens. The men obediently stacked arms and filled their canteens at the Palo Alto watering hole while Taylor coolly sat on Old Whitey, working on a chaw of tobacco. Such a demeanor before a much larger force awed Taylor's young officers.[18]

Returning to their posts, the Americans advanced toward Arista's troops until a final drum ruffle brought them to a halt eight hundred yards from the Mexican line. Enemy bayonets and lances glistened in the afternoon sun, flags and *banderíns* (pennants) snapped in the breeze.[19]

The Mexicans opened fire first. While Arista had over 1,000 more men, he was woefully deficient in artillery. His gun crews were poorly trained, and their powder and shot immediately proved inferior. Their first copper cannonballs bounced yards away from the *yanqui* lines, the Americans easily turning or jumping to avoid them. Taylor ordered his artillery to return fire.[20]

With unerring accuracy, American artillery fired into Arista's ranks with impunity. Desperate to silence them, Arista ordered Torrejón's cavalry to charge. Once they were in range, Taylor's 8th Infantry, in time-honored fashion, formed a hollow square and fired into the lancers. Meade later recounted how the "ineffectual attempts to charge our lines . . . were met by our squares coolly, and repulsed with heavy loss." Just above the American infantry, Ringgold's "flying artillery" poured fire on the Mexican horses and dragoons. His endless drilling and the nimbleness of his maneuverable guns more than proved their worth that day.[21]

Meade saw plenty of action that afternoon, galloping between the American lines with new orders, then racing back to await Taylor's next dispatch. Aides on errands were popular targets for the enemy. Upon returning to Taylor's perch, one officer on the general's staff had his horse shot out from under him. Meade had never seen that before.[22]

Taylor originally believed the bayonet would prevail, but Palo Alto was an artillery battle. Burning wadding from the guns soon started brushfires; by three o'clock the prairie grass was a sea of flame. Thick smoke "concealed us from each other," Meade reported, blinding and choking both sides so badly, the battle stopped altogether.[23]

An hour later the fighting resumed, both sides pinwheeling until they were practically at right angles from their original lines. Now the Mexican artillery had its own deadly effect: "Some five horses and men were killed at various times right close to me," Meade recounted. While moving his flying artillery, Ringgold was thrown from his horse by a Mexican barrage that tore both his thighs apart.[24]

The fighting concluded at dusk. "Night closed," Meade wrote Margaret, with the Army of Occupation "on the ground they [the Mexicans] occupied when the action commenced."[25]

Lacking daylight and ammunition, Arista prudently retreated. In terms of casualties, it had been no contest: four Americans were dead, with over 40 wounded. Mexican numbers were much higher, Arista estimating 102 killed, 129 wounded, and 26 missing. Taylor sent his wounded back to Port Isabel, where a naval surgeon did his best to save Ringgold's life; he died several days later.[26]

That night, as remnants of the grass fire still burned brightly and howling coyotes tore apart corpses on the field, Meade wrote to Margaret by lantern light that he and his comrades "fully expected to renew the contest next morning."[27]

The smoke had cleared by sunrise on May 9, but the day would be hot and humid. Several miles from Palo Alto, Arista had found ground far better suited for his battered army along the Port Isabel–Matamoros Road: a bow-shaped, shallow resaca, a dried-up channel that had once been a small lake or tributary to the ever-changing whims of nature on the Rio Grande. The resaca was at least ten feet deep and two hundred feet across—easy, Arista believed, to defend against a *yanqui* assault. The Mexicans called the field Resaca del Guerrero; the Americans, Resaca de la Palma. Arista dispatched a courier to Matamoros with orders for the garrison he had left there to join him immediately.

As Taylor's army advanced, Meade found himself with soldiers trying to make their way through the chapparal, "thick thorny bushes" that "tear your clothes to pieces in trying to get through them." Just past noon, Taylor's advance guard came within range of Arista's guns.

When the Mexicans opened fire, thousands of birds of all different colors fled the trees and filled the sky, their screeching an unnerving accompaniment to the sound of the guns.[28]

At the end of the day, Resaca de la Palma was a complete victory for the Americans. Once again, Taylor's guns (particularly Ringgold's Flying Artillery, now commanded by Lieutenant Randolph Ridgely) were lethally effective, and Taylor's infantry and cavalry distinguished themselves. Meade praised "our gallant little force" in a letter home: while pursuing Arista's men to the Rio Grande, Meade and the other Americans took heart, having "the gratification of seeing our flag waving in triumph over our little field work." Fort Texas withstood the siege, but at a price. Major Jacob Brown was killed during the fighting. Taylor renamed the earthworks Fort Brown. It is now the site of Brownsville, Texas.[29]

Taylor hesitated to enter Mexico, believing it required a declaration of war. Days later he changed his mind. On May 18, borne by a flotilla of small boats manned by Mexican fishermen, Taylor's army crossed the river. Instead of gunfire they were greeted by a delegation of Matamoros's leading citizens: Arista had fled, his battered army "in full retreat for Monterey [sic]," Meade wrote. It would be four months before Taylor and Meade beheld that magnificent fortress city—four frustrating, fatal months.[30, 31]

In Washington, "the cup of forbearance has been exhausted," Polk declared, adding that Mexico "has invaded our territory, and shed American blood upon American soil." He asked Congress for a declaration of war. The vote for war was overwhelming. Polk made Winfield Scott supreme commander of U.S. forces bound for Mexico. Scott spent the summer making plans for a grand campaign should one be required.[32]

Matamoros soon lost its luster for Meade. "The most pleasing view of it," he sardonically wrote, "is from the other side" of the Rio Grande. Taylor gave assurances to Matamoros's citizens that both their property and laws would be respected; he wanted the Mexicans to understand that the United States was at war with the Mexican government, not the Mexican people. For the first week, all went well.[33]

And then the volunteers began arriving.

In late May, 8,000 Louisianans began arriving at Point Isabel. With recruiters' assurances of plentiful plunder and easy women awaiting them in Mexico still fresh in their ears, they willfully disobeyed Taylor's orders that vandalism and other crimes would not be tolerated. Soon the guardhouses were filled with drunken volunteers. Their worst habit was their love of shooting their guns in camp. "The bullets come whizzing by us as thick as in an action," Meade wrote Margaret, "and I really consider spending a day in my tent, uninjured, equivalent to passing through a well-contested action." Nor did the newcomers' lack of a work ethic escape Meade's wrath. "Gentlemen from Louisiana, owning plantations and negroes," he thundered, "came here as common soldiers, and then revolt at the idea of drawing their own water and cutting their own wood, and in fact, they expect the regulars, who have to take care of themselves, to play waiters to them."[34]

But the later arrival of the Texas volunteers gave Meade and other regular army officers even more concerns, with their "thirst to gratify personal revenge . . . [I]f we advance with them into the interior," Meade believed, "they will exasperate the people against us, causing them to rise *en masse*, and if so there is no telling when the war will end." The atrocities committed by the mostly Protestant Texans eclipsed those of the Louisianans: killing priests, raping nuns, and destroying churches. For many Texans, the Alamo had not been forgotten, after all.[35]

In June, Taylor was ordered by Secretary of War Marcy to "capture and hold Monterrey," and by Winfield Scott to march up "the high road to the capital of Mexico." That "high road" began just *past* Monterrey. Taylor replied that the 1,000-mile trek from Matamoros to Monterrey would best succeed with a small army. Meade was one of the engineers sent to scout the possibility of making the journey by both land and water. Taylor embarked with a force of 7,000 regulars and volunteers.[36]

Harsh weather, bad drinking water, and the challenge of going both by boat and overland plagued the journey to Monterrey. At the town of Camargo, Taylor lost over 1,000 volunteers to dysentery, diarrhea, even measles. On August 19, Meade departed with General William Worth's 1st Brigade as chief engineer to Cerralvo, halfway to Monterrey. He found the town "prettily placed in the valley of a mountain stream," its residents "most kindly," its fruit and pecan trees a daily temptation after the poor food and water of past weeks. Meade found the same pleasant climate and resources at Marín. "Were I single, I should be tempted to spend my days in the lovely climate," he whimsically wrote Margaret.[37]

A city of 10,000 residents, Monterrey enjoyed natural defenses. It lay in the shadow of the Sierra Madre range, with a series of promontories, high hills, and the Santa Catarina River to protect it. In addition, a network of forts and redans ringed the city, covering every possible route of attack. Its strongest fortification was an unfinished cathedral converted into a citadel looming over Monterrey's north end. Its citizens mostly lived in handsome one-story stucco houses with flat parapet roofs, giving them a garrison-like countenance and a fine defense for riflemen. The streets were straight, intersected at 90-degree angles, making it easy to move troops and ammunition. Earthworks were dug, loopholes were drilled, sandbags were piled.[38]

The Mexican army's new commander, Pedro de Ampudia (having replaced Arista after his two defeats), believed Monterrey unconquerable. His cavalry had dogged Taylor's march, as much to intimidate as to scout. Ampudia had 7,000 soldiers, 3,000 rancheros, and forty-two cannons against Taylor's just over 6,200 men.[39]

On September 18 the Americans arrived before Monterrey, where the engineers found an almost idyllic campsite with plenty of water and pecan trees. The next morning Taylor ordered the mounted Texans to accompany him to get a closer look at the Mexican defenses. Meade rode with them. They were soon in range, and the Mexicans fired an artillery salvo. When one cannonball bounced over Taylor's head and another just missed Meade, Taylor and company calmly trotted away.[40]

Careful to stay out of range, Meade and the other engineers spent the rest of the day scouting and sketching the details of Ampudia's defenses. The field map Meade gave Taylor clearly showed that Monterrey's defenses were stronger on Taylor's left flank (east) than his right (west).[41]

At a council of war that night, Taylor decided to split the army in two, on either side of the Saltillo Road, which ran by the river going west. General Worth, with John C. "Jack" Hays's Texas Rangers, would make demonstrations before the hills on the right of Monterrey, while Taylor and his other generals—David Twiggs, William O. Butler, and Texas governor J. Pinckney Henderson—would attack from the northeast. Worth would have 2,000 men for his attack. The plan was risky: Taylor was splitting his smaller force before Ampudia's larger numbers. Once again Meade was assigned to Worth, who bragged to all that he would "earn a grade or a grave" at Monterrey.[42]

On Sunday afternoon, September 20, Worth, Meade, and fifty Texans rode southwest, swinging around Independencia Hill to the Saltillo Road to reconnoiter again. They spent the night shivering under a cold rain. Before dawn on the twenty-first, "As we were turning the corner of the road entering the valley," Meade recollected, "the enemy showed himself with a large cavalry force, some two thousand, with some five hundred infantry . . ." The Battle for Monterrey commenced.[43]

Worth had his troopers dismount and massed them behind a fence, supported by flying artillery. The Mexican horsemen charged: officers swinging sabers, lancers' weapons leveled, guidons whipping in the wind. The first salvo of the flying artillery, rifles, and shotguns smashed into the Mexican cavalry, killing and wounding rider and horse indiscriminately. The few Mexicans still on horseback retreated. The Saltillo Road was open to Taylor and closed to Ampudia. "The town," Worth prematurely reported to Taylor, "is ours."[44]

As Worth's aide, Meade sat mounted next to him, watching dismounted Texas Rangers and infantry regulars wade waist-deep through the cold Santa Catarina River, then scale and seize four-hundred-foot Federación Hill. After a boisterous cheer, the Americans turned a captured gun toward nearby Fort Soldado. When their first shot smashed the fort's last cannon, the Mexicans fled. "By night we had taken two of the four positions, and encamped in the gorge," Meade wrote Margaret, proudly adding, "So much for our operations."[45]

On the left, Taylor's day ended with high casualties and little success. One fort, La Tenería ("the Tannery"), was taken. "The slaughter," Meade wrote, "was terrific": there were 394 casualties. Taylor's force saw no action the following day.[46]

Worth's troops did. After shivering through another night of bone-chilling rain, Worth's men stormed Independencia Hill. By sunrise, Meade saw them driving the Mexicans back to the Bishop's Palace. When the Stars and Stripes rose above it, Taylor's soldiers threw their caps and lustily cheered.[47]

On the morning of the twenty-third, Worth sent Meade from the Bishop's Palace to scout out the enemy defenses: "I ascertained the enemy had abandoned all that portion of the town in our direction, and had retired to the central plaza of the town, where they were barricaded, and all the houses occupied by their infantry." Most of Ampudia's men were massed in the city square, his guns covering the main streets, riflemen on the roofs, the side streets barricaded.[48]

Taylor's men came under a constant barrage of gunfire. Lieutenant Ulysses S. Grant described the streets as "commanded from all directions of artillery" with "a volley of musketry and a discharge of grape-shot" an ongoing, deadly reality. The fighting was by inches, with heavy losses. But while Taylor's men were fighting on the street, Worth's soldiers did not advance in the open. Instead, Meade and the other engineers were engaged with picks and crowbars to break down house walls, allowing Worth to send his sharpshooters to man the roofs; sheltered by the parapets, they picked off any Mexican who showed his head. Resistance, like the houses, crumbled.[49] By nightfall, Worth's troops were one square from the central plaza. Meade expected "close quarters the next day," but General Ampudia did not engage, surrendering Monterrey on September 24. Taylor's terms were generous: the surrender of Monterrey and the withdrawal of Ampudia's army forty miles south (minus all weapons but one cannon and officers' sidearms) in exchange for an eight-week armistice.[50]

While Worth reported that Meade performed with "intelligent zeal and gallantry" at Monterrey, Meade realized how lucky he had been during those three days. "Many of our brave fellows slept in a nameless grave," he confided to Margaret. The realization that survival in battle is often a matter of luck was not lost on Meade, allowing him "to cling to hope of once more being reunited to you," he told Margaret. "Tell the boys," he concluded, "I will give them a long story about it all, when I get back."[51]

In Washington, Polk was livid over Taylor's truce. The general "had the enemy in his power," he groused. To Polk, Taylor had fought three days for nothing; he could have ended the war if he had either kept fighting or forced Ampudia to surrender.[52]

Political machinations now took center stage regarding the war. For months, Polk had debated sending Winfield Scott to take over command of the war effort in Mexico. Initially, both saw no reason for the general to rush south. But as Taylor piled up victory after victory, Scott began gnashing his teeth, and after Taylor's triumph and armistice at Monterrey, Polk saw Scott as the lesser of two evils, if not of two Whigs. On November 19, Polk offered Scott command of the expedition to take Vera Cruz. Taylor was ordered to send his 2,000 regulars to Tampico as part of Scott's new army.[53]

Polk was also working stealthily to ascertain if former Mexican *presidenté* Antonio López de Santa Anna—then an exile in Cuba—should get Polk's assistance in returning to Mexico. He hoped restoring Santa Anna to power would result in willingness to end the war, in return for millions of U.S. dollars for the lands north of the Rio Grande.[54]

In between his favorite pastime of watching cockfights, Santa Anna assured American diplomats in Havana that he would broker a peace deal. Polk ordered Commodore David Conner's squadron off the Gulf of Mexico to allow Santa Anna to "pass freely" through its blockade. His return ended Mariano Paredes's rule. Arriving in Vera Cruz in

August, Santa Anna made his way to Mexico City, where an extravagant reception awaited the one-legged expatriate.[55]

To Polk's embarrassment, Santa Anna immediately declared he had returned to fight the Americans, not make peace with them. Polk's abetting Santa Anna's return—and his dream of buying all Mexican territory above the Rio Grande with dollars—now looked to be an embarrassing nightmare. Mexico's vast territory would still be purchased with blood.

Meade was sharing quarters in a vacant Monterrey mansion with Lieutenants John Pope and Jeremiah Scarritt in January 1847 when he and Taylor's 2,000 regulars were ordered to Tampico. Taylor, with his decimated force, would remain in Monterrey, where rumors spread that Santa Anna was coming with 25,000 troops. "Old Rough and Ready" wished Meade well. "I must confess," Meade wrote, "I regretted exceedingly parting with the old man."[56]

Scott's fleet of two hundred ships arrived in Tampico on February 18; visiting the town the following day, he paid little attention to its amenities. Scott was Taylor's antithesis, impeccably decked out in full uniform adorned with epaulettes. He posed a challenge for the average doorway with his height and width.[57]

Despite his towering presence and rank, Scott did not make a favorable impression on Meade or the other officers detached from Taylor's army. "He seemed to be quite insensible to everything but his own expedition," Meade informed Margaret. When Taylor's officers told Scott of "the critical condition in which we believe General Taylor to be," Scott dismissively answered, '*Men of straw, men of straw,*' and took no further notice." To Meade and his comrades, "Old Fuss and Feathers" was no "Old Rough and Ready."[58]

As Scott sailed for Vera Cruz, and while Meade awaited further orders, Taylor and his small army were in the fight of their lives at Buena Vista, due south of Monterrey. Santa Anna's 15,000 troops attacked Taylor's 4,700 over February 22–23. On the evening of the twenty-third, the Mexicans lit hundreds of campfires and left the battlefield. "My great regret now is that I was separated from General Taylor," Meade wrote, rejoicing at his general's "brilliant achievement." It was Taylor's last battle in the war.[59]

On March 6, Scott clambered up the gangplank of a small steamer, the *Petrita*, to personally see Vera Cruz's defenses from the water. In addition to Commodore David E. Conner and Scott's generals (including Worth), the entire contingent of engineers, including Meade, was also aboard. Scott wanted his officers and engineers to do a firsthand reconnaissance. A high seawall protected the city with more than one hundred guns (most from U.S. foundries, purchased before the war). The most formidable defense was San Juan de Ulúa, a fortress three-quarters of a mile from Vera Cruz, with another 125 guns. It was obvious to everyone aboard the *Petrita* that the safest approach would be a landing on Collado Beach, several miles southeast.[60]

Passing between Vera Cruz and San Juan de Ulúa, Conner sailed too close to the fortress. With their spyglasses, the engineers could see Mexican gun crews man their batteries and sponge their guns before seeing a cloud of smoke, followed by one cannon roar after another. Conner slowed the *Petrita* to gauge their marksmanship. After they "fired some eleven shells; luckily quite ineffectually," as Meade put it, the *Petrita* steamed out of range.[61]

Meade was furious at such risky bravado: "Having aboard all the general officers of the army, one shot, hitting the vessel and disabling it, would have left us a floating target to the enemy." It was the closest Meade came to being directly fired upon at Vera Cruz. "I have been pretty much a spectator," he bemoaned as the siege began. It was clear that Totten's engineers would handle all topographical work.[62]

Eleven days later, Meade wrote Margaret from New Orleans, "having been, as you will see by the enclosed document, ordered to Washington by General Scott, or in other words, *honorably discharged*." Throughout Scott's Mexican campaign he would rely as heavily on one of the other engineers aboard the *Petrita* that day as Taylor had done with Meade. That would be Captain Robert E. Lee.[63]

Unlike George Meade, Robert E. Lee did not have to wait months for his first full battle. That happened just days after his arrival in Vera Cruz.

He believed himself to be "the last man ordered" to Mexico and was disappointed he was not assigned to Taylor, the general doing the fighting at the time. He was to meet General John E. Wool's division in San Antonio. His overland trip introduced Lee to both Texas's "intolerable heat" and its insects. "I have got such a taste of prairie flies," he wrote, "that I determined to travel by night." He reached San Antonio on September 21. At his first officers' dinner, Lee's mess chest made a bigger impression than he did. It had belonged to George Washington and was passed around the table to the delight of Lee's messmates.[64]

On Wool's march into Mexico, Lee rode ahead with a small detachment of Illinois volunteers, repairing roads and building small bridges. By October 11 they had crossed the Rio Grande, spending a peaceful Christmas in Saltillo. Lee's cheerful letter to his children—"If [Santa Claus] only leaves for you one half of what I wish, you will want for nothing"—hid his homesickness from them.[65]

On January 19, 1847, Lee turned forty. A daguerreotype shows that his hairline had migrated somewhat from his forehead but was still dark and thick. A mustache draped over his lips, and his eyes shone with an expression of reserved optimism. Wool, impressed with Lee's reports, had already made him acting inspector general. Lee did not have his new responsibilities for long. Orders arrived from Vera Cruz: General Scott wanted Lee to join his engineers. After boarding a transport for the island of Lobos, the rendezvous for Scott's forces, Lee was assigned a stateroom with his old friend Joseph E. Johnston. By the time Lee reached Vera Cruz, he had been assigned to Scott's staff, along with his former supervisor, Joseph Totten.[66]

After the near-disastrous *Petrita* cruise, Lee and the other engineers began laying the groundwork for the siege of Vera Cruz. The cannons Lee was placing were not army stock; Scott's heavy guns and mortars were still stateside. Lee transferred guns from the American warships, their weight (6,300 pounds) and small wheels making transportation laborious. Mexican cavalry patrols and the violent storms off the Gulf of Mexico delayed but did not stop the engineers' work. Nor did the sand fleas, which often were more trouble than enemy dragoons. Scott wanted the siege over quickly, before the *vomito-negro*—yellow fever—arrived with the warmer weather, as it was sure to kill more Americans than the Mexicans ever could. Scott began firing sporadic salvos from the emplaced guns on March 19, to no great effect.[67]

Two incidents happened during Lee's pre-siege duties. One evening, returning from a reconnaissance with First Lieutenant Pierre G. T. Beauregard, a startled sentry fired his pistol at Lee, the ball passing between his chest and arm, singeing his uniform. When the man stated he was with a nearby artillery battery, the two officers walked him back to his guns, concluding he was either green, scared, or deserting.[68]

While accompanying Scott inspecting emplacements, a lieutenant was spotted walking alone—in flagrant disobedience of Scott's order that all officers remain in camp unless on duty. The young man claimed ignorance. Lee icily ordered him to return to camp. Later Lee sought him out to apologize for his attitude. The lieutenant, George B. Mc-Clellan, insisted he had taken no offense.[69]

On March 22, Scott sent an ultimatum to Vera Cruz *commandante general* Juan Morales to surrender. He refused. There were a considerable number of foreigners within the walls; they, too, refused to leave. Scott opened fire with what guns were ready, while the navy's warships did the same. Mexican guns responded immediately in a mutual bombardment.[70]

On the night of the twenty-third, another storm struck, but Lee kept the sailors who had brought the guns ashore working, much to their displeasure. By morning, the siege began in earnest. When the gun crews came ashore, Lee was astonished to see Commander Sydney Smith Lee among them. The joy in seeing his brother was more than mixed with the dread of Smith becoming a casualty. Lee directed the naval gunners' fire on Vera Cruz, just seven hundred yards away. After eighteen years in the army, Lee was in his first battle.[71]

In between salvos, Lee kept an eye on Smith:

No matter where I turned my eyes reverted to him, and I stood by his gun
whenever I was not wanted elsewhere. Oh! I felt awfully, and am at a loss
what I should have done had he been cut down before me. I thank God he
was saved.[72]

By four o'clock the ammunition had run out. Scott's ring of cannons had blasted the Vera Cruz walls and panicked the civilians. When another battery launched forty Congreve rockets over the crumbling walls, with their high-pitched screaming before exploding into houses and streets, panic became terror.[73]

The bombardment resumed on March 25 when the consuls of Great Britain, France, and Prussia appealed to Scott for a partial truce to allow civilians time to leave. Scott refused: Had he not warned them of what was to come if Morales did not surrender? The cannonading continued through the night, until Morales's second-in-command, General J. J. Landero, proposed a "convention" to arrange terms. Now Scott ordered a ceasefire.[74]

Like Taylor, Scott provided generous terms to Landero, promising "absolute freedom of worship" for Mexican citizens. When American volunteers were brought before Scott for looting and rape, he proclaimed martial law and had them whipped, even hanging one of them. But all his pre-siege assurances and post-siege actions to win over the Mexican people could not make amends for the hundreds of men, women, and children killed in the shelling of Vera Cruz. "My heart bled for the inhabitants," Lee wrote. Scott's easy victory did not cow Santa Anna: "Vera Cruz," he blustered, "calls for vengeance!"[75]

With 8,500 soldiers, Scott set out from Vera Cruz on April 12, marching northwest on the National Road, the same route Hernán Cortés had taken in 1519. The line of march of his three divisions stretched for miles. The army entered the Valley of Mexico, a series of deep descents into ravines, numerous rivers to cross, and the ever-present possibility of ambush from Santa Anna—wherever he was.[76]

In fact, Santa Anna was fairly close. After his return to Mexico City, he raised a new army of 12,000 and marched west on the National Road. He stopped at Cerro Gordo ("Fat Mountain"), 1,000 feet high, just left of the highway. Santa Anna's soldiers dug in, placing batteries on the cliffs and forcing Scott to make a frontal assault. Slaughter, Santa Anna believed, awaited the Americans.[77]

As Scott approached Cerro Gordo, he sent chief engineer Major John L. Smith and Lee to scout the terrain. Lee spent days and nights exploring and finding pathways that would allow Scott to flank Santa Anna's positions, his men widening paths with picks, shovels, and axes and painstakingly hauling artillery behind Santa Anna's line. On one reconnaissance, Lee went so far beyond the others that he found himself alongside a detachment of enemy soldiers filling their canteens at a brook. Ducking behind a log just behind a wide bush, Lee lay dead-still as the Mexicans idly chattered. He didn't move until nightfall, then skulked back to Smith's party.[78]

The battle on April 17 did not go as planned: timed assaults went completely awry, but the firing from Lee's battery emplacements saved General Twiggs's force from being annihilated. When Scott's assault on the Mexican left flank failed, Lee galloped to join Colonel Bennet C. Riley's 2nd Brigade, attacking and taking a Mexican battery. The second day's battle was a complete success for Scott. In Santa Anna's hasty retreat down the ravines, he left one of his spare wooden legs. The rest of him remained undaunted, ready to fight again. Scott marched out on the National Road and camped outside of Puebla, seventy-five miles from Mexico City.[79]

Scott's force, already small, got even smaller. The one-year enlistment of thousands of volunteers was ending; to his dismay, 80 percent of them chose to go home. Anxious to get them back before the *vomito-negro* season returned, Scott sent them to Vera Cruz. He also abandoned his supply line, now 150 miles long and frequently prey for guerrillas and bandits. In London, Arthur Wellesley, 1st Duke of Wellington, was aghast. "Scott is lost! He has been carried away by his successes!" he declared. "He can't fall back on his base!"[80]

Scott's favorite soldier saw it differently. Lee believed sending the volunteers home ahead of schedule was another example of Scott's earning soldiers' loyalty by looking out for them—hardly what Meade had seen in Scott's "men of straw" comment. Lee called Scott "a great man on great occasions . . . [H]is judgment is sound as his heart is bold & daring." In Scott, Lee had found the role model his father could never have been.[81]

Scott was promised 20,000 fresh troops by Polk, but newly arrived troops only brought his number to 14,000 (including 2,500 down with dysentery). By August 5 he resumed his campaign, marching into the mountains. There, on August 10, they beheld the twenty-mile-wide, bowl-shaped Valley of Mexico and its focal point, Mexico City. Four centuries earlier, Cortés and his *conquistadores* had stood in the same place, the spectacular view taking away, for a brief moment, the reason they had come so far: to conquer. Now came the Americans' turn to feel the same.[82, 83]

A Mexican sixteen-pounder's roar let Mexico City know the *yanquis* were close. Santa Anna gave a speech to the crowd: "Blinded by pride," the Americans would certainly be defeated at last. To ensure victory, he issued a new "reform," drafting everyone from sixteen to sixty years of age for the city's defense.[84]

Realizing that Santa Anna's outer perimeter defenses required taking before an attack on Mexico City, Scott sent Lee and the other engineers to find a weak point. Accompanied by Beauregard, Lee took a scouting party west, where they discovered a slim road through some marshland that led to a lava field, fifteen miles in area, called the *pedregal*, a "raging sea of molten rock" covered over by black basalt, a petrified igneous rock of molten lava. Traveling across such terrain by foot or horse was so challenging that Santa Anna had left the *pedregal* completely undefended. Lee came upon a "mule path" running northwest to the San Angel Road above Padierna that led to the villages of San

Angel, Coyocán, and Churubusco. Lee told Scott the path could be broadened into a road that infantry, artillery, and cavalry could use to flank Santa Anna again. Scott agreed, sending Lee back with three lieutenants, five hundred troops, and the necessary tools to turn centuries-old lava into a pathway to victory.[85]

Over the next twenty-four hours Lee crossed the searing *pedregal* three times: getting the path widened within hours, reconnoitering behind enemy lines, crossing the *pedregal* during a drenching evening thunderstorm to report the latest American positions to Scott. During the ensuing Battle of Churubusco, Lee led two separate fighting forces against the enemy and also directed the placement and firing of batteries. By day's end he had gone without sleep for forty hours.[86]

At one point during the fighting, a loud cheer suddenly erupted from the ranks, but not from watching the enemy flee. General Scott had arrived. Lee later recalled the "loud and boisterous" welcome he received: "It must have shaken the 'halls of Montezuma,'" he wrote. Soldiers surrounded Scott's mount, deafening him with their cheering. For all Scott's self-importance, they knew he was not about to risk their lives needlessly. Never had Lee witnessed such adulation for a general.[87]

By day's end, Churubusco was another victory for Scott but his costliest battle of the war: over 1,000 casualties. The bloodiest fighting occurred at San Mateo, whose defenders included the remnants of the San Patricio Battalion, mainly comprising Irish and Irish American soldiers from Taylor's army who had earlier crossed the Rio Grande at Matamoros. Knowing they would be hanged as deserters, they were the last to surrender that day; their stubborn resistance included tearing down every white flag a Mexican officer raised.[88]

As the sun set, Santa Anna, "possessed by a black despair," as one onlooker noted, led the remnants of yet another vanquished army into Mexico City for one final stand against the Americans that now seemed futile.[89]

After Churubusco, Scott demanded Santa Anna surrender the city, not his army. Scott hoped Santa Anna would remember his assurances to

Polk that he would make peace if placed in power. After a brief palaver, an armistice took effect, and Scott ensconced himself at the Bishop's Palace at Tacubaya, one mile from a hill called Chapultepec. Santa Anna, meanwhile, rebuilt his army once again, seizing any boy or old man who could carry a weapon. When Scott got word that Santa Anna was melting church bells and casting cannons in the hillside buildings on Molino del Rey, he canceled the armistice.[90]

There were no less than eight entrances into Mexico City. Raised causeways ran through the surrounding wetlands. Water-filled ditches acted like a moat before each causeway ended at a *garita*—a small plaza with compact buildings used for customhouses and tax collecting. Now each *garita* was a fortified battery, its guns placed to slaughter with impunity. A hill on the east, El Peñón, and Lake Texcoco on the northeast were equally fortified. Scott was confined to two alternatives: attack over the three causeways to the south or from the west, where the Garita de San Cosmé and the Garita de Belén were protected by fortress Chapultepec.[91]

On September 9, Scott and Lee rode around the outskirts of Mexico City. Through their spyglasses, they watched Mexican soldiers wheeling more artillery onto the *garitas*; there would be close to a dozen at each gate before they were through. On September 11 Scott called a council of war in the village of La Piedad. He planned a direct attack on Chapultepec, believing it less fortified than it looked, while the soggy grounds to the south would slow an attack before the Mexican guns there.[92]

To some officers' surprise, Lee objected. Combining deference with firmness, he said an attack at the San Antonio Gate to the south would have the greatest chance of success and the smallest casualty count. When Scott put the decision to a vote, four generals and three engineers sided with Lee; only two agreed with Scott.[93]

Chapultepec ("Grasshopper Hill") rose two hundred feet above Mexico City. The ground had been sacred to the Aztecs; the original castle had been home to generations of their princes, its walls literally enclosing the Halls of Montezuma. After Cortés, Spanish viceroys used it as a summer home, and by 1847 it was Mexico's military academy. A high wall surrounded the castle and an expansive terrace clogged with cannons. To the west, the wall encircled groves of cypress trees. The road to the castle was lined with sandbags and batteries. Finally, looming over the western hillside was a higher retaining wall that could only be scaled with ladders. The garrison was commanded by Major General Nicolás Bravo Rueda. He needed at least 2,000 men to man the walls, but Santa Anna had given him eight hundred, including the academy cadets.[94]

Scott sent Lee and George McClellan to place four batteries of sixteen- and twenty-four-pounders before Chapultepec. Finding the ground sodden, their party built wooden platforms for the batteries while under fire from Mexican guns. A fourteen-hour bombardment was unleashed on Chapultepec on September 12, cannonballs smashing the thin walls quicker than the garrison could fill the holes with sandbags. At night, scores of Mexican soldiers deserted, the cadets remaining at their posts, determined to defend Chapultepec to the last man.[95]

Scott had ordered an all-out assault on Chapultepec at sunrise. Lee, who again had not slept in two days, repaired and readied the batteries for the attack. At 6 a.m. the American bombardment was renewed, two hours of solid shot hammering what was left of the fortress walls while other guns pelted the soldiers beneath the cypress groves with grape and canister. Lee was mounted next to Scott, who had abandoned fuss and feathers for a simple broad-brimmed hat to shade himself from the hot sun. When the bombardment stopped at 8 a.m. and the troops began their assault, Scott sent Lee to lead General Gideon Johnson Pillow's troops from Molino del Rey; when Pillow was wounded, Lee got him to a field hospital. The full assault commenced.[96]

It was a brutal, bloody clash, with a new twist in the war: the Mexicans had buried land mines, most of which did not explode. Lee was grazed by a musket ball, but he was lucky. Another eight hundred Americans were casualties that day, many while climbing scaling ladders ("like goats," one Mexican soldier recalled) to the top of the high wall and fighting hand to hand.

The cadets were particularly brave. As Mexican soldiers fled for their lives once resistance became hopeless, six cadets were killed at their posts, one cadet jumping to his death with his academy's flag in his arms.[97]

Other Americans distinguished themselves that day. Seizing one of the Mexican flags, Lieutenant James Longstreet was wounded, but his comrade, George Pickett, picked up the flag. Lee's old friend Joe Johnston led one attack, while one of the batteries in the morning salvo was commanded by Lieutenant Thomas J. Jackson. Lieutenant D. H. Hill found "the havoc among the Mexicans was horrible in the extreme," he recalled, with American soldiers "shouting 'give no quarter.'" Hill noticed that "none was asked by the Mexicans." Finally, the remaining Mexicans gave up the fight.[98, 99]

It had been fifty-six hours since Lee had slept, and his stamina was long spent. His work finished, he rode back to Scott and fell from his horse. Scott had him taken back to camp. As Lee slept that night, Santa Anna and his remaining troops abandoned Mexico City.[100]

The next morning Scott marched his army triumphantly into the city but soon learned that although he occupied it, he had not conquered it. Before leaving, Santa Anna had released thousands of prisoners who joined the poorest of the city's citizens, *léperos*, becoming angry mobs, sacking the palace and sniping at their new conquerors. Scott imposed martial law, sending the flying artillery through the streets with orders to destroy any houses that were the source of gunfire. Such measures convinced the Mexicans to lay down their arms. Scott then ordered his army to be "sober, orderly, and merciful."[101]

Once again, Scott lavished Lee with praise. "Captain Lee, Engineer, so constantly distinguished, also bore important orders from me (September 13) until he fainted, from a wound and the loss of two nights sleep at the batteries." Lee was promoted to brevet colonel, his third brevet promotion since Vera Cruz.[102]

With hostilities halted save for sporadic guerrilla actions, Lee began assessing the war, his role in it, and its consequences in letters to friends and family. Earlier, he had crowed to MacKay that "this Mexican affair is a glorious thing for West Point"; now he grew guilty about both defeating Mexico and conquering the land. "It is true we bullied [Mexico]," he admitted to Mary, and "Of that I am ashamed." And while "we drubbed her handsomely," he wondered what would happen "if we should refuse to accept the territory we have forced her to relinquish & fight her three more years more to compel her to take it back." That, he sarcastically added, "would be marvelously like us."[103]

Unlike many of his comrades, he was not captivated by the Mexican people. He found the residents of the capital "idle worthless & vicious." A few of his letters showed a latent streak of Manifest Destiny. Once a treaty was signed, "open the ports of European immigration. Introduce free opinions of government & religion. Break down the power & iniquity of the church. It is a beautiful country," he told MacKay, "& in the hands of the proper people it would be a magnificent one."[104]

Lee soon bristled over his brevet promotions not being made permanent, particularly in pay. For the past ten years his captain's salary had been less than $1,200 a year. He knew, he told his father-in-law, that Lieutenant John Charles Frémont had been raised three grades, to a lieutenant colonel, and his friend Joe Johnston from lieutenant to lieutenant colonel. He soon came to believe that his promotions were being stalled by President Polk, who was suspected by many an officer of favoritism and partisanship. Despite Lee being so honorably mentioned in Scott's reports, the fact that Scott was an arch-Whig might have affected Lee's chances of permanent promotion.[105]

Scott's campaign was initially applauded at home and abroad. In London, an awestruck Duke of Wellington hailed Scott as "the greatest living general." Now all that was left was for peace commissioner Nicholas Trist to get Polk's treaty signed by somebody, Santa Anna's departure having left, for a time, a leaderless country.[106]

While arguments continued in Congress over the justness of "Mr. Polk's War," Lee sadly witnessed the dissolution of Scott's relationship with his generals. At a court of inquiry, Scott was falsely accused of a bribery scheme regarding peace negotiations.[107]

To his dismay, Lee was called as a witness by both parties. "We are our own trumpeters," he wrote cynically to his old friend MacKay. "It is so much more easy to make heroes on paper than in the field." The affair vindicated no one, but it did give Polk what he yearned for: the chance to recall Scott.[108]

As usual, Lee publicly cloaked his disappointment over Scott's removal but privately vented his anger. "The great cause of our success
was in our leader," he told Smith Lee, crediting Scott's "stout heart,"
"bold self reliance," and "indomitable courage" for the army's victories.
Lee wanted to come home, and Scott had approved, but the new
commander, Major General William O. Butler, rescinded Lee's request.
Scott departed Mexico in April 1848, while an embittered Lee remained.[109]

The Treaty of Guadelupe Hidalgo, engineered by Trist (with few of
Polk's proposed ultimatums), was signed on February 2, 1848. Finally,
on June 9, Lee boarded the steamship *Portland* at Vera Cruz. He had
been away for twenty-one months.[110]

While Lieutenant Meade's first battle in the Mexican War came in May
1846 and Captain Lee's in March 1847, Congressman Lincoln's first
congressional speech was made in December 1847.

By mid-October 1847, congressman-elect Lincoln had rented his
Springfield house and settled what cases he could, signing off "Yours in
haste" on a letter regarding one that remained unresolved. Then, with
bags packed, the Lincoln family began its lengthy journey to Washington, D.C. They arrived on December 2.[111]

Not yet fifty years old, Washington, D.C., was becoming what John
F. Kennedy would later call "a city of southern efficiency and northern
charm." On a visit in 1842, Charles Dickens had called it a "City of
Magnificent Intentions," with "spacious avenues, that begin in nothing, and lead nowhere."[112]

After a brief stay at the royally named but dilapidated Indian Queen
Hotel, the Lincolns took up residence at Mrs. Ann Sprigg's boardinghouse, just across from the Capitol. It was home to arch-abolitionist
congressman Joshua Reed Giddings of Ohio, the unofficial headquarters of Whig decision-makers, and a way station on the Underground
Railroad. After supper, wives and children retired to their rooms while
congressional boarders (counting Giddings and Lincoln, there were
nine) talked politics, particularly the politics of slavery. The tall, broad

Giddings earned his nickname the "Lion of Ashtabula" as much for his defiant antislavery oratory as for his imposing presence.[113]

Lincoln soon ingratiated himself with the widow's boarders. One, Samuel C. Busey, "learned to know and admire him for his simple and unostentatious manner, kind-heartedness, and amusing jokes," describing how

> when about to tell an anecdote during a meal he would lay down his knife and fork, place his elbows on the table, rest his face in his hands, and begin with the words "that reminds me" and proceed. Everybody prepared for the explosions sure to follow.[114]

The freshman congressman was appointed to the Committee on Post Office and Post Roads and the Committee on Expenditures in the War Department. The former was by far more important and hit home for the former postmaster. Daily mail delivery was rarely achieved, leading to grave consequences, particularly for lawyers. Delays in legal correspondence during a trial or hearing easily fouled up a circuit-riding lawyer's schedule. Lincoln's second committee, even during wartime, rarely met at all.[115]

"As you are all anxious for me to distinguish myself, I have concluded to do so before long," Lincoln assured both Billy Herndon and his Illinois friends. On December 6, Lincoln crossed First Street, passed the iron-rail fence around Capitol Park, and continued until he reached the Capitol steps on the east front to be sworn in.[116]

The House of Representatives held its sessions in what is now Statuary Hall, designed as a rectangular room with rounded sides, but reconstruction after the conflagration started by British soldiers in 1814 turned it into what is now a large semicircle. Congressmen sat in curved rows; a gallery above them was rarely crowded save for during important debates, when women dominated attendance. Above the chamber *The Car of History*, a sculpture depicting Clio, the Muse of History, stood before the Chariot of Time, its wheel a working clock, alongside a profile of George Washington. The members' chairs were atop a floor of black-and-white tile that contributed to the dreadful acoustics. Again Dickens put it best:

"It is an elegant chamber to look at, but a singularly bad one for all purposes of hearing." Lincoln, a "back-bencher," sat in the last row.[117]

As the cacophony from speeches, hand-clapping summonses to pages, and a persistent hum of muffled conversation from congressmen and guests rose to the ceiling, representatives frequently reviewed their correspondence while an exasperated colleague pleaded for attention. Boring orators no sooner started a speech when others, in unison, pulled out newspapers to read.[118]

On December 22, Lincoln first tested the chamber's acoustics by introducing a resolution on the war. After citing Polk's declaration of May 11, 1846, that Mexican forces "invaded *our territory*, and shed the blood of our fellow *citizens on our own soil*!" Lincoln requested that Polk "inform this House" where the exact spot was: a not-so-cloaked accusation that the war had started under false pretenses and with Polk's blessing.[119]

Lincoln's resolution was not so much bravado as toeing the Whig line. The war on the battlefields was over; all that remained was getting a peace treaty signed. But Democrats, aware that the country's mood was vacillating over the conflict, were not about to give the Whigs any ground on this issue. Once in session, "their very first act in congress was to present a preamble declaring that war existed by the act of Mexico," Lincoln wrote to Usher F. Linder, an ardent Illinois Democrat, and "the Locofocos here will not let the whigs be *silent*." Lincoln, the sole Whig representative from Illinois, decided not to be quiet.[120]

Lincoln's first attempt to "distinguish" himself backfired, winning him more guffaws from Democrats than praise from fellow Whigs, particularly in Illinois, where the war remained popular. Whig newspapers praised his resolutions as "based on facts," but Democratic publications had a field day. The *Illinois Globe* called him "the pettifogging lawyer." That was kind; the *Illinois State Register* accused him of encouraging "moral traitors," while the *Chicago Times* accuse him of "giving aid and comfort to the Mexican enemy." From the White House, Polk delivered the most stinging rebuke to Lincoln: he simply ignored him.[121]

Lincoln remained undeterred, supporting Massachusetts congressman George Ashmun's amendment declaring the Mexican-American War as "unnecessarily and unconstitutionally begun by the President."

Again Democratic politicians and editors pounced. Lincoln's home newspaper, the *Springfield Register*, noted that 1,000 men from his district had fought in Mexico; now their congressman questioned their sacrifices. Another publisher was even more blunt: "The mark of Cain is on him."[122]

Then, on January 12, 1848, a nervous Lincoln rose to make his first major speech in the House, a combination of legal argument and biblical oratory. He began by dismissing resolutions proposed by Illinois Democrat William A. Richardson supporting Polk's version of the start of the war. "The whole of this—issue and evidence—is, from beginning to end, the sheerest deception," Lincoln stated, later adding,

> . . . *I have sometimes seen a good lawyer, struggling for his client's neck, in a desperate case, employing every artifice to work round, befog, and cover up, with many words, some point arising in the case, which he* dared *not admit, and yet* could *not deny.*

For Lincoln, there was only one thing for Polk to do. "Let him answer with *facts*, and not with arguments. Let him remember he sits where Washington sat, and so remembering, let him answer as Washington would answer." If he did, Lincoln said, he would "be most happy to reverse the vote I gave the other day." However, if Polk "*can* not, or *will* not do this," then the president would "be deeply conscious of being in the wrong; that he feels the blood of this war, like the blood of Abel, is crying to Heaven against him." Lincoln compared Polk's contradictory arguments to "the half insane mumbling of a fever dream."[123]

Once again, partisanship shaped opinions on his speech. The Illinois newspaper the *Quincy Whig* placed him "in the front rank of the best speakers in the House." Democratic response was correspondingly critical, none more so than that of the *Springfield Register*, which called his speech "treasonable" and Lincoln "Benedict Arnold."[124]

Among his supporting arguments in the speech was an aside regarding the Declaration of Independence: "Any people any where, being inclined and having the power, have the *right* to rise up and shake off the existing government, and form a new one that suits them better.

This is a most valuable, a most sacred right . . ." Putting Jefferson's ideas in his own words made sense to Lincoln in 1848. It would be a discordant echo for him in 1860.[125]

Although he had committed to serving just one term in Congress, "it was very pleasant to learn," he told Herndon, "that there are some who desire I should be reelected." When a concerned Herndon wrote him questioning both Lincoln's votes on the war and his remarks, Lincoln was defensive. "I will stake my life," he declared, "that if you had been in my place, you would have voted just as I did." Regarding his stance on the war, Lincoln's conscience was clear, yet with each speech against it his political future was clear as well. Weeks into his new job, "Spotty" Lincoln looked to be a one-term congressman.[126]

Among the Whigs sitting through Lincoln's maiden speech was the representative from Massachusetts's Twelfth District. John Quincy Adams was eighty years old, a recent stroke victim, and frequently seen asleep at his congressional desk. "Old Man Eloquent" had led the Whig opposition to the war and its fight to abolish slavery. On February 21, during a debate over honoring veteran officers of the war, Adams slumped from his chair. "Mr. Adams is dying!" someone cried, and he was carried to House Speaker Robert C. Winthrop's office. He died in that room two days later. Lincoln, as the sole Whig from Illinois, was placed on the "Committee of Arrangements" for Adams's services in the congressional chamber.[127]

Nearly every American event of note, from the American Revolution to the Mexican War, was entwined somehow in Adams's life. He had been a diplomat and politician, secretary of state and president, and served his country since 1781, having met every president since Washington. It is not known whether, in his last weeks, he had met the sixteenth.

For the remainder of his term, Lincoln returned to the House floor to chastise Polk and the Democrats over the war. When they accused the Whigs of lack of support for the war effort, Lincoln struck back hard:

It is not true that we have always opposed the war. With few individual exceptions, you have constantly had our votes here for the necessary supplies. And, more than this, you have had the services, the blood, and the lives of our political brethren in every trial and on every field. The beardless boy and the mature man—the humble and the distinguished, you have had them. Through suffering and death, by disease, and in battle, they have endured, and fought, and fell with you. Clay and Webster each gave a son, never to be returned . . . [B]esides other worthy but less known whig names, we sent Marshall, Morrison, Baker, and Hardin . . . In that fearful, bloody, breathless struggle at Buena Vista . . . of the five high officers who perished, four were whigs.[128]

Once Lincoln learned that his unpopularity at home came mostly from Democrats, he started switching his focus to the war's impact on the spread of slavery, and thence to slavery itself.

Another change came that spring: Mary and the boys returned to Springfield. She had hoped to find in Washington a social calendar befitting her image of a congressman's wife. "Mary was full of fun and an airy sort of badinage, very puzzling to a dull-witted person," her niece Katherine Helm stated during this time. "She kept in touch with current events and could forecast many a political outcome."[129]

It was not to be. Most congressmen left their families at home. Almost immediately, her daily lot of cramped confinement with two rambunctious boys, along with complaints from boarders about them (and, at times, Mary herself), made her departure inevitable. Later, Lincoln confessed that "when you were here, I thought you hindered me some in attending to business; but now, having nothing but business . . . I hate to stay in this old room by myself."[130]

He did not linger "in this old room" long. Now he could tarry at the House to his heart's content and participate in boardinghouse post-dinner debates to the end. Giddings dominated the sessions, especially when Duff Green, a newspaper publisher, walked down from his home to loudly defend the Southern lifestyle. As before, Lincoln interspersed his viewpoint with anecdotes to keep the temperature down.[131]

He had, by this time, won over both his Whig colleagues and the press. He was already a popular raconteur at the House's post office, where, newspaperman Benjamin Perley Poore recalled,

> *his favorite seat was at the left of the open fire-place, tilted back in his chair, with his long legs reaching over to the chimney jamb. He never told a story twice, but appeared to have an endless repertoire of them . . . always pertinently adapted to some passing event. It was refreshing to us correspondents, compelled as we were to listen to so much that was prosy and tedious, to hear this bright specimen of Western genius tell his inimitable stories.*[132]

Among his new friends was a diminutive Whig from Georgia. Alexander H. Stephens's background was similar to Lincoln's. His mother had died when he was an infant, his father and stepmother dying of pneumonia when he was fourteen. Despite his lifetime of health issues, Stephens possessed a brilliant mind and innate determination. Now in his fifth year in Congress, Stephens was a fervent opponent of the war, and Lincoln watched the "slim, pale-faced, consumptive" Stephens give "the very best speech . . . I have ever heard," telling Herndon, "My old, withered, dry eyes, are full of tears." Stephens, in turn, discovered Lincoln had "a very strong, clear, and vigorous mind." They made an odd couple in appearance but were united in their goals, save one: slavery. They joined five other junior congressmen in declaring their support for Zachary Taylor for president and were soon dubbed the "Young Indians."[133]

The awkward newcomer to Congress had also honed his speaking persona. Mixing his remarks with an occasional witty (or biting) aside, Lincoln's high-pitched Midwestern tones could cut through the poor audibility of the chamber. With his left hand behind his back to control his coattails, his right free for gestures or pointing at friend or foe, he constantly roamed the aisles until his remarks were finished, prompting a Democrat to wonder if Lincoln would "charge mileage on his travels."[134]

His "travels" soon became reality. In June, he accompanied other congressional Whigs to Philadelphia for their convention. He had already decided that Clay was unelectable and declared his support for

Zachary Taylor. To Billy Herndon he added that "Taylor's nomination takes the locos on the blind side. It turns the war thunder against them."[135]

Lincoln found Philadelphia in the throes of adapting to the Industrial Revolution. Factories were replacing storefronts and shops; manufacturing ownership promised new wealth accompanied by an influx of menial labor. The rise of a Black upper class, combined with the daily arrival of thousands of Irish immigrants, resulted in violent riots by nativist mobs. Mayor John Swift had his hands full providing a peaceable city for his fellow Whigs.[136]

The Illinois Whig had never witnessed such a scene. "All the hotels were crowded to overflowing . . . [B]oarding houses were full—and private families largely quartered on," an Alabama attendee wrote. "All seemed mad with excitement on politics—such gesticulating, and jabbering, you never saw or heard—Babel could not have beat it far in noise and confusion."

Delegates convened at the Chinese Museum in Philadelphia, whose galleries were crammed with 3,000 spectators every day. Taylor's nomination, a foregone conclusion to Lincoln, was met with near disdain by Northern Whigs. The thought of nominating a slaveholder was anathema to many. Horace Greeley, publisher of the *New York Tribune*, believed Taylor's "unqualified devotion to slavery" made it indecent to choose him. "We may elect him," Greeley warned, "but we destroy the Whig party." On the fourth ballot, Taylor finally prevailed.[137]

Lincoln became a stalwart member of the Whig executive committee, a bloc of congressmen working during the recess "to supply every section of the country with useful information." None of his colleagues outdid Lincoln's efforts on Taylor's behalf in their goal to get out the vote.[138]

The Whigs had every reason to be concerned about the race. Weeks after his nomination, Taylor had yet to accept it. And now there was a third party to contend with: Northern Whigs, disillusioned that a slaveholder was their nominee, formed the Free Soil Party. Among their ringleaders were Salmon Chase, Charles Sumner, and Lincoln's fellow boardinghouse tenant Joshua Giddings. Their presidential candidate was Martin Van Buren, with John Quincy Adams's son Charles Francis as their vice presidential candidate.[139]

Democrats selected Lewis Cass, a War of 1812 veteran and Andrew Jackson's secretary of war who had diligently seen to it that the Indian Removal Act of 1830 was carried out. Cass was an early proponent of popular sovereignty, originally a tenet summarized as consent of the governed but fast becoming a solution to the free-state-versus-slave-state issue: Let the voters in the state or territory decide. Cass was a "doughface," a decades-old term describing a Northern politician supporting Southern policies.[140]

Lincoln was invited to go to Boston to speak on Taylor's behalf. After a sumptuous dinner hosted by former governor Levi Lincoln Jr., his distant cousin, Lincoln took to the hustings. Local newspapers described him as "a very tall and thin figure, with an intellectual face, showing a searching mind, and cool judgment." They gave detailed reports on his speeches throughout the state, calling one "replete with good sense, sound reasoning, and irresistible argument." After reciting his reasons for supporting Taylor, he derided the Free Soilers' rationale for splitting the party: "We can't go for General Taylor because he is not a Whig, Van Buren is not a Whig; therefore we go for him."[141, 142, 143]

At a rally in Boston, Lincoln sat alongside William H. Seward, former governor of New York and now a candidate for the Senate. Seward averred that "all Whigs agree—that Slavery shall not be extended into any Territory now free" and called for its abolishment in Washington, D.C. Not to be outdone, Lincoln followed him with a ninety-minute speech that "for sound reasoning, cogent argument and keen satire, we have seldom heard equalled," according to the *Boston Atlas*. After he concluded, "the audience gave three cheers for Taylor and Fillmore, and three more for Mr. Lincoln."[144]

Seward was less impressed, calling Lincoln's remarks "a rambling story-telling speech, putting the audience in good humour, but avoiding any extended discussion of the slavery question." They shared a room the next evening in Worcester, where Lincoln told Seward his bold call to end slavery hit home. "I reckon you are right," he told Seward. "We have got to give it more attention hereafter."[145]

Once back in Springfield, Lincoln traversed Illinois, asking potential Free Soil voters not to waste their votes, as he "doubted Van Buren would get even one State." On Election Day, Taylor won decisively, gaining 47 percent of the total vote. Lincoln was right: Van Buren did not win one state. The slaveholder and hero of a war the Whigs had opposed gave the Whigs their last presidential victory.[146]

On November 26, Lincoln traveled back to Washington alone, contemplating William Seward's eloquent and stubborn antislavery convictions. Lincoln was now halfway through his congressional term. What would he do with the rest of it?

With Quincy Adams's death, Giddings assumed his mantle as the de facto leader of the antislavery movement in Congress. Despite his rupture with the Whigs, he and Lincoln remained friendly. One night at Mrs. Sprigg's, three armed men broke in, gagged and shackled Henry Wilson, a Black waiter, in front of his wife, then dragged him to a "slave pen" and sent him to New Orleans to be sold. When the widow's boarders learned of the incident, Giddings drew up a resolution for a committee to investigate the assault and kidnapping of Wilson. It lost, 94–88.[147]

The new congressional session was just underway when New York's Daniel Gott proposed a resolution abolishing slavery in Washington. The measure's preamble, written by Horace Greeley, derided slave trading as "notoriously a reproach to our country throughout Christendom and a serious hindrance to the progress of republican liberty among the nations of the earth." Finding such phrases certain to raise the bilious indignation of their Southern colleagues, Lincoln and three Northern Whigs joined the majority in tabling Gott's proposal, prompting Giddings to accuse them of "support of the slave trade."[148]

As the House debate over slavery grew more rancorous, Lincoln came up with a solution. Giddings joined him in a courtesy call to Mayor William Winston Seaton on January 9. Lincoln also solicited the opinion of Joseph Gales, veteran publisher of the *National Intelligencer*. Both men gave him their endorsement. Seaton humorously remarked that Lincoln's solution might prove so popular that Seaton was sur-prised Giddings supported it.[149]

On January 10, Lincoln rose and introduced "A bill for an act to abolish slavery in the District of Columbia by the consent of the white people of said District, and with compensation to owners." His bill was rife with conciliatory conditions: those enslaved in the District would be freed if their owners applied and received "full value"; enslaved owned by federal officials could be brought into the District if the own-ers were on "public business"; and any fugitive enslaved—runaways—would be arrested and returned to their owners. A referendum would be voted on in April by "every free white male citizen" to vote on Lin-coln's proposal.

Lincoln then announced he "was authorized to say, that of about fifteen of the leading citizens of the District to whom this proposition had been submitted, there was not one but who approved of the adop-tion of such a proposition."[150]

If Lincoln anticipated this last remark would help win votes, he quickly learned he was mistaken. Numerous Democrats jumped to their feet, shouting "Who are they?" and "Give us their names!" Their clamor soon became a veritable storm directed at Lincoln.

Either because he did not have their permission to name them or because he did not want their support of his proposal revoked if he did, Lincoln did not answer. At that moment his proposal was doomed. "I learned," he later recalled, "that many leading southern members of Congress, had been to see the Mayor and the others who favored my Bill and drawn them over to their way of thinking."[151]

He had read the mood of the citizens correctly, but not the will of the Whigs in the House. While Northern Whigs might have gone along with Lincoln's proposal, the Southern Whigs' collective wrath cowed even Giddings. Meanwhile, fervent antislavery proponents pilloried Lincoln; Wendell Phillips later branded him "the Slave-Hound of Illi-nois" for his clause regarding fugitive slaves. "Finding that I was aban-doned by my former backers, and having little personal influence," Lincoln noted, he "dropped the matter knowing that it was useless to prosecute the business at that time."[152]

The next day the Widow Sprigg's congressional boarders "remained in the dining room after tea, and conversed upon the subject of Mr. Lincoln's bill to abolish slavery," Giddings entered in his diary. "It was approved by all; I believe it as good a bill as we could get at this time, and am willing to pay for slaves in order to save them from the Southern market . . ."[153]

Southern congressmen and senators took delight in publicly eviscerating Lincoln's proposal. Tennessee congressman Andrew Johnson later warned that if Lincoln's proposal was approved, "it will be followed in the states"—a veritable domino theory on the potential spread of emancipation.[154]

Lincoln sought freedom for the enslaved in Washington by appealing to Northerners' sympathy and moral certitude while hoping to circumvent Southerners' intransigent belief that Black enslavement was a legal right by paying for the freedom of the enslaved. Giddings was correct: Lincoln's plan of gradual emancipation and compensation was the best chance for ending slavery in Washington, which was why the proslavery bloc desperately wanted to kill it. Lincoln's first major attempt to right a wrong that had preyed on his mind since his youth had failed. He was not the Great Emancipator yet, but he had finally started down the path.

The second session of the contentious Thirtieth Congress battled into the wee hours of March 4. An appropriations bill to keep the government running through 1849 soon had so many amendments attached to it, including several on slavery, that both houses were at loggerheads. With Congress set to adjourn in hours, the threat of a government shutdown loomed. Finally, the bill, stripped of extraneous modifications, passed both houses. Congress adjourned at 7 a.m. Lincoln's hour on the national stage was officially over.[155]

March 4 was usually Inauguration Day, but as it fell on a Sunday in 1849, Taylor chose to be sworn in on the fifth, a typically damp, gray, blustery March day. Crowds clogged every street, blocking the parade to the Capitol for over an hour. Despite an evening snowstorm, the

Whigs celebrated with three inaugural balls. Lincoln was one of 230 organizing sponsors of one affair, as was Robert E. Lee. Lincoln stayed until at least 3 a.m. His friend Elihu Washburne recalled, "It would be hard to forget the sight of that tall and slim man, with his short cloak thrown over his shoulders, starting for his long walk home on Capitol Hill, at four o'clock in the morning."[156]

His term over, Lincoln had two tasks remaining before his departure. On March 7, he returned to the Capitol and descended the east stairs next to the Senate chamber and entered the Supreme Court chamber, a fifty-foot-by-seventy-five-foot room, ornate in design, with a vaulted ceiling. Behind the bench, a lunette depicting Justice grasping scales and a sword watched over proceedings, accompanied by a winged male holding the Constitution in one hand and pointing at it with the other, and an eagle guarding lawbooks. The chamber was badly lit, perpetually damp, and poorly ventilated. The gallery was often fully occupied during important cases or when someone of note was arguing a case. (Daniel Webster's appearances packed the place.) Many a congressman appeared as an attorney before the court and then returned to his congressional duties upstairs.[157]

The case, Lewis v. Lewis, had begun when Lincoln was ten years old: a dispute over a poorly prepared deed filed in 1819 concerning land in Ohio. The case boiled down to the statute of limitations in Illinois and an ongoing lawsuit from William Lewis against Thomas Lewis over one hundred acres. Lincoln represented the defendant, Thomas.[158]

Just turned forty, Lincoln had been admitted to the bar of the Supreme Court right before the proceedings began. With his long hair, bushy eyebrows, and grim expression, Chief Justice Roger B. Taney, ten days shy of his seventy-second birthday, was an ominous presence. Oral arguments took two days. Lincoln asserted that the statute of limitations had expired; therefore, William Lewis was not entitled to collect damages. Five days later the court delivered its decision. Lincoln lost. Taney wrote the majority opinion holding for the plaintiff, while Justice John McLean's dissent supported Lincoln's argument.[159]

Lincoln's last act before leaving Washington took place on March 10 when he appeared at the patent office on F Street to make an application for his floating machine. In May he was notified that Patent No. 6,469, for "Buoying Vessels Over Shoals," had been registered and issued. He is the only president to have received a patent for an invention.[160]

After farewells to Giddings, Stephens, and other colleagues, Lincoln boarded a westbound train on March 20 at the same dingy station where he and his family had arrived in 1847. He reached Springfield on March 31, welcomed by friends and family but at loose ends over what he wanted to do next.[161]

Once home, Lincoln pursued an appointment as commissioner of the General Land Office, a bureaucratic position that guaranteed financial security—it paid $3,000 a year—but would hinder his law practice. Offered both the secretaryship and later governorship of Oregon Territory, Lincoln turned both down despite his old law partner John T. Stuart's urging that he accept the latter. Oregon would soon be a state, Stuart argued, and return Lincoln to Washington as a senator. Lincoln said he would take the post if Mary consented. She did not.[162]

Losing the commissioner's position due to political infighting and the Oregon opportunity to Mary's rebuff left Lincoln with one recourse. He "went to the practice of law with greater earnestness than ever before," stating years later that "I was losing interest in politics."[163]

But was that completely true? If Billy Herndon's oft-cited remark that Lincoln's ambition "was a little engine that knew no rest" is accurate, returning to his practice allowed him to wait for another opportunity to present itself. To win the presidency, the Whigs had cleaved themselves to a slaveholding Southerner. Lincoln had been the only Whig member of Illinois's congressional delegation; perhaps, in 1849, he realized he had gone as far as he could go politically—for now.[164]

The Mexican-American War had done much to mold Meade, Lee, and Lincoln. Battle after battle had demonstrably shown the two officers the importance of what they had learned at West Point and given them a chance to demonstrate both their courage and resourcefulness. The examples of their generals—Taylor for Meade, Scott for Lee—stayed with them throughout their careers, impressing on them what they did right in leadership and tactics and to be careful to avoid what they did not do well. Both being remarkably talented engineers, Meade and Lee witnessed repeatedly the importance of taking—and holding—the high ground on a battlefield.

For two years, Lincoln saw firsthand the inner workings of the federal government and came to understand how effective a speaker he could be and how disunited the United States was regarding war and slavery. And from the congressional chamber to Mrs. Sprigg's dining room, from Giddings to Seward, he realized his innate detestation of slavery must be welded to his oratorical gifts.

Three different roads awaited these men. The 1850s beckoned.

FIVE

THE LIGHTHOUSE BUILDER,
THE RAIL-SPLITTER,
AND THE MARBLE MODEL

He did not know it yet, but after two years of war Lieutenant George Meade was about to begin his happiest years in the United States Army.

After a journey of three weeks from New Orleans, Meade arrived in Washington in April 1847. The visit was twofold: to settle the accounts of his late engineering comrades, Captain William G. Williams and Lieutenant Jacob E. Blake, and help sell his mother's Georgetown home. She had purchased a house just blocks away from his in Philadelphia.[1]

It was during Meade's reunion with his family in Philadelphia that his nephew, Richard Meade Bache, discovered his uncle's gift for story-telling. "He had the gift of clear statement . . . how a certain gun was placed at the battle of Resaca de la Palma at a critical juncture of the fight," Bache later recalled. Honors from his hometown included Philadelphia's gift of "a beautiful and costly sword, as a tribute to his gallant conduct." Meade was given his old assignment to finish the lighthouse at Brandywine Shoal. Little had been done in his absence, but there was one positive development: Colonel J. J. Abert, still commander of the Corps of Topographical Engineers, had successfully obtained funding to complete the first screw-pile lighthouse in the United States. Meade reveled in his return to the project, once again taking soundings daily and studying the tides, currents, winds, and other factors with an engineer's meticulous concentration.[2]

The work was arduous. Nine pilings made of hammered iron were transported one at a time to the shoal by a small supply boat and loaded aboard a drilling raft, then eased through a hole in the raft until it struck bottom. Next, a windlass—a cylindrical mechanism with a crank—turned the piling into the seabed until the flanges were secured at the proper depth. By autumn, the foundation was deemed sturdy enough to withstand the coming winter, during which Hartman Bache sent Meade to the Florida Keys, where Bache was surveying reefs and islands for a network of new lighthouses.[3]

The Florida Keys stretch 185 miles in a southwestern arc starting fifteen miles south of Miami at Virginia Key, through Key West, to the Dry Tortugas. On charts, the symmetrical curve of the keys looks like a finger gesturing, *Come closer*, but Spanish sailors soon learned how treacherous they were. Upon sighting them, the conquistador Juan Ponce de Léon called the keys the "Martyrs" due to the sorrowful gazes of the Calusa and Tequesta tribes, whose expressions might have been due to de Léon's arrival. Many a galleon, her hold full of the riches wrought from the forests, mountains, and Indigenous peoples whose lands were now the "Spanish Main," was dashed by jagged coral reefs, ran aground on sandbars or shoals, or foundered in one of the hurricanes that tossed the great ships like a tosspot in an eddy. Small wonder that Daniel Elfrith's 1631 manuscript guide to the Caribbean (unpublished until 1944) instructed pilots that "they must knowe the head of [the] Martirs."[4] Over the centuries, innumerable ships had met their fate along the keys, inspiring bands of men, soon known as wreckers, to make sail for the derelict vessels, salvaging anything of value from them.[5]

The Louisiana Purchase in 1803 created a surge in sea traffic as new American mercantile firms shipped goods from New Orleans to the United States and Europe. By the 1850s, between $300 million and $400 million worth of goods passed annually through the Florida Straits. With the increase in potential victims, wreckers soon began using false lights to lure their prey into the reefs, particularly Carysfort Reef, considered the most dangerous along the archipelago. For decades, insurance companies had sued in courts to reclaim salvage while urging Congress to establish an admiralty court at Key West and build lighthouses along the keys. Congress passed measures for both in the 1820s; by 1848, construction of lighthouses along the keys was approved, hence Bache's request for Meade to join him in Florida and help select sites for the new lighthouses.

With some of the keys barely above sea level, it was originally thought that screw-pile construction would be the norm. Meade's initial observations convinced him that the classic heavy brick lighthouse structure might be suitable for some sites. He returned to Philadelphia to work in harness with Bache on plans.[6]

Meade was already collaborating with Isaiah William Penn Lewis, a Philadelphia engineer known as "I.W.P.," on Brandywine Shoal's foundation. The large pilings for the project were made by the Southwark Foundry, Merrick & Towne, near the same Philadelphia shipyard that had seen the birth of both the Continental and U.S. Navies. The first attempt at securing the structure at the shoal failed; the combination of fierce winds and tide made it shake uncontrollably. Meade realized that if the pilings were driven into the seafloor diagonally, the result would be an integrated support base, and he made the correction. The lighthouse's frame soon rose above Brandywine Shoal.[7]

In the fall of 1849, Meade was summoned again to Florida, not by Bache but by General David E. Twiggs, who was in need of a topographical engineer. There was a threat of an outbreak of hostilities by the Seminoles still remaining in Florida. Meade reported to Twiggs at Fort Brooke in Tampa Bay. In Mexico, Meade had considered Twiggs a martinet. "No good feeling existed between them," Meade's son George later recalled.

Meade found Fort Brooke much the same as when he had last seen it in 1836. He was to survey the Florida territory, choosing sites for a line of forts from Fort Brooke across the peninsula to Fort Pierce on Florida's east coast. After a lengthy enumeration of Meade's mission, Twiggs asked what he needed in manpower and supplies. Meade's answer, "two men and a mule," was a far easier request than Twiggs had expected. The next morning, Meade and one assigned soldier mounted up; with one mule in tow, they set off to cross Florida.[8]

  Sixty miles from Fort Brooke, Meade chose ground along the Peace River over another selected site. Skeptical, Twiggs rode out to see it for himself and surprisingly agreed. For four months Meade crisscrossed central Florida south to Lake Okeechobee, providing Twiggs with cartographical maps and details. "Meade is doing good work, and putting on no staff airs," Twiggs reported. The frostiness between the men ended; in February 1850, Twiggs cited Meade's "cheerful intelligence which insured success," naming the fort after Meade.[9]

On one return to Fort Brooke, Meade met another Philadelphian, two years out of West Point. But let Lieutenant John Gibbon tell us:

> *Late one afternoon, rode a horseman attended by a single orderly. He was a gaunt, thin man, with a hatchet face and a prominent aquiline nose. He introduced himself as Lieutenant Meade, Topographical Engineers, just from a reconnaissance on the hostile border. He was wet, tired, and hungry. It was my good fortune to be able to offer dry clothes, food, and a bed of blankets.*[10]

Gibbon's and Meade's careers would intersect again, particularly at Gettysburg.

Meade returned to Philadelphia in early 1850, weeks after the birth of his third son, Spencer. Come springtime he was back at Brandywine Shoal, where he discovered that ice floes had damaged the lighthouse. He constructed an iron fence around the shoal, secured by screw-piles that broke up the ice. As summer progressed, so did the keeper's house, its conical design now fact and not idea. By September the first lighthouse of its kind in the Western Hemisphere just needed a lens.[11]

Once more Meade provided an engineering breakthrough. The light source was a third order Fresnel lens, named after the French engineer and physicist who had helped prove the wave theory of light. It was a network of prisms enclosed in a six-foot brass frame that looked to some like a giant beehive and to others like an immense fly's head. Meade fell in love with its design; once installed, he was overjoyed with the results. "This marvelous contrivance darts forth its dazzling flash," he reported, "and revolving as it flashes, only intermits its light still more to startle the beholder . . . A cast iron column, or pedestal, sustains the whole structure . . . Motion is given to this by a handsome piece of clock-work."[12]

Once completed, Brandywine Shoal Lighthouse rose forty-six feet and was hardly handsome but completely practical. In 1851 an experiment was performed by an ad hoc committee whose members set out by boat one evening to a point fifteen miles from the Brandywine Shoal lighthouse, putting them 6¼ miles from Cape Henlopen's lighthouse and 8¾ miles from Cape May's. The latter two were equipped with a tried-and-true system of reflectors and lamps. Despite their significant advantage in height, the Fresnel lens at the shoal shone far more brilliantly than the others. A new era in lighthouse construction and design had arrived.[13]

Meade's success at Brandywine Shoal was not lost on Colonel Abert in Washington, who sent him in late 1851 to Florida's Carysfort Reef, six nautical miles east of Key Largo, to oversee completion of another screw-pile lighthouse designed by I.W.P. The reef was named for HMS *Carysfort*, one of dozens of ships lost there. By 1849 the reef had become a financial windfall for wreckers; insurance rates for ships passing the Florida Keys equaled those imposed on vessels sailing around Cape Horn.[14]

Construction on the lighthouse began in 1848, with the frame built in Philadelphia, disassembled, and shipped to Tavernier, a small settlement of mariners, ne'er-do-wells, and wreckers at the southwest tip of Key Largo. Meade soon discovered the coral reef was not solid enough to support the lighthouse. To secure the pilings, six-foot circular cast-iron disks were needed. By 1851, two other officers had already attempted to complete the task but come up short.

Meade resumed construction despite storms and oppressive heat as well as financial and equipment challenges. A promised Fresnel lens never arrived, so Meade substituted an old-fashioned lamp and reflector lens. Completed on schedule, the narrow, 117-foot, red-painted

cylindrical tower was surrounded by a fifty-foot skeleton, its open structure guaranteeing its durability. Carysfort Light was lit on March 10,
1852. It was during this assignment that Meade received his first lieutenant's commission.[15]

Before departing, Meade assigned the lighthouse keepers a new
task: to board any wrecks or ships in distress and aid them "by piloting
or the supplying of sustenance." He requested that two rowboats and
one sailboat be assigned to the keepers for that purpose.[16]

He returned to Philadelphia to both work on lighthouse design and
visit his seriously ill mother, who died on March 22, 1852. Eight months
later his father-in-law, John Sergeant, died, another sad blow.[17]

In 1853, Meade was ordered to Sand Key, six nautical miles southwest of Key West. Meade departed alone; unlike Robert and Mary Lee,
Meade and Margaret believed the family was better off remaining at
home. They now had four children, ranging from eleven to one year old:
John Sergeant, George Gordon Jr., Margaret Butler, Spencer, and Sarah
Wise. While he was in Florida, Margaret gave birth to another daughter, Henrietta.[18]

In 1852, Congress replaced the outdated sixty-year-old Lighthouse
Service with the United States Lighthouse Board, under the direction
of the Topographical Bureau. The board consisted of senior naval
officers, army engineers, and civilian experts. Meade was named an
engineer of the Seventh District, including Florida. The Sand Key
lighthouse was his first assignment under the new program.

As at Carysfort, there had been a previous lighthouse at Sand Key,
a sixty-foot brick structure with a small home for the keeper and
family, but the edifice proved problematic during hurricane season.
One storm in 1844 washed away most of the island. The keeper at the
time, Joshua Appleby, a former wrecker, remarked to U.S. Navy lieutenant William A. Pease that some future tempest "would sweep all
to destruction." Sadly, his prediction came true; in October 1846,
Appleby and his daughter's family—along with their dwelling and the
lighthouse—vanished in a hurricane that another officer called "the
most destructive of any that ever visited these latitudes in the memory
of man."[19]

The foundation for the new lighthouse had been laid in 1852 by I. W. P. Lewis himself, a screw-pile base ten feet beneath Sand Key's surface. Meade and his team arrived on a schooner in January 1853 to complete the project. The smallness of the key and its fragility were challenging enough, but the lighthouse required completion before the hurricane season. Nor could Meade rush or cut corners: the tragedy of '46 could easily have been repeated in the keys.[20]

By springtime, the skeleton emerged above the delicate key's sand, fastened securely to Lewis's fifty-foot-wide base and the seventeen two-foot-long screws supporting it. Construction of the lighthouse immediately followed as Meade's team dealt with storms, rough tides, and the incessant hum of mosquitoes and flies feeding off their arms and necks. In early summer, a 121-foot lighthouse, with nine twelve-foot-square rooms for dwelling and machinery, was finished. All that was left to do was install the light itself.[21]

That was easier said than done. Once the lamp was placed inside the Fresnel lens, it proved difficult to use. Its oil came from a mechanism that required winding by the lighthouse keeper. Seeing this, Meade installed one of his own making: a five-wick hydraulic lamp. A hand pump sent oil into a tank in the lighthouse dome, and gravity fed the lamp enough oil to keep it aglow.[22]

Meade's simple solution worked. Sand Key first shone its light across the waters on July 20. The Lighthouse Board approved Meade's design; his lamp would be installed in American lighthouses until kerosene replaced whale oil. That October, Meade was ordered to demonstrate the "Meade Hydraulic Lamp" at the 1853 Crystal Palace Exhibition in New York City. He replied, "I will cheerfully attend to this business with two provisions: first, that it is made a matter of duty, and second, that it is not to cost me anything."[23]

Leaving Sand Key in autumn 1853, Meade happily reported: "The work was closed, and all parties returned to their homes without the slightest accident, or without a serious case of illness." The true proof of his success at Sand Key came in 1856, when another hurricane decimated Key West and the nearby keys. The Lighthouse Board reported that

*many lives were lost and much property was destroyed . . . [T]he sand
island, upon which the Sand Key light-house was, with the wooden buildings, wharf, and boats, was destroyed, leaving, however, the lighthouse
tower uninjured.*

Over the next twenty years, hurricanes would continue attacking Sand Key, taking everything, including Sand Key, away—except
Meade's lighthouse.[24]

Meade's successes led to his promotion to superintendent of the Seventh Lighthouse District, including Florida. Every lighthouse planned
for the keys now came under his direct supervision. He left Philadelphia
and family again in early 1854 to resume his tasks.[25]

Meade was justifiably proud of his designs, particularly the one for
Coffins Patches, also known as Sombrero Key or "Sombrero Shoals" by
the Lighthouse Board, six miles from Marathon. Initial plans for a
brick-and-mortar structure were abandoned for the more reliable design that worked at Carysfort and Sand Key. The octagonal skeleton
and the red cast-iron tower, towering 142 feet above the reef, were the
tallest of Meade's lighthouses in the keys.[26]

During these years, Meade encountered two men who would play
significant roles in his life. The first was Lieutenant William Franklin
Raynolds, who had graduated fifth in West Point's class of 1843. (Fellow
cadet Ulysses S. Grant ranked twenty-first.) Raynolds had served as a
topographical engineer under both Taylor and Scott in the Mexican-
American War; now he was assigned to Meade to assist in lighthouse
construction.[27]

The other gentleman was Massachusetts-born Theodore Lyman,
twenty-three, whose father had been mayor of Boston. The Harvard-
educated Lyman was embarking on a career as a naturalist and was part
of a survey of Florida's coastline led by famed professor Louis Agassiz.
Lyman met Meade in Key West in 1856 and the two quickly became
friends, their conversations on engineering and science lasting well into
the evenings. Seven years later they would meet again under harsher
circumstances.[28]

Completion of Sombrero Light was placed in Raynolds's capable hands. By then, Meade had been given more responsibilities by the Lighthouse Board; Bache was reassigned to the West Coast, and the Board wanted Meade to assume leadership of the Fourth District as well as the Seventh. As the Fourth District covered New Jersey and Delaware, Meade happily accepted. It brought him closer to home, at least half the time.[29]

Many a coastal area along the mid-Atlantic shore had been given the dubious nickname "the Graveyard of the Atlantic." Barnegat, on Long Beach Island, New Jersey, certainly fit the bill. An early colonial newspaper reported in 1705 how three sloops "were cast away near Barnegat by the late easterly storms." One hundred and fifty years later, little had changed; in April 1854, the clipper *Powhatan*, carrying 311 German immigrants, fell victim to a horrific snowstorm, slammed into the Barnegat Shoals, and was carried by the gale south to Surf City, where one last, huge wave smashed into the *Powhatan*, drowning everyone aboard. "Bodies are constantly washed ashore along the coast of New Jersey, from Long Beach down to Absecom [*sic*]," the *New York Daily Times* grimly reported.[30]

The tragedy hastened the board's determination to build three lighthouses from Barnegat down to Cape May, the southernmost point on New Jersey's coastline. The first was to be near Atlantic City, a newly named town whose leaders hoped to create a vacation destination for Philadelphians. Meade produced plans for handsome masonry lighthouses.

Bache had originally selected a site some 1,400 feet from the ocean in the nearby village of Absecon. Construction commenced in June 1855. Logistical challenges arose immediately. Atlantic City lacked commercial wharves; supplies could only come from the railroad. Topography also provided a challenge: excavation for the foundation had reached a depth of eight feet when water from the surrounding marshlands flooded the dig, halting work until a train brought a massive steam-powered pump that could remove 12,000 gallons per hour.[31]

When the lighthouse was completed, it stood at a height of 171 feet, the tallest in New Jersey. Nearly 600,000 bricks were used for the tower and two dwellings for the keeper and his assistants. Its lamp was lit on January 15, 1857; by year's end the Lighthouse Board reported, "On this part of the coast of hitherto frequent and appalling shipwrecks, since the exhibition of this light, a period of ten months, there have been no wrecks in the vicinity." Meade's next assignment lay thirty miles north, at Barnegat.[32]

Upon visiting Barnegat, Meade not only found that the old lighthouse's light was inadequate but that the inlet's channel was "so winding and shifting" that "a light at this point is of no use at all." Meade researched the past winter's record of shipwrecks and ordered the keeper, James Fuller, to keep daily count of the ships that passed each day: an average of four hundred "square-rigged vessels and steamers." Meade believed the same number sailed by at night, giving him an accurate estimate of "the number of lives and amount of property whose safety is dependent on being furnished with the most efficient aid to navigation."[33]

Meade designed a lighthouse like Absecon Light, estimating the cost at $45,000. Construction commenced in late 1856 as waves continued to erode the nearby location of the old lighthouse. Later, when that structure collapsed into the water, Meade ordered construction halted and moved nine hundred feet south. Barnegat lighthouse, just three feet shorter than Absecon Light, was lit on New Year's Day 1859.[34]

By then Meade's design for the new Cape May lighthouse was approved and construction underway. But that was done under Raynolds's watchful eye. The army had other plans for George Meade.

Beginning in 1855, a flurry of changes in Lieutenant Meade's life took place. That year Margaret gave birth to their seventh child, a son named William. For several months in 1856, Meade was dispatched to Detroit to assist Lieutenant Colonel James Kearney with the ongoing Great Lakes survey, a fifteen-year-old project to provide the most accurate soundings and charts to improve navigation, maritime commerce, and safety on the Great Lakes and connected waterways. A promotion in May, in recognition of his successes with lighthouses, put captain's bars on Meade's shoulders.[35]

Meade was busy with several lighthouse projects in 1857 when he received orders on May 20 to replace Kearney and lead the Great Lakes survey. This time Meade would not travel alone: Margaret and the children would accompany him.[36]

The family traveled to New York City, then up to Albany, where George and Margaret crammed their seven children and baggage aboard a packet on the Erie Canal. From Buffalo a steam-powered ship carried them across Lake Erie and up the Detroit River to Detroit itself.[37]

Detroit was booming. Factories and warehouses clogged the waterfront, and houses could not be built fast enough. Thousands of immigrants swelled the population. Many of them encountered Detroit's richest citizen, eighty-eight-year-old Joseph Campau, who habitually greeted newcomers on his daily constitutional. By 1854 a railroad linked Detroit to New York City. Ships carrying iron ore and copper now passed through the new locks at the Sault Ste. Marie Canal, linking Lakes Huron and Superior. Ohio congressman Joshua Giddings, Lincoln's boardinghouse colleague, was among the first to see the opportunity the Great Lakes provided and the need for a thorough survey.[38, 39]

But the Great Lakes posed economic hazards for merchants and life-threatening dangers for sailors. Powerful gales swept across the vast waters, with immense waves sweeping seamen off the decks and sending vessels to watery graves. Soundings were needed, as well as sites for safe harbors and lighthouses. In 1841, Congress allocated funds for the United States Lake Survey.[40]

The Mexican-American War interrupted the survey, but by 1856 it was well underway. Counting Kearney's two stints, Meade was the fifth officer to take charge. The Great Lakes region covered 95,000 square miles of water, with a coastline of more than 6,000 miles. Named "Superintendent (or Superintending) Engineer, Survey of the Northern & Northwestern Lakes," a title nearly as long as his assignment, Meade went to work.[41]

For the next three years Meade and a handpicked crew of military and civilian engineers worked tirelessly, "bringing to light all hidden dangers; obtaining the evidence and capacity and depth of water in all the harbors and rivers and consequently the most practicable mode of improving them; furnishing the evidence of the wants of navigation in reference to lighthouses, beacons and buoys and the proper sites for same." From Saginaw Bay in the "Thumb Region" of Michigan's Lower Peninsula to the bottom of Lake Huron, Meade scoured old charts and maps, convinced the longitude lines were wrong, and began correcting them.[42]

Earlier, Professor C. A. Young of Western Reserve College in Ohio had come up with a new method of determining longitude. Young proposed setting up observation points at two stations, east and west, to observe the meridian passage of the stars using an electric observatory clock at one station. To Meade, this procedure lacked complete accuracy. His solution was simple: use *two* clocks, one at each station, to monitor a star's passage across the night sky. Meade's idea worked, allowing his crew to determine longitude much quicker and more accurately than previously.[43]

The challenge of accurately gauging the configuration of the bottom of Lake Huron was solved when Meade ran measuring lines completely across the bottom. By the end of 1859, Meade had placed nineteen weather stations across the Great Lakes, improving communications to warn ships by semaphore of coming storms. Reporting that work on Saginaw and Thunder Bays had been completed as well as "a considerable portion of Lake Huron," Meade added that "there are two portions of the lake region not yet surveyed that require immediate attention . . . Lake Superior and the north end of Lake Michigan."[44]

Meade's requests for necessary funds from Congress were now answered with sizably smaller amounts. The Panic of 1857 was reaching a crescendo of bank failures nationwide. Among the closures was the Bank of Pennsylvania, where the Meade family had the monies from the sale of Meade's mother's home and most of his father's art collection. While in Mexico, Meade had boasted to Margaret of "ample means to support us." Now his captain's pay would be stretched very thin indeed. He would never brag about "ample means" again.[45]

The Meades enjoyed their years in Detroit. They made friends among his staff and their families as well as among neighboring families, frequently attending social affairs. Meade's junior officers liked and respected him. He saw his time in Detroit as an opportunity to add to his oldest son John Sergeant's education, buying him a horse to ride and putting him on the surveyors' work details.[46]

Yet, for all "the quiet and happy days" spent in Detroit, Meade saw that his successes were contributing to the growing divide between North and South. When Meade and family had clambered aboard that Erie Canal packet, trade with the western states had approached 80 percent of the canal's total revenues. Meade's improvements on the Great Lakes only added to the profits from Northern trade by water. "What is good for the Lakes is good for the country," one congressman crowed. Midwestern legislators now had staunch allies in their Northeastern colleagues as New England shoes, textiles, and furniture found markets westward. Goods borne on the Mississippi were being outpaced by Northern waterways, which were connected to the North's ever-expanding railroads, their tracks making a large spider's web on maps compared with the few railways in the South. And Southerners— that is, white Southerners—resented this.

Economically, cotton was "king" in the South. Eli Whitney's cotton gin had made the crop more lucrative while increasing the need on plantations for more enslaved persons. In the North, abolitionists were gaining in numbers and support, culminating in the birth of the Republican Party, an alliance of probusiness and antislavery politicians. Farther west, "Bleeding Kansas" abandoned town hall debates for civil war, pitting antislavery "Jayhawkers" and "Red Legs" against "Border Ruffians" and "Bushwhackers." During the years when Meade was making water routes safer in the North and South, slavery was tearing the fabric of the country apart.

Later, Meade would wistfully write Margaret how he held "some glimpse of hope that the storm might pass away," but this storm was human, not meteorological. In 1860, Meade supported the Constitutional Union Party, voting for their presidential candidate, John Bell. By the spring of 1861, Meade was also in charge of the survey of the

St. Louis River channel, the very area where Captain Robert E. Lee had worked a quarter century earlier. Meade was aboard the steamship *Search*, selecting sites for triangulation stations and soundings of Lake Superior, when word reached Detroit on April 14 that Fort Sumter, in Charleston Harbor, had been bombarded and had surrendered. The happiest years of Meade's army career were over.[47]

Having turned down opportunities in Oregon and failed to win the Land Office commissioner's position in 1849, Abraham Lincoln returned to his law practice. "I am not an accomplished lawyer," he wrote after his return home, but notes for a proposed lecture on his occupation reveal the lofty standards he set for himself that ended with a Lincolnesque conclusion: "If you cannot be an honest lawyer, resolve to being honest without being a lawyer."[48]

In July 1849, Mary lost her hero and father, Robert Todd, followed months later by the death of her beloved maternal grandmother. But neither death compared with the infinite sorrow awaiting the Lincolns when Eddie was felled by consumption (tuberculosis). For two months the little boy fought a losing battle to breathe, dying on February 1, 1850. Lincoln took Eddie's death hard, Mary's caterwauling a discordant sound passersby easily heard. She stopped eating and remained in her bedroom. "Eat, Mary, for we must live," Lincoln pleaded. "We" included Robert as well, just six years old, his closest companion now gone. Ten months later, another brother, William, would be born.[49]

News of Thomas Lincoln's serious illness did not compel Lincoln to visit his father in 1851. "My business is such that I could hardly leave home now," he told his stepbrother, John. "If we could meet now," he resignedly told Johnston, "it is doubtful whether it would not be more painful than pleasant." Tom Lincoln died five days later.[50]

Lincoln was right about his business. His office was, in a word, unkempt: one small desk, one cluttered table, several wooden chairs, a couch, and an ancient stove—all rarely dusted—atop flooring where plants from seeds Lincoln and Herndon dropped grew in the accumulated dirt. Blinds were unnecessary, as the windows were so dirty they almost hid the change of seasons. Despite such self-imposed, unattractive surroundings, Lincoln's practice began to flourish.[51]

He especially enjoyed riding the circuit. His friend John T. Stuart remembered him carrying Euclid, Shakespeare, Burns, and Poe in his satchel to read in between trials. "After Supper he would Strip—go to bed—get a Candle—draw up a chair or table and read till late at night . . ." Stuart remembered. "He never read poetry as a thing for pleasure, Except Shakespear [sic]—he read Poe because it was gloomy."[52]

When court was in session, county seats frequently saw the roads into town clogged with villagers coming to watch the trials. Assaults, divorces, adultery, libel—the court was not just a shrine of justice but a theater of entertainment, particularly when a neighbor was involved. Lincoln once defended a man accused of carnal knowledge of a pig, its owner certain that the forthcoming piglets were sure to resemble the defendant.[53]

Lincoln often represented women in divorce cases, knowing soon-to-be ex-husbands rarely contested them. His fees frequently went unpaid, as husbands often had deserted their wives. Murder cases were rare. Lincoln had several of them, assisting in the prosecution occasionally, but mostly representing defendants. One of them, Melissa Goings, was a seventy-seven-year-old woman who had killed her husband. The trial was not going Lincoln's way when a recess was called. Afterward it was discovered that Mrs. Goings had escaped, somehow making it to the Pacific. When the bailiff accused Lincoln of abetting her flight, he mildly protested: "I didn't run her off. She asked me where she could get a good drink of water, and I told her there was mighty good water in Tennessee."[54]

As Lincoln's reputation spread, he went on retainer with the Illinois Central Railroad and other Midwestern rail companies. In one case that went to the Illinois Supreme Court, he blocked McLean County's attempt to tax the Illinois Central by citing *McCullouch v. Maryland,* the landmark Supreme Court case that established the division of powers between the federal and state governments. The court held for the railroad.[55]

In the 1850s, slavery was argued over at dinner tables, in taverns, at picnics, and in the halls of Congress. It strained family ties and ended friendships. But nothing, not even the Fugitive Slave Act, had the impact of Harriet Beecher Stowe's *Uncle Tom's Cabin*. It flew off bookstore shelves in the North even as it increased anti-Northern animosity in the South. Stowe became the victim of hate mail and death threats, among them a package with the ear of an enslaved person enclosed. Lincoln reportedly carried "a well-worn copy" with him. Still, he held back on any in-depth discussion of slavery.[56]

On January 23, 1854, while Lincoln was holed up in his dingy office, preparing for the Illinois Central–McLean County case, Stephen Douglas was introducing a bill in the Senate chamber that split the Kansas-Nebraska territory in two: the northern half, Nebraska, to be admitted as a free state; Kansas, the southern half, as a slave state.[57]

News of the Kansas-Nebraska Act spread like prairie wildfire through the North, with thousands signing petitions to overturn the new law. Marches and protests in hamlets, towns, and cities became commonplace. Douglas, pleased with himself, had warned that repealing the Missouri Compromise "would raise a hell of a storm," and he was right. There was one political consequence he had not considered: his victory reawakened a sleeping Illinois giant.

Lincoln was riding the circuit when he learned of the Kansas-Nebraska Act's passage. His roommate, T. Lyle Dickey, a Douglas supporter, remembered Lincoln sitting on the edge of his bed, lost in thought. They discussed the news into the wee hours when Dickey, exhausted, fell asleep. He awoke to find Lincoln still sitting on his bed. "I tell you Dickey," he remarked, "this nation cannot endure half-slave and half-free." If indeed that famous line was first uttered in a tavern bedroom, it certainly resonated with its speaker. At the state library in Springfield, he pored over remarks and debates on slavery found from state and congressional records. Herndon was struck by Lincoln's sudden passion. "The day of compromise," Lincoln told him, "has passed."[58]

On October 4, at the Illinois State Fair in Springfield, Lincoln entered the stifling statehouse chamber wearing a plain shirt with no collar, sweating as much from the heat as nervousness. He began "in a slow, hesitating manner, but without any mistakes," young reporter Horace White recalled. For three hours Lincoln took his audience back in time, to every document and bill dealing with slavery from the Northwest Ordinance of 1787 to the Kansas-Nebraska Act, which Lincoln claimed upended the balance between free states and slave states. His diagnosis was simple: "No man is good enough to govern another man, *without that other's consent.*" His remedy lay with "the sheet anchor of American republicanism. Our Declaration of Independence says: 'We hold these truths to be self-evident: that all men are created equal . . .'"[59]

After cheers and applause washed over Lincoln, two abolitionists, Ichabod Codding and Owen Lovejoy (the abolitionist Elijah's brother), announced a spontaneous meeting that evening to form the Illinois Republican Party. Lincoln did not attend their meeting, viewing the fledgling party as mostly arch-abolitionists. Among Lincoln's remarks against slavery were comments unpalatable to the abolitionists, from "I have no prejudice against the Southern people" to "I mean not to ask a repeal, or modification of the fugitive slave law." The lanky Whig was not a Republican. Not yet.[60]

A major reason for his reluctance was his decision to run for an elective office that fall. He returned to the hustings with a renewed vigor, easily winning election as state representative from Sangamon County. But that was not the office he wanted. "I have got it in my head to try to be U.S. Senator," he declared; *that* was the office he wanted. The 1854 election was the Whigs' last hurrah: with five "anti-Nebraska" Democrats

elected to the state senate, the selection of a Whig senator by the legislature looked possible. A blizzard delayed the legislature's selecting a
senator until February 8, 1855. Lincoln looked like a shoo-in.[61]

That morning a proud Mary Lincoln sat next to Julia Trumbull, one
of Mary's bridesmaids whose husband, Lyman, another anti-Nebraska
Democrat about to switch parties, had been elected to Congress. For six
ballots Lincoln led the other candidates but never got a majority. Realizing that the seat would go to a staunch Democrat, Lincoln withdrew,
urging supporters to support Trumbull, who won on the tenth ballot.
Mary never spoke to Julia Trumbull again. Lincoln was sure he had
made the right decision. "The agony," he told a friend, "is over at last."[62]

Eighteen fifty-five continued to be a character-building year for Lincoln. Invited by Pennsylvania attorney George Harding to assist him in
a patent infringement case brought by the mighty McCormick Harvesting Machine Company, Lincoln showed up weeks later for the trial
taking place in Cincinnati. Harding had neglected to tell Lincoln he
was not needed, having hired Ohioan Edwin M. Stanton, who had a
thriving law practice in Pittsburgh. Encountering Lincoln in the hotel
lobby, Stanton drew Harding aside; "Why did you bring that d——d
long armed Ape here?" he muttered. Harding and Stanton proceeded
to the courthouse, leaving a mortified Lincoln standing there. Instead
of leaving, Lincoln unpacked. With rapt attention, he marveled how
"these college-trained men" dominated the courtroom. Afterward,
Lincoln would eat dinner alone, as Harding and Stanton supped a few
feet away. He learned much during that week in Cincinnati and tucked
away his impressions of Stanton.[63]

In May 1856, three violent events further split the country to the core.
On May 20, Missouri senator David Atchison, vowing "to kill every
God-damned abolitionist in the Territory," led eighty Missouri border
ruffians into the town of Lawrence, an antislavery stronghold, smashing

presses, burning buildings, and killing one citizen while federal marshals watched or assisted in the town's sacking. In Washington, South Carolina congressman Preston Brooks, cane in hand, entered the Senate chamber on May 22 and nearly beat Massachusetts senator Charles Sumner to death for remarks he had made about Brooks's cousin, South Carolina senator Andrew Butler. Two days later, religious zealot and arch-abolitionist John Brown led four sons and two other followers in the dead of night to proslavery Pottawatomie Creek, Kansas. With broadswords, they hacked to death five proslavery men before their families. The guerrilla war in "Bleeding Kansas" continued unabated.[64]

By 1856, Lincoln's viewpoint of the nascent Republican Party had changed. With the Whigs finished and the Know-Nothings too bigoted, Lincoln decided to join the Illinois Republican Party. His name appeared at the top of a petition of 129 Sangamon County citizens calling for a convention of Republicans in Illinois. They were abolitionists, conservative Whigs, and disgruntled Democrats, all sharing a hatred of slavery and the Kansas-Nebraska Act. Lincoln, a member of the nominating committee, subtly made recommendations for moderate candidates; even the platform bore his imprimatur.[65]

On May 29, Lincoln strode to the convention's dais to address the delegates. He kept his audience spellbound; reporters, to a man, were so enthralled, they neglected their job. There is not even a shorthand account of what became known as the "Lost Speech." One scribe summarized Lincoln's remarks this way: *"The Union must be preserved in the purity of its principles as well as the integrity of its territorial parts.* It must be 'Liberty and Union, now and forever.'"

In Philadelphia, Republicans nominated "the Pathfinder," war hero John C. Frémont, for president. An absent Lincoln received 110 votes for vice president but lost out to former New Jersey senator William L. Dayton. They faced Democrats James Buchanan and John C. Breckinridge and the American (Know-Nothing) Party ticket of Millard Fillmore and Andrew Jackson Donelson. Buchanan won decisively, including in Bloomington, Illinois, that November. But Lincoln's slate for state positions also won handily, including the governorship. Lincoln's efforts at the Bloomington convention bore fruit for the Republican Party, and for Lincoln as well.[66]

"At night attended a large & pleasant party at Lincoln's," a neighbor noted in his diary on February 5, 1857. Abe and Mary extended five hundred invitations for the affair, and three hundred attended, their modest home near bursting with guests, laughter, song, and cigar smoke. Mary, who loved parties, was thrilled; Lincoln, who did not, saw this as a first step toward the 1858 Senate race.[67]

On March 6, after a year of deliberations, the Supreme Court announced its decision in the Dred Scott case. Scott, an enslaved man, had been suing for his freedom in a case that finally wound up in Chief Justice Roger Taney's lap. By a vote of 7–2, Scott was denied his freedom, for Blacks were "not included, and were not intended to be included, under the word 'citizens' in the Constitution." But Taney did not stop there. He declared that slavery was legal in every state and territory. Nor did the listed rights in the Declaration of Independence pertain to Blacks in America, being "so far inferior that they had no rights which the white man was bound to respect . . ."[68]

Before the Dred Scott decision, the Supreme Court had been the national arbiter, keeping North and South on a tenuous but equal footing. Now the court had taken sides, ripping the frayed fabric of the Union. Taney expected the Dred Scott decision would settle the issue of slavery. He could not have been more wrong. In Springfield, Stephen Douglas triumphantly endorsed the Dred Scott decision, warning that the Republicans' goal was the "amalgamation between superior and inferior races." Lincoln was in the crowd that night.[69]

Three months later Lincoln addressed the Dred Scott decision and the stark difference between the two parties. "The Republicans inculcate, with whatever of ability they can, that the negro is a man; that his bondage is cruelly wrong, and that the field of his oppression ought not to be enlarged. The Democrats deny his manhood, deny, or dwarf to insignificance, the wrong of his bondage." It was the only speech he made that year.[70]

While Lincoln was garnering support among Republicans for his second Senate run in 1858, Douglas was confronted with Buchanan's support of the Lecompton Constitution in Kansas. It gave Kansans the choice between being admitted as a slave state or a free state banning future importation of the enslaved but protected slaveholding Kansans from losing theirs. Douglas opposed the measure as it corrupted his creed of "Popular Sovereignty," giving voters the right to decide whether or not to allow slavery in their territories. Buchanan and Southern politicians were appalled. "I made Mr. James Buchanan," Douglas confided to a Republican, "and by God, sir, I will unmake him."[71]

At Springfield on June 16, Lincoln accepted the Republican nomination for senator, the eleventh line of his acceptance speech containing words that had been weaving through his thoughts for years, from the Gospel of Saint Mark: "A house divided against itself cannot stand." State senator Norman B. Judd missed hearing the address but later chided Lincoln. "Had I seen—that Speech I would have made you Strike out that house divided part." Lincoln took no offense and sent Judd to invite Douglas to a series of debates. Douglas refused.[72, 73]

Undeterred, Lincoln began shadowing Douglas during the latter's whistle-stop speeches across the state. Douglas traveled in the personal coach of Illinois Central's vice president, George B. McClellan, while Lincoln often rode the same train, seated in a public car. At practically every stop, Douglas saw Lincoln's looming presence in the crowds, announcing after Douglas's remarks that he would make his own speech, often to laughter and applause. Finally, after reading barbed rebukes in newspapers over Douglas's refusal, he and Lincoln agreed over dinner to seven debates across the state. Douglas had one condition: that Lincoln cease showing up at his remaining campaign events.[74]

Politically, accepting Lincoln's challenge made no sense: Douglas was far better known. But he had seen Lincoln's impact on crowds; better to share a stage with him than for Douglas's absence to be Lincoln's topic. Plus it got Lincoln off his train.[75]

"History furnishes few characters whose lives were so near parallel as those of Lincoln and Douglas," Herndon recollected, and he was right. Since their first meeting in Vandalia in 1834, the two men's paths had been inextricably entwined. Douglas's career had been far more successful; his only loss to Lincoln was Mary Todd. Now, with their eyes on Douglas's Senate seat in 1858 and the presidency in 1860, they were about to capture the attention of the entire country.[76]

Just five feet four, Douglas "had a large head, surmounted by an abundant mane, which gave the appearance of a lion prepared to roar or crush his prey," one onlooker recalled. His stentorian tones frequently carried him and his audience to great heights. One journalist later recalled Lincoln's "thin, high-pitched, falsetto" voice "that could be heard a long distance," his "accent and pronunciation peculiar to his native State, Kentucky." For fifty-five days, these two most disparate men traveled their state in what would become the most legendary of American debates. Thousands of citizens attended to have their own beliefs reinforced, questioned, and changed, as did their fellow Americans elsewhere, devouring their local newspapers to do the same.[77]

The night before their first encounter, in Ottawa, Illinois, on August 21, gave everyone an idea of what was in store. Some 12,000 people crammed Ottawa's streets. Out-of-towners came by special trains, others on boats filled to the gunwales traveling the Fox and Illinois Rivers or the Michigan Canal. That night, countless campfires on the outskirts of town resembled army encampments. Douglas arrived in a grand coach, accompanied by marching bands and hundreds of followers waving banners and signs. Lincoln arrived by train, "three great cheers" given as he stepped on the platform.[78]

Douglas, dressed in an elegant suit, his long hair perfectly coiffed, expanded his broad chest as he acknowledged the cheers. Lincoln, in a better suit than usual, was equally appreciative. A photographer had recently captured him with a stern expression, squinting beneath his tousled hair, his high cheekbones accentuated and his jaw tightly clenched. This was not the usual expression of the affable storyteller. Lincoln had come to do battle.[79]

Douglas began with a reminiscence. "We were both comparatively boys, and both struggling with poverty in a strange land. I was a school-teacher," he stated, and Lincoln "a flourishing grocery-keeper"—a euphemism for selling liquor. After some chuckles from the crowd, Douglas went on the offensive:

> We are told by Lincoln that he is utterly opposed to the Dred Scott decision . . . for the reason he says it deprives the negro of the rights and privileges of citizenship . . . I ask you, are you in favor of conferring upon the negro the rights and privileges of citizenship? . . . Do you desire to turn this beautiful State into a free negro colony . . . [and for Black people] to become citizens and voters, on an equality with yourselves? . . . [T]hen support Mr. Lincoln and the Black Republican party, who are in favor of the citizenship of the negro.

During Lincoln's rebuttal, a heckler shouted, "Give us something besides Dred Scott." Lincoln replied, "Yes; no doubt you want to hear something that don't hurt," to laughter and applause. Then he went to work, his remarks bringing cheers:

> When he says that the negro has nothing to do with the Declaration of Independence . . . Judge Douglas is going back to the era of our Revolution, and to the extent of his ability, muzzling the cannon which thunders its annual joyous return. When he invites any people willing to have slavery, to establish it, he is blowing out the moral lights around us.[80]

Who won the debate depended on what newspapers one read. The *Chicago Times* joyfully reported that "Republicans hung their heads in shame" over Douglas's "excoriation" of Lincoln. The hometown *Ottawa Republican* declared that "Lincoln won the field." Northern newspapers heralded Lincoln's efforts: the *New York Evening Post* calling Lincoln "a champion"; the small-town *Muscatine Journal* labeling Douglas "a dead cock in the pit."[81]

At Freeport, Lincoln asked, "Can the people of a United States Territory, in any lawful way, against the wish of any citizen of the United

States, exclude slavery from its limits prior to the formation of a State Constitution?" An exasperated Douglas, struck by a watermelon rind, laid out his case:[82]

"In my opinion the people of a Territory can, by lawful means, exclude slavery from their limits, prior to the formation of a State Constitution . . . It matters not what the Supreme Court hereafter decide . . . [T]he people have the lawful means to introduce it or exclude it as they please."

Douglas's reply became known as "the Freeport Doctrine" in the North, and "the Freeport Heresy" in the South.[83]

At Charleston, Lincoln was asked if he truly favored "perfect equality between the negroes and white people." He answered:

I am not, nor ever have been, in favor of bringing about in any way the social and political equality of the white and black races . . . I have not nor ever have been in favor of making voters or jurors of negroes, nor of qualifying them to hold office, nor to intermarry with white people . . . [T]here is a physical difference between the white and black races . . . I as much as any man am in favor of having the superior position assigned to the white race.[84, 85]

As much as his loathing of slavery and belief that the rights in the Constitution and Declaration of Independence were color- (if not gender-) blind, these remarks accurately reflected who Lincoln was in 1858. His advocacy of equality under the law was a radical idea for a white American, but Lincoln did not—would not—go as far as Lovejoy and other abolitionists—not if he wanted to win.

The last debate was at Alton on October 15. Both men were physically drained, having given dozens of speeches in between the debates; Douglas could hardly speak above a whisper, reiterating that "the signers of the Declaration of Independence had no reference to negroes at all when they declared all men to be created equal. They did not mean negro, nor the savage Indians, nor the Feejee Islanders, nor any other barbarous race."[86]

In one of his better arguments, a weary Lincoln called slavery "the eternal struggle between these two principles . . . The one is the common right of humanity and the other the divine right of kings . . . It is the same spirit that says, 'You toil and work and earn bread, and I'll eat it.'"[87]

The debates over, Lincoln returned to campaigning. Buoyed by enthusiastic crowds, he wrote Norman Judd, "I now have a high degree of confidence that we shall succeed." On Election Day, November 2, a driving rain covered Illinois but did not deter the voters: Lincoln won by 3,800 votes. But the vote that mattered lay in the legislature, and the Democrats held fifty-four seats to the Republicans' forty-six. Douglas's reelection was assured. "Let the voice of the people rule," he exclaimed.[88]

Lincoln reacted with gallows humor, grace, and grit. "I feel like the boy who stumped his toe," he told visitors. "I am too big to cry and too badly hurt to laugh." To a friend he wrote, "I am glad I made the late race. It gave me a hearing which I could have had in no other way."[89]

He closed that letter with the gloomy phrase "I now sink out of view." But Mary still believed in Abe's destiny. Years later, a former hired servant of the Lincolns told Billy Herndon that Mary was certain "she would be the mistress of the White House."[90]

Over the winter of 1858–59, Lincoln licked his wounds from his defeat. He did urge Republicans to "keep the faith," but he rebuffed suggestions of a presidential candidacy in 1860, telling one newspaperman, "I do not think myself fit for the presidency." He was fifty now and seemed more interested in speaking about the "Discoveries and Inventions" of America's technological advances.[91]

But the political itch returned that spring. A publisher's offer to print his speeches from the debates was eagerly accepted, and he spent the summer and fall addressing Republican gatherings in different states. He was in Elmwood, Kansas, recounting the "strife and bloodshed" Kansans endured, calling John Brown's recent attack on Harpers Ferry both lawless and futile, and advocating "a peaceful way of settling these questions." Two days later, John Brown was hanged in Virginia.[92]

On February 27, 1860, Lincoln spoke before 1,500 at the Cooper Union for the Advancement of Science and Art in Manhattan, a veritable temple of intellectualism. When William Cullen Bryant ended his introduction saying, "I have only, my friends, to pronounce the name of Abraham Lincoln," the hall exploded with cheers.[93]

With those twelve words, Lincoln discovered his popularity, the growing public faith in his message, and that he was, at last, a living part of his country's history. *I have only, my friends, to pronounce the name of Abraham Lincoln.* He had become his own tough act to follow. There were no anecdotes or humorous asides. In a brilliant presentation under the twenty-seven chandeliers lighting the auditorium, Lincoln linked America's past actions with its present crisis before lifting his audience's hearts: "Let us have faith that right makes might, and in that faith, let us, to the end, dare to do our duty as we understand it."[94]

One spectator called Lincoln "the greatest man since St. Paul"; Northern and Western newspapers lavished him with praise. His triumph resulted in more speeches throughout New England. "Twenty-five years ago I was a hired laborer, mauling rails, at work on a flatboat," he marveled. Lincoln's trip accomplished more than he had hoped for, but he remained unexcited on the surface. "The taste *is* in my mouth a little," he confided to Lyman Trumbull—one of history's grander understatements.[95]

Since 1859, Lincoln and his friends had subtly—at times—greased the political wheels to increase his odds for the Republican presidential nomination, including getting the party bosses to hold the national convention in Chicago. At the state convention on May 10, Lincoln's cousin John Hanks burst through the doors toting two weather-worn rails with a banner stating they were "made in 1830 by John Hanks and Abe Lincoln." Lincoln's grin cloaked his humiliation at Hanks's antics. "I think I could make better ones than these now!" he dryly joshed. Despite Lincoln's mortification, Hanks's stunt proved a godsend: the image of a log cabin birth and frontier upbringing far surpassed that of a lawyer representing the railroads. And while "Honest Abe" and "Old Abe" were affectionate nicknames, they paled in comparison to the "Rail Splitter."[96]

By May 16, it seemed that every train in the United States was in or heading for Chicago. Ribbons of locomotive smoke could be seen for miles. Chicagoans, anxious to show off their city, sent welcoming committees and brass bands to meet the arriving delegates, newspapermen, and spectators. With hotels filled to overflowing, even pool halls served as hostelries, with mattresses spread atop the felt tables. Among the sources of evening entertainment was the popular comedy *Our American Cousin* at the McVicker's Theatre.[97]

There were four major presidential candidates. New York senator William H. Seward led the list, followed by former Ohio governor Salmon P. Chase, former Missouri congressman Edward Bates, and Lincoln. Several others including Pennsylvania senator Simon Cameron rounded out the field. The convention was held in the grand wood-framed hall nicknamed the "Wigwam," seating 10,000. Lincoln's campaign manager, David Davis, led Lincoln's supporters in buttonholing delegates. When Lincoln heard that Davis had approached Cameron, whose candidacy was a nonstarter, about throwing his Pennsylvania bloc of voters Lincoln's way, the candidate sent Davis one simple command: *"Make no contracts that will bind me."* Davis ignored it, telling his camp, "Lincoln ain't here and don't know what we have to meet."[98]

The Wigwam was filled to the rafters on May 18 when the 466 delegates cast their first ballots. Seward received 173½ votes, Lincoln 102, the rest 50 or less. It was evident to all inside the Wigwam that this was now a two-man race. Back in Springfield, a nervous Lincoln busied himself playing fives, an early game of handball, before pacing from his office to his friend James Conkling's law office. Lincoln gained ground in the second ballot and overtook Seward on the third. Later in the day he received a wire: "TO LINCOLN YOU ARE NOMINATED."[99]

In Springfield that afternoon, cannons boomed salutes; that evening a marching band led hundreds of townsfolk to Eighth and Jackson Streets. In his gracious remarks, Lincoln said he would "invite the whole crowd" into his house "if it was large enough." One supporter shouted, "We will give you a larger house on the fourth of next March!"

Lincoln formally accepted the nomination on May 19, with Maine senator Hannibal Hamlin his running mate. He would make but one speech, in Springfield on August 8. According to tradition, he would not campaign for himself.[100]

The unified Republicans faced a divided field. In April, the Democrats had a civil war instead of a convention, pitting Douglas Northerners against Southern "fire-eaters." They reconvened in Baltimore in June, picking up where they had left off. Douglas won the nomination, but the fire-eaters held a third session, nominating Vice President John Breckinridge. Earlier, the new, conservative Constitutional Union Party had convened in Baltimore, choosing Tennessee senator John Bell for president over Texas governor Sam Houston and Massachusetts politician, diplomat, and stem-winding orator Edward Everett for vice president.[101]

The coming contest was actually two different elections, one pitting Lincoln against Douglas in the North while in the other Bell and Breckinridge fought over the South. The trick was to come up with the 152 electoral votes that would give Lincoln a majority. To his surprise, his best campaigner was Seward, who stumped vigorously on Lincoln's behalf.[102]

The weather on Election Day 1860 was perfect: cool and sunny. The boom of cannon fire woke residents at sunrise. Springfield had good reason to celebrate with two citizens on the ballot for president of the United States. That afternoon Lincoln strode to the courthouse to vote; as he left, an onlooker shouted, "You ought to vote for Douglas, Uncle Abe, he has done all he could for you." Lincoln won Springfield over Douglas by 69 votes.[103]

Well after midnight, church bells pealed, and hordes of townsfolk came out in their nightshirts and robes to cheer their neighbor. The throng parted as Lincoln headed home to tell his anxious wife the news. "Mary," he cried, "we are *elected*!"[104]

Perhaps Mary was not surprised. "The man I marry will be president of the United States," she had bragged in her youth, spurning accomplished, ambitious Stephen Douglas for the gangly backwoodsman turned lawyer. Mary Todd had made the right decision after all.

Lincoln had won the majority of electoral votes (180) but less than 40 percent of the popular vote (1,865,908), still a better figure than his opponents. In the South, Lincoln received just 2.1 percent of the popular vote, an omen of things to come.

The next four months would be hectic for Lincoln and brutal for the country he was to lead. John George Nicolay agreed to stay on as Lincoln's assistant; he brought on board his former classmate John Hay to assist him. Lincoln made one significant decision purely for appearance. Grace Bedell, eleven years old, had written to Lincoln from New York, hoping he would win the election and suggesting growing a beard would help, for "you would look a great deal better for your face is so thin." Whether Lincoln's decision to become the first bewhiskered president was due to Ms. Bedell's entreaty is up to the reader.[105]

As Southern fire-eaters and newspapers clamored for secession, efforts in the new congressional session to patch up the Union surfaced. The most significant came from Kentucky senator John Crittenden, who proposed amendments to the Constitution guaranteeing Southerners a free hand regarding slavery, principally by restoring the Missouri Compromise line, dividing free and slave states to the Pacific, in direct opposition to both Lincoln's and the Republicans' vow to stop the spread of slavery.[106]

When influential Republicans, led by Seward, embraced the Crittenden Compromise, Lincoln made his opinion clear. "Let there be no compromise on the question of *extending* slavery," he wrote Senator Trumbull, and to Illinois congressman Elihu Washburne: "Hold firm, as with a chain of steel." Crittenden's ploy failed.[107]

On December 20, New York boss Thurlow Weed met Lincoln in Springfield, where the latter reiterated that "no state can, in any way lawfully, get out of the Union, without the consent of the others." Later they learned by telegraph that South Carolina had seceded from the Union that very day. By February 1, 1861, six other states would follow

South Carolina's lead: Mississippi, Florida, Alabama, Georgia, Louisiana, and Texas.[108]

Before leaving Springfield, Lincoln went to see his stepmother, Sarah. Despite his assurances, she was certain she would never see him again. Before departing, he paid his respects at his father's grave site, promising to send a more fitting stone. He never did.[109]

February 11 was bitter and damp in Springfield as Lincoln and family took a carriage to the railroad depot. More than 1,000 neighbors saw them off. Lincoln asked for silence, took off his hat, and spoke extemporaneously from his heart:

> *No one, not in my situation, can appreciate my feeling of sadness at this parting. To this place, and the kindness of these people, I owe everything. Here I have lived a quarter of a century, and have passed from a young to an old man . . . I now leave, not knowing when, or whether ever, I may return, with a task before me greater than that which rested upon Washington . . . To His care commending you, as I hope in your prayers commending me, I bid you an affectionate farewell.*[110]

With tears in both Lincoln's and his listeners' eyes, he boarded the four-car train, never to return. The next day Lincoln turned fifty-two.

The train took a winding route to Washington: everyone in the North was anxious to see the new president. The journey was more of a whistle-stop tour, with Mary joining her husband in the rear car as he made brief remarks at each stop. In Westfield, New York, Lincoln found Grace Bedell, hopped off the train, and—to the crowd's and Grace's delight—gave her a quick kiss after showing off his beard.[111]

In Philadelphia, Lincoln was met by Allan Pinkerton, a railroad detective with serious news of a plot to assassinate Lincoln when he changed trains in Baltimore. Pinkerton wanted Lincoln to take another train immediately and go through Baltimore in the dead of night. Lincoln refused. Speaking to a crowd at Independence Hall, he declared to cheers, "I would rather be assassinated on this spot than to surrender it."[112]

When he learned from Seward's son that General Scott had also learned of the plot, Lincoln agreed to Pinkerton's plan. Leaving his family to travel as scheduled, Lincoln donned a floppy felt "Kossuth" hat and an overly long coat and boarded the special train. It reached Washington at 6 a.m. The press had a field day covering the "Flight of Abraham," including one version of him dressed in women's clothes. President Buchanan's attorney general, Edwin Stanton, picking up his disgust with Lincoln from years ago, said the legendary rail-splitter had "crept" into the capital. The *Baltimore Sun* contemptuously called it the "Underground Railroad Journey."[113]

Washington seemed partly constructed and half-empty. The Capitol Dome was half-done, looking like a giant uncompleted wedding cake, while at the mall the Washington Monument was also incomplete, a half-grown obelisk casting its shadow over piles of wood and rubble—the two projects labored over daily by enslaved laborers and free Black artisans. Most Southern congressmen and senators—now ex-congressmen and ex-senators—had gone home.[114]

The Lincolns took a suite in the Willard Hotel. Stephen Douglas was among the first to greet him: "I am with you, Mr. President and God bless you." In a split second, their decades-long rivalry ended. "God bless you, Douglas," Lincoln said with emotion, adding, "The danger is great, but with such words and friends why should we fear? Our Union cannot be destroyed."[115]

On March 3 a storm struck Washington, D.C. At night it departed as suddenly as it had come; the sun rose over a raw morning, fierce winds sending a wall of dust through unpaved Washington streets, stinging and covering those among the 30,000 visitors who had no lodging. Hotels, boardinghouses, and taverns were overcrowded; the Willard Hotel, the city's largest, laid 475 mattresses in the hallways. By noontime, clear skies and warm weather prevailed.

In a suite at the Willard, Lincoln was dressing for the occasion as never before: an expensive black cashmere suit that actually fit, new boots, a gold-tipped cane, and a new silk stovepipe hat. As he dressed, Robert read his father's inaugural aloud, handing it to him when a phrase did not ring true enough.[116]

There was a martial presence on the streets due to a warning of a plot to blow up the speakers' stage, constructed at the Capitol's east portico. At noon a carriage carrying Buchanan and Senators James Pearce of Maryland and Edward Dickinson Baker of Oregon, the latter Lincoln's good friend, arrived at the Willard to pick up the president-elect. A cheering crowd greeted Lincoln; one spectator thought he looked "calm, easy," and "sedate," while Buchanan appeared "pale and wearied." They were escorted by a company of cavalry down Pennsylvania Avenue as sharpshooters watched from the rooftops, part of the thousands of troops Scott had placed along the parade route and at the Capitol.[117]

The inaugural party entered the Capitol through the north entrance. When they appeared at the east portico, cheers and musical fanfare rang out. Mary and her sons sat behind Lincoln, who sat with Buchanan, Douglas, and Chief Justice Roger Taney. Senator Baker approached the podium and simply said, "Fellow citizens, I introduce to you Abraham Lincoln, president-elect of the United States."[118]

Before Lincoln took to the podium, Douglas gallantly held his hat. At "Fellow citizens of the United States," the crowd cheered wildly. When it quieted, Lincoln spoke to the matter at hand:

> In your hands, my dissatisfied fellow countrymen, and not in mine, is the momentous decision of civil war . . . We are not enemies, but friends. We must not be enemies. Though passion may have strained, it must not break our bonds of affection. The mystic chords of memory, stretching from every battlefield, and patriot grave . . . will yet swell the chorus of the Union, when again touched, as surely they will be, by the better angels of our nature.[119]

After the applause died down, Taney, looking like "a galvanized corpse," administered the oath of office for the seventh and last time. That evening at Lincoln's inaugural ball, Mary, wearing an exquisite blue gown and adorned in gold and pearls, danced a lively quadrille with Douglas. Lincoln left the affair around one; Mary continued partying.[120]

On his first day in office, Lincoln was handed a message from Major

Robert Anderson: Fort Sumter's provision would only last six weeks. In January, the supply ship *Star of the West* had been fired on by Citadel Academy cadets, forcing her to turn back before reaching the fort. Lincoln asked advice from his cabinet and General Scott. Seward and Scott both urged Lincoln to give up the fort. Scott asked Lincoln to resuscitate Crittenden's Compromise. At one point Seward took the lead when a possible solution arose: surrendering Fort Sumter if Virginia remained in the Union.[121]

Lincoln was steadfast. Evacuating Fort Sumter "will convince the rebels that the administration lacks firmness." He proposed not sending reinforcements but simply "food for hungry men" and relaying this to the new Confederate States of America president, Jefferson Davis. He sent a letter to South Carolina's governor, Francis Wilkinson Pickens, declaring his intentions.[122]

Now came Davis's turn to feel public pressure. Lincoln's message was clear: in *Davis's* hands, not *his*, lay the momentous decision of civil war. Lincoln soon learned Davis's answer. At 4:30 a.m. on April 12, Confederate general Pierre G. T. Beauregard ordered his aide, Colonel James Chesnut Jr., to open fire on Fort Sumter. The gods of war had won over the better angels of America's nature.[123]

On April 17, the day after Virginia finally seceded, Lincoln asked Francis P. Blair Sr., Postmaster Montgomery Blair's father, to meet with Colonel Robert E. Lee. Lincoln wanted him to lead the United States Army against Virginia and the other Confederate states.[124]

As with Odysseus, the first to recognize the weary Lee on his return home from the Mexican War was the family dog. Spec, a terrier, leapt happily off the porch, barking joyfully as Lee dismounted his horse at Arlington's front steps. Once in the hallway, he was surrounded by children, happily picking up one and kissing him before discovering he was a friend of Robert's, much to his son's embarrassment.[125]

It was June 1848. Lee had been gone twenty-one months. He was not surprised to be "hardly recognizable" to the younger children, "but some of the older ones gaze with astonishment and wonder" at "the furrows in my face and the white hairs in my head." He was more upset over President Polk's reduction of both the size and budget of the army now that the war was over. Lee had considered leaving the army before. Over the next decade, doing so would occur to him more frequently.[126]

After a brief stint at engineering headquarters in Washington, Lee was tasked with building Fort Carroll, the latest defense for Baltimore Harbor. The Lees were popular in the city, young Robert recalling his father "as a great favourite . . . especially with ladies and little children." Through Jefferson Davis, an offer to command an army of Cuban rebels was offered him, but serving in another country's army held no appeal at all. By late summer 1852, the walls of Fort Carroll were taking shape, but another officer would have to finish construction. As before in his career, Lee was being sent elsewhere before his task was finished, this time to West Point to replace Captain Henry Brewerton as the academy's superintendent.[127]

Lee balked at the assignment. His oldest son, Custis, was attending the academy, and there would soon be another Lee on the rolls, Smith's son Fitzhugh; there would be enough Lees at West Point. But Secretary of War Charles Conrad rejected his request. Lee reported to West Point on September 1, certain he would fail. "The Supt. can do nothing right and must father every wrong," he grumbled to P. G. T. Beauregard, confiding, "I shall get away from it as soon as I can." The "Marble Model" cadet would be the "Marble Model" superintendent.[128]

To Lee's delight, Mary agreed to come along. The stone-built superintendent's home was large and roomy, with gardens and stables. One night a week the Lees invited groups of cadets for dinner. Both Robert and Mary became particularly fond of a friend of Custis's: a plain-looking but engaging Virginian, James Ewell Brown ("Jeb") Stuart. On some occasions, Lee broke out Washington's silverware, thrilling his guests as he had in Mexico.[129]

Lee was determined to make changes in policies, personnel, and property, but soon discovered, as he suspected, that a superintendent often encountered a brick wall of tradition.

The absence of a qualified pool of instructors nettled him, especially finding a strong instructor for mathematics. Lee requested funds for a new riding center, stables for the artillery and dragoon horses, a new wharf, and new quarters for the officers and non-service engineers. Seeking ways to increase cash flow, he sought permission to allow a treasure hunter to dig up a supposed cache on the academy grounds. As the treasure would have been owned by the United States, Lee felt 50 percent of the findings should have gone to the academy.[130]

The cadet who never had a demerit spent a fair amount of time with problem cadets, the meddling politicians who appointed them, and their interfering parents. His letters were clear, tactful, and firm when required. Many a parent was told their son could not get leave for Christmas or a sister's wedding. Often the reason was exams and the need to "maintain his present high standing in his class." Those were the easy ones. In one instance a cadet assaulted the captain of the mess hall. "The 9th Article of War makes such conduct a Capital Offence," Lee decided, recommending a court-martial.[131]

Lee would offer resignation from the academy as a better alternative than being discharged. One cadet, James McNeill Whistler, declined resignation. The son of an academy graduate, James showed his later renowned artistic talents in engineering class by adding two boys sitting on his diagram of a bridge. Told to remove them, he placed them on-shore; told again, he removed them from the drawing but added two gravestones. "In the opinion of his particular Professor," Lee wrote Whistler's mother, "every lesson he loses will be a disadvantage to him." Lee kept her updated on her son's status; at one point Whistler ranked thirty-second in his class but first in drawing. To Lee's chagrin, Whistler flunked out of West Point. Later, his painting *Arrangement in Grey and Black No.1* made his mother immortal. For the rest of his life, he always spoke kindly of Lee.[132]

No cadets made Lee prouder or gave him more gray hairs than his two relations. In 1854 his son Custis graduated first in his class, besting his father's placement. Fitzhugh, Smith's son, was another story. Caught twice with classmates sneaking back to the academy (once after a night of drinking), Fitzhugh was court-martialed twice. Like Custis, Fitzhugh's classmates' support saved him the first time; Secretary of War Jefferson Davis did so on the second occasion. A charismatic rascal, Fitzhugh graduated forty-fifth out of forty-nine in the class of 1856. By then his uncle was no longer at the academy to congratulate him.[133]

Lee was soon chafing to leave West Point. He maintained his pleasant but distant expression walking the Plain—the small plateau along the Hudson—and interacting with officers, cadets, and families. Yet underneath Lee's friendly countenance he was ready for something different, and he got it: a promotion to lieutenant colonel in the newly formed United States Cavalry. Lee would be going west again.[134]

The new states were in need of government protection. Native American tribes were not about to leave their homelands without a fight; in Kansas, Northern and Southern settlers added bloodshed to the issue of slavery, giving their home the unwanted nickname "Bleeding Kansas." Lee was assigned to the new 2nd Cavalry as second-in-command under Colonel Albert Sidney Johnston and put in charge of Camp Cooper.[135]

Johnston's subordinates included George Stoneman, John Bell Hood, and Fitzhugh Lee. Known as "Jeff Davis's Pets," the 2nd received the best of everything, including Kentucky-bred horses. The mounts were, to some, better bred than the new recruits; about 40 percent of them did not finish their training. "So great are the facilities offered for escape by passing steamers" that search parties stood little chance of capturing them. "I had rather they would run now than in battle," Lee declared. He grew frustrated with commanding men who did not want to be commanded.[136]

Camp Cooper sat on the Clear Fork, a western tributary of the Brazos River, in the Llano Estacado ("Staked Plains"), the vast array of mesas in the Southwest. The camp comprised several rows of tents; there were groves of pecan and elm trees at the riverbank, but the land became dry and bare just yards from Clear Fork. There was no stable for the mounts, just a picket line. "We are situated on the Commanche Reserve, with the Indian camps below us on the river whom the Govt. is intending to humanize," Lee wrote Mary. "I fear it will be an uphill battle."[137]

About six hundred Comanches were in the camp Lee mentioned; another reserve across the Brazos held nearly 1,000. The cavalry's tasks were to keep the warriors from raiding and keep resentful, fearful whites from any violent outburst as well. Lee had 12 officers and 226 mostly green troopers for the job.

One day Katum'seh, leader of the Commanche Reserve, rode into camp to meet Lee. "We have had a long talk, very tedious on his part and very sententious on mine," Lee wrote Mary. "I hailed him as a friend," Lee added, "but would meet him as an enemy the first moment he deserved it." Lee repaid Katum'seh's visit the next day, just as government provisions arrived. Lee watched the warriors and boys "riding in and out of camp all day. Their paint and ornaments make them more hideous than nature made them."

In June and July, Lee and his men rode 1,600 miles over fifty days in pursuit of raiding Comanches, finding evidence of Comanche attacks but no warriors. Returning to Camp Cooper, Lee came upon a small party of Comanches—several men and one woman—and pursued them for two hundred miles. The men were killed; Lee returned the woman to the tribe south of the camp "where her father resides."[138]

By summer's end, Lee was assigned to a tour of Western and Southern forts, where he was expected to sit on a series of courts. But in October he received a telegram from Arlington: his father-in-law had died.[139]

The morass of financial issues Custis had ignored, the deterioration of Mary's health, and daily guilt over his absences reawakened Lee's inner turmoil over leaving the army. "I have at last to decide the question," Lee informed Johnston, "whether to continue in the Army all my life, or to leave it now." At Arlington, he found Mary incapacitated with rheumatoid arthritis, a disease that constantly advances through the body, with no cure. She had never fully explained her condition to her husband in her letters. Seeing her this way broke his heart. "I fear Mary will never be able to accompany me in my wandering life."[140, 141]

Lee was also shocked at Arlington's deplorable state. In his letters to Mary, he had advised her on financial matters but was never convinced that she grasped the idea of balancing the books. Over and over again he politely remonstrated with Mary how "it is unpleasant to give checks on Banks & not have the funds to meet them. People may think I am endeavouring to swindle." Lee never, ever forgot who his father was.[142]

Apparently, neither had Parke Custis. Lee, first named among four executors, surmised that Mary, being the only child, would inherit the bulk of her father's estate, but Custis followed the tradition of a man's male heirs being first and foremost, bequeathing most of his holdings to his grandsons. Arlington went to Mary for the rest of her life, and then to her son Custis. Two other farms, White House (Martha Washington's former home) and Romancoke, went to Lee and Mary's other sons, Rooney and Rob. Lee's daughters were to receive $10,000 each. Other pieces of real estate were to be sold. And Parke Custis's son-in-law? An empty lot in Washington, D.C., was given "to him and his heirs forever."

Once the executors had seen to the above duties, Custis had one last stipulation: "I give freedom to my slaves, the said slaves to be emancipated by my executors . . . the said emancipation to be accomplished in not exceeding five years from the time of my decease."[143]

Custis's debt was massive. All of his estates were plainly in disrepair; it would cost thousands to fix them. The properties Custis wanted sold would not come close to the $40,000 Custis had promised Lee's daughters. Without help from his sons—Custis was serving in California, Rooney was part of an expedition against the Mormons, and Rob was only fourteen—Lee faced all this alone.[144]

It seemed a monstrous practical joke. Lee had more than lived up to his father's military heroics while shunning Light Horse Harry's egregious financial habits. Now he was saddled with his dilettante father-in-law's debtors and the daunting task of keeping the Custis name out of the financial gutter. Parke Custis had not trusted Lee enough to bequeath him anything of real worth but trusted him to fix everything

Custis had neglected during his life. Chasing Comanches in Texas looked safer than settling debts in Virginia.[145]

"What am I to do?" he plaintively and rhetorically asked a cousin. "Everything is in ruins & will have to be rebuilt," and to do that immediately the money would have to come from Lee himself, using what funds he had after paying the harshest of Parke Custis's creditors. Embarrassed over his plight, Lee applied for an extension of his leave—a request he would ask for repeatedly over the next two years—and began the expensive and thankless task of salvaging another father's false legacy.[146]

Over the next two years Lee succeeded in making renovations and restitutions, steadily paying off Parke Custis's debts, often interrupted to attend courts of inquiry in Washington and West Point. In the spring of 1859, Rooney, who had resigned his commission, was married at White House and moved in. Looking ahead to returning to his post, Lee wangled a transfer for Custis to join the Corps of Topographical Engineers in Washington, allowing him to move into his future inheritance and care for his mother. In the waning months of 1859, all three estates were in better shape than Parke Custis had left them, and Lee began setting aside money from the farms' harvests to pay the $40,000 Custis had promised his granddaughters. Lee was learning firsthand that "a farmer's work is never done."

As he began his campaign to restore the estates, Lee hoped those running White House and Romancoke "will be considerate & kind to the Negroes" and "will be firm & make them do their duty." He certainly expected to do the same.[147]

At the time of Custis's death, he owned 196 men, women, and children. Once Lee informed them their emancipation would not take place for five years, men and women he hired out often ran away; the rewards and bounties Lee was forced to pay added to his debt. Lee considered one man, Reuben, "a great rogue & rascal whom I must get rid of in some way." Lack of docility by the housekeepers at Arlington angered Mary, calling them "a host of idle & thankless dependents." One runaway fled with a jewelry box containing valuables of Martha Washington. Lee's daughter, Agnes, described her personal gardener, a young

Black, as "much fonder of play, than work," an apt description of herself and her sisters.[148]

The Lees could not grasp that once the enslaved at Arlington learned about their promised freedom, the promise meant nothing to many if it could not happen that day. In a letter to Mary, Lee called slavery "a moral & political evil in any country" but insisted that "Blacks are immeasurably better off here than in Africa, morally, socially & physically." Lee believed freedom for Blacks was up to "a wise and merciful Providence." In the meantime, "the systematic & progressive efforts of certain people of the North"—i.e., abolitionists—would only end in "a civil & servile war."[149]

The worst incident regarding Arlington's enslaved persons, at least publicly for Lee, occurred in 1859. Wesley Norris, then twenty-nine, his younger sister Mary, and their cousin, George Parks, fled Arlington, bound for Pennsylvania. They were ten miles from freedom when they were apprehended in Westminster, Maryland, jailed, returned to Arlington, and immediately brought before Lee.

What happened next has been the subject of conjecture for 150 years. When Lee "demanded the reason why we ran away, we frankly told him that we considered ourselves free," Norris attested. Lee "told us he would teach us a lesson we would never forget . . ." He explained:

> We were tied firmly to posts by a Mr. Gwin, our overseer, who was ordered by Gen. Lee to strip us to the waist and give us fifty lashes each, excepting my sister, who received but twenty; we were accordingly stripped to the skin by the overseer, who, however, had sufficient humanity to decline whipping us; accordingly Dick Williams, a county constable, was called in, who gave us the number of lashes ordered . . . Gen Lee than ordered the overseer to thoroughly wash our backs with brine which was done.

After a week in jail, Norris and Parks were hired out to work on railroad construction; Mary was hired out for domestic work.

Lee was unpleasantly surprised to learn that word of this incident had traveled north, first appearing in the *New York Tribune*, whose version stated that when the "slave-whipper" refused to flog Mary Norris,

Lee did it himself. While the *Alexandria Gazette* called the *Tribune*'s version a "malicious fabrication," Lee did not publicly reply but vented to Custis Lee that the *Tribune* "has attacked me for my treatment of your grandfather's slaves" and that Parke Custis "has left me an unpleasant legacy." He would not respond to outsiders until 1866, after Norris's account was published in several papers. "The statement is not true," he stated.[150]

On October 17, 1859, Lieutenant Jeb Stuart was at the War Department on 17th Street NW. Stuart was fresh from a tour of duty in "Bleeding Kansas," where he had once crossed paths with John Brown. That day Stuart overheard that "the Harpers Ferry armory was in possession of a mob of rumor said over 3000 men." Stuart immediately volunteered his services and was ordered by Secretary of War John B. Floyd to ride to Arlington and fetch Lee. Upon their return to Washington, Lee was given command of a company of marines to retake the arsenal. Stuart, as Lee's aide, went by train to Harpers Ferry.[151]

Harpers Ferry sits at the confluence of the Potomac and Shenandoah Rivers in the Blue Ridge Mountains along the Maryland-Virginia border. A hub of early American commerce, canals and the railroad only added to the town's importance. The arsenal had been built at George Washington's behest; since 1800 it had produced thousands of firearms for the army.

Lee and Stuart arrived late that night to learn that the raiders were far fewer in number than rumored. Armed townsfolk and local militia had thwarted the raiders' plans, killing several of them; the remainder were now holed up in the armory's firehouse, a solid brick structure with oak doors. Thirteen hostages were also inside. The ringleader was someone named Smith.[152]

At seven o'clock the next morning, Lee sent Stuart to the firehouse under a flag of truce to demand the raiders' surrender. When "Smith" came to the door, Stuart immediately recognized "Old Osawatomie Brown," something nobody else there could have done. Once he realized Brown had no intention of coming out, Stuart "left & waved my cap," his signal to Lee to commence the attack. Minutes later, most of Brown's raiders were dead, Brown was wounded, and his raid over.

The firehouse secure, Lee and the marines kept a mob from lynching Brown and the other survivors. "It appears that the party consisted of nineteen men—fourteen white and five black," Lee reported, adding that Brown "avows that his object was the liberation of the slaves of Virginia, and of the whole South . . . The blacks whom he forced from their homes in this neighborhood, as far as I can learn, gave him no voluntary assistance."[153]

On December 2, Lee and his troops watched Brown ascend the wooden steps to the hangman's platform. Among those present were Major Thomas J. Jackson, an instructor at the Virginia Military Institute; Edmund Ruffin, a slaveholding intellectual and firebrand; and John Wilkes Booth, a young actor anxious to see Brown's execution. The trapdoor was sprung. "Brown hung at eleven o'clock. Died easy— everything quiet," one newspaper reported.

It was soon evident that everything was *not* quiet. Brown's failed raid had further rent the country. The Southern press was nearly unanimous in its condemnation of both Brown and the North, while most Northern newspapers condemned Brown's actions. But after Brown's hanging, that changed. "We thank God for the grace of God vouchsafed in him," the *New York Daily Herald* celebrated, while the *Liberator*, quoting Macbeth, proclaimed about Brown's execution: "We have scotch' d the snake, not killed it."[154]

After two years as unofficial master of Arlington, Lee was ordered twelve days after Brown's execution to return to Texas and his duties there. Despite his ailments, he led troopers in pursuit of Comanche and Kiowa raiding parties and into Mexico to stop bandit raids in southern Texas. Eventually, Lee reported to Governor Sam Houston that "there are no more disturbances on this frontier."[155]

As rumors of secession by the Southern states wafted through Texas, Lee blamed politicians, calling them "the most difficult to cure of all insane people" and declaring, "If the Union is dissolved I shall return to Virginia and share the fortune of my people." In December, he received word that he would be transferred to the War Department. Lee had just read Edward Everett's *The Life of George Washington* and was caught in the irony that the country Washington and Lee's father had risked everything to create was being torn apart.[156]

As the president of the new Confederate States of America, Jefferson Davis, prepared to arrest army garrisons in the South, Lee received orders to report to General Scott as soon as possible. On April 17, 1861, Lee received two more missives, one from Scott requesting another meeting and the second from Francis P. Blair Sr., father of Lincoln's postmaster general. That same day, unbeknownst to Lee, delegates at a convention in Richmond voted to secede.[157, 158]

The following day, Lee crossed the Long Bridge over the Potomac to find gun crews placing cannons and carts full of cannonballs and grapeshot at the Washington end of the bridge. The city's streets were teeming with uniformed riders galloping back and forth with orders. The nation's capital was preparing for war against half the nation.[159]

Lee arrived at Blair's home, across the street from the White House. A former newspaperman, Blair, horseshoe bald, with penetrating eyes, got right to the point. "I come to you on the part of President Lincoln," he said, "to ask whether any inducement that he can offer will prevail on you to take command of the Union Army?" It was Scott's idea; having been called the best soldier of his generation, he wanted to turn his beloved army over to the best soldier of the next.[160]

Lee, speaking "as candidly as I could," replied, "Mr. Blair, I look upon secession as anarchy. If I owned the four million slaves in the South I would sacrifice them all to the Union; but how can I draw my sword upon Virginia, my native state?"

Lee next met with a downcast Scott privately for over two hours. Scott could empathize with Lee over his dilemma, but only so far. If Lee did not accept Lincoln's offer, Scott said, duty dictated that Lee resign.[161]

Lee did not return immediately to Arlington. Instead, he went to the

Navy Yard to find his brother, Smith, who faced the same predicament as did other Lees, starting with Lee's son Custis. At this point Custis advocated placing guns at Arlington, all pointed south.[162]

That night Mary Lee, confined in her wheelchair on Arlington's first floor, could hear her husband pacing on the second. Here was the son of Light Horse Harry, who had risked his life and disfigurement defending his beliefs, and the husband of Martha Washington's great-granddaughter, whose whole life had been devoted to serving the United States. If he accepted Lincoln's offer, the new Confederate government would confiscate Arlington and the other estates now belonging to his sons; if he refused command, there was the very real risk that the Union Army would do the same. Smith Lee's wife summed it up best in almost Shakespearean terms: "taking sides, *North or South,* to fight against his own people or *for* them," or "to fight against *your State,* where your kindred children were, or *with them.*"[163]

Later that day, Scott received a letter from Lee tendering his resignation and thanking Scott for his "uniform kindness and consideration." He ended the letter with its most difficult sentence to write—and the most difficult sentence Scott would read: "Save in defense of my native State, I never desire again to use my sword."[164]

SIX

"AND THE WAR CAME"[1]

I n the wee hours of June 28, 1863, as Colonel James Hardie interrupted Meade's slumber to inform him his world had changed, Lee
was asleep in Pennsylvania, surrounded by the largest army he could
muster. About 70,000 Confederates, in gray or butternut unforms, had
marched with him, their expectations high that this Northern invasion
would be more successful than the last.

In Washington, Lincoln slept little that night, but that had become
his habit over the past two years. Now it was exacerbated by the very
real threat of the man whose record in campaigns against the Army of
the Potomac was four victories and a draw. And Lincoln's new commander had never led an army before.[2]

What was about to take place in the following days was a direct result of the roles these three men had played over the past two years and
the decisions they had made through the course of their lives. Now the
decisions they would make—and not make—would change the course
of American history.

"A ceaseless patter" of rain fell on Detroit on April 18, 1861, but it did
not stop thousands of citizens from coming out to cheer Detroit's Light
Guard, Scott's Guard, and Hussars as they paraded to the post office,

where it was announced that every soldier—army regulars, militiamen, and volunteers—would return to the post office the next day, to "take anew their oath of allegiance to the United States, its constitution, government, and flag."[3]

That evening, during a meeting of the six army and naval officers in town, Meade argued that taking this oath flew in the face of the oath they had already taken as U.S. Army regulars. The officers agreed, signing resolutions stating that "the oaths of allegiance that we have taken" were as binding "at the present as on the day we swore them." Meade considered the matter closed, but Michigan senator Zachariah Chandler, a staunch antislavery advocate, saw their refusal as anti-American and political fodder for himself. The resignation of two of Meade's Southern officers to join the Confederacy only made things worse. "Old Zach," as Meade disdainfully called him, would be his "bitterest foe" in Congress for years to come.[4]

It vexed Meade to see less experienced officers like John Pope promoted to volunteer brigadier generals. Letters to the Corps of Topographical Engineers headquarters requesting a field command and a trip east to meet with fellow Pennsylvanian Simon Cameron, now Lincoln's secretary of war, yielded no results. In addition to being opposed by Chandler, he was thwarted for the best of reasons. Professor Joseph Henry of the U.S. Lighthouse Board wanted Meade and his engineering brilliance right where he was. Seeing her husband's frustrations, Margaret reached out to other family connections.[5]

Meade was on the verge of accepting a colonelcy in a Michigan regiment when he learned that Margaret's intercessions had won out. Pennsylvania senator David Wilmot got him an appointment as a volunteer brigadier general and travel to Washington for further orders from Major General George B. McClellan. Since the Mexican-American War, Meade's attitude toward politics and politicians had ranged from skepticism to anathema. Thwarted by politicians in his efforts to obtain a leadership position in the war with Mexico, it was ironic that his new aspiration was assisted by other politicians.[6]

On April 23, Robert E. Lee, a private citizen for three days and dressed in civilian garb, waited in the rotunda of the Virginia State Capitol to be admitted to the Virginia State Convention to accept the state's offer to lead its military forces. The building's façade eerily resembled the columned entryway to Arlington; inside these walls, his father had served as governor. Dominating the chamber was Houdon's majestic statue of Washington mounted on a marble pedestal, his left arm resting on a draped column, his gaze extending above and beyond the activities about to take place. Now Light Horse Harry's son was about to be cheered for leaving the army and the country Washington had led to accept the challenge of rebelling against it.[7]

The chamber's doors soon opened and Lee was escorted in. Convention president John Janney bid Lee a hearty welcome. "Your mother, Virginia, placed a sword in your hand," he declared, and, "you are at this day, among living Virginians, 'first in war,'" thereby tying Lee to both his father by quotation and Washington by example. "Profoundly impressed," when offered the command of Virginia's forces, Lee accepted, pledging to "devote myself to the service of my native state." Cheers and congratulations followed.[8]

Shortly afterward Lee was asked to meet with Lincoln's old friend Alexander Stephens, now the Confederate vice president. President Jefferson Davis had sent Stephens from Alabama to gauge both Virginia's and Lee's loyalty to the new country. After seeing Lee's magisterial charisma firsthand at the Capitol, Stephens believed Lee could have stopped the vote to join the Confederacy just "with a look."[9]

Stephens was even more a skeletal appearance than when he and Lincoln had been congressional colleagues, but he was still passionate about his views, particularly about the Confederate States of America: "Its foundations are laid, its cornerstone rests, upon the great truth that the Negro is not equal to the white man; that slavery, subordination to a superior race, is his natural and normal condition." Stephens returned to Alabama believing Lee "came out of the crucible, pure and refined gold."[10]

Lee found a general attitude of cockiness on Richmond's streets and in the newspapers. The city was a major link to the South, a railroad terminus with a thriving industry: ordnance, ammunition, and other war matériel would soon be sent to the Deep South and west to the states on the Mississippi. Lee took a room at the Spotswood Hotel and was given an office at the Virginia Mechanics' Institute. He immediately tore into his assignments, organizing regiments, procuring munitions and uniforms, and selecting campsites. Needing competent trainers, he gave the work to Virginia Military Institute students and sent one of the graduates, now Colonel Thomas Jackson, to assume command at Harpers Ferry.[11]

Unlike many Virginians, Lee was no firebrand when it came to the prospect of war. Where they expected "a very short and decisive struggle," Lee's new aide, Lieutenant Walter H. Taylor, recollected, Lee voiced "apprehensions of a prolonged and bloody war," confiding to Mary that "the war may last 10 years." Private suspicions about his loyalty soon became public. After meeting with Lee, one D. G. Duncan, an acquaintance of Confederate secretary of war LeRoy Pope Walker, accused Lee of treachery.[12]

Arlington was now too geographically close to Lee's former country for Mary's comfort. "You have to move and make arrangements to go to some point of safety," he told her. "Keep quiet while you remain and in your preparation. War is inevitable, and there is no telling when it will burst around you." To her consternation, Arlington soon became the headquarters of the Union Army's commanding general, Irvin McDowell, who assured her that "on your return you will find things as little disturbed as possible." It was an otherworldly setting, the bustle of a general's office surrounded by empty picture frames on the walls; Lee had told Mary to take the paintings with her.[13]

By June, President Davis was in Richmond, soon the Confederacy's capital. Lee turned over responsibility for Virginia's army and naval force to the Confederate government. "I do not know what I shall do," he told Mary. Davis and his family had also taken rooms in the Spotswood Hotel. He soon found Lee's knowledge of military affairs and needs invaluable, but Lee's pessimism about the coming war was an obstacle to giving him what he wanted: a field command. Davis gave Lee a brigadier general's rank but no brigade.[14]

Davis had a more pressing command issue: Who was to lead a Confederate army? By this time General Joe Johnston was commanding a sizable force at Harpers Ferry and Davis sent for the hero of Fort Sumter, Brigadier General Pierre G. T. Beauregard, to command the army at Manassas, 22,000 strong. Beauregard immediately requested that Johnston's 9,000 troops join him. Lee privately objected to Johnston abandoning Harpers Ferry, but Davis approved.[15]

April 1861 found the four Lincolns adjusting to life in the White House. Family residence was on the second floor at the west end. Lincoln chose a small bedroom, while Mary took the largest. She soon had a trusted confidante: Elizabeth Hobbs Keckley, a seamstress whose talents allowed her to buy both her and her son's freedom from slavery. Willie and Tad shared a room across the hall. The boys soon had the run of the place, running roughshod up and down both floors. They were a contrasting pair: the intelligent, reflective Willie and the hyperactive, prankish Tad. The hallway to Lincoln's office and the rest of the White House was overrun daily by job seekers, tourists, and newspapermen, who thought nothing of pestering all four of the Lincolns for favors or positions.[16]

As spring passed into summertime, Lincoln became more acquainted with the talents and foibles of his cabinet. He had wanted its members to reflect both his country's geography and his party's fluidity. He succeeded in both, but at the expense of unity. No less than four of them—William Seward (State), Salmon Chase (Treasury), Edward Bates (attorney general), and Simon Cameron (War)—had lost the Republican presidential nomination to Lincoln and remained convinced of their superiority to the new president. Rounding out the cabinet were former Democrats Montgomery Blair (postmaster general) and Gideon Welles (Navy) and Republican Caleb B. Smith (Interior).

Beneath their veneer of courtesy toward each other lurked resentment, jealousy, even enmity. But Lincoln believed their talents outweighed their vices, especially when war became a reality. "I had no right to deprive the country of their services," he told the *Chicago*

Tribune's co-owner and editor, Joseph Medill. Lincoln's appointments guaranteed contentious sessions, but he knew the country would benefit from the results. "He was one of the men," Medill later wistfully remarked, "who could do such things."[17]

On April 12, Lincoln met three commissioners from the Virginia Convention of 1861, also known as the Secession Convention, which was still debating whether or not to leave the Union. The commissioners were sent to learn from Lincoln himself what his intentions were for the Confederacy. The following day, as word arrived that Fort Sumter had been bombarded, Lincoln's reply to the commissioners picked up where his inaugural address left off. Those forts and other properties of the federal government "within the states, which claim to have seceded" still remained federal property "as much as they did before the supposed secession." When Fort Sumter fell, he called up 75,000 militia to end the rebellion; days later, he ordered a naval blockade of the Confederate coastline.[18]

It would be at least a week before any significant militia force arrived. To add to his logistical worries, any militia traveling by train from states north of Maryland had to come through Baltimore, a powder keg of Confederate sympathizers, with Confederate flags flying everywhere. The Potomac divided Washington from the latest rebel state but "lies surrounded by the soil of Maryland," Lincoln acknowledged. A sense of fear gripped the city. The danger had become so threatening that "every scrap and show of military force was welcome," Lincoln's secretary, John Hay, recalled.

The first troopers arriving in Washington were the "Frontier Guard": 120 Kansans led by Senator Jim Lane, a former Jayhawker. Lane, "brandishing a sword of irreproachable brightness," drilled his troops in the East Room of the White House "under the light of the gorgeous chandeliers." Hay found the new volunteers "a combination of Don Quixote and Daniel Boone." General Winfield Scott assigned them as presidential bodyguards and they bivouacked "on the brilliant-patterned velvet carpet." Hay found the situation surreal.[19]

Reality returned the next day when the 6th Massachusetts Infantry Regiment reached Baltimore. They were soon attacked by a mob armed with bricks, paving stones, knives, and pistols, and calling the militia-men "n——r thieves." When police finally broke up the fighting, four soldiers were dead and three dozen wounded, one mortally. Nine citizens were killed and dozens wounded. During the fighting, Mayor George William Brown wired Lincoln, "Send no troops here. We will endeavor to prevent all bloodshed," and that peace could be preserved if Northern troops avoided Baltimore. Most Maryland citizens and politicians made it clear they wanted no out-of-state militia or federal soldiers in Maryland, period.[20]

Lincoln summoned Brown and Governor Thomas Holliday Hicks to come immediately to Washington "by special train," acerbically adding he would arrange for one. While "for the future, troops *must* be brought here," General Scott proposed that they "march them *around* Baltimore, and not through it." When a delegation from Baltimore's YMCA confronted Lincoln, demanding that Northern militiamen and federal soldiers stay out of Maryland altogether, Lincoln was equally stubborn. Their "great horror of bloodshed" did not include "those who are making war on us," adding:

> You would have me break my oath and surrender the Government without a blow . . . Our men are not moles, and can't dig under the earth; they are not birds, and can't fly through the air . . . Keep your rowdies in Baltimore . . . [T]ell your people that if they will not attack us, we will not attack them . . . [21]

Lincoln was well aware that another theater of the war was just down the street at the Capitol. Democratic supporters of the Confederacy from non-secessionist states—not yet called "Copperheads"—were making their resistance to Lincoln well-known. Congressman Daniel W. Voorhees of Indiana summed up the opposition that Lincoln faced. "*I will never vote for one dollar, one man, or one gun to the administration of Abraham Lincoln to make war upon the South,*" he declared.[22]

After they reached Washington, the 6th Massachusetts camped in the Senate chamber, and several of the wounded called on Lincoln at the White House. He had kept his composure throughout the month, never giving a hint of the dread he felt inside that the troops promised him by Pennsylvania, New York, and Rhode Island were not coming. "I begin to believe," Hay recalled him saying, "that there is no North. The Seventh [New York] regiment is a myth. Rhode Island is another. You are the only real thing." In private he aired his despondency to Hay and Nicolay. "Why don't they come! Why don't they come!"[23]

In fact, they *were* coming. On April 25, New York's 7th Regiment marched down Pennsylvania Avenue, their band playing as thousands lined the streets, cheering their arrival. By May 1, over 13,000 militiamen were in Washington. Two days later, Lincoln called for 42,034 volunteers to enlist in the U.S. Army and Navy for three years "unless sooner discharged."[24]

On April 27, Lincoln authorized Scott "to suspend the writ of Habeas Corpus for the public safety." The writ, requiring that an arrested person be brought before a judge to justify incarceration, is found in Article I of the Constitution, thereby being under the legislative branch. It cannot be suspended except "when in Cases of Rebellion or Invasion the public safety may require it." With Congress absent until July, Lincoln, as commander in chief, gave Scott the order.[25]

He also made a point of visiting the troops. Genuinely moved by their patriotism, he wanted these men and boys to see how much they personally meant to him. Some found him coarse or were unimpressed by his informality. "He looks like a good honest man," one Rhode Island soldier commented. A Minnesotan wrote home that "'Old Abe' has confidence in us, and *we shall not betray it*." The supreme irony of Lincoln's policy—that a war was required to force those Americans whose states had left the Union to *remain* in the Union—would mean that many of these young volunteers—and hundreds of thousands that would follow—would shed *their* blood, not his. And he knew it. Throughout American history, the exhortation by politician and citizen alike to "support the troops" was empty sloganeering. Lincoln's support of the troops was constant and unwavering.[26]

In May, the tragedy that many a soldier would pay the last full measure became personal for Lincoln. His former law clerk, Elmer E. Ellsworth, twenty-four, had returned to his home state of New York and raised a volunteer regiment mostly composed of firemen. They called themselves the 11th New York Zouaves, inspired by the French light infantrymen in North Africa, with red shirts and caps and gray jackets and baggy trousers. Ellsworth was their colonel.[27]

On May 24, the Fire Zouaves crossed the Potomac to take Alexandria. Upon reaching the town, Ellsworth and Corporal Francis Brownell entered the Marshall House Hotel to take down a Confederate flag flying atop a dormer. As Ellsworth came down the steps clutching the banner, the hotel's owner, James Jackson, fired his shotgun point-blank at Ellsworth, killing him instantly. Brownell summarily shot and bayoneted Jackson.[28]

News of Ellsworth's death spread rapidly. Flags flew at half-staff as far away as Kentucky and Indiana. Northerners had their first martyr of the war. Lincoln was distraught; newspapermen found him in tears. A public viewing was held in the East Room; thousands waited in line to pay their respects. The captured flag, stained with his blood, was given to Mary Lincoln. In a letter to Ellsworth's parents mournfully lauding his "fine intellect," "indomitable energy," and "good heart," Lincoln closed: "May God give you that consolation which is beyond all earthly power." It was his first letter to loved ones of the fallen. Far too many would follow.[29]

Washington's stifling summer heat and humidity took its toll on the arriving soldiers. Dysentery broke out in the camps; men who bathed in the Potomac came out of the water dirtier than when they waded in. On July 4, Lincoln, Scott, and other dignitaries watched as regiments passed in review, followed by cannon salutes and fireworks that evening.[30]

The following day Lincoln sent his first message to the recently arrived Congress. He asked for at least 400,000 men and $400 million. Congress, now overwhelmingly Republican as a result of Southern secessions, gave him more than he asked for. Lincoln's intuition told him this would not be a brief conflict with little bloodshed but carnage on a scale unthought of in the North and South alike. "This is essentially a People's contest," he believed, and that "the people will save their government, if the government itself will let them." For decades, civil war loomed over the country. Now it had come, and Lincoln believed, as Robert E. Lee did, that "the Peoples" of the North and South would not resolve their differences with a mere battle or two.[31]

"FORWARD TO RICHMOND!" was the daily banner headline of Horace Greeley's *New York Tribune*. Greeley was not leading public sentiment for battle so much as acknowledging it. The *Richmond Enquirer* headline "To Arms! To Arms!" reflected the Confederacy's collective itch to fight. As politicians and the public on both sides clamored for action, Lincoln, Davis, and their generals knew the Blue and Gray were too green to start killing each other. Yet, on July 20, McDowell led his army of 35,000 south to meet Beauregard's 22,000 and Johnston's 9,000 along a winding stream called Bull Run near Manassas, Virginia.[32]

That same day, Lincoln visited the War Department. "He was dressed in a common linen coat, had on a straw hat, & pushed along the crowd," one observer noted. "No one seemed to know who he was." The only elected president to possess a patent was already fascinated with the telegraph's wondrous capabilities; relaying messages from the battlefield to Washington to the battlefield, thereby revolutionizing the science of war, was just one of them.[33]

Four young men manned the telegraph office, and Lincoln would come to know them well. "We had heard of him as 'Old Abe the rail-splitter,' and he seemed to us uncouth and awkward . . ." David Homer Bates, one of the four, later recalled. "But as afterward I saw Lincoln almost daily, often for hours at a time," Bates and the others "came to think of him as a very attractive and, indeed, lovable person." If Lincoln was not in his office during the war, odds were that he was at the telegraph office to "read over the telegrams, beginning at the top, until he came to the one he had seen at his previous visit."[34]

On Sunday morning, July 21, a mass exodus of Washingtonians took carriages, hacks, buckboards, and chaises to witness McDowell win the war. The high volume of picnic lunch orders could not be met; the price of bottles of wine soared 300 percent. Socialites and politicians, including Senator Zachariah Chandler, Meade's nemesis, were among the sightseers, as was Mathew Brady, his wagon covered by dark cloth to record for posterity the Union victory. Before long, cannon fire could be heard in Washington, interrupting a church service Lincoln was attending.[35]

The Battle of Bull Run, as Northerners called it (the South would call it "Manassas"), looked at first to be a Union triumph, but by late afternoon Beauregard and Johnston's forces were routing McDowell's. The retreat soon became a rout. Throughout the night and into the following morning, soldiers—some frightened, some angry, some ashamed—mixed with the civilians, who learned that battles were not meant for picnicking. Chandler and his colleagues made a beeline to the White House; Brady returned with a souvenir sword but without his wagon full of valuable equipment (and no pictures); and McDowell bypassed his Arlington headquarters for the stronger defenses of Washington.[36]

Greeley dropped the *New York Tribune*'s large headline, declaring, "It is best for the country and for mankind that we make peace with the rebels." Lincoln responded to the humiliating defeat with alacrity, signing two bills, each calling for the enlistment of 500,000 volunteers. He also wanted the defeated army "reorganized as rapidly as possible."[37]

What Lincoln, the country, and mankind did not need was a negotiated peace but a new general—and fast. At 2 a.m. on July 22, Major General George B. McClellan, commanding a small army in western Virginia, received a wire from the War Department: "Circumstances make your presence here necessary . . . [C]ome hither without delay."[38]

McClellan had graduated second in his class at West Point in 1846; among his friends were George Pickett and A. P. Hill. After the Mexican War he was sent to observe the Crimean War, designed a cavalry saddle, and served as an executive for both the Illinois Central and Ohio and Mississippi Railroads. In 1859 he married Ellen Marcy, daughter of Major Randolph B. Marcy, once McClellan's commanding officer and now his chief of staff.

McClellan catapulted to fame ten days before Bull Run at Rich

Mountain in western Virginia, where his 7,000 troops whipped a Confederate force of 1,300. Considering McDowell's failure at Bull Run, and with seventy-five-year-old Winfield Scott overweight, gout-ridden, and unable to mount a horse, McClellan seemed the perfect antithesis of both defeat and old age. Lincoln gave him command of the brand-new Division of the Potomac, consisting of McDowell's army and Washington's defenses. To his wife, Ellen, he boasted that he would "crush the rebels in one campaign."[39]

The army McClellan was to lead was no army at all, "only a mere collection of regiments cowering on the banks of the Potomac." He wasted no time making it into what became the Army of the Potomac. His rigorous drilling, strict disciplinary measures, and weeding out of incompetent officers had immediate results. Parade ground reviews instilled pride among the troops and calmed fearful Washingtonians. Within three months the Army of the Potomac *was* an army. Morale soared among soldiers and citizens alike. He was cheered on campgrounds and city streets, his soldiers affectionately calling him "Little Mac."[40]

But "Little Mac's" successes began to fuel his large ego. He viewed Scott's ideas as obsolete and Scott as either "a dotard or a traitor," spoiling Lincoln's hopes that a mentor-pupil relationship could develop. McClellan found Lincoln's visits to his headquarters on fashionable Lafayette Square tedious and thought nothing of having Lincoln wait for hours in McClellan's drawing room, for Lincoln had "nothing very particular to say, except some stories to tell." The initial admiration Radical Republicans bestowed on him vanished once they learned that McClellan would not turn his soldiers into emancipators. "Help me to dodge the n——r," he implored his friend, New York lawyer Samuel L. M. Barlow. McClellan took heart when Lincoln chastised General John Frémont for issuing an emancipation proclamation in Missouri, believing the edict was illegal (and certain to be unpopular among many Northerners). "The Presdt.," McClellan believed, "is perfectly honest and sound on the n——r question."[41]

McClellan's luster was besmirched on October 21 after a Union colonel crossed the Potomac and was soon attacked by Confederates at Ball's Bluff. The colonel was killed; most of the Union casualties drowned trying to cross the Potomac to safety. McClellan was at the White House when Captain Thomas Eckert of the telegraph office handed him the telegram detailing the defeat. McClellan did not mention its contents to Lincoln. On a subsequent visit to the telegraph office, Lincoln read the wire. The dead colonel was Senator Edward Baker, Lincoln's dear friend and late son Edward's namesake.

The next day McClellan dryly admitted to Lincoln that "the affair of yesterday was a more serious one than I had supposed." To others, including his wife, he denied any responsibility. "The man *directly* to blame for the affair was Col. Baker." According to David Homer Bates, Lincoln had watched Baker depart Washington from the telegraph office's windows. As with Ellsworth's death, Lincoln was inconsolable.[42]

When he had assumed command, McClellan told Lincoln that "the rebels have chosen Virginia as their battle-field—and it seems proper for us to make the first great struggle there." By November he believed his army should "either go into winter quarters, or to assume the offensive with forces greatly inferior in number" to Confederates in Virginia. He had created an efficient fighting force but did not want to use it until its total strength was over 200,000.[43]

Another casualty of Ball's Bluff was Lieutenant John "Willie" Grout of the 15th Massachusetts, whose drowned body washed up in Washington, D.C. A family friend, Henry Stevenson Washburn, wrote a poem memorializing Grout called "The Vacant Chair." Within weeks it was put to music with a mournful, gripping chorus:

We shall meet, but we shall miss him
There will be one vacant chair.
We shall linger to caress him
While we breathe our ev'ning prayer.[44]

By the end of 1861, the song was sung by both sides of the war.

One week after Bull Run, Jefferson Davis sent Lee to northwest Virginia to assess the training and needs of three small Confederate "armies." Part of Lee's westward journey was through familiar ground. "I passed over in the summer of 1840, on my return to St. Louis," he wrote Mary. "If any one had then told me that the next time I travelled that road would have been on my present errand, I should have supposed him insane." Lee found soldiers who were physically sick and others sick of being soldiers, led by generals who had little control over the troops and argued with each other. Lee, without a proper uniform or authority, exhorted the generals to cooperate. Behind his back, officers and soldiers gave him his first wartime nickname, "Granny Lee."[45]

On September 12, Lee took the three separate forces into battle at Cheat Mountain. Due to rain, difficult terrain, and inexperienced officers and soldiers, his plan for a five-pronged assault on Union forces fell apart. Three days later Lee withdrew, his first battle ending in defeat. For the next several weeks he sought a chance to redeem himself, with no luck. The papers, having had "high hopes" for Lee's success, now rebuked him. He earned another sobriquet: "Evacuating Lee." He returned quietly to Richmond on October 31.[46]

President Davis next sent Lee to Charleston and Savannah with full authority to oversee defensive improvements. Lee privately called it "another forlorn expedition" but, using tact instead of bluster, got the results from politicians and military officers that Davis wanted. When he returned to Richmond in March 1862, both ports were well fortified with a system of earthworks and floating batteries.[47]

That year, Lee complied with Parke Custis's will, calling for Arlington's enslaved persons to be emancipated. He directed his son Custis to hire out "the Arlington people" and those enslaved at the other estates. With Arlington in Union hands, Lee saw a gloomy financial future for himself and Mary. "I expect to be a pauper if I get through the war," he told Custis.[48]

Upon his arrival at the Union Army encampment in Maryland, Brigadier General George Meade made an immediate impression on his commanding officer. Meade was "one of my early appointments as brigadier general," McClellan later wrote. He considered Meade "an excellent officer; cool, brave, and intelligent" and "an honest man." McClellan assigned Meade to Brigadier General George A. McCall's Pennsylvania Reserves, in command of the 2nd Brigade, encamped at Tenallytown, eight miles north of Washington.[49]

Meade found the 2nd Brigade campsite, introduced himself to his officers, and then paid his respects to the other brigade commanders: Generals John F. Reynolds of the 1st and Edward O. C. Ord of the 3rd. Ord, Reynolds, and Meade were old friends, having served under Taylor together. Each brigade numbered about 4,000 men—more than Taylor had commanded during most of his time in Mexico. McCall had a trio of experienced, no-nonsense commanders.[50]

Meade purchased a horse recently wounded at Bull Run for the hefty price of $150. Named "Old Baldy" for the white patch on his face, the large bay-colored stallion had white stockings to match. He was a difficult ride, with a rolling gait too fast for a walk or trot yet easily broke into a gallop. He would be Meade's principal ride for the rest of the war, to the consternation of his aides, who had trouble keeping up with him.[51]

Hopes of a winter offensive ended when McClellan came down with typhoid and Meade was given ten days' leave to visit his family. He possessed a cautious optimism for the coming year. "If our men will fight," he told Margaret, "we must whip them so badly and distress them so much that they will be compelled to accept terms of peace dictated by us."[52]

For Meade and the Army of the Potomac, 1862 picked up where 1861 had left off. Most of the men, from generals to privates, were beginning to chafe at the inactivity. In February, clamor for McClellan to act became the talk of the camp as well as the country. Meade acknowledged the "rabid feeling . . . against McClellan" but remained optimistic, at least to Margaret. Citing the recent victories in Tennessee at Forts Henry and Donelson under Brigadier General Ulysses S. Grant, Meade believed "it will not be long before the other side will have enough of it."[53]

While Northerners cheered Grant's twin triumphs, Lincoln was dealing with a family crisis. In early February, Willie and Tad were stricken
with a "bilious fever"—likely, typhoid—that hit Willie particularly
hard. "It was sad to see the poor boy suffer," Elizabeth Keckley wrote.
"Always of a delicate condition, he could not resist the inroads of the
disease." Both Lincoln and Mary kept constant watch as, in Mrs. Keckley's words, Willie "grew weaker and more shadow-like." White House
events were canceled. Tad later rallied, but Willie died on February 20.
"Well, Nicolay, my boy is gone—he is actually gone," Lincoln told his
secretary, before bursting into tears.[54]

Four days later, the funeral of "the interesting boy whose death had
stricken so many hearts" was held in the East Room, attended by congressmen, cabinet members, foreign dignitaries, even McClellan and
his aides. Outside, a sudden, violent storm assaulted Washington, up-
rooting trees and tearing off roofs. The "beautiful edifice" of the Baptist Church, with its 179-foot spire, was "totally destroyed." The
National Intelligencer reported that "many tears fell on the coffin."[55]

Mary Lincoln was stricken with incapacitating depression and hysterical grief. Lincoln did his best to control his own deep sadness, run
a wartime government, and keep watch over little Tad and Mary. Mrs.
Keckley recalled that Lincoln took Mary after one of her hysterical
outbursts and "gently led her to the window" and "pointed to the luna-
tic asylum," solemnly warning her that if she could not control her grief,
"we may have to send you there."[56]

One wonders how often the Lincolns heard "The Vacant Chair"
after the funeral and how the second verse affected them:

> At our fireside, sad and lonely,
> Often will the bosom swell
> At remembrance of the story
> How our noble Willie fell.[57]

Now, without a shot fired, the Lincolns had two vacant chairs.

The winter saw little fighting by armies but plenty of infighting in Lincoln's cabinet. Members had pointedly singled out Simon Cameron's inept leadership and awarding of government contracts. For months, Lincoln had turned a seemingly blind eye to Cameron's failings, but when Cameron openly supported the arming of runaway enslaved men in his part of Lincoln's annual message to Congress, Lincoln had enough. "This will never do!" he declared, for the question of arming enslaved men "belongs exclusively to me!" In his message, Lincoln urged that those enslaved who sought refuge from Union forces "must be provided for in some way," even suggesting a return to the idea of colonization.[58]

To replace Cameron, Lincoln turned to a prestigious Washington lawyer and Democrat who had ghostwritten Cameron's report and, years earlier, publicly derided Lincoln in Ohio during the *McCormick v. Manny* case: Edwin McMasters Stanton. Lincoln's decision to leave their first encounter in the dustbins of memory would prove its worth over the next three years. Lincoln sent Cameron into political exile as his minister to Russia.[59]

One of the first things Stanton did as secretary of war was to take control of the telegraph office away from McClellan, moving it next to his own. Lincoln had already issued General War Order No. 1, ordering "a general movement of the Land and Naval forces of the United States against the insurgent forces" to commence on February 22—George Washington's Birthday. The orders were meant for all commanding officers, particularly the commanding officer of the Army of the Potomac.[60]

McClellan was excellent in turning 120,000 farm boys, urbanites, and young idealists into a well-trained army, the largest ever seen in the Western Hemisphere. He had grand designs to take the entire force by boat down the Chesapeake to Fort Monroe, on the peninsula between the James and York Rivers. From there he planned to march toward Richmond after taking Yorktown by siege.[61]

At first, Lincoln objected to McClellan's plan. To him it appeared that McClellan was abandoning the North's capital to capture the South's. McClellan agreed to leave the 1st Corps in northern Virginia to deter any Confederate attacks. After discussion, both men got their way. On March 17, the first transports carrying 100,000 soldiers to Fort Monroe departed Alexandria. The 1st Corps remained in northern Virginia to protect Washington. McClellan promised Stanton "happy and glorious results."[62]

Meade, left behind, was unsure. Regarding McClellan's soured relationship with Lincoln and Congress, he believed "it is pretty well settled that Old Abe will not cut his head off till [McClellan] has had a chance." As for the coming campaign? "It is very hard to know what is going to be done, or what the enemy will do."[63]

In the spring of 1862, Lee was overseeing rings of defensive breastworks and trenches dug around the city's seven hills, giving him a third nickname among the soldiers and Lee's political detractors: "King of Spades." "Disasters seem to be thickening all around us," Lee wrote. In addition to Grant's victories, Ambrose Burnside had won a battle for New Bern, North Carolina. On the Kentucky side of the Mississippi, John Pope took Island No. 10 and its 7,000-man garrison. By May 1, New Orleans was in Union hands. The war was but a year old, and already the Confederacy was in danger of losing the Mississippi.[64]

But the costliest blow, in terms of lives, came in Tennessee, near a Methodist meetinghouse called Shiloh Church. Over two days more than 100,000 men fought, bled, and died in the largest battle yet on the North American continent. When it was finished, Grant had won another victory against Confederates under Albert Sidney Johnston and P. G. T. Beauregard. Union casualties numbered over 13,000, Confederate losses nearly 11,000. The grisly totals would soon be eclipsed on a regular basis. Among the dead was Johnston, Lee's former commander and Davis's dear friend.[65]

With the actual war going badly on all fronts save in the Shenandoah Valley, there was an internal war heating up between Joe Johnston and Jeff Davis. The two had never been close, and for the past two months dislike and distrust had increased. Johnston despised Davis's interference in his plans; Davis thought Johnston's refusal to discuss them bordered on insubordination.[66]

The most propitious decision Lee took during this time regarded another secretive general whose passion for lemons and religion was mixed with visionary strategies and a love for battle. Thomas J. Jackson was "Mad Tom" to his VMI cadets, but had earned the name "Stonewall" after his brigade's defense at Bull Run. That spring, Jackson led his 20,000-man army in a brilliant campaign up and down the Shenandoah Valley. With forced marches, swift attacks, and well-picked defenses, Jackson defeated three different Union armies in five different battles, denying McClellan the reinforcements he constantly called for.[67]

"Always mystify, mislead, and surprise the enemy" was Jackson's credo. Lee was ecstatic over Jackson's triumphs. "I think if it were possible to reinforce Jackson it would change the character of the war," he told Davis.[68]

By May, McClellan was finally taking the offensive, with hundreds of transports sending his massive army up the James River to take Richmond and end the war. Soon Union gunboats were bombarding Confederate batteries below Petersburg.[69]

On May 14, Davis called an emergency meeting of his cabinet at the "Confederate White House," a handsome three-story building, and asked Lee to attend. Davis wanted to discuss what options the government had as McClellan's forces edged slowly but surely toward Richmond. When the discussion turned to abandoning Richmond, Lee interrupted. "Richmond must not be given up—it shall not be given up!" Decades later, Postmaster General John H. Reagan swore there were tears in Lee's eyes; never before had he seen Lee speak so emotionally.[70]

Lee never disclosed what went through his mind before his defiant outburst. Whether it was anger at the real possibility of defeat, frustration at his desk assignment, or the very thought of what he had given up to be in this room, we will never know. But, for nearly three years, Richmond would not be "given up."

Joe Johnston had already pulled his 75,000-man army back along the Richmond defenses Lee had designed. Heavy rains slowed McClellan's progress; by May 30, McClellan's force straddled the Chickahominy River. Davis, and the public, demanded action.[71]

On May 31, as a bedridden McClellan was battling malaria, Lee was riding to Johnston's encampment when he heard the echoing gunfire of a major battle: Johnston was attacking McClellan at a crossroads called Seven Pines. Lee and Davis found Johnston as his forces were driving McClellan's back toward the Chickahominy. Johnston soon galloped off toward the battlefield.

Hours later, a courier returned to tell Lee and Davis that Johnston was seriously wounded with a musket ball in his shoulder and a shrapnel wound in the chest. It would take weeks, if not months, for him to recover. As Lee and Davis rode back to Richmond together at dusk, Davis told Lee to take command of the army.[72]

McClellan was now opposed by the very officer who had coolly upbraided him when he was a shavetail lieutenant in Mexico. But that was an earlier McClellan and an earlier Lee; upon hearing of Lee's taking field command, the Young Napoleon was dismissive, believing Lee "likely to be timid & irresolute in action." He was not the only one to think so.[73]

The new commander of what would be forever called the Army of Northern Virginia was now fifty-five years old. He had grown a beard during the past year that added to his already austere presence; his three stars were plainly pinned to the collar of his colonel's jacket. News of his appointment was met with every negative emotion from concern to condemnation. The *Richmond Examiner* derided Lee as "a general who had never fought a battle." Recent nicknames returned in conversations and the newspapers.[74]

But one insider disagreed. Colonel Joseph Christmas Ives had worked with Lee in Richmond as a member of Davis's staff. He was riding with Major Edward Porter Alexander, who had read the press's attacks on Lee. Outnumbered and outgunned by McClellan, Alexander knew the only way to defeat "Little Mac" was with a commander with "audacity," and he pointedly asked Ives if Lee was the right man. "Alexander, if there is one man in either army, Federal or Confederate, who is head & shoulders, far above every other one in either army in audacity that man is Gen. Lee, and you will very soon have lived to see it. Lee is audacity personified."[75]

Lee met with his generals on June 3. He did not say much, but the others did. As one after another argued for a closer defensive line before Richmond, given McClellan's superiority in both firepower and manpower, Lee had had enough: "If we leave this line because they can shell us, we shall have to leave the next for the same reason."[76]

Command of this army also gave history and legend the consistent presence of one of the five horses Lee would ride throughout the war. "Among the soldiers this horse was as well known as his master," Lee's son Rob recollected. "He was a handsome iron-gray with black points— mane and tale very dark—sixteen hands high, and five years old." Lee loved Traveller. "He carried me through the seven days battle around Richmond . . . to the final days at Appomattox Court House," he told Agnes after the war.[77]

By June 25, Lee had reorganized the army into six large divisions and strengthened Richmond's defenses. He sent General J. E. B. Stuart, his former student and aide at Harpers Ferry, "to make a secret movement to the rear of the enemy" and "destroy his wagon trains." Most important, he asked—not ordered—Jackson "to deceive the enemy & impress him with the idea of your presence" in the Shenandoah Valley and then steal away with his army to join Lee's at Richmond. All this was done with little if any interference by McClellan.[78]

Stuart's successful ride around McClellan's army gave Lee invaluable information: McClellan's right wing was "up in the air"—wide open to an attack. By June 25, Lee had 92,000 men, the largest force he would have in the war. McClellan's numbered about 105,000. Since

March, Lee had seen McClellan's lack of initiative and rightfully concluded it was not so much caution as habit. McClellan had planned and replanned everything for his siege of Richmond. He had discounted one option: a full-scale rebel attack, which was just what Lee decided to do.[79]

The Seven Days' Battles began at Oak Grove on the twenty-fifth, when McClellan attacked Benjamin Huger's thin defensive line, just four miles from Richmond. It was McClellan's last attack in the campaign; for the next four days, Lee attacked McClellan at Mechanicsville, Gaines' Mill, Savage's Station, and Garnett's and Golding's Farm. During those battles Lee's plans often fell apart due to miscommunication and inexperience. Only Gaines' Mill was an actual victory for Lee. "We have again whipped secesh badly," McClellan crowed after Mechanicsville, but despite having "not lost a single foot of ground" to the Confederates, McClellan fell back four miles toward Gaines' Mill. He had won a victory and lost his grandiose campaign on the same day.[80]

Despite heavier losses than McClellan's, Lee kept the pressure on. "The rebel force is stated at 200,000 . . ." a despondent McClellan wired Secretary of War Edwin M. Stanton. The sixth day's fighting would take place at Glendale and White Oak Swamp.[81]

When McDowell's force was ordered to the Shenandoah to stop Jackson, the Pennsylvania Reserves were left at Fredericksburg; orders came on June 9 for them to join McClellan. The transports carrying the Reserves docked at McClellan's supply base, White House—Rooney Lee's estate on the Pamunkey River. The Reserves were now assigned to the 5th Corps under Brigadier General Fitz John Porter. On June 18, Meade marched his men to their position on the front lines behind Beaver Dam Creek, north of the Chickahominy River. Meade's brigade was just five miles from Richmond.[82]

Meade's brigade saw plenty of action during the Seven Days' Battles, particularly on June 30.

He arose at dawn to join his aides at breakfast when McClellan arrived to post his forces: west of Malvern Hill to the north, then east to White Oak Swamp. Meade's Reserves were in the center at New Market Road. McClellan then rode back to his headquarters on Turkey Island, near Malvern Hill, the last anyone near Glendale saw of him that day. After breakfast, Meade and Captain Alanson M. Randol rode up a ridge behind the Union line. From there they saw enemy pickets and a small cavalry detachment less than a mile away. Meade and Randol galloped back to the line of defense.[83]

The troops they spotted were Major General James Longstreet's. McCall's division was down to 6,000 men that one Reserves historian described as "fitter subjects for the hospital than for the battlefield." At 2 p.m., Longstreet's artillery opened fire. The Battle of Glendale began.[84]

The Confederate assault began on the Union left. Using three of his regiments to support Randol's six guns, Meade galloped back and forth on Old Baldy, "encouraging & cheering them by word and example," as Randol later recalled. At one instance, the fighting was hand-to-hand. By dusk, the Reserves, outnumbered and exhausted, slowly began giving way to the enemy.[85]

Suddenly, Meade winced, swinging in his saddle and catching himself before being dismounted. Confederate firing paused as they re-formed ranks for another attack as Meade walked Old Baldy over to Randol. "I am badly wounded in the arm and must leave the field," he said quietly to Randol. "Fight your guns to the last, but save them if possible."[86]

Meade rode stiffly to the rear, giving orders to the officers he passed by. His forearm bleeding profusely, he slowed Old Baldy to a walk and became aware of another, deeper pain in his hip and back, and searched for another wound. He turned command over to Colonel Horatio G. Sickel of the 3rd Regiment before seeing Dr. Isaac Stocker, the division's surgeon. Stocker reached up to catch Meade from falling. Meade's saddle was soaked in blood. He had been shot in his right hip.[87]

The field hospital was a madhouse, cacophonous with the moans, cries, and pleas of the wounded and dying lying next to those comrades who only minutes earlier had been alive. Surgeons worked frenetically with saws as much as scalpels. There was no sign of transportation to

Harrison's Landing, the Army of the Potomac's base on the James River; fear, sometimes voiced, sometimes silent, gripped those who knew they faced capture and prison if not treated before the army left the field.[88]

Meade was eventually taken to McClellan's encampment. By now his physical pain was mixed with mental anguish. What could be worse for a general than to be shot in the back? The surgeon confirmed for him that a sniper's bullet hit him while he was turned in the saddle. Meade was placed on a transport bearing wounded officers to Washington and then to Philadelphia, penning a note to Margaret before departure: "After four days' fighting, last evening, about 7 p. m., I received a wound in the arm and back . . . [M]y wounds are not dangerous, though they require immediate and constant medical attendance."[89]

Glendale was a missed opportunity for the commanders of both armies. Once again, Lee's plans were not successfully carried out by his corps commanders, and the defense by Meade's Reserves and other Union soldiers kept Longstreet from dividing the Yankee forces. McClellan's absence, and his failure to turn his command over to one of his field generals, damaged his reputation both with Lincoln and posterity. "Never in his military career was he so derelict of his duty," historian Stephen W. Sears wrote.[90]

"It was only the stubborn resistance offered by our division, prolonging the contest till after dark, and checking till that time the advance of the enemy, that enabled the concentration during the night of the whole army on the James River, *which saved it*," Meade later told McCall. Porter heartily agreed.[91]

As Meade's transport headed up the Chesapeake, he could hear cannon fire from the last of the Seven Days' Battles at Malvern Hill. With a written medical leave in his pocket, Meade headed home.

Malvern Hill is 150 feet high, with long, sloping, open ground bordered on either side by creeks, ravines, and woods. Atop the hill is a plateau that was broad enough for four divisions and 150 guns placed by Union artillery chief Colonel Henry Jackson Hunt; four more divisions and 100 guns were in reserve. Seeing the Union position, General Daniel

Harvey "D. H." Hill advised Lee that "if McClellan is there in strength, we had better leave him alone." Fitz John Porter was in command of the Union forces as senior officer; that morning McClellan had boarded the *Galena* and disappeared, claiming he wanted to personally inspect the defenses at Harrison's Landing.[92]

On the morning of July 1, Lee rode with Longstreet to inspect the Union position. A direct assault on Malvern Hill looked futile. But later that morning Longstreet told Lee there were two knolls on the Confederate right where enough cannons could be placed; they might damage Union artillery and weaken the Union line. Lee, desperate for a clear victory, agreed. Drive "those people," as Lee called the Union Army, off Malvern Hill and they could be thoroughly beaten in their retreat to Harrison's Landing, where McClellan had even better defenses. The attack would commence after an artillery bombardment from the knolls.[93]

But it was Colonel Henry Hunt's well-trained gun crews that opened fire first. Their massed salvos smashed Confederate cannons, whose sporadic replies proved ineffective. A Union soldier watched Confederates prostrate on the ground trying to avoid incoming shells. "Frequently, some poor fellow picks up his leg or arm, and hobbles off to the rear; then some fellow, less fortunate, had *to be* picked up," he grimly recalled.[94]

Finally, Lee ordered the assault. With meager artillery fire to cover them, the Confederate troops were slaughtered. Malvern Hill was an utter defeat. Union casualties numbered 3,214, while the Confederate number was 5,355. Lee had wanted each of the Seven Days' Battles to be the decisive one; from a tactical standpoint, Malvern Hill was the worst.

Hard rain fell on July 2 as Union forces retreated from Malvern Hill. Outside of one lone cannon from Stuart's cavalry firing at McClellan's position on July 3, the Peninsula Campaign was over. "I fear [McClellan] is too secure under cover of his boats to be driven from his position," Lee told Davis on July 4.[95]

There was a pattern to the Seven Days' Battles: a technical Union victory followed by a Union retreat. Lee's goal of driving McClellan from

Richmond was accomplished. He had absorbed the lesson sadly learned by American generals since Washington: complex plans for victory rarely succeed once the battle is joined. Lee also read the price of his attacks in the casualty lists. More than 20,000 Confederates were killed, wounded, missing, or captured, compared to 16,000 Union soldiers and officers. Lee had driven McClellan's massive army from Richmond but at a human price the South could ill afford.[96]

Lee was praised in the Southern newspapers and publicly congratulated his army for their "courage, endurance, and soldierly conduct" while acknowledging his victory "has cost us many brave men." As white Virginians read his remarks, enslaved men ascended Malvern Hill with picks and shovels to bury the dead.[97]

According to telegrapher David Homer Bates, Lincoln came to the telegraph office after the Seven Days' Battles and asked Captain Thomas Eckert for some paper "to write something special." Eckert lent him his desk, gave him a sheaf of paper, an inkwell, and a "small barrel pen" the cipher operators used. Each visit, Lincoln "would look out the window a while and then put pen to paper," not minding the clatter of the telegraphers. Eckert assured the president he would keep his writing locked up and that no one, including himself, would look at it. Lincoln told Eckert "he had been able to work at my desk and command his thoughts better than at the White House."[98]

On Sunday, July 13, Lincoln attended the funeral of Edwin M. Stanton's infant son—a sad reminder of Willie's death five months earlier. Lincoln had asked William Seward and Gideon Welles to accompany him. Seward brought his daughter, Frances.[99]

As the carriage made its way to Stanton's summer residence in Georgetown, Lincoln threw a vocal lightning bolt into the conversation. "On this ride," Welles wrote later that day, Lincoln first mentioned "emancipating the slaves by proclamation in case the Rebels did not cease to persist in their war." He assured Seward and Welles that he had "dwelt earnestly on the gravity, importance, and delicacy of the movement" and believed it to be "a military necessity . . . [W]e must free the slaves," he believed, "or be ourselves subdued . . ."[100]

When Lincoln asked their opinions, Seward spoke for both men, calling Lincoln's declaration "so vast and momentous" that it required "mature reflection before giving a decisive answer." Lincoln "desired us to give the question special and deliberate attention," for he believed "something must be done."[101]

Welles obeyed the president. Whenever emancipation was raised in cabinet meetings, Lincoln "had been prompt and emphatic in denouncing any interference by the General Government," and his cabinet agreed. But now, Welles saw Lee's success in Virginia and "the formidable power and dimensions of the insurrection" looked "to destroy the Union." Welles came to realize, as Lincoln already had, that the moral reasons for emancipation were now intertwined with politics and war: "The slaves, if not armed and disciplined, were in the service of those who were, not only field laborers and producers, but thousands of them were in attendance upon the armies in the field, employed as waiters and teamsters, and the fortifications and intrenchments were constructed by them."[102]

When a cabinet meeting in the White House library "to take some definitive steps in respect to the military and slavery" ran overlong on July 21, Lincoln called for another on the twenty-second to resume discussion. Once seated, Lincoln began to read the document he had been working on at the telegraph office: his first draft of the Emancipation Proclamation.[103]

Only Seward and Welles had known of Lincoln's intention. The others sat in stunned silence. Lincoln insisted that "the time had arrived when decisive action must be taken" but "wished to know our views"— and he got them. Stanton and Bates were completely in favor; Welles and Caleb Smith remained silent. Blair voiced his opposition. Chase, the most adamant member when it came to emancipation, worried it went too far and could lead to massacres in the South and push the border states into the Confederacy.[104]

Finally, Seward spoke in support of Lincoln's startling policy but wisely added a cautionary thought. The Union's "repeated reverses" on the battlefield would be interpreted at home and abroad as "our last *shriek,* on the retreat." Would the proclamation not be better served after "the eagle of victory takes his flight?" Lincoln bowed to Seward's sagacity and put the proclamation aside, knowing that the victory he needed would have to be won in the East, preferably against Lee.[105]

Meade arrived in Philadelphia by boat on July 4. The *Philadelphia Inquirer*'s Independence Day edition displayed a large map detailing the Seven Days' Battles, a sidebar mentioning "General Mead [*sic*], of Pennsylvania was severely wounded." The bullet that had struck his hip just missed hitting his spinal cord when it exited. It would plague Meade off and on for the rest of his life.[106]

He maintained a quiet convalescence, happy to be with his wife and children and welcoming friends and family. The most welcome visitor was his Black valet, John Marley, who showed up with Old Baldy and Meade's personal effects, save his sword. Marley had heard that Meade had died and believed he was bringing everything back as keepsakes for his family.[107]

Anxious to return to his brigade, Meade boarded a steamship on August 11. When he reached the 3rd Corps camp at Fredericksburg, he was greeted with cheers from his men and was visibly moved. "They had more opportunity of knowing what I did and what I am than my superior officers," he wrote Margaret.[108]

Lee, meanwhile, took advantage of the lull in fighting near Richmond to finish reorganizing his forces. The Seven Days' Battles had given him opportunity to see his generals in action, and he proceeded to remove those he found unreliable. He established two large corps to be commanded by Jackson and Longstreet. Historians have long remarked how the two men each possessed one-half of Lee: Jackson personified Lee's "audacity," while Longstreet displayed a grounded unflappability in the heat of battle.[109]

Lincoln, weary of McClellan, removed him as general in chief of the armies and replaced him with Major General Henry Halleck, commander of the Western Department and called "Old Brains" as much for his high forehead and open-eyed gaze as for his military smarts. Lincoln hoped Halleck would establish order and authority over the army in general and generals in particular, only to wind up calling Halleck "a first rate clerk." Halleck was not the only western general summoned east. Major General John Pope was given command of the new "Army of Virginia," consisting of Banks's, Frémont's, and McDowell's forces. By mid-July, Lee's army and Richmond were between two Union forces. McClellan was still on the peninsula, less than twenty-five miles from Richmond.[110]

Pope was the best general Pope ever saw. "I have come to you from the West, where we have always seen the backs of our enemies," he informed his troops. "Success and glory are in the advance, disaster and shame lurk in the rear." These soldiers, mostly veterans, found Pope's condescension revolting. Fitz John Porter openly called Pope "an Ass."[111]

But Radical Republicans in Congress liked Pope's seizure of Virginians' livestock and food, demanding loyalty oaths from male civilians and warning Southerners that any damages done to his supply wagons would be met with extreme reprisals, including execution. He also indiscriminately seized Confederate "property," including the enslaved, a measure supported by both Stanton and Lincoln.[112]

Lee, enraged over Pope's actions, determined not so much to defeat Pope as to humiliate him. He sent Jackson's corps north to Gordonsville to gauge Pope's strength while at the same time retesting McClellan's resolve. Skirmishes along the Seven Days' battle sites had failed to pull McClellan from Harrison's Landing, but on August 3, General in Chief Halleck ordered him to move up to Aquia Landing, near Fredericksburg, to assist Pope or defend Washington. Lee soon learned that one hundred transports were bringing up Porter's corps to join Pope. The race to defeat Pope before McClellan's larger army arrived was on. And Lee was ready for it. "I want Pope to be suppressed," Lee told Jackson, and left it to him to decide when and how to do it. He also sent a missive to Halleck assuring him that if Pope was going to kill civilians, Lee would execute a like number of captured officers.[113, 114]

In a bold move, Lee split his army. Two weeks after fighting an inconclusive battle with two divisions of Pope's army at Cedar Mountain on August 9, Jackson marched northwest. Pope believed he was returning to the Shenandoah Valley. Instead, Jackson turned east and struck the Union supply base at Manassas; what his men could not eat, wear, or carry, they burned. Meanwhile, Stuart's cavalry raided Pope's telegraph post at Catlett's Station, learning that McClellan and Pope were indeed joining forces. By the twenty-ninth, Lee and Longstreet were through Thoroughfare Gap in the Bull Run Mountains. Lee, returning to his younger days in Mexico, rode out with a reconnaissance party and was grazed on the cheek by a sharpshooter's bullet: one half-inch closer and he would have been the late Robert E. Lee.[115]

Pope, finding Jackson at Bull Run, began a vicious assault. The rebel line held; when Jackson reconfigured his defenses, Pope erred again, believing Jackson was retreating. That evening he sent a dispatch that victory was at hand. August 30 broke hot and humid. For Pope it would get even hotter. Jackson's men repelled another strong attack; in the afternoon, Longstreet's guns opened fire and then his infantry made an unstoppable attack on Pope's left while Jackson's weary soldiers made their own counterattack. By nightfall, Pope's army had left the battlefield.[116]

As at First Bull Run, the Pennsylvania Reserves had admirably stood up to enemy fire. "We have been, as usual, out-manoeuvred and outnumbered, and though not actually defeated, yet compelled to fall back on Washington," Meade bitterly acknowledged. However, "everything now has changed," Meade wrote Margaret from Arlington. "McClellan's star is again in the ascendant, and Pope's has faded away." Having shown his mettle, Meade hoped to be awarded his own division. As for Lee's army, "I hardly think they will adventure to attack Washington, yet I believe they will try to get into Maryland."[117]

In a letter to Horace Greeley, Lincoln wrote, "If I could save the Union without freeing *any* slave I would do it, and if I could save it by freeing *all* the slaves I would do it; and if I could save it by freeing some and leaving others alone, I would also do that." Now Lincoln, to save the Union, reappointed the one man who had most vexed him thus far in the war and who would take delight in Lincoln's embarrassment at having to give him a second chance. Facing the evil of two lessers, Lincoln removed Pope from the field for McClellan.[118]

After routing Pope, Lee and his army were praised in the South and feared in the North. For the first time since he had taken command, Confederate casualties were sizably smaller than those of Union forces: 7,298 to 14,462. One unlisted casualty was the Confederate commander himself. During a heavy rain on the thirty-first, Lee, wearing a poncho and rubber overalls, was holding Traveller's reins when the horse "spooked" and reared. Lee slipped in the mud, trying to grab the reins and fell, spraining both hands and breaking a bone in one. For several weeks, splints and a sling confined him to traveling by ambulance.[119]

Lee now believed the time had come "for the Confederate Army to enter Maryland." He acknowledged to Davis that his army lacked ordnance, the horses and mules were in poor condition, and his men lacked clothing; many were "destitute of shoes." Lee remained concerned over his lack of ammunition, especially for his artillery; he had not forgotten Malvern Hill. Yet he was convinced "we cannot afford to be idle."[120]

There were ample reasons for his proposal. In marching into western Maryland during harvest time, he would not require the long, easily attacked supply line carrying food Virginia farmers did not have. There was also an international reason: European nations, frustrated at the Northern blockade's effect on their economies, were also unimpressed with Northern defeats. A successful Northern invasion by Lee might result in European recognition of the Confederacy. Lee saw entering Maryland as an opportunity to gauge Marylanders' sympathy and possibly add another star to the Confederate flag, but he had his eye on the Mason-Dixon Line: "Should the results of the expedition justify it, I propose to enter Pennsylvania." With assurances to Davis that "a respectable force" would remain to defend Richmond, Lee was sure of Davis's approval.[121]

By September 1862, Davis was as beleaguered on all sides in Richmond as Lincoln was in Washington. The conscription act seemed to instill more pleas for exemptions than recruits, with generals and governors demanding more men. Inflation was clobbering both the economy and morale: "Turkeys were thirty dollars apiece," Confederate diarist Mary Chesnut bemoaned. Armies and the public grew hungry while tons of food rotted on station platforms or sidelined boxcars. And Davis's wife, Varina, like her counterpart Mary Lincoln in Washington, possessed the innate talent of stirring up trouble with his aides, generals, and generals' wives.[122]

One solace Davis had was Lee, not just for his victories but in his consideration of Davis. This was not happenstance. While Lee had learned thoroughness in engineering from Gratiot and bold tactics from Scott, he had also witnessed the fragility of their relationships with their civilian commanders in chief. Since 1861, Lee had made it a point to keep Davis informed of activities, plans, and ideas. For that, Davis stood by him after Cheat Mountain. Now he trusted Lee implicitly.[123]

Davis not only approved Lee's plan but made it part of a three-pronged autumn offensive: Lee invading Maryland, Major General Braxton Bragg's army invading Kentucky, and Major Generals Earl Van Dorn and Sterling Price retaking Corinth. Lee planned to take 55,000 men and a letter "To the People of Maryland," written by Lee himself, declaring that "the people of the South have long wished to aid you in throwing off this foreign yoke"—that would be the United States government—"and enjoy the inalienable rights of freemen" the Confederacy had to offer.[124]

By September 7, all of Lee's divisions had crossed the Potomac. They entered Frederick, Maryland, with bands interspersing the joyous tunes "Dixie" and "Bonnie Blue Flag" with "Maryland, My Maryland." But instead of their regal-looking commander riding his handsome steed, followed by soldiers in well-pressed uniforms, Frederick's townsfolk saw Robert E. Lee stiffly clamber out of an ambulance. Nor did his broadside have the effect he had hoped. The appearance and condition of his soldiers were both frightening and pitiful; there was no rejoicing among most Marylanders—and no signs of enlisting. Lee was forced to maintain a supply line stretching back to Culpeper, over eighty miles south.[125]

On September 9, Lee issued Special Order No. 191, splitting his army into four segments after it had marched west from Frederick to Middletown. Jackson would take three divisions, cross the Potomac, and retake Harpers Ferry. The rest of the army was soon separated, taking different passes through South Mountain, the vast northern extension of the Blue Ridge Mountains. The move was risky, but Lee knew his opponent. His army would reunite at Boonsboro or farther north at Hagerstown, where Lee would lead it into Pennsylvania.[126]

Lee believed it would be at least two weeks before the snail-like McClellan would discover his whereabouts and pursue him. He soon learned he was wrong.

Upon reassuming command, McClellan relieved McDowell of 3rd Corps, replacing him with Major General Joseph Hooker and renumbering it 1st Corps, including Reynolds's division. With "The Rebels on the Aggressive," as the *Philadelphia Inquirer* warned, Pennsylvania governor Andrew Gregg Curtin requested that the War Department send John Reynolds back to Pennsylvania to command the state militia. Command of the Pennsylvania Reserves went to Meade. By September 13, McClellan was in Frederick. Meade joined McClellan's meeting with other generals and local dignitaries.[127]

The meeting was still in session when a courier burst in: a corporal had found a paper wrapped around three cigars in the tall grass outside of Frederick. It was "Special Order No. 191"—the full details of Lee's plans. The Young Napoleon exulted, "Now I know what to do!"[128]

McClellan's braggadocio was heard by a Marylander with Confederate sympathies who galloped off to find J. E. B. Stuart at Turner's Gap. Stuart dispatched a rider to Lee in Hagerstown bearing the awful news. Realizing that McClellan could take each portion of his separated army piecemeal, Lee ordered his generals to block the passes of South Mountain. It is one of the war's ironies that McClellan, given Lee's plans, acted slowly; Lee, learning this, moved with all speed.[129]

On the fourteenth, McClellan moved his troops westward, sending Hooker's corps to Turner's Gap in South Mountain. Starting as a low ridge on the Potomac, South Mountain runs north into Pennsylvania, where it grows higher and expands. A series of gaps runs through it, and these were held by smaller numbers of Confederate forces. Hooker's corps marched toward Turner's Gap. In a full day of desperate fighting, Meade's division took the pass and pursued the retreating Confederates to Antietam Creek. Hooker's report that day praised Meade's "great intelligence and gallantry." Meade, in a rare instance of chest-thumping, let Margaret know "I gained great credit."[130]

The Battle of South Mountain ended with McClellan's forces holding the mountain gaps and Lee's forces retreating to Sharpsburg, a hamlet settled by German and Dutch settlers. After viewing the line of hills west of Sharpsburg and Antietam Creek, Lee decided to stand and fight. His line stretched four long miles, from the Potomac on his left to Antietam Creek on his right. Defenses along these hills were high groves of trees, clusters of thick rock, and a few stone walls. A sunken road in the center was the closest thing to the trenches Lee usually ordered dug. Below his line were three bridges spanning the creek, with only the southernmost within range of Confederate guns. He did not have a large enough force to adequately defend such a line: "Our great embarrassment is the reduction of our ranks by straggling," Lee informed Davis. By the fifteenth, Lee's army had lost 15,000 men. Since his defensive position was on the high ground, and that behind Antietam Creek, Lee may have been optimistic enough to think McClellan could be thoroughly whipped right where Lee was standing.[131]

By the time Jackson arrived on the sixteenth, McClellan's far larger army was across Antietam Creek. An attack that day might have overwhelmed Lee's smaller force. But the Young Napoleon was still George McClellan; once again he believed he faced superior numbers and spent the day and evening reviewing his plans. McClellan's golden opportunity vanished as if it had never existed.[132]

Daybreak came with a drizzling rain as McClellan began his first attack, including Meade's division. He sent a brigade against Jackson's men waiting in a massive cornfield by a whitewashed German Baptist church called "Dunker" by the town because of the churchgoers' enthusiastic baptisms. Soon, hundreds of Meade's troops lay dead or wounded, covered in cornstalks shot to pieces. "It was never my fortune to witness a more bloody, dismal battlefield," one officer recalled. And the battle was only an hour old. It would seesaw all day long.[133]

A second Union assault smashed Jackson's men at Dunker Church, only to be driven back by a vicious Confederate counterattack. As the fighting intensified, the sunken road by the church filled with corpses from both sides, giving it the nickname "Bloody Lane." At one point Meade was struck in his thigh by a spent piece of grapeshot, while Old Baldy was shot through the neck. Around 1:30, Meade received a hasty order from McClellan: 1st Corps's commander, Major General Joseph Hooker, had been wounded; McClellan wanted Meade to assume command with orders that "it is absolutely necessary that the right should be held." By late afternoon Meade's division had little ammunition or stamina left. He withdrew it to a ridge to let the men refill their canteens and cartridge belts before returning to combat. Their long day of fighting was over, but the battle had one more act before sunset.[134]

Throughout the morning, Lee had been astride Traveller while an aide, holding the reins, led the horse where Lee wanted to go. As the tide of battle ebbed and flowed, Lee sent in what reserves he had, maintaining his composure as American soldiers below him, wearing blue or gray, killed and wounded each other indiscriminately while praying for survival. Since dawn, Lee had moved his forces as if they were on a human chessboard, taking troops from an idle area to plug in the gaps where fighting took place. "The battle ebbed & flowed with terrific slaughter on each side," Longstreet recalled. By midafternoon, there were no reserves to speak of. At this point in the battle, the Army of Northern Virginia was ripe for the taking.[135]

McClellan had ample reserves to make another all-out attack on Lee's center and break the Confederate line. Instead, he turned his attention to Lee's right and sent Major General Ambrose Burnside's 9th Corps across the southernmost bridge—the last Union attack. At first, the fighting was going Burnside's way. Defeat was becoming a reality for Lee when he spotted a cloud of dust moving toward Antietam. "What troops are those?" he asked. An artillery lieutenant offered his telescope to Lee, who presented his bandaged hands. Looking through the scope, he sang out, "It is A. P. Hill, from Harpers Ferry."[136, 137]

Hill's counterattack on Burnside began just before Burnside was about to smash the remnants of Lee's right. Burnside fell back, recrossing the bridge that has borne his name ever since. There would be no more fighting. "Night put an end to a bloody day," Edward Porter Alexander recalled, with the Confederates "worn & fought to a perfect frazzle."[138]

Many of Lee's officers and soldiers anticipated he would take advantage of darkness and leave the battlefield. Lee did not. "We were so badly crushed that at the close of the day ten thousand fresh troops could have come in and taken Lee's army and everything it had," Longstreet believed. But Lee remained in his position all the next day, daring McClellan to attack—and knowing he would not. McClellan wired Halleck, "Send all the troops you can." Smart enough to not push his luck, Lee and his battered army slipped into Virginia that night.[139]

At dawn on the nineteenth, "we moved forward," Meade told Margaret, "when lo! The bird had flown." Antietam was the bloodiest day of the war: the Army of the Potomac suffered 12,410 casualties, the Army of Northern Virginia 10,317. With Lee gone, McClellan declared victory. "Those in whose judgment I rely tell me that I fought the battle splendidly & that it was a masterpiece of art," he crowed to Halleck. "Maryland & Penna. are now safe."[140]

Lincoln, desperate for a victory in the East, agreed.

— SEVEN —

EMANCIPATION AND INVASION

Antietam was no smashing triumph, but for Lincoln it was victory enough, and he put it to effective use. He called a cabinet meeting on September 22, opening with a joke that fell utterly flat (at least Seward laughed). Then Lincoln, as Chase put it, "took a graver tone." In his diary, Welles wrote that Lincoln "had made a vow, a covenant, that if God gave us the victory in the approaching battle, [Lincoln] would consider it an indication of Divine will, and that it was his duty to move forward in the cause of emancipation." After discussion and what Welles called "one or two unimportant amendments" from Seward, the proclamation was published the next day:

> That on the first day of January, in the year of our Lord one thousand eight hundred and sixty-three, all persons held as slaves within any state, or designated part of a state, the people whereof shall then be in rebellion against the United States, shall be then, thenceforward, and forever free . . .[1]

While Lincoln and his cabinet were concerned about public acceptance of the proclamation, the first reaction was a happy one. On the twenty-fourth, a large crowd serenaded the president at the White House. After joshing with his audience and explaining his decision, Lincoln said, "I can only trust in God I have made no mistake," prompting spontaneous applause and encouraging comments from the crowd. He added, "I only ask you, at the conclusion of these remarks, to give three hearty cheers to all good and brave officers and men who fought these successful battles" that allowed him to issue the proclamation.[2]

The reaction of those brave officers and men to the proclamation was mixed. Since the war began there had been mistreatment and outright atrocities on Blacks by Union soldiers. One soldier wrote after Antietam that Lincoln's proclamation "meets with denouncement among the men of the Army . . . We must first conquer & then its [sic] time enough to talk about the *dam'd n——s.*" Yet many who willingly volunteered to fight for the Union soon added ending slavery to their mission. "I have never been in favor of the abolition of slavery," a Massachusetts soldier wrote, "and now I go in for a war of emancipation and I am ready and willing to do my share of the work." A war-weary Illinois soldier was revitalized: "My hopes are somewhat revived since Old Abe has come out with his proclamation . . . [E]very boddy [sic] knows slavery was the cause of this war . . . [N]ow let us put an end to it."[3]

The hero of the hour told his wife that he believed Lincoln's proclamation "an accursed doctrine." To a friend, McClellan complained that, with "one stroke of a pen," Lincoln was "changing our free institutions into a despotism." Such was the general's mood when his commander in chief came for a visit.

On October 2, President Lincoln and a coterie of advisers visited McClellan's encampment outside Sharpsburg. "I had the distinguished honor of accompanying him to the battlefield, where General McClellan pointed out to him the various phases of the day, saying here it was that Meade did this and there Meade did that; which all was very gratifying to me," Meade happily informed Margaret.[4]

Meade did not share the opinion of Lincoln and many Republicans that McClellan should have pursued Lee after he crossed the Potomac. "If there is any common sense in the country, it ought to let us have time to reorganize and get into shape our new lines," Meade wrote Margaret, "and then advance with such overwhelming numbers that resistance on the part of the enemy would be useless." At Antietam, Meade's division "took a great many prisoners," describing them as "tired of the war."[5]

If Confederates were tired of the war, Meade was tired of Congress. "They do not, or will not, send from Washington the supplies absolutely necessary for us to have before we can move," he grumbled. "I have hundreds of men in my command without shoes, going barefooted, and I can't get a shoe for a man or beast . . . Our artillery horses and train animals have been literally starving, and have been suffering for the want of forage, and our men for the want of clothing, and yet we can't get these things."

The main thing, at least to Meade, was that "Maryland is free, and their audacious invasion of our soil put an end to." It was the first time he used that result as an eminent justification for pausing before pursuing a fleeing enemy. The next time would help undo his reputation.[6]

By mid-October, Meade believed that "McClellan's position is most precarious," adding, "if he does not advance soon and do something brilliant, he will be superseded." He was correct: on November 7, as a snowstorm raged, Brigadier General Catharinus P. Buckingham arrived at McClellan's headquarters to remove him from command. His replacement was Major General Ambrose E. Burnside. "I am sorry for him," McClellan condescendingly remarked.[7]

One wonders if McClellan ever saw the irony of Antietam. In giving Lincoln the slimmest of victories, he gave the president what he needed to do the very thing McClellan did not want done: the "accursed doctrine" forever called the Emancipation Proclamation.

Gone this time for good, McClellan's influence among the Army of the Potomac—especially its generals—would last until 1864. "Little Mac" had created a fissure between the mostly West Point–trained generals who admired McClellan's strategies but chafed at his reluctance to fight and the politically appointed ones who allied themselves with the

Radical Republicans in Washington. Meade was in the first camp. "The army is filled with gloom and greatly depressed," he wrote Margaret."[8]

Burnside immediately returned to the pre-McClellan "On to Richmond" offensive but from northern Virginia instead of the James River. Meade saw Halleck's influence in this, wanting the Army of the Potomac constantly between Washington and Lee's army. Burnside restructured the army into three "Grand Divisions" of two corps each, with Meade assigned to the Left Grand Division under Major General William B. Franklin.[9]

Jefferson Davis's hopes that his triple offensive would be successful were dashed across the board. After Antietam, Major General Earl Van Dorn's attack on Corinth, Mississippi, on October 4 was repulsed by Major General William S. Rosecrans with great losses. Four days later, in Perryville, Kentucky, Major General Braxton Bragg's army was defeated by Union forces under Major General Don Carlos Buell, sending Bragg back to Tennessee.[10]

Once home, the Army of Northern Virginia started to replenish itself. Custis Lee informed Davis that roads in northern Virginia were "full of stragglers." Lee came back from Maryland with less than 40,000 men; now the return to the army of so many veterans who had deserted before Antietam was staggering. Along with new recruits, the army swelled to over 78,000 by December. Lee made Jackson and Longstreet lieutenant generals. Jackson had been called "Stonewall" since First Bull Run; after Antietam, Lee began calling Longstreet "my old war horse." He also sent Stuart on another daring ride around McClellan's army. His route took him as far north as Chambersburg, Pennsylvania, sending alarms throughout the mid-Atlantic right before the 1862 midterm elections.[11]

In October, Lee learned that his daughter Annie had died of typhoid. Her death was naturally a tremendous blow to her father. "To know that I shall never see her again on earth, that her place in our circle which I always hope one day to rejoin is forever vacant is agonizing in the extreme," he told Mary. More sad news came from home in

December: Rooney's wife had given birth to a daughter, Charlotte, who soon passed away. "God's will be done," Lee wearily wrote, calling the infant "a bright angel in Heaven."[12]

Ambrose E. Burnside cut an imposing figure: a six-footer with a face too big for his balding head. Thick muttonchops that soon inverted his name often camouflaged a pleasant grin. Beneath Burnside's demeanor was a general who knew himself far better than Lincoln or Halleck did. Burnside "openly says he is not fit for the position." Burnside was right.[13]

As November's rain became December's snow, Meade hoped the army would go into winter quarters, but Burnside decided to march on Fredericksburg, midway between Washington and Richmond and a transportation junction both by land and water. Logistical failures came with him: pontoon bridges to cross the Rappahannock did not arrive promptly, giving Lee enough time to bring up his army and establish a seven-mile-long defensive line along the heights to the west of Fredericksburg. Unlike Antietam, Lee had more than enough troops to oppose Burnside. "We hold the hills around the city," Lee reported. He could not have chosen better ground.[14]

The engineer in Meade believed every day without pontoons further guaranteed defeat. "We will break down, lose all our animals, experience great suffering [and if] the enemy are at all energetic, meet with a check, if not disaster." Even his long-anticipated promotion to major general did not raise his spirits.[15]

The pontoons finally arrived, but Burnside again hesitated. His plan of building five bridges in awful weather, in full view of Lee's army, followed by the crossing of 100,000 men and artillery, and climaxed by a frontal attack on the Confederates firmly emplaced on the heights above Fredericksburg seemed pure idiocy. When asked by Burnside what he thought, Lieutenant Colonel Joseph H. Taylor was blunt: "The carrying out of your plan," Taylor insisted, "will be murder, not warfare."[16]

Sleeping Confederates were awakened at 2 a.m. on December 11 when construction on the bridges commenced. Those built for Meade's division on the Union left were completed with little difficulty, but those under construction before Fredericksburg met constant sniper fire from the town. At 1 p.m., Union artillery opened fire on Fredericksburg, smashing brick buildings and setting wooden homes afire. That night much of the town was put to the torch as looting Union soldiers smashed everything from china plates to pianos.[17]

A heavy fog hung over Fredericksburg on the morning of the thirteenth, as Meade's division prepared to lead the assault on Lee's right flank, with Major General Abner Doubleday's division on his left and Brigadier General John Gibbon's division on his right. Across an open field 1,000 yards away, along a wooded ridge, was Stonewall Jackson's corps. They could hear Meade's division band playing, the steady rhythm of foot soldiers marching, the rattle of swords in scabbards, the noise of horses and caisson wheels signaling the placement of Union guns.[18]

As the fog lifted, Meade sent out a skirmish line, followed by his three brigades. "The rebel batteries open on Meade," Captain Joseph R. Orwig of the 131st Pennsylvania Volunteers later recalled, "but Meade's men are pressing forward and gaining ground steadily." Meade's attack was interrupted by a two-hour duel between Confederate and Union artillery; when a final Union cannonball smashed a rebel caisson, causing an explosion, Meade resumed his offensive.[19]

Around 1:30, Meade's Pennsylvanians slammed into A. P. Hill's division on the wooded ridge and broke the Confederate line, seizing two regimental flags and several hundred prisoners. After detaching enough troops to march the prisoners back to the Union line, Meade expanded the attack on his left and right, widening the breach. A minié ball pierced Meade's hat; while Meade was ordering a half-crazed Yank to keep moving, the man turned his gun on Meade, who struck him so hard with the flat of his sword that it broke. Meade's men surged forward, attacking Brigadier General Maxcy Gregg's 1st South Carolina Brigade. Gregg, believing them Confederates, told his men to hold their fire. In seconds Gregg fell, mortally wounded. One Confederate unit was shot to pieces while the rest fled. Meade's men continued into the woods.[20]

Both Lee and Burnside watched Meade's success unfold. Lee reacted immediately. Within minutes, fresh Confederate forces met

Meade's tiring soldiers in the woods. Their arrival inspired the rest of the Confederate line; soon Meade's men were fighting an enemy assault from three sides. On Meade's right, Gibbon had a difficult fight on his hands. When Meade looked for Doubleday on his left, he saw no blue uniforms.[21]

Burnside's Left Grand Division major general, William B. Franklin, had ordered Doubleday to stay put that morning to protect the army's left flank in the event of attack. Behind Doubleday, Meade saw Brigadier General David B. Birney's division. Twice Meade sent a courier to get Birney's assistance, and twice he was denied. Now Meade galloped back himself.[22]

He wasted no time with formalities: "General, I assume the authority of ordering you up to the support of my men." When Birney hesitated, Meade fired a volley of profanity at Birney that one staff officer later said would "almost make the stones creep." Birney ordered up two brigades, hardly adequate help. Meade returned to the battle with Major General Reynolds, both encouraging their troops as best they could. Seeing that all his division had gained was now impossible to hold, Meade ordered a retreat. Frustrated beyond measure at the results of such a deadly day, Meade angrily vented to Reynolds, "Did they think my division could whip Lee's whole army?" Then, pointing to the living remainder of his bloodied soldiers, he added, "There is all that is left of my division."[23]

Meade had led roughly 4,500 men in his attack; by day's end his casualties totaled 1,853—a loss of 40 percent. It is impossible to know if Franklin—or, more important, Burnside—had seized the moment when Meade's men broke Lee's line, the results of Fredericksburg would have turned out differently. "My men went in *beautifully*," Meade told his wife. He would have been gratified to read what Captain Orwig wrote about him at Fredericksburg forty years later: "General Meade was possibly the best general in the Army of the Potomac that day."[24]

Soon afterward, line after line of the Army of the Potomac began advancing up Marye's Heights, muskets loaded, each line moving in perfect synchronization until it was in range of thousands of Confederate muskets and 306 field guns on the heights above them. It was Malvern Hill in reverse on an even bloodier and more wasteful scale. On the Confederate left, Longstreet's men had dug earthworks. "A chicken cannot live on that field when we open on it," Edward Porter Alexander told Longstreet. Fourteen brigades marched courageously up Marye's Heights. Retreating survivors left their dead, dying, and wounded on the ground as the sun set and a bitter winter night set in.[25]

It was at Fredericksburg where Lee famously said to Longstreet, "It is well that war is so terrible—we should grow too fond of it." Burnside's casualties totaled 12,653, nearly 1,300 of them killed. Lee lost 5,377 men, 608 of whom died. After a tormented, sleepless night, with the freezing Union soldiers dying and the wounded calling for their mothers, comrades, or God, Burnside decided to personally lead another attack with his old 9th Corps. Cooler heads prevailed. On the stormy night of the fourteenth, the Army of the Potomac abandoned Fredericksburg, leaving Burnside's reputation behind with the men he sacrificed.[26]

"Last night we had the humiliation to be compelled to return this side of the river . . . that we never should have crossed . . ." Meade wrote home. He requested leave for Christmas, but when Burnside told Meade of his intention to give him command of the 5th Corps, he decided to stay. "Burnside, I presume, is a dead cock in the pit," he told his wife, adding, "and your friend Joe Hooker (fighting Joe) is the next on the list . . ."[27]

"I have the honor to report that the army of Genl. Burnside recrossed the Rappahannock last night, leaving the dead & some of the wounded on this side," Lee informed Secretary of War James A. Seddon on the sixteenth. He sent a less gruesome letter to Mary, thanking God for "His discomfiture of our numerous foes" and ending with "They went as they came, in the night."[28]

Eighteen sixty-two began with Confederate doubts about Lee's military skills and his loyalty; it ended with him a national, almost godlike figure. Comparisons with Washington and even King Arthur were made; Lee politely demurred. In 1863, "a young French officer, full of vivacity, and ardent for service with me," entered Lee's camp. Instead of drawing parallels to young Lafayette and Washington, Lee let nature and the winter weather take its course. "I think the appearance of things will cool him," he wryly wrote Mary. "If they do not, the night will, for he brought no blankets."[29]

His officers and soldiers loved him. Most came from far humbler surroundings and lacked much, if any, education. They saw him treat Jefferson Davis and the rawest recruit with equanimity. At Fredericksburg, Lee stayed in a tent with "his military family at sunrise & at dusk in the evenings, with their tin plates & cups freezing to their fingers out of doors enjoying their sup & rough biscuit." As with Washington, his soldiers fought for him as much as for their cause. Edward Porter Alexander put it best: "We looked forward to victory from him as confidently as to successive sunrises." The men took to calling him "Marse Robert," the colloquialism for "Master."[30]

On December 29, Lee rode into Fredericksburg and walked into the county courthouse, a Gothic structure with a minaret-like tower. Since the war started, it had been used as a barracks, a signal station, and a holding center for captured runaways. Two weeks earlier it had served as a makeshift hospital.[31]

Lee had official legal business that day. Upon meeting a justice of the peace, he produced a deed of emancipation. It named every enslaved person owned by his father-in-law, George Washington Parke Custis, whom Lee could remember (he would add to the list those he forgot over the next month), as well as any enslaved persons he had hired out. Those named were declared "forever free from slavery."[32]

It would be a challenging task to fulfill, so he turned to his son Custis for assistance: "Liberate Harrison, Reuben & Parks as soon as you can. Give to them any wages they have earned this year." As to the enslaved that were at Arlington and Alexandria, "They are already free & when I can get to them I will give them their papers." He was determined "to manumit all the people of your Grd. Father, whether on the several estates or not." Upon learning a year later there were still "people at the White House & Romancoke," he wanted them to "get their free papers . . . their families if they choose or until they can do better Can remain at their present homes. I do not know what to do better for them."[33]

Lee and his family were slaveholders no longer. He was technically two months past his five-year deadline but three days before January 1, 1863, when Lincoln's Emancipation Proclamation went into effect. Freeing the family's enslaved persons reflected Lee's desire to fulfill what Parke Custis's will dictated. But his expressed concerns for the men, women, and children owned by the family did not signal a moral shift in his attitude toward enslaved or free Blacks.[34]

On New Year's Day 1863, Lincoln issued his definitive version of the Emancipation Proclamation, exempting the border states and those parts of Virginia and Louisiana under Union control, asking the enslaved in those territories to "abstain from all violence." But it also called emancipation "an act of justice, warranted by the Constitution." And it declared that such persons of suitable condition—Black males—"will be received into the armed service of the United States to garrison forts, positions, stations, and other places, and to man vessels of all sorts in said service." What historian James McPherson called "the *bête noire* of southern nightmares"—armed Blacks—was soon to be a reality.[35]

"As our case is new, so must we think anew, and act anew," Lincoln declared in his 1862 message to Congress. He meant it.

Meade's promotion to lead 5th Corps put him under Major General Hooker and propelled him one giant step further into the entwined world of military and congressional politics. He would be replacing Major General Daniel Butterfield. Just thirty-one, Butterfield had been working for the American Express Company (cofounded by his father) in New York when war broke out. His rise in rank was meteoric; his valor at Gaines' Mill during the Seven Days' campaign earned Butterfield the Congressional Medal of Honor. His musical composition of several notes for bugle to sound lights out, called "Taps," has been used by the military ever since. The young, balding Butterfield possessed both physical courage and astute political skills, as Meade would soon discover.[36]

On Christmas Eve, Meade reported for duty to Hooker and found Butterfield with him. After Butterfield departed, Hooker told Meade, "There was no other officer in the army I would prefer to you," but he was backing Butterfield's request to rescind Meade's promotion. The next day Butterfield invited Meade to have Christmas dinner with him, along with 5th Corps's division and brigade commanders. Afterward, Meade spoke alone with Butterfield, empathizing with his disappointment and telling of his similar experience. Butterfield angrily replied that Burnside had assured him *"positively* and *distinctly"* that Butterfield's promotion was "permanent." Taken aback, Meade said Butterfield's anger should be directed at Burnside, delicately adding that he actually outranked Butterfield. They parted amicably, Meade certain that "the first ice was broken."[37]

Meade had mixed emotions about leaving the Pennsylvania Reserves. "They all as a Division loved you as a commander," one private wrote Meade. They collected $1,500 for a new sword and sash. "I would much prefer the men giving their money to their wives, or, if they are not so blessed, to the widows and orphans that the war has made," he modestly told his wife.[38]

In January, Burnside launched another campaign, as much to vindicate himself for Fredericksburg as to engage Lee. The army broke camp and began crossing the Rappahannock to flank the Confederates, but Burnside's combination of poor judgment and bad luck dogged him yet. On January 20, a drizzle became a storm, a storm became a deluge, and finally the deluge became a howling nor'easter. After days of mud sucking the shoes off their feet, Burnside's infantry came up with a fitting lullaby:

Now I lay me down to sleep
In mud that's many fathoms deep;
If I'm not here when you awake,
Just hunt me up with an oyster rake.

For Burnside, "the game was up," Meade wrote. Days later, his troops were cutting down trees to build eight miles of "corduroy roads" to get artillery and infantry back to Burnside's original encampment.[39]

With the "Mud March" over, Burnside told Meade he intended to rid his army of Hooker, Butterfield, Franklin, and other detractors, promising Meade command of the Left Grand Division once Hooker was ousted. The commander who had given the Union Fredericksburg and the Mud March threatened to resign should Lincoln and Stanton disagree with Burnside's purge. Instead, Lincoln transferred Burnside to Ohio, replacing him with Hooker, as Meade had predicted weeks before. "Hooker is a good soldier," Meade wrote, but worried that his cronies, especially Butterfield and Major General Dan Sickles ("intellectually more clever than Hooker"), would easily manipulate Hooker for their own interests and at Hooker's expense.[40]

A West Point graduate breveted three times for courage in the Mexican War, Hooker was despised by Winfield Scott for taking part in the cabal to remove Scott from command. When Fort Sumter fell, he was an unsuccessful farmer in California. Knowing he had no chance of getting a command from Scott, Hooker went to Washington carrying a letter of recommendation from Lincoln's friend Edward Baker. Lincoln gave him a brigadier's appointment to command volunteers.[41]

Like Butterfield, Hooker rapidly ascended the ladder of command. According to some narratives, he benefited from a New York typesetter's error during the Peninsula Campaign: after the reporter wired "Fighting—Joe Hooker" in describing the day's battle, the typesetter omitted the dash, and one of the war's popular nicknames was born. The handsome New Englander's charm was mixed with bluster, a love for intrigue, and the inability to know when to shut up.[42]

Hooker revitalized an army that was homesick, poorly led, and in bad health. He personally attended drilling exercises and inspections; improved and enforced sanitation policies; set up a system of furloughs; eliminated Burnside's system of "Grand Divisions"; and did his best to eliminate the considerable number of obscene books found in soldiers' tents. Hooker's appointing Butterfield as his chief of staff worried Meade, but everything else Hooker did filled Meade with hope and enthusiasm.[43]

In February, Meade visited Washington, meeting with other generals and politicians. One night, upon returning to the Willard Hotel, he found himself ambushed by Brigadier General Andrew Porter, McClellan's provost marshal. Porter's apparent envy of Meade's promotion, combined with his sharing McClellan's anathema for the Emancipation Proclamation, made for an unwelcome conversation, as Meade recounted to Margaret:

> *I went in to the private parlor where McClellan was dining, and found a party of some dozen or more, all officers but one, a Mr. Cox, Democratic member of Congress from Ohio. Among the party were Andrew Porter, Sykes, Buchanan, General Van Allen and others . . . The subject of conversation at the table was general, and referred principally to military matters and pending acts of legislation. My friend [Porter] who doubtless had heard of my confirmation and was in consequence disgusted, said he heard I was to be given an* Army Corps of N——s. *I laughingly replied I had not been informed of the honor awaiting me, but one thing I begged to assure [Porter] that if the n——s were going into the field and really could be brought heartily to fight, I was ready to command them, and should prefer such duty to others that might be assigned me. As this was a fair hit at [Porter]'s position, it silenced him, and I heard nothing further.*[44]

Meade's use of the N-word was common in the army; his turning the tables on the envious and sarcastic Porter was not.

In April, Hooker staged a "Grand Review" for the Lincolns—and Lee's watchful eye—at Falmouth Heights, across the Rappahannock from Fredericksburg. A snow squall delayed the gala, but the next day 15,000 cavalrymen, guidons lowered and sabers raised, passed in review. That night Meade enjoyed dinner with the Lincolns, Hooker, and other officers. (Mary Lincoln "seems an amiable sort of personage," Meade confided to Margaret.) The next day, Lincoln inspected Meade's encampment, followed by 85,000 infantrymen, bayonets glistening, parading past their commander in chief. Hooker had instilled purpose and confidence among the soldiers not seen since McClellan's early months as commander.[45]

Hooker's accomplishments aside, Meade was still wary of his entourage. When Sickles did not invite Meade to a ball he hosted, Meade felt relieved, not snubbed. Stanton opined that there were actually two Hookers: the dashing, handsome "Fighting Joe" on the battlefield, and the "Fighting Joe" whose swagger was mixed with a loose tongue and immature disdain for his superiors. As for Hooker's personal activities, "The Army of the Potomac was a place to which no self-respecting man liked to go and no decent woman could go. It was a combination of barroom and brothel," Charles Francis Adams Jr. recollected.[46]

One day at camp, under a flag of truce, a Confederate courier delivered a sad letter to Meade from his nephew, Frank Ingraham, now a private in the 21st Mississippi Regiment. Ingraham's brother Ned and his sister Appoline's husband had both been killed in the war. Frank's letter stated that "his mother and the rest . . . wish to be remembered to his yankee relatives."[47]

Hooker's planned spring offensive was simple, shrewd, and reflective of a general with an army more than twice the size of his enemy's. Reynolds's and John Sedgwick's corps would remain before Fredericksburg to keep Lee occupied while Hooker took the rest of his army above Fredericksburg and cross the Rappahannock before marching through the large, dense forest called the Wilderness, until reaching the clearing called Chancellorsville, thereby forcing Lee to fight on ground of Hooker's choosing. "The enemy must ingloriously fly," Hooker boasted, "or give us battle on our own ground, where certain destruction awaits him."[48]

Hooker had an even more lopsided number of troops than he assumed. In February, Lee had sent Longstreet and two of his divisions down to cover Norfolk and any Union incursions into North Carolina. As Hooker's forces began their movements, Lee did not order Longstreet's return at the double-quick but merely asked "whether any of the troops you have in Carolina can be spared from there?" As April closed, Hooker had 133,868 soldiers and 413 guns at his disposal; Lee had 60,892 soldiers and 220 pieces of artillery. One heavy blow from Hooker, at the right time and place, could crush Lee's army.[49]

Lee was not himself: the stress of winter weather and mud along with inadequate supplies, a faulty war department, and family health and financial issues finally affected his health. "Old age & sorrow is wearing me away," he confided to Mary on March 9. Four days later he came to Richmond to see both Jefferson Davis and Mary. By the time he returned to camp at Hamilton's Crossing, he was deathly ill. Not wanting to alarm Mary, he told her, "I have been suffering from a heavy cold which I hope is passing away."[50]

It did not. Camp doctors, fearing Lee was truly passing away, moved him to a house close to camp for his comfort. He "suffered a good deal of pain in my chest, back, & arms. It came on in paroxysms," he wrote Mary, adding that the doctors did eventually "pronounce me tolerably sound." He continued to call it "a bad cold" to family, but it was likely either a heart attack or the onset of cardiovascular disease. Lee returned to camp on April 16, telling Mary, "I am feeble and worthless & can do but little"—hardly the best condition of a general knowing a major battle was imminent.[51]

On April 27, Meade mounted Old Baldy and led 5th Corps in advance of the Army of the Potomac. After crossing the Rappahannock on one pontoon bridge, they found the Rapidan swollen from rain. The men forded it on foot, holding their rifles firmly on the extra clothing, ammunition, and food atop their caps while mounted cavalry stood downstream to save any soldier who lost his footing in the strong current. When Meade arrived at the ford, the men burst into cheers. Throughout their march, 5th Corps broke into song:

> *The Union boys are moving on the left and the right,*
> *The bugle call is sounding, our shelters we must strike,*
> *Joe Hooker is our leader, he takes his whisky strong,*
> *So our knapsacks we will sling and go marching along.*[52]

Once Meade reached the Chancellor House, he dispatched cavalry to reconnoiter. When Major General Henry Slocum arrived, Meade could not contain himself. "This is splendid, Slocum," Meade crowed. "Hurrah for Old Joe; we are on Lee's flank and he doesn't know it." The generals set up headquarters in the Chancellor House, to the consternation of the ladies of the house, who derided the Yankee brass as they moved up to the second floor while Hooker's entourage took over the first.[53]

Lee had taken to calling his opponent "Mr. F.J. Hooker" in his correspondence, as if Hooker's first name were "Fighting." But Lee recognized the seriousness of F.J.'s intentions. Responding to Hooker's movements, Lee wired the Confederate war department that he planned to hold Fredericksburg with part of his force, using the rest to drive Hooker back across the Rapidan.[54]

May 1 opened with perfect weather. Hooker ordered Meade to advance his corps, then ordered him back to Chancellorsville just as 5th Corps had taken high ground at the Zoan Church ridge. "My God," Meade reportedly groused, "if we can't hold the top of a hill, we certainly can't hold the bottom of it!" Instead of taking the bold initiative his plan warranted, Hooker wavered, giving Lee the opportunity to take the offensive. Realizing the presence of Sedgwick and Reynolds at Fredericksburg was a decoy, Lee divided his much smaller force, leaving token resistance at Fredericksburg and taking the fight to Hooker instead of the other way around. To the consternation of Meade and other corps commanders, Hooker abruptly ordered them to assume defensive positions. "It's alright," Hooker told Major General Darius Couch. "I have got Lee just where I want him." Years later, Couch remarked that "I retired from his presence with the belief that my commanding general was a whipped man."[55]

Around midnight of May 2, two generals held one of the most famous councils of war, lit by a single fire. Sitting on hardtack boxes, Lee and Jackson discussed what to do with Hooker. They were soon joined by Stuart, who had news. Hooker's left brushed against the Rappahannock, but Fitzhugh Lee had found Hooker's 11th Corps on the right completely open without any natural protection, or even a regiment covering the flank. Lee decided to send Jackson on a march around Hooker's army to attack his exposed flank. Jackson agreed.[56]

Throughout the night, while Lee and Jackson occasionally catnapped in the clearing with their saddles for pillows, maps were drawn, guides were found, and plans were made. Stuart would screen Jackson's march. When Lee asked Jackson how many troops he intended to take, he calmly replied, "With my whole command." When Lee asked, "What will you leave me?" Jackson tersely replied, "The divisions of Anderson and McLaws."

Two divisions. This meant Lee would be facing Hooker's 100,000-man force with barely 15,000. Lee agreed. It was the third time he had divided his army: Longstreet in February; Major General Jubal Early, with 10,000 facing Sedgwick at Fredericksburg; and now Jackson taking 26,000 on his risky march. "It was, therefore, imperatively necessary to strike—to strike boldly, effectively, and at once," Lee's aide Taylor later recalled. And the perfect general for such an assignment was two feet away from Lee, sitting on a hardtack crate.

"Well," Lee replied, "go ahead."[57]

That crisp morning Lee mounted Traveller and watched by the roadside as 2nd Corps and three regiments of Stuart's cavalry, along with supply wagons filled with ammunition (no food), 108 fieldpieces, caissons, and ambulances, departed camp, marching into the thick Wilderness in complete silence. By the time A. P. Hill's division brought up the rear, Lee went back to direct the remainder of his army, feigning preparations for attack to keep Hooker focused on his front.

All day long Hooker received reports that a large force of Confederates was moving first east and later north, some two miles from Major General Oliver Otis Howard's 11th Corps on Hooker's right. At one point Hooker believed he was being flanked and sent a message to Howard to prepare for an attack from the west, not the south. Howard acknowledged but only set up a token resistance. When General Birney of 3rd Corps spotted Jackson's movement coming across the Union center, he warned his commander, General Sickles, who launched an attack on Jackson's rear that Hill's division rebuffed. Sickles then reported to Hooker, now at Chancellorsville, that Lee was retreating.[58]

The *West Point Atlas for the American Civil War* describes the Wilderness as "extremely thick and overgrown . . . The entire area was an obstacle to maneuver." For hours, Jackson and his men moved through the morass of trees, underbrush, and swamp, the wagons rolling over the poor roads they found. By 5:30, Jackson's corps had formed lines at the Orange Turnpike Road as he watched atop his Morgan horse, Little Sorrel, next to Brigadier General Robert E. Rodes. Once satisfied with their formation, Jackson ordered Rodes to attack.[59]

Howard's 11th Corps, with its large number of German immigrants, seemed blissfully ignorant as the sun was setting. While some soldiers were stacking arms, resting on knapsacks, or playing cards, cattle were being slaughtered behind the lines for fresh meat while a German band played "Come Out of the Wilderness." Suddenly a stampede of deer, foxes, and rabbits burst through camp, followed by "the crash of Jackson's guns and the 'Rebel yell' from more than twice ten thousand throats," Captain Hartwell Osborn of the 55th Ohio vividly recalled. Some spades and clubs were soon red as well as black.[60]

Of all the acoustic anomalies during the war, few had deadlier consequences than here. Confederate bugle calls went unheard by 11th Corps. Over the next ninety minutes, Jackson's Confederates slaughtered Howard's men, driving them back toward Hooker's headquarters, nearly two miles away. Stacked muskets were left where they stood; artillery, facing south instead of west, was turned east, to fire at the soldiers in blue. At his campsite, Howard saw scores of his soldiers, "some with arms and some without running or falling." Confederate colonel David McIntosh later described the attack as "a solid wall of gray, forcing their way through the timber and bearing down upon them like an irresistible avalanche."[61]

At 6:30, Hooker was meeting with two captains on the Chancellor House porch, discussing his plans for attacking Lee's "retreat," when they heard shouts and gunfire heading their way. A captain peered through his looking glass and cried, "My God! Here they come!" The three officers mounted horses and galloped westward and were soon engulfed by fleeing soldiers, wagons, and horses. Rallying most of the men seemed pointless; orders shouted in English were gibberish in German ears. Hooker soon understood he was in the midst of an utter rout of his right flank and began organizing a resistance: bringing up guns, sending riders galloping off to other corps commanders for reinforcements, and forming a solid line of defense. Hooker then directed cannon and musket fire that shuddered and stopped Jackson's attack. At last, Fighting Joe Hooker had shown up.[62]

That evening Hooker redirected his line of battle, placing Sickles, Slocum, and Couch's corps in a U-shaped defense of the heights around Chancellorsville, with Meade and Reynolds on an extension on the west and Howard's battered and dispirited men on another running northeast. As the Army of the Potomac moved into its new positions that night, Jackson and his aides probed his enemy's line, looking for the opportunity to make a night attack, rarely done and rarely successful. In the darkness, "not two rods from [his] troops," as Captain James Power Smith recalled, Confederate pickets fired at his scouting party. Jackson was struck twice in his left arm and carried back to a field hospital where a surgeon amputated the arm.[63]

Fighting began at dawn on May 3, with J. E. B. Stuart taking command of Jackson's corps and picking up where Jackson had left off, attacking

Couch at the Union center. When Couch requested Meade's assistance, he sent Colonel Alexander S. Webb's brigade into the fray. To everyone's surprise, Webb's men overran a segment of Stuart's line, taking prisoners and weapons. Stuart had no reserves to draw from. Seeing this, Meade and Webb rode back to the Chancellor House to get Hooker's permission to counterattack Stuart with Meade's 5th and Reynolds's 1st Corps. They found Hooker lying on his cot after a segment of a porch pillar had knocked him senseless.[64]

Under Lee's direction, Stuart, supported by Edward Porter Alexander's artillery, had attacked Hooker relentlessly. When word reached Lee that Sedgwick had taken Marye's Heights and was heading to Lee's rear, he dispatched a division to hold Sedgwick at bay. After Hooker came to, he ordered the army to withdraw and head a mile north toward the Rapidan. On the fourth, Lee divided his army yet again, sending another division to join an attack against Sedgwick, who had crossed the Rappahannock that night.[65]

While some accounts of what followed stated that Hooker was still dazed when Meade and Webb arrived, Meade later disagreed. Meade and Webb noticed that there were fresh Union forces on the end of Hooker's line that far outnumbered Lee's divided army. "I have never known anyone so vehemently to advise an attack on the field of battle," Webb later recalled of Meade's insistence. But Hooker ignored Meade's request. All Meade could do the rest of the day was listen to the battle being fought elsewhere.[66]

After Hooker abandoned Chancellorsville on May 3, Lee rode into the clearing with his aide, Colonel Charles Marshall, who vividly described the scene:

> The fierce soldiers with their faces blackened with the smoke of battle, the wounded crawling with feeble limbs from the fury of the devouring flames, all seemed possessed with a common impulse. One long, unbroken cheer . . . rose high above the roar of battle, and hailed the presence of the victorious chief . . . I thought that it must have been from such a scene that men in ancient days rose to the dignity of gods.[67]

That night, Hooker held a council of war where Meade passionately reiterated his desire to attack. Couch, Reynolds, Slocum, and Howard—the latter anxious to get a chance to redeem himself—supported Meade, while Hooker, Butterfield, and Sickles voted to retreat; Couch changed his mind, realizing any attack would fail under Hooker's command. On May 5, as torrential rains returned, the Army of the Potomac, defeated again, made another mud march back to Falmouth.[68]

Hooker had already left.[69]

Before retreating, Hooker had privately told Meade, "in the most desponding manner, that he was ready to turn over to me the Army of the Potomac; that he had enough of it, and almost wished he had never been born." Meade was "flattered," but once Hooker met with Lincoln "he seems in better spirits"—and that was fine by Meade. "I do not desire the command," he unequivocally informed Margaret. When Couch asked Meade to join other generals in asking Lincoln to remove Hooker, he refused. Meade believed that "Hooker has one great advantage over his predecessors in not having any intriguer among his subordinate generals." Meade could read topography as well as anyone, but he was very, very wrong about this.[70]

Encouraging news about Jackson's recovery was soon replaced with gloom: pneumonia had set in. Jackson died on May 10. "It is a terrible loss. I do not know how to replace him," Lee wrote Custis. The casualties at Chancellorsville were sobering: Hooker lost 17,287 men to Lee's 12,764. To dampen emotions among the men, Hooker banned newspapers in the camp. He at first acknowledged his failure—"To tell the truth, I just lost faith in Joe Hooker," he admitted—but soon looked for a scapegoat. While the retreat ended fighting with Lee, Meade now faced a fight with Hooker.[71]

It happened this way. On May 8, Lincoln and Halleck came to Falmouth to meet with Hooker and his generals individually. Lincoln said he was not looking to affix blame on anyone, just for the details of the short campaign. Meade was respectful but distant, not wanting to say anything negative about Hooker, but when Lincoln declared his belief that Chancellorsville "would be more serious and injurious than any other previous act of the war," Meade agreed. "When it comes to be known that it might and should have been avoided, I think the country will hold some one responsible," Meade told Margaret, stating the obvious.[72]

Ironically, the despairing Hooker who left Chancellorsville seemed rejuvenated after *his* meeting with Lincoln and Halleck. Lincoln remained circumspect. Hooker had many friends in Congress, among them members of the Joint Committee on the Conduct of the War, including Michigan senator Zachariah Chandler, who earlier had harped on Meade's opposition to a loyalty oath back in Michigan. Hooker was safe with these men. Chandler, accompanied by Senators Benjamin Wade and Henry Wilson, arrived at Hooker's encampment to make an unofficial investigation. They declared Hooker blameless for Chancellorsville; the fault lay among his corps commanders.[73]

Politicians found visits to the army's encampments to be excellent opportunities to show public support, glean information, and wield (or attempt to wield) influence. On May 12, Pennsylvania governor Andrew Curtin made such a visit. With Hooker in disfavor with the public and possibly Lincoln, Curtin hoped to promote Reynolds or Meade to succeed him. Whatever Reynolds told Curtin is lost to history. Not so Curtin's conversation with Meade, who found the governor "very much depressed. I tried to put him in better spirits," he told Margaret.[74]

Curtin "drew out of me opinions such as I have written to you about General Hooker," Meade wrote, listing in detail the disappointments he and other generals had felt during and after the battle, including Meade's stated opposition to leaving the battlefield at Hooker's council of war. "This opinion was expressed privately, as one gentleman would speak to another," Meade added; it was "never intended for the injury of General Hooker, or for any other purpose than simply to make known my views."[75]

Curtin "made known" Meade's views—and then some. Stopping in Washington on his way home, he told anyone and everyone, including Lincoln, that Hooker was persona non grata in his own army and with Meade in particular. After Curtin left, Lincoln summoned Hooker to the White House, telling him that some of his corps commanders were "not giving you their entire confidence. This would be ruinous, if true." Before Hooker left Washington, he learned that Darius Couch's cabal against Hooker was the talk of the Capitol; later, an acquaintance of Curtin's told him of Meade's remarks. Hooker returned to camp on the fifteenth and immediately summoned Meade.[76]

Hooker wasted no time confronting Meade about his conversation with Curtin. If he had expected Meade to be cowed, he learned otherwise. Keeping his own temper in check, Meade admitted he had spoken with Curtin privately and that Curtin had had no right to use Meade's name; that his remarks to Curtin had been in confidence. Furthermore, Hooker "had no right to complain of my expressing my views to others," as Meade had made these remarks to Hooker at the time the events were occurring. Hooker then "assented and expressed himself satisfied with my statement." Meade believed the matter settled.[77]

Of course, it was not. Hooker was soon after Meade. The *New York Herald* reported that four corps commanders had opposed Hooker's retreat, news that was sure to spread through the camp despite Hooker's banning newspapers (but not newspapermen). According to John Gibbon's recollection, Hooker now told Meade "he understood him to be in favor of a retreat"; in fact, Hooker said he had reported this to Washington.

"Why?" asked Meade. "I voted to remain."

"I know you did," replied Hooker, "but you coupled that vote with the expression of an opinion that we *could* not retire and as I knew we could and the result proved that we could, I consider that you voted to retreat!"[78]

Meade's reply came just short of calling Hooker a liar. He found Hooker's language an "ingenious" interpretation of the truth and assured Hooker he would publicly deny it. Meade intended to ask the other corps commanders for their recollections of that night. And while "it could only be known to himself and his God," Meade believed Hooker "had made up his mind to withdraw the army" before he called for the council of war. "I am sorry to tell you I am in open war with Hooker," he sadly, and angrily, informed Margaret.[79]

Meade asked for statements from the other corps commanders. Reynolds stated that Meade's "opinion was decided and emphatic." Sedgwick was already on the record calling Meade "the proper one to command the army." Couch met with Lincoln to say he wanted a transfer if Hooker remained in command but would happily serve under Meade, and Howard stood by Meade's account. Only Hooker's friend Sickles colored the story, stating that Meade had wanted to fight on but changed his mind once Hooker's "clear conviction became apparent." Sickles also got his letter into the *Herald*. Rumors circulated that Hooker would have Meade relieved, but no investigation into the dispute between the two generals was made.[80]

By June, Meade had calmed down and was even conciliatory to Hooker, at least in his letters home, hoping Hooker "may find a chance to assume the offensive and reverse matters." He relished telling Margaret about Lincoln's remark to Reynolds about dismissing Hooker: "The President said he was not disposed to throw away a gun because it misfired once; that he would pick the lock and try it again."[81]

On May 14, Lee, still a bit thin and wan-looking from his illness, went to Richmond to meet with Davis and his cabinet to discuss the status of the war. Davis, still recovering from "neuralgia in the head" and plagued by abscessed teeth, was furious over Lincoln's Emancipation Proclamation, which proved to not just Davis but many in the South that the Republicans' aim—if not Lincoln's—had been abolition all along. He called the enslaved "an inferior race" and "peaceful and contented laborers" who were now "doomed to extermination." He was as dissatisfied with Seddon's performance as secretary of war as Lee was. Supplies for the armies and the public were disappearing, thanks to the Union blockade of Southern ports and the need for farmers to be shouldering muskets rather than pushing plows.[82]

Inflation ran amok. By 1863 the Confederate dollar was so worthless that tobacco farmers refused to take it in exchange for supplying tobacco to Stuart's cavalry. The Confederate Congress passed new taxes, taking 10 percent of wheat, corn, rice, cotton, oats, potatoes, bacon, and beef for the armies. This was a challenge for plantation owners but devastating to rural farmers, who could not feed their own families. Soldiers' wives were openly rebelling. When a mob of Richmond women, some carrying knives and shouting "bread or blood," squared off with the police, Davis mounted a wagon and pleaded with them not to lower themselves by plundering. As the police loaded their weapons behind him, Davis promised them food and they dispersed.[83]

Despite Lee's string of victories, the South's future looked bleak, particularly at Vicksburg, the Confederacy's last bastion on the Mississippi, besieged by a Union army under Ulysses S. Grant. Vicksburg's force of 30,000 was commanded by Meade's Philadelphia fellow West Pointer John C. Pemberton, whose Virginia-born wife and years of service in the South had led him to join the Confederate army. By May 14, Grant's stranglehold on the fortress-like city on the bluffs that Lincoln had steered a flatboat past as a young man was tightening.

(The week before, another Philadelphia-born woman, now a staunch Confederate, fled her mansion, Ashwood, as her front yard became part of the Battle of Port Gibson. When the battle ended, Union major general James B. McPherson "dined comfortably at my table, *but not with me*," while his "whole division camped and fed in and around the yard." The woman was Elizabeth Meade Ingraham, Meade's older sister.)[84]

At the presidential mansion in Richmond, Lee listened as Davis and Seddon suggested he continue his defense of Richmond and send Longstreet's corps west to join Bragg in another Kentucky invasion before marching to Vicksburg to relieve Pemberton. Lee dismissed the idea. Instead, he suggested Johnston, whose army of 25,000 was also in Mississippi, go to Pemberton's aid. Lee wanted to invade Pennsylvania, and now was the time to do it.[85]

He had compelling reasons: "Our resources in men are constantly diminishing," he argued, and "conceding to our enemies the superiority claimed by them" was a tacit admission of eventual defeat. Yet a battle won in Pennsylvania might finally force Lincoln to end the war.

Lee was absolutely certain that this was the right course. Only one cabinet member, Postmaster John H. Reagan of Texas, disagreed: lose Vicksburg, he argued, and you cut the Confederacy in two. Even Longstreet came around to Lee's point of view. "The prospect of an advance changes the aspect of affairs entirely," he acknowledged. After all, who was going to differ on strategy with "Marse Robert"?[86]

His battle in the Confederate White House done, Lee now confronted another challenge: Who could replace Jackson? "Our army would be invincible if it could be properly organized," he confided to Major General John Bell Hood. "But there is the difficulty—proper commanders." On May 20 he revealed his solution to Davis. "I have for the past year felt the corps of the army were too large for one commander," Lee believed. "The loss of Jackson from the command of one half the army seems to me a good opportunity to remedy this evil." Lee reorganized the divisions into three corps, under Longstreet, Richard S. Ewell, and A. P. Hill, each containing three divisions.[87]

Ewell, "Old Bald Head" to his soldiers, was a West Point graduate who had served in the Mexican-American War. Forty-six years old, he had lost a leg at Second Bull Run. Ambrose Powell Hill, thirty-seven, had distinguished himself at Cedar Mountain and Antietam; he'd quietly fought a battle with gonorrhea contracted while at West Point. Hill had known Jackson since the academy, and the two had never gotten along. After Hill's heroics at Antietam, Jackson had him arrested for insubordination.[88]

Ewell was given Jackson's corps; the new 3rd Corps went to Hill, whom Lee now called "the best soldier of his grade with me." The two joined Longstreet as lieutenant generals. Lee was convinced "there never were such men in an army before" as the Army of Northern Virginia, but he was not so rosy about his corps commanders. "I do not know where to find better men than those I have named," he confided to Davis, and began making plans and preparations to invade the United States once more. On June 3, Lee's army began its march northward. Years later, Edward Porter Alexander would recall the irony of the departure date: "It was just a month to the very hour almost that Pickett's charge at Gettysburg was repulsed."[89]

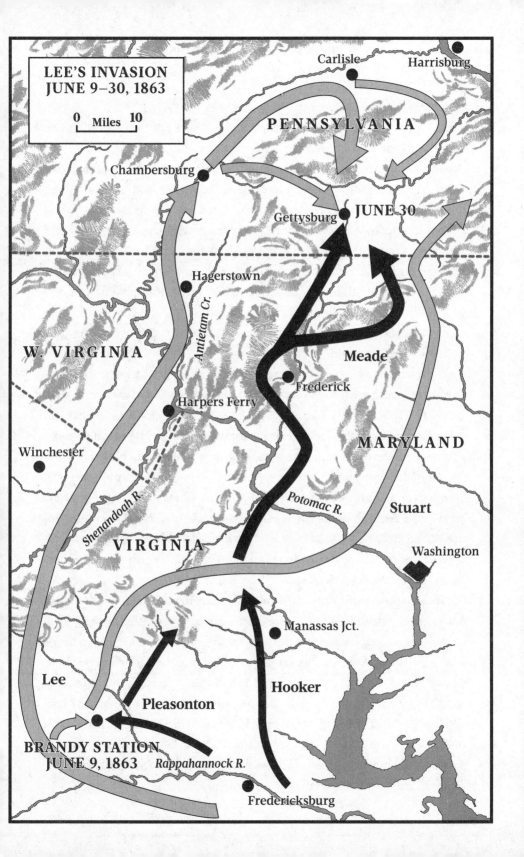

LEE'S INVASION
JUNE 9–30, 1863

0   Miles   10

Carlisle

Harrisburg

PENNSYLVANIA

Chambersburg

Gettysburg

JUNE 30

Hagerstown

Antietam Cr.

W. VIRGINIA

Harpers Ferry

Frederick

Meade

Winchester

MARYLAND

Shenandoah R.

Potomac R.

Stuart

VIRGINIA

Washington

Lee

Manassas Jct.

Pleasonton

Hooker

BRANDY STATION
JUNE 9, 1863   Rappahannock R.

Fredericksburg

The Army of Northern Virginia's 75,000 soldiers did not march alone into Maryland and Pennsylvania; thousands of enslaved persons, most owned by officers, were brought along. They were butchers, cooks, hostlers, and blacksmiths; others were trained as nurses and body servants; the rest were laborers setting up campsites and digging latrines. Most of their owners were confident they would steadfastly remain loyal and not run off; the other owners hoped they were right.[90]

Lee left his headquarters on June 6, catching up with the army the following day at Culpeper, southwest of Brandy Station. "The country here looks very green & pretty notwithstanding the ravages of war," Lee told Mary. His comment on the peaceful countryside was fitting, as peace was on his mind.[91]

That same day he wrote a lengthy letter to Davis addressing the possibility of peace with the North. Lee believed the bellicosity from firebrand newspapermen and politicians "weaken[s] the hands of a peaceful policy on the part of the Federal Government and give[s] much encouragement to those [Northerners] who urge a continuance of the war." Sensing the war's unpopularity on both sides, and recognizing the fraught state of his new country, Lee wanted Davis's approval for a new strategy: a decisive victory in the North—and any victory would be decisive, he believed—followed by "giving all the encouragement we can . . . to the rising peace party of the North." Victory first, Lee argued, peace and independence afterward.[92]

In the predawn hours of June 9, Union brigadier general Alfred Pleasonton, with Hooker's entire cavalry corps, two infantry brigades, and four artillery batteries, attacked Stuart's strung-out encampments around Brandy Station. Stuart's recently appointed adjutant general, Major Henry Brainerd McClellan, found Stuart "incredulous concerning the presence of the enemy," but he rallied his forces in what became the largest cavalry engagement ever fought in North America. By day's end, Pleasonton had retreated, but not without bloodying and embarrassing Stuart, who succeeded in keeping Pleasonton from learning how close and strong Lee's force was at Culpeper.[93]

Lee watched some of the battle from a distance; he did not want to commit any guns or infantry lest he tip Hooker off about the number of troops at Culpeper, which would be a sure sign to Hooker that Lee was marching north. Two of his sons, Rooney and Rob (now Rooney's aide), had been in the fight, with Rooney shot in the leg. He was sent, along with Rob, to Hickory Hill to recover.[94]

The campaign began in earnest on June 10, with Lee sending Ewell up the Shenandoah Valley. Six days later, Longstreet began moving northward, with Hill a day behind him. On the fourteenth, Ewell won a splendid victory at Winchester, capturing most of the garrison there. On the twenty-fifth, Lee crossed the Potomac into Maryland.[95]

Four days earlier, Lee had issued General Order No. 72, consisting of six rules for the behavior of his army "while in the enemy's country." First and foremost: "No private property shall be injured or destroyed by any person belonging to or connected with the army, or taken, except by the officers hereafter designated." The next five rules covered requisitions of "stores and supplies" and a compensation policy for them, carried out by "the Chiefs of the Commissary, Quartermaster, Ordnance and Medical Departments of the Army." He wanted to show "those people" that Robert E. Lee was not John Pope or Ambrose Burnside.[96]

The first commandment of Lee's orders met with different responses from his men. Major General Isaac R. Trimble, riding with Lee, called it "that humane order, one of the noblest records of the war, the recollection of which should cause the cheeks of Northern generals and people to kindle with shame, when in contrast with their orders and their conduct in the South." Captain Robert Emory Park of the 12th Alabama praised his commander's "utmost forbearance and kindness to all."[97]

But the reaction of most of their comrades in arms was just the opposite. Major General Lafayette McLaws thought the order too strict in light of the Union Army's destruction of Virginians' property and possessions. Anything requisitioned or seized outright was to be paid for with Confederate dollars or vouchers. Many civilians "packed nearly all their packable goods—I have packed nothing," Chambersburg resident Rachel Cormany wrote in her diary on June 15. She elected to stay with her baby, hoping her husband, serving in the Army of the Potomac, might pay her a visit. The next day, in Mercersburg, saw the "removal of goods by the merchants, of the horses by the farmers," and the "hiding and burying of valuables." The "Greybacks" arrived on the nineteenth, stealing horse and cattle from the defenseless community.[98]

Ewell's corps entered Chambersburg to his band playing "The Bonnie Blue Flag." After a brief but fruitless negotiation between the town's merchants and Ewell, the seizing of supplies began. "The Rebs are plundering the stores. [S]ome of our merchants will be almost if not entirely ruined," Rachel Cormany wrote. Citizens of Chambersburg and other Pennsylvania towns bore witness to stores emptied of anything of use, with the Confederates "taking horses and cattle, carrying off property and destroying buildings." In one instance an officer entered a church service brandishing his pistol and threatening to shoot anyone who left the service before his men had rounded up the horses waiting outside.[99]

In Mercersburg, Confederate money, as worthless in the South as it was in the North, was handed to shopkeeper, homeowner, and farmer alike. "They emptied Mr. Fitzgerald's cellar of sugar, molasses, hams, etc. and enjoyed the candies, nuts, cigars, etc. at Mr. Shannon's," Dr. Philip Schaff reported, and "drove their booty, horses, cattle, and about five hundred sheep . . . So the Southern chivalry have come down to sheep stealing," a woman bitterly told a Confederate officer as he departed with three hundred of hers. "I want you to know we regard sheep thieves as the meanest of fellows," she said defiantly. "They burned the barn of a farmer in the country who was reported to have fired a gun, and robbed his house of all valuables," Schaff added.

When Brigadier General John D. Imboden was accosted by a Pennsylvanian after requisitioning "five thousand pounds of bacon, thirty barrels of flour, shoes, hats etc. to be furnished by eleven o'clock," the imposing general replied for all to hear, "You have only a little taste of what you have done to our people in the South. Your army destroyed all the fences, burnt towns, turned poor women out of house and home, broke pianos, furniture, and family pictures, and committed every act of vandalism." Taking a breath, he concluded, "I thank God that the hour has come when this war will be fought on Pennsylvania soil."[100]

Upon learning of these transgressions against his orders, Lee issued another on June 27. After fulsomely declaring his "marked satisfaction" over "the conduct of the troops," Lee expressed concern over the "instances of forgetfulness on the part of some" that could tarnish "the unsullied reputation of the army . . . [W]e cannot take vengeance for the wrongs our people have suffered," he declared, as that belonged to "Him to whom vengeance belongeth," and ordered officers to "arrest and bring to summary punishment" the few perpetrators, who actually numbered in the thousands. "We make war only upon armed men," Lee unequivocally stated.[101]

While the "instances of forgetfulness" continued, there was a sizable portion of the population in Maryland and Pennsylvania who were exempt from Lee's exhortations, and the Army of Northern Virginia, from major general to private, knew it. Be they enslaved Marylanders, runaways, or freeborn, African Americans living or hiding along the routes of the army's northward march knew they were not safe. On June 15, Rachel Cormany saw

> contrabands . . . coming as fast as they could on all & any kind of horses, their eyes fairly protruding with fear—teams coming at the same rate . . . men without hats or coats—some lost their coats as they were flying, one darky woman astride of a horse going what she could . . . All reported that the rebels were just on their heels.[102]

The next day, Mrs. Cormany watched Confederates "hunting up the contrabands & driving them off by droves. O! How it grated on our hearts to have to sit quietly & look at such brutal deeds . . . [T]hey were driven by just like we would drive cattle. One woman was pleading wonderfully with her driver for her children—but all the sympathy she received from him was a rough 'March along'—at which she would quicken her pace again."[103]

In nearby Mercersburg, Schaff watched the "flight of the poor ne-groes to the mountains from fear of being captured by the Rebels and dragged to the South." On a "slave hunt" one rainy afternoon, Confed-erates promised "they would burn down every house which harbored a fugitive slave, and didn't deliver him up in twenty minutes . . . They succeeded in capturing several contrabands, among them a woman and two little children."[104]

When another twenty-one Blacks were captured and claimed as Virginia slaves, Schaff, "positively assured" an officer "that two or three were born and raised in this neighborhood." Schaff, standing by "women and children, sitting with sad countenances on their faces on the stolen store boxes," accosted the officer. "Do you not feel bad and mean in such an occupation?" The man replied that "he felt very com-fortable. They were only reclaiming their property which we had stolen and harbored." Schaff hid his servant, Eliza, and her little boy in the grain fields by day, sneaking her back in his house for a meal after dark before sending her back before sunrise. (Eliza's grown daughter and two children were captured in town and sent to Virginia.)[105]

With his lieutenant generals giving orders to their subordinates re-garding Lee's silence over the best way to get the "contrabands" back to Virginia, Lee still had to know what was going on. His two general orders do not mention Black Americans. The reason was simple. In response to Lincoln's Emancipation Proclamation, and the Union Army now enlisting Blacks, the Confederate Congress had issued a proclamation of its own in May rejecting Lincoln's right to free the en-slaved anywhere while permitting Southerners, including the army, to seize any Blacks and send them to any Confederate state and have them sold as slaves.[106]

And there was profit to be made in Lee's army's actions. Those sent back to Richmond were auctioned and sold. Schaff summed up what he witnessed as "a most pitiful sight, sufficient to settle the slavery ques-tion for every humane mind."[107]

———————

LINCOLN AS A FLATBOATMAN ON THE MISSISSIPPI RIVER.

This depiction of a young Lincoln bound for New Orleans was published in Chicago's *Republican Standard* in 1860. *Library of Congress*

BY HEWLETT & RASPILLER,
On Saturday, 14th April, inst.
At 1-2 12 o'clock, at Hewlett's Exchange,
WILL BE SOLD,

24 HEAD OF SLAVES,

Lately belonging to the Estate of Jno. Erwin, of the parish of Iberville. These Slaves have been for more than 10 years in the country, and are all well acclimated, and accustomed to all kinds of work on a Sugar Plantation. There are among them a first rate cooper, a first rate brick maker, and an excellent hostler and coachman. They will be sold chiefly in families.

TERMS----One year's credit, payable in notes endorsed to the satisfaction of the vendor, and bearing mortgage until final payment. Sales to be passed before Carlisle Pollock, Esq. at the expense of the purchasers.

Fielding, aged 27 years, field hand,
Sally, aged 24 do. field hand and cook,
Levi, aged 26 years, cooper and field hand, }
Aggy, do. 24 do. house servant and field hand. } 15..
James, do. 6 do.
Emeline, 8 do.
Stephen, 3 do.
Priscilly, 1 do. } 21 00

Bill, aged 24 years, field hand,
Leah, do. 22 do. field hand, } 16 00
Rosette, do. 3 do.
Infant child.

Alfred, aged 22 years, brick maker, servant and field hand,
Charlotte, do. 20 years, house servant and field hand, } 18 00
Infant.
Forrester, aged 41 years, hostler, house servant and field hand. }
Mary, aged 22 years, field hand and cook. } 18 00

Harry, aged 24 years, field hand, } 14 00
Charity, aged 24 years, field hand,
Polly, aged 22 years, house servant and seamstress, } 800
Sam, aged 2 years,
Bedford, aged 14 years, field hand, } 700
Mahaly, aged 12 years, field hand, } 500.
11..00

A broadside of a New Orleans slave auction.
Library of Congress

THE YOUNG LINCOLNS

Library of Congress   *Library of Congress*

THE YOUNG LEES

William Edward West, 1838,   *Fort Monroe National Monument,*
National Park Service   *National Park Service*

Above:
Portrait of George Meade at twenty years of age, artist unknown, from the book Meade of Gettysburg *by Freeman Cleaves, 1960*

Right:
Portrait of Margaretta (Sergeant) Meade, artist unknown, from the estate of her great-grandson

Left: In Mexico, Meade found much to admire in General Zachary Taylor.
Half-plate daguerreotype of Zachary Taylor, unknown, possibly Maguire of New Orleans

Right: As did Lee with his commander, General Winfield Scott.
Robert Walter Weir, ca. 1855, National Portrait Gallery

Meade served courageously as an aide to Taylor in the Mexican-American War, starting at Palo Alto. *Battle of Palo Alto, Carl Nebel, 1851*

By the Battle of Chapultepec, Lee's courage and resourcefulness proved invaluable to Scott. *Battle of Chapultepec, Carl Nebel, 1851*

Lee as he appeared as superintendent of West Point.
Library of Congress

This photograph of Lincoln, from 1854, reflects both his physical presence and toughness.
Library of Congress

Meade's lighthouses (this one is in Absecon, New Jersey) were both well-designed and enduring. Many of them were in service well into the twentieth century. *Skip Willits*

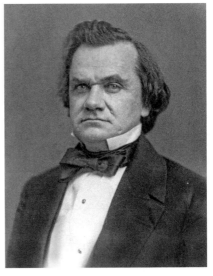

Lincoln's opponent in 1858, incumbent Senator Stephen A. Douglas, the "Little Giant."
Julian Vannerson, Library of Congress

The unfinished U.S. Capitol seemed a symbol of the country's division in 1861. *Library of Congress*

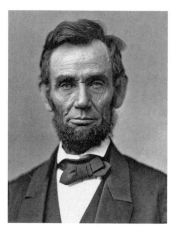

Above: Alexander Gardner's photograph, taken days before Lincoln's trip to Gettysburg, reveals both the stress of the Civil War and Lincoln's inner strength. *Library of Congress*

Right: Major General George B. McClellan made the Army of the Potomac a well-trained fighting force—then tested Lincoln's patience beyond measure by failing to lead it successfully. *Matthew Benjamin Brady, ca. 1860–1865, National Archives and Records Administration*

Francis Bicknell Carpenter, "First Reading of the Emancipation Proclamation by President Lincoln." *Collection of the United States Capitol*

MANAGER LINCOLN. "Ladies and Gentlemen, I regret to say that the Tragedy, entitled *The Army of the Potomac,* has been withdrawn on account of Quarrels among the leading Performers, and I have substituted three new and striking Farces or Burlesques, one, entitled *The Repulse at Vicksburg,* by the well-known, popular favorite, E. M. STANTON, ESQ., and the others, *The Loss of the Harriet Lane* and *The Exploits of the Alabama*—a very sweet thing in Farces, I assure you—by the Veteran Composer, GIDEON WELLES."
(*Unbounded Applause by the* COPPERHEADS.)

Throughout the war, Lincoln was skewered by both the northern and southern newspapers, even across the Atlantic by the British publication *Punch.* This 1863 cartoon is from *Harper's Weekly.* *"Manager Lincoln," January 31, 1863, Thomas Nast,* Harper's Weekly

Above: It's estimated that several hundred Black Americans, both free and those who escaped from the Confederate states, were seized and sent south to be enslaved. *"Negroes Being Driven South by the Rebel Officers," November 1862, by* Harper's Weekly

Right: Meade's predecessor, Major General Joseph Hooker, found himself pursuing Lee into Maryland and Pennsylvania. *Brady-Handy photograph collection, Library of Congress, Prints and Photographs Division*

Below: Robert E. Lee on Traveller, the best-known war horse in American history. *Photograph by Michael Miley, 1866*

Top: Major General George Meade assumed command of the Army of the Potomac while Lee's army was already in Pennsylvania. *Library of Congress*

Middle: Meade's favorite mount, Old Baldy, survived several battlefield wounds and was often as irascible as his rider. Meade loved him. *Library of Congress*

Bottom: Gettysburg town square, ca. 1863. *Library of Congress*

Top left: Gettysburg was 2nd Corps Lieutenant General Richard S. Ewell's first battle as a corps commander. It did not go well for him. *Library of Congress*

Top right: Lieutenant General James Longstreet was Lee's senior commander. His caution—or "reluctance"—to fight at Gettysburg, criticism of Lee after the war, and service in President Grant's administration made him an anathema in the South. *Library of Congress*

Bottom left: The dashing Major General J. E. B. Stuart had known Lee since his days as a West Point cadet. His ride around the Union army's east flank in late June left Lee blind to the whereabouts of the Union army. *Library of Congress*

Bottom right: Major General George Pickett brought his division to Gettysburg late on July 2, worried he might miss the fighting. *Library of Congress*

The first line of defense for the Union army at Gettysburg was led by Brigadier General John Buford *(seated)*, whose cavalry fought a delaying action on foot on the morning of July 1. *Matthew Brady, National Archives at College Park*

Left: Major General John F. Reynolds, 1st Corps commander, first viewed the high ground at Gettysburg earlier in the war. *National Park Service, Franklin and Marshall College Library*

Right: Along with Reynolds, Major General Winfield Scott Hancock of 2nd Corps had Meade's complete support and trust. *Library of Congress*

Left: Major General Dan Sickles saved his public reputation by brazenly insisting the truth of his actions at Gettysburg was "fake news," and that he was the true hero at Gettysburg. He derided Meade's leadership at Gettysburg to his dying day. *National Archives at College Park*

Right: Major General George Sykes succeeded Meade as commander of 5th Corps and saw plenty of action on July 2. *Library of Congress*

Left: As a shavetail lieutenant serving in the 1840s, John Gibbon gave fellow lieutenant George Meade shelter and blankets in the Florida wilderness. Fifteen years later, Brigadier General Gibbon would command Meade's center during Pickett's Charge. *Library of Congress*

Center: Meade, having earlier replaced Major General Butterfield as 5th Corps commander, inherited Butterfield as chief of staff on June 28. Later, Butterfield stated that Meade wanted to retreat from Gettysburg. *Library of Congress*

Right: Major General Abner Doubleday took over 1st Corps when John Reynolds was killed. Sent back to his division by Meade the next day, he later joined Sickles, Butterfield, and Hooker in their assault on Meade, aided by their congressional cronies. *Library of Congress*

"Death of General Reynolds" by Peter Frederick Rothermel.
The State Museum of Pennsylvania, Pennsylvania Historical and Museum Commission

"Sharpshooters at Round Top" by Peter Frederick Rothermel.
The State Museum of Pennsylvania, Pennsylvania Historical and Museum Commission

Meade meeting with his commanding officers in Leister House to discuss strategy near midnight on July 2. *"Council of War at Gettysburg" by James Edward Kelly, U.S. Army Military History Institute*

Top: Hancock at Gettysburg by Thure de Thulstrup. Hancock is mounted on a brown horse *(center).* *"Hancock at Gettysburg" by Thure de Thulstrup, Library of Congress*

Middle: Artist Alfred R. Waud's depiction of Hancock's old friend, Confederate Brigadier General Lewis A. Armstead, his slouch hat atop his sword. Seconds later, he fell mortally wounded. *Library of Congress*

Bottom: Union dead at Gettysburg. Alexander Gardner titled this picture (taken by his associate Timothy H. Sullivan) "A Harvest of Death." *Library of Congress*

Left: Young Tillie Pierce, who later published her vivid account of the battle. *Public Domain*

Right: Basil Biggs *(center)*, the Black farmer and veterinarian of Gettysburg who organized the exhumation and reburial of the Union dead at the new National Cemetery at Gettysburg. *Adams County Historical Society*

Top: Bodies of Union soldiers being exhumed at Gettysburg. *Gettysburg National Military Park*

Bottom: Crowd arriving for the Inauguration Ceremony of the National Cemetery at Gettysburg. *Library of Congress*

Above: The only photograph of Lincoln at Gettysburg finds him in the upper center. *Matthew Benjamin Bady, National Archives at College Park*

Below left: Levin C. Handy's portrait of Robert E. Lee, 1869, one year before his death. *Library of Congress*

Below right: One of the last photographs of Lincoln, taken by Alexander Gardner in February 1865. The trace of a smile might stem from the passage of the Thirteenth Amendment days earlier. *National Portrait Gallery*

Bottom right: This photograph of George Gordon Meade was taken in 1872, the year of his death. *Wenderoth, Taylor & Brown, Philadelphia*

"We have again outmanoeuvred the enemy, who even now don't know where we are or what are our designs," Lee told General Trimble as they rode northward. His army's advance into Maryland and Pennsylvania was going smoothly enough; indeed, Hooker would not know Lee's whereabouts for days. At the same time, Lee did not know where Hooker was until he read the Yankee newspapers of June 28. That information was supposed to come from Stuart and his cavalry, but Lee did not know where Stuart was, and Stuart did not know where Lee was.[108]

The fault lay with both men. It was raining hard the night of June 23 when a courier found Stuart at Rector's Crossroads (now Atoka), Virginia, after days of skirmishing with Union cavalry. Stuart, sleeping in the rain with his men, was awakened to read Lee's orders:

If General Hooker's army remains inactive, you can leave two brigades to watch him, and withdraw the three others, but should he not appear to be moving northward, I think you had better withdraw this side of the mountain to-morrow night, cross at Shepherdstown next day, and move over to Fredericktown.

You will, however, be able to judge whether you can pass around their army without hinderance, doing them all the damage you can, and cross the river east of the mountains. In either case, after crossing the river, you must move on and feel the right of Ewell's troops, collecting information, provisions, &c.[109]

Near the close of his dispatch Lee urged "the sooner you cross into Maryland, after to-morrow, the better." The orders were specific and unspecific at the same time and just what Stuart wanted. Still smarting over the embarrassment at Brandy Station, Stuart was eager to restore his reputation, particularly with the press and public, and these orders were discretionary enough, in Stuart's mind, for him to make yet another ride around the Union army. And that is what he did.[110]

Hooker finally broke camp on the Rappahannock, marching north while keeping his army between Lee and Washington. Initially, Lincoln had hopes that there was still some fight in Fighting Joe. "This is his opportunity," Gideon Welles thought. Lincoln agreed—at first. "We cannot help beating them, if we have the man." But Hooker, already bristling at being under Halleck, insisted the garrison at Harpers Ferry be put under his command. When Halleck refused, Hooker offered to resign. With Lee threatening Pennsylvania, Lincoln accepted Hooker's offer and turned to a Pennsylvanian. Halleck sent Colonel Hardie to find George Meade.[111]

Once Meade saw there was no arguing with Hardie over his appointment, Meade sent for his newest staff member, his son George. At West Point, George had spent more time racking up demerits than plaudits. In 1862 he joined the 6th Pennsylvania Cavalry, "Rush's Lancers," their name honoring a weapon the war and Virginia woods made obsolete. Young George proved to be a fearless cavalryman. "The more I see of the regiment, the better satisfied I am with George's being in it," Meade told Margaret. "The officers, as a body, are very much superior to any others." In June, father had son reassigned to his staff with the rank of captain.[112]

While young Meade went to procure a mount for Hardie, his father went to General Gouverneur Warren's tent and woke him up. Warren, chief of engineers, was someone Meade both liked and trusted. He asked Warren to become his chief of staff. Warren declined, with compelling reasons that Meade accepted. The Army of the Potomac was widespread, and Warren, like Meade, did not know everyone's whereabouts. Plus Butterfield at least knew the job, and with a battle with Lee more a "when" than an "if," Meade realized Warren lacked enough time to familiarize himself with the position. Meade decided to keep Butterfield for the time being.[113]

At daybreak, young Meade had found a horse for Hardie, and the three men rode to Hooker's headquarters. They found Hooker in full regalia, having learned Hardie was in camp and sensing why. After salutes, Hardie handed him an envelope informing Hooker he was being transferred to the defenses of Baltimore. Hooker summoned Butterfield, and the three generals reviewed the state of the army. Meade was aghast to learn that Hooker "had no intimation of any plan" to locate the enemy. All that was certain was that Lee had marched through Hagerstown and up the Cumberland Valley. After several perfunctory disagreements about where to move the army, Meade left Hooker's tent and returned to his own.

It was only 7 a.m.; Meade had been up three hours but it felt like three years. "Well, George," he sighed to his son, "I am in command of the Army of the Potomac."[114]

In Washington, Lincoln anxiously awaited word from Halleck that Meade had received and accepted his orders. Later that afternoon in the telegraph office, Lincoln wired General Couch outside of Harrisburg. "What news now? What are the enemy firing at four miles from your works?"

Couch telegraphed back hours later. While enemy forces "are burning bridges on the Northern Central road," the Confederates "have not up to this time made any show of attack in force." Couch did not know why.

That same day, Lee was planning an attack on Harrisburg but changed his mind when he learned from Ewell that a large Union force had crossed the Potomac. Lee notified Longstreet, A. P. Hill, and Ewell of his change in plans, sending similar instructions to each of them. He gave direct orders to Ewell: "I desire you to move in the direction of Gettysburg."[115]

By 1863, Gettysburg was a thriving town in south-central Adams County. It was also a network of nearly a dozen major roads that led in every direction, connecting towns from Carlisle and Chambersburg to Philadelphia. Its population was 8 percent Black, and Black residents owned 1% of the land, but those of age held working-class jobs in the town and on surrounding farms. (The 1860 census showed that no Blacks lived in the almshouse.) McAllister's Mill served as a station on the Underground Railroad, but Gettysburg had its share of anti-abolitionist, proslavery factions as well. One of the stalwart members of the Adams County Anti-Slavery Society was Congressman Thaddeus Stevens.[116]

When word reached Gettysburg that Lee's army was in Pennsylvania, its Black citizens sought to avoid the fates of those African Americans in Chambersburg. Years later, one white resident recalled their flight: "I can see them yet, men and women with bundles as large as old-fashioned feather ticks slung across their backs, almost bearing them to the ground . . . Children also, carrying their bundles and striving in vain to keep up with their seniors . . . children stumbling, falling, and crying."[117]

Not all of Gettysburg's Black citizens left right away. Basil Biggs, a tenant farmer on the Crawford farm, held off. On July 1, as the Confederates were taking over the town, Biggs galloped away on a borrowed horse.[118]

The eyewitness quoted above, fifteen-year-old Matilda "Tillie" Pierce, was a student at the Young Ladies' Seminary in Gettysburg. Her literary class was in session on Friday afternoon, June 26, when the cry "The Rebels are coming!" could be heard. From the school's front portico they saw "a dark dense mass, moving toward town." The girls ran for home as Major General Jubal Early's division, having easily routed a hastily organized militia, took over Gettysburg. Tillie described them as "clad in rags, covered with dust, riding wildly, pell-mell down the hill toward our home!"[119]

While Early demanded $100,000 worth of supplies, Confederate soldiers seized the livestock, including the Pierce family's horse. Mrs. Pierce begrudgingly gave them bread and apple butter. "We frequently saw the Rebels riding our horse up and down the street until at last she became so lame she could hardly get along," Tillie sadly recalled. Before leaving town, the rebels torched the railroad cars and bridge and destroyed the track.

Four days later, on June 30, "a great number of Union cavalry began to arrive," Tillie recollected. It was Brigadier General John Buford's division. Tillie, her sister, and their friends serenaded them, endlessly repeating the chorus of "The Battle Cry of Freedom." The events of the past five days convinced Tillie "that some great military event was coming pretty close to us. As we lay down for the night, little did we think what the morrow would bring forth."[120]

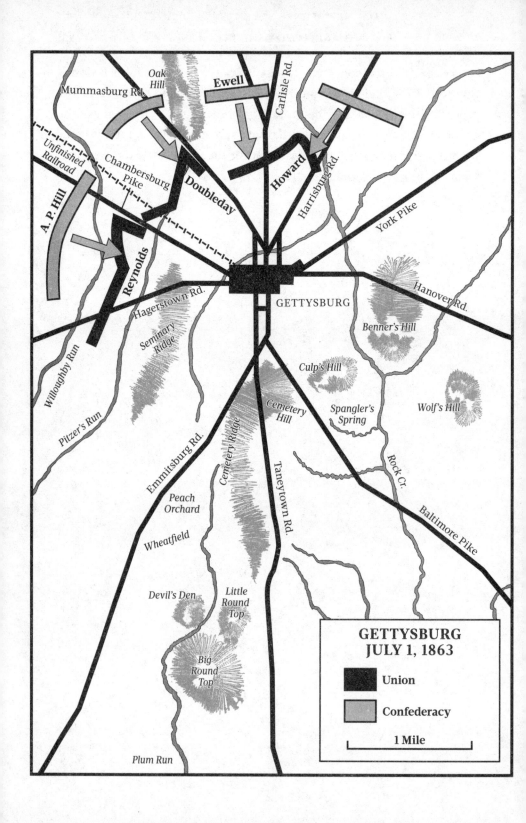

Mummasburg Rd.

Oak
Hill

Ewell

Carlisle Rd.

Unfinished
Railroad

Chambersburg
Pike

Doubleday

Howard

Harrisburg Rd.

A. P. Hill

York Pike

Reynolds

Hagerstown Rd.

Hanover Rd.

GETTYSBURG

Benner's Hill

Willoughby Run

Seminary
Ridge

Culp's Hill

Pitzer's Run

Cemetery
Hill

Spangler's
Spring

Wolf's Hill

Emmitsburg Rd.

Cemetery Ridge

Taneytown Rd.

Rock Cr.

Peach
Orchard

Baltimore Pike

Wheatfield

Devil's Den

Little
Round
Top

Big
Round
Top

Plum Run

**GETTYSBURG
JULY 1, 1863**

Union

Confederacy

1 Mile

WEDNESDAY, JULY 1

W hen Tillie Pierce awoke early on July 1, the temperature was already in the 70s. Neither Tillie nor the rest of the town had slept much. "It was impossible to become drowsy with the events of the previous day," she later wrote.[1]

One observer called the sunrise that day "a blood red dawn." Professor Michael Jacobs, who remained in Gettysburg despite the potential danger, would note the weather for each day of the coming battle less colorfully but with more accuracy: July 1 was "cloudy, with a gentle southern breeze." The temperature at 7 a.m. was 72 degrees. It would get warmer.[2]

In Washington, Lincoln arose early as usual. Couch's late-night telegram was the last bit of information he had received regarding the whereabouts of the armies of Meade and Lee. Before turning in on the thirtieth, Lincoln replied to former Pennsylvania congressman Alexander K. McClure's telegram from Chambersburg urging the president to appoint McClellan a third time to lead the Army of the Potomac, calling it "an imperative necessity." Three years earlier, in Chicago, McClure had wrested Pennsylvania's delegates from Cameron to Lincoln, giving him the presidential nomination. Surely Lincoln would heed

McClure's advice. Lincoln refused with biting logic: "Do we gain any-thing by opening one leak to stop another?"[3]

The three potential target cities of Lee's invasion—Washington, Philadelphia, and Baltimore—had been preparing for the worst. Washington, already ringed with forts, was still gripped in anxiety. Philadelphia's mayor, Alexander Henry, proposed "encampments of minute men" and drilling all able-bodied males should Lee's invaders approach. In Baltimore, Major General Robert C. Schenck imposed martial law. He also informed Lincoln that the "4,000 able-bodied negroes at work on the fortifications" surrounding Baltimore wanted "to fight for the Government"; Schenck wanted to "create a regiment of sappers and miners" and "have it done immediately, while the humor is on them."[4]

Lincoln's hope that more reports would soon come over the wire at the War Department's telegraph office was quickly dashed. "When Meade's headquarters were pushed beyond [Hagerstown] through the necessity of Lee's advance, we lost telegraphic connection altogether," telegrapher David Homer Bates recalled. "Lincoln was in the telegraph office hour after hour during those anxious days and nights." He knew Lee's army was in Pennsylvania; beyond that, Lincoln was in the dark.[5]

He was not alone. The greatest battle fought in North America would begin before either commanding general saw the battlefield. They were both hours away, so both men were forced to rely on the judgment and actions of their subordinates until they could arrive at the scene.

Outside Gettysburg, Brigadier General John Buford waited for the rebel soldiers certain to arrive that morning. "He is a man of middle height with a yellow moustache, and a small triangular eye; his expression is sinister, though his reputation is the contrary," an aide of Meade marveled. "He has a great reputation for cool daring, and is good hearted." Buford was about to exhibit his "cool daring" this morning.[6]

Buford saw for himself the lay of the land surrounding Gettysburg. Four major ridges lay west of town across three miles: Seminary Ridge, named for the Lutheran seminary; McPherson Ridge, named after the McPherson family's farm; Herr Ridge, alongside Herr's Tavern; and Schoolhouse Ridge, the westernmost of the four.

But it was the ground just south of Gettysburg that most impressed Buford, particularly five-hundred-foot-high Cemetery Hill. More of a plateau, it was the perfect site for massed artillery. Facing north, Culp's Hill lay on the right; to the left of Cemetery Hill, Cemetery Ridge ran south toward two other high points, Little Round Top and Big Round Top.

At a time when Meade was hoping to bring Lee to a fight in Maryland at Pipe Creek, just north of Frederick, and Major General John Reynolds and 1st Corps were still a two-hour march away, Buford determined to dismount his two brigades and fight the vastly superior Confederate infantrymen heading his way on foot. Buford posted Colonel William Gamble's brigade just west of Gettysburg along Seminary Ridge in anticipation of Lieutenant General A. P. Hill's arrival and sent Colonel Thomas C. Devin's brigade to the north and east of the ridge in the event Ewell's corps came calling. Buford sent out mounted sentries four miles west and northwest of Gettysburg to give him ample warning of an enemy advance. Second Lieutenant Marcellus Jones of the 8th Illinois Volunteer Cavalry led one of those units.[7]

In Taneytown, Maryland, a courier found Meade awake at dawn and handed him a much-needed topographical map of Pennsylvania. For months, Second Lieutenant Washington Augustus Roebling had spent his daylight hours in a hot-air balloon; it was he who had first spotted Lee's move northward and relayed it to Meade. When no topographical map could be found among the army's engineers, Roebling remembered his father had left one in Trenton, New Jersey, and was dispatched to retrieve it forthwith. After a ten-day round trip on horseback (including a night spent hiding in a cave from Confederate cavalry), Roebling handed the map to Meade, giving him at least secondhand knowledge of Pennsylvania's terrain.[8]

Roebling's map was about the only bit of good news Meade received that morning. In the orders of his Pipe Creek Circular, Meade had given his corps commanders thorough instructions explaining his plan to use that ground, if possible, to meet Lee. Located twenty miles southeast of Gettysburg near Westminster, Maryland, Pipe Creek offered good terrain to defend and put Meade's army directly between Lee and Washington and Baltimore. He had spent much of the night and predawn hours responding to a stack of wires sent to the army's telegraph post at Frederick. Once the Baltimore & Ohio tracks were repaired and trains were running, Meade learned that Halleck had not received his proposed plans for more than a day. Furthermore, Major General William H. French had disobeyed both Meade's and Halleck's orders; he was not marching his garrison from Harpers Ferry to join Meade. Hours later, another courier brought Meade a sheaf of telegrams, including one from Stanton informing him that French had blown up the Harpers Ferry magazine, spiked its guns, and awaited Meade's orders.[9]

Meade also received a message from Buford, originally sent to Pleasonton and Reynolds in the predawn hours, updating them on the whereabouts of the enemy. A. P. Hill's corps was nine miles away from Gettysburg at Cashtown, Longstreet's corps was behind Hill's at Chambersburg, and Ewell's corps was marching south to Gettysburg from Carlisle. "I have many rumors and reports of the enemy advancing on me from toward York," Buford added. As with Reynolds, Major General Winfield Scott Hancock, and Brigadier General Gouverneur K. Warren, Meade completely trusted Buford and considered him the best gatherer of information in the army.[10]

Finally, another flurry of telegrams arrived from army railroad supervisor and Brigadier General Herman Haupt, Meade's old classmate. The wires had originally been sent to Halleck, who relayed them to Meade. Haupt's most recent message informed Halleck that railroad spies assured him that Lee's "point of concentration" was, indeed, Gettysburg. And if "Meade could not at once get his forces in hand" before Lee had his full army together, "he could be crushed."[11]

If Meade did not appreciate Haupt making suggestions on a situation he knew little or nothing about, at least he was spared what Haupt was saying to others miles away. Haupt went even further in his forecast of doom to one officer: "Lee has just received the intelligence that Hooker has been relieved and Meade put in command. He knows that our Army Corps are scattered, and that Meade cannot get the reins in hand for some days at least." Haupt was certain Lee would "concentrate with all possible expedition and fall, with a largely superior force, upon our isolated Army Corps and overwhelm them successively . . . [N]othing but the interposition of Providence can save us."[12]

With reports convincing him that "the enemy is moving in heavy force on Gettysburg," Meade sent out new orders in the event "circumstances render it necessary for the Commanding General to fight the enemy to-day"; Meade wanted the corps within striking distance of each other. He ordered Hancock's 2nd Corps to Taneytown, or possibly Emmitsburg, Maryland, or even Gettysburg, depending on the morning's developments; Sickles's 3rd Corps to Emmitsburg; Sykes's 5th Corps to Hanover; and Slocum's 12th Corps to Two Taverns, on the Baltimore Pike just five miles southwest of Gettysburg. This put his entire army in positions to support Major Generals John Reynolds and Oliver Otis Howard—already marching north toward Gettysburg—while keeping it within reach of Pipe Creek, if circumstances allowed Meade to confront Lee there.[13]

At 7 a.m., Meade responded to Halleck's and Stanton's telegrams. "The point of Lee's concentration and the nature of the country, when ascertained, will determine whether I attack him or not. Shall advise you further today."[14]

At Cashtown, Confederate major general Henry Heth's division broke camp at 5 a.m. Minutes later it was marching toward Gettysburg. Among Heth's brigadiers was James Johnston Pettigrew of North Carolina, scion of a wealthy family of Huguenot descent. A South Carolina politician and author, he had served briefly in Giuseppe Garibaldi's war for Italian independence. His broad forehead and long goatee gave him an intellectual appearance. He'd been wounded during the Seven Days' Battles and was a cousin of Union brigadier general John Gibbon.

On June 30, Heth had sent Pettigrew on a reconnaissance toward Gettysburg. If he found no sign of Union forces, Pettigrew was to "search the town for army supplies," especially shoes. As Pettigrew got close to town, he spied Buford's cavalry and immediately reported back to Heth in Cashtown, announcing what he had discovered as A. P. Hill, fresh from Chambersburg, joined them.[15]

To Pettigrew's surprise, Hill dismissed this discovery: those Yankee horsemen were more likely "a detachment of observation." Then Hill continued: "I am just from General Lee, and the information he has from his scouts corroborates what I have received from mine—that is, the enemy are still at Middleburg and have not yet struck their tents." Hearing that, Heth asked Hill if he had any objections to his marching his division smack-dab into Gettysburg to "get those shoes!" Hill replied, "None in the world." Now Heth's entire division was heading to Gettysburg in search of free shoes.[16]*

Three miles west of Gettysburg, along Marsh Creek, Second Lieutenant Marcellus Jones of the 8th Illinois Volunteer Cavalry anxiously watched for rebel forces. An early mist had set in, making his task difficult. He and his troopers were the farthest from Gettysburg. Buford had ordered them to prepare to fight dismounted. Accordingly, they formed a thin line on the high ground above the creek, one cavalryman holding the reins of four horses while his three comrades readied their carbines and waited for the Confederates.

Jones heard the enemy before he saw them. As they came out of the mist, Jones borrowed a carbine from a trooper and fired the first shots of the Battle at Gettysburg.[17]

---

*Author's note: There are historians who believe that Heth came up with the "shoe story" years after the battle as an excuse for why he began to engage Buford's cavalry that morning. There was no shoe factory in Gettysburg. As for there being a supply of shoes in town, wouldn't Early's soldiers have taken them? Perhaps, as James McPherson notes, "The Confederates may have *thought* there were shoes; several of them later said so." Let the reader decide (McPherson, *Hallowed Ground*, 35–36).

Back in Gettysburg, Buford ran up the stairs to the cupola at the Lutheran seminary. Earlier he had sent his signal officer, Lieutenant Aaron
Jerome, there for observations. Beneath its wooden canopy, the cupola
provided a panoramic view of the grounds around Gettysburg. Buford
"seemed anxious," Jerome recalled, "even more so than I ever saw him."

Buford's edginess was warranted. Heth's division far outnumbered
his 2,500 cavalrymen. For the next hour, his galloping back and forth
to where he positioned his men was interrupted by further ascensions
to the cupola. On one quick ride into town, he encountered a 1st Corps
staff officer sent by Reynolds for an update on the situation. Not knowing the man, Buford ordered him to return to his troops. "Why, what is
the matter, General?" he naively asked. Just then a cannon boomed in
the distance. "That," Buford replied, "is the matter."[18]

Ascertaining "the nature of the country" was Reynolds's job. On the
night of the thirtieth his 1st Corps was four miles away at Marsh Creek
when he received Meade's order to "get all the information" possible,
taking Howard's 11th Corps with him. Meade told Reynolds to "advance on Gettysburg" without suggesting Reynolds *fight* at Gettysburg.
Once there, Meade gave Reynolds the freedom to "fall back without
waiting for the enemy or further orders. Your present position was given
more with a view to advance on Gettysburg than a defensive point."[19]

Now, this morning, Meade needed more information from Reynolds. Having "no time to learn the condition of the army as to morale
and proportionate strength," Meade asked for Reynolds's opinion on
this as well, for Reynolds knew "more of the condition of the troops in
your vicinity and the country" than Meade did.[20]

Reynolds began his march toward Gettysburg at 8 a.m. "[T]he
weather still being muggy and disagreeable, and making the roads very
bad in some places," twenty-one-year-old Captain Stephen Minot Weld
of the 18th Massachusetts wrote that day. Shortly after 10 a.m., "as
the sun breaks out above," drummer boy Harry Kieffer of the 150th

Pennsylvania was struck by "a magnificent view" from a high ridge. Suddenly the Pennsylvanians spotted "a puff of smoke in midair," followed by "the faint and long-coming 'Boom' of the exploding shell . . . something is going on yonder, away down in the valley," Kieffer observed.[21]

Upon hearing the artillery fire, Reynolds acted immediately. After sending 1st Corps into what Keiffer would call "four miles of almost constant double-quicking," Reynolds galloped through Gettysburg to locate Buford. He found him directing a fierce defense by his outnumbered cavalrymen against a strong force of rebel infantry. Seeing Buford in the cupola, Reynolds sang out, "What's the matter, John?" "The devil's to pay," Buford replied, telling Reynolds the rebels were in the woods "and I am unable to dislodge them."[22]

Interrupted by the sounds of gunfire and artillery blasts coming from McPherson Ridge, Buford informed Reynolds that once he'd heard the firing along his picket line, he ordered Gamble and Devin to form a line of battle on Herr Ridge, high enough above the woods and farmlands to give his outnumbered troopers some advantage in the coming fight. His artillery commander, Second Lieutenant John H. Calef (just one year out of West Point), spread his three-inch rifles across the line of battle, giving the illusion that there were two batteries on the field instead of merely one. "The enemy's infantry advanced rapidly, and the musketry and artillery fire soon became extremely warm," Calef reported. His gunners' efforts, along with the effective fire from the cavalrymen's carbines, slowed Heth's attack. There were also rebel soldiers from Ewell's corps coming down from the north. Buford's cavalrymen faced being overwhelmed, sooner rather than later.

Reynolds exhorted Buford to hold on; Brigadier General James Wadsworth's division was coming double-quick, and the rest of 1st Corps would follow. Calling for his staff, Reynolds told Weld "where the road started for Taneytown" and "to ride with the greatest speed I could." Weld was to inform Meade "that the enemy were coming in strong force, and that [Reynolds] was afraid they would get the heights on the other side of town before he could; that he would fight them all through the town, however, and keep them back as long as possible."[23]

"The heights on the other side of town" meant Cemetery Hill. While commanding the Pennsylvania Militia in late 1862, Reynolds had seen Cemetery Hill and the natural defenses on either side (Culp's Hill and Cemetery Ridge). Reynolds's adjutant, Captain Joseph G. Rosengarten, would later insist that Reynolds "first appreciated the strength of Cemetery Hill," suggesting his general, like Wellington when he first studied the ground at Waterloo a year before that battle, saw Cemetery Hill and "kept it in his pocket." Meade did not know it yet, but his hope of fighting at Pipe Creek was over.[24]

Reynolds dispatched other couriers besides Weld. Rosengarten had already been sent into town to inform residents to stay inside. Now Reynolds sent word for Sickles to come up and for Howard to march to Gettysburg "with all possible speed." Buford, meanwhile, sent his own message to Meade: "I am positive that the whole of A. P. Hill's force is advancing."[25]

That morning, A. P. Hill lay on his cot, fighting severe intestinal pains. While he had approved of Heth's entering Gettysburg, his latest orders to Heth were succinct: "Do not bring on an engagement."[26]

Unwittingly, that was exactly what Heth did. Believing that the enemies in Gettysburg were militia and that "they would run as soon as we appeared . . . I was careless and marched with my batteries in advance." His soldiers shared his overconfidence. The Confederates were two miles from Gettysburg and the officer was watering his horse in a creek when he heard musket fire. "'Tis only an accidental discharge," he thought.[27]

Sighting Buford's men, Heth told an artilleryman to "send a few shells over there and drive them out . . . [T]o my astonishment we had one sent back right in our teeth." Heth got his infantry in position and commenced an attack on Buford's dismounted cavalry.[28]

For two hours, Buford's troopers grudgingly gave ground, falling back from McPherson Ridge in good order against the much larger and better-armed Confederates. It was carbines against muskets, light cavalry cannon against infantry, until the first brigades from Brigadier

General Wadsworth's division arrived. The leading brigade comprised regiments from Wisconsin, Indiana, and Michigan whose courage under fire in battle after battle had earned them the nickname the "Iron Brigade." Wadsworth relieved Buford, sending his exhausted cavalrymen out of range.[29]

By now Hill's corps was getting closer to Gettysburg, but instead of attacking en masse he sent his troops in piecemeal. The fighting that ensued dwarfed the magnitude of Heth's clash with Buford; this was the beginning of an all-out battle, one that neither commanding general had had in mind, nor was yet even present to see.

That morning Lee awoke before dawn with a confidence that belied the fact that Stuart was still unaccounted for. Any information Lee received on his cavalry commander and Meade's army came from Northern newspapers. Their reports, anxiously telling readers information that was frequently at least two days old, were usually accompanied by a map on the front page showing where Meade's widespread army or Stuart's cavalry had last been seen. Also, that morning Longstreet sent the spy Harrison out on another errand to learn the whereabouts of part, if not all, of Meade's army.[30]

Lee "was in his usual cheerful spirits," Longstreet recalled, "and called me to ride with him." With most of Longstreet's corps following— Major General George Pickett's division was left behind to guard the supply train—the two generals and their aides headed for Cashtown, eight miles from Gettysburg. They were well on their way when they heard the rumblings of artillery. As the sound of the guns increased, Lee and his aides left Longstreet, spurring their horses into a sustained canter.[31]

Shortly after 11 a.m., his horse in a lather and his uniform soaked in sweat, Weld galloped into Meade's headquarters at Taneytown. After receiving Reynolds's message to Meade, the general exclaimed, "Good

God! If the enemy get Gettysburg, we are lost." Realizing that Butter-field had not yet sent the circular regarding concentrating at Pipe Creek, Meade exploded, shocking Weld: "Then he—to speak in plain English—roundly damned the Chief of Staff, whom he had inherited from his predecessor, for his slowness in getting out orders. He said that two or three days before, he had arranged for a plan of battle, and it had taken so long to get the orders out that now it was all useless.

"After this tirade," Weld recalled, Meade "summoned all his aides out to hurry up Hancock and all the other commands" to their assigned towns. When Weld replied that General Reynolds "would barricade the streets of Gettysburg and hold the enemy back as long as he could," Meade exclaimed, "Good! That is just like Reynolds."[32]

Still, Meade either did not or could not change his plans—not yet. He assumed that Reynolds was still following the orders of the day before to fall back from Gettysburg to Emmitsburg if the Confederates had already taken the former town. If Reynolds did this now, using the Emmitsburg Road instead of the Taneytown Road, a gap between Meade's forces would present itself, an open invitation to split his army if A. P. Hill and Ewell chose to do so. As delivered by Weld, Reynolds's verbal message to Meade did not suggest that the rest of the army should move on Gettysburg. Learning of Ewell's advance, Meade sent orders to General Couch in Harrisburg "to throw a force in Ewell's rear." To prevent the gap he feared, Meade sent new orders to Hancock at 12:30 to "proceed with your troops out on the direct road to Gettysburg from Taneytown," thus filling in the gap. If Reynolds was covering that road, Hancock was to withdraw to nearby Frizellburg, across the state line in Maryland, in accordance with Meade's Pipe Creek Circular.[33]

For Meade, Pipe Creek was becoming a pipe dream. Yet, if he could not fight on ground of his choosing, he was confident of two things. In Reynolds and Hancock, he had two men he trusted implicitly to pick another site. The other factor was Lee's situation. Untethered by a supply line, Lee's army was happily living off the land, enjoying the bounty of unlucky Pennsylvania farmers. But that prevented Lee from choosing the battlefield. The Army of Northern Virginia, traveling on its stomach, was forced to keep moving for a steady supply of food, fodder, and horses.

Around 1 p.m. another of Reynolds's aides, Major William Riddle, galloped into Taneytown with the latest message from Gettysburg. John Reynolds had been shot in the head; Riddle did not know whether he was dead or alive.[34]

Back at Gettysburg, the fighting spread to McPherson's farm, just past the woods that Heth's division was penetrating. Reynolds, on horseback, had been placing the Iron Brigade in position when the Confederates seized McPherson's barn in the midst of an intense firefight. "Forward for God's sake," Reynolds shouted to his soldiers, "and drive those fellows out of the woods." He was moving into the woods with the 2nd Wisconsin when a Confederate soldier took aim and fired, the bullet striking below Reynolds's ear, killing him instantly.[35]

Upon learning of Reynolds's death, Major General Abner Doubleday assumed command of 1st Corps. Initially, things went well for him: 1st Corps beat back one Confederate attack on the Chambersburg Pike and another assault from a brigade coming through the woods. But Hill's corps significantly outnumbered Doubleday's. As morning gave way to afternoon, Doubleday's losses mounted, principally among the Iron Brigade. One of its regiments suffered 80 percent casualties.[36]

Doubleday, whose first battle of the war was at Fort Sumter, kept plugging the holes in his line until 1:30 when a new, equally lethal challenge came on his right flank. It was Major General Robert Rodes's division, part of Ewell's corps, making a near-perfect attack.

Just as things looked overwhelming, Major General Oliver Otis Howard's 11th Corps arrived from the south, coming at the double-quick in response to Reynolds's messages. Being senior to Doubleday, Howard now became the fourth Union general commanding the field. "God helping us," he said, "we will stay here till the army comes." Leaving one division on Cemetery Hill, a few hundred yards from Gettysburg, Howard sent his men to meet Rodes.

At first Howard's men held sway. His mostly German-speaking soldiers were anxious to reclaim their reputation lost at Chancellorsville. With bilingual officers translating Howard's orders as fast as he shouted them, 11th Corps slowed Rodes's attack enough for Howard to establish a semicircular line of defense running north to south, with Schurz's division on the north at the Heidlersburg road and running west to Doubleday's troops down to the Hagerstown road—a two-and-a-half-mile line they could hold, providing no other Confederates showed up.[37]

The news that Reynolds had fallen hit Meade hard. He not only trusted Reynolds's judgment implicitly; the two had been friends for years. Meade listened as Major James Cornell Biddle related what happened and then sent for the only other general Meade believed he could trust at the battlefront in his absence.[38]

No one in the Union Army possessed a more commanding presence than Major General Winfield Scott Hancock. Not yet forty, Hancock had a thick head of dark hair, a broad forehead, piercing eyes, a Roman nose, and a thick goatee, all above broad shoulders and a muscular frame. "Authority was in his open face," one officer said admiringly. Another West Pointer and Pennsylvanian, Hancock had served in the Mexican-American War and afterward in outposts from the Midwest to California. Twice wounded in the past year, his heroic leadership (spiced with his colorful profanity) during the Peninsula Campaign had earned him the nickname "Hancock the Superb."[39]

Meade now sent a dispatch and map to Hancock. He was to turn command of 2nd Corps over to Brigadier General John Gibbon and "assume command of the corps there assembled," and furthermore, "if you think the ground and position there a better one to fight a battle under existing circumstances, you will so advise," Meade adding that he would "order all the troops up." Meade had already sent Warren to find out about Reynolds; Hancock and Warren were the remaining two generals he trusted to ascertain not just what was going on but where to fight Lee. Between Warren's topographical expertise and Hancock's fighting skills, Meade had sent the best people he could to make any judgments for him.[40]

Why didn't Meade leave Taneytown to see the fighting for himself? There were two reasons. The first regarded communications. All the corps commanders knew he was in Taneytown; should any of them have discovered rebel movement in their vicinity, or found themselves under attack, they would have immediately sent word there; relaying those messages farther north to Gettysburg would have delayed any decisions required by Meade regarding their situation. The other, of course, was his lingering preference to have it out with Lee at Pipe Creek.[41]

It was well past midday before Lee found Hill and scolded the still ailing general. "A general engagement was to be avoided" until the rest of Lee's army came up, he crossly remarked. Hill honestly replied that he did not know what was happening and painfully mounted his horse to find out. "I cannot think what has become of Stuart," Lee thought aloud. "I ought to have heard from him long before now . . . I am in ignorance as to what we have in front of us here. It may be the whole Federal Army, or it may be only a detachment." Minutes later, Heth rode toward them to explain that the supposed Yankee militia was Buford's cavalry, now joined with Reynolds's 1st Corps. After Hill related what had taken place that morning and that he had already sent in more of his soldiers in support, Lee remained steadfast. "I do not wish to bring on a general engagement today," he repeated. "Longstreet is not up."[42]

Then Lee turned Traveller into a grassy field. Taking out his field glasses, he gazed eastward to the sounds of the battle. The smoke from the guns had thinned enough to let him see Seminary Ridge and the heights just past the town. Lee saw Rodes's division attacking Doubleday's force while Heth implored Lee to let him rejoin the battle. "Wait awhile," Lee coolly replied, "and I will send you word when to go in."[43]

At this point Lee's earlier order for his army to coalesce that day paid off in a way he could not have foreseen. Soon one division after another began arriving, just in time to win what was becoming a major battle. Another of Ewell's divisions came in from York, commanded by Major General Jubal A. Early, whom Lee affectionately called "my bad old man." Now, with Ewell's corps coming into the fight, the Union defense led by Doubleday and Howard faced attacks on two sides, at right angles to each other: Hill from the west, Ewell from the north.

With Early heading straight for Howard's exposed right, the Yankees were caught between Ewell's and Hill's forces. Ewell's 3rd Division should be coming up soon, and Longstreet's corps would arrive before dark. There were now four Confederate divisions present on the field. Now Lee changed his mind about not making a full-scale fight. He ordered both Hill and Ewell to attack at once. The decision to fight at Gettysburg, in limbo since Reynolds's death, was made.[44]

Jubal Early loved a fight and wasted no time getting into this one. He immediately launched an attack on Howard's right flank, just as Jackson had at Chancellorsville. This time, however, Howard's soldiers saw it coming and put up a stiff but brief resistance. Outnumbered—and poorly deployed—there was little they could do. "The fighting became severe and reinforcements were called for," Howard recollected, but there were no reinforcements: the other corps of the Army of the Potomac were still miles away. While Howard's rear guard put up a valiant defense, grudgingly giving up one yard and then another, the rest of 11th Corps soon fled. Many men raced to Cemetery Hill to join those comrades (and artillery) Howard was keeping there in reserve while the rest bolted through Gettysburg, where heavy, fog-like smoke from artillery fire cloaked the streets.[45]

The flight of 11th Corps opened another opportunity, this one for A. P. Hill. Once Howard's right broke and the "Dutch Corps" fled, Doubleday's right was instantly exposed, and rebel soldiers swung around to hit 1st Corps's rear while the rest of Hill's men continued their frontal assault, spearheaded by the 26th North Carolina going straight at what remained of the Iron Brigade's 24th Michigan. "The fighting was terrible," Confederate major J. T. Jones recalled. "The two lines were pouring volleys into each other at a distance not greater than twenty paces." In the quickening slaughter that ensued, fourteen Carolinians, officers and privates alike, picked up their bullet-riddled ensign when it fell and ran toward the decimated Iron Brigade. Every one of them was killed, ensign in hand.[46]

Doubleday rallied his men at Seminary Ridge, but they, too, were heavily outnumbered and far too exhausted to put up another spirited defense. When 1st Corps broke, its elements made for Gettysburg, where chaos soon reigned. Street-to-street fighting was as dangerous to friend as to foe, with Confederate artillery sending shells flying into the streets, one slamming into the schoolhouse of the Young Ladies' Seminary. Once the Union soldiers reached the southern end of town, they made their way to Cemetery Hill just as Hancock, the fifth field commander of the Army of the Potomac, arrived on the scene.[47]

As the sun slowly dropped through the afternoon, Meade started pacing. By the time he received a report from Howard that he had reached Gettysburg, Howard's corps was already being attacked. Meade watched General John Gibbon lead 2nd Corps's march north to Gettysburg. Meade sent orders to Major General John Sedgwick to come at once to Taneytown and sent a courier to Sykes in Hanover to march through the night to Gettysburg as well. Now all Meade could do was wait to hear from Hancock.

Sitting astride Traveller, Lee watched Doubleday's and Howard's soldiers flee Gettysburg and scramble up Cemetery Hill. The Yankees were now on a curving stretch of high ground that began with Culp's Hill on Lee's left; then Cemetery Hill, just south of Gettysburg and Cemetery Ridge, stretching over a mile southward; and then two hills below the ridge, called the Round Tops. Lee sent orders to Ewell to immediately attack the Union forces atop Cemetery Hill: "Press those people and secure the hill if possible," Ewell's aide-de-camp, Captain James Power Smith, recalled.[48]

But Ewell and his staff were in Gettysburg. "The square was filled with Confederate soldiers, and with them were mingled many prisoners," Smith recalled.

Ewell was "simply waiting for orders." Both Early and Rodes had already pleaded with him to attack Cemetery Hill—or, at the very least, send a rider to Lee to ask for orders. Ewell sent Smith, who soon galloped back. Lee "regretted that his people were not up to support him" but "wished [Ewell] to take the Cemetery Hill if it were possible."[49]

If it were possible. As Reynolds did with Meade's last message, Ewell saw Lee's orders as a suggestion, not a command. But unlike Reynolds, Ewell did not take any initiative: his corps had been marching and fighting all day and were tired and thirsty. The recent loss of a leg might also have added to his caution. They had driven the Yankees off the defensive line where they had first found them, and then out of Gettysburg.

Had Jackson been at Gettysburg with Lee, he would have attacked. One reason Jackson would have sent his men up Cemetery Hill was because his first thought would have been that the *Yankees* were not only tired and thirsty but defeated. Taking Cemetery Hill would have proved his point. But Ewell was not Jackson. Ewell saw the formidable enemy defense on the high ground first. Jackson would have seen dispirited, scared Yankees ready to break and run.

There was no officially designated second-in-command in either army, but if there had been, Longstreet would easily have been Lee's and, with Reynolds dead, Hancock would have been Meade's. Longstreet and Hancock arrived at the battlefield around the same time.

Hancock's ambulance rumbled up toward Cemetery Hill around 4:30. From there he beheld thousands of Union soldiers falling back from Seminary Ridge, driven back by the one-two punch of Hill's corps from the west and Ewell's from the north. Some were still fighting as they retreated, but many more were running through Gettysburg for the safety of Cemetery Hill. As Hancock left the ambulance, there was a visible hum from the soldiers close by. Hancock's mere presence instilled a confidence in the battered soldiers that seemed to emanate from him. Mounting his horse, he rode to find Howard and Doubleday.[50]

The three generals' versions of what transpired next were as different as they were: "I rode directly to the crest of the hill where General

Howard stood and said to him that I had been sent by General Meade to take command of all the forces present," Hancock recalled, and Howard "acquiesced in my assumption of command."[51]

Howard recollected that "Hancock greeted me in his usual frank and cordial manner and used these words: 'General Meade has sent me to represent him on the field.' I replied, 'All right, Hancock. This is no time for talking. You take the left of the pike and I will arrange the troops to the right.' He said no more, and moved off in his peculiar gallant style . . . It did not strike me then that Hancock, without troops, was doing more than directing matters as a temporary chief of staff for Meade."[52]

Doubleday's version was completely different. In his account, Hancock immediately told Howard he was "placed in command of both corps." Howard got flustered, and Hancock offered to show him his orders. "I do not doubt your word, General Hancock, but you can give no orders here while I am here." In Doubleday's version, it was Hancock who "acquiesced," telling Howard he would "second any orders you have to give."[53]

The three differing accounts might reflect the egos, tension, and exhaustion from a long, bitter day, but there is an eyewitness who had no ego to bruise. According to an equally exhausted Buford, Hancock "made superb disposition to resist any attack that might be made." No further attack came that day.[54]

After Hancock—with Howard, Doubleday, and Gouverneur Warren beside him—placed the troops and guns, he fulfilled his second task for Meade. He observed Culp's Hill to the northeast, rocky and tree covered; Cemetery Hill, with its plateau-like top, ideal for artillery; Cemetery Ridge, running for a mile and a half southward; and, finally, the Round Tops. It was Lee's view in reverse, both literally and figuratively. Unlike Lee, Hancock liked what he saw very much and sent a dispatch immediately to Meade:

> *When I arrived here an hour since, I found that our troops had given up the front of Gettysburg and the town. We have taken up a position in the cemetery, which cannot be well taken; it is a position, however, easily*

turned . . . [T]he battle is quiet now. I think we will be all right until
night . . . [W]e can fight here . . .[55]

A couple of hours after Lee rode toward the sound of the guns, Longstreet rode ahead of his corps to find Lee and see for himself what the conditions were. He found Lee had set up headquarters on Seminary Ridge and was "engaged at the moment," so Longstreet dismounted, handed his horse's reins to a soldier, and "drew my glasses and made a studied view of the position upon which the enemy was rallying his forces, and the lay of the land surrounding." He saw the high ground from Culp's Hill to the Round Tops, "all marking the position clearly defensive."

But Longstreet dismissed his usual caution, for he noticed beyond the Round Tops what "the lay of the land surrounding" offered the Army of Northern Virginia. He could not wait to tell Lee. When the two met, the usually unflappable Longstreet excitedly said, "We could not call the enemy to position better suited to our plans. All that we have to do is to file around his left and secure good ground between him and his capital. This," Longstreet later wrote, "was thought to be the opinion of my commander as much as my own" from the instant that Lee and Longstreet first discussed invading Pennsylvania.

According to Longstreet, Lee "had announced beforehand that he would not make aggressive battle in the enemy's country." To Longstreet, the Union position on July 1 gave Lee the opportunity to do just that: after an effective feint keeping Meade on his hills and ridge, and a quick march at night to the east to find similar terrain closer to Washington that *Lee* could easily defend, Meade would have no choice but to attack, and it would be Fredericksburg all over again. Then, maybe then, the war would be over.[56]

But Lee's reply stunned Longstreet. "Striking the air with his closed hand, [Lee] defiantly said, 'If he is there to-morrow I will attack him.'" Longstreet, as deferentially as possible, defied Lee: "If he is there to-morrow it will be because he wants you to attack." Then Longstreet gave Lee an alternative: "If that height has become the objective, why not take it at once? We have forty thousand men less the casualties of the day; [Meade] cannot have more than twenty thousand." For a split second, the habitually defensive-minded Longstreet was possessed by Stonewall Jackson.[57]

It was then that Lee made his open-ended order to Ewell. Calling Ewell "the subordinate," Longstreet believed Ewell "did not care to take upon himself a fight that his chief would not venture to order." One wonders what would have happened had Lee, as Meade had done with Reynolds and Hancock, given Longstreet command of Ewell's corps and told *him* "if practicable" to take Cemetery Hill.[58]

Fifteen years later, Hancock answered one of Gettysburg's many what-ifs: the consequences for the Army of the Potomac had Ewell attacked Cemetery Hill as the sun began setting. "If the Confederates had continued the pursuit of General Howard on the afternoon of the first of July, at Gettysburg, they would have driven him over and beyond Cemetery Hill," Hancock averred, while adding that "After I arrived upon the field, [and] assumed the command . . . I do not think the Confederate force then present could have carried it."[59]

Lest the reader believe this braggadocio, Union Army colonel John B. Bachelder—"the historian of Gettysburg," as Confederate James Power Smith called him—echoed Hancock's belief:

> *There is no question but that a combined attack on Cemetery Hill made within an hour, would have been successful. At the end of an hour the troops had been rallied, occupied strong positions, were covered by stone walls, and under the command of General Hancock, who in the meantime had reached the field, they would, in my opinion, have held the position against any attack from the troops then up.*[60]

So the first day's fighting ended. It was a major battle by itself; combined casualties approached 16,000. As night fell, the moans and cries of the wounded still lying on the fields of battle were mixed with the clank of canteens, the neighs of horses, and the squeaking of caisson wheels as thousands of soldiers from both armies joined their physically spent comrades, many too tired to sleep, all wondering what the next day would bring.

The morning of July 1 had begun with two commanding generals miles away from the onset of a battle fought on ground that neither wanted. By day's end, portions of Lee's army had succeeded in driving portions of Meade's army all the way back to the very ground that Buford, Reynolds, Howard, and finally Hancock thought was as close to perfect for the Army of the Potomac to defend as any other, including Pipe Creek. The Army of Northern Virginia had done what it had done so many times before: driven the Army of the Potomac from its defensive lines. But this time the rebels had driven the Yankees to the very ground that would change the course of the battle.

Before Meade left Taneytown for Gettysburg, he dispatched a courier to Frederick, hoping the telegraph there was still operational. It was. At 6 p.m. the telegrapher wired a thorough report to Halleck, and thereby Lincoln, on the day's events:

> *The First and Eleventh Corps have been engaged all day in front of Gettysburg. The Twelfth, Third, and Fifth have been moving up, and all, I hope, by this time [are] on the field. This leaves only the Sixth, which will move up to-night. General Reynolds was killed this morning early in the action. I immediately sent up General Hancock to assume command. A. P. Hill and Ewell are certainly concentrating; Longstreet's whereabouts I do not know. If he is not up to-morrow, I hope with the force I have concentrated to defeat Hill and Ewell. At any rate, I see no other course than to hazard a general battle. Circumstances during the night may alter this decision, of which I will try to advise you. I have telegraphed Couch that if he can threaten Ewell's rear from Harrisburg without endangering himself, to do so.*[61]

Four hours and twenty minutes later, Halleck received the telegram. He and Lincoln would not hear directly from Meade again until July 3.

Sometime after midnight, Meade and his staff reached Cemetery Hill, riding through the rear entrance of the cemetery. When told by several corps commanders that they were on good ground, Meade replied that "he was glad to hear it, because it was too late to leave it."[62]

After meeting with his commanders, Meade, with his son George and another aide, walked the grounds. Although it was too dark to make out the finer points of his army's position, Meade could make out Hancock's battery placements. The twinkling of thousands of sputtering campfires over on Seminary Ridge looked like fireflies. Young George recalled how the summer night's silence was "interrupted only by the low voices of [Meade's] companions, the growl of some tired soldier as he changed his uneasy position on the ground, or the occasional ping of a bullet fired by some restless spirit on the picket line."[63]

Years later, General Francis A. Walker, then a lieutenant colonel, wrote about Meade's decision to send Hancock to Gettysburg:

> It is difficult for us, now, to appreciate what this decision meant, on the part of Meade. Himself but three days at the head of the army, he was sending an officer, who had but three weeks before left his division, to assume command of three corps, over two officers who were his seniors. When one remembers how strong is the respect for rank among the higher officers, and how greatly the oldest commander is subject to the public sentiment of his army, this act of General Meade becomes one of the boldest in the history of our war. That it was also one of the most judicious, is abundantly established. No other man . . . arriving on that field of disaster, could have done what Hancock did in checking the rout, in establishing order, in restoring confidence, and in making the dispositions which caused Lee to postpone his contemplated assault on Cemetery Hill.[64]

Looking at his father's grim expression, young George wondered whether Meade had turned his thoughts to Reynolds, "his trusted friend, fallen at the beginning of that day's fight," and to the "ten thousand men upon whom he could no longer count." From corps commander to green private, thousands of soldiers under the absent Meade's command had died that day so that he could walk the high ground south of Gettysburg after midnight and decide his army's fate.[65]

In Gettysburg that afternoon, Tillie Pierce's neighbor, a Mrs. Schriver, came to the Pierce house. She was leaving Gettysburg with her two daughters for her father Jacob Weikert's farm off Taneytown Road, and offered to take Tillie with them. "As it was regarded a safer place for me than to remain in town, my parents readily consented that I should go," Tillie later wrote.

The farm was nestled on the eastern slope of Round Top.[66]

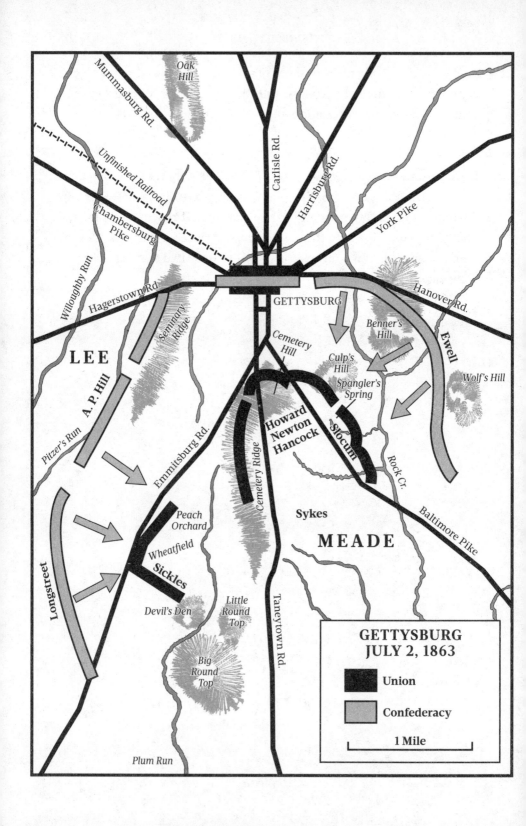

Oak
Hill

Mummasburg Rd.

Unfinished Railroad

Carlisle Rd.

Harrisburg Rd.

York Pike

Chambersburg
Pike

Willoughby Run

Hagerstown Rd.

Seminary Ridge

GETTYSBURG

Hanover Rd.

LEE

A. P. Hill

Pitzer's Run

Emmitsburg Rd.

Cemetery
Hill

Benner's
Hill

Culp's
Hill

Spangler's
Spring

Wolf's Hill

Ewell

Howard
Newton
Hancock

Slocum

Cemetery Ridge

Rock Cr.

Peach
Orchard

Sykes

Baltimore Pike

Longstreet

Wheatfield

Sickles

Devil's Den

Little
Round
Top

Taneytown Rd.

MEADE

Big
Round
Top

Plum Run

**GETTYSBURG
JULY 2, 1863**

███ Union

███ Confederacy

1 Mile

— N I N E —

THURSDAY, JULY 2

"FIRST BATTLE IN PENNSYLVANIA!" was the *Philadelphia Inquirer*'s banner headline on July 2. The sparse report mentioned Reynolds's death and that "portions of the fighting have been very severe, and attended with heavy losses."[1]

Tillie Pierce recollected that July 2 "dawned bright and clear" over the Weikert farm, and "the hot rays of the July sun soon fell upon the landscape." The sight of more troops arriving after their overnight marches—and seemingly endless wagons and caissons bringing more artillery and ammunition—gave Tillie pause. Slowly, she and Beckie Weikert returned to ladling water for the passing soldiers as they marched toward a dangerous and unknown future.[2]

Sometime that morning—Tillie called it "forenoon"—"Three officers on horseback came riding up to the gate. The centre one kindly requested me to give him a drink. I asked him to please excuse the tin cup I then held in my hand. He replied: 'Certainly, that is all right.'" The infantrymen in line for their water took on a respectable silence. After his drink, the officer thanked Tillie "very pleasantly." As the three began to ride away, the nearby soldiers gave three cheers. The officer Tille had given the water to "turned his horse about, made me a nice bow, and then saluted the soldiers" before galloping away.

"Who did you say that officer was?" she asked a nearby soldier. He replied, "General Meade."[3]

"The morning was pleasant, the air was calm, the sun shone mildly through a smoky atmosphere, and the whole outer world was quiet and peaceful," Professor Michael Jacobs noted. "There was nothing to foretoken the sanguinary struggle that was to close the day."[4]

Those Confederates who had spent the night sleeping on the town's streets began preparing for the next round of fighting. "They commenced barricading Middle street, on its south side, from the Seminary Ridge on the west to Stratton street on the east," Jacobs wrote. "They also broke down the fences, on the north side, in order to enable them to bring up reinforcements and to send back their men, without subjecting them to a raking street fire from ours."[5]

On Seminary Ridge, Lee awoke around 4 a.m. in his headquarters, the small fieldstone home of Gettysburg widow Mary Thompson. She refused to leave, so Lee would meet with Confederate officers and take his meals there but spend the next nights in his tent, pitched just outside. The previous day, the widow's acreage had been fought over by Generals Rodes's and Pender's divisions against Doubleday's 1st Corps. This morning Lee began forming a plan of attack if the Army of the Potomac was still on the heights south of town.[6]

The stars were still shining in the early-morning hours when General Longstreet arrived at Lee's headquarters. When Longstreet asked for orders, Lee replied he had none for him yet: Confederate soldiers were still marching into camp. Nor had Lee yet heard from Stuart, and therefore he knew nothing of the enemy's movements. Finally, "as soon as it was light enough to see," Lee and Longstreet clearly saw that "the enemy was found in position on his formidable heights awaiting us."[7]

They were. Meade was not going anywhere. Through their field glasses, Lee and Longstreet saw fresh Union troops arriving, bolstering the Yankee position, while behind them the same thing was happening for the Confederate forces on Seminary Ridge: Longstreet had assured Lee that two of his three divisions would be at Seminary Ridge in time for the day's fighting. By midmorning, the only absent Confederates were Stuart's cavalry, two of Ewell's divisions, and Longstreet's last division, commanded by Major General George Pickett.[8]

Lee did not need Longstreet to remind him of Meade's formidable position. The engineer who had redirected the path of the mighty Mississippi and whose keen observations had contributed to victories from Cerro Gordo to Chancellorsville knew topography as well as any man in either army. Despite Meade's strong position, in Lee's mind and heart, the Army of Northern Virginia could do anything its commander asked of it and would do so today.

Longstreet repeated the proposal he had made to Lee the night before, but with a wrinkle. Longstreet still wanted the army to go around Meade's line to the south, but instead of heading east for better ground he suggested flanking Meade's left and attacking him from the rear. Lee again refused, and for sound reasons: lacking knowledge of the whereabouts of all of Meade's army, and without Stuart, Longstreet's proposal for a long march followed by a flanking attack might be disastrous—they could very well be heading into a trap. Again Lee said no, but he did send Captain Samuel R. Johnston, of his engineering staff, to reconnoiter Meade's left.[9]

A. P. Hill and Heth soon arrived, as did Longstreet's division commanders, Major Generals John B. Hood and Lafayette McLaws. Along with Lee, they discussed plans while sitting on a couple of logs. Perched atop a tree branch, British colonel Arthur James Lyon Fremantle and a Prussian army observer were entranced as Longstreet and Hood took out their pocketknives and began "the truly American custom of *whittling* sticks" as they deliberated. At one point Longstreet took Hood aside. "The general [Lee] is a little nervous this morning. He wishes me to attack. I do not want to do so without Pickett," Longstreet added. "I never like to go into battle with one boot off."[10]

Earlier, Lee had finally learned of Stuart's whereabouts. He had been in Carlisle, thirty miles north of Gettysburg. Even if Stuart's horses had been sired by Pegasus, they would not arrive in time to assist with that day's attack.[11]

Captain Johnston returned from his reconnaissance and told Lee he saw no sign of Union strength on Meade's left flank, and the Round Tops were unoccupied. Now Lee ordered Longstreet to march southward behind Seminary Ridge and find a suitable position to attack Meade's left. Once Ewell heard Longstreet's attack, he could commence an assault on Cemetery Hill and Culp's Hill. A. P. Hill, stationed at the Confederate center, would keep his divisions at the ready to assist Longstreet or Ewell. It would be en echelon—one attack after another— hopefully forcing Meade to move troops to one front at the expense of what would be the next. Taking both flanks would collapse Meade's line and win the battle. Couriers went galloping down the Chambersburg Pike to get Longstreet's corps to Seminary Ridge on the double.[12]

"General Lee—with coat buttoned to the throat, sabre-belt buckled round the waist, and field glasses pending at his side—walked up and down in the shade of the large trees near us, halting now and then to observe the enemy," Hood later recalled. Lee was preoccupied with the one factor he could not control: geography. Later that morning he would tell Ewell that "the enemy have the advantage of us in a shorter and inside line," he remarked, "and we are too extended."[13]

Before dawn, across a half mile of open farmland, Meade was also up and about early. A small, white-painted, two-room farmhouse behind Cemetery Ridge had been selected for his headquarters. As with Lee's, a widow owned it, but, unlike Mrs. Thompson, Lydia Leister and her two youngest children had left Gettysburg before the battle. The house's size was offset by its closeness to the battlefield, allowing orders and messages to be dispatched and received quickly.

We do not know whether Meade slept at all the previous night, but he was riding Old Baldy before sunup, surveying his line again. With him were Howard, Henry Hunt, and Captain William H. Paine of Warren's staff. The early-morning light let Meade clearly see the soundness of Hancock's choice of ground. Like Lee, the former lighthouse builder and Great Lakes surveyor knew topography as well as any man in either army. Like Hancock, Meade liked what he saw.

Their inspection finished, Meade and company tied their horses to

the white picket fence before Leister House and went inside. Over coffee, Meade took a map where Paine had sketched the field and wrote
the corps assignments as Butterfield and assistant adjutant general,
Brigadier General Seth Williams arrived. Meade sent couriers to Gibbon and Sykes to hurry it up. A rider brought Meade news that General Andrew Atkinson Humphreys's division, part of 3rd Corps, had
fought a rebel brigade on its way. Soon, Major General John Newton
and his division from Sedgwick's 6th Corps arrived. Meade took Newton outside for a private conversation. The full-faced, bearded Newton
had had a distinguished engineering record after West Point. Meade
wanted him to replace Doubleday as commander of 1st Corps.[14] Newton balked—Doubleday outranked him—but Meade insisted. Halleck
had given him complete authority to make any changes he deemed necessary. Howard had privately told Meade that Doubleday did not handle the previous day's fighting well.

As Meade and Newton conversed, *New York Herald* correspondent
George Hosmer approached them just as a rebel bullet flew between the
two generals. Startled, they took it for a chance shot and continued
talking until Hosmer directed their attention to a tall church belfry in
Gettysburg manned by rebel sharpshooters. The three quickly moved
out of range.[15]

Meade's decision to return Doubleday to his division obviously did
not go well with Doubleday—nor, for that matter, with the men of 1st
Corps. One soldier later praised Doubleday's "skill and courage which
even the dullest private could not help commending." A sullen Doubleday resumed command of his division. He would exact his revenge on
Meade later.[16]

The army's line of defense and Newton's acceptance increased
Meade's confidence for the coming day's fight, but he faced two other
challenges that morning: supplies and respite for his soldiers. Meade
could give them neither. They desperately needed a meal, as did the
army's horses and mules. The need was not only immediate but massive: most of his roughly 90,000 soldiers had hastily marched four to
fifteen miles in the past day and had not eaten since. There were also
about 30,000 horses and mules with Meade's army, each requiring

fourteen pounds of hay and between nine and twelve pounds of oats daily, as well as a steady supply of iron and coal for blacksmiths to forge shoes and nails.[17]

Meade's soldiers and artillery needed ammunition; his men needed fresh clothing. Most of all, they needed shoes. The story of Gettysburg's vast supply of shoes—and Early and Heth going to Gettysburg to get them—is part of the battle's folklore. The fact that, after long days of marching over rough, rocky roads and in rain-made muck and mud from Virginia through Maryland to Pennsylvania, 25 percent of Meade's army was shoeless is not nearly as well-known. As historian Kent Masterson Brown points out, "Men cannot undergo forced marches and then effectively engage the enemy when they are shoeless and lack adequate clothing and socks."[18]

Brigadier General Rufus Ingalls had served as quartermaster for the Army of the Potomac since August 1862, with years of prior experience in that capacity before the war broke out. The stocky, bearded Ingalls repeatedly proved his worth, no matter who led the army. Like Hancock, Reynolds, and Warren, Meade trusted Ingalls, who corresponded by telegraph with Quartermaster General Montgomery C. Meigs in Washington for supplies and forage. He arranged with Meigs for supplies to arrive by rail at Westminster and Union Bridge, twenty miles southeast of Gettysburg, near Pipe Creek. "Supplies of shoes are on the cars," Meigs promised.[19]

Meanwhile, General Herman Haupt was doing everything possible to facilitate both supplies and communications for Meade and his army. Within two days he had tracks replaced, bridges repaired, a supply depot built, and a steady schedule of trains delivering supplies to Union Bridge and returning east with cars full of wounded soldiers. With the telegraph cut and communications slowed to a crawl, Haupt even arranged a veritable pony express, sending couriers every three hours to gallop seven miles to the next relay post day and night. Haupt's organizational skills and accomplishments were nothing short of breathtaking.[20]

Meade was considering every possibility that the day might bring. He sent Gouverneur Warren and Henry Slocum on reconnaissance to see if a large assault by 12th and 5th Corps (once Sedgwick arrived) on

Lee's left, originating from Culp's Hill, could succeed. Both generals urged Meade to forget it: with Sedgwick still miles away, Slocum told Meade, "I do not think we could detach enough troops for an attack to insure success," adding, "I do not think the ground in my front, held by the enemy, possesses any peculiar advantage to him." Slocum was right on that account. That ended, for Meade, any thought of an attack that morning.[21]

Years later, Hunt recalled what Meade did next:

It was clearly now to his advantage to fight the battle where he was, and he had some apprehension that Lee would attempt to turn his flank and threaten his communications,—just what Longstreet had been advising. In this case it might be necessary to fall back to the Pipe Creek line, if possible, or else to follow Lee's movement into the open country. In either case, or in that of a forced withdrawal, prudence dictated that arrangements should be made in advance, and General Meade gave instructions for examining the roads and communications, and to draw up an order of movement.

Meade sent Butterfield to the cramped second room at Leister House to review the maps and officers' sketches and see what roads would serve the army best if a withdrawal proved necessary. Years later, after recounting this contingency plan, Hunt added another observation: "General Butterfield, the chief-of-staff, seems to have considered an order absolute for the withdrawal of the army without a battle."

Hunt also came through for Meade on another issue that day. 1st Corps had left its entire artillery behind in its haste to get to the battle-field. Unbeknownst to Hooker or Meade, Hunt had ordered an ammunition column to join the artillery reserve; the column carried twenty rounds per gun in the army. Hunt's resourcefulness would serve Meade well this day.[22]

Once each corps commander arrived, Meade assigned him his place along the line of defense. With Sedgwick's 6th Corps still on the march, Meade held Sykes's 5th Corps in reserve. Slocum's 12th Corps was already ensconced on Culp's Hill. On Slocum's left, where the line began to curve, Wadsworth's division was stationed. To his left, Howard's 11th Corps remained on Cemetery Hill, linked with Newton and 1st Corps, on the right side of Cemetery Ridge. Linking with Newton was Hancock's 2nd Corps. Finally, beginning where Cemetery Ridge descended to its lowest level and from there to the Round Tops, was the Union's left flank, where Meade assigned Major General Daniel Sickles.

George Sykes was "career army": a disciplinarian with a steady record of accomplishments since the Mexican-American War, during which he was breveted for his gallantry at Cerro Gordo. He had a hawklike profile above a thick, dark beard. Sykes had led the rearguard action at Bull Run and had been in every major engagement in the Virginia theater and Maryland ever since. Not yet thirty-six, the graying, mustachioed Henry W. Slocum was senior general in rank among the Army of the Potomac's corps commanders but accepted Meade's promotion with grace. His intelligence and courage would come in handy at Gettysburg.

Daniel Edgar Sickles, Meade's only corps commander who was not a West Point graduate, was a forty-three-year-old New Yorker (he constantly insisted he was younger) and the son of a wealthy real estate speculator who had given him everything but a moral compass. Spoiled, selfish, and ambitious, young Sickles fell in love with politics more for image than service. He became a lawyer and was elected to the New York State Assembly. His sycophantic ways led him to an amanuensis's position for James Buchanan during his years as minister plenipotentiary to Great Britain. Upon his return to the states, Sickles was elected to Congress.[23]

Beneath Sickles's veneer of charm was a habitual penchant for boastful lies. George Templeton Strong, a prominent New York attorney and socialite, called Sickles "an unmitigated blackguard and profligate." In 1852, Sickles married sixteen-year-old Teresa Bagioli, whose father was a successful music teacher to children of upper-crust New York families. Fidelity, like honesty and decency, held no allure for Sickles, who maintained a string of affairs behind Teresa's back—or so he thought. Seven years later, he learned otherwise in Washington, discovering that his wife was having an affair of her own, a profound embarrassment for the pompous lothario.[24]

Unable to abide being treated by Teresa the way he had treated her, Sickles caught the lovers in a tryst at his posh Lafayette Square home. Grabbing his revolver, Sickles followed her lover out the door and shot the man to death across the street from the White House. The murder caused a nationwide scandal. Teresa's lover was Washington's district attorney, Philip Barton Key, Francis Scott Key's son.[25]

Sickles was immediately jailed. "The Honorable Dan Sickles has attained the dignity of homicide," Strong wrote in his diary back in New York, before predicting what he expected anytime Sickles got in trouble: "Probably he will not be even indicted."[26]

Strong's prediction was wrong. Sickles *was* indicted. From his cell he put together a defense team for the ages, including Edwin M. Stanton. The trial made front-page headlines across the Atlantic to Europe and over the Pacific to Australia. As it progressed, Strong made a second forecast: "I predict they [the jury] will acquit without leaving the box." This time Strong called it pretty close. After a seventy-minute deliberation, Sickles became the first American acquitted of murder due to "mental unsoundness"—what we call temporary insanity today.[27]

Acquittal made Sickles a free man but a pariah everywhere. With his career and reputation as dead as Key was, Sickles desperately wanted a second chance—not for redemption, but to once again be Dan Sickles.[28]

If the election of Republican Abraham Lincoln in 1860 brought about the Civil War, it could also be said that it gave Democrat Dan Sickles the opportunity of a lifetime. Immediately after the fall of Fort Sumter he raised five volunteer regiments, calling them the "Excelsior Brigade." Already an honorary major in the New York militia and aware that a brigade commander merited a general's rank, Sickles faced obvious opposition from New York politicians loath to taint themselves with him. Instead, they sought to eviscerate the brigade, technically depriving Sickles of the title he craved.

So Mr. Sickles went to Washington. Knowing that Lincoln needed support from patriotic Democrats, Sickles wangled a meeting, asking the president to make the Excelsiors U.S. volunteers rather than a New York brigade. After months of political wrangling, Sickles got everything he wanted. Parading his brigade before Lincoln, Sickles told him that he had paid all the expenses to raise, arm, clothe, and feed the Excelsiors. That was news back in New York, especially to his old friend Captain William Wiley, whom Sickles stuck with a bill totaling $283,000. The Excelsiors were assigned to Hooker's 3rd Corps. Consistent lathering of Hooker's ego guaranteed good press for Sickles, whom Hooker praised as an "intrepid chief."[29]

That was not Meade's opinion. While he did have carte blanche from Halleck to make whatever personnel changes he wanted to guarantee success, he did not replace Sickles as he did Doubleday. Having no knowledge of what action Lee would take that day, Meade felt compelled to keep Sickles at the head of 3rd Corps, just as he kept Butterfield as chief of staff. Meade could only hope that Sickles would make no errors during the coming fight.

After Meade assigned his corps commanders their stations, Captain George Meade found his father "in excellent spirits." Father sent son to visit Sickles to see if 3rd Corps was getting in position. George found 3rd Corps camped north of Little Round Top, where he was told by the corps's artillery chief, Captain George E. Randolph, that Sickles, exhausted by his forced march, was resting in his tent. Randolph took Meade's message into the tent and came out telling George that "General Sickles was in some doubt as to where he should go." Captain Meade galloped back to Leister House.[30]

Meade's "excellent spirits" vanished upon hearing Sickles's message. He sent his son galloping back to Sickles to tell him to "go into position on the left of Second Corps" and "prolong his line" to include troops on the Round Tops and relieve Brigadier General John W. Geary's cavalry there. Meade wanted Sickles's troops "in position as quickly as possible." This time Captain Meade delivered the message personally to Sickles. Captain Meade found "the tents about to be struck" and "the general just mounted." Before departing, Randolph asked him to have Hunt come and check his artillery positions.[31]

Once Sickles arrived at his assigned post, he began causing trouble. Cemetery Ridge dropped precipitously between Hancock's position and Little Round Top. Sickles later described it as "a low, marshy swale and a rocky wooded belt unfit for artillery & bad front for infantry." He plainly saw higher ground a half mile east where a peach orchard bloomed along the Emmitsburg road. Just two months before, at Chancellorsville, Sickles had been ordered to withdraw from high ground at Hazel Grove, allowing the rebels to place artillery and rake 3rd Corps with devastating effect.[32]

Sickles decided that the higher ground at the Peach Orchard was the place for 3rd Corps without considering the potential dangers of breaking Meade's defensive line. Taking Major Henry E. Tremain with him, Sickles went to see Meade to argue his case.[33]

Once at Leister House, Sickles made a spirited argument to send his troops a half mile to the high ground at the Peach Orchard on the Emmitsburg road. From there he would send his line southwest to Little Round Top. Taking Sickles out to the front porch, Meade gestured to Little Round Top and again told Sickles his line would start on the right, linking with Hancock's 2nd Corps, and then run due south to the Round Tops. Sickles, not to be deterred, and possibly with Chancellorsville in mind, maintained that his choice of ground was excellent for artillery: better, he argued, that Meade's army possess it than Lee's. He asked Meade to send another officer to review the ground and if he could place his troops at the best possible site. "Certainly," Meade replied, "within the limits of the general instructions I have given you; any ground within those limits you choose to occupy, I leave to you." Meade ordered Hunt to accompany Sickles and Tremain to see the ground Sickles wanted and report back to him.[34]

"I had been as far as Round Top that morning, and had noticed the unfavorable character of the ground," Hunt recollected years later about the portion of Sickles's assigned ground. When he and Sickles reached the Peach Orchard, Hunt understood why Sickles coveted it. But Hunt also saw that Sickles's proposed move "would so greatly lengthen our line—which in any case must rest on Round Top, and connect with the left of the Second Corps—as to require a larger force than the Third Corps alone to hold it," especially if the Confederates already were in the woods east of it.[35]

As Sickles ordered a reconnaissance of the woods, "a cannonade was opened at Cemetery Hill," and Hunt decided to return to headquarters. When Sickles asked if he could move 3rd Corps to the Peach Orchard, Hunt replied, "Not on my authority: I will report to General Meade for his instructions." Hunt told Meade he "could not advise" him to accept Sickles's line "and suggested Meade 'examine it himself.'" Meade agreed to do so.[36]

While Sickles focused on the Peach Orchard, Tremain focused on "the high ground on the left," Little Round Top, remarking to Hunt and Sickles that "that would be a good place for some guns." Tremain later wrote that "I did not then realize its significance." As Hunt departed, "a lively skirmish fire" opened on Sickles's picket line.[37]

After Sickles and Hunt left him, Meade received messages just before noon from Lieutenant Aaron B. Jerome at the signal station on Little Round Top. Jerome was watching the action taking place in the woods beyond the Peach Orchard. "The rebels are in force, and our skirmishers give way," he reported, adding that one mile west of Little Round Top "the woods are full of them." Ninety minutes later, signal officer Captain Paul Babcock Jr. informed Meade that "a heavy column of enemy's infantry" was "moving from opposite our left toward our right." This was Longstreet's corps.[38]

"Our march seemed slow," Longstreet later wrote, blaming "the conduct of our reconnoitering officer"—Johnston. "To save time, I ordered the rear division to double on the front." Longstreet, with no cavalry to ride ahead to scout his enemy's line, told Hood to "select scouts in advance, to go through the woodlands" and "give information of the enemy, if there." The absence of cavalry hindered Longstreet's advance, but Longstreet's sluggish start could also have been due to his reluctance to make this fight in the first place.[39]

Thanks to some bungled orders, Meade soon found himself in the same position. Buford's exhausted cavalry was patrolling the Emmitsburg road. On June 30, he had told Pleasonton that "my men and horses are fagged out." Since then, neither Buford's men nor his horses had been fed, and many of his horses needed shoeing. He requested his men be sent to Westminster for refitting. That morning, Meade ordered Pleasonton to relieve and replace them.[40]

Pleasonton sent orders to Buford relieving him without adding that he *remain* in position until his replacements arrived. Buford, seeing Sickles's corps approaching the Emmitsburg road, assumed they were relieving him and immediately led his exhausted brigades to Westminster. Learning this, Meade sent Pleasonton two quick messages: the first, that he "has not authorized the entire withdrawal of Buford's force"; the second, "that a force be sent to replace it, picketing and patrolling the Emmitsburg Road." Pleasonton did not send orders to Brigadier General David M. Gregg to send another cavalry replacement for Buford's until 1:45. When the fighting started, both Meade and Longstreet would be without cavalry.[41]

Soon Meade had another visit from Tremain, his horse in a lather after galloping from Sickles's headquarters. Tremain was to report the latest reconnaissance from Sickles's front and went inside Leister House to see Meade. When Tremain mentioned that Sickles needed more artillery, Meade replied that "generals were always expecting attacks on their own fronts." Tremain felt "frosted" by Meade's offhand comment until the general added that "if General Sickles needed more artillery . . . the reserve artillery could furnish it." Tremain left, neglecting to tell Meade that Sickles was no longer alongside Hancock on Meade's planned line that ran to Little Round Top. He had moved to the Peach Orchard.[42]

The 3rd Corps, led by skirmishers, had marched forward to the drummers' cadence, Sickles sitting confidently on his steed, flags snapping in the wind, artillery bringing up the rear. Hancock was not impressed, believing Sickles's advance "would be disadvantageous" to his soldiers. "Wait a moment," he dryly said to his aides. "You will see them marching back."[43]

Before 3 p.m. Meade learned that Sedgwick's 6th Corps was on the Baltimore Pike and should soon arrive. He drafted a report for Halleck:

> *I have concentrated my army at this place to-day. The Sixth Corps is just coming in, having been marching since 9 p.m. last night.*
>
> *The army is fatigued. I have to-day, up to this hour, awaited the attack of the enemy. I have a strong position for defensive. I am not determined, as yet, on attacking him till his position is more developed. He has been moving on both my flanks, apparently, but it is difficult to tell exactly his movements . . . Expecting a battle, I have moved all my trains to the rear. If not attacked, and I can get any positive information of the position of the enemy which will justify me in so doing, I shall attack. If I find it hazardous to do so, or am satisfied the enemy is endeavoring to move to my rear and interpose between me and Washington, I shall fall back to my supplies at Westminster. I will endeavor to advise you as often as possible . . . I feel fully the responsibility resting upon me, but will endeavor to act with caution.*[44]

As Haupt's relay stations were not yet in place, and because of other logistical issues, Halleck and Lincoln would not get Meade's message until the following morning.

Around 3 p.m., Meade summoned his corps commanders for an update on their positions and needs. All of them were at Leister House except Sedgwick and Sickles, whom Meade summoned a second time. The meeting was just underway when General Warren entered, telling Meade that Sickles was moving his entire corps out to the Peach Orchard. The words were no sooner spoken when the sound of cannonading and musketry came from the left.[45]

Meade acted immediately. He ordered Sykes to return to 5th Corps, now on the Baltimore Pike, and head immediately to the Union left to assume the positions Sickles had abandoned, telling Sykes to "hold it at all hazards" and that he would soon join him on the field. After telling Warren and his aides to get mounted, Meade sent an aide to have Old Baldy saddled. It was high time to see Sickles.[46]

While Meade waited for Old Baldy, Sickles himself, accompanied by Tremain, came riding up to Leister House. Meade, his Irish temper up, stopped Sickles in mid-dismount. Captain William Paine witnessed the exchange: "I never saw General Meade so angry," Paine remembered. "In a few sharp words," Meade "ordered General Sickles to retire his line to the position he had been instructed to take." Once Old Baldy arrived, Meade would follow Sickles to personally see that Sickles went to where he had been ordered, now for the fourth time.[47]

Noting Meade's impatience over waiting for Old Baldy, General Pleasonton sang out, "Take my horse, General. He is right here."[48] Meade accepted his offer. This steed was even more difficult to ride than Old Baldy, to whom Meade was accustomed. The orneriness of Pleasonton's horse was due to his bridle; the animal was usually fitted with a snaffle bit, which allows the rider to apply direct pressure equally proportionate to the rider's hands. That afternoon, Pleasonton's horse was fitted with a curb bit, which works with leverage, requiring a lighter touch from the rider. A simple yank on a curb bit applies far more pressure due to its leverage design. Most cavalrymen used a snaffle bit. If Meade had his hands figuratively full with Sickles, he now had them overfilled with Pleasonton's horse.[49]

Once on Cemetery Ridge, Meade was aghast at what he saw. Warren would later tactfully damn Sickles's line, saying his "troops seemed very badly disposed." As Meade, Warren, and their aides approached, Sickles rode over to meet them.[50]

Meade wasted no time asking Sickles to "indicate his general position." Sickles's reply was barely out of his mouth when Meade snapped back that this was *not* the line he had tasked the New Yorker to defend. Turning his back to Sickles, Meade angrily gestured toward Hancock's left flank and Little Round Top. For the last time Meade cuttingly stated that *that* was the assigned line of 3rd Corps. Looking over 3rd Corps's new line, Meade icily said, "General Sickles this is neutral ground, our guns command it as well as the enemy's. The very reason you cannot hold it applies to them."[51]

Undaunted, the politician now confronted the topographical engineer. He told Meade he could hold this line but would, of course, need support: "I have made these dispositions to the best of my judgment." Meade's lifetime habit of not tolerating fools put an end to any civil tone. *"General Sickles,* this is in some respects higher ground than that in the rear, but there is still higher ground in front of you, and if you keep on advancing you will find constantly higher ground all the way to the mountains."[52]

To Meade it was not a question of *if* Sickles would be overwhelmed but *when.* A penitent Sickles now offered to march his men back to his assigned line. Just then Confederate artillery began shelling Sickles's troops. Shouting over the barrage, Sickles asked if he should still extricate his soldiers from his error. "I wish to God you could," Meade shouted back, "but the enemy won't let you withdraw!"[53]

Meade sent Warren and his aides galloping to Little Round Top to see what, if any, troops were stationed there. Meade and Sickles were still together when a Confederate shell slammed into the ground near them. Whether it had been hit, was spooked, or was tired of Meade's painful tugs on its mouth, Pleasonton's horse reared and plunged. "Nothing was possible to be done with such a beast except to let him run . . ." The embarrassed commanding general had no choice but to run the fear out of Pleasonton's mount, leaving behind a general he could not control any better than Pleasonton's horse as a great battle began with his defensive line sabotaged by insubordination.[54]

At Confederate headquarters, an anxious Robert E. Lee wondered what was holding up Longstreet's attack. Captain Justus Scheibert, a visitor from the Prussian army who had first met Lee back in May, later wrote that

> Lee at Chancellorsville . . . (where I had the honor of being at his side in
> the brunt of the struggle), was full of calm, quiet, self-possession, feeling

that he had done his duty to the utmost, and had brought the army into the most favorable position to defeat the hostile host. In the days at Gettysburg this quiet self-possessed was wanting. Lee was not at ease, but was riding to and fro, frequently changing his position, making anxious enquiries here and there, and looking careworn. This uneasiness during the days of battle was contagious. [55]

One of the victims of "this uneasiness" was Longstreet, who "passed us once or twice, but he had his eyes cast to the ground, as if in a deep study," Captain David Augustus Dickert of Company H, 3rd South Carolina Regiment of Infantry, recalled. The 3rd was part of Brigadier General Joseph B. Kershaw's brigade in Major General Lafayette McLaws's division. A South Carolina lawyer, politician, and slaveholder who had served in the Mexican-American War, and was beloved by his soldiers, the forty-one-year-old Kershaw had thick eyebrows that seemed to protect his eyes and a drooping mustache that did the same for his mouth.

Longstreet "had more the look of gloom than I had ever noticed before . . . There seemed to be an air of heaviness hanging around all." There was more than just contagious unease. There was also exhaustion, hunger, and empty canteens. The two divisions Longstreet was sending into battle had been marching since before sunup. [56]

After giving orders to Longstreet and A. P. Hill, Lee rode into Gettysburg to find Ewell, who was to make a show of force on Meade's right that could become a full attack if the opportunity arose. According to Ewell's aide, Captain James P. Smith, Lee found Jubal Early "ready to scale Cemetery hill, and eager for the order to advance." Years later, Alexander insisted that Ewell's corps was in an "awkward place . . . there was no reasonable possibility of his accomplishing any good on the enemy's line in his front & where his artillery was of no service." [57]

As morning approached noontime, Lee grew irritable and anxious. "What can detain Longstreet?" he edgily asked while in Gettysburg. "He ought to be in position by now." Smith thought Lee "exceedingly impatient." [58]

The fault lay not so much with Longstreet as with his guide. Johnston's report indicated that there was no significant Union force before them, but when the Confederates came to Black Horse Tavern, they "could clearly see the flags of Union signal men in rapid motion" on Little Round Top. They had been spotted, and any hope of surprise was lost. Longstreet, who later wrote of his "manifesting considerable irritation," ordered the corps to march through "the rough character of the country," the numerous fences and ditches along the way further delaying the attack.[59]

From what Johnston had reported, 1st Corps would find itself on open ground alongside the Emmitsburg road. Instead it found a series of farms—more "fences and ditches"—including that of Reverend Joseph Sherfy, which included the Peach Orchard. Across the road, Longstreet rode up to Major General Lafayette McLaws and asked him, "How are you going in?" McLaws answered, "That will be determined when I can see what's in my front." Johnston's scouting debacle only reinforced Longstreet's displeasure with his orders.[60]

Longstreet, recollecting Johnston's report of no Union force at this point, replied, "There is nothing in your front; you will be entirely on the flank of the enemy." McLaws then stated he would continue forward and attack the Yanks. "That suits me," Longstreet answered, and rode away. It took some time for McLaws to form a line of battle for his 6,000 soldiers; when finished, he dismounted, walked to a grove of trees, and took a good look to see if Johnston's report was correct.[61]

Years later McLaws wrote, "The view presented astonished me." His "view" was of "the enemy massed in my front, and extended to my right and left as far as I could see." It was Sickles's 3rd Corps. What Johnston had seen in the early-morning hours was not what McLaws— and the rest of 1st Corps—now faced: a superior enemy force. "They were suddenly confronted with superior forces, in position and ready to fight." This, to McLaws, upended everything. Instead of a surprise attack on the Union left, 1st Corps faced slugging it out with an enemy force that far outnumbered it. But when McLaws brought this to Longstreet's attention, he got another dismissive reply, admitting the presence of Union forces while discounting their strength: "There is no one in your front but a regiment of infantry and a battery of artillery."[62]

On McLaws's right, Hood was having his own problems with Lee's orders. His scout came back to him with a correct assessment of the Union army's strength and position. Hood's scouts saw that the two Round Tops were unoccupied. If Hood obeyed Lee's orders and attacked the Union forces to the north, he would face Major General David B. Birney's division ensconced at Devil's Den and a neighboring wheat field. If Hood's troops attacked, they would face deadly fire from their right at Devil's Den and before them as they assaulted Birney's line in the wheat field. Hood saw that if he made this attack, "it must be at a fearful sacrifice."[63]

But Hood saw the golden opportunity that lay before him by going around the Round Tops and attacking the Union forces in their rear, behind Cemetery Ridge. Hood sent a courier to Longstreet requesting approval of Hood's new plan. Longstreet refused: "General Lee's orders are to attack up the Emmitsburg road." Hood sent another officer with a stronger message: "Nothing could be accomplished by such an attack." Longstreet's reply was the same. Finally, Hood sent Colonel Harry Sanders to Longstreet for one last plea, asking Longstreet to see for himself. He did. "We must obey the orders of General Lee," Longstreet told Hood, who then "rode forward with my line under a heavy fire." Hood obeyed and disobeyed at the same time. He did attack, but east toward Devil's Den and, eventually, the Round Tops.[64]

Forty-two years after the Battle of Gettysburg, Ewell's aide James P. Smith stated that "slow and recalcitrant as he was, Longstreet's battle on the second day, was in itself a great success." "Recalcitrant" might be too prejudicial a word, and "great success" an overstatement. But while Longstreet was slow to attack, once he did, it was fearsome. The battle for Meade's left began in earnest.[65]

Hood split his division into two lines: the right led by Brigadier General Evander M. Law and the left under Brigadier General Jerome B. Robertson. Law's men soon came under fire by Union sharpshooters on Big Round Top. Law sent the 15th and 14th Alabama Regiments, under Colonel William C. Oates, to take them out and take the hill.[66]

Hours earlier, when Lee left Ewell to find out what was delaying

Longstreet's advance, he had been told Longstreet's troops were "in motion." While Lee waited for Longstreet, a captured Union sergeant approached under guard. In questioning him, Lee learned he belonged to "a division which had taken position in the Peach Orchard." That would be Sickles's troops. "It was now apparent," Lee's aide, Colonel Armistead L. Long, wrote, "that the advantage of position was lost by delay, and the enemy had been permitted to concentrate a greater part of his forces."[67]

It was past 1 p.m. and Lee's "impatience again urged him to go in quest of Longstreet." A mile down the road, Lee found Hood's division waiting for McLaws's countermarch. Lee returned to Seminary Ridge. After Longstreet's heavy cannonade commenced, Lee spoke occasionally with A. P. Hill or Long but mostly "sat quite alone on the stump of a tree. During the whole time the firing continued, he sent only one message and received only one report," Colonel Fremantle marveled. Meanwhile, a brass band "began to play polkas and waltzes, which sounded very curious, accompanied by the hissing and bursting of shells."[68]

That afternoon, Jeb Stuart rode up Seminary Ridge with his aides, leaving his cavalry and 125 captured supply wagons miles behind him. The wayward cavalier's meeting with Lee, according to one aide, was "painful beyond description." Seeing Stuart's sorrowful expression, Lee relented. There was nothing Stuart could do for Lee that day; there would be plenty for his cavalry to do the next.[69]

At 7 p.m., Lee finally received the one message that Fremantle alluded to. It was from Longstreet: "We are doing well."[70]

Back in Washington, Lincoln had ridden out to the Soldiers' Home, the unofficial summer retreat of the president. Built in the 1840s, the "cottage" was more a mansion and became a summer home for James Buchanan. It was part of a rambling estate less than two miles from downtown Washington, a welcome respite from the humidity and the heat, political and otherwise, of the capital. Mary Lincoln loved the place: "We are truly delighted with this retreat, the drives & the walks around here are so delightful." Lincoln frequently rode a horse out to the Soldiers' Home accompanied by a cavalry escort. Lincoln's friend and bodyguard, Ward Hill Lamon, constantly worried about Lincoln's security there; in 1864, while riding alone, someone would fire a gun at him, putting a bullet through his hat and spooking his horse.[71]

On July 2, the Lincolns were returning with an escort of cavalry to the White House after an overnight stay, Lincoln on horseback and Mary in a carriage. As they were heading down a winding road, the driver's seat gave way, throwing him to the ground. The panicked horses broke off in a run; Mary, trying to rein them in, was also thrown, landing on her back and cutting her head on a sharp stone. She was rushed to the closest hospital, where her wound was treated and dressed; then she was taken back to the Soldiers' Home.

It turned out the carriage had been sabotaged: "A plan had been concerted by Secessionists to take the life of the President . . . [T]he screws that held the driver's seat in place, had been removed by unknown hands." Mary had a painful night, and it would get worse. Lincoln now was bedeviled with taking care of Mary, his White House daily duties, and his constant urge to be at the telegraph office.[72]

After a struggling climb over boulders while Union soldiers poured fire on from behind the rocks above, Oates's soldiers finally reached the summit of Big Round Top, at 305 feet the highest point of the Union line. Slowly but surely the Yanks began a slow retreat back down the craggy hill. Oates recalled the crag-filled peak as "thicker than gravestones in a city cemetery." Oates's men were nearly dehydrated from the intense heat and lack of water. He let his men rest while he walked through the woods to get a view of the battlefield to his north.

Oates was ecstatic. He could see clear to Cemetery and Culp's Hills, back to Cemetery Ridge, and then to Little Round Top just before him. To him, Big Round Top was "a Gibraltar I could hold against ten times the number of men I had." Bring up some axmen and artillery pieces, and Oates could slaughter the entire Yankee line.[73]

Just then, Captain Leigh Richmond Terrell of Law's staff reached the hilltop with news: Hood was seriously wounded, carried from the field with a shattered left forearm, leaving Law commanding the division. Law wanted Oates to leave Big Round Top and attack Little Round Top. Once at the bottom, Oates was joined by Law's 4th Alabama and the 4th and 5th Texas Regiments. They immediately began their ascent.[74]

After reaching Little Round Top, Gouverneur Warren ordered the captain of a rifle battery to fire a round into the woods below, which immediately became alive with the movement of enemy soldiers. Warren promptly dispatched one aide to Meade, urging him to send an entire division to Little Round Top immediately while Lieutenant Ranald Mackenzie galloped over to Sickles, requesting the general send a brigade to defend the ground Meade had ordered him to defend in the first place.[75]

Sickles refused. With his corps now all alone a half mile from the Union line, he needed every soldier. Mackenzie then rode over to Sykes, who was moving toward the Peach Orchard to assist Sickles. Sykes ordered Brigadier General James Barnes to send a brigade of his division to Little Round Top. There, Warren was standing with a signal officer when shots rang out and musket balls began buzzing past them just as the signal officer was folding up his flags. Warren watched with admiration as the man "kept waving them in defiance" of the approaching rebels.[76]

The first arrival Warren saw was Lieutenant Charles E. Hazlett and Captain Augustus P. Martin of the 5th Corps artillery brigade. Hazlett placed his guns at the crest of the hill. While unsure of his accuracy at that elevation, Hazlett believed the sound of his guns would encourage Union troops, declaring, "My battery's of no use if this hill is lost."[77]

At the same time, the first brigade from Sykes's corps commanded by young Colonel Strong Vincent of Pennsylvania, began the steep march up Little Round Top. "The enemy's artillery got range of our columns as we were climbing the spur, and the crashing of the shells among the rocks and treetops made us move lively along the crest," one

Union officer recalled. Vincent commanded four regiments: the 44th New York, the 16th Michigan, the 83rd Pennsylvania, and the 20th Maine. Handsome and Harvard educated, Vincent immediately began assigning positions to the regiments. When the 20th Maine arrived, Vincent put them on his left and told their commander, Colonel Joshua Lawrence Chamberlain, to "hold that ground at all hazards." Vincent was just finishing the placement of his regiments among the rocky terrain when Oates's men burst through the woods.[78]

The Confederates rushed at what Oates called "a zigzag line of boulders" behind which Vincent's soldiers knelt and stood. "They poured into us the most destructive fire I ever saw," Oates recalled. "Our line halted, but did not break . . . As men fell their comrades closed the gap, returning the fire most spiritedly." Chamberlain remembered the rebels "pushed up to within a dozen yards of us before the terrible effectiveness of our fire compelled them to break and take shelter." Then it began all over again.[79]

For the next hour, attack followed attack, with the Alabama and Texas regiments being repelled again and again as casualties mounted on both sides. One of the casualties was Oates's brother John, who later died from his wounds. On the Union left, Chamberlain's men were getting low on ammunition while Oates's men moved closer to flanking his line with each assault. The brief breaks in this seemingly never-ending contest gave neither Yank nor Reb any respite. Instead, those still standing on both sides quickly removed the wounded—with both sides carrying fallen friend and foe alike.

At the same time, other soldiers scrambled, snatching ammunition from cartridge boxes from the dead and wounded and seizing any muskets lying on the ground. One Union private later called the fight "a terrible medley of cries, shouts, cheers, groans, prayers, curses, bursting shells, whizzing rifle bullets and clanging steel." At times both sides were so close their musket barrels almost touched. "The dead and the wounded clog the footsteps of the living," Quartermaster Sergeant Howard L. Prince of the 20th Maine declared.[80]

On the last Confederate assault, Chamberlain, with one-third of his men dead or wounded, counterattacked with a bayonet charge, the 20th

Maine sweeping down Little Round Top like a swinging gate, linking them with the remnants of the 83rd Pennsylvania and the 44th New York. It took Oates by surprise, especially when he found himself flanked. "While one man was shot in the face," Oates recalled, "his right-hand or left-hand friend was shot in the side or back." Oates intended to "sell out as dearly as possible" but changed his mind. At his signal, the remaining Confederates "ran like a herd of wild cattle."[81]

While Chamberlain's success has become well-known, it by no means ended the fighting. To his right, Vincent's other regiments were being hard pressed by Robertson's 4th and 5th Texas. On Vincent's right flank, the 16th Michigan, under Lieutenant Colonel Norval E. Welch, had fewer than 250 men. During one attack, when the Texans looked to overwhelm the 16th, Vincent attempted to rally the soldiers of the 16th as the 44th New York, "coming promptly to its support," reestablished the line. "Don't give an inch," Vincent urged his men, before being struck down from a bullet to his groin and carried off the field.[82]

As combat continued, Gouverneur Warren again rode back in search of reinforcements. Finding the 140th New York at the rear of Brigadier General Stephen H. Weed's 5th Corps, he learned their commander, Colonel Patrick H. O'Rorke, was getting ready to reinforce Sickles. "Never mind that, Paddy," Warren shouted. "Bring them up on the double-quick—don't stop for aligning. I'll take full responsibility." Leaving Lieutenant Roebling to show O'Rorke the way, Warren found Weed at the head of his brigade, on his way to join Sykes. As Warren explained the situation at Little Round Top, Weed immediately ordered his other regiments to turn around and follow O'Rorke's regiment.[83]

O'Rorke led his men at the double-quick up the east face of Little Round Top. Once at the crest, he leapt off his horse, handed the reins to his sergeant major, and cried, "Down this way, boys!" The 140th came right behind them. "Our men poured down the rocks in their jaunty but tattered Zouave uniforms," Captain Joseph M. Leeper remembered. The 140th slammed into the Texans and soon had them flying, but O'Rorke did not live to see it. Standing tall in the open, urging his men onward, O'Rorke was shot through the neck, falling dead without a word.[84]

General Stephen Weed reached Little Round Top just as the 140th and Vincent's brigade sent the Confederates piling down the hill for the last time. A rebel sniper took aim at him just as he ordered his bugler to sound officer's call. The minié ball passed through both of Weed's shoulders, severing his spine and puncturing his lungs. "I am cut in two," he whispered, then asked to see Hazlett.

The artilleryman rushed to his dying friend, who asked him to see that any debts to fellow officers were paid. As Weed struggled to pull his friend closer, another sniper's rifle rang out, and Hazlett fell across Weed, dead from a bullet to his brain. Weed was carried off the field to the Weikert farm, "dead as Julius Caesar," as he had predicted.[85]

"Thus had fallen our brigadier, the commander of the battery which we supported, and our gallant young colonel," Lieutenant Porter Farley of the 140th New York Volunteers mourned. He would later call the sacrifice at Little Round Top by 140th "the supreme event of its existence."[86]

"If I had one more regiment we would have completely turned the flank and have won Little Round Top, which would have forced Meade's whole left to retire," Oates believed. He called it "Another lost opportunity."[87]

Once the battle for Little Round Top was over, Lieutenant Roebling galloped to find Meade and "gave him at least a ray of comfort" about Little Round Top. Meade and his aides rode over to have a better view of the rest of the day's fighting.[88]

That afternoon, thousands of officers and soldiers had been killed, wounded, or captured, all fighting for a hill few Americans outside of Gettysburg had ever heard of. The Confederate attempt to take Little Round Top was over.

When Lieutenant Farley reached the crest of Little Round Top, he later recalled "a never-to-be-forgotten scene burst upon us":

A great basin lay before us full of smoke and fire, and literally swarming with riderless horses and fighting, fleeing, and pursuing men. The air was saturated with the sulphurous fumes of battle and was ringing with the shouts and groans of the combatants. The wild cries of charging lines, the rattle of musketry, the booming of artillery, and the shrieks of the wounded were the orchestral accompaniments of a scene very like hell itself . . . The whole of Sickles' corps, in that ill-chosen hollow, were being slaughtered and driven before the impetuous advances of Longstreet.

Farley and the 140th then turned their attention to the "bloody work . . . at our very feet."[89]

The Round Tops were secure, but the ground below now became contested territory. An hour before the Confederate assaults on Little Round Top, a division of Hill's corps joined Longstreet's ongoing assault on Meade's left. At one point Union infantry was so bloodied that only some gun crews and their batteries were left on the field. As another attack commenced, Hancock sent in the 1st Minnesota to assist; it held the Confederates back, but at the cost of 80 percent of its men. Just north of this fighting, a handful of Hill's men briefly captured some Union guns but were driven back before they could turn them to fire on the Yanks.

Devil's Den, a harsh wasteland of large boulders and unsettling passageways, got its name from the Loch Ness Monster of Gettysburg, an eight- to fifteen-foot snake rumored for decades to call the area's crevices and caves home. Just east of Little Round Top, it is the base of Houck's Ridge, which runs north through Rose Woods. There, six guns of the 4th New York Battery under Captain James E. Smith supported Brigadier General J. H. Hobart Ward's brigade, part of Major General David Birney's division. The brigade included the 124th New York Regiment, nicknamed the "Orange Blossoms" for both their county and the orange ribbons they wore.[90]

In the artillery duel that preceded Longstreet's attack, it was a shell from Smith's battery that crippled Hood. Now Brigadier General Henry L. Benning's Georgia brigade and Robertson's last Texas regiment were massing to attack. Ward, who had survived the siege at Fort Texas during the Mexican-American War, ordered his soldiers to hold their fire until the enemy was two hundred yards away. As the Confederates attacked, Ward's first volley decimated the rebel line and drove it back. Then the 124th charged. The furious sounds of battle, one New Yorker recalled, "were the notes of the song of death which greeted the grim reaper, as with mighty sweeps he leveled down the richest field of scarlet human grain ever garnered on this continent." Like many a regiment at Gettysburg, the overwhelmed 124th New York was nearly wiped out.[91]

Now the 1st Texas and the 15th Georgia Regiments attacked the 4th New York Battery. Low on canister, Captain Smith roared orders over the gunfire to his gun crews: "Give them shell! Give them shot! Damn them, give them anything!" A shot smashed into the Texas line, but it kept coming. "For God's sake, men, don't let them take my guns away!" Major James Cromwell led a charge with some of the remaining 124th, driving back the rebels again. "The day is ours!" he cried, and then was shot dead off his horse. Then came Colonel Augustus Van Horne Ellis's turn. "My God! My God, men! Your major's down; save him! Save him!" he cried, standing in his stirrups and brandishing his sword before he, too, was killed.[92]

The fighting now disintegrated from regiment against regiment to man to man, a Yank prowling behind a boulder on one side while a Reb on the other side crept around the rock, bayonet at the ready. As more Confederates entered the maze called Devil's Den, Union resistance vanished. Ward led what was left of his brigade to Houck's Ridge; Smith came away with only one gun, and that one disabled.[93]

Late that afternoon, Tillie Pierce heard some of the soldiers saying, "The Rebels are on this side of Round Top, coming across the fields toward the house, and there will be danger if they get on the Taneytown Road." Tillie ran out to the south side of the Weikert house and saw "the Rebels moving rapidly in our direction."

With the barn filling up with the wounded and dying, Tillie steeled herself as to what was coming their way when "suddenly, I heard the sound of fife and drum coming from the other side of the barn. Then some of our soldiers shouted, 'There are the Pennsylvania Reserves!' And sure enough, there they were, coming on a double-quick between the barn and Round Top, firing as they ran.[94]

"The Confederates faced towards them, fired, halted, and then began to retreat. I saw them falling as they were climbing over a stone wall and as they were shot in the open space. The firing lasted but a brief time when the Confederates were driven back . . ."[95]

It was not until about 5:30 p.m., as Hood's corps threatened the Round Tops and Devil's Den, that Longstreet commenced the second part of Lee's en echelon attack. Longstreet could clearly see that Sickles's line was too long for Sickles's corps to adequately defend. On Longstreet's left, Major General David B. Birney's division was stretched thin from Devil's Den northwest to the high ground at the Peach Orchard that Sickles coveted. To Birney's right, Brigadier General A. A. Humphreys's division ran northward up the Emmitsburg road, with the Trostle and Weikert farms behind his line.[96]

Leading the attack was Brigadier General Joseph B. Kershaw. Longstreet walked with him up to the Emmitsburg road. "Looking down from this road," Kershaw reported, "a large wheat field could be seen." With a shout and wave of his hat, Longstreet set Kershaw into battle.[97]

The Union force facing them in Rose Woods and the Wheatfield was the 38th New York, led by Colonel Régis de Trobriand, a balding, handsome Frenchman descended from aristocracy. A poet, editor, and expert duelist, he had sent two of his five regiments to aid Ward at Devil's Den; now his remaining three were about to be attacked by two Confederate brigades. Next to him was the 17th Maine, behind a stone wall just south of de Trobriand's line. They soon had company, courtesy of Sykes's 5th Corps: Brigadier General James Barnes, with three brigades. They took a position on de Trobriand's right.[98]

Once across the Emmitsburg road, three of Kershaw's regiments drove north to attack the enemy at the Peach Orchard while the other two jumped the stone wall before them to join Brigadier General George "Tige" Anderson's men (of Hood's division) as they advanced toward the Wheatfield. They were instantly subjected to withering fire from Union batteries that David Augustus Dickert later called "cannon crowned battlements."[99]

De Trobriand's thinning ranks held fast; when Kershaw and Anderson's men were joined by a Georgia brigade under the command of Brigadier General Paul J. Semmes, they faced another assault. Semmes was bringing his men up when he fell, mortally wounded, stopping his Georgians in their tracks for a few seconds before they regrouped to continue their attack.[100]

The fierce fighting continued. When the 17th Maine's soldiers, thinned out and exhausted by hand-to-hand fighting with Anderson's Georgians, began to withdraw, Birney rode over and ordered them to return to their line. They did not. De Trobriand, his heavy French accent murdering his English while the Confederates were murdering his men, ordered his men to fall back.

Meade and his staff were with General Sykes, watching the loss of life and battleground as the Confederates broke that part of Sickles's line, chasing the Yankees through the plush Wheatfield. Their joyous pursuit came to a quick end with a volley of Union muskets fired by soldiers of Brigadier General John C. Caldwell's division, hurriedly dispatched by Caldwell's corps commander, Hancock.[101]

One division, commanded by Major General McLaws, struck Sickles on the west while Hood's division slammed into Sickles from the south. Soon the Confederate attack became three-sided as Sickles's line began crumbling. He was mounted and a quarter mile north of the Wheatfield when he was struck by solid shot. Looking down, he saw that his right leg was nearly torn off below the knee, hanging by a patch of skin. Aides got him off his mount, and Sickles turned his command over to Major General David Birney. After instructing a drummer boy on how to apply a tourniquet, he was carried off the field sitting on a litter, calmly smoking a Havana cigar.[102]

In fighting as bitter and costly as any during this bitter and costly war, 3rd Corps gave up the Wheatfield and the Peach Orchard at great cost to the enemy. Many of them headed to Devil's Den, piling up rocks for makeshift breastworks. Meade sent 5th Corps into the fray just as a line of Confederates assembled at the bottom of Little Round Top. At this point in the battle, nearly 8,000 men lay dead or wounded across the battlefield. Thanks to Sickles's costly misjudgment, Meade's left flank was not so much "up in the air" as nonexistent, compelling Hancock to throw unit after unit into the breach to prevent a Confederate breakthrough.[103]

On Meade's right, Ewell's men made four sharp attacks up Culp's Hill, but Slocum's 12th Corps held their ground, also at great cost. On their last assault before darkness set in, the rebels took a line of Union trenches high enough on the hill to hold its westernmost part, guaranteeing a fight for the Union right flank the next day.[104]

The day's fighting was not yet over. As he had the day before, Jubal Early attacked Union troops, clambering up a ravine between Culp's Hill and Cemetery Hill, where several Louisiana regiments seized artillery belonging to Howard's 11th Corps, sending one Yankee brigade fleeing. Meade's line was just about to break when Hancock sent a brigade to the rescue, their counterattack driving Early's men back into the ravine and to Seminary Ridge.[105]

The second day's fighting was now over. With so many Confederate attacks coming so close to breaking Meade's lines, it resembled an American Waterloo, with Meade, like Wellington, skillfully moving troops in time to fill in the breaks and maintain his line. But, unlike Waterloo, there was neither another army to assist Meade nor a conclusive end to the battle. Another bloody day of fighting loomed. Casualties for July 2 were about 9,000 on each side, for a total of 35,000 over the two-day conflict, making Gettysburg already the costliest battle of the war.[106]

Despite its late start, Longstreet's offensive had come within a whisker of succeeding. Lee could not possibly withdraw now. Too much blood and ammunition had been spent. The victory he came to Pennsylvania for had to happen here, the next day.

By nightfall, the Weikert farmhouse was a field hospital. "The scene had become terrible beyond description," Tillie recalled. "The orchard and space around the buildings were covered with the shattered and dying and the barn became more crowded." That night, Tillie scurried between the kitchen and the wounded, bringing them fresh bread and beef tea. At one point, candle in hand, she sat beside a badly wounded man and asked him what she could do for him:

> *The poor man looked so earnestly into my face, saying, "Will you promise to come back in the morning to see me." I replied: "Yes, indeed." . . . [T]he poor wounded soldier's eyes followed me, and the last words he said to me were: "Now don't forget your promise."*
>
> *"No indeed," and expressing the hope that he would be better in the morning, bade him good night.*[107]

Near midnight, Meade assembled his corps commanders, and Butterfield, Warren, Birney, Gibbon, and others converged on lantern-lit Leister House for a council of war. After making their reports, Meade asked for opinions: Should they stay and fight? After some discussion, the decision was made to stay and defend their position. Meade agreed, not bothering to tell them he had already wired Halleck that he intended to do just that.

As the fatigued officers left the house, Meade called Gibbon aside. "If Lee attacks tomorrow," he assured Gibbon, "it will be in your front." When Gibbon asked why, Meade explained that Lee's attacks on the right and left had failed and that Lee would believe Meade's center was weakened from reinforcing the flanks.[108]

Meade knew—he just knew—what awaited him. The only thing he got wrong with Gibbon was using the word "if."

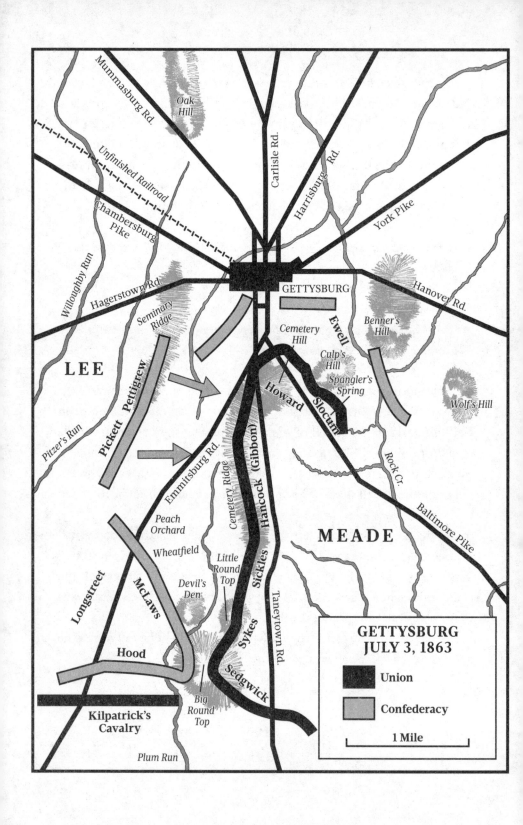

Mummasburg Rd.

Oak Hill

Carlisle Rd.

Harrisburg Rd.

York Pike

Unfinished Railroad

Chambersburg Pike

Willoughby Run

Hagerstown Rd.

Hanover Rd.

GETTYSBURG

Benner's Hill

Seminary Ridge

Cemetery Hill

Ewell

LEE

Culp's Hill

Spangler's Spring

Wolf's Hill

Pickett Pettigrew

Howard

Slocum

Pitzer's Run

Emmitsburg Rd.

Cemetery Ridge

Hancock (Gibbon)

Rock Cr.

Peach Orchard

Baltimore Pike

MEADE

Wheatfield

Little Round Top

Sickles

Devil's Den

McLaws

Longstreet

Sykes

Taneytown Rd.

Hood

Sedgwick

Kilpatrick's Cavalry

Big Round Top

Plum Run

GETTYSBURG
JULY 3, 1863

■ Union

Confederacy

1 Mile

— T E N —

FRIDAY, JULY 3

"T he sun was high in the heavens when I awoke," Tillie Pierce later
recalled about July 3. "The first thought that came into my mind,
was my promise of the night before." She headed down the narrow stairs of the Weikert farmhouse basement to check on the wounded
soldier:

> *As I entered, the soldier lay there—dead. His faithful attendant was still
> at his side. I had kept my promise, but he was not there to greet me. I hope
> he greeted nearer and dearer faces than that of the unknown little girl on
> the battlefield of Gettysburg.*

The dead man's comrade then informed Tillie that the dead soldier
was General Stephen Weed, carried from Little Round Top to the
Weikert farmhouse the previous day. Upon going outside, she saw two
large cannons in the yard, the gun crews telling her "there would likely
be hard fighting around the house; and that if we remained, we would
be in the midst of flying bullets and shell." Shortly afterward, Tillie and
the Weikerts climbed into carriages and were driven to the safety of
Sedgwick's 6th Corps just as Confederate shells began screaming overhead, the prelude to the most famous charge in American history.[1]

From the very start, Robert E. Lee's plans for July 3 went awry.

The fighting on July 3 began in earnest before sunrise on Culp's Hill. Both Union and Confederate lines had been reinforced overnight; those soldiers sent from Slocum's 12th Corps to the Union left had returned, and Ewell had doubled his forces, waiting per Lee's plan to attack once the main Confederate offensive commenced on the Union center.

Overnight, Slocum had repositioned twenty guns on Baltimore Pike to maximize their chances for success against Major General Edward "Allegheny" Johnson's Confederates, now occupying 12th Corps's lower trenches on Culp's Hill. Slocum's soldiers were itching to fight; they had spent hours building those defenses and resented that they now protected the rebels.

At 4:30 a.m., Slocum launched an artillery bombardment on the Confederates in the trenches on the south slope and on the Confederate troops in the woods behind them. Union guns had the Confederates in a cross fire; for a moment, confusion reigned—but only for a moment. Lee had reinforced Johnson's force to a number far greater than Slocum's. At the same time Brigadier General John Geary's men charged down the hill, Johnson sent his men charging uphill, revealing the superior numbers Johnson had that morning.

The fighting continued for seven hours. Years later, Slocum's son summed it up best: both sides were "composed of similar veterans" who were "possessed with the same determination to make [a] favorable record, and fought accordingly." For the rest of the morning, attack was followed by counterattack; ground taken at great cost was retaken at great cost. In one charge, the 2nd Maryland Confederate Infantry squared off against the Union's 1st Maryland Regiment, "neighbors against neighbors."[2]

At 10 a.m., after several charges had been repulsed, including one made by the famed Stonewall Brigade, the last rebel attack was repulsed. Johnson withdrew, leaving Culp's Hill permanently in Union hands. 12th Corps's victory was the first disruption of Lee's planned offensive that day.

During the fighting on Culp's Hill, a sergeant from the 4th Ohio spotted on his left

> *an American citizen of African descent [who] had taken position, and with a gun and cartridge box, which he took from one of our dead men, was more than piling hot lead into the Graybacks. His coolness and bravery was noticed and commented upon by all who saw him. If the negro regiments fight like he did, I don't wonder that the Rebs and Copperheads hate them so.*[3]

The sergeant's small narrative listed his name as "Corine" when the *Cincinnati Daily Gazette* published it on July 14. Thirty years later, Dr. August Zeitler, a former sergeant major of the 109th Pennsylvania, published a different account in the *National Tribune*. His regiment was among fighting behind a wooded area of half-grown oaks, when

> *suddenly there appeared among us from the rear a young negro, without uniform, but with a musket and a cartridge-belt. He spoke to no one, but moved steadily and rapidly towards the front, soon passing beyond the line. Scores of men yelled at him to come back, that he would be killed, but he gave no heed. He sought no cover, but with a calm dignity advanced to midway between the contending lines. Here he halted, leaned his gun against a tree, which he climbed. Forty feet or more in the air he rested. Now he could see over and beyond the enemy's breastworks, and his purpose was clear. The significance of his action was noted by all, for he was doing the right thing at the right time.*
>
> *For [a] full three minutes the negro surveyed the ground. Then he leisurely descended from his perch, and as calmly and fearlessly as before retraced his steps. He gave us information to the effect that the enemy was massing and maneuvering behind the breastworks as if to charge us, and then he disappeared.*
>
> *Half an hour elapsed in anxious suspense. Then the enemy appeared*

in serried lines, their banners waving brightly. Now the muskets from
thousands of men volleyed, defiantly Union cheers answered rebel yells,
and the third day's battle at Gettysburg was fairly on.[4]

No one knows if both reports concern the same man, whose name
is unknown to us. Historian Allen C. Guelzo wondered if he was a civilian teamster, a refugee, or a member of an Adams County company
of Black volunteers denied admission to the 54th Massachusetts, then
in South Carolina. Several other experts believe the man could have
been Randolph Johnston, a twenty-two-year-old Gettysburg resident
itching to fight the Confederates.[5]

Among the fallen during those three days was a Confederate soldier
who grew up in Gettysburg, became a carriage maker, and went to
Virginia when the business moved. A private in the 2nd Virginia infantry, John Wesley Culp was killed on or nearby the hill that bore his
family's name.

In those predawn hours, Jeb Stuart led a cavalry force of 5,000 three
miles east of Gettysburg on the York Pike, then headed south before
turning west. His four brigades, under Brigadier Generals Fitzhugh
Lee and Wade Hampton III and Colonels John Chambliss and Milton
J. Ferguson, made their way through the woods, heading to Cress
Ridge. Although both his troopers and horses were exhausted, Stuart
wanted to surprise the Yanks; wishing to atone for being surprised at
Brandy Station, he hoped today's attack would win back Lee's approval
after his prolonged disappearance.[6]

As a former cavalry commander, Lee knew that Stuart's troops, exhausted from hard riding, fighting, and lack of food and forage, were in
no condition to make a full-scale attack on Meade's infantry. The ob-
jectives of Stuart's actions that day were either a strike to bolster Lee's
left or seizure of the Baltimore Pike, the main supply road for Meade's
army.[7]

Once on Cress Ridge, Stuart looked through his field glasses and
saw "a large force of enemy cavalry" two miles away at the intersection

of Hanover and Low Dutch Roads. At the same time, the element of surprise was lost when troopers from Hampton's and Fitzhugh Lee's brigades rode across open terrain and were instantly sighted by Union pickets. Soon the "large force" was galloping toward Cress Ridge. Stuart ordered four light guns to fire a salvo, the prearranged signal letting Lee know the cavalry was in position.[8]

The Union cavalry consisted of two brigades under Colonels John B. McIntosh and J. Irvin Gregg. They were under the command of Gregg's cousin, Brigadier General David McMurtrie Gregg, who also had a brigade of Michigan regiments attached to him from General Hugh Judson Kilpatrick's cavalry. Their commander, just twenty-three years old, was General George Armstrong Custer, last in his class at West Point and first to get into a fight, if he had his way.[9]

Stuart might just as well have paraded to Cress Ridge, for Gregg had been tipped off about his coming by Union scouts that morning. Gregg, knowing the size of Stuart's force, asked Custer to stay when the latter received orders to return to Meade's left flank; Gregg assured him he would countermand Custer's orders. Never one to leave a fight if he could help it, Custer stayed.[10]

Initially the confrontation was limited to skirmishers and artillery fire from both Gregg and Stuart. Custer's West Point friend and artillery commander, Lieutenant Alexander Pennington, ordered one of his gunners to hit an enemy gun. "I will try," he answered. After adjusting his piece, he fired. The shell sped across the field and flew down the muzzle of the rebel gun, the explosion causing instant wreckage and carnage.[11]

Gregg and Stuart kept pawing at each other until suddenly, at 1 p.m., an impossibly fast, thunderously loud volley of cannon fire was heard two miles distant: the Confederate bombardment of Cemetery Ridge was underway. With a skirmish line of dismounted cavalrymen leading the way, Stuart now advanced onto the farmland owned by John Rummel. Rebel sharpshooters sprinted into Rummel's barn and began picking off Yankee soldiers, Union captain William Brooke Rawle recalled. In response, Captain Alanson Randol brought up his horse artillery, and pounded away at the barn, allowing a skirmish line of dismounted Yankees to overrun the rebels fighting from Rummel's fences and outbuildings. Stuart then counterattacked and retook the farm, putting both sides back in their former positions. The rest of the fighting on Rummel's farm would mostly be on horseback.[12]

That morning it was Lee who came to see Longstreet instead of waiting for Longstreet to come to him. Picking up where he had left off the previous morning, Longstreet told Lee that his scouts had again reconnoitered Meade's left flank, and he again advocated moving the Army of Northern Virginia to the right and thereby compel Meade to do the attacking. Again Lee said no and gave the same reasons as the day before: logistics and lack of a supply train made Longstreet's proposal unworkable. Lee wanted Pickett's fresh division to lead an attack on Meade's center, supported by Hood's and McLaws's divisions.[13]

As tactfully as possible, Longstreet protested. Those two divisions were exhausted and thinned out from the previous day's attack. Lee agreed; instead, Heth's division and two brigades from Pender's division, both from Hill's corps, would join Pickett's division, giving Longstreet 15,000 men for the assault. Longstreet responded that those units only had 13,000, having lost men in the battle already; that "thirty thousand men was the minimum of force necessary for the work"; and that "such force would need close co-operation on other parts of the line." When he added that Lee was expecting the men "to march a mile under long-range musketry," Lee said, "The distance is not more than fourteen hundred yards."

Years later, in his article "Lee's Right Wing at Gettysburg," Longstreet recounted his reply more dramatically:

> *I have been a soldier, I may say, from the ranks up to the position I now hold. I have been in pretty much all kinds of skirmishes, from those of two or three soldiers up to those of an army corps, and I think I can safely say there never was a body of fifteen thousand men who could make that attack successfully.*[14]

Lee's expression said more to Longstreet than a thousand words. "The general seemed a little impatient at my remarks, so I said nothing more. As he showed no indication of changing his plan, I went to work at once to arrange my troops for the attack."[15]

Meade got little or no sleep after his officers' meeting near midnight at Leister House, but the sounds of battle from Culp's Hill before dawn woke everyone for miles around. "Meade was receiving reports in the little house, coming occasionally to the door to address a hasty inquiry to someone in the group of staff officers under a tree," correspondent Whitelaw Reid of the *Cincinnati Gazette* reported. Meade was "quick and nervous in his movements, but calm, and as it seemed to me, lit up with the glow of the occasion, [and] looked more the General, less the student," Reid observed.[16]

Once the fighting had stopped at Culp's Hill, Meade once again ordered Slocum to send troops over to Cemetery Ridge to act as reinforcements for the attack Meade anticipated. Soon he had troops from 1st, 3rd, and 6th Corps in place on the front lines or at the ready. From Meade's right to left, Slocum still held Culp's Hill, with Howard's 11th Corps remaining at Cemetery Hill; Hancock's 2nd Corps at Cemetery Ridge; Birney with what remained of 3rd Corps in the place Meade had assigned to Sickles on July 2; Sykes's 5th Corps across from Devil's Den and the Wheatfield; and John Sedgwick's 6th Corps at the Round Tops.[17]

Aside from the fighting at Culp's Hill, only a brief skirmish over a barn in no-man's-land that morning interrupted the silence over the battlefield, the air growing heavier with humidity as the sun rose. A few minutes of Confederate artillery fire followed, shells screaming past Leister House. Meade, standing outside, came to the door and calmly told his aides the house was in range and suggested they head up the hill to the stable. The cannonade followed them. Union gunners began returning fire; after a few minutes it ceased.

Lieutenant Franklin Aretas Haskell remembered that peaceful interlude vividly:

The clouds became broken, and we had once more glimpses of sky, and fits of sunshine—a rarity, to cheer us . . . All was silent there—the wounded horses were limping about the field; the ravages of the conflict were still fearfully visible—the scattered arms and the ground thickly dotted with the dead—but no hostile foe . . . [T]hen ensued the hum of the army . . . They looked like an army of rag-gatherers . . . They packed their knapsacks, boiled their coffee and munched their hard bread, just as usual—just like old soldiers who know what campaigning is; and their talk is far more concerning their present employment—some joke or drollery—than concerning what they saw or did yesterday.[18]

John Gibbon took the opportunity to invite Meade to join him, Winfield Scott Hancock, and other officers for a brunch of boiled chicken and potatoes. Meade at first declined, saying he must remain at his headquarters to receive reports from the field. But Gibbon, seeing that Meade looked "worn and haggard," insisted he "keep up his physical strength" and that they would be eating within sight of Leister House. Meade relented. He soon joined a veritable picnic of officers sitting on blankets in a small peach orchard along the hillside. "We all had a most hearty and well relished dinner," Haskell recalled.[19]

Meade found time to write a short letter to Margaret:

All well and going on well with the Army. I had a great fight yesterday, the enemy attacking and we completely repulsing them; both Armies shattered. To-day at it again, with what result remains to be seen. Army in fine spirits and every one determined to do or die. George and myself well. Reynolds killed the first day. No other of your friends or acquaintances hurt.[20]

Then, for Meade, it was back to work.

In Washington, a fretful Lincoln was torn between the telegraph office and his wife's bedside. "We are happy to say that Mrs. Lincoln is much better to-day, and not as seriously injured as was first feared," the *Eve-*

ning Star reported on July 3. But she was seriously injured indeed. She was in great pain. An infection soon set in. Unable to help her clinically, and near stir-crazy with the telegraph line cut, the resourceful husband sent her to the Soldiers' Home to be cared for there, allowing him to have a bit less guilt spending day and night at the telegraph office.[21]

There, he also took time to send a terse wire to Robert at Harvard ("Don't be uneasy. Your mother very slightly hurt by her fall," adding at the bottom "Please send at once.") and to wire Ambrose Burnside in Cincinnati, sparing one Private John Downey from execution for desertion.[22]

"Except in equipment, I think a better army, better nerved up to its work, never marched on a battlefield," Colonel Edward Porter Alexander wrote of the Army of Northern Virginia after the war. "But many of our infantry still carried smooth-bore muskets, and our artillery ammunition was inferior, especially that of rifles . . . How our rifled batteries always envied our friends in the opposition their abundant supply of splendid ammunition!" That morning, Alexander was asked to use all his skills not only to make the Confederacy's poorer artillery equal to the Union's superior ordnance but to defeat it.[23]

At the end of the attacks on July 2, Alexander had found Longstreet and gotten his orders for the next day. "They were, in brief, that our present position was to be held, and the attack be renewed as soon as Pickett arrived, and he was expected early." Alexander could not wait until morning:

> There was a good deal to do meanwhile. Our sound horses were to be fed and watered, those killed and disabled were to be replaced from the wagon-teams, ammunition must be replenished, and the ground examined and positions of batteries rectified. But a splendid moon made all comparatively easy, and greatly assisted, too, in the care of the wounded, many of whom, both our own and the enemy's, lay about among our batteries nearly all night.

Finally, at 1 a.m., Alexander "made a little bed of fence rails" and slept two hours. "At 3 I began to put the batteries in position."[24]

By midmorning, Alexander had about 150 guns. As he continued placing them, he noted how "the enemy, aware of the strength of his position, simply sat still and waited for us." Once the infantry columns were assembled, Longstreet wanted two guns fired to signal the bombardment. At noon, Alexander took one of Pickett's couriers with him and found a favorable point for observation just left of the line of guns. Minutes later he got a message from Longstreet:

> *Colonel: If the artillery fire does not have the effect to drive off the enemy, or greatly demoralize him, so as to make our efforts pretty certain, I would prefer that you should not advise Gen. Pickett to make the charge. I shall rely a great deal on your good judgment to determine the matter & shall expect you to let Gen. Pickett know when the moment offers.*

Longstreet's orders "startled" Alexander. "If that assault was to be made on General Lee's judgment it was all right," Alexander thought, "but I did not want it on mine." The incongruity that a twenty-eight-year-old colonel of artillery should overrule his commander in chief—and Robert E. Lee to boot—was not lost on Alexander if it was on Longstreet. "I will only be able to judge the effect of our fire on the enemy by his return fire, for his infantry is but little exposed to view and the smoke will obscure the whole field," he immediately replied.[25]

Longstreet had fervently hoped that Lee would change his mind about this attack. He did not. If Longstreet, seeing his superior unmoved, hoped a subordinate could take the mournful burden of what was to come off Longstreet's shoulders by countermanding Lee's orders, he was mistaken. Alexander soon got another message from him: "Let the batteries open."[26]

When Alexander got this message, he was with General Ambrose R. Wright of Hill's corps. Wright laced their discussion with grim humor. "It is not so hard to *go* there as it looks; I was nearly there with my brigade yesterday. The trouble is to *stay* there. The whole Yankee army," Wright concluded, "is there in a bunch."[27]

Alexander decided to check Pickett's mood and thoughts on what was to come. "He seemed very sanguine," Alexander felt, "and thought himself in luck to have the chance." Alexander sent another messenger to Longstreet: "General: When our artillery fire is at its best, I shall order Pickett to charge." He returned to his place with the guns.[28]

Longstreet believed he had conveyed to Alexander his objections, but "there was no alternative . . . General Lee had considered and would listen to nothing else . . ." The show was on. "At exactly one o'clock by my watch, the two signal guns were heard in quick succession," Alexander later wrote. "In a minute every gun was at work."[29]

Following his meal, Meade paid a visit to John Sedgwick's headquarters at the base of Little Round Top. From there, he and Warren rode to the summit. Through his binoculars Meade watched the deployment of scores of Confederate guns before Seminary Ridge. The attack he had predicted at midnight was coming. The two generals galloped down the north slope and made for Leister House, where they found Hancock, Gibbon, and Haskell still chatting. In minutes, two Confederate cannons fired, the shells smashing onto the grounds near Gibbon's division. All of Hancock's 2nd Corps hit the ground, those nearest the low stone wall taking shelter behind it.[30]

Seconds later, 150 Confederate guns belched in near unison with a deafening, continuous roar that lasted nearly two hours. In minutes they were joined by the one hundred guns Hunt and Meade had placed on Cemetery Ridge. Some rebel shells smashed trees and plowed earth, while others smashed into caissons, artillery, horses, and men. Gun crews could not hear each other or even the sound of their own cannons, while the high-pitched screams of men and neighing horses added to the audial terror. "Who can describe such a conflict as is raging around us?" Haskell thought at the time, and later described the terror perfectly:

The thunder and lightning of these two hundred and fifty guns and their
shells, whose smoke darkens the sky, are incessant, all pervading, in the

air above our heads, on the ground at our feet, remote, near, deafening,
ear-piercing, astounding; and these hailstones are massy iron, charged
with exploding fire . . . These guns are great infuriate demons, not of the
earth, whose mouths blaze with smoky tongues of living fire, and whose
murky breath, sulphur-laden, rolls around them and along the ground,
the smoke of Hades. These grimy men, rushing, shouting, their souls in
frenzy, plying the dusky globes and the igniting spark, are in their league,
and but their willing ministers.

Haskell chillingly added, "We thought that at the second Bull Run, at the Antietam and at Fredericksburg on the 11th of December, we had heard heavy cannonading; they were but holiday salutes compared with this."[31]

Leister House was well within range of rebel guns. Bursting shells killed and maimed horses, smashed the steps and porch, and ripped into the house. One solid shot just missed Meade as he stood in the doorway.[32]

"The thunder of the guns was incessant, for all ours had now opened fire and the whole air seemed filled with rushing, screaming and bursting shells," Gibbon recalled. As other officers shouted to orderlies for their mounts, Gibbon ran back to his division on Cemetery Ridge.[33]

Back at Leister House, Meade looked askance at his aides' efforts to find safety someplace, anyplace. "Gentlemen, are you trying to find a safe place?" he asked with a grin. "You remind me of the man who drove the ox-team which took ammunition to the heavy guns on to the field of Palo Alto. Finding himself within range, he tilted up his cart and got behind it. Just then General Taylor came along, and seeing this attempt at shelter, shouted, 'You damned fool, don't you know you are no safer there than anywhere else?' The driver replied, 'I don't suppose I am, general, but it kind o' feels so.'"[34]

Meanwhile, Hunt was riding from battery to battery and back to the artillery reserve, ordering fresh batteries and ammunition be sent to Cemetery Ridge, but *after* the Confederate bombardment, not during. To his surprise, the Confederate fire "was more dangerous behind the ridge than on its crest . . . Most of the enemy's projectiles passed overhead, the effect being to sweep all the open ground in our rear . . . a mere waste of ammunition" by the Confederates. The smoke of the cannonade had grown so thick that Alexander could not accurately see what he was *not* hitting.[35]

During the bombardment, Hancock noticed some of his soldiers prostrate on the ground, digging into it with their fingernails as if trying to escape the cacophony and the chance of being mutilated. As he mounted his horse, Hancock's aides joined him, one carrying the corps pennant. At a slow walk, they moved along the 2nd Corps line, oblivious to the screaming shells above and around them. When an aide told him the risk was too great for a man of his rank, he replied, "There are times when a corps commander's life does not count." It was dangerous, foolhardy, and just what many of the men needed to steel themselves.[36]

Eventually, Meade determined that Leister House was more death trap than headquarters and moved his staff to a barn across Taneytown Road. They were no sooner settling in there when a shell smashed into the barn, sending a jagged shard of wood into Chief of Staff Dan Butterfield's chest, just below his heart. Meade sent Butterfield to a surgeon and moved to Slocum's headquarters on Powers Hill, well within sight of Leister House and the Union center. From there he sent orders to Hunt and all the artillery commanders to cease firing. They would need every bit of ammunition for what was to come their way. Hunt, thinking likewise, had also ordered his gunners to cease fire.[37]

But that was not the only reason Meade wanted the counter-barrage stopped. He wanted the enemy attack to come sooner, not later. Hunt felt the same way. Stop firing and the Rebs might conclude the Yanks were being driven off the high ground. Meade was at Powers Hill when the enemy bombardment suddenly stopped.[38]

Across Seminary Ridge, Alexander's massed Confederate artillery continued its deafening barrage of the Yankee center, even though he could

no longer *see* the center. Nor could he see that the longer his bombardment continued, the less accurate it became. Since the end of the battle,
military and armchair historians, national park guides, and professional
soldiers alike have debated what happened to cause the declining accuracy of Confederate guns. Theories range from the guns' recoil creating
ruts, thereby lowering the wheels, to the explosion that closed the Richmond arsenal in March, compelling the government to get its shells
from other arsenals, their fuses a tad slower than what Alexander and
the other artillerists had been using.[39]

As Hunt ordered shattered, useless Union guns withdrawn, Alexander saw through his binoculars several batteries leaving the field. He
was running out of ammunition and wanted to save what he had to
cover the coming attack. Union guns had taken their toll on Alexander's
batteries and gun crews, and close to five hundred infantrymen lay dead
in the woods behind him from Union shells.[40]

Alexander was to give Pickett the order to charge. At first, he could
not bring himself to do it: "It seemed madness to launch infantry into
that fire, with nearly three-quarters of a mile to go at midday under a
July sun." But some hope returned to Alexander when he saw the Union
guns being withdrawn. "We Confederates often did such things as that
to save our ammunition for use against infantry, but I had never seen
the Federals withdraw their guns simply to save them up for the infantry fight. So I said, 'If he does not run fresh batteries in there in five
minutes, this is our fight.'" Quickly, Alexander sent a dispatch to Pickett: "For God's sake, come quick, or we cannot support you."[41]

Longstreet rode up to Alexander for an update. "I explained the situation, feeling then more hopeful, but our artillery ammunition might
not hold out for all we would want." A frustrated Longstreet barked,
"Stop Pickett immediately and replenish your ammunition." Alexander
told him that was impossible: "It would take too long, and the enemy
would recover from the effect our fire was then having."[42]

Longstreet could no longer hold back his frustration. "I don't want
to make this attack. I would stop it now but General Lee ordered it and
expects it to go on. I don't see how it can succeed." Alexander "did not

dare offer a word. The battle was lost if we stopped . . . There was a chance, and it was not my part to interfere."[43]

Years after the Civil War ended, James Longstreet could still smile when he thought or wrote about Major General George E. Pickett's "wondrous pulchritude and magnetic presence." Like Custer, Pickett had graduated last in his West Point class; other officers under Longstreet deemed that ranking appropriate. But Pickett was brave and anxious to make a name for himself. After being wounded during the Seven Days' fighting, he and his division saw little action. Today was his great chance for glory.[44]

With Alexander's dispatch in hand, Pickett galloped over to Longstreet. "General," he asked in an anxious tone, "shall I advance?" Longstreet, as if thinking that what was to come was not at all present in Pickett's mind, could only nod his head in silent assent.[45]

In the woods behind Alexander's guns, Lieutenant John H. Lewis was resting on the ground with his fellow infantrymen when Brigadier General Lewis Armistead cried, "Attention, second battalion! Battalion of direction forward; guides center; march!" Lewis watched as Armistead calmly walked twenty paces ahead of his brigade and prepared to lead his Virginians across the open field.[46]

Watching a number of enemy batteries being hitched up, Longstreet assumed they were being removed from the field, giving him "glimpse of unexpected hope." Soon the columns came out of the woods "on elastic springing step." Longstreet recalled:

> General Pickett, a graceful horseman, sat lightly in the saddle, his brown locks flowing quite over his shoulders. Pettigrew's division spread their steps and quickly rectified the alignment, and the grand march moved bravely on. As soon as the leading columns opened the way, the supports sprang to their alignments. General Trimble mounted, adjusting his seat and reins with an air of grace as if setting out on a pleasant afternoon ride. When aligned to their places solid march was made down the slope and past our batteries of position.[47]

With the cessation of artillery fire, the heavy smoke from the bombardment had begun to thin out, and the hot July sun reclaimed its command of the sky. The valley between Seminary Ridge and Cemetery Ridge was, for a moment, the eye of a human hurricane: an eerie, ominous peace that gave no clue of the carnage that was to come.

Looking westward from Cemetery Ridge, Hancock's 2nd Corps watched as the last fresh troops of the Army of Northern Virginia, along with six brigades from A. P. Hill's corps (rested after July 1), emerged from the woods behind Seminary Ridge to form ranks before making the nearly mile-long attack against them. The Confederate line of attack stretched from north to south about a mile. "Their lines were formed," Hancock admirably noted, "with a precision and steadiness that extorted the admiration of the witnesses of that memorable scene."[48]

The cavalry was off fighting miles away to break into the Union rear; hundreds of artillerymen had just finished the first part of their assignment. Now came the infantry's turn, as had been the case for every pitched battle since the Iron Age: be they armed with clubs, spears, swords and shields, or rifles, muskets and bayonets, it had always been up to the infantry to settle things.[49]

Lines formed, the Confederates began marching past Alexander's guns—about 13,000 of them—in the tradition of Roman legions and Napoleon's Old Guard. Their legend of invincibility preceded them as they marched silently. No rebel yells emanated from Southern throats, just line after line after line of armed men, so used to winning these battles that their leaders felt their silence would be more chilling this day than their legendary battle cry.[50]

The Confederates kept marching in silent unison. Alexander's guns could not resume firing at the Union line until the Confederate infantry had passed them, while Hunt's artillery waited for the rebel lines to get closer. The first line reached the Emmitsburg Road, running diagonally across the path of attack. Across the road, the open farmlands rose and fell, interrupted by post-and-rail or Virginia worm fences. Now Armistead placed his black felt hat atop his sword so his brigade could see him, encouraging his men to close ranks and keep marching. He was half a mile away from Hancock. For more than two years he had hoped for a reunion with his best friend from the prewar days, but not like this.[51]

The Confederates' target was the same copse of ten-foot-high trees on Cemetery Ridge that Lee had sighted that morning. Seven months earlier, Lee had watched as the Army of the Potomac, in crisp wool uniforms more dazzling than his soldiers' meager gray and butternut clothing this day, made a similar advance against his men behind the stone wall at Marye's Heights. Now it was his army's turn. It was not a charge but a march—an orderly, awe-inspiring march, incredibly beautiful to behold . . . until the guns opened fire.[52]

Once the Confederates crossed the road, they came within range of Union muskets. To the south, the right wing of Pickett's division crossed a field that exposed them to a brigade of Vermont infantry and several batteries of Hancock's guns on their right. A massive, collective groan came from the rebel lines as volleys of musket fire and grape and canister ripped into the Confederate lines, not only slowing their advance but crippling them from having any impact on the assault. The same thing was happening on Pickett's northern flank. There, an Ohio brigade found a defensive position past Hancock's line and poured fire into the Confederates while Union soldiers directly ahead of the approaching Confederates put them in a north-and-east cross fire.[53]

Now came Hunt's moment. Once the Confederates were within two hundred yards, dozens of Yankee cannons poured grape and canister into the rebels, whose collective moans intensified and multiplied as large segments of the Confederate lines simply disappeared.[54]

Hunt was at the front line, riding his favorite horse, named Billy, through Gibbon's division. The Confederate line suddenly halted; now the Union soldiers were in range of *their* muskets. A deadly volley struck down dozens of 2nd Corps soldiers, four of the minié balls striking Billy from his head down to his legs and killing him.[55]

For all the destruction on the Confederate flanks, the center of the attack kept coming. "The crash of shell and solid shot, as they came howling and whistling through the lines, seemed to make no impression on the men," Lewis remembered. "Great gaps were being made in the lines, only to be closed up, the gallant Armistead still in the lead, his hat working down to the bottom of his sword." By now the Confederates were running, stopping only to fire as they moved forward. What was left of Pickett's division made a left oblique line, placing it squarely before the Union center. Those few hundred Confederates had come a long, costly way to the stone wall. Now, for a moment, they outnumbered the Yanks and were within walking distance of the grail that was the copse of trees.[56]

Of a battery of six guns alongside the trees, only two were still in action. The battery's commander, Lieutenant Alonzo Cushing, got off one more lethal blast of grapeshot before he was killed. Led by Armistead, about two hundred of Pickett's men knelt before the stone wall, firing point-blank into the Union line as it fell back. Then they jumped over the wall to turn around Cushing's last cannon, the rebel yell sounding once again.[57]

From Seminary Ridge, Lee could see nothing of the attack; the heavy smoke of battle cloaked everything. Longstreet had sent out a brigade to reinforce Pickett, but they could not see their objective. Blinded like his commanding generals, Alexander's guns, firing to protect Pickett's men, hit them instead.

On a borrowed horse, Hancock was riding toward the stone wall, unaware how close his friend Armistead was, when he was shot in the thigh. Gibbon had already fallen from a shoulder wound. With a handful of men, including Lewis, Armistead cried, "Come on, boys, give them cold steel! Who will follow me?" They broke the Union line amid bitter, hand-to-hand fighting at an indentation in the Union line that became known as the "Angle."[58]

Armistead no sooner laid his hand on one of Cushing's guns when he fell mortally wounded from a shot fired by a 72nd Pennsylvania soldier. In seconds, the 69th Pennsylvanians joined the 72nd in overwhelming the Virginians, who were killed, wounded, or surrendered. Among those captured was Lieutenant John H. Lewis.[59]

Hancock's wound was bleeding profusely, but before leaving the field he dictated a message: "Tell General Meade that the troops under my command have repulsed the enemy's assault and that we had gained a great victory."[60]

Meade had already left Powers Hill to get back to Leister House, accompanied by Lieutenant Ranald Mackenzie. As they rode closer, Meade spotted several staff members, including his son, walking toward them instead of riding. At Leister House he found the reason: sixteen dead horses were strewn across the Leister yard. Meade and Mackenzie continued toward the stone wall, passing hundreds of Confederate prisoners. At least two thousand of their comrades lay dead before the stone wall, along with hundreds of Meade's soldiers. Finding a gunner from Cushing's battery, Meade asked, "Have they turned?"

"Yes," the soldier replied. "See, General Hays has one of their flags."

"I don't care for their flag," Meade fired back. "Have they turned?"

"Yes sir. They are just turning."[61]

Meade continued forward until he came upon Lieutenant Haskell, who took in Meade's appearance for posterity: "His soft black felt hat was slouched down over his eyes. His face was very white, not pale, and the lines were marked, and earnest, and full of care."

Meade wasted no time on greetings. "How is it going here?"

"I believe, General, the enemy's attack is repulsed." Meade stared for a second, and Haskell repeated, "The attack has been repulsed."

"Thank God," Meade replied.

After Haskell informed him that Gibbon had been wounded, Meade said, "The troops should be reformed as soon as possible and . . . they should hold their places as the enemy might be mad enough to attack again . . . If they attack again, charge him in the flank and sweep him from the field, do you understand?" Then Meade headed for Cemetery Hill.[62]

Those Confederates unharmed, or whose wounds did not prevent them from walking, made their way back across the field now covered with the bodies of their dead comrades in arms, assisting those lying wounded if they could get to their feet.

Instead of the din of battle, they heard only occasional gunfire and, for a moment, the collective cry, "Fredericksburg! Fredericksburg!" coming from the parched throats of the Pennsylvania regiments that had held their line and won the day. "Fredericksburg! Fredericksburg!" For the Army of the Potomac, it was an exultant, exhausted cheer, or taunt—the cry of an army that at last knew success; for the Army of Northern Virginia, it was a vindictive cry at best, an insulting jeer at worst. Both sides understood what it meant.

A mile away, on Seminary Ridge, Lee rode Traveller out to meet the survivors of the greatest mistake of his life, giving them the simplest of explanations. "It is all my fault," he said repeatedly with true emotion. "It is I who have lost this fight, and you must help me out of it the best way you can. All good men must rally." Most took his words to heart. There were still over three hours of daylight left, more than enough time for Meade to strike.[63]

Back at Cress Ridge and Rummel's farm, the battle between Confederate and Union cavalries ensued with a series of headlong charges by both sides. The two cavalries, galloping toward each other with incredible speed, crashed into each other "with a sound like the falling of timber." Horses were upended, slamming into the ground and crushing their riders. Hand-to-hand fighting was commonplace, a melee of slashing sabers, pistols at point-blank range, and carbine volleys from dismounted troopers. Each charge added another layer of choking dust on horse and rider. During the fighting, Hampton was nearly captured after sustaining a saber wound, the blood blinding him. Custer had one horse shot from under him and jumped on another one, his saber finding more than one victim that day. On one desperate charge, he rallied his troopers, shouting, "Come on, you Wolverines," then galloped four lengths ahead of them as they raced to catch up.[64]

At last, those horses and riders still standing or mounted were too spent for another round. Stuart led his surviving brigades away, making one point clear: "I held such a position," he wrote, that "commanded a view of the routes leading to the enemy's rear." Had Pickett's charge succeeded, Stuart believed he was in "precisely the right position to discover it and improve the opportunity."[65]

Afterward, Colonel Gregg believed that if his men had failed and Stuart's cavalry had carried the field, "disastrous consequences might have resulted." But Stuart's "plans were disarranged" by the smaller Union cavalry force. "His was to do," Gregg summarized, "ours to prevent."[66]

It fell to General Hunt to sum up the chronology of those three desperate days: "Thus the battle of Gettysburg closed as it had opened, with a very creditable cavalry battle."[67]

After watching Longstreet make his troop dispositions for the day's assault, Colonel Fremantle and Captain Scheibert had ridden over to the Lutheran seminary to view the attack from the cupola. They no sooner got there than Alexander's bombardment started. They found themselves in an artillery cross fire from both armies as countless shells whistled menacingly over their heads. They decided to take the Hagerstown road out of Gettysburg to return to Longstreet's base. They were accompanied briefly by a young boy on horseback who was not scared of the artillery duel at all. "This urchin took a diabolical interest in the bursting of the shells, and screamed with delight when he saw them take effect," Fremantle recalled. "I never saw this boy again, or found out who he was."[68]

The two foreign officers found the road "lined with Yankee dead, and as they had been killed on the 1st, the poor fellows had already begun to be very offensive," Fremantle wrote. As they made their way back to Seminary Ridge, they came across "a melancholy procession" of wounded Confederates. While some hobbled on crutches, Fremantle saw others "walking alone on crutches composed of two rifles, others were supported by men less gravely wounded to the rear." All the while the Union artillery's heavy fire broke off large tree branches above them, many striking the disabled and limping rebels. "It was as if nature itself was against them," Fremantle reflected.

When they found Longstreet, Fremantle, believing the attack was still ongoing, said, "I wouldn't have missed this for anything." Longstreet cut him off with a derisive laugh and replied, "The devil you wouldn't! I would like to have missed it very much; we've attacked and been repulsed: look there!" he said, pointing westward. At last, Fremantle got a view of the day's fighting: "small broken parties, under a heavy fire of artillery," making their way back to Seminary Ridge.[69]

After his brief outburst, Longstreet began rallying officers and soldiers to prepare for a Yankee counterattack. "No person could have been more calm or self-possessed than General Longstreet under these trying circumstances." After taking a drink of whiskey from Fremantle's flask, he left to find McLaws to make sure his battered corps was getting ready for the counterattack Longstreet expected. Fremantle and Scheibert went in search of Lee.[70]

As more sad and weary Confederates returned from the failed attack, Lee continued rallying and encouraging them, doing his best to take the weight of the defeat off their shoulders: "It is all my fault." To the unscathed or slightly wounded soldiers, he asked that they "bind up their hurts and take up a musket." Fremantle saw "badly wounded men take off their hats and cheer him." Lee told him, "This has been a sad day for us, Colonel—a sad day; but we can't always expect to gain victories." Fremantle was awed by how Lee's words and presence turned these men around. "Longstreet's conduct was admirable," he wrote, but "that of General Lee was perfectly sublime."[71]

Then Pickett approached, his face a mask of irrepressible sadness. He was accompanied by his aide, Captain Robert Bright. Lee took Pickett's hand and, in a calm, but strong tone, said, "General Pickett, place your division in rear of this hill, and be ready to repel the advance of the enemy should they follow up their advantage." Captain Bright was struck by Lee's change of vocabulary: he always called Union soldiers "those people." Pickett was nonresponsive, as if in shock. Using a kinder tone, Lee, still holding Pickett's hand, said, "Your men have done all that men could do, the fault is entirely my own."

Pickett lifted his head off his chest. "General Lee, I have no division now."[72]

Meade arrived at Cemetery Hill to learn that Gregg's cavalry had turned Stuart back. He was also handed Hancock's message. Meade's reply was heartfelt: "Say to General Hancock that I regret exceedingly that he is wounded and that I thank him for the Country and for myself for the service he has rendered today." Once his staff officers joined him, Meade rode with Generals Warren and Pleasonton over to Little Round Top to review Sykes's position. He was greeted by such strong cheers from the "battered but unbowed" soldiers on Cemetery Ridge that the enemy mistook the cheers for a coming charge. From Seminary Ridge, Alexander's guns fired a salvo or two across the field, and the still retreating Confederates from Pickett's charge opened fire with their muskets, wounding Meade's horse and killing his son's, the second horse Captain Meade lost that day.[73]

Meade strongly considered "advancing on my left, and making an assault on the enemy's lines." He ordered Sykes to send out a skirmish line, which met with strong resistance. Pleasonton, meanwhile, ordered Hugh Judson Kilpatrick's 3rd Cavalry Division to attack the Confederate lines south and west of Little Round Top. Kilpatrick's horsemen staged a combine mounted and on-foot assault, but without infantry support it was a catastrophe. Seeing both actions thwarted, Meade concluded that Lee's army had lost the day but not their spirit.

Lieutenant Roebling later wrote that the army's divisions were either scattered across the Union line or so intertwined with others that it would have been long past sundown before an offensive could have gotten underway. Taking into account the fact that most of his men had not eaten in days, not hours, and realizing the logistics of a successful offensive required Sedgwick's 6th Corps to march a mile up, form a line of attack, and move in coordination with Sykes's soldiers could not be accomplished before sunset, Meade decided not to attack Lee. His physically spent army had done enough soldiering over the past three days.[74]

An equally weary Gouverneur Warren agreed. "We were much shattered," he later told the Joint Committee on the Conduct of the War, "and there was a tone among most of the prominent officers that we had saved the country for the time, and that we had done enough." Further-more, "we might jeopardize all that we had won by trying to do too much."[75]

Later, Pleasonton stated he urged Meade "to order a general ad-vance of his whole army in pursuit of the enemy." There is no proof that Pleasonton made that statement to Meade, and Pleasonton's own order to Kilpatrick—and the disastrous results—should be taken into account in regard to Meade's decision to stay put on Cemetery Ridge. It is also the first in a long series of questionable accounts and actions that would eventually question Meade's leadership and judgment at Gettysburg, from petulant and lying officers to Meade's commander in chief smear-ing his reputation and, as time passed, relegating him to being a foot-note.[76]

Late that night, Lee summoned Brigadier General John Imboden to meet with him. Imboden's cavalry brigade had arrived at Gettysburg only on July 3, after days of destroying railroad bridges. He and his horsemen saw no action that day. Lee did not arrive at his quarters un-til 1 a.m., "riding alone at a slow walk." Imboden was in shock at the effort it took Lee just to dismount, then "threw his arm across the sad-dle to rest, and fixing his eyes upon the ground leaned in silence and almost motionless upon his equally weary horse." Imboden watched in embarrassed silence before he spoke. "General," he said quietly, "this has been a hard day on you."[77]

"Yes, it has, been a sad, sad day to us," Lee mournfully replied, and resumed his uncomfortable silence. Then he said, "I never saw troops behave more magnificently than Pickett's division of Virginians did to-day in that grand charge upon the enemy," before reciting the what-ifs of the afternoon. "And if they had been supported, as they were to have been—but for some reason not yet fully explained to me, they were not—we would have held the position . . . and the day would have been ours . . . . Too bad! *Too bad!* Oh! TOO BAD!"

Imboden never forgot Lee's "manner, and his appearance . . . of mental suffering." Finally, "all emotion was suppressed," and Lee got to the point of his summons of Imboden. "We must now return to Virginia," Lee told him. Imboden's brigade would escort the wagon train of wounded back home. He and Lee spent the next hour reviewing the roads, what light artillery was available to make for Williamsport, Maryland. The brief crack in the "Marble Model's" composure had passed, but Imboden never forgot it.[78]

That night in Washington, Secretary of the Navy Gideon Welles visited the War Department telegraph office and found the president there as usual, waiting quietly but anxiously for news from Meade. "Lincoln was in the telegraph office hour after hour during those anxious days and nights," telegrapher David Homer Bates recalled. Welles left at 11 p.m. He was roused from slumber at midnight. A brief telegram had arrived for Welles "stating that the most terrible battle of the War was being fought at or near Gettysburg" and that "everything looked hopeful." It was simply signed "Byington."[79]

Lincoln quickly read it and asked, "Who is Byington?" None of the telegraphers knew. "Ask the Secretary of the Navy," one suggested. Welles returned, told Lincoln that the sender was Aaron Homer Byington, owner of the *Norwalk Gazette* and occasional reporter for the *New York Tribune*. Welles "informed the President that the telegram was reliable." It was not detailed news but encouraging enough for Lincoln to remain hopeful and Welles to go back to bed.[80]

Darkness was setting in when Meade and his aides returned to Leister House to find it, too, was now a hospital. They rode down Taneytown Road, stopping at a grove of trees. Meade, physically spent himself, finally dictated the telegram that Lincoln and Halleck had been anxiously waiting for:

The enemy opened at 1 p.m. from about 150 guns, concentrated upon my left and center, continuing without intermission for about three hours, at the expiration of which time he assaulted my left center twice, being upon both occasions handsomely repulsed, with severe loss to him, leaving in our hands nearly 3,000 prisoners; among the prisoners, Brigadier-General

Armistead and many colonels and officers of lesser rank. The enemy left
many dead upon the field and a large number of wounded in our hands.

The loss upon our side has been considerable. Major-General Hancock
and Brigadier-General Gibbon were wounded. After the repelling of the
assault, indications leading to the belief that the enemy might be with-
drawing, an armed reconnaissance was pushed forward from the left, and
the enemy found to be in force. My cavalry have been engaged all day on
both flanks of the enemy, harassing and vigorously attacking him with
great success, notwithstanding they encountered superior numbers, both of
cavalry and infantry. The army is in fine spirits.[81]

His message of victory sent, Meade sought a spot to rest on and
settled on a flat boulder. A newspaperman thought him "stooping and
weary, his slouched hat laid aside so that the breeze might fan his brow."
Soon afterward the wind picked up and a furious thunderstorm struck,
drenching the hapless soldiers. Young George looked over to find his
father sitting ramrod straight on his boulder, weathering yet another
storm.[82]

Meade's wire reached the army telegraph office in Washington at
6:10 a.m. the next day, the Fourth of July. Lincoln was likely still there.

ELEVEN

THURSDAY, NOVEMBER 19

O nce the sounds of Pickett's charge subsided, Tillie Pierce and the Weikerts returned to the Weikert farmhouse: "As we drove along in the cool of the evening, we noticed that everywhere confusion prevailed. Fences were thrown down near and far; knapsacks, blankets and many other articles, lay scattered here and there." Nothing she observed along the way prepared her for what she and the Weikerts saw as they approach the farm. "As we passed on toward the house, we were compelled to pick our steps in order that we might not tread on the prostrate bodies."[1]

They found the house filled with wounded soldiers and tried to make themselves useful. Mrs. Weikert took all the muslin and linen she thought she could spare, and the girls tore it into bandages for the surgeons.

Later, when Tillie went outside, she saw a pile of amputated limbs higher than the fence. Her grim account of July 3 ended with: "Twilight had now fallen; another day had closed, with the soldiers saying that they believed this day that the Rebels were whipped, but at an awful sacrifice."[2]

A heavy thunderstorm raged that night, the thunder replacing the seemingly endless boom of cannons that afternoon. As the rain stopped that morning, the sun broke through the clouds. It was Saturday—the Fourth of July. Slowly, cautiously, those Gettysburg citizens that had remained in town opened their doors to find the Confederates gone. They were joined by handfuls of Union soldiers from 1st and 11th

Corps who had hidden in basements, attics, and barn lofts to avoid capture. "How happy everyone felt; none but smiling faces to be seen," young Jennie McCreary wrote. "It was indeed a joyful 'Fourth' for us."[3]

Other residents were not so jubilant. The streets were littered with the tangible articles of war: muskets, knapsacks, swords, and bayonets. "There lay with the slain all sorts of debris," Lutheran seminary student Henry Eyster Jacobs recalled, including letters and photographs of loved ones. Jennie McCreary's younger brother, Albertus, walked the battlefield with his father, searching for a missing cow. Father and son walked among "dead soldiers lying around thick, dead horses, and cow skins and heads," the latter's "bodies much swollen, the feet standing up in the air." The stench of death was overwhelming: "Every one went about with a bottle of pennyroyal or peppermint oil," he remembered.[4]

Those Black citizens of Gettysburg who had not fled before the battle commenced either hid out in the nearby hills, away from the battle, or stayed in town, doing what they could to show the rebels they were unfit to be seized and sent south to an auctioneer's block. One white resident recalled their transformation "into limping, halting, and apparently worthless specimens of humanity" once a Confederate was sighted. The damage both armies did to property did not discriminate between the races, but few had it worse than those Black families whose farms were on or near Cemetery Hill. They found their homes and barns battered by artillery, their personal belongings stolen or smashed, their fields of wheat and barley trampled, and their livestock stolen if not already eaten.[5]

The task of rebuilding their lives and homes, plus caring for the wounded of both armies, the burial of thousands of dead soldiers, the burning of thousands of livestock carcasses, and keeping their own health in the midst of stench and putrefaction, seemed insurmountable.

"VICTORY!! WATERLOO ECLIPSED!!" was the *Philadelphia Inquirer*'s jubilant headline once news of Meade's victory was verified. Most Southern papers merely reported Lee's departure from Pennsylvania. The *Richmond Enquirer* initially refused to use the word "defeat" while admitting, "We were unable to carry the heights beyond and below Gettysburg." Those Confederate officials who got the news in private were

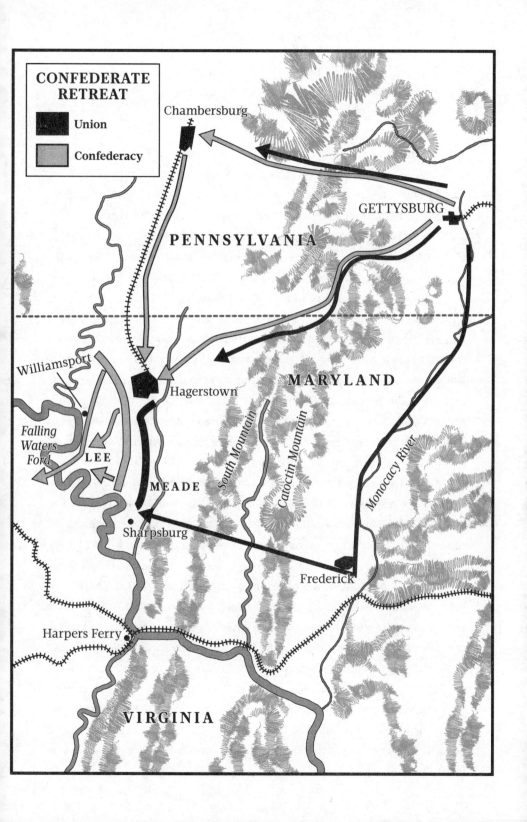

CONFEDERATE RETREAT

■ Union
▬ Confederacy

Chambersburg

GETTYSBURG

PENNSYLVANIA

Williamsport

Falling Waters Ford

LEE

MEADE

Hagerstown

MARYLAND

South Mountain

Catoctin Mountain

Monocacy River

Sharpsburg

Frederick

Harpers Ferry

VIRGINIA

less circumspect. "The news from Lee's army is appalling," one war department clerk wrote.[6]

The morning of the Fourth saw scattered gunfire from pickets. Meade could see Lee's army still on Seminary Ridge, daring him to attack the Confederates just as Lee had done with McClellan at Antietam. But there would not be a fourth day of heavy fighting. Meade saw through Lee's bluff: "expecting that flushed with success, I would attack them when they would play their old game of shooting us from behind breastworks— a game we played this time to their entire satisfaction," he noted.[7]

Around 8 a.m., Meade was handed a message from Lee requesting a prisoner exchange. It was an offer Meade could not accept: Halleck had ended the practice six weeks earlier. Meade suspected that Lee's message was a telltale sign that he was about to retreat. That afternoon, Meade was convinced Lee would soon be retreating. He notified General Couch in Frederick, Maryland. While "this army is resting from its severe conflict and rapid marches . . ." Meade told Couch, "as soon as it can be definitely ascertained that Lee is retiring into the Valley, I shall move rapidly in a southerly direction."[8]

Meade faced other difficult challenges besides Lee. His men had not been fed in days and desperately needed shoes; the horses had no hay and desperately needed shoeing. Supply wagons had been taken off the roads to get artillery and ammunition to the battlefield. The loss of horses numbered in the thousands. Round-the-clock burial details were formed, but Meade found himself "compelled to employ citizens to bury the enemy's dead." To make matters worse, the train bridges from Harrisburg to Gettysburg had been burned. Until they were repaired, the only way to get more than 10,000 wounded from both sides and 5,000 rebel prisoners to Baltimore would be over the Baltimore Pike.[9]

That afternoon, Meade issued an order congratulating the army on its victory but cautioning that "our task is not yet accomplished" and would not be until he and the army made "greater efforts to drive from our soil every vestige of the presence of the invader." Those two phrases would come back to haunt Meade sooner rather than later.[10]

The only rumbling over Gettysburg came that evening when yet another thunderstorm raged while Meade met with his generals again. The steady downpour soaked Meade as he led his generals in a slog to a nearby house. In addition to Meade, there were a dozen generals present, including corps commanders Howard, Newton, Sedgwick, Slocum, and Sykes, along with Generals David Birney, heading 3rd Corps in place of Sickles; and Brigadier General William Hays, heading 4th Corps in place of Hancock and Gibbon. Also present were Generals Pleasonton and Warren and wounded chief of staff Butterfield.

Meade opened the meeting by reiterating his earliest orders from Halleck "to cover Washington and Baltimore." By a vote of five to three the generals determined to remain in position to see if Lee would retreat or remain on Seminary Ridge. Once that was ascertained, the cavalry would harass Lee's communications and rear guard. Sedgwick and his fresh 6th Corps would leave Gettysburg, with Warren commanding an advance division, and march west to find Lee. Once they learned of Lee's whereabouts, Meade would follow with the rest of the army south, staying east of South Mountain, and turn west to cut off Lee's escape.[11]

Sometime after the meeting, Meade's aide-de-camp, Major James Cornell Biddle Jr., wrote an optimistic letter to his wife: "The corps commanders appear very satisfied with Meade. I think there is more unity among them than ever before."[12]

At 10 a.m. on the Fourth, a telegram was issued by the War Department to the press and public:

> *The president announces to the country that news from the Army of the Potomac, up to 10 p.m. of the 3rd, is such as to cover that Army with the highest honor, to promise a great success to the cause of the Union, and to claim the condolence of all for the many gallant fallen. And that for this, he especially desires on this day, He whose will, not ours, should ever be done, be everywhere remembered with profoundest gratitude.*[13]

No one in the country was more grateful for the news than the army's commander in chief. The Army of the Potomac had finally won a decisive victory, and Lincoln's approval for appointing Meade seemed to erase the president's disappointments—and despair—from his predecessors. He now hoped for further good news from Meade at Gettysburg and from Grant at Vicksburg. But as triumphant as his message read, it was parsed: the most optimistic word in the telegram was "promised." Nowhere did he use the word "victory."

Nor was he happy with Meade's victory statement to the army. "You know," Lincoln told Halleck, "I do not like the phrase, 'Drive the invaders from our soil.'" To him, the entire country was "our soil"; that was his original premise in fighting this war. After two years of deficient commanding generals—particularly McClellan—Lincoln's joy over Meade's triumph was mixed with skepticism that he would pick up where "Little Mac" left off. (Welles called it "a little of the old lagging infirmity" from McClellan's day.) Lincoln told Halleck to keep after Meade. Over the next two weeks, telegraph wires sang with messages between the two generals.[14]

Meade's vocabulary seemed to set the tone for Lincoln's opinion of him, but Meade was not McClellan. On July 5, he notified Halleck that Lee had begun his retreat and that "all my available cavalry are in pursuit." He instructed Sedgwick to march west, find Lee, and "fire on his force . . . Time is of great importance," and promised him support from Sykes. His orders stressed that Sedgwick's pursuit and reports be thorough. "I can't give orders without explicit information from you," he told "Uncle John."[15]

In Washington, the news that followed Meade's July 4 statement increased Lincoln's hopes for another battle with Lee. Late in the evening of the Fourth, General Couch wired Halleck that Lee's pontoon bridge had been "utterly destroyed." And, on July 7, Lincoln learned that Meade's West Point roommate and fellow Philadelphian, Confederate lieutenant general John Pemberton, had surrendered his 29,000-man army and the city of Vicksburg to U. S. Grant on July 4. That day Halleck had already sent Meade a congratulatory wire that he had been appointed a brigadier general in the regular army "to rank from July 3, the date of your brilliant victory." Hours later Meade heard from him again. "I have received from the President the following note, which I respectfully communicate," wrote Halleck:

> *We have certain information that Vicksburg surrendered to General Grant on the 4th of July. Now, if General Meade can complete his work, so gloriously prosecuted thus far, by the literal or substantial destruction of Lee's army, the rebellion will be over.*[16]

Halleck did not need to tell Meade that the pressure was on. Lincoln's note said enough, but by the time Meade received it, his army was already slogging through miles of mud—a punishing march under a steady downpour, each step in the muck taking them closer to Lee. One soldier described the road assigned Sykes's 5th Corps as "one immense hog-wallow the entire distance."[17]

Brigadier General John Imboden did not possess the cavalier-like appearance of a cavalry commander. He had neither the flowing hair or beard nor the feathered or gaudy outfits of a Stuart or Custer. He wore a simple gray uniform and kept his dark hair short and his mustache trimmed. Before the war he had been a teacher of deaf children before becoming a lawyer and politician. As an artillery commander earlier in the war, his left eardrum was punctured by cannon fire.[18]

On the morning of the Fourth, Imboden received his orders from Lee along with a large envelope to be given to Jefferson Davis. He was to take the wounded from Cashtown, bypass Chambersburg, and make for Williamsport. There he would ford the Potomac and escort the train to Martinsburg in the Shenandoah Valley.[19]

At 4 p.m., under driving rain, the unharmed Confederates bade farewell to their wounded comrades as Imboden's forlorn caravan, some seventeen miles long, began its return home. "There was no abatement in the storm," Imboden recalled:

Canvas was no protection against its fury, and the wounded men lying upon the naked boards of the wagon-bodies were drenched. Horses and mules were blinded and maddened by the wind and water, and became almost unmanageable. The deafening roar of the mingled sounds of heaven and earth all around us made it almost impossible to communicate orders . . . [M]any of the wounded in the wagons had been without food for thirty-six hours . . . Very few of the wagons had even a layer of straw in them, and all were without springs . . . The jolting was enough to have killed strong men . . . From nearly every wagon as the teams trotted on, urged by whip and shout, came such cries and shrieks as these: "My God! Will no one have mercy and kill me?"[20]

For four days, Imboden led the wagon train to its destination. With orders not to stop until he reached Williamsport, Imboden was forced to abandon any wagons that broke down—and those wounded in them—on the roadside. Despite Confederate cavalry protecting both sides of his train, Imboden's wagons soon became targets for Union cavalry and Union townsfolk. "After a great deal of desultory fighting and harassments," Imboden's train reached Williamsport, only to find that the torrential rains had made the Potomac impossible to cross. That was not all: he soon learned that the pontoon bridge his train was to cross at Falling Waters, six miles downstream, had been destroyed by Pennsylvania cavalry. Looking across the Potomac, Imboden could see Virginia.

On July 6, a Yankee cavalry force of 4,000 under General John Buford approached Williamsport. "Our situation," Imboden declared, "was frightful." With the swollen river behind him, Imboden had two infantry regiments, two cavalry brigades, a few pieces of artillery, and little ammunition to fight with. He placed his guns on the neighboring hills and made a defensive line, even arming his seven hundred teamsters. The next day Imboden, with assistance from Wade Hampton's and Fitzhugh Lee's cavalry brigades, drove Buford back. Over the next three days, Jeb Stuart's horsemen held off the Union cavalry at nearby Boonsboro and both cavalry and infantry forces at Funkstown. The Confederates now held the crossings.[21]

After Imboden's train departed Gettysburg, Lee began the retreat of the remainder of his army as darkness fell on the Fourth. Hill's 3rd Corps started the march on Fairfield road, followed by Longstreet's 1st Corps and then Ewell's 2nd Corps as Lee's rear guard. Unlike his march northward and the first two days of battle, Stuart's cavalry resumed their role as Lee's "eyes and ears"; the chastised cavalier would do his utmost to restore Lee's regard for him. They marched back to the South Mountain passes that first brought them to Pennsylvania.[22]

Edward Porter Alexander found the retreat "very slow & tedious . . . stopped by the thing in front of you stopping—it may be a few seconds; it may be a half hour." The wind and rain blinded the teamsters. Lee and Longstreet shared a van on the way to Hagerstown. Their conversation about the battle was polite, Lee quietly insisting the defeat was his responsibility, while Longstreet refrained from any criticism. Upon reaching Hagerstown, they learned of the pontoon bridge's destruction at Falling Waters. Lee's engineers would have to build a new one, while Lee's army would have to hold off the Army of the Potomac.[23]

On July 5, Lincoln took his son Tad to 248 F Street to visit Dan Sickles. They found the general still on the same stretcher that had taken him from the battlefield to the train and now at this residence. His attending physician feared Sickles's condition would worsen by moving him to a bed. Lincoln and Tad found him with two of his officers. One, Lieutenant Colonel James Rusling, described Sickles as "in much pain . . . weakened and enfeebled from loss of blood" yet "with a cigar between his fingers, puffing it leisurely."[24]

After their perfunctory greetings, "Mr. Lincoln sat down crossing his prodigious arms and telescopic legs" and "soon fell to cross examining General Sickles as to all phases of the recent combat." When Lincoln asked how Sickles had come to lose his leg, Lincoln "jollied" him, certain Sickles would soon "be out and up at the White House, where they would always be glad to see him." After discussing the "great casualties at Gettysburg" (Rusling added Lincoln felt the Union victory "equaling if not exceeding Wellington at Waterloo"), Lincoln asked Sickles what Meade proposed to do with his victory.

On the surface, Lincoln's question seemed matter-of-fact, but Lincoln wanted Sickles's opinion. He had met Meade but had not gotten to really know him. Lincoln did not know, nor could he have, that his visit to Sickles—and his question—gave Sickles a consequential opportunity if not an outright gift. No one in Washington, including Lincoln, knew that Sickles had disobeyed Meade's orders on July 2, abandoning his assignment on the defensive line for the higher ground that nearly proved disastrous for the army (and Sickles, had that cannonball struck him several inches higher). Meade and generals like Hancock were sure to damn Sickles's disobedience. But now, from the same stretcher that had carried him off the field, Sickles could bypass his commanding officer and tell the commander in chief about the true hero of Gettysburg: one Daniel Sickles.

The one-legged general "answered Mr. Lincoln in detail, but warily." Rusling did not write down what Sickles said, but years later summed up Sickles's account thusly: "He certainly got his side of the story of Gettysburg well into the President's mind and heart that Sunday afternoon; and this doubtless stood him in good stead afterward."[25]

Sickles soon was well enough to visit the White House, further ingratiating himself to both the president and Mary Lincoln. Gideon Welles was present at one visit when Lincoln asked Sickles if Hancock had chosen the battleground at Gettysburg. "Sickles said he did not, but that General Howard and perhaps himself"—meaning Sickles— "were more entitled to that credit than any others." It was really Sickles who had "arrived later, between five and six p.m., and liked the position. General Meade arrived on the ground soon after, and was for abandoning the position and falling back."

Welles was well aware of Sickles's habitual braggadocio. "Allowance must always be made for Sickles when he is interested . . ." Welles wrote in his diary. Sickles would get plenty of allowance from both Lincoln and his wife. He relished holding court with the newspapermen, politicians, and socialites in Washington, accusing Meade of weak character, poor judgment, and outright cowardice. The battle had been won not on July 3 but on July 2, and by Dan Sickles.[26]

Despite his army's exhaustion, its staggering casualties, and its lack of everything from shoes to horses to seasoned corps commanders, Meade genuinely wanted to catch Lee. "I think we shall have another battle before Lee can cross the river," he wrote Margaret from Frederick on July 8. "For my part, as I have to follow and fight him, I would rather do it at once and in Maryland than to follow into Virginia." He then confided in her about the stress he was under, recounting ten days of sleepless nights, not changing his clothes, no full meal, and the "mental anxiety" he had kept to himself. "Indeed," he concluded, "I think I have lived as much in this time as in the last thirty years."

Two days earlier, on July 6, Sedgwick's 6th Corps had been within two miles of Lee's rear guard at Fairfield. When the Confederates opened fire, Sedgwick answered with a lengthy barrage from his light artillery. Meade was anxious to join Sedgwick, but "my army is assembling slowly," he told Halleck on July 8. "Be assured I most earnestly desire to try the fortunes of war with the enemy on this side of the river . . ." he continued, but added a caveat: "I expect to find the enemy in a strong position, well covered with artillery, and I do not desire to imitate his example at Gettysburg, and assault a position where the chances were so greatly against success." He promised that "all that I can do under the circumstances I pledge to do."[27]

Halleck's terse response was one of restrained exasperation. "The opportunity to attack [Lee's] divided force should not be lost. The President is urgent and anxious that your army should move against him by forced marches." The wire brought back the snapping turtle in Meade, particularly the dismissive line of "forced marches," caustically informing Halleck that Lee's "whole force is in position between Funkstown and Williamsport." Halleck was conciliatory—"Do not understand me as expressing any dissatisfaction"—replying with Washington rumors that Lee had a new pontoon bridge to cross and had been using it for two days. Meade waited a day to reply. His army was assembling; the

Potomac was still too high for Lee to cross. "I think the decisive battle of the war will be fought in a few days," he added. Meade was right: Lee's army could not possibly have crossed the Potomac. Not yet.[28]

Realizing his army had no chance of crossing the river without a new pontoon bridge, Lee looked to the best way for his army to survive until a new bridge was constructed. The terrain around Williamsport gave him that opportunity. While "there was no very well defined & naturally strong line," as Alexander later recalled, the combination of ridges and marshes between them had caught the eyes of Confederate engineers. Lee, too, found it appealing; the old engineer set the men to building breastworks and selected artillery positions, working day and night. When completed, Lee's army had a nine-mile line to defend. Long but forbidding, Lee's defense rivaled Meade's fishhook at Gettysburg or Lee's line on Marye's Heights in Fredericksburg.[29]

Lee then ordered his engineers to get to work on another bridge. As they took every piece of wood to the riverside sawmills, Lee issued a general order that ranks with Thomas Paine or Shakespeare's *Henry V*: "Once more you are called upon to meet the enemy from whom you have torn so many fields—names that will never die . . . Soldiers! your old enemy is before you! Win from him honor worthy of your righteous cause . . ."[30]

Over the next three days, Meade carefully arranged his troops and wondered how his new promotions would fare. Before departing Gettysburg, he had replaced the wounded and unwanted Butterfield as chief of staff with the capable general Andrew A. Humphreys. Meade left Brigadier General William Hays in charge of 2nd Corps but ended General David Birney's brief time leading 3rd Corps with the more experienced William H. French, returning Birney to his division. Meade already had engendered some resentment from Butterfield, Howard, Doubleday, and Sickles; now Birney joined the list. For all their talents, the generals Meade retained or promoted were not as good as the men

Meade needed and missed the most. "The loss of Reynolds and Hancock is most serious; their places are not to be supplied," he confided to Margaret.[31]

On July 10, Meade notified Halleck that he was preparing to advance on Lee. Ironically, Halleck urged him to delay; he was sending reinforcements from other Union forces. Once they arrived, "hurl upon the enemy all your forces, good and bad." On the twelfth, General Howard, on Meade's right flank, crossed the Antietam River. Sighting Williamsport, he saw for himself how well positioned Lee's army was and informed Meade. Nevertheless, Meade intended to "attack them to-morrow, unless something intervenes to prevent it."[32]

That same day, Lieutenant Ranald Mackenzie sent a note to Warren from the Potomac: "The river has fallen here 18 inches in the last twenty-four hours, and is still falling." Furthermore, a "citizen" had assured Mackenzie that fording the Potomac was "now practicable for the infantry." Warren immediately took it to Meade. Taking Warren and Humphreys along, Meade rode toward Williamsport to see Lee's defenses for himself. He found Lee to be "strongly intrenched [sic]." Humphreys believed there were no "vulnerable points." Returning to camp, Meade called for a meeting with his corps commanders. At 8 p.m. they met in his tent; he was camped near the rocky ridge called the Devil's Backbone.[33]

Meade saw that Lee's position was "a very strong one" and that Lee "was prepared to give battle and defend it if attacked . . . [N]evertheless, I was in favor of moving forward and attacking the enemy and taking the consequences; but that I left it to their judgment, and would not do it unless it met with their approval." Only Howard and General Wadsworth (General Newton was ill) sided with Meade. The others— French, Hays, Sedgwick, Slocum, and Sykes—all were against an attack. Meade acquiesced but still ordered an examination of Lee's position the next morning.

Ironically, as Meade's generals were talking him out of attacking Lee at Williamsport, General Longstreet questioned Lee's decision to cross the Potomac for Virginia. From the time the Army of Northern Virginia crossed the Mason-Dixon Line, Longstreet had constantly advocated what Lee originally planned: an invasion comprising defensive battles.

Now, as Lee's line of defense at Williamsport took shape, Longstreet saw the opportunity to again argue for a defensive battle, with Lee holding the high ground. This time Meade had the outer curve, while the Confederates held the inner defensive lines. It would be, as Meade's generals feared, another Fredericksburg, or Gettysburg in reverse. Plus artillery supplies had been transported across the Potomac shortly after Imboden's arrival. A victory here would certainly turn the tables on Meade, Halleck, and Lincoln.[34]

Lee said no. While his men were itching for another fight with the Yankees, Lee had made his mind up. The evacuation would begin on the evening of July 13. Just as he was getting the army and his hundreds of wagons ready, another storm struck. "The rain fell in sheets, during the entire night," Longstreet recalled. On the fourteenth, Buford's cavalry attacked General Harry Heth's division, still on the Maryland side of the Potomac as Lee's rear guard. By afternoon the remnants of Lee's army were back in Virginia. In a few days the army was right back at Culpeper Court House, where the march northward had begun.[35]

It was raining on July 13, when Meade and Humphreys again rode over the grounds before Lee's defenses. Meade sent out several divisions to find a weak point, and by late afternoon he was convinced there was none. He wired Halleck of his decision.[36]

An incensed Halleck wasted no time replying. "You are strong enough to attack and defeat the enemy before he can effect a crossing. Act upon your own judgement . . . Do not let the enemy escape." After all, "councils of war never fight." Once again the heavens opened up. It rained all night.[37]

The next morning, July 14, Meade ordered the army out in full reconnaissance, ready to attack, only to find there was no enemy *to* attack. Making the best use of the rain and darkness, Lee had gotten his army across the Potomac and back to Virginia. Meade wired Halleck that the Confederate lines had been evacuated and he would "immediately put my army in pursuit, the cavalry in advance." His closing sentence would only add to what he must have known would be an eruption of anger in Washington: "Your instructions as to further movements, in case the enemy are entirely across the river, are desired."[38]

Halleck's reply was brutal. "The escape of Lee's army without another battle has created great dissatisfaction in the mind of the President," he scolded. That was an understatement. Meade immediately answered Halleck's reprimand. "The censure of the president, conveyed in your dispatch of 1 p.m. this day, is, in my judgment, so undeserved that I feel compelled most respectfully to ask to be immediately relieved from the command of this army." Halleck replied with a tepid non-apology: his telegram "was not intended as a censure, but as a stimulus to an active pursuit" and "not deemed a sufficient cause for your application to be relieved." Meade returned to updating Halleck on his activities and observations.[39]

Lincoln learned about Lee's escape before a cabinet meeting on July 14. It was one more challenging development for him to deal with. "We have accounts of mobs, riots, and disturbances in New York and other places in consequence of the Conscription Act," Welles noted. When the meeting broke up, Welles joined Lincoln as the president headed to see Halleck. Lincoln told Halleck he "had dreaded yet expected this . . . There is bad faith somewhere," Lincoln continued, describing his frustration with Meade and Meade's generals. "What does it mean, Mr. Welles? Great God! What does it mean?"[40]

To his secretary, John Hay, he bitterly remarked that "we had only to stretch forth our hands and they were ours. And nothing I could say or do could make the army move." To his son Robert, Lincoln vented further: "If I had gone up there I could have licked them myself." But it was to Hay that Lincoln made his greatest insult to Meade: "This is a dreadful reminiscence of McClellan." But the rising bile inside Lincoln still needed an outlet, and that was a damning letter to Meade himself:

You stood and let the flood run down, bridges be built, and the enemy move away at his leisure . . . [Lee] was within your easy grasp, and to have closed upon him would, in connection with our other late successes, have ended the war . . . [T]he war will be prolonged indefinitely . . . Your golden opportunity is gone, and I am distressed immeasurably because of it.

Writing the letter proved a catharsis for Lincoln. Instead of mailing it—or, worse, wiring it to Meade—he added one more line: "To Gen. Meade, never sent, never signed."[41]

One wonders if Lincoln would have had a different viewpoint had he personally seen at least the horrific aftermath of the three days at Gettysburg: the devastation of the land, the unburied corpses, the bloated carcasses of horses, and the thousands of wounded . . . From Lincoln's writings and discussions with Halleck and his cabinet, it appears he gave no serious thought that an attack on Williamsport could have evened the score for Lee and left Philadelphia, Baltimore, and Washington in jeopardy a second time. The fact that Meade's fellow West Point generals, several of them accomplished engineers like Meade, agreed with his decision not to attack Lee at Williamsport meant nothing to Lincoln. Besides, he already had a firsthand account of Meade as a commander from another Gettysburg general, Dan Sickles.

At daybreak on July 18, with the piercing sounds of bugles and the ruffle of drums, Meade's army crossed the Potomac, some of the troops sardonically singing "Carry Me Back to Old Virginny." Meade soon had fewer men to command when Halleck ordered him to send troops to New York City to maintain order after the Draft Riots. An attempt to pick a fight in July came to naught at Manassas Gap on July 23. On the night of the thirty-first, with the armies on opposite sides of the Rappahannock, Meade sent a combined infantry and cavalry force to threaten the rebel flank, but Lee withdrew behind the Rapidan. "The government insists on my pursuing and destroying Lee," he vented to Margaret. "The former I can do, but the latter will depend on him as much as me."[42]

In the midst of his frustration over Meade, Lincoln had received a letter from General Howard defending Meade to the president (something Meade certainly did not expect from Howard). Lincoln sent Meade both Howard's letter and his reply. Where he was "deeply mortified" at Meade's failure to bag Lee, he was "now profoundly grateful for what was done, without criticism for what was not done. Gen. Meade has my confidence as a brave and skillful officer and a true man."[43]

In one respect, Meade and the Army of the Potomac had at least lived up to Meade's July 4 message. They did succeed in driving Lee "from our soil."

Lincoln's displeasure over Meade's pursuit of Lee was soon replaced with a more immediate crisis. July 11 had been slated as the first day of the draft under the Conscription Act. All men between the ages of twenty and forty-five were ordered to register for the new draft, but there was a loophole. Anyone could be exempted if they either found a willing substitute or paid $300. Lincoln opposed the clause, but his argument had fallen on deaf ears in Congress. The draft, as Carl Sandburg noted, made the conflict "a rich man's war and a poor man's fight."[44]

Tensions simmered for two days, but on the thirteenth, "when less than two dozen names had been called," a mob of five hundred attacked the draft officer, destroyed the large selecting wheel and the conscription lists, and then torched the building. What the *New York Times* called "A Day of Infamy and Disgrace" turned into four days of lawbreaking and violence not seen before in the United States. Blacks were beaten, burned, or lynched by Irish immigrants, longshoremen, firemen, and Nativist gangs. An orphanage caring for Black children was burned and countless stores and homes looted. By the time Meade's assigned regiments arrived to establish order, over a thousand residents had been wounded or killed.[45]

In August, Lincoln summoned Meade to Washington for some fence-mending. Most of Lincoln's cabinet had never met him; Postmaster General Montgomery Blair knew Meade from their West Point days but they had not seen each other since. Meade "gave some details of the Battle of Gettysburg clearly and fluently," Welles noted. "I was as well or better pleased with him than I expected I should be." Meade was equally pleased. "The manner in which I was received and treated in Washington by all with whom I came in contact"—including Lincoln—"was certainly most gratifying to me," he wrote Margaret. "I really believe I have the confidence of all parties, and will continue to retain it, unless some disaster should overtake me." He returned to headquarters hoping "to look upon the future in the most favorable light."[46]

Lee's army, what was left of it, had been shattered at Gettysburg. "We had a nice time going into Pa.," one Virginian remarked, "but coming out was quite the contrary." He was one of the lucky ones: roughly one in three Confederates was among the killed, wounded, missing, or captured. "It is believed the enemy suffered severely," Lee earlier informed Davis, "but our own loss has not been light." Before leaving Williamsport, he learned that his son Rooney had been captured at Hickory Hill, while convalescing from his wound received at Brandy Station. "We must bear this additional affliction with fortitude & resignation," he wrote Mary.[47]

Once the army was south of the Rappahannock, Lee sent his assessments to Davis. While "the men are in good health and spirits," his needs were much like Meade's: shoes and clothing for the men and shoes for the horses. By the end of the month, the Southern newspapers that had printed rumors of victory had gotten the facts. The *Charleston Mercury* called Lee's invasion "foolish and disastrous." Southern politicians now felt bold enough to criticize Lee publicly. Alabama senator Clement C. Clay decried Lee's "utter want of generalship."[48]

The general who said on Seminary Ridge "This is all my fault" had already begun to change both his admission and his rhetoric upon leaving Gettysburg, starting with Mary. "You will have learned before this reaches you that our success at Gettysburg was not as great as reported," he wrote on July 12. To Davis he noted that "the Army of the Potomac had been thrown north of that river, the forces invading the coasts of North Carolina and Virginia diminished, their plan of the present campaign broken up," thereby keeping the fight out of Virginia for at least a few weeks. After Davis sent him the *Charleston Mercury* clipping, Lee made a subtle but firm defense. "No blame can be attached to the army for its failure to accomplish what was projected by me . . . I am alone to blame . . . [I]n my opinion [the army] achieved under the guidance of the Most High a general success, though it did not win a victory . . . I do not know what better course I could have pursued."[49]

But by August 8, Lee had had enough. After reflecting on the "discontent in the public journals," he offered his resignation:

> *No one is more aware than myself of my inability for the duties of my position. I cannot even accomplish what I myself desire. How can I fulfill the expectations of others? In addition I sensibly feel the growing failure of my bodily strength . . . a younger and abler man than myself can readily be attained.*[50]

Davis's answer to Lee's request was simple. "To ask me to substitute you by some one in my judgment more fit to command . . . is to demand an impossibility," he wrote. As unpopular as Davis was in the Confederacy, he was not about to remove the South's hero. Lee agreed to stay on.[51, 52]

Once in Richmond, Lee learned that Davis really wanted Lee to assume command of the western forces. The loss of Vicksburg was followed by General Braxton Bragg's being outmaneuvered by General William S. Rosecrans and forced to abandon Tennessee. Lee tactfully but sternly declined, citing a recent "heavy cold," an "attack of rheumatism," as well as lack of knowledge of the Army of the Tennessee and the geography. In truth, he wanted no part of this. Longstreet was not so averse. "I think it is time we had begun to do something in the west," he argued, and suggested sending "one corps of this army" to Tennessee. Taking one from Lee's army would have put an end to any offensive plans for Lee; Longstreet hoped the corps to head west would be his.[53]

It was. With Longstreet gone, Lee's army was down to 46,000 men. He had no choice but to play defense. "The enemy is aware of Longstreet's departure," he told Davis on September 23, and "Genl Meade is strengthening himself daily." He forebore telling Davis that his cold and rheumatism were likely severe angina, if not another coronary.[54]

———

From September into November, Lee and Meade engaged in a deadly game of poker with their soldiers as human chips, raising the stakes and calling each other's bluff, only to take turns folding. Several skirmishes and small battles were fought and two prospective major battles ended before both generals committed their full forces. At Bristoe Station on October 14, Meade's strong defensive line compelled Lee to withdraw. On November 26, Meade crossed the Rapidan, desperate to silence the wagging tongues in Washington. Over the next several days, both Meade and Lee failed to take advantage of opportunities. On November 30, an assault by 5th Corps (now led by General Warren) was called off at Mine Run; as at Williamsport and Fredericksburg, Lee's defenses were unassailable.[55]

Meade was acutely aware that Mine Run was probably his last chance to fight Lee before winter set in. "I shall always be astonished at the extraordinary moral courage of General Meade," one aide wrote, "which enabled him to order a retreat, when his knowledge, as an engineer and soldier, showed that an attack would be a blunder . . . [H]e had only to snap his fingers, and that night would probably have seen ten thousand wretched, mangled creatures, lying on those long slopes . . ." Meade was certain his decision not to sacrifice his soldiers pointlessly would result in his being relieved of command.[56]

The campaigns of the Army of Northern Virginia and the Army of the Potomac for 1863 were over. Both went into winter quarters not too far from where they had been a year earlier. That Christmas, thousands of families, in the North and South, had an empty chair at their table. But on the generals' maps, it looked as if nothing had changed, as if both armies had never been to Gettysburg.

As July melted into August, the most pressing issue for Gettysburg's citizens was the corpses of soldiers from both armies either buried in shallow graves or not buried at all. Army burial details made little dent in the growing number of corpses over three days.

Among the thousands of human bodies swelling under the scorching summer sun were thousands of dead horses. Within three days the stench must have been unbearable. No bandana or perfume or toilette water could overcome the reeking odor. Despite the summer heat and humidity, windows were nailed shut and doors closed; it was better to swelter indoors than to be constantly vomiting. "My clothes smell of death," one resident wrote.[57]

Pressure to do something fast came from local Pennsylvania politicians and those of other states, all wanting their fallen properly buried but balking at the expense of shipping so many coffins home. It fell to Pennsylvania governor Andrew Gregg Curtin and David Wills, a local lawyer with connections in Harrisburg, to produce a solution. Wills proposed a Soldiers' National Cemetery, to be placed at Cemetery Ridge between Taneytown Road and the Baltimore Pike. Governor Curtin approved, and Wills bought the land for $2,471.87. He then contacted horticulturalist William Saunders to design the layout. To oversee the exhumation, identification, and reburial of more than 3,300 bodies, Wills reached out to a contractor, Franklin W. Biesecker, whose winning bid was less than $1.75 per body. The trick for Biesecker was to find cheap enough labor that would allow him to get the job done and still make a profit.[58]

After the Battle of Gettysburg ended, Basil Biggs, a prominent member of the Black community in Gettysburg who had fled on a borrowed horse on July 1, returned to his tenant farm on Marsh Creek to find that the three days of bloody conflict had ruined him. The farmhouse was a makeshift hospital, the carpets, floors, and furniture soaked in blood. Walking his acreage, he found at least forty-five shallow graves, all for Confederate soldiers. His livestock was slaughtered and his barley and wheat crops destroyed. The forty-three-year-old man and his family had escaped Lee's army of slave hunters but not the consequences of their presence.[59]

Since childhood, Biggs had exhibited resilience in the face of adversity. Born to a free family in Carroll County, Maryland, in 1819, his mother died when he was four and he was hired out for thirteen years of hard labor. His mother left him $400, earmarked for education, but the boy never saw it. According to the obituary writer for the *Gettysburg*

Compiler after Biggs's death in 1906, "The only education he received was how to work with his hands." A photograph of him as an older man among his family shows a pensive person with a strong jawline and broad shoulders, his eyes looking away from the camera as if lost in thought or remembrance.[60]

By the time Biggs married Mary Jackson in 1843, he was a teamster with an uncanny knack for working with animals. His skills in animal husbandry prompted him to get work among the Carroll County farms as a veterinarian. He must have been good at it: horses, cows, and oxen were staples for a successful farm and not cheap to purchase.[61]

By 1858, Basil and Mary had five children. The Fugitive Slave Act was eight years old, and Biggs's reputation among the farmers and townsfolk meant nothing to the gangs of bounty hunters who rode in from other parts of Maryland or Virginia. That year Basil decided to take his family to Pennsylvania, a free state where they should have been safer.[62]

The move allowed Biggs's children to have what Biggs himself had been denied: a formal education. In Maryland, Black children were barred from all public schools. In Pennsylvania, Black children were allowed to attend public schools if there were no Black private schools in the community. By 1860, Biggs had hired a hand to help with the farming and maintained a thriving veterinary practice. He also used his farm as a way station for the Underground Railroad.

Now Biggs was just one more Gettysburg farmer ruined by the war. His claim for damages—from livestock and furnishings to eight tons of hay and shelves of jellies—came to $1,506. With no harvest, and with the animals of other farmers for miles around seized or eaten, Biggs faced ruin.[63]

Enter Franklin Biesecker. Knowing Biggs was a man of influence in the Black community, Biesecker subcontracted his services, giving him the authority to hire other African Americans and begin the Sisyphean task of mass exhumation and reburial. The work commenced on October 27, after Saunders's landscaping plan was laid out. Among the eight to ten men Biggs had on hand was thirteen-year-old Leander Warren, who with some friends had watered the horses of Union soldiers on July 1.[64]

Under Biggs's leadership, his crew developed a routine. In the morning the burial team picked up coffins at the train depot, loaded them on two wagons, and then went across the battlefield and backyards, searching for shallow graves. The cadavers were exhumed, inspected, and placed in a coffin. Once all the coffins were filled, Biggs and another driver hauled them to the new cemetery for burial. Those bodies initially buried deep enough or in clay could still be identified by a scar, an insignia, or letters or other documents. Those buried in shallow graves or sandy sediment were usually too decomposed. There was a telltale sign that indicated which side a soldier had fought on: Confederate uniforms were made of cotton; Union ones of wool.[65]

What these men went through emotionally, day after day, was never recorded. Whether they mentally blocked out what they were dealing with—whether they worked in grisly silence—is unknown. In just three weeks there were nearly 1,000 reburied soldiers in neat rows near the large stage constructed for the dedication scheduled for November 19. There were still 2,500 more to reinter; their remains were moved out of sight until the ceremony was over. Then Biggs and his detail would resume their work. It took four more months to complete.[66]

David Wills had hoped for an earlier dedication, but his handpicked speaker, the renowned orator Edward Everett, demurred. His speech would be a detailed recounting of the battle, and he needed more time for research and heroic anecdotes. Everett asked for, and got, November 19 as the dedication date. Lincoln received an invitation from Wills on November 2 inquiring whether the president would like to make a "few appropriate remarks." Lincoln accepted.[67]

The invitation extended was perfunctory and not an afterthought. It put Lincoln in a delicate position. Presidents usually were (and are) the principal speakers at events. Wills had picked the imposing Everett for a myriad of reasons. Everett had spent decades in public oratory, honing his skills first as a Unitarian pastor and then as a distinguished politician and diplomat; at age twenty-five he spoke at a U.S. Capitol service in the midst of debates resulting in the Missouri Compromise.

His theme? "Brethren, the Time Is Short." Everett's speechifying was a combination of language, stentorian tones, a still-handsome visage at sixty-nine, and great—if subtle—acting. He was a born crowd-pleaser.[68]

Lincoln gave no thought at all to surpassing Everett's flamboyancy. He knew his speech should serve as a coda to Everett's stem-winder. For him, as always, the quality of his remarks was far more important than the quantity. He had excelled at this for decades. On the surface, the trip was a political opportunity to meet with Northern governors and other politicians whose support he would need in the presidential election just a year away. But he also saw his trip to Gettysburg as a chance to articulate his evolving vision—not of his policies but of his beliefs. And, following Everett, he must do so as succinctly as possible.[69]

After Lincoln's death, Mary told Lincoln's old law partner, Billy Herndon, that while her husband "never joined a Church . . . still, as I believe, he was a religious man by nature." Now, in these days before leaving for Gettysburg, she noticed he had become even more reflective than usual: "He first seemed to think about the subject [of religion] when our boy Willie died, and then more than ever about the time he went to Gettysburg."

As he worked on his speech, the president told Ward Hill Lamon that "he greatly feared that he would not be able to acquit himself with credit, much less to fill the measure of public expectation." Lincoln did not want his audience to just *hear* what he said; he wanted them to *think* about what he said.[70]

He was familiar with Western history's great speeches: Pericles's eulogy over the dead Athenian warriors, the Sermon on the Mount, the orations of Antony and Henry V from Shakespeare, the insightful remarks of Edmund Burke, and the declamations of Webster and Clay. He may also have recalled Sam Wilkeson's moving words from the battlefield in the *New York Times*.

How was Lincoln to sum up the reason for this event and combine it with a lifetime of incidents and experiences that shaped who he now was: the shackled droves of enslaved Blacks approaching the auction block in New Orleans; his speeches opposing the Mexican-American War in Congress; his debates with Stephen Douglas across Illinois; his speech at Cooper Union; his election to the presidency, which had brought forth this Civil War; his Emancipation Proclamation; the long-awaited Union victories at Gettysburg and Vicksburg; and the inclusion of Black soldiers joining the fight for the preservation of the Union—and for their own equality as American citizens?

And, perhaps, the words from his first major speech at the Young Men's Lyceum, a quarter century ago: "If destruction be our lot, we ourselves must be its author and finisher." How to combine all this—resolve all this—in a speech to last only a few minutes?[71]

On the evening of the seventeenth, Lincoln invited William Saunders to the White House. Saunders showed Lincoln the plans for the cemetery and reported on its progress. "He took much interest in it, and asked about the surroundings, about Culp's Hill, Round Top, etc., and seemed familiar with the topography of the place although he had never been there," Saunders marveled, gratified that Lincoln seemed much pleased with the arrangement of the graves.[72]

Lincoln's son Tad was extremely sick, and Mary had not wanted her husband to go anywhere; the slightest head cold or fall brought their dead son Willie to mind for both parents. But Lincoln felt he had to go and was willing to incur his wife's wrath. For Lincoln, this event was too important, historically as well as politically. Edwin Stanton had arranged for Lincoln to leave Washington at 6 a.m. on the nineteenth and depart Gettysburg that same evening at 6 p.m. Lincoln refused. "I do not like this arrangement," he told Stanton, comparing it to "a mere breathless running of the gauntlet." He insisted that he leave the day before the ceremony and return the day after, negating the slightest chance of a delay or missing the event altogether. Stanton complied.[73]

Around noon on November 18, Lincoln boarded a four-car Baltimore & Ohio train, accompanied by Secretary of State Seward, aides John Nicolay and John Hay, and a free Black named William Henry Johnson, who had been with Lincoln as his valet since his Springfield years. A brass band took over one of the cars; journalists did not report if they spent the trip rehearsing.[74]

He had "found time to write about half the speech," he told one friend before departing Washington. Accounts abound that he wrote it during the train ride, using the top of his stovepipe hat as a desk, or on an envelope. John Nicolay later attested that Lincoln did not write a word on the train, just enjoyed the random conversations with his companions, spiked, of course, with his anecdotes. Nicolay, writing thirty years later, presented what might be considered the most accurate version:

> *There is no decisive record of when Mr. Lincoln wrote the first sentences of his address. He probably followed his usual habit in such matters, using great deliberation in arranging his thoughts, and molding his phrases mentally, waiting to reduce them to writing until they had taken satisfactory form.*

There was outside pressure on Lincoln for such precaution in this case, with the invitation specifying his being limited to "a few appropriate remarks." Brevity in speech and writing was one of Lincoln's marked characteristics, but in this instance there existed two other motives: one, the knowledge that Everett would easily speak over an hour; the other, the want of opportunity even to think leisurely about what he might desire to say.[75]

Boarding the train, Lincoln was preoccupied and quiet, but as the train got farther away from Washington, he grew more relaxed. To the delight of his fellow passengers, he proceeded to entertain them with yarns and jokes; at one stop, a small girl handed him a bouquet of flowers and received a kiss in appreciation. Stopping at Hanover, Lincoln stepped out on the platform for a brief but humorous word with the crowd. "Well, you had the rebels here last summer," he said, asking, "Did you fight them any?"[76]

The train pulled into Gettysburg at 5 p.m. "All the hotels as well as the private houses were filled to overflowing," the *New York Times* reported. Lincoln's decision to change traveling arrangements proved wise: Governor Curtin had arranged for a special train to take him, six other governors, and various dignitaries from Harrisburg that day at 2 p.m. Due to breakdowns and delays, their thirty-mile trip took nine hours; they arrived in Gettysburg after 11 p.m., having missed an elaborate dinner at David Wills's home.[77]

Wills and Everett met Lincoln at the station and escorted him to the Wills house. (Lincoln's entourage "were entertained elsewhere," Nicolay wrote.) Lincoln's dinner was interrupted by a welcome telegram from Stanton: "Mrs. Lincoln informed me that your son is better this evening." Since the afternoon the streets had been teeming with visitors and townsfolk intermingling with regimental bands and glee clubs. A large crowd gathered outside Wills's home and began calling for the president to come out and speak to them.[78]

Lincoln eventually obliged, thanking them for coming by and citing "several substantial reasons" for not making any remarks that evening. "The most substantial of these is that I have no speech to make," he said, drawing a laugh from the crowd. "In my position it is somewhat important that I should not say foolish things." At this a heckler added, "If you can help it." Lincoln saw the barb as a chance to keep the crowd with him and exit at the same time: "It very often happens that the only way to help is to say nothing at all," he replied, and the crowd laughed with him as he went back inside.[79]

The following morning Nicolay found Lincoln in his room, where Lincoln "finished his address during the short leisure he could utilize for this purpose before being called to take his place in the procession . . ."[80]

Before breakfast, Lincoln went with Seward to visit the battlefields by carriage, while Lamon, placed in charge of security, assigned horses to each dignitary to ride over to the cemetery. It was a beautiful day, warm by November standards. The procession began at 11 a.m., an hour later than scheduled, Lincoln being one of the reasons. Mounting a chestnut-colored horse, Lincoln, "attired in black with white gauntlets upon his hands," was immediately "besieged by a crowd eager to shake hands with him." Around his stovepipe hat was a crepe ribbon in memory of his son Willie. After a cordon of Lamon's handpicked marshals separated the crowd from the president, everyone in the procession either rode a horse or walked to the cemetery.[81]

It took fifteen minutes for the procession to reach the ground. A crowd of 9,000 formed a semicircular ring before the platform and took on an air of dignified silence; this event was more funeral than celebration. Lincoln received a military salute before sitting in the front row on the platform, next to Seward and Everett. After what some found a tedious prayer by U.S. House of Representatives chaplain Thomas H. Stockton and perfunctory remarks by several governors, Everett rose to speak. For two hours he held sway over the crowd, reciting a rousing, emotional account of history from ancient Greece to Cromwell and the Founding Fathers and a detailed dramatic account of the three-day battle, including both praise for Meade and empathy for his failed pursuit after the battle:

> *The struggle of the last two days resembled, in many respects, the battle of Waterloo; and if, in the evening of the third day, General Meade, like the Duke of Wellington, had had the assistance of a powerful auxiliary army to take up the pursuit, the rout of the Rebels would have been as complete as that of Napoleon.*[82]

In his acclaimed *Lincoln at Gettysburg: The Words That Remade America*, Garry Wills wrote that "Lincoln no doubt watched closely how the audience responded to passages that absolved Meade of blame for letting Lee escape."[83]

At one point during Everett's oration a spectator watched as Lincoln "took out his steel-bowed spectacles, put them on his nose, took two pages of manuscript from his pocket, looked them over and put them back." After two hours, Everett finished with a flourish: "In the glorious annals of our common country, there will be no brighter page than that which relates to THE BATTLES OF GETTYSBURG." The crowd politely applauded. Lincoln stood and shook Everett's hand and congratulated him. After a solemn hymn, Lincoln rose again to speak. "The President was greeted with most enthusiastic cheering," one journalist noted. When order was restored, he approached the front of the platform.[84]

George Gitt was fifteen years old in 1863; before the procession arrived at the cemetery, he had hidden himself under the platform, emerging from underneath as the dignitaries took their seats "and stationed myself before my hero." Now, with the hymn concluded, he watched in awe as "the flutter and motion of the crowd ceased the moment the President was on his feet. Such was the quiet that his footfalls,

I remember very distinctly, woke echoes. And with the creaking of the boards, it was as if some one were walking through the hallways of an empty house."[85]

Reaching the small table for each speaker's use, Lincoln paused to pull out his spectacles and then held the two sheets of paper that bore his remarks. Speaking slowly and clearly, his high-pitched voice and Kentucky accent carried his words over the crowd:

> *Four score and seven years ago our fathers brought forth on this continent a new nation, conceived in Liberty, and dedicated to the proposition that all men are created equal.*
>
> *Now we are engaged in a great civil war, testing whether that nation, or any nation so conceived, and so dedicated, can long endure. We are met on a great battlefield of that war. We have come to dedicate a portion of that field as a final resting place for those who here gave their lives that that nation might live. It is altogether fitting and proper that we should do this.*
>
> *But in a larger sense, we can not dedicate—we can not consecrate—we can not hallow—this ground. The brave men, living and dead, who struggled here, have consecrated it, far above our poor power to add or detract. The world will little note, nor long remember, what we say here, but it can never forget what they did here. It is for us the living, rather, to be dedicated here to the unfinished work which they who fought here, have, thus far, so nobly advanced. It is rather for us to be here dedicated to the great task remaining before us—, that from these honored dead we take increased devotion to that cause for which they here gave the last full measure of devotion— that we here highly resolve that these dead shall not have died in vain— that this nation, under God, shall have a new birth of freedom—and that government of the people, by the people, for the people, shall not perish from the earth.*[86]

His speech had been interrupted by applause five times, but its brevity, and how it closed, left Lincoln standing in uncomfortable silence. John R. Young, a Philadelphia reporter, paused writing his shorthand and leaned across the aisle. "Is that all?" he whispered.

"Yes," Lincoln replied, "for the present."[87]

— TWELVE —

AFTERMATH

In his *Recollections*, Lamon wrote that, upon concluding his speech, Lincoln expressed "deep regret that he had not prepared it with greater care. He said to me on the stand, immediately after concluding the speech: 'Lamon, that speech won't *scour*! It is a flat failure, and the people are disappointed.'" With the phrase "won't *scour*," Lincoln referred to the failure of a dull plow; he felt his remarks would not be well regarded. John Hay, despite a hangover from a long night of socializing and imbibing with fellow Republicans, thought otherwise. He thought Lincoln spoke "in a firm, free way, with more grace than was his wont."[1]

But no one understood Lincoln's words better than the one-armed Union captain in attendance. When Lincoln stated that the world "can never forget what they did here," the veteran "broke down and buried his head in his handkerchief. With tears still in his eyes, he said quietly to no one and everyone, 'God Almighty Bless Abraham Lincoln.'"[2]

That night, Lincoln boarded his special car, and the train pulled out of the Gettysburg station to cheers. "No trains were permitted to leave town until after the President's departure, and thousands of citizens were unable to leave for their homes" until the next morning—a security precaution Americans would get used to and endure whenever a president came to call.[3]

On the ride home, Lincoln began feeling poorly. By the time the train reached Washington he was deathly ill; he had contracted small-pox. Upon learning he was contagious, he dryly remarked, "Now I have something I can give everybody." His old valet, William Henry Johnson, was not so lucky, dying from the disease two months later.[4]

Lamon's recollection of Lincoln's disappointment was offset by the reports many newspapermen wired to their editors. "Mr. Lincoln sat down amid a scene of wild and lengthened excitement," the *Philadelphia Inquirer*'s reporter noted. Most Northern papers shared the *Inquirer*'s praise. The *Springfield* (MA) *Republican* said Lincoln's "little speech" was "a perfect gem . . . Turn back and read it over, it will repay study as a model speech. Strong feelings and a large brain are its parents." Horace Greeley thought that "our national literature contains no finer gem than that little speech." Even Everett was awed by what he heard, telling Lincoln, "I should be glad, if I could flatter myself that I came as near to the central idea of the occasion in two hours, as you did in two minutes."[5]

Northern Democratic-leaning papers reported otherwise. "We pass over the silly remarks of the President; for the credit of the Nation we are willing that the veil of oblivion shall be dropped over them and that they shall no more be repeated or thought of," the *Harrisburg Patriot and Union* decreed. The *Chicago Times* easily deduced what Lincoln had done and was appalled by it, declaring that Gettysburg's dead Union soldiers "were men possessing too much self-respect to declare that negroes were their equals, or were entitled to equal privileges."[6]

The predominantly positive response to Lincoln's address was one of several pieces of good news for Lincoln in November. The elections in the North had gone very well for the Republicans, and although Meade and Lee had come to a stalemate in Virginia, Ulysses S. Grant, now commanding the western armies, won victories at Lookout Mountain and Missionary Ridge, driving Bragg's army out of Tennessee.[7]

Lincoln was just back from Gettysburg when he got a letter from Michigan senator and Radical Republican Zachariah Chandler, a constant critic of Lincoln with a reputation even a neutral publication described as "openly partisan and despotic." Chandler wanted to make sure Lincoln took a "bold *radical* campaign" in light of Republican and

Union successes, and rid himself of the moderate likes of William Seward. "You are today Master of the situation if you stand firm . . . Conservatives & traitors," Chandler threatened, "are buried together." Lincoln, ailing and exhausted, answered in peevish politeness: "I hope to 'stand firm' enough to not go backward," he told Chandler, "and yet not go forward fast enough to wreck the country's cause."[8]

Eighteen sixty-four gave Lincoln plenty of chances to prove he would stand firm when necessary and move toward ending the war. He brought Ulysses Grant east, making him the first lieutenant general since George Washington, putting him in charge of all Union armies. Grant turned over operations in the western theater to Major General William Tecumseh Sherman, while Grant stayed with the Army of the Potomac. While Meade remained officially the army's commanding officer, it would be Grant in actual charge, as the Army of the Potomac and its old foe, the Army of Northern Virginia, slugged it out over the remainder of the war.

Lincoln was forever battling the Radicals in Congress over Reconstruction policies. They countered his 1863 "Proclamation of Amnesty and Reconstruction" with the far harsher Wade-Davis Reconstruction Bill, which Lincoln killed with a pocket veto. In August, the Democrats nominated George McClellan as their candidate for president, demanding "that immediate efforts be made for a cessation of hostilities [so that] peace may be restored"—meaning a complete rejection of Lincoln's actions and policies, including the Emancipation Proclamation.[9]

The pressure to abandon his goals of reuniting the states and ending slavery was enormous. "There have been men who have proposed to me to return to slavery the black warriors of Port Hudson & Olustee to their masters to conciliate the South," he said. "I should be damned in time & in eternity for so doing." He remained adamant that "no human power can subdue this rebellion without using the Emancipation as I have done." But by the end of August, he told his cabinet: "It seems exceedingly probable that this Administration will not be re-elected."[10]

But Sherman and his army took care of that. McClellan had been the Democratic candidate for three days when Sherman sent a wire to

Lincoln's second home, the telegraph office: "Atlanta is ours, and fairly won." Atlanta—along with Admiral Farragut's victory in Mobile Bay, Alabama, and Major General Philip Sheridan's successes in the Shenandoah Valley—gave the commander in chief a luster that not only surpassed the days of Gettysburg and Vicksburg but won him a resounding victory. The Democrats were confident that "Little Mac's" old army would vote for him; the soldiers voted overwhelmingly for Lincoln.[11]

His first term closed with his skillful passage of the Thirteenth Amendment, ending slavery forever in the United States. On Inauguration Day 1865, he equated his address at Gettysburg with his eloquent hopes for a postwar America:

With Malice towards none, with charity for all, with firmness in the right, as God gives us to see the right, let us strive on to finish the work we are in; to bind up the nation's wounds; to care for him who shall have borne the battle, and for his widow, and his orphan—to do all which may achieve and cherish a just and a lasting peace among ourselves, and with all nations.[12]

Lincoln knew that Lee's surrender to Grant at Appomattox would surely be followed by Joe Johnston's to Sherman. On Good Friday, April 14, he had breakfast with his son Robert, who presented him with a photograph of Robert E. Lee. "It is a good face," Lincoln said. Elizabeth Keckley, Mary's dressmaker, later remarked that Lincoln's "face was more cheerful than I had seen for a long while." A cabinet meeting followed, with Grant as a guest. The men discussed Reconstruction policies in detail; Lincoln whimsically "found it providential that this great rebellion was crushed just as Congress had adjourned." That night he went into Ford's Theatre and history.[13]

After lying in state in the East Room of the White House and in the Capitol rotunda, Lincoln's coffin was placed on a funeral train draped in black, with a large photograph of the president mounted above the locomotive's cowcatcher. For two weeks, the nine-car train wound its way from the Eastern seaboard to Springfield, Illinois, letting Americans pay homage to their fallen leader. In Philadelphia, a hearse pulled by eight black horses brought Lincoln's remains from the Broad Street train station to Independence Hall, to lie in state for two days.[14]

Four years earlier, on Washington's Birthday, Lincoln had raised the flag of the United States in front of Independence Hall. "I never had a feeling politically that did not spring from the sentiment embodied in the Declaration of Independence," he said to a cheering crowd that cold February day. Now, passing a flag at half-staff, thousands of mourning citizens waited to enter the East Wing of the hall, where the Declaration had been proposed, debated, passed, and signed, to pay their final respects to the sixteenth president of the United States.[15]

Abraham Lincoln sailed through the challenges of his public life, tacking back and forth through the hardships, triumphs, tragedies, and joys with the Declaration of Independence as his North Star. And, as president, he had done the same for his country, navigating it through the very worst of storms. Walt Whitman was right: the ship of state never had—and may never have—a better captain.

Robert E. Lee turned fifty-seven in January 1864. The previous year, begun with so much hope after Fredericksburg, had seen Lee's greatest strategic triumph at Chancellorsville followed by his greatest strategic defeat at Gettysburg. He was in better health but not by much; though his heart was weaker, "I am pretty well & comfortable enough in my tent," he assured Mary.[16]

The winter months were hard on his soldiers. They were shoeless and starving. "If we were supplied with tools and materials, from one-third to one-half of the army could be shod by the system of brigade shoemakers," he complained. When he learned that many other Confederate armies, most not currently in harm's way, were regularly well fed, he grew livid: "I have been mortified to find that when any scarcity existed this was the only army in which it is found necessary to reduce the rations," he bluntly informed Commissary General Lucius Northrop. When he failed to receive what his men needed, he appealed once again to their patriotism. "Soldiers! You tread with no unequal step the road by which your fathers marched through suffering, privations and blood to independence," he declared, asking them not to forget "their high resolve to be free."[17]

Yet, despite his own poor health and the deprivations of his soldiers, Lee was more than ready to cross the Potomac again. "We are not in a condition, & never have been, in my opinion, to invade the enemy's country with a prospect of permanent benefit. But we can alarm & embarrass him to some extent," he told Davis, hoping a third time would be the charm. Three months later, as the weather warmed and the Army of the Potomac grew by the thousands, he wanted to "move right against the enemy on the Rappahannock."[18]

Technically, the Army of the Potomac was still under Meade's command. In reality, the commander was the new lieutenant general in charge of all Union armies. For the rest of the war, Ulysses S. Grant spent day and night with the Army of the Potomac, and his orders to Meade were simple: "Lee's army will be your objective point," Grant stated. "Wherever Lee goes, there you will go also." By May, the long-awaited major battle between the Army of Northern Virginia and the Army of the Potomac was about to take place in the same area where both armies had fought a year earlier: the Wilderness around Chancellorsville.[19]

Over the next six weeks, Lee's 66,000 men more than held their own against the 120,000 soldiers in Grant and Meade's army. In previous years, the Battles of the Wilderness, Spotsylvania Court House, the North Anna, and particularly Cold Harbor would have resulted in Confederate victories against any of the Union Army's commanders before Gettysburg. But despite significantly higher casualties than Lee's forces suffered, Grant kept ordering Meade to march his army south and east until they reached the James River and Petersburg. "If he gets there," Lee told Jubal Early in May, "it will just be a mere question of time."[20]

Situated on the Appomattox River, Petersburg lay twenty-three miles south of Richmond. Its population of 18,000 was evenly divided between white and Black residents; one-third of the latter were free. It was the railway hub of Virginia. Grant beat Lee there, but a staunch defense by the troops in Petersburg bought enough time for Lee's army to arrive. The siege was a long one—over nine months—during which each army extended its line of trenches, often just yards apart. Petersburg was a precursor to World War I. Confederate trenches seemed unassailable.[21]

At 4:40 on July 30, a deafening explosion blasted a giant hole in the Confederate trenches on the east defensive line. A regiment of Union miners from Pennsylvania had dug a tunnel 510 feet long beneath the rebel trenches and detonated 8,000 pounds of gunpowder. When the billowing smoke and clouds of dirt, debris, and bodies settled, there was a five-hundred-foot gap in the line and a hole two hundred feet by seventy feet and twenty-five feet deep—a man-made crater. Lee rode immediately to the scene, directing reinforcements along the perimeter of the hole. Instead of attacking around the crater, Union troops charged into it, including two divisions of U.S. Colored Troops. As Lee watched, Confederates poured deadly musket and mortar fire into the hapless assailants. Lee rode off before most of the surviving Union soldiers surrendered; many of the Black troops were presumed executed. Union casualties came to roughly 4,400.[22]

Trench warfare continued into autumn, as did the issue of Black soldiers. In October, Lee and Grant exchanged a series of messages regarding a prisoner exchange. Lee looked to "alleviating the sufferings of our soldiers" and offered an exchange "man for man." Grant replied that "among those lost by the armies operating against Richmond were a number of colored troops." Before further negotiations commenced on the subject, Grant asked if Lee intended "delivering these men the same as white soldiers." Lee said he "intended to include all captured soldiers of the United States of whatever nation and color under [his] control."[23]

However, there was a stipulation. "Deserters from our service and negroes belonging to our citizens are not considered subjects of exchange and were not included in my proposition." Grant's reply summed up the difference between the two armies, the two governments, and the two countries:

I have to state that the Government is bound to secure all persons received into her armies the rights due to soldiers. This being denied by you in the

persons of such men as have escaped from Southern masters induces me to
decline making the exchanges you ask.[24]

As 1865 began, things looked bleak across the Confederacy. Atlanta had fallen; in November, Sherman had marched to the sea, giving Lincoln a "Christmas present" of captured Savannah; and Lee's dwindling army did not have enough soldiers to man the trenches of Petersburg much longer. Lee, unknowingly taking Lincoln's advice to "think anew and act anew," raised the question of Black troops wearing Confederate butternut. "We must decide whether slavery is extinguished by our enemies, and the slaves used against us, or use them ourselves at the risk of the effects which may be produced upon our social institutions." When asked his opinion, Lee came right to the point: "My opinion is that we should employ them without delay."

Lee believed the "long habits of obedience and subordination" would make good soldiers out of male slaves and suggested rewarding Black recruits with a bounty and "a well-digested plan of gradual and general emancipation"; after all, "we should not expect slaves to fight for prospective freedom when they can secure it by going to the enemy." Not only would it "greatly increase our military strength," but "it would disappoint the hopes which our enemies base upon our exhaustion, deprive them in a great measure of the aid they now derive from black troops, and thus throw the burden of the war upon their own."

Lee's idea met with praise in some circles, skepticism in others, and denunciation by many. For him, emancipation for enslaved men was a pragmatic solution, not a moral step forward. As historian Allen C. Guelzo put it, Lee believed this "a time for slaves to fight in defense of their own enslavement."[25]

At this point it was too late. By February, he had less than 45,000 men to Grant's 110,000. The siege could only be broken by the Army of the Potomac. "I think Gen. Grant will move against us soon," he confided to Mary. An "alarming number of desertions" left "a very bad effect on the troops that remain." By this time only the most loyal soldiers were left—far too few to even barely man the miles of trenches— and their loyalty was not to the Confederacy but to their general. When

Lee resigned his commission in the U.S. Army in April 1861, he had foreseen what the outcome of a civil war would be. Now, in March 1865, he was living it.[26, 27]

At 4 a.m. on April 1, an all-out assault on the rebel lines by the Army of the Potomac began the final fighting between the two armies. The following day A. P. Hill was killed, shot through the heart. Learning of this brought Lee to tears. "He is now at rest," he sorrowfully said, "and we who are left are the ones to suffer." Hours later he wired Davis: "I think it will be necessary to move tonight." Once darkness fell, campfires were lit and bands began playing to cloak the sound of a stealthy retreat as the Army of Northern Virginia abandoned their trenches, marching west along the Appomattox River and leaving both Petersburg and Richmond to the Army of the Potomac. Among the Virginians left in Petersburg was Lee's daughter Agnes.[28]

At dawn on April 9, the rebels attacked the Yankees in a short battle near Appomattox Station in one last effort to break away that ended in a Confederate retreat. It was Lee's last fight. April 9 was Palm Sunday. In churches north and south that morning, worshippers heard the words of St. Matthew: "Put up again thy sword into his place: for they that take the sword will perish by the sword." Lee was finally ready to do just that.[29]

That morning Lee asked Grant for "an interview in accordance with the offer" Grant had made regarding terms of surrender. Lee's note was given to Meade, who immediately granted a truce. Lee, Colonel Charles Marshall, and orderly Joshua O. Johns rode into the village of Appomattox Court House, where Wilmer McLean offered Lee his stately brick home as a meeting place. A crowd of Union soldiers and town residents began gathering in the yard. Lee went inside; a half hour later, Grant and an entourage of aides and generals followed.[30]

Lee wore his simple uniform, with a sash and his sheathed sword; Grant arrived in his own plain and mud-spattered uniform. Grant opened the conversation recollecting that they had met during the Mexican War; Lee remembered they had but could not recall Grant's features. After some uncomfortable small talk, Lee brought them to the subject at hand. Grant discussed his generous terms and Lee asked him to put them in writing. Reaching into his pocket, Lee pulled out his wire-rimmed spectacles and scanned over the articles of agreement. After some discussion clarifying certain phrases, Lee said, "This will have the best possible effect on the men."

After Grant offered rations for Lee's troops, Lee and his companions departed. As he mounted Traveller, Grant and his officers doffed their hats. Lee did the same. "We all appreciated the sadness that overwhelmed him," one officer recalled. Grant wanted no raucous celebrations, no artillery salutes. There had been enough gunfire by the Army of the Potomac.[31]

When the rebel soldiers saw Lee and his two companions heading toward them, they rushed forward to greet him. They loved him, and would have died for him as so many of their comrades had done. The next day he sent a message praising their "unsurpassed courage and fortitude," and including the generous terms of surrender he had agreed to, and his prayer "that a Merciful God will extend to you His blessing and protection."[32]

At the end of the war, Lee faced crises on three fronts. The first was domestic. He had lost a daughter during the war; one son had been seriously wounded, while another was taken prisoner. By 1865, Mary was confined to a wheelchair. To Robert's chagrin and Mary's everlasting resentment, their home, Arlington, was no longer an estate but an army cemetery, some of the graves dug within a few feet of the house. Legally, Robert and Mary still owned Arlington, but they would be dead for years before the U.S. government finally made a settlement.

The second was his role in the war. On June 7, Lee was indicted by the federal government for treason. He turned to Grant for assistance. He believed that he and other officers of the Army of Northern Virginia were protected by the U.S. government under the terms of their surrender. Grant agreed and declared to President Andrew Johnson that he would resign in protest if Johnson failed to honor Grant's word. Johnson backed down.[33]

The third was how to spend his final years. The solution came from an unthought-of source: a financially strapped college in Lexington, Virginia. Its board of trustees offered Lee the presidency of the school, named Washington College. They proposed a salary of $1,500 a year and housing. Lee accepted. In September, he saddled Traveller and made the four-day trip alone. "The scenery was beautiful all the way," he wrote Mary.[34]

He exceedingly hoped this might literally be a new beginning. "Life is indeed gliding away and I have nothing of good to show for mine that is past," he wrote Mary. "I pray I may be spared to accomplish something for the benefit of mankind and the honour of God." For Lee, Washington College was exactly that: the last five years of his life were as different as they could have been from the first fifty-eight. Robert Jr. marveled at the president's house. Lee had furnished it with everything from "a handsomely carved piano" and even "carpets rescued from Arlington . . . We were all very grateful and happy—glad to get home— the only one we had had [after] four long years."[35]

Lee expanded the curriculum, increased the faculty, embarked on the construction of housing for the faculty and a campus chapel, and increased the endowment with his fundraising. He met every student and learned their foibles as well as their talents. When Lee warned a problem student that his lack of effort guaranteed failure, the boy shot back, "But, General, you were a failure." Lee's remark surprised him: "Yes," Lee replied, "but let us hope you will be more fortunate than I." When the college faculty and students marched with the cadets of the Virginia Military Institute, Lee quietly but deliberately stayed out of step.[36, 37]

As the 1860s ended, Lee's health steadily declined. In April 1870, he and Agnes went to Georgia, stopping at Cumberland Island to pay respects to Light Horse Harry's grave. Lee's condition worsened: "The pain in my chest, along the heart bone, is ever present." He returned to Savannah, where a large crowd welcomed him. The trip taxed his stamina. "I wish I were back," he cryptically wrote Mary.[38, 39]

His health worsened further over the summer; a visit by train to Baltimore to see a doctor sapped his strength. "I never recollect having suffered so much," he confided to Mary. The doctor's diagnosis was "rheumatic excitement." He told Lee to "guard against cold" and "try lemon juice and watch the effect." He was back in Lexington for the start of the school year.[40]

On September 28, Lee returned to the house in the rain from a vestry meeting. "You have kept us waiting for a long time," Mary gently rebuked, and offered him a cup of tea. Lee stood at the head of the table and did not say a word, eventually sitting in his chair ramrod straight "with a sublime air of resignation," not answering his wife or daughters. They hurriedly sent for doctors and put him to bed. It is likely he had suffered a stroke. He lingered for two weeks, unwilling or unable to answer any entreaties. "The silence was awful!" Mildred recalled. On October 12, Mary was in her wheelchair, holding his hand, when he passed away.

Legend has it that Lee, like Stonewall Jackson, reached out to A. P. Hill right before he died, ordering him to "come up" and then quietly giving the old order to break camp: "Strike the tent."[41]

As 1864 began, Meade found himself fighting a war on two fronts. Despite his frustration at not getting a chance to fight Lee before wintertime, 1863 had ended on a hopeful note. While Republican newspapers called for the return of Hooker after Mine Run and the difficulties with drafted soldiers and substitutes, the Army of the Potomac's winter camp at Culpeper was relatively quiet. Meade was buoyed by letters from recuperating generals Gibbon and Hancock, the latter warmly and simply telling Meade: "I have faith in you."[42]

The rumors that Meade would be replaced soon ended. Colonel Theodore Lyman, the naturalist Meade had met in his lighthouse-building days, was impressed that Meade "is in excellent spirits and cracks a great many jokes and tells stories. You can't tell how different he is when he has no movement on his mind, for then he is like a firework, always going bang at someone, and nobody knows who is going to catch it next . . ." Meade spent his birthday, December 31, with Lincoln, discussing one of Meade's pet peeves: the constant pardons of soldiers sentenced to death for desertion and other criminal offenses sent to Meade by Lincoln. Meade's suggestion to commute death sentences to hard labor at Fort Jefferson, in the Dry Tortugas, was approved. The next day he and Margaret attended the annual New Year's Day reception at the White House; Meade took delight in "how affable" Stanton was to Margaret. "A bright day ushers in the year," Gideon Welles recorded in his diary.[43]

On March 4, Meade returned to Washington to discuss his plan for reorganizing the Army of the Potomac. He wanted to maintain the size of the army but with just three corps. Upon arriving, he found the streets abuzz over "grave charges by Sickles and Doubleday" made to the Joint Committee on the Conduct of the War regarding Meade during the battle at Gettysburg.[44]

By this time the committee was dominated by chairman Benjamin Wade and Zachariah Chandler. Both were also suspicious of many of the West Point generals, often questioning their loyalty, although they were highly supportive of Hooker, hoping they could help restore both "Fighting Joe's" reputation and command. After their treatment by Meade at Gettysburg, Hooker's cronies Sickles and Butterfield were happy to help. And Chandler had his own axe to grind, as he was still seething at Meade's refusal to renew his oath at Chandler's behest, in 1861.[45]

The committee interviewed Sickles on February 25, and he gave them more than they had hoped for. Under oath, Sickles testified that Meade had wanted to retreat from Gettysburg as soon as he arrived; that he issued no orders to Sickles on July 2; that Sickles had saved the day by his move a half mile east of the fishhook line; and that removing Hooker three days before the battle was "a misfortune to the army" as "the rank and file had entire confidence in General Hooker."[46]

Doubleday followed Sickles on March 1, still resentful of being relieved of commanding 1st Corps after John Reynolds's death. He testified that Meade removed him because he wanted to put his friends in command and place the blame on Doubleday and Oliver Howard had the battle been lost. Knowing his audience, Doubleday delivered a wound: "No man who is an anti-slavery man or an anti-McClellan man can expect decent treatment in that army as at present constituted."

Doubleday had damned Meade twice without using his name. The legend that Doubleday invented baseball has been laid to rest, but Doubleday was quite inventive this day.[47]

A third officer, Brigadier General Albion P. Howe—a man with a reputation for quarreling with his superiors—testified that Meade was among those "who do not like the way the negro question is handled," insisting that "copperheadism" was "the root of the matter" with Meade and other generals tainted by the Radical Republicans for their connection with McClellan.[48]

That was enough for Wade and Chandler, who demanded Lincoln and Stanton remove Meade from command. When Lincoln asked whom they would recommend to replace Meade, they replied that "they would be content with General Hooker." Furthermore, "it would be their duty to make the testimony public." In the Senate chamber, Chandler's friend and fellow Radical Morton S. Wilkinson of Minnesota accused Meade of ordering a retreat on July 1. Such was the firestorm Meade found himself in upon his arrival in Washington. From Brandy Station, Colonel Charles Wainwright called the witnesses "a pretty team!—Rascality and Stupidity."[49, 50]

Meade arrived at the Capitol determined to defend his reputation. Ushered into the ornate Senate Committee on Territories Room, he found only Wade and a clerk present. Wade began by telling Meade that the committee was not looking to besmirch Meade's conduct and character but merely to collect testimony and documents to tell the story of the war. It was a lie, and Meade bought it. Wade was "very civil," he assured Margaret. Meade then gave a three-hour "succinct account" of the battle and its aftermath. In fact, it was *too* succinct; Meade, not wanting "to cast any censure on General Sickles," stated that Sickles's technically insubordinate refusal to place his troops where Meade had directed was "what [Sickles] thought was for the best," adding, "but I differed with him in judgment." Had the committee's investigation been an actual battle, Meade had just left his defensive line as open as Sickles had done to Meade's on July 2.

Meade got his first clue to how naive he had been at his very next stop, meeting Stanton at the War Department. The secretary informed

Meade of the plot to replace him with Hooker. Stanton assured him "there was no chance of their succeeding." Meade tried to put this "melancholy state of affairs behind him," he told Margaret, but it stung that "persons like Sickles and Doubleday can, by distorting and twisting facts, and giving a false coloring, induce the press and public . . . to take away the character of a man who up to that time had stood high in their estimation." Still, "the truth will slowly and surely be made known." Meade returned to headquarters.[51]

Back in Washington, Wade and Chandler took testimony from Generals Pleasonton and Birney, the former claiming he had urged Meade "to order a general advance on the enemy" after the repulse of Pickett's charge. Birney testified that he had wanted to attack Lee's rear guard but received no orders. He called Meade's actions after Gettysburg "a succession of useless advances and rapid retreats."[52]

But the most damaging salvo came in the March 12 issue of the *New York Herald*, in which the writer, under the pseudonym "Historicus," laid waste to Meade's reputation and the truth about Gettysburg, declaring, "My only motive is to vindicate history, do honor to the fallen, and justice to the survivors when unfairly impeached."

If not a product of Sickles himself, the lengthy diatribe had been written by someone in possession of Sickles's testimony and with a similar enmity toward Meade. The *Herald*'s readers learned how General Sickles saw the necessity of occupying the elevated ground; that Sickles could wait no longer for orders from General Meade; that he went to secure that vital position; that his great aim was to prevent the enemy from getting between his flank and the Round Top; and that, had General Meade been more copious in his report and less restricted as to his own important acts, the necessity for this communication would not have existed.[53]

An apoplectic Meade demanded a court of inquiry "that the whole subject may be thoroughly investigated and the truth made known." If that was denied, Meade wanted the "authority to make use of and publish such official documents as in my judgment are necessary for my defense."[54]

Learning of Meade's counterattack, Sickles wrote Chandler to subpoena Dan Butterfield, certain his old crony and drinking pal would testify against Meade. He did, telling the committee among other things that Meade's first task upon arriving at Gettysburg was "to prepare an order to withdraw the army from that position." By this time Generals Warren, Humphreys, Hancock, Gibbon, Hunt, and Sedgwick had come forward. Some spoke solidly on Meade's behalf; others, including Hancock and Hunt, were more evenhanded.

Warren told the truth: that Sickles had left Little Round Top unoccupied. ("I do not think General Sickles would be a good man to fight an independent battle," he added.) Hancock subtly testified that Sickles's disregard for Meade's orders to defend the Union line to Hancock's left was "disadvantageous to us." Gibbon stated that Meade's orders of July 2 were very clear. ("I understood [Sickles's] position to be on the left of our line extending . . . in the direction of Round Top hill on our left flank.") Humphreys declared that Meade's original placement of Sickles's 3rd Corps was "undoubtedly" correct and that "we should have suffered very severely" had Meade decided to attack Lee at Williamsport.[55]

Meade made two more appearances before the committee, bringing documents from other officers backing up his accounts of what had occurred at Gettysburg. He denied ever wanting to retreat from Gettysburg, saying that "it was my desire to receive an attack of the enemy, and fight a defensive rather than an offensive battle," believing "my chances of success were greater." He was right, but his use of the word "defensive," taken out of context, was used against him by politician and general alike. A second attack by "Historicus" in the *Herald* on April 4 derided Meade's "inglorious failure" for not capturing Lee's army.[56]

Meade's request for a court of inquiry was denied. Halleck told Meade that he, too, believed that the Historicus articles were written or dictated by Sickles, but Meade could not prove he was the author, and Sickles's "controlling or giving color to the New York press" meant that

Meade could not win this fight. "Ignore him entirely," Halleck advised: Sickles's attacks would not "injure your military operation in the slightest way."[57]

Meade strongly disagreed; after all, he was the one being libeled, not Halleck. He believed Sickles might at least have "the manliness" to acknowledge that he had written the articles—or name the man who had. Meade did not want "such slanders as have been circulated to pass unnoticed." His reply to Halleck was answered by their commander in chief, who had been slandered himself, beyond belief, for years:

> It is quite natural that you should feel some sensibility on the subject; yet I am not impressed, nor do I think the country is impressed, with the belief that your honor demands, or the public interest demands, such an inquiry. The country knows that at all events you have done good service . . . [I]t is much better for you to be engaged in trying to do more, than to be diverted, as you necessarily would be, by a court of inquiry.
>
> Yours truly,
> A. Lincoln.[58]

"The main point of my request has been avoided," Meade told Margaret, but "I am bound to be satisfied." As at Gettysburg, he would take the high ground, while Sickles, other generals, and politicians like Wade and Chandler would continue doing otherwise as far as Meade was concerned.[59]

Meade returned to camp in April, happy to be out and away from Washington politics. He was even happier with Grant, who "agrees so well with me in his views, I cannot but be rejoiced at his arrival," he told Margaret. While "my share of the credit will be less" during the coming campaign, Meade wanted to "continue quietly to discharge my duties, heartily cooperating with him and under him." In turn, Grant was impressed with Meade. During the Battle of Spotsylvania he wrote Stanton, recommending that Meade and William Tecumseh Sherman be promoted to major generals in the regular army. "General Meade has more than met my most sanguine expectations," he noted, adding, "I would not like to see one of these promotions without seeing both."[60]

But as the Overland Campaign continued, human nature took its course, starting with both generals' staffs. Grant's came east with a string of victories under their belts, while the Army of the Potomac had Gettysburg and little else. Grant's aides looked down on their peers and "talked and laughed flippantly about Lee and his army." Wait and see, Theodore Lyman thought. Soon the field generals' personalities came into play.[61]

As the campaign progressed, from the Wilderness to Cold Harbor, Meade's authority lessened. The Overland Campaign was Grant's strategy, and the soaring casualty lists made Meade recollect his decision not to fight at Williamsport and Mine Run. "I feel a satisfaction in knowing my record is clear . . . In every instance that we have attacked the enemy in an entrenched position, we have failed, except in the case of Hancock's attack at Spotsylvania . . . I think Grant has had his eyes opened, and is willing to admit now Virginia and Lee's army is not Tennessee and Bragg's army."[62]

During the fighting at Cold Harbor, Meade read a short article in the *Philadelphia Inquirer* by reporter Edward Cropsey that lauded Meade's role in the Overland Campaign thus far: "He is as much the commander of the Army of the Potomac as he ever was . . . He is entitled to great credit for the magnificent movements of the army since we left Brandy [Station] . . . [I]n a word, he commands the army." But then Cropsey recounted how Meade "was on the point of committing a great blunder unwittingly . . . Grant assumed the responsibility and we are still 'On to Richmond.'"[63]

An irate Meade accosted Cropsey. What was this "great blunder" and who was his source? Cropsey told Meade that "the talk of the camp" was that he had pleaded with Grant to recross the Rapidan after the Battle of the Wilderness. Meade called that "a base and wicked lie." Meade expelled Cropsey from the camp, but not before placing him backward on a mule with the sign "libeler of the press" hung around his neck and paraded through the camp to "The Rogue's March."

Meade learned afterward that Cropsey's article had been reprinted across the country. The remaining camp reporters got even: unless the story would put Meade in a bad light, they refused to mention him at all in their papers. Over the next year, Grant, Sherman, Hancock, Sheridan, and Custer saw their names emblazoned on the front pages and later in the history books.[64]

Trouble with Meade's subordinates in the first days before Petersburg resulted in trouble with Grant afterward. When Gouverneur Warren hesitated on a planned assault on the Confederate line, Meade reprimanded him on his failure to obey orders. An issue with John Gibbon over his division's defeat at Reams' Station frayed their two-decade friendship.

But the worst issue was with Ambrose Burnside and the Crater catastrophe. Meade opposed it from the first but reluctantly authorized it. The 4th Division from Burnside's 9th Corps, consisting of Black troops, had been specifically trained to lead the assault after the explosion. Meade, certain that Radicals and abolitionists would believe they were sent into a suicide mission if the risky endeavor failed, countermanded Burnside and ordered that a white division lead the attack. The disastrous results ended with Burnside and Meade publicly bickering over who was to blame. Once again the Joint Committee on the Conduct of the War led a full investigation. While Meade received a degree of blame for the ill-fated action, the weight of it went to Burnside, who was relieved of his command. Meade was blamed for not allowing the Black troops to lead the assault and for taking over the "entire direction" of the plan after it was in place—a political accusation with no merit. It had lingering effects for Meade, who was finally promoted to major general in the regular army only after that honor had gone to Sherman, Sheridan, and Hancock.[65]

When Grant proposed to consolidate the Union forces in the Shenandoah Valley under one commander, he informed Meade that he had submitted the latter's name as the new army's commander. Meade said he was ready to accept any orders given to him; this was a chance to get out from under Grant's shadow. But there was not a Gibbon, Hancock, or Humphreys among the generals he would be commanding, and so he declined. But in September, when Grant offered the post to

Sheridan—and Sheridan accepted—Meade reconsidered. He regretted that "this opportunity of distinction was denied me" but had only himself to blame. "My time I suppose had passed," he glumly recorded, "and I must now content myself with doing my duty unnoticed."[66]

Seven months later, when Lee met Grant at the McLean House, Meade was moving his army east of Appomattox Court House, about to attack the remnants of Lee's remaining force when he received word that Lee had surrendered. "We gave three cheers and then more for General Meade," Colonel Lyman recalled:

> *Such a scene followed as I can never see again. The soldiers rushed, perfectly crazy, to the roadside . . . threw up their hats and hopped madly up and down! . . . The noise of the cheering was such that my very ears rang. And there was General Meade galloping about and waving his cap with the best of them!*[67]

Had Grant given Meade the choice of the McLean House or that roadside, Meade would have happily stayed with his men, sharing the news they—and their comrades no longer present—had fought and prayed for. "His name was yelled and screamed in a way I never dreamt any man's could be," his son told Margaret. Peace allowed him to visit with old comrades from another war an eternity ago. Meeting Meade, Lee joshed, "What are you doing with all that grey in your beard?" Meade's answer matched Lee's question: "You have to answer for most of it!"[68]

The postwar years were not kind to George Meade. Feted with grand parties in Philadelphia, a prominent place in the Army of the Potomac's Grand Review in Washington, and an honorary degree from Harvard, Meade was deemed a hero in his hometown, if not the rest of the country. When Reconstruction began, he took command of the Military Division of the Atlantic, based in Philadelphia. His report after an inspection tour of Virginia and the Carolinas stressed that "the great change in the labor question"—a tacit reference to slavery—"would require time for both races to realize and conform to." He advocated "military control" to "compel mutual justice from both parties," a tactfully worded phrase that cloaked his reluctance to use Black troops to maintain order, as they would face openly hostile Southerners.[69]

One challenge he faced did not come from the South but up north when armed Irish Americans from the Fenian Brotherhood—an Irish American organization dedicated to Ireland's independence—raided into Canada from New York. With a detachment of troops, Meade intercepted them returning across the Niagara River and convinced them that returning home was better than imprisonment. Secretary of War Stanton extolled Meade's "calm, patient and firm method of dealing with this matter so as to avoid any possible collision or bloodshed . . ."[70]

In August 1866, Meade succeeded his old roommate from the Mexican War, John Pope, to run the Department of the South, headquartered in Atlanta. Pope was seen by white Georgians as a Radical. Meade was known to be otherwise. One Southern paper in an article titled "God Bless Andrew Johnson!" claimed that in Meade "we may hope to escape from Negro bondage; with him it is not a crime to be white." Meade hoped to be judicious and fair and was also cautious. He replaced one Georgia mayor who was thwarting the investigation into the murder of a white Georgian working with Black delegates at the Georgia convention, but the killers, presumed Ku Klux Klan members, went free. In the town of Camilla in southwest Georgia, a political meeting ended in a riot; nine Black men were murdered. When Meade learned of it, he immediately led troops to Camilla but arrived too late.[71]

Although handed "almost unlimited powers" and "determined from the first to ignore all partisan considerations," Meade was tired of what he called "the animosity of both sides, without having the benefit of the sympathy of either." One last political injury remained: upon his inauguration as president, Grant made Sherman general in charge of the army and then passed over Meade and made Sheridan lieutenant general. Meade took the snub extremely hard, telling Margaret, "It is useless to repine what cannot be remedied." One week later, Meade ended his assignment commanding the Department of the South; Sherman was returning him to the Department of the Atlantic. Meade was coming home.[72]

Philadelphia made him a commissioner of Fairmount Park. Residents would see him riding Old Baldy, often with one of his daughters. He planned bridle paths and clearings as assiduously as he had designed lighthouses, or the fishhook at Gettysburg. He was a cofounder of the Lincoln Institution, which cared for orphans and widows of the war, and attended soldiers' reunions when his health permitted. Bouts of pneumonia and the increasing pains from old wounds—particularly those received at the Battle of Glendale—began to take their final toll. On October 31, 1872, he and Margaret went out for their daily walk when he complained about severe pains in his side. A doctor was summoned; it was the onset of another attack of pneumonia. It was his last; six days later, he quietly said, "I am about crossing a beautiful wide river, and the opposite shore is coming nearer and nearer." He died with his family around him.[73]

"The Dead Chieftain," as the *Philadelphia Inquirer* called him, was buried on November 11 with full military honors. Grant and Sherman attended the service at St. Mark's Episcopal Church; over 50,000 citizens lined the streets as over a thousand troops marched behind the hearse, a saddled, riderless Old Baldy taking part. A steamboat, the *Undine*, draped in black, carried the coffin across the Schuylkill River to the Laurel Hill Cemetery.[74]

Nine years earlier, Meade had taken command of an army yet to win a decisive battle against an opponent who had never lost one. Since then, not only his generalship had been called into question but also his integrity, the result of which cast him into the shadows of history. His funeral was the largest yet seen in Philadelphia, but the rest of the country, including the Northern states, were well on their way to forgetting him.

By the time of Meade's death, the prediction he had made to Margaret five months after his dramatic victory had become reality: "I suppose after awhile it will be discovered that I was not at Gettysburg at all."[75]

One-legged Dan Sickles outlived Lincoln, Lee, and Meade by decades. He had returned to Congress after the war and served under the Grant administration as minister to Spain. Mark Twain paid him a visit in January 1906. "Sickles is eighty-one years old now . . . [W]e sat there in the general's presence, listening to his monotonous talk—it was about himself, and is always about himself . . . [T]he general valued his lost leg above the one that is left." Twain was convinced, if given the chance, "he would part with the one that he has got."[76]

He was now obsessed with becoming a lieutenant general, lobbying for that with the passion of Historicus. His version of the Battle of Gettysburg was being taught to a fourth generation of admirers. But his carefully burnished false claims and attacks on the long-dead George Meade were still mixed with scandals: his stint on the New York Monuments Commission ended with accusations of embezzlement; rumors of yet another affair and his mishandling of relatives' monies shocked the public, but not enough to keep on winning the Battle of Gettysburg.[77]

One thing kept him going: a statue of himself on the battlefield. As a congressman, he was a driving force in preserving the battlefield as a national monument. By 1913, he knew his days were numbered but was determined to return to Gettysburg for the fiftieth anniversary of the battle in July. He arrived in his wheelchair with a small entourage.

The heat was oppressive. Three veterans died; the *New York Times* called for "closing all saloons" and banning the sale of liquor during the festivities. 3rd Corps veterans told him how they had seen him being carried off the field fifty years before.[78]

The story soon spread that Sickles was with Joe Twitchell, the Excelsior Brigade chaplain and both Sickles's and Twain's close friend. Some wrote that Twitchell consoled Sickles over the lack of a statue; others say a lady told Sickles it was a shame that, on a battlefield clustered with statues, there was no monument to Sickles. He is said to have uttered that "the whole damned field" was his monument. He died on May 3, 1914.

There is still no statue of Sickles at Gettysburg.

Black men from Gettysburg were among the 180,000 who fought in Black regiments in the last two years of the war. Their heroism largely went unnoticed. Some died at the Battle of Olustee in Florida and at the Crater in Petersburg. Those veterans who survived the war and passed away years later were buried in "colored" graveyards. The Black community in Gettysburg founded "the Sons of Good Will," who cared for the old and sick in the community, made sure the dead were properly honored and buried, and held annual celebrations on New Year's— "Emancipation Day." Basil Biggs served as treasurer.[79]

In 1865, Biggs bought a farm on Cemetery Hill. Once he and the family settled in he began renovations. A grove of trees on his new property seemed a practical source for fences, new buildings, even firewood to keep Mary and his children warm in the winter. As he began sawing away John Bachelder, the town historian, hastened up the hill to beg Biggs to spare the trees. They were the "copse of trees" Lee had pointed to as Pickett's goal: the trees that survived the endless volleys and cannonades on July third. Biggs left the trees standing.[80]

Over the decades, the battlefield has gone through substantial changes. Most recently, the Gettysburg National Tower, which dwarfed the nearby statue of Meade, was demolished in 2000; the legendary Electric Map, its white light telling the audience "You are here," was removed, but the equally famous Cyclorama has been restored. The success of the book *The Killer Angels* by Michael Shaara and the movie *Gettysburg* increased interest in Joshua Lawrence Chamberlain, James Longstreet, Lewis Armistead, and Winfield Scott Hancock. The concerted effort to return the battlefield to the way it looked in 1863 is a constant work in progress. While ghost tours remain popular, some ideas never get off the ground: the souvenir John Wilkes Booth bobblehead dolls did not have a very long shelf life.

Most significant has been the change in emphasis from the decades-long theme "High Watermark" to the recent "A New Birth of Freedom." In making that change, the park's leadership, park rangers, and tour guides have taken the focus from looking backward to a "Lost Cause" to the words Lincoln spoke that could only have *been* spoken because Meade's army had won. The park, like the Civil War, remains what the Reverend Theodore Hesburgh called it: "unfinished business."[81]

The battlefield has changed; Lincoln's words have not. The ebb and flow of American history gets Americans closer to his "new birth of freedom" and at times takes Americans further away. Dr. Barbara Fields said it best in Ken Burns's documentary: "The Civil War is still going on, it's still being fought, and regrettably it can still be lost." There have been moments in American history since Lincoln's time where "the better angels of our nature" have been sent into exile, when the pendulum of history swings too far toward a past that was never as good as "the mystic chords of memory" recall, forsaking the present and the fleeting opportunities it gives Americans to better their country and the rest of the world.

In 1838, a month before his twenty-ninth birthday, Lincoln foresaw those periodic challenges. "At what point then is the approach of danger to be expected? I answer, if it ever reach us, it must spring up amongst us. It cannot come from abroad. If destruction be our lot, we must ourselves be its author and finisher. As a nation of freemen, we must live through all time, or die by suicide."[82]

Twenty-five years later, at Gettysburg, Robert E. Lee and his army came very close to a victory that would have reinforced the belief of white supremacy and might have succeeded in forever splitting the United States in two. There is irony in the fact that Lee was stopped by an army led by a man who loved building lighthouses. George Gordon Meade's victory allowed Abraham Lincoln to give a short but perfect speech, welding Thomas Jefferson's proposition "that all men are created equal" with Lincoln's "new birth of freedom."

Each generation of Americans is given "a new birth of freedom" and the opportunity and responsibility of living up to Lincoln's challenge. If that sounds too hard for individuals, one can always remember Lincoln's collective and confident solution that a government of, by, and for the people offers its citizens.

"The remedy," Lincoln said, "is in our hands."

Our hands.

— ACKNOWLEDGMENTS —

I first encountered the Civil War in 1956 in Wildwood, New Jersey. My dad took my cousin Jay and me to see Walt Disney's *The Great Locomotive Chase*, starring Fess Parker as Union spy James J. Andrews. If memory serves, the film ends with Parker in jail, about to be hanged. I had last seen Fess in 1955 as Davy Crockett on television, swinging his rifle "Old Betsy" at a host of actors playing Mexican soldiers at the Alamo. It was Fess Parker who taught me, as Gordon Lightfoot later stated, that "Heroes . . . often fail."

Five years later, Dad took me over Easter vacation on a whirlwind tour of the Virginia battlefields and then to Gettysburg. My mother and two brothers came along—not sure they enjoyed it as much as I did. My dad also introduced me to the wonderful books of Bruce Catton and Carl Sandburg's *Lincoln* works.

In high school I discovered my grandmother's family Bible, from which came Elizabeth Curtis's moving poem that opens this book. It was not until researching this project that I learned that Cpl. Richard J. Curtis is buried at Fredericksburg, thanks to retired Sgt. Ted (Hal) Myers, who has dedicated his retirement years to traveling to battlefields and cemeteries, where he discovers the resting places of thousands of veterans from American wars. Thanks, Sergeant Myers.

This is my third book with the Penguin family, and my second with Dutton. As before, my thanks go to president Ivan Held and publisher John Parsley. Thanks also to text designer Laura Corless, production editor Janice Barral, marketer Caroline Payne, publicist Hannah Poole, and assistant editor for audio Katie Lakina. For the third time, my thanks to Steve Meditz, associate director of art/design, for coming up with a cover so good that once more I can only hope the text lives up to his design. Further thanks go to the renowned editor Roger Labrie for his unstinting efforts and spot-on suggestions, and to copy editor David Chesanow, who ably picked up where Roger left off. Thanks are also due to Penguin Random House audio producer Nick Martorelli and narrator Vas Eli for their terrific work on this book's audio version. And my gratitude to Peter Brigaitis and Marie Nuchols for their tackling a pretty challenging index.

All of thus was coordinated by associate editor David Howe, whose organizational skills were truly taxed (I hope he hasn't aged too greatly). And to Messrs. Held, Parsley, and Howe, my appreciation for their patience with this project.

I first met Lieutenant Colonel Carmen Bucci when he was six years old as he was drawing planes, tanks, and soldiers. After graduating from the United States Military Academy, he kindly gave me *West Point Atlas for the American Civil War* (or "Dirt" as the cadets call it) and *The 1862 Army Officer's Pocket Companion*. For this project, he pointed me in the right direction more than once to find sources that were invaluable to this undertaking. Many thanks, sir.

Two great historians from Temple University have kept me on the right course for years: Dr. James Hilty and Dr. Gregory J. Urwin. Jim's been teaching me history since 1970; Greg's been tag-teaming with him since 2003. Both gentlemen are accomplished authors themselves and have read all or parts of all four manuscripts over the years. Even Job would've lost patience with me by now. I owe them a debt that can never be repaid.

Greg kindly connected me with Temple University's CENFAD (Center for the Study of Force and Diplomacy); its director, Dr. Alan McPherson; and former Thomas J. Davis fellow Joseph Edward Johnson. At CENFAD's "All Roads Lead to Gettysburg" seminar, I had the honor of discussing the battle and its consequences with a host of experts, including PhD candidate Rachel Barbara Nicholas, Dr. Peter Miele, Dr. Jill Ogline Titus, and Dr. Jennifer M. Murray, whose forthcoming book, *Meade at War*, will be the first in-depth biography of him in decades, and will be his definitive biography for years to come.

Other old friends continue to assist, no matter what the topic. Craig Symonds, so kind with his advice for years on the American Navies, walked with me every step on this project, thanks to his books *Gettysburg: A Battlefield Atlas* and *American Heritage History of the Battle of Gettysburg*. Scott Harris, executive director of the museums of the University of Mary Washington, shared his Civil War knowledge and a wealth of sources that helped immeasurably. Dan Hinchen at the Massachusetts Historical Society, J. J. Ahern at the University of Pennsylvania, and Bruce Kirby at the Library of Congress, all kept me on course. Thanks also to staff members at the New York Historical Society, the New York Public Library, and the Virginia Historical Society.

And I always find helping hands at the Historical Society of Pennsylvania, where emeritus librarian Lee Arnold is both a dear friend and valuable source of information, as is Chris Damiani, who got me through some tough post-Covid times with the Society's vast Civil War–era treasure trove, especially the Meade Family Papers. I made a new friend in Dr. Anthony "Andy" Waskie, president of the General Meade Society, who helped find an array of documents and photographs. Thanks also to Mary Procopio, archivist and curator at the Adams County Historical Society, particularly regarding background on Basil Biggs.

Derrick Pratt with the Erie Canal Museum explained the watery route George Meade and family took to reach Detroit. The prolific author Eric Jay Dolin was an engaging conversationalist, sharing his extensive knowledge of lighthouses over dinner at Philadelphia's Sansom Street Oyster House (if you want a nice challenge, climb the winding stairs of the Absecon Lighthouse, designed by George Meade, near Atlantic City). John Heckman, "The Tattooed Historian," happily shared his vast array of Gettysburg lore and knowledge. Presidential historian Bill Haldeman, a PhD still on "the front nine" career-wise, was a fine sounding board on Lincoln and Gettysburg. I am also indebted to Dr. William C. "Jack" Davis, who has written at length over the decades on the Civil War, Lincoln, and Lee. His ear and advice are greatly appreciated.

My thanks to Bob and Robin Stiles, with fond memories of sailing Cheetah Cats in our younger days. Now they share their passion for our history as Revolutionary War reenactors and have attended countless presentations over the years. And thanks also to Bob's brother, Bill, and his wife, Kelly, who took me aboard their boat to see Brandywine Shoal Lighthouse one raw November morning.

Philadelphia Inquirer columnist Jenice Armstrong is a dear friend and excellent writer who often serves as our city's social conscience. A graduate of Howard University (founded by Union general Oliver Otis Howard), Jenice was a wonderful help with the text and sources of this book. She is a living embodiment of Frederick Douglass's exhortation: "Agitate! Agitate! Agitate!"

I owe special thanks to Brent Howard, who edited the last two books for me, and is now embarking on a new adventure in his publishing career. A true friend as well as a great editor, he always inspired me to do . . . better.

No one, in any field, can have a finer agent and advocate than Jim Donovan. An award-winning writer himself, he is both a good listener and benevolent taskmaster, empathetic and exact. These are just four reasons why I call him "Coach," and count him as one of the best friends I've ever had.

My niece, Kim Haemmerle, was an immense help in searching for more information on our ancestor Elizabeth Curtis. Once again, my son, Ted, an acclaimed artist whose work has appeared around the world in print, television, and film, provided the maps for the Gettysburg campaign. And once again, my daughter, Courtney, was always there for the right turn of phrase and sharing her twenty-first-century technological knowledge whenever her twentieth-century father couldn't fix his own PC.

Finally, there's Cyd, our in-house editor and grammarian. Words cannot adequately describe these last fifty-five years. No one has ever had a better companion to walk through life with.

To all of the above, my thanks. The merits of this book are shared among you; its errors are mine alone.

—ABBREVIATIONS KEY—

B&L: *Battles and Leaders of the Civil War*

CCL: Charles Carter Lee

CW: *The Collected Works of Abraham Lincoln*

CWDBD: *Civil War Day by Day*

CWPGBM: *Civil War Papers of George B. McClellan*

FO: Founders Online

GGM: George Gordon Meade

HI: *Herndon's Informants*

HL: *Herndon's Lincoln*

HSP: Historical Society of Pennsylvania

JCCW: Joint Committee on the Conduct of the War

L&L: *Life and Letters of George Gordon Meade*

LDBD: *Lincoln Day by Day*

LFDA: Lee Family Digital Archive

LFP: Lee Family Papers

LOC: Library of Congress

MCL: Mary Anna Randolph Custis Lee (Mrs. Robert E. Lee)

MFP: Meade Family Papers

MM: Margaretta "Margaret" Meade (Mrs. George Meade)

NA: National Archives

NRHP: National Register of Historic Places

OR: *War of the Rebellion*

PMHB: *Pennsylvania Magazine of History and Biography*

REL: Robert Edward Lee

SHSP: *Southern Historical Society Papers*

SSL: Sydney Smith Lee

USMA: United States Military Academy Library and Archives

UTA: University of Texas at Arlington

UVA: University of Virginia

VHS: Virginia Historical Society

VMHB: *Virginia Magazine of History and Biography*

VMHC: Virginia Museum of History and Culture

WHH: William Henry Herndon

ZT: Zachary Taylor

— NOTES —

FOREWORD

1. *The Holy Bible, Containing the Old and New Testaments, Together with the Apocrypha* (Philadelphia: John E. Potter, late 1850s), property of the author; "John E. Potter and Company," Timothy Shay Arthur website, http://t.s.arthur.com.
2. "26th Pennsylvania Regiment," Pennsylvania Volunteers of the Civil War website, www.pa-roots.com.
3. William C. Davis, *Lincoln's Men: How President Lincoln Became Father to an Army and a Nation* (New York: Touchstone, 1999), 38; Claire Prechtel-Kluskens, "A Reasonable Degree of Promptitude," National Archives (hereafter NA), *Prologue Magazine* 42, no. 1 (Spring 2010), www.archives.gov/publications/prologue/2010/spring/civilwarpension.html.
4. Tom Wheeler, *Mr. Lincoln's T-Mails: How Abraham Lincoln Used the Telegraph to Win the Civil War* (New York: Collins, 2006), 14, 110, 116–18.
5. Don E. Fehrenbacher, ed., *Lincoln: Speeches and Writing 1859–1865* (New York: The Library of America, 1989), vol. 2, 411–12, to Joseph Hooker, 1/26/63; Roy Basler, ed. *The Collected Works of Abraham Lincoln*, 8 vols. plus index (hereafter *CW*) (New Brunswick, NJ: Rutgers University Press, 1953), VI, to Joseph Hooker, 5/6/63, 12:30 a.m., and fn1.
6. Noah Brooks, *Washington, D.C. in Lincoln's Time* (New York: Century Company, 1894), 61.
7. Fehrenbacher, *Lincoln*, 453–54, to Joseph Hooker, 6/10/63; Wheeler, *Mr. Lincoln's T-Mails*, 118.
8. Clifford Dowdey and Louis H. Manarin, eds., *The Wartime Correspondences of Robert E. Lee* (Boston: Little, Brown, 1961), to General Samuel Cooper: Battle Report of Chancellorsville Campaign, 9/23/63, 458–72; Edward B. Coddington, *The Gettysburg Campaign: A Study in Command* (New York: Touchstone, 1997), 5–7; James McPherson, *Battle Cry of Freedom: The Civil War Era* (New York: Oxford University Press, 1988), 646–47; Allen C. Guelzo, *Gettysburg: The Last Invasion* (New York: First Vintage Books, 2013), 18–22.
9. Dowdey, 482, to James Seddon, 5/10/63; 497–98, to Seddon, 5/30/63; 507–9, to Jefferson Davis, 6/10/63.

10. *Lincoln*, 395, Annual Message to Congress, 12/1/61; E. B. Long with Barbara Long, *The Civil War Day by Day: An Almanac* (hereafter *CWDBD*) (Philadelphia: Da Capo Press; New York: Doubleday, 1985), 70–71, 5/6/63 entry; Doris Kearns Goodwin, *Team of Rivals: The Political Genius of Abraham Lincoln* (New York: Simon & Schuster, 2005), 363–64, 532.
11. Allen C. Guelzo, *Robert E. Lee: A Life* (New York: Alfred E. Knopf, 2021), 292.
12. Charles F. Benjamin, "Hooker's Appointment and Removal," *Century Magazine* 33 (November 1886): 106–11; Richard A. Sauers, *Gettysburg: The Meade-Sickles Controversy* (Washington, D.C.: Brassey's, 2003), 5.
13. Constance McLaughlin Green, *Washington, vol. 1, Village and Capital, 1800–1878* (Princeton, NJ: Princeton University Press, 1962), 242–46; Edna M. Colman, *Seventy-Five Years of White House Gossip: From Washington to Lincoln* (New York: Doubleday, Page, 1925), 271–73.
14. Captain George Gordon Meade (ret.), ed., *The Life and Letters of George Gordon Meade, Major General, United States Army* (hereafter *L&L*), 2 vols. (New York: Charles Scribner's Sons, 1913), vol. 2, 12–13, George Gordon Meade (hereafter GGM) to Margaret Meade (hereafter MM), 6/29/63.
15. *L&L*, vol. 2, 12–13.
16. *L&L*, vol. 2, 13.
17. *L&L*, vol. 2, 11–12, GGM to MM, 6/29/63; Freeman Cleaves, *Meade of Gettysburg* (Norman: University of Oklahoma Press, 1960), 123–24.
18. *L&L*, vol. 2, 10–12, Orders; GGM to Halleck, 6/28/63.
19. *L&L*, vol. 2, 12–13, GGM to MM, 6/29/63.

ONE: SON OF THE PRAIRIE

1. *CW* I, 1.
2. *CW* I, 455–56, to Solomon Lincoln, 3/6/48.
3. Fehrenbacher, *Lincoln*, vol. 1, 177–78; Fehrenbacher, *Lincoln*, vol 1, 106–8, to Jesse W. Fell ("Enclosing Autobiography"), 12/20/59.
4. David S. Reynolds, *Abe: Abraham Lincoln in His Times* (New York: Penguin Press, 2020), 19–24.
5. Reynolds, 24–25; John Amos Johnson, "Pre-Steamboat Navigation on the Lower Mississippi" (PhD diss., Louisiana State University, 1963), 116–27, 292.
6. Carl Sandburg, *Abraham Lincoln: The Prairie Years, and the War Years* (New York: Harcourt, Brace, 1954), 4.
7. Sandburg, 4–7; Reynolds, 26–27.
8. *Lincoln*, vol. 2, 106–8.
9. *Lincoln*, vol. 1, 160–67, "Autobiography Written for Campaign," June 1860.
10. Reynolds, 26–28; Tim McGrath, *James Monroe: A Life* (New York: Dutton, 2020), 60.
11. *Lincoln*, vol. 1, 160–67; Reynolds, 26–27; Sandburg, 9.

12. *CW* IV, 60–67, "Autobiography Written for John L. Scripps," ca. 6/60; Fehrenbacher, *Lincoln*, vol. 1; Reynolds, 29.

13. *Lincoln*, 161.

14. *Lincoln*, 161; Doris Kearns Goodwin, *Team of Rivals: The Political Genius of Abraham Lincoln* (New York: Simon & Schuster, 2005), 47–48; Reynolds, 29; Sandburg, 11–12; Noah Brooks, *Abraham Lincoln, and the Downfall of American Slavery* (New York: G. P. Putnam's Sons, 1894), 31; Allen Walker Read, ed., *Funk & Wagnalls New International Dictionary of the English Language* (Garden City, NY: 1987), 808.

15. *CW* I, "The Bear Hunt," before February 28, 1847.

16. *Lincoln*, vol. 2, 161; Reynolds, 30.

17. Reynolds, 31.

18. Reynolds, 34; Goodwin, 53.

19. *CW* IV, 48–49, remarks to the Republican State Convention, Decatur, IL, 5/9/60; "Learn the Skill of Rail-Splitting," *Mother Earth News* (online); Richard Lawrence Miller, *Lincoln and His World: The Early Years, Birth to Illinois Legislature* (Mechanicsburg, PA: Stackpole Books, 2006), 98.

20. *Lincoln*, vol. 1, 107, to Jesse W. Fell ("Enclosing Autobiography"), 12/20/59; Reynolds, 15–17; Douglas L. Wilson and Rodney O. Davis, eds., *Herndon's Informants: Letters, Interviews, and Statements About Abraham Lincoln* (hereafter *HI*) (Chicago: University of Illinois Press, 1998), 107–8, Sarah Bush Lincoln (William Henry Herndon—hereafter WHH—interview), 9/8/65.

21. Reynolds, 47.

22. Reynolds, 47, 87; William Henry Herndon and Jesse William Weik, *Herndon's Lincoln: The True Story of a Great Life* (hereafter *HL*) (Springfield, IL: Herndon's Lincoln Pub. Co., 1889), vol. 1, 107–8.

23. *HI*, 111–15, Nathaniel Grigsby (WHH interview), 9/12/65.

24. *HI*, 111–15, Nathaniel Grigsby (WHH interview), 9/12/65; Richard Campanella, *Lincoln in New Orleans: The 1828–1831 Flatboat Voyages and Their Place in History* (Lafayette: University of Louisiana at Lafayette Press, 2010), 32–33.

25. Johnson, 112–14; Reynolds, 88.

26. Johnson, 116–27, 292; Josephine E. Phillips, "Flatboating on the Great Thoroughfare," *Historical and Philosophical Society of Ohio*, bulletin 5, no. 2 (June 1947): 21, "Flatboat Reminiscences," Captain Miles A. Stacy.

27. Johnson, 122–23; Ron Fisher, John Hess, et al. *Into the Wilderness* (Washington, D.C.: National Geographic Society, 1978), 91; Mark Twain, *Life on the Mississippi* (Boston: James R. Osgood, 1883), 21.

28. Johnson, 162–71.

29. Johnson, 202–21; Sandburg, 19.

30. Johnson, 298–99.

31. Johnson, 296–97.

32. *HL*, vol. 1, "Autobiography," 162.

33. Johnson, 200; Reynolds, 89.

34. William C. Davis, *The Coming Fury: The Battle of New Orleans and the Rebirth of America* (New York: Caliber, 2019), 5–7; Sandburg, 19.
35. Quote from Miller, 107.
36. *HL*, vol. 1, Herndon, 162; Reynolds, 88–89.
37. *HL*, vol. 1, 162.
38. Reynolds, 92.
39. Reynolds, 93–94; Eleanor Atkinson, "The Winter of the Deep Snow," in *Transactions of the Illinois State Historical Society for the Year 1909* (Springfield: Illinois State Historical Society, 1909), 47–53.
40. Atkinson, 57–53; Miller, 98–99.
41. *CW* IV, 62–64.
42. *CW* IV, 63; Sandburg, 22.
43. Sandburg, 22.
44. *CW* IV, 63–64; Reynolds, 94; Sandburg, 22–23.
45. Reynolds, 94.
46. Reynolds, 112, 116; Josiah G. Holland, *The Life of Abraham Lincoln* (Springfield, MA: Gurdon Bill, 1866), 40–41; Josephine Craven Chandler, "New Salem: Early Chapter in Lincoln's Life," *Journal of the Illinois State Historical Society* 22, no. 4 (1930): 505.
47. *HI*, Henry McHenry interview, 369; *CW* IV, 65, "Autobiography Written for John L. Scripps," ca. 6/60; Reynolds, 119–21.
48. *HI*, 369, 386; *CW* I, 2, "Petition to Sangamon County Commissioners' Court for Appointment of a Constable," 3[/11]/31.
49. *HI*, 369. According to one observer, "Offutt was inclined to yield, as there was a score or more of the Clary's Grove Boys against him and Mr. Lincoln . . . But Lincoln said they had not won the money and should not have it" (quote from Miller, 122).
50. Reynolds, 112–13; John G. Nicolay and John Hay, *Abraham Lincoln: A History* (New York: Century Co., 1912), vol. 1, 101.
51. *CW* IV, 65, "Autobiography Written for John L. Scripps," ca. 6/60; James M. McPherson, *Abraham Lincoln* (New York: Oxford University Press, 2009), 5.
52. R. D. Monroe, "Indian Fighting and Politics in New Salem, 1831–36," Northern Illinois University Digital Library, Lincoln/Net, https://digital.lib.niu.edu/illinois/lincoln/newsalem.
53. Reynolds, 121–22; *HI*, 390; Miller, 159; *CW* I, 9–10, "Receipt for Arms," 4/28/32, 10–11, "Muster Roll of Lincoln's Company," 5/27/32.
54. *HI*, 362, 372; Reynolds, 124–25; Miller, 161.
55. *HI*, 48, 339; Reynolds, 124.
56. *CW* I, 509–10, "Speech in the House of Representatives on the Presidential Question," 7/27/48; *CW* IV, 4, 64, "Autobiography," ca. 6/60.
57. Reynolds, 103–4, 115–19; quote from Miller, 124.
58. Emanuel Hertz, ed., *The Hidden Lincoln: From the Letters and Papers of William H. Herndon* (New York: Viking, 1938), 571; Reynolds, 126.

59. *CW* I, 5–9, "Communication to the People of Sangamo County," 3/9/32.
60. *CW* I, 5–9; U.S. Senate: The Civil War: The Senate's Story, https://www.senate
.gov/artandhistory/history/common/civil_war/MorrillLandGrantCollegeAct
_FeaturedDoc.htm#:~:text=First%20proposed%20when%20Morrill%20
was,law%20on%20July%202%2C%201862.
61. Reynolds, 186–87.
62. *CW* I, 20–21, "Appraisal of New Salem Lots Owned by Henry Sinco," 10/25/33,
Certificate of Survey for Russell Godbey," 1/14/34, 24–26, "To the County
Commissioners' Court," 6[/2]/34 and 11/4/34; Reynolds, 133; McPherson, 7.
63. Benjamin P. Thomas, *Lincoln's New Salem* (Carbondale: Southern Illinois
Press, 2021), 118–19; Reynolds, 134–35.
64. Reynolds, 134–35.
65. Roy Morris Jr., *The Long Pursuit: Abraham Lincoln's Thirty-Year Struggle with
Stephen Douglas for the Heart and Soul of America* (New York: Smithsonian
Books/Collins, 2008), 15.
66. *CW* IV, 65, "Autobiography Written for John L. Scripps," ca. 6/60; quotes from
Miller, 296–97, and Thomas, 116–17.
67. *CW* I, 1, 73, fn1, "Amendments Introduced to Illinois Legislature (to Senate
Bill Permanently Locating the Seat of Government of the State of Illinois)";
Reynolds, 136–37.
68. *CW* I, 73–75, Various Bills, Amendments, and Reports Introduced to the Il-
linois State Legislature, 1/21–2/13/37; Reynolds, 136–37; Thomas, 131.
69. Thomas, 131; Richard Lawrence Miller, *Lincoln and His World: Prairie Politician, 1834–1842* (Mechanicsburg, PA: Stackpole Books, 2008), 181–82; United
States Congress, "William Lee D. Ewing," *Biographical Directory of the United
States Congress.*Mr. Miller points out in his book that there was an upside to
Ewing's threat of a duel: such conflicts were only conducted between "gentlemen." For all his name-calling, Ewing ironically raised "the coarse and vulgar
fellow" to gentleman's status (Miller, *Prairie Politician*, 1820).
70. *Sangamo Journal*, 1/29/41.
71. *HI*, 73, James Short to WHH, 7/7/65, 242–43, Mentor Graham to WHH,
4/2/66; Thomas, 121.
72. *HI*, 253, John McNamar to G. U. Miles, 5/5/66; Thomas, 122–23; Reynolds, 157.
73. *HI*, 236, George U. Miles to WHH, 3/23/66; Miller, *Prairie Years*, 2–3, Robert Rutledge to WHH, 11/18/66; 408–9, Rutledge to WHH, 11/21/66.
74. *HI*, 591, 606, WHH interview with Elizabeth Herndon Bell, 8/24/83 and 3/87;
Miller, 40–41.
75. *Sangamo Journal*, 6/13/35; *Chicago American*, 8/15/35; Miller, 42–43.
76. Miller, 44.
77. *HI*, 23, John Hill to WHH, 6/6/65, 128, Elizabeth Abell, 2/15/67; William
Knox, "Mortality."
78. Quoted from Lewis Gannett, "The Ann Rutledge Story: Case Closed?" *Journal of the Abraham Lincoln Association* 31, no. 2 (Summer 2010): 40. Gannett's

article is a detectivelike piece, taking a hard-eyed look at the reminiscences of Lincoln's acquaintances regarding Lincoln and Ann Rutledge.

79. Gannett, 40. Gannett's article goes into great detail.

80. *HI*, 253, McNamar to G. Miles, 5/5/66. In this letter, McNamar added a postscript of the tragedy. "I never heard [any] person say that Mr. Lincoln addressed Miss Ann Rutledge in terms of courtship, neither her own family nor my acquaintances otherwise."

81. *HI*, 556–57, Elizabeth Abell interview, 2/15/67.

82. *HI*, 243, Mentor Graham, 4/2/66, 250, L. M. Green, 3/3/66, 265, Mary Owens Vineyard, 374, Caleb Carman, 10/12/66; Miller, 98–99; Reynolds, 154–55.

83. *CW* I, 117–19, "To Mrs. Orville H. Browning," 4/1/38.

84. *CW* I, 117–19.

85. *CW* I, 117–19. One wonders if Lincoln's public rudeness was an act. While he certainly was no Lothario, he had more than his share of female friends, something he did receive some ribbing about from the likes of the Clary's Grove Boys and others.

86. *CW* I, 117–19; Miller, 156–58.

87. *CW* I, 119, and 78–79, to Mary S. Owens, 5/7/37; Northern Illinois University Digital Library, Mary Owens Vineyard to WHH, 5/23/66.

88. *HI*, 255–56, Mary Vineyard, 5/23/66, 262, Vineyard, 7/22/66; Reynolds, 155.

89. *CW* I, 74–76, "Protest in Illinois Legislature on Slavery," 3/3/37, fn2.

90. *CW* I, 74–76.

91. *CW* I, 108–15, Address Before the Young Men's Lyceum of Springfield, IL, 1/27/38; *Marietta Intelligencer*, 10/25/39; Miller, 32.

92. *Marietta Intelligencer*, 10/25/39; Miller, 321.

93. *Sangamo Journal*, 8/2 and 10/25/39.

94. Quotes from Miller, *Prairie Politician*, 441.

95. Miller, *Prairie Politician*, 436–37; Michael Burlingame, *An American Marriage: The Untold Story of Abraham Lincoln and Mary Todd* (New York: Pegasus Books, 2021), 9–11.

96. Justin G. Turner and Linda Levitt Turner, *Mary Todd Lincoln: Her Life and Letters* (New York: Knopf, 1972), 588, Mary Todd Lincoln to Eliza Stuart Steele, 5/23/71; lawsuit quote from Miller, 439.

97. *HI*, 440.

98. Goodwin, 95.

99. Turner and Turner, 8; Reynolds, 162.

100. *HI*, 438.

101. Turner and Turner, 293, Mary Todd Lincoln to Josiah G. Holland, 12/4/65; *HI*, 623, Elizabeth and Ninian Edwards, 7/27/87; Goodwin, 94–95; Reynolds, 161.

102. Goodwin, 94–95; Reynolds, 161.

103. *HI*, 443, Elizabeth Todd Edwards, 1/10/66; Turner and Turner, 15, 17, Mary Todd to Mercy Levering, 7/23/40, 20, Todd to Levering, 12[/15]/40, 446–49.

104. Turner and Turner, 200; *HI*, 443–44, Elizabeth Todd Edwards interview,

1865–66; Turner and Turner, 18, 20, Mary Todd Lincoln to Mercy Ann Levering, 7/23 and 12[/15?]/40; Goodwin, 97.

105. Goodwin, 97.

106. *HI*, 430, Joshua F. Speed to WHH, 11/30/66, 443, Elizabeth Todd Edwards interview, 1865–66; Goodwin, 96–97.

107. *HI*, 430–31, Speed to WHH; 443–45, Elizabeth Todd Edwards.

108. *HI*, 474, Joshua Speed, 1865–66; *CW* I, 228–29, AL to John Stuart, 1/20 and 1/23/41; Goodwin, 99.

109. *HI*, 304, Speed to WHH, 1/7/66.

110. Goodwin, 99–101; Turner and Turner, 18, 20, Mary Todd to Mercy Ann Levering, 7/23/40, 25, 27, Todd to Levering, June 1841.

111. Quotes on Logan from Miller, 467–71; *CW* I, 230–52, Various Amendments Debates, and Speeches in Illinois Legislature, 1/25–2/27/41, 254–58, AL to Joshua Speed, 6/19/41, 265, to Speed, 1[/3?]/42, 267–68, to Speed, 2/3/42, 269–70, to Speed, 2/13/42.

112. *CW* I, 1, 304, Family Record in Abraham Lincoln's Bible, 11/4/42–4/4/53; *HI*, 251, James Matheny, 5/3/66; Miller, 533.

113. *HI*, 443, Elizabeth Todd Edwards interview, 1865–66.

114. *HL*, 270; McPherson, 12.

115. *CW* I, 306–7, to Alden Hall, 2/14/43, 307, to Richard S. Thomas, 2/14/43.

116. *CW* I, 1, 309–18, Campaign Circular from Whig Committee: Address to the People of Illinois, 3/4/43; Morris, 33–34.

117. Lincoln Home, National Historic Site, Illinois, https://www.nps.gov/liho/index.htm; Goodwin, 105.

118. Reynolds, 212–14; Morris, 40.

119. *CW* I, 352–53, to Robert Boal, 1/7/46, 353–54, to AR-Billings F. James, 1/14/46, 355, to John Bennett, 1/15 and 1/16/46, 356–58, to John Hardin, 1/19/46, 359, to N. J. Rockwell, 1/21/46, 359–60, to Benjamin F. James, 1/27/46, 360–66, to John J. Hardin, 2/7/46, 365–66, to AR-Billings F. James, 2/9/46.

120. *CW* I, 382–83, Handbill Replying to Charges of Infidelity, 7/31/46; *HI*, 388–90, John B. Weber (interview), 11/1/66; Reynolds, 288–89.

121. Reynolds, 288–89.

122. Morris, 41.

123. *CW* I, 389–91, to Joshua F. Speed, 10/22/46.

TWO: SON OF THE SOUTH

1. Stephen E. Ambrose, *Duty, Honor, Country: A History of West Point* (Baltimore: Johns Hopkins University Press, 1966), 157; Michael Korda, *Clouds of Glory: The Life and Legend of Robert E. Lee* (New York: HarperCollins, 2014), 30.

2. Korda, 7–9; Guelzo, *Lee*, 14–16.

3. NA, Founders Online (hereafter FO), Henry Lee Jr. to General George Washington, 1/20/78; *Pennsylvania Packet*, 1/28/78; Guelzo, *Lee*, 20–21; Korda, 7–9.

4. NA, Lee to Washington, 3/31/78, and Washington to Henry Laurens, 4/3/78.

5. Guelzo, 20–21; Korda, 8–9.

6. NA, FO, Washington to Lee, 7/9/79 and 1/9/80.

7. Paul Nagel, *The Lees of Virginia: Seven Generations of an American Family* (New York: Oxford University Press, 2007), 166; Korda, 10–12.

8. NA, FO, Washington to Lee, 5/6/93; Lee to Washington, 5/18/93; Albert H. Tillson, "Charles Carter," *The Dictionary of Virginia Biography*, from the Encyclopedia Virginia website; Theodore R. Reinhert and Judith A. Habicht, "Shirley Plantation in the Eighteenth Century: A Historical, Architectural, and Archaeological Study," *Virginia Magazine of History and Biography* (hereafter *VMHB*) 92, no. 1 (January 1984): 35–39; Korda, 11.

9. Korda, 12.

10. NA, FO, Washington to Lee, 4/2/97.

11. Guelzo, 26; Korda, 12–13; Nagel, 195–96.

12. Clifford Dowdey, *Lee* (New York: Skyhorse Publishing, 2015; originally published by Little, Brown, 1965), 26–27; Gene Smith, *Lee and Grant: A Dual Biography* (New York: McGraw-Hill, 1984), 6–7.

13. Dowdey, 33, 42.

14. *Annapolis Maryland Republican*, 7/1/12; Paul A. Gilje, "The Baltimore Riots of 1812 and the Breakdown of the Anglo-American Mob Tradition," *Journal of Social History* 13, no. 4 (Summer 1980): 548–52; *Annapolis Maryland Republican*, 7/1/12; *Niles Weekly Register*, 8/8/12; "Account of the Latest Riots," *Interesting Papers Illustrative of the Recent Riots at Baltimore* (Philadelphia, 1812), 55–59; Gilje, 555–56; Guelzo, 29; Korda, 15.

15. Guelzo, 30; General Henry Lee to C. C. Lee, 4/19/17, from Henry Lee, *Memoirs of the War in the Southern Department of the United States* (New York: University Publishing Company, 1869).

16. Robert E. Lee (hereafter REL), "Biography of the Author," from Henry Lee, *Memoirs*, 78.

17. Guelzo, 32; Smith, 22–24; Emily V. Mason, *The Life of General Robert E. Lee* (Baltimore: John Murphy, 1874), 22.

18. Guelzo, 32; Korda, 20; REL to Anna Fitzhugh, 6/6/60, in Francis Raymond Adams Jr., "An Annotated Edition of the Personal Letters of Robert E. Lee" (doctoral thesis, University of Maryland, 1955), 638; REL to Mary Custis, quoted from William C. Davis, *The Crucible of Command: Ulysses S. Grant and Robert E. Lee; The War They Fought, the Peace They Forged* (Philadelphia: Da Capo Press, 2014), 8.

19. Ann Hill to Charles Carter Lee (hereafter CCL), 7/17/16, Charles Carter Lee Collection, Major Henry Lee Papers, Virginia State Library; Ann Hill Lee to Sydney Smith Lee (hereafter SSL), 4/10/27, Jessie Ball duPont Library, Stratford Hall, Stratford, VA; Davis, *Crucible*, 4–6.

20. REL to William B. Leary, 12/15/66, from Captain Robert E. Lee, *Recollections and Letters of General Robert E. Lee* (New York: Doubleday, 1904), 417.

21. Davis, *Crucible*, 6–7.
22. Davis, *Crucible*, 10–11; Mason, 22; REL to John C. Calhoun, 2/28/24, in Elizabeth Brown Pryor, "Rediscovered: Robert E. Lee's Earliest-Known Letter," *VMHB* 115, no. 1 (2007): 108–10.
23. Pryor, "Rediscovered," 108–10; Dowdey, 42.
24. Dowdey, 43.
25. Douglas Southall Freeman, *Robert E. Lee: A Biography*, vol. 1 (New York: Scribners, 1934), 52–57; Korda, 33.
26. Greta G. Hughes and Richard Owen, "The Grand Duke Bernhard's Visit to West Point, 1825: From *Reise durch Nord Amerika* of the Grand Duke Bernhard of the House of Saxe-Weimar-Eisenach," *New York History* 26, no. 1 (January 1945): 81; Guelzo, *Lee*, 37–38.
27. Hughes and Owen, 85.
28. Cazenove G. Lee Jr., "Ann Hill Carter," *VMHB* 16, no. 3 (July 1936): 419.
29. Quote from Davis, *Crucible*, 26.
30. Historical Society of Pennsylvania (hereafter HSP), Dreer Collection, George Washington to David Stuart, 8/13/98; G.W.P. Custis to Washington, 5/29/97, in "Letters from G.W.P. Custis to George Washington, 1797–1798," *VMHB* 20, no. 3 (July 1912): 298–99.
31. Guelzo, *Lee*, 45–46; "George Washington Parke Custis," Arlington House, nps.gov.
32. Murray Nelligan, "The Building of Arlington House," *Journal of the Society of Architectural Historians* 10, no. 2 (1951): 11–15; William George Rudy, "Interpreting America's First Grecian Style House: The Architectural Legacy of George Washington Parke Custis and George Hadfield" (master's thesis, University of Maryland, 2010), 35–36; Benson J. Lossing, "Arlington House: The Seat of G.W.P. Custis, Esq.," *Harper's New Monthly Magazine* 7, no. 40 (1853): 433–55; William Buckner McGroarty, "A Letter and a Portrait from Arlington House," *William and Mary Quarterly* 22, no. 1 (January 1942): 46–48. Custis did show his mettle in 1814, serving on a gunnery crew at the Battle of Bladensburg.
33. Rose Mortimer Ellzey MacDonald, *Mrs. Robert E. Lee* (Boston: Ginn and Company, 1939), 18–24; Portrait of Mary Anna Randolph Custis by Auguste Jean-Jacques Hervieux, Arlington House, nps.gov; Smith, 27; Arlington House, the REL Memorial, nps.gov; https://encyclopediavirginia.org/maria-syphax/.
34. Quoted from Robert E. L. Debutts Jr., "Lee in Love: Courtship and Correspondence in Antebellum Virginia," *VMHB* 115, no. 4 (2007): 488–90, Mary Custis to Edward George Washington Butler, no date (possibly 8/10/27); Sally Nelson Robins, "Mrs. Lee During the War—Something About 'The Mess' and Its Occupants," in *Gen. Robert Edward Lee: Soldier, Citizen, and Christian Patriot*, ed. R. A. Brock (Richmond, VA: Royal Publishing Co., 1897), 322–23.
35. A. L. Long, *Memoirs of Robert E. Lee: His Military and Personal History* (New

York: J. M. Stoddart, 1886), 71; Guelzo, *Lee*, 41; Davis, *Crucible*, 26–27, 509, endnotes 16 and 17.

36. John Howard Brown, ed., *Lamb's Biographical Dictionary of the United States*, vol. 5 (Boston: Federal Book Company, 1903), 387–88.

37. "Cadets Arranged in Order of Merit, in Their Respective Classes, as Determined at the General Examination, in June 1829," *Official Register of the Officers and Cadets of the U.S. Military Academy, June 1829* (West Point, NY: United States Military Academy Library and Archive (hereafter USMA), 1884), 6; Guelzo, *Lee*, 47.

38. Jessie Ball DuPont Library, Ann Lee to SSL, 4/10/29; Freeman, *Lee*, vol. 1, 87; Guelzo, *Lee*, 47–48. Professor Guelzo mentions that Lee's mother probably had tuberculosis.

39. Virginia Historical Society (hereafter VHS), George Bolling Lee Papers, Catharine Mildred Lee to Mary Custis, 8/22/29; Debutts, 490, 510, REL to Mary Custis, 1/10/31.

40. DeButts, 525–26, REL to Mary Custis, 12/28/30.

41. DeButts, 525–26.

42. University of Virginia (hereafter UVA), Lee papers, REL to CCL, 9/22/30; National Park Service, Arlington House, Mary Custis to Hortensia Monroe Hay, 10/14/30; Davis, *Crucible*, 34; Debutts, 491.

43. VHS, Lee Family Papers (hereafter LFP), Mary Anna Randolph Custis prayer diary, July 1830 entry; UVA, Papers of REL, 1830–1870, REL to CCL, 9/22/30; Debutts, 491–95.

44. DeButts, 529–30, REL to Mary Custis, 1/10/31.

45. Debutts, 527, REL to Mary Custis, 12/28/30 and 537–38, 4/3/31; Davis, *Crucible*, 49.

46. Debutts, 528–31, REL to Mary Custis, 1/10/31; "harassed" quote from Guelzo, *Lee*, 51.

47. Debutts, 511, 532–35, REL to Mary Custis, 3/8/31; 539–40, REL to Mary Custis, 5/13/31.

48. DeButts, 535–36, REL to Mary Custis, 4/3/31; Guelzo, *Lee*, 53.

49. DeButts, 539–40, REL to Mary Custis, 5/13/31, 542–44, 6/5/31; 546–48, 6/12/31; 548–50, 6/21/31; 575, fn203; Korda, 55; quote from Emory Thomas, *Robert E. Lee* (New York: Norton, 1995), 64. Mary Custis did not wear a white wedding dress; that custom came later in the nineteenth century.

50. VHS, LFP, 1824–1918, REL to Mary Custis Lee (hereafter MCL), 6/30/64; REL to Andrew Talcott, 7/13/31, Robert Edward Lee Papers, Virginia Museum of History and Culture (hereafter VMHC); Guelzo, *Lee*, 54.

51. DeButts, 544–45, Mary Lee Custis and Mary Custis to REL, 6/11/31 (based on 6/12/31 postmark); 545, REL to Mary Custis, 6/12/31; Davis, *Crucible*, 38.

52. DeButts, 540, REL to Mary Custis, 5/13/31; George Green Shackelford, ed., "Lieutenant Lee Reports to Captain Talcott on Fort Calhoun's Construction on the Rip Raps," *VMHB* 60, no. 3 (July 1952): 458–87.

53. DeButts, 465, REL to Capt. Talcott, 12/7/32; 468, 6/11/33; 469, 7/3/33; Freeman, *Lee*, vol. 1, 96–97.

54. William L. Andrews and Henry Louis Gates, eds., *Slave Narratives* (New York: Library of America, 200), "The Confessions of Nat Turner," 252–53.

55. VMHC, LFP, REL to Mary Fitzhugh Custis, 9/4/31; *Ninth Annual Report of the American Society for Colonizing the Free People of Color of the United States* (Washington, D.C.: Way & Gideon, 1826), 11–12; Davis, *Crucible*, 47; Guelzo, *Lee*, 55–56.

56. DeButts, 544–45, Mary Fitzhugh Custis and MCL to REL, 6/11/31; VMHC, REL to MCL, 6/2/32; REL to Talcott, 4/10/34; Guelzo, *Lee*, 56–57; MacDonald, 40–41.

57. REL to CCL, 9/28/32, REL Papers, Small Special Collections Library.

58. Mary Custis to MCL, 10/6/31, Custis Family Papers, VMHC; REL to CCL, 5/2/36, REL Papers, UVA.

59. Quote from Thomas, 77.

60. REL to MCL, 8/21/35; Norma B. Cuthbert (and REL), "To Molly: Five Early Letters from Robert E. Lee to His Wife," *Huntington Library Quarterly* 15, no. 3 (May 1952): 271–73.

61. REL to CCL, 8/2/36; REL Papers, UVA; Thomas, 84–85; Shackelford, 469, REL to Talcott, 7/3/33.

62. REL to MCL, 4/24/32, LFP, VMHC; REL to Talcott, 11/17/35, Shackelford, 481, REL to MCL, 6/6/32; Cuthbert, 264–65; REL to Jack MacKay, 6/6/34, 10/27/37, Letters of REL Georgia Historical Society; Thomas, 73.

63. VMHC, REL to Talcott, 11/1/34, 475–76; 11/28/34, 472.

64. REL to Talcott, 2/13/36, Talcott Papers, VMHC; REL to Charles Gratiot, 3/18/35; Thomas, 81.

65. REL to MCL, 9/2/35, Cuthbert, 274–75; Guelzo, *Lee*, 65; Thomas, 82–84; Shackelford, 481–83, REL to Talcott, 11/17/35 and 6/22/36.

66. VMHC, REL to Talcott, 2/2/37; Talcott Papers, VMHC.

67. VMHC, REL to Talcott, 6/29/37; Thomas, 84–85.

68. Lee Papers, Georgia Historical Society, REL to Jack MacKay, 10/2/37.

69. Twain, 145, 181.

70. Stella M. Drumm, "Robert E. Lee and the Improvement of the Mississippi River," *Missouri Historical Society Collections* 6, no. 2 (February 1929): 158–59; Freeman, *Lee*, vol. 1, 145–46; Thomas, 86–87.

71. Edgar P. Richardson, "The Athens of America," in *Philadelphia: A 300-Year History*, ed. Russell Weigley (New York: W. W. Norton, 1982), 237–38; Florence E. Dorsey, *Master of the Mississippi: Henry Shreve and the Conquest of the Mississippi* (Boston: Houghton Mifflin Company, 1941), 211; James H. Lemly, "The Mississippi River: St. Louis' Friend or Foe?" *Business History Review* 39, no. 1 (Spring 1965): 10.

72. Guelzo, *Lee*, 68–69. One of Shreve's many accomplishments was piloting a steamboat from Pittsburgh laden with munitions for General Andrew Jackson's force in New Orleans. Shreve made the passage in a remarkable nineteen

days, arriving the day after the Battle of New Orleans—a remarkable effort nonetheless (*American Telegraph*, 3/29/15).

73. Guelzo, 69; First Lieutenant B. C. Dunn, "Maj. Gen. Montgomery Cunningham, Meigs," *Professional Memoirs, Corps of Engineers, United States Army, and Engineer Department at Large* 6, no. 28 (July–August 1914): 337; Russell F. Weigley, *Quartermaster General of the Union Army: A Biography of M. C. Meigs* (New York: Columbia University Press, 1959), 32–33; quote from Robert O'Harrow Jr., *The Quartermaster: Montgomery C. Meigs: Lincoln's General, Master Builder of the Union Army* (New York: Simon & Schuster, 2016), 8.

74. REL to MCL, 8/5/37, LFP, VMHC; REL to Talcott, 8/25/37, Talcott Papers, VMHC; Drumm, 159; Thomas, 87.

75. REL to MCL, 8/5/37, LFP, VMHC; REL to CCL, 10/8/37, REL Papers, Small Special Collections Library; REL to Jack MacKay, Lee Papers, Georgia Historical Society; Guelzo, *Lee*, 69–70; Thomas, 88–89.

76. Frank Leverett, "The Lower Rapids of the Mississippi River," *Journal of Geology* 7, no. 1 (January/February 1899): 1–3; John Fletcher Darby, *Personal Recollections of Many Prominent People Whom I Have Known* (St. Louis: G. I. Jones, 1880), 228.

77. REL Papers, Small Special Collections Library, REL to CCL, 10/8/37, Guelzo, *Lee*, 69; Thomas, 91.

78. REL Papers, Small Special Collections Library; Lee Report, 12/6/37, *Executive Documents*, 25th Congress, Second Session, vol. 1, no. 39.

79. MacDonald, 75–79; Freeman, *Lee*, vol. 1, 149; Guelzo, *Lee*, 70–72; Thomas, 93.

80. Guelzo, 70; Drumm, 163–64.

81. REL to CCL, 12/24/38, Lee Papers, UVA; REL to Talcott, 1/8/39, Talcott Papers, VMHC; REL to Horace Bliss, 3/29/39, LFP, VMHC; Freeman, *Lee*, vol. 1, 160–69; Thomas, 94–95; MacDonald, 78.

82. Darby, 229–30; Thomas, 95–96; Guelzo, *Lee*, 74–75.

83. REL, "The Erection of a Pier in the Mississippi River near St. Louis," 10/21/39, *Executive Documents of the 46th Congress*, vol. 1, 145–46; Thomas, 96–97; Guelzo, *Lee*, 75.

84. REL to CCL, 1/30, 2/23, and 8/22/40, UVA, LFP; Death Certificate of Ann Robinson McCarty Lee, LFP, Jessie Ball duPont Library, Stratford Hall; Cazenove Garner Lee Jr., *Chronicle: Studies of the Early Generations of the Lees of Virginia* (New York: New York University Press, 1957), 91; Guelzo, *Lee*, 75; Thomas, 97–98.

85. Freeman, *Lee*, vol. 1, 178; REL to MacKay, 7/23/40, Screven, 44; Darby, 230.

86. REL to Jack MacKay, 10/22/37, Georgia Historical Society.

87. "Joseph Gilbert Totten," *Professional Memoirs, Corps of Engineers, United States Army, and Engineer Department at Large*, vol. 3, no. 10 (April–June 1911): 313–14; Julian L. Schley, "Some Giants of the Corps of Engineers," *Military Engineer* 30, no. 171 (May–June, 1938): 182; "Preserving Fort Jefferson," National Park Service, Department of Interior.

88. REL to Fred Smith, 8/12/39, LFP, VMHC; Freeman, *Lee*, vol. 1, 184–87.

89. REL to MCL, 4/18/41, REL Papers, UVA; Thomas, 102–3.

90. MacDonald, 83–85; Lee, *Recollections*, 6–9.

91. REL to Custis Lee, 11/30/45, LFP, VMHC; REL to Kayser, 6/16/45, "Letters of Robert E. Lee to Henry Kayser, 1838–1846," Missouri Historical Society, *Glimpses of the Past* 3 (January–February 1936), 38; Thomas, 104–7.

92. REL to Jack MacKay, 3/18/45, Screven, 49; Freeman, *Lee*, vol. 1, 194; Guelzo, *Lee*, 79–80; REL to Dr. Adam Thomas, 4/30/42, and REL to C. S. Brainerd, 5/21/42, Archives of the REL Memorial Foundation, Papers of the Lee Family, Jessie Ball duPont Library, Stratford Hall.

THREE: SON OF THE NORTH

1. *L&L*, vol. 1, 11; Isaac R. Pennypacker, *General Meade* (New York, D. Appleton, 1901), 13.

2. *L&L*, vol. 1, 13.

3. R. W. Meade, "George Meade Born in Philadelphia, Province of Pennsylvania," *American Catholic Historical Researches* 6, no. 3 (July 1989): 98–107; "The Children of George Meade," *The Pennsylvania Magazine of History and Biography* (hereafter *PMHB*) 5, no. 1 (January 1988): 47–50; Susan Klepp, "Meade, George," American National Biography; Christopher S. Stowe, "A Philadelphia Gentleman: The Cultural, Institutional, and Political Socialization of George Gordon Meade" (PhD diss., University of Toledo, 2005), 26–35.

4. *L&L*, vol. 1, 8; Rossiter Johnson, "Meade, Richard Worsam," in *The American Cyclopaedia: A Popular Dictionary of General Knowledge*, ed. George Ripley and Charles A. Dane, vol. 11 (New York: D. Appleton, 1875), 310; File: Portrait of Richard Worsam Meade, by Vicente Lopez y Portana, Spanish, 1815, oil on canvas, Meadows Museum, Southern Methodist University; Portrait of Margaret Coates Butler Meade by George Augustus Baker (after Gilbert Stuart), Frick Reference Library, New York.

5. NA, FO, Richard W. Meade to Thomas Jefferson, 12/8/02; Thomas P. Hughes, *American Ancestry: Giving the Name and Descent, in the Male Line, of Americans Whose Ancestors Settled in the United States Previous to the Declaration of Independence, A.D. 1776*, vol. 10 (Albany, NY: Joel Munsell's Sons, 1895), 110–11.

6. Dorothy C. Barck, ed., *Diary of William Dunlap (1766–1839): The Memoirs of a Dramatist, Theatrical Manager, Painter, Critic, Novelist, and Historian*, vol. 2 (New York: New York Historical Society, 1930), 432, 450; NA, FO, Jonathan Williams to James Madison, 2/24/06; William Duane to Jefferson, 6/5/24.

7. NA, Jefferson to Yznardi, 7/1606; Yznardi to Jefferson, 11/8/06; James Morton Smith, ed., *The Republic of Letters: The Correspondence Between Thomas Jefferson and James Madison, 1776–1826*, vol. 3 (New York: W. W. Norton, 1995), 1436, Jefferson to Madison, 8/28/06, 1489–90, Jefferson to Madison, 8/19/07; W. Herman Bell, ed., "A Captain in Captivity," *New England Quarterly* 14, no. 1 (March 1941): 122.

8. REL, "The Erection of a Pier," 145–46; Thomas, 96–97; Guelzo, *Lee*, 75.

9. Cleaves, 3–4; "Archives of the Parish of Nuestra Señora de Rosario, Fourth Book of Baptismal Registry," 43, Meade Family Papers (hereafter MFP), HSP.

10. *L&L*, vol. 1, 10–11; *The Case*, 12–13; FO, NA, Meade to James Leander Cathcart, 2/2/16; Film, *Castillo de Santa Catalina*, Andalucia.com; Library of Congress (hereafter LOC), American State Papers, *Foreign Affairs*, vol. 4, 145, fn8, *Daily National Intelligencer*, 6/26/26; Cleaves, 6.

11. LOC, Senate Executive Proceedings, 2:534.

12. American State Papers, *Foreign Affairs*, vol. 4, 151; Massachusetts Historical Society, Adams Family Papers, Charles Francis Adams, ed., *Memoirs of John Quincy Adams*, vol. 4, 104, 6/26/18 entry; Cleaves, 6–7.

13. American State Papers, *Foreign Affairs*, vol. 4, 155; Adams, *Memoirs*, vol. 4, 104; Tom Huntington, *Searching for George Gordon Meade: The Forgotten Victor of Gettysburg* (Mechanicsburg, PA: Stackpole Books, 2013), 11–12.

14. U.S. Court of Claims, Reports from the Court of Claims, Submitted to the House of Representatives During the First Session of the Thirty-Sixth Congress, 1859–60, vol. 3, 36th Congress, 1st Sess. (Washington, D.C.: Thomas Ford, Printer, 1860), Letter of Margaret Coates Butler Meade, 1/17/19, 134; McGrath, 425, 432, 435–36.

15. U.S. Court of Claims, 122–136. The Court of Claims report is dozens of pages long, a masterwork in semantics, obfuscation, and conjecture until it denies Meade's claim, where the court becomes the voice of clarity.

16. Johnson, "Meade, Richard Worsam"; *New York Times*, "People Who Never Tire. Old Government Claims and the Claimants," 8/11/1878; Cleaves, 8.

17. Cleaves, 9; *L&L*, vol. 1, 11; Charles H. Bowman Jr., "Manuel Torres, a Spanish American Patriot in Philadelphia, 1796–1822," *PMHB* 94, no. 1 (1970): 53.

18. *L&L*, vol. 1, 12; John J. Maitland, "St. Mary's Graveyard, Fourth and Spruce Streets, Philadelphia. Records and Extracts from Inscriptions on Tombstones," *Records of the American Catholic Historical Society of Philadelphia*, vol. 3 (1888), 258.

19. "Death of Gen. Roumfort," Special Dispatch, *New York Times*, 8/3/1878; George Lehman, Artist, "American Classical Military Academy at Mt. Airy, Germantown," Library Company of Philadelphia; Quote from *L&L*, vol. 1, 12.

20. *L&L*, vol. 1, 12; GGM to MM, 1/20/46, 51–52.

21. HSP, MFP, Will of Richard Worsam Meade; *L&L*, vol. 1, 13; Cleaves, 9.

22. Cleaves, 9–10; Donn Piatt, "Salmon P. Chase," *North American Review* 143, no. 361 (1886): 600; Mary Merwin Phelps, *Kate Chase, Dominant Daughter: The Life Story of a Brilliant Woman and Her Famous Father* (Whitefish, MT: Literary Licensing, 2012), 4–5.

23. *L&L*, vol. 1, 10–11.

24. Cleaves, 9–10; *L&L*, vol. 1, 51–52, GGM to MM, 1/20/46.

25. Cleaves, 9; McGrath, 435–38; George Cullum, *Biographical Register of the Officers and Graduates of the U.S. Military Academy at West Point, N.Y., from Its Establishment in 1802 to 1890 with the Early History of the United States Military Academy* (New York: Houghton, Mifflin, 1891), 157.

26. Cleaves, 10–11.

27. NA, Meade Letters, MM to John Eaton, 3/13/30.

28. NA, Frederick Hall to MM, 1/28/31.

29. *L&L*, vol. 1, 51–52, GGM to MM, 1/20/46.

30. F. A. Mahan, "Professor Dennis Hart Mahan," *Professional Memoirs, Corps of Engineers, United States Army, and Engineer Department at Large* 9, no. 43 (February 1917): 72–73; Ethan S. Rafuse, "'To Check . . . the Very Worst and Meanest of Our Passions': Common Sense, 'Cobbon Sense,' and the Socialism of Cadets at Antebellum West Point," *War in History* 16, no. 4 (November 2009): 416–17.

31. Rafuse, 416–17.

32. Quote from William B. Skelton, *West Point: Two Centuries and Beyond* (Abilene, TX: McWhinney Foundation Press, 2004), 29–30; Michelle Sivilich, "A Proposed Model to Investigate the Role of Education in the Success of Military Strategy in Florida During the Second Seminole War (1835–1842)," *Historical Archaeology* 46, no. 1 (2012): 63.

33. *L&L*, vol. 1, 15; Herman Haupt, *Reminiscences of General Herman Haupt* (Milwaukee: Wright & Joys, 1901), 310; Cleaves, 11–12; Pennypacker, 13; U.S. Military Academy Records, 1817–1837.

34. Rafuse, 416–17.

35. Marvin J. Anderson, "The Architectural Education of Nineteenth-Century American Engineers: Dennis Hart Mahan at West Point," *Journal of the Society of Architectural Historians* 67, no. 2 (June 2008): 222–23, 226–27.

36. *L&L*, vol. 1, 15–16.

37. *L&L*, vol. 1, 15–16; Cleaves, 11–12; "West Point Officers in the Civil War—Class of 1835," *The Civil War in the East*, https://civilwarintheeast.com/west-point-officers-in-the-civil-war/class-of-1835/.

38. Cleaves, 13. "Commodore" is an honorary title given the senior captain of a squadron.

39. HSP, Meade Papers, Dallas to Meade, 2/7/80; *L&L*, vol. 1, 17; *Army and Navy Chronicle*, 10/8/35 and 10/15/35; Cleaves, 13; *Key West Inquirer*, 9/19/35; Gail Swanson and Jerry Wilkinson, "Florida Hurricanes of the Last Millennium," KeysHistory.org, https://www.keyshistory.org/hurricanelist.html.

40. Pennypacker, 14; "West Point Officers in the Civil War—Class of 1835."

41. HSP, Meade Papers, Sandy Dallas to Captain George Meade, 2/7/80; *Army and Navy Chronicle*, 1/28/ and 2/25/36; Cleaves, 13–14.

42. George M. Brooke and James W. Covington, "The Establishment of Fort Brooke: The Beginning of Tampa," *Florida Historical Quarterly* 31, no. 4 (1953): 275; Richard Meade Bache, *Life of General George Gordon Meade: Commander of the Army of the Potomac* (Philadelphia: Henry T. Coates, 1897), 9–10.

43. LOC, A. A. Humphreys, "Address of A. A. Humphreys on the Military Service of the Late Maj. Gen. George Gordon Meade" (Washington, D.C., 1872).

44. John Bemrose, *Reminiscences of the Second Seminole War*, ed. John K. Mahon (Gainesville: University of Florida Press, 1966), 78–79; John Eisenhower, *Agent of Destiny: The Life and Times of General Winfield Scott* (New York: Free Press, 1997), 157–58; Eric Jay Dolin, *Brilliant Beacons: A History of the American Lighthouse* (New York: Liveright, 2016), 88–91.

45. Eisenhower, *Agent of Destiny*, 150.

46. Eisenhower, 152–53.

47. Eisenhower, 156–59; John Missail and Mary Lou Missail, *The Seminole Wars: America's Longest Indian Conflict* (Gainesville: University Press of Florida, 2004), 111–14.

48. Lt. Joseph R. Smith to his wife, 1/20/38, from John K. Mahon, ed., "Letters from the Second Seminole War," *Florida Historical Quarterly* 36, no. 4 (1958): 336–37.

49. Cleaves, 13–14; HSP, Meade Papers, "Letter from Troy, New York," 3/26/65. The marine's name is not known; he signed it "Medicine Chest."

50. Cleaves, 14; HSP, Meade Letter Book, "Appointments, Assignments, and Reports," 4/8/36.

51. Paul D. Lack, "An Urban Slave Community: Little Rock, 1831–1862," *Arkansas Historical Quarterly* 41, no. 3 (1982): 258–65. "Living out" did not live very long. After years of fearing the possible effects of separate housing, town officials banned it in 1856, forcing enslaved Blacks to return "to the homestead of their owners" (Lack, 265).

52. *L&L*, vol. 1, 14; Cleaves, 14.

53. *Army and Navy Chronicle*, 7/21 and 11/3/36; Bache, 10–11; *L&L*, vol. 1, 18; Cleaves, 14–15.

54. Stephen Ambrose, *Upton and the Army* (Baton Rouge: Louisiana State University Press, 1964), 142; Ambrose, *Duty, Honor, Country*, 116–18; Huntington, 13.

55. Ambrose, *Duty, Honor, Country*, 123–24; Sidney Forman, "The First School of Engineering," *The Military Engineer* 44, no. 298 (1952): 112.

56. Bache, 10; Cleaves, 15; *L&L*, vol. 1, 18.

57. Cleaves, 15; Alice Whitman, "Transportation in Territorial Florida," *Florida Historical Quarterly* 17, no. 1 (1938): 44–48.

58. HSP, Meade Papers, Captain W. H. Chase to Meade, 4/19/37; Meade to Secretary of War Joel Poinsett (undated).

59. Walter M. Lowrey, "The Engineers and the Mississippi," *Louisiana History* 5, no. 3 (Summer 1964): 238–39.

60. LOC, Humphreys, "Address"; Matthew T. Pearcy and Andrew Atkinson Humphreys, "Andrew Atkinson Humphreys' Seminole War Field Journal," *Florida Historical Quarterly* 85, no. 2 (Fall 2006), 6/23 and 7/23/36 entries, 228–30.

61. LOC, Humphreys, "Address"; *L&L*, vol. 1, 14–15.

62. Bache, 557–58; *L&L*, vol. 1, 15–16.
63. "The Late Honorable John Sergeant of Philadelphia," *American Law Register* 1, no. 4 (February 1853): 193–98; *L&L*, vol. 1, 19.
64. Cleaves, 16; *L&L*, vol. 1, 16–17; 37–48, GGM to MM, 2/18/46; Bache, 562–63.
65. Bache, 557.
66. HSP, Meade Assignment Book, Meade Papers, Col. J. J. Abert to Meade, 8/18/40; Cleaves, 16–17; *L&L*, vol. 1, 20; Pennypacker, 15; George J. Gill, "Edward Everett and the Northeastern Boundary Controversy," *New England Quarterly* 42, no. 2 (1969): 204–5; J. Chris Arndt, "Maine in the Northeastern Boundary Controversy: States' Rights in Antebellum New England," *New England Quarterly* 62, no. 2 (1989): 217–18.
67. *L&L*, vol. 1, 16–17.
68. *L&L*, vol. 1, 16–17; Sidney George Fisher, "The Diary of Sidney George Fisher, 1841," *PMHB* 77, no. 2 (April 1953), January 4, 1841 entry, 198.
69. VMHC, Meade to (Mrs.) Sarah Wise, 8/9/41; Cleaves, 17.
70. *L&L*, vol. 1, 17; B. H. Wise, *The Life of Henry A. Wise of Virginia, 1806–1876* (New York: Macmillan, 1899), 91, 103, 367.
71. *L&L*, vol. 1, 17–18; quote from Cleaves, 18.
72. Wayne C. Wheeler, "A Lighthouse for Brandywine Shoal," *The Keeper's Key* (Summer 1999), courtesy of the U.S. Lighthouse Society.
73. Dolin, 104–7; George Rockwell Putnam, *Lighthouses and Lightships of the United States* (Boston: Houghton Mifflin Company, 1917), 41–43. For more information on the fascinating subject, the author happily recommends Mr. Dolin's book.
74. Dolin, 104–9; U.S. H.R. Doc. 24, 1838, 70.
75. Dolin, 119; U.S. Coast Guard website, Brandywine Shoals Light; Anyplace America website, Brandywine Shoal Topographical Map; Kraig Anderson, "Brandywine Shoal Lighthouse," Lighthouse Friends website; Wheeler, "Lighthouse."
76. James Blaney, "Alexander Mitchell (1780–1868): Belfast's Blind Engineer," History Ireland website; Wheeler, "Lighthouse"; Dolin, 119; *L&L*, vol. 1, 18.
77. Blaney, "Alexander Mitchell"; Wheeler, "Lighthouse"; Dolin, 119; *L&L*, vol. 1, 22.
78. *L&L*, vol. 1, 22; Cleaves, 18.
79. Bache, 562–63.
80. Bache, 560.
81. *L&L*, vol. 1, 24–25, GGM to MM, 8/15/45; Cleaves, 19.

FOUR: MEXICO AND WASHINGTON

1. William H. Goetzmann and William N. Goetzmann, *The West of the Imagination* (New York: W. W. Norton, 1986), 71–74.
2. Julius W. Pratt, *A History of the United States Foreign Policy* (Englewood Cliffs, NJ: Prentice-Hall, 1955), 226–27; David A. Clary, *Eagles and Empire: The*

United States, Mexico, and the Struggle for a Continent (New York: Bantam Books, 2009), 43–44.

3. U.S. Congress, House Executive Document No. 60, 30th Congress, 1st Session, *Messages of the President of the United States with the Correspondence, Therewith Communicated, Between the Secretary of War and Other Officers of the Government: The Mexican War* (Washington, D.C.: Wendell and Van Benthuysen, 1848), No. 60, 90, William Marcy to Zachary Taylor (hereafter ZT), 1/13/46; John S. D. Eisenhower, *So Far from God: The U.S. War with Mexico* (New York: Random House, 1989), 48–50; David Nevin, *The Mexican War* (New York: Time-Life Books, 1978), 22.

4. K. Jack Bauer, *Zachary Taylor: Soldier, Planter, Statesman of the Old West* (Baton Rouge: Louisiana State University Press, 1985), 152; Clary, 108; Ulysses S. Grant, *Memoirs of U. S. Grant*, vol. 1 (from *Memoirs and Selected Letters*) (New York: Library Company of America, 1990), 65.

5. *L&L*, vol. 1, 24–25, GGM to MM, 8/15/45, 29–33, GGM to MM, 9/4, 9/5, and 9/18/45; Bauer, 117–18; Clary, 71. LOC, Illustration of Corpus Christi campground, from Nevin, *Mexican War*, 20–21.

6. *L&L*, vol. 1, GGM to MM, 9/5 and 9[?], 1845; Clary, 68–69; Eisenhower, *So Far from God*, 29–30.

7. *L&L*, vol. 1, 31, GGM to MM, 9/18/45. Damon Manders, *Engineers Far from Ordinary: The U.S. Army Corps of Engineers in St. Louis* (St. Louis: U.S. Army Corps of Engineers, 2011), 44–45; Jeff Leen, "A Civil War General's Journey from Goat to Hero," *Washington Post*, 9/13/13.

8. *L&L*, vol. 1, 35.

9. Gregory J. Urwin, *The United States Cavalry: An Illustrated History, 1776–1944* (Norman: University of Oklahoma Press, 1983), 74–75; Cleaves, 22; Eisenhower, 51; Todd H., "Ringgold Military Saddle Patent [Oct. 7, 1844]," Military Horse, June 10, 2023, https://www.militaryhorse.org/ringgold-saddle-patent/.

10. *L&L*, vol. 1, 94–96, GGM to MM, 5/19/46; Grant, 61; Clary, 81–85; Nevin (illustration), 62.

11. *L&L*, vol. 1, 63–64, GGM to MM, 4/13/46; 72–74, GGM to MM, 4/21/46; 75–78, GGM to MM, 4/22/46; U.S. Congress, House Executive Document 60, 139–40, General Pedro de Ampudia to ZT, 4/12/46; Taylor to Ampudia, 4/12/46; Eisenhower, 63–64; Cleaves, 23; *National Intelligencer*, 5/7/46.

12. Eisenhower, 65; quote from Clary, 97–98.

13. NA, Letters Received, RG 94 Adjutant General's Office, Dept. of War, Sam Walker to ZT, 5/2/46; Clary, 105–6; James B. Donovan, "Two Sams and Their Six-Shooter," *Texas Monthly* (April 2016): 90–91. Walker had fought in the Seminole Wars. While in the army, in 1842 he marched with three hundred Texans into Mexico after the Battle of Salado Creek only to be captured and sentenced to death by General Santa Anna. Spared execution, he was imprisoned and beaten for six months before he escaped and joined the Texas Rangers in 1843.

14. Clary, 105; *L&L*, vol. 1, 83, GGM to MM, 5/2/46.

15. *L&L*, vol. 1, 83; Clary, 106–7; Grant, 65.

16. Clary, 106–8; Grant, 65.

17. ZT to Adjutant General and AO Order 58, both May 7, 1846; ZT to Adjutant General, AO Order; U.S. Congress, House Executive Document 60, 294–95; *L&L*, vol. 1, 83–87, GGM to MM, 5/5 and 5/7/46.

18. Nevin, 38; Eisenhower, 76–77; *L&L*, vol. 1, 87–91, GGM to MM, 5/9/46.

19. *L&L*, vol. 1, 88–91, GGM to MM, 5/9/46; French quote from Eisenhower, 77; Mexican witness quote from Clary, 108.

20. Clary, 108–9.

21. Eisenhower, 79; Nevin, 39; Grant, 66–67.

22. *L&L*, vol. 1, 89–91, GGM to MM, 5/9/46.

23. *L&L*, vol. 1, 89–91; Clary, 110.

24. *L&L*, vol. 1, 89–91; Grant, 67; Nevin, 39; Eisenhower, 79; Clary, 110–11.

25. *L&L*, vol. 1, 90–91.

26. *L&L*, vol. 1, 92–94, GGM to MM, 5/15/46; Nevin, 42–43; Grant, 67.

27. *L&L*, vol. 1, 92–94; Clary, 110–11; Eisenhower, 81; Bauer, 159.

28. Smith, 45–46, letter dated 5/10/46.

29. *L&L*, vol. 1, 87–91, GGM to MM, 5/9/46.

30. *L&L*, vol. 1, 91–92 and 92–94, GGM to MM, 5/11/ and 5/15/46; Smith, 53–55, 5/19/46.

31. *L&L*, vol. 1, 94–96, GGM to MM, 5/19/46.

32. Richardson, *Messages*, vol. 5, 2287–93, Polk's War Message, 5/11/46; *Congressional Globe*, 29th Congress, 1st Session, 794–95, 5/11/46; Walter Borneman, *Polk: The Man Who Transformed the Presidency and America* (New York: Random House, 2008), 204–7.

33. *L&L*, vol. 1, GGM to MM, 5/19/46. Meade also sought to assuage Margaret that he remained a faithful husband. "You must not be concerned about the pretty girls, for I will frankly confess as yet I have seen but one sufficiently good looking to stop me, and she evinced no disposition to cultivate my acquaintance."

34. *L&L*, vol. 1, 100–3, GGM to MM, 5/27/46; *L&L*, vol. 1, 103–7, GGM to MM, 5/28/46. Taylor not only had trouble keeping his soldiers out of trouble in town but also between themselves. Throughout the war, fights broke out between the troops, especially between nativist Americans and Irish immigrants. In one instance, a brawl between the Kennesaw Rangers and Savannah's Irish Greens escalated from fisticuffs to bullets after one Ranger called one of the Irish "a d—d Irish son of a b—h." When the melee was finally broken up, wounds ranged from missing teeth to an officer's bullet wound in the neck. Many U.S. newspapers duly reported the incident, although ethnicity and geography intermingled with accuracy. "Justice to the Greens" was the clarion call of the *Savannah Republican*, while the *Illinois State Register* ignored the taunting and blamed alcohol. *Savannah Republican*, 9/7/46; *Illinois State Register* (Springfield), 9/18/46.

35. *L&L*, vol. 1, 117–21, GGM to MM, 6/28/46; Clary, 141. In his book *Eagles and Empire*, David A. Clary notes that, while most of the Army regulars were Irish Catholic, nearly all their officers were Protestants who were disdainful of their Catholic troops. While Taylor and Polk went to great lengths to assure Mexican citizens that their religious beliefs would be protected—Polk even asked Archbishop John Hughes of New York to make similar assurances—Taylor's officers thought nothing of ordering their Catholic soldiers to attend services where a Presbyterian minister harangued them about the faith (Clary, 141). Taylor aptly summed his experience with his Texas volunteers: "On the day of the battle," he wrote, "I am glad to have the Texas soldiers with me, for they are brave and gallant; but I never want to see them before or afterward" (Nevin, 64).

36. *L&L*, vol. 1, 117–21, GGM to MM, 6/28/46.

37. *L&L*, vol. 1, 130–32, GGM to MM, 8/3/46; 131–36, 8/13/46; 136–37, 8/18/45; 130–131, GGM to MM, 9/17/46; Clary, 162–63; Bauer, 175–76.

38. *L&L*, vol. 1, 146–56, GGM to MM, 9/27/46; HSP, Meade Papers, Sketch of Monterrey, 9/46; Bauer, 176–77; Clary, 192; Eisenhower, 120–21; Nevin, 68–69.

39. Clary, 192.

40. Eisenhower, 125–26.

41. Eisenhower, 129; HSP, Meade Papers, Sketch of Monterrey by GGM.

42. Clary, 193–94; Eisenhower, 125–26. "This plan was unclear," K. Jack Bauer writes in his biography of Taylor, citing Worth, William W. S. Bliss, and Brevet Major Joseph K. F. Mansfield (another engineer senior to Meade) as probable officers. "It is too complex, sophisticated, and radical to have been developed by Taylor, all of whose battle plans were relatively simple and extremely conservative" (Bauer, 178).

43. *L&L*, vol. 1, 132–40, GGM to MM, 9/27/46.

44. *L&L*, vol. 1, 132–40. During the short battle, a woman known to history as Dos Amades ("Two Sweethearts") donned a dead lancer captain's uniform, rallied the lancers, and led them on another brave but futile charge. "There's an example of heroism worthy of the days of old!" one American officer cried. "It has remained for Mexico to produce a second Joan d'Arc!" (Clary, 195).

45. *L&L*, vol. 1, 132–40, GGM to MM, 9/27/46; Eisenhower, 131–33; Clary, 194–97.

46. *L&L*, vol. 1, 132–40; Bauer, 179; Clary, 186–97; Eisenhower, 134–38.

47. *L&L*, vol. 1, 132–40; Eisenhower, 140; Nevin, 76.

48. *L&L*, vol. 1, 132–40; Bauer, 181–83; Clary, 198–99; Eisenhower, 140–41; Nevin, 76–77.

49. Nevin, 77; Grant, 78; *L&L*, vol. 1, 132–40; Wallace, 166.

50. Bauer, 182–83.

51. *L&L*, vol. 1, 139–41; HSP, Meade Papers, J. C. Pemberton to Adjutant General R. Jones, 3/31/47.

52. Borneman, 246.

53. Eisenhower, *Agent of Destiny*, 256–57. Polk's public support of Scott cloaked his behind-the-scenes efforts to have Congress create the rank of lieutenant general—three stars to Scott's two—and give that command to Democratic senator Thomas Hart Benton.

54. Borneman, 229–30.

55. Nevin, 78; Eisenhower, *So Far*, 152–53.

56. *L&L*, vol. 1, 174–75, GGM to MM, 1/24/47.

57. *L&L*, vol. 1, 195–201, GGM to MM, 2/3/47.

58. *L&L*, vol. 1, 184–85, GGM to MM, 2/21/47.

59. *L&L*, vol. 1, 211–12, GGM to MM, 3/25/47; Eisenhower, 178–91.

60. *L&L*, vol. 1, 187–91, GGM to MM, 3/8/47; Eisenhower, 258–59; Nevin, 137.

61. *L&L*, vol. 1, 187–91.

62. *L&L*, vol. 1, 191–92, GGM to MM, 3/13/47; 192–93, GGM to MM, 3/25/46.

63. *L&L*, vol. 1, 193–95, GGM to MM, 4/9/47.

64. LOC, Debutts–Ely Letters, 46, REL to MCL, 9/21/46; and 12/25/46; J. William Jones, *Life and Letters of Robert E. Lee: Soldier and Man* (New York: Neale, 1906), 50; Korda, 107–8.

65. VHA, LFP, REL to MCL, 11/4/46; REL to MCL, 10/11/46, and REL to Fitzhugh and Custis Lee, 12/24/46; both found in Fitzhugh Lee, *General Lee: A Biography of Robert E. Lee* (New York: Appleton, 1913), 33–34; Eisenhower, 167; Guelzo, *Lee*, 88; Thomas, 117.

66. Lee, *Biography*, 34–35; Thomas, 119; Lee, *Biography*, 35; J. William Jones, *Personal Reminiscences of General Robert E. Lee* (Richmond, VA: U.S. Historical Society, 1989), 371–73, REL to My Dear Boys, 2/27/47.

67. Clary, 298; Eisenhower, *Agent of Destiny*, 242; Guelzo, 90.

68. Thomas, 121; T. Harry Williams, ed., *With Beauregard in Mexico: The Mexican War Reminiscences of P. G. T. Beauregard* (New York: Da Capo Press, 1969); Davis, *Crucible*, 63.

69. Davis, *Crucible*, 63.

70. Clary, 298; Eisenhower, *Agent of Destiny*, 241.

71. Eisenhower, *Agent of Destiny*, 241–42; Nevin, 140.

72. Lee, *Biography*, 36–57, REL letter.

73. Lee, *Biography*, 56–57; Clary, 299; Thomas, 122. Scott's earlier public statement of winning the minds of Mexican civilians ended with the first salvo at Vera Cruz. The walls were a target, true, but so was the town—and therefore its citizens. His public promise to avoid harming civilians, as opposed to his actions, made the newspapers in the United States as well as in Mexico and Europe. The cries and screams of the wounded within Vera Cruz's crumbling walls were heard in the American camp. "It really goes to my heart to be compelled to do my duty when I know that every shot either injures or seriously distresses the poor inoffensive women and children," one heartsick American officer wrote (Clary, 299–300).

74. Eisenhower, *Agent of Destiny*, 243.

75. Eisenhower, *Agent of Destiny*, 245; Long, *Memoirs of Robert E. Lee*, 69–70; Clary, 303–5.

76. Eisenhower, *So Far*, 267–69; quote from Korda, 131.

77. Clary, 320–21; Eisenhower, *Agent of Destiny*, 251–52.

78. Eisenhower, *Agent of Destiny*, 252–59; Eisenhower, *So Far*, 277–78. Guelzo, *Lee*, 90; Davis, *Crucible*, 64; Lee, *Biography*, 37–38, Letter from REL, 4/25/47; Korda, 136–39.

79. Eisenhower, *Agent of Destiny*, 254–57; Korda, 136–39.

80. Eisenhower, *Agent of Destiny*, 260–61; Winfield Scott, *Memoirs of Lieut.-Gen. Scott, LL.D., Written by Himself*, vol. 2 (New York: Sheldon, 1864), 460; Korda, 141.

81. United States Military History Institute, REL to John Mackay, 10/2/47; Davis, *Crucible*, 65. Ironically Grant, like Meade, preferred Taylor to Scott. Taylor, he thought, "knew how to express what he wanted to say in the fewest well-chosen words" (Grant, 138–39; Davis, *Crucible*, 67).

82. Eisenhower, *So Far*, 303; Eisenhower, *Agent of Destiny*, 260–65; Guelzo, 93.

83. Nevin, 178.

84. Clary, 303, 344–45.

85. Nevin, 178; Korda, 141; Eisenhower, *So Far*, 316–19; Guelzo, 93–95.

86. LFP, VHS, REL to Major J. L. Smith, 8/21/47; Lee, *Biography*, 40; Guelzo, 95; Thomas, 132–33.

87. Quote from Guelzo, 95; Thomas, 132.

88. Clary, 354–55; Tom Mahoney, "50 Hanged and 11 Branded: The Story of the San Patricio Battalion," *Southwest Review* 32, no. 4 (Autumn 1947): 373–77.

89. Clary, 356; Smith, 205, E. Kirby Smith to his wife, 8/22/47.

90. Clary, 303, 325–27; 356–57; Nevin, 201; Eisenhower, *Agent of Destiny*, 287–89. "We are in a strange situation," Captain E. Kirby Smith wrote his wife, "a conquering army on a hill overlooking the enemy's Capital, which is perfectly at our mercy, yet not permitted to enter it, and compelled to submit to all manner of insults from its corrupt inhabitants." Smith was "much afraid that peace cannot be made, but this satisfaction remains to us, that the world must always see that, though always victorious, we have ever extended the olive branch, always ready to sheathe the sword" (Smith, 208, letter to his wife, 8/22/47). Smith continually added to this letter well past its date. He next wrote his wife on September 7, before the battle at Molino del Rey. "Tomorrow will be a day of slaughter. I firmly trust and pray that victory may crown our efforts though the odds are immense. I am thankful that you do not know the peril we are in. Good Night," he closed. Smith was killed the next morning (Smith, 215–17, Smith to his wife, 9/7/47).

91. Nevin, 203.

92. Eisenhower, *Agent of Destiny*, 291.

93. Eisenhower, *Agent of Destiny*, 291–93; Williams, 68–74; Clary, 368. Scott was not as cocksure as he pretended to be. "I have my misgivings," he muttered to General Ethan Allen Hitchcock (Eisenhower, *Agent of Destiny*, 293).

94. Eisenhower, *Agent of Destiny*, 293; Scott, *Memoirs*, "Report No. 34," 511–34, 9/18/47; Nevin, 210–11.

95. Eisenhower, *So Far*, 338–39. Bravo had begged for reinforcements from Santa Anna, who had visited Chapultepec the morning of the twelfth. He refused, believing the full attack would come from the south.

96. VHS, LFP, REL to Major J. L. Smith, 9/15/47; LOC, Senate Executive Documents, 30th Congress, 1st Session, vol. 1, 375–425, "Scott's Report of the Battle for Mexico City." Pillow's being "wounded" was called into question at an inquiry.

97. Clary, 371; Eisenhower, *So Far*, 341; Nevin, 214–15.

98. Eisenhower, *So Far*, 341; Nevin, 211.

99. Nevin, 211; quote from Clary, 371.

100. VHS, LFP, REL to Major J. L. Smith, 9/15/47; Guelzo, 98; Thomas, 136.

101. Guelzo, 98; Scott Order, 9/22/47, from Eisenhower, *Agent of Destiny*, 300–1; Eisenhower, *So Far*, 346.

102. Thomas, 136; Allen C. Guelzo, "'War Is a Great Evil,'" *Southwestern Historical Quarterly* 122, no. 1 (July 2018): 76.

103. Mexican War Collection, University of Texas at Arlington (hereafter UTA), REL to MacKay, 6/21/46; VHS, REL to MCL, 2/13/48.

104. UTA, REL to MacKay, 10/2/47; VHS, LFP, REL to Anna Fitzhugh, 4/12/48; Davis, *Crucible*, 71; Thomas, 137.

105. VHS, LFP, REL to George Washington Parke Custis, 2/13/48.

106. VHS, LFP, REL to George Washington Parke Custis, 2/13/48; Korda, 154.

107. *New Orleans Delta*, 9/10/47; VHS, REL Papers, Lee to MacKay, 10/2/48; Eisenhower, *Agent of Destiny*, 310–15.

108. VHS, REL Papers, REL to MacKay, 10/2/48.

109. Lee Family Archive, REL to CCL, 2/13 and 5/15/48; to SSL, 3/4/48.

110. Lee Family Archive, REL to CCL, 2/13 and 5/15/48; to SSL, 3/4/48.

111. *CW* 1, 405–6, to Buckner S. Morris and John J. Brown, 10/19 and 10/21/47; 406–7, Lease Contract Between Abraham Lincoln and Cornelius Ludlum, 10/23/47.

112. Charles Dickens, *American Notes for General Circulation and Pictures from Italy* (London: Chapel & Hall, 1892), 163, 168–69, 177; Green, 172–73.

113. Papers of the Abraham Lincoln Digital Library, Abraham Lincoln Presidential Library and Museum, Ann G. Sprigg, https://papersofabrahamlincoln .org/persons/SP47523; Bytes of History, http://bytesofhistory.com/Collec tions/UGRR/Sprigg_Ann/Sprigg_Ann-Biography.html; Burlingame, *An American Marriage*, 260; George W. Julian, *The Life of Joshua Giddings* (Chicago: A. C. McClurg, 1892), 238.

114. Samuel C. Busey, *Personal Reminiscences and Recollections of Forty-Six Years' Membership in the Medical Society of the District of Columbia and Residence in This City* (Philadelphia: Dornan, Printer, 1890), 25–28. Busey was a medical student who became a devout member of the American Party (aka the "Know-Nothings") and went on to specialize in childhood diseases (George M. Kober,

"Samuel Clagett Busey, 1828–1901," *Proceedings of the Washington Academy of Sciences* 5 [1903]: 373–79).

115. George Watterston, *New Guide to Washington* (Washington, D.C.: Robert Farnham, 1842), 209, 211–12; Chris DeRose, *Congressman Lincoln: The Making of America's Greatest President* (New York: Threshold, 2013), 100.

116. *CW* I, 420, to WHH, 12/13/47; Jon Meacham, *And There Was Light: Abraham Lincoln and the American Struggle* (New York: Random House, 2022), 98.

117. Stephen Minot Weld, *War Diary and Letters of Stephen Minot Weld, 1861–1865* (Cambridge: Riverside Press, privately printed, 1912), 882–83; Henry Hope Reed, *The United States Capitol: Its Architecture and Decorations* (New York: W. W. Norton, 2005), 91–94.

118. Michael Burlingame, *Abraham Lincoln: A Life*, 2 vols. (Baltimore: Johns Hopkins University Press, 2008), vol. 1, 263; *CW* I, 417, Endorsement: Chester Butler et al. to Robert E. Horner, 12/7/47; 417–18, (two letters) to James K. Polk, 12/8/47; 419, to James K. Polk, 12/11/47.

119. *CW* I, 420–22, "Spot" Resolutions, 12/22/47.

120. *CW* I, 457–58, to Usher F. Linder, 3/22/48. Linder and Lincoln were on opposite sides of the political fence but had maintained an amicable relationship as lawyers on the Illinois circuit. Linder first encountered Lincoln when he led the "Long Nines" campaign to relocate the capital from Vandalia to Springfield. The term "Locofocos" came from New York and described the "Equal Rights Party" wing of the Democrats who supported Jackson and Van Buren; deriving their name from a self-igniting cigar (F. Byrdsall, *The History of the Loco-Foco or Equal Rights Party* [New York: Clement & Packard, 1842], 13, 26–27).

121. Burlingame, *A Life*, vol. 1, 265–66; *Illinois State Register* (Springfield), 1/14/48.

122. Burlingame, *A Life*, vol. 1, 265–66, *Congressional Globe*, 30th Congress, 1st Session, 95 (1/3/48); *Illinois State Register* (Springfield), 1/14/48.

123. *Congressional Globe*, 30th Congress, 1st Session, 95 (1/3/48); *CW* I, 431–42, Speech in the United States House of Representatives: The War with Mexico, 431–42. Italics are from the text.

124. *Illinois State Register* (Springfield), 3/10/48; Burlingame, *A Life*, vol. 1., 268–69; Goodwin, 122.

125. *CW* I, 438.

126. *CW* I, 430–31, to WHH, 1/8/48; 446–48, to WHH, 2/1/48.

127. LOC, "Order of Procession for the Funeral of Hon. John Quincy Adams," 2/24/48.

128. *CW* I, 501–16, Speech in the House of Representatives on the Presidential Question, 7/27/48. Lieutenant Colonel Henry Clay Jr. had died at the Battle of Buena Vista. Major Edward Webster, the senator's son, died of typhoid in Mexico City in January 1848 (Gilder Lehrman Institute of American History, Daniel Webster to Daniel Fletcher Webster, 3/4/48). Fourteen years later, Colonel Daniel Fletcher Webster was killed on August 30, 1862, at the battle of Second Bull Run.

129. Katherine Helm, *The True Story of Mary, Wife of Lincoln* (New York: Harper & Brothers, 1928), 114, 116.

130. *CW* 1, 465–66, to Mary Todd Lincoln, 4/16/48.

131. Busey, 25–28; Reynolds, 298; Gretchen Garst Ewing, "Duff Green, John C. Calhoun, and the Election of 1828," *South Carolina Historical Magazine* 79, no. 2 (1978): 126–27; Wyndham D. Miles, "Washington's First Medical Journal: *Duff Green's Register and Library of Medical and Chirurgical Science, 1833–1836,*" *Records of the Columbia Historical Society* 69/70 (January 1969): 114–15.

132. Allen Thorndike Rice, ed., *Reminiscences of Abraham Lincoln by Distinguished Men of His Time* (New York: North American Review, 1888), 216–19.

133. Myrta Lockett Avar, ed., *Recollections of Alexander H. Stephens: His Diary Kept When a Prisoner of War at Fort Warren, Boston Harbour, 1865* (New York: Doubleday, Page, 1910), 3–10, 21; *CW* I, 448, to WHH, 2/2/48; Burlingame, 274–75; Reynolds, 208–9.

134. Reynolds, 221.

135. *CW* I, 452, to Thomas Flournoy, 2/17/48; 476–77, to WHH, 6/12/48; Goodwin, 125.

136. Elizabeth M. Geffen, "Industrial Development and Social Crisis, 1841–1854," in *Philadelphia: A 300-Year History,* ed. Russell Weigley (New York: W. W. Norton, 1982), 307, 345–59; Benjamin C. Bacon, *Statistics of the Colored People of Philadelphia* (Philadelphia: Elwood, 1856), 15–16; Alexander K. McClure, *Old Time Notes of Philadelphia,* vol. 1 (Philadelphia: John C. Winston, 1905), 203; *National Intelligencer,* 6/7/48; DeRose, 174–75.

137. *National Intelligencer,* 6/9 and 6/12/48; Malcolm C. McMillan, "Joseph Glover Baldwin Reports on the Whig National Convention of 1848," *Journal of Southern History* 25, no. 3 (August 1959), 371; New York Public Library, Greeley Papers, Greeley to Schuyler Colfax, 4/3/48; Burlingame, 276.

138. Burlingame, *A Life,* vol. 1, 276; *CW* I, 517–18, Whig Circular Letter, 8/17/48.

139. Eisenhower, *Agent of Destiny,* 240–41.

140. Eisenhower, 241; Goodwin, 125.

141. *HI,* 697, Edward L. Pierce to JWW (Jesse W. Wilk), 2/12/90; Burlingame, 306; Ralph Waldo Emerson, "Ode," Eduard C. Lindeman, ed., *Basic Selections from Emerson* (New York: New American Library, 1954), 138–40.

142. *CW* II, 1–5, *Boston Daily Advertiser,* Speech at Worcester, MA, 9/12/48; 5, *Boston Atlas,* Speech at Boston, MA, 9/15/48; 6, *Lowell Daily Journal,* Speech at Lowell, MA; 6–9, *Taunton Daily Gazette,* 9/23/48.

143. *CW* II, 3.

144. *CW* II, 5; Burlingame, 283.

145. Burlingame, *A Life,* vol. 1, 282–83.

146. *CW* II, 11, Speech at Chicago, IL, 10/6/48; 11–13, Debate at Jacksonville, IL, 10/21/48; 14, Speech at Lacon, IL, 11/1/48; DeRose, 202–9.

147. DeRose, 112–13; *Congressional Globe,* 1/17/48; *House Journal,* 1/17/48.

148. *Congressional Globe,* 12/18/48; Burlingame, 288.

149. LOC, Abraham Lincoln Papers, James Quay Howard's notes of an interview with Lincoln, 5/60; Burlingame, 289.

150. *CW* II, 20–22, Remarks and Resolution Introduced in United States House of Representatives Concerning Abolition of Slavery in the District of Columbia, 1/10/49.

151. LOC, Abraham Lincoln Papers, James Quay Howard's notes of an interview with Lincoln, 5/60; Burlingame, 289.

152. Burlingame, *A Life*, vol. 1, 289; Wendell Phillips quote in Albert Beveridge, *Abraham Lincoln: 1809–1858*, vol. 2 (Boston: Houghton Mifflin, 1928), 185; Meacham, 110.

153. Burlingame, 290.

154. DeRose, 228.

155. DeRose, 238–44. Mr. DeRose's book, *Congressman Lincoln: The Making of America's Greatest President*, goes into detail about our country's near first government shutdown.

156. Borneman, 338–39; Bauer, 256–58. Rice, 19–20.

157. Reed, 105–7; Watterston, 33.

158. *Lewis v. Lewis*, 48 U.S. 776 (1849): U.S. Supreme Court, 48 U.S. 7 How. *Lewis v. Lewis* 776 776 (1849), https://supreme.justia.com/cases/federal/us/48/776/.

159. DeRose, 249; Arielle Gordon, "The Time Abraham Lincoln Argued a Case at the Supreme Court," Boundary Stones, December 16, 2020, https://boundarystones.weta.org/2020/12/16/time-abraham-lincoln-argued-case-supreme-court. Besides Taney and McLean, the other justices were James Moore Wayne, John Catron, John McKinley, Peter Vivian Daniel, Samuel Nelson, and Levi Woodbury. *Lewis v. Lewis* has been cited in federal courts at least thirty times since 1849 (DeRose, 250).

160. *CW* II, 32–36, Application for Patent on an Improved Method of Lifting Vessels over Shoals, 3/10/49; Watterston, 65; DeRose, 207–8; Reynolds, 317–18.

161. Earl Schenck Miers, ed., *Lincoln Day by Day: A Chronology, 1809–1865*, (hereafter *LDBD*) 3 vols. (Washington, D.C.: U.S. Lincoln Sesquicentennial Commission, 1960), vol. 2, 9–10.

162. *HI*, 479–80, John T. Stuart (WHH interview), 1863–66; Burlingame, 296–300; Meacham, 111; Reynolds, 319–20; Thomas F. Schwartz, "An Egregious Policial Blunder: Justin Butterfield, Lincoln, and Illinois Whiggery," *Papers of the Abraham Lincoln Association* 8 (1986): 9–19.

163. *CW* IV, 60–67, "Autobiography Written for John L. Scripps," ca. 6/60.

164. *CW* IV, 12–13; Don E. Fehrenbacher, *Prelude to Greatness: Lincoln in the 1850s* (New York: McGraw-Hill, 1964), 2021.

FIVE: THE LIGHTHOUSE BUILDER, THE RAIL-SPLITTER, AND THE MARBLE MODEL

1. *L&L*, vol. 1, 203–4.

2. HSP, Assignment Book, MFP, Col. Abert to Meade, 4/22/47; Cleaves, 45;

https://www.nps.gov, US Mexican War Soldiers and Sailors Database. Mexico War Soldiers, 1846–1848; Bache, 559–60; Wheeler, 5.

3. Cleaves, 46; *L&L*, vol. 1, 200; Lieutenant Colonel J. D. Kurtz and Captain Micah R. Brown, *Report on the Effects of Sea-Water and Exposure upon the Iron-Pile Shafts of the Brandywine Shoal Lighthouse* (Washington, D.C.: Government Printing Office, 1874), 5–6, Lt. Col. J. D. Kurtz to Brig. Gen A. A. Humphreys, 12/3/73; Miles, 29; Anthony Waskie, PhD, "Meade and Lighthouses," General Meade Society, https://generalmeadesociety.org/about-george-g-meade/meade-and-lighthouses/.

4. Frederick Webb Hodge, ed., *Bulletin 30: Handbook of American Indians North of Mexico*, 2 vols. (Washington, D.C.: Bureau of American Ethnology, 1907), vol. 1, 195; H. Robert Morrison and Christine Eckstrom Lee, *America's Atlantic Isles* (Washington, D.C.: National Geographic Society, 1981), 181; Stanley Pargellis and Ruth Lapham Butler, "Daniell Ellffryth's Guide to the Caribbean, 1631," *William and Mary Quarterly* 1, no. 3 (1944): 299, fn79.

5. Dorothy Dodd, "The Wrecking Business on the Florida Reef, 1822–1860, *Florida Historical Quarterly* 22, no. 4 (April 1944): 171–72.

6. Dodd, 175; *L&L*, vol. 1, 200; Cleaves, 46.

7. *L&L*, vol. 1, 200; Miles, 29; Wheeler, 6.

8. HSP, Meade Papers, General Orders No. 41, Major General Twiggs to Lieutenant Meade, 11/7/49; *L&L*, vol. 1, 201.

9. HSP, Meade's Report to Brevet Major William W. Mackall, Adjutant General, 12/13/49; General Orders No. 12, Mackall by order of Major General Twiggs, 2/12/50; *L&L*, vol. 1, 201; Cleaves, 46–47.

10. General John Gibbon, *An Address on the Unveiling of the Statue of Major-General George G. Meade in Philadelphia, October 18th, 1887* (Philadelphia: Allen, Lane, & Scott's Printing House, 1887), 3.

11. Miles, 29.

12. Samuel Rhoads and Enoch Lewis, "The Fresnel Light," *Friends' Review* 7 (1854): 87; Dolin, 120–21, 138; Leslie Blanchard, "Focus on Lighthouses," *Technology and Culture* 19, no. 4 (October 1978): 805, published by the Johns Hopkins University Press and the Society for the History of Technology; Linda M. Scott, "The Fresnel Lens: Our Shining Star," *Cape May Magazine*, High Summer 2022, https://www.capemaymag.com/feature/the-fresnel-lens-our-shining-star/.

13. Blanchard, 805; Wheeler, 7; "Brandywine Shoal Lighthouse, Delaware Bay, NJ," Delaware Bay Lighthouse Keepers & Friends Association, https://www.delawarebaylightkeeper-friend.org/brandywine_shoal.htm. Meade's lighthouse was not replaced until 1914 when a new lighthouse, made of reinforced concrete, was erected (Wheeler, 8–9).

14. Dolin, 121; *National Geographic Magazine* 24 (January 1913), 251; vol. 80 (December 1941), 807; Putnam, 106–9; *Pensacola Gazette*, 6/10/26; Dodd, 173, 179–80.

15. "Carysfort Light," U.S. Coast Guard website, https://www.history.uscg.mil/carysfort-reef-light/; Dolin, 121; *L&L*, vol. 1, 204; NA, National Register of Historic Places (hereafter NRHP), Carysfort Lighthouse, 1984.

16. Love Dean, *Lighthouses of the Florida Keys* (Sarasota: Pineapple Press, 1998), 140–41; "Extracts from Report of Lt. G.G. Meade to the Secretary of the Light House Board," 7/31/52, 2–3.

17. Rhoads and Lewis; *L&L*, vol. 1, 204; Cleaves, 48.

18. *L&L*, vol. 1, 204; Putnam, 108–9; "Meade Family Genealogy," General Meade Society, chrome-extension://efaidnbmnnnibpcajpcglclefindmkaj/https://generalmeadesociety.org/wp-content/uploads/2015/09/genealogy.pdf.

19. Amy K. Marshall, "Frequently Close to the Peril: A History of Buoys and Tenders in the U.S. Coastal Waters, 1789–1939" (thesis presented to the Faculty of East Carolina University, April 1997), 15; NA, *Journal of the Light House Board*, Record Group 26, Entry 1, vol. 1, 2.

20. *L&L*, vol. 1, 205; Putnam, 109.

21. *L&L*, vol. 1, 205.

22. *L&L*, 205–6; Taylor, 7; NA, NRHP, Sand Key Lighthouse, 1972.

23. NA, NRHP, Sand Key Lighthouse, 12/19/72; Waskie, "Meade and Lighthouses."

24. *L&L*, vol. 1, 206; Taylor, 7–8.

25. HSP, Meade Papers, George G. Meade, Lieutenant, Topographical Engineers, to Lieut. T. A. Jenkins, U.S.N., Capt. E.L.F. Hardcastle, U.S.A., Secretaries of Lighthouse Board, Washington D.C., 1854–55; quoted in "Rebecca Shoal, FL," Lighthouse Friends, https://www.lighthousefriends.com/light.asp?ID=1837#google_vignette.

26. HSP, Meade Papers, "Iron Pile Lighthouse, to be erected on Coffins Patches, Florida Coast, U.S."; *L&L*, vol. 1.

27. James L. Morrison, *The Best School: West Point 1833–1866* (Kent, OH: Kent State University Press, 1998), 62–63; Josh Liller, "Bright Ideas #3: William Raynolds," *U.S. Lighthouse Society News*, August 6, 2020, https://news.uslhs.org/2020/08/06/bright-ideas-3-william-raynolds/.

28. George R. Agassiz, ed., *Meade's Headquarters, 1863–1865: Letters of Colonel Theodore Lyman from the Wilderness to Appomattox* (Boston: Massachusetts Historical Society, 1922), 4–6.

29. *L&L*, 207–8; Edward Rowe Snow, *Famous Light of America* (New York: Dodd, Mead, 1955), 11; Sauers, 11.

30. Snow, 120, 132–33; *Boston News-Letter*, 5/7/1705; *New York Daily Times*, 4/21/54.

31. *L&L*, vol. 1, 207; "Absecon Light," Lighthouse Friends, https://www.lighthousefriends.com/light.asp?ID=379#google_vignette.

32. Snow, 126; Putnam, 82; "George Gordon Meade Built Lighthouses and Surveyed the Great Lakes Before the Civil War," Magic Masts and Sturdy Ships, https://magicmastsandsturdyships.weebly.com/george-gordon-meade-built-lighthouses-and-surveyed-the-great-lakes-before-the-civil-war.html; "Absecon Light."

33. *L&L*, vol. 1, 207; "Barnegat Light," Lighthouse Friends, https://www
.lighthousefriends.com/light.asp?ID=380#google_vignette; NA, NRHP, Barnegat Lighthouse, 1/25/1971; Putnam, 133–34; Timothy Van Staden, "George
Gordon Meade's Lighthouses," Postcard History, July 4, 2023, https://
postcardhistory.net/2023/07/george-gordon-meades-lighthouses/.

34. "Barnegat Light."

35. Meade Family Genealogy; *L&L*, vol. 1, 207–8; Henry P. Beers, "A History of
U.S. Topographical Engineers," *The Military Engineer* 34, no. 201 (July 1942):
348–49.

36. Gustav J. Person, "Captain George G. Meade and the Great Lakes Survey,"
Defense Technical Information Center (Accession Number ADA560277,
12/01/2010), 45–46.

37. Person, 46; "Moving to Michigan in the 1800s," *Detroit News*, 2/10/2016. With
thanks to Derrick Pratt, Director of Education and Public Programs at the
Erie Canal Museum, for his expertise and time.

38. "Boom Town Detroit (1820–1860)," Detroit Historical Society, https://de
troithistorical.org/learn/timeline-detroit/boomtown-detroit-1820-1860.

39. Marc Egnal, *Clash of Extremes: The Economic Origins of the Civil War* (New
York: Hill and Wang, 2009), 101–2; Person, 44.

40. Person, 45; U.S. 27th Congress, 2nd Session, House Document 2, "Annual
Report of the Bureau of Topographical Engineers," 15 November 1841, 146,
167; Beers, 348–49.

41. *L&L*, vol. 1, 208–10; Ira A. Hunt Jr., "The Lake Survey and the Great
Lakes," *Military Engineer* 51, no. 141 (May–June 1959), 184; "George Gordon
Meade Built Lighthouses and Surveyed the Great Lakes Before the Civil
War."

42. Captain George G. Meade's Report of September 18, 1857, 35th Congress, 1st
Session, Senate Exec. Doc. No. 920, 286; *L&L*, vol. 1, 210; Cleaves, 50.

43. Cleaves, 50; HSP, Professor C. A. Young to Captain George G. Meade, 4/28/59;
Person, 45.

44. Person, 45; *Report of the Survey of the North and Northwest Lakes by Capt. George
G. Meade, Being Appendix I of the Report of the Chief Topographical Engineer,
Accompanying Annual Report of the Secretary of War 1858* (Washington, D.C.:
Lemuel Towers, 1859), 14–15; Susan Powers, "Orlando Poe and the United
States Lake Survey," including "Transcription of a letter from Captain George
Meade to Orlando Poe, describing survey work to be done at Betsie Lake,
Michigan, March 24, 1859," Michigan in Letters, May 17, 2010, http://www
.michiganinletters.org/2010/05/.

45. *L&L*, vol. 1, 42, GGM to MM, 12/25/45; Cleaves, 50.

46. *L&L*, vol. 1, 212–13; Cleaves, 50–51.

47. HSP, MFP, GGM to MM, 10/29/62; *L&L*, vol. 1, 214–15; NA, Geo. G.
Meade, Capt. Top. Engr. to W. H. Hearding, Asst. Survey of the Lakes, Detroit, Michigan, 6/15/61; Cleaves, 51.

48. *CW* II, 57–59, to Joseph Gillespie, 7/13/49; 65, to Thomas Ewing, 9/27/49; 81–82, Fragment: Notes for a Law Lecture, 7/1/50.

49. Reynolds, 329–31; Turner and Turner, 40; *LDBD*, vol. 2, 45, 75–76; *CW* I, 304, Family Record in Abraham Lincoln's Bible; *CW* II, 76–77, to John D. Johnston, 2/23/50; Ruth Painter Randall, *Mary Lincoln: Biography of a Marriage* (Boston: Little, Brown, 1953), 141; Goodwin, 131.

50. *CW* II, 76–77, to John D. Johnston, 2/23/50, and 96–97, 1/12/51; Meacham, 121–22.

51. Burlingame, vol. 1, 310.

52. *HI*, 64, John Stuart interview, late 1865; 519, John Stuart interview, 12/20/66; Goodwin, 130.

53. Reynolds, 249–50; Burlingame, vol. 1, 313.

54. Burlingame, 342; Reynolds, 249.

55. *CW* II, 194, to Mason Brayman, 5/4/53; 202, to Thomas P. Webber, 9/12/53; 205, to Brayman, 10/3/53; Reynolds, 258; Burlingame, 336; Carlton J. Corliss, *Abraham Lincoln and the Illinois Central Railroad: Mainline of Mid-America* (n.p.: Illinois Central Railroad Company[?], 1950); Lincoln's rail pass, "Abraham Lincoln in McLean County," McLean County Museum of History, https://mchistory.org/digital-exhibits/abraham-lincoln-in-mclean-county/the-varied-caseload-of-a-lincoln-attorney; David A. Pfeiffer, "Lincoln for the Defense: Railroads, Steamboats, and the Rock Island Bridge," *Railroad History*, no. 200 (Spring–Summer 2009): 48–51.

56. Sidney Blumenthal, *The Political Life of Abraham Lincoln*, vol. 2, *Wrestling with His Angel.* (New York: Simon & Schuster, 2017), 125; Goodwin, 161.

57. Goodwin, 161–63; Morris, 68–71; Allan Nevins, *Ordeal of the Union*, vol. 2, *A House Dividing, 1852–1857* (New York: Charles Scribner's Sons, 1947), 154–56; McPherson, 15–16.

58. *HI*, 238–39, Samuel C. Parks to WHH, 3/25/66; 504–5, T. Lyle Dickey to WHH, 12/8/66; Goodwin, 164; Morris, 74; *HL*, vol. 2, 365–66; Frederick Trevor Hill, *Lincoln the Lawyer* (New York: Century, 1906). Dickey would later state to William H. Herndon that Lincoln used the same phrase in his "lost speech" at Bloomington on May 29, 1856 (*HI*, 504–5).

59. *Missouri Republican*, 10/6/54; *Missouri Democrat*, 10/6/54; Graham A. Peck, "New Records of the Lincoln-Douglas Debate at the 1854 Illinois State Fair: The Missouri Republican and the Missouri Democrat Report from Springfield," *Journal of the Abraham Lincoln Association* 30, no. 2 (Summer 2009): 32–33; *LDBD*, vol. 2, 129; Horace White, *The Lincoln and Douglas Debates: An Address Before the Chicago Historical Society, February 17, 1914* (Chicago: University of Chicago Press, 1914), 7–8; Morris, 74; *CW* II, 240–46, Speech at Springfield, IL, 10/4/54, *HL*, vol. 2, 368–69; White, 10–11.

60. *CW* II, 255, 260, Speech at Peoria, IL, 10/16/54; 288, to Ichabod Codding, 11/27/54; *HL*, vol. 2, 368–69; Burlingame, 393; Morris, 75.

61. *CW* II, 286, to Charles Hoyt, 11/10/54; to Jacob Harding, 11/11/54; 287–88,

to Noah W. Matheny, 11/25/54; 288, to Thomas J. Henderson, 11/27/54; 289, to Elihu N. Powell, 11/27/54; 290, to Joseph Gillespie, 12/1/54; 292, to John McLean, 12/6/54; 292, to Herbert Fay, 12/11/54; 292–93, to Elihu B. Washburne, 12/11/54; *HI*, 182–83, Joseph Gillespie to WHH, 1/31/55.

62. *LDBD*, vol. 2, 137–38; *Illinois Journal*, 1/23/55; *CW* II, 304–6, to Elihu B. Washburne, 2/9/55; Goodwin, 170–72.

63. *CW* II, 314–15, to Peter H. Watson, 7/23/55; *HI*, 655, William M. Dickson to WHH, 4/17/88; Goodwin, 173; Morris, 79. In the *McCormick v. Manny & Co.* case, Judge McLean held for Manny. McCormick appealed to the Supreme Court, which upheld McLean's decision ("Decision of the Supreme Court," from *Scientific American*, May 1858).

64. Morris, 81–85; David M. Potter, *The Impending Crisis, 1848–1861* (New York: Harper & Row, 1976), 199–201; Nevins, 384–85; Goodwin, 183–84; Meacham, 151–53.

65. *CW* II, 320–23, to Joshua Speed, 8/24/55; 340, Call for Republican Convention, *Illinois State Journal*, 5/10/56; Mitchell Snay, "Abraham Lincoln, Owen Lovejoy, and the Emergence of the Republican Party in Illinois," *Journal of the Abraham Lincoln Association* 22, no. 1 (Winter 2001): 90–95; Walter B. Stevens, *A Reporter's Lincoln* (St. Louis: Missouri Historical Society, 1916), 34–35; Reynolds, 431–33. Some of Lincoln's friends, including John T. Stuart, were shocked that Lincoln's name was on the list. In fact, Herndon had written it, as Lincoln was on the circuit in Pekin, Illinois. The conservative Stuart chastised Herndon, saying "You have ruined him." Stuart and Herndon both reached out to Lincoln, who wired Herndon: "All right, go ahead. Will meet you—radicals and all" (*CW* II, 5/10/56, 340, fn; *HL*, vol. 2, 382–3).

66. *CW* II, 346, to John Van Dyke, 6/27/56; 381, to Richard Thorne, 11/13/56; *LDBD*, vol. 2, 175–76.

67. *CW* II, 388, Invitation, 2/5 [1857], fn2; *LDBD*, vol. 2, 189–90. The Lincoln household was not a haven of domestic bliss; Mary's emotional struggles and Lincoln's moods saw to that. On one occasion a gentleman watched dumbstruck as Mary, brandishing a butcher knife, chased Lincoln around the yard. Passersby coming along the side yard stopped Mary's pursuit, giving Lincoln a chance to disarm her, spinning her toward the back door, and pushing her inside. "There, damn it now, stay in the house and don't disgrace us before the eyes of the world," Lincoln scolded (*HI*, 727–28, Stephen Whitehurst [WHH interview] [1885–89]).

68. *CW* II, 387–88, Fragment on the Dred Scott Case, 1/57; Gossie Harold Hudson, "Black America vs. Citizenship: The Dred Scott Decision," *Negro History Bulletin* 46, no. 1 (1983): 26–28; John Bassett Moore, ed., *The Works of James Buchanan, Comprising His Speeches, State Papers, and Private Correspondence*, vol. 10, 1856–1860 (Philadelphia: J. P. Lippincott, 1910), 105–6; Goodwin, 189; Meacham, 153; NA, *Dred Scott v. Sandford Decision.*

69. *Richmond Enquirer*, 3/13/57; *Philadelphia Bulletin*, 5/5/57; Goodwin, 189–90;

Douglas R. Egerton, *Year of Meteors: Stephen A. Douglas, Abraham Lincoln, and the Election That Brought On the Civil War* (New York: Bloomsbury, 2010), 39–40.

70. *CW* II, 409, Speech at Springfield, IL, 6/26/57.

71. Egerton, 40–42; quote from Morris, 96–98.

72. Burlingame, 461–69; *CW* II, "A House Divided": Speech at Springfield, IL, 6/16/58; 484–502, Speech at Chicago, IL, 7/19/58; 504–21, Speech at Springfield, IL, 7/17/58; Morris, 102–3. Judd was not alone in criticizing Lincoln's use of "A House Divided." "Numbers of his friends, distant from Springfield, on reading his speech, wrote him censorious letters; and one well informed co-worker predicted his defeat" (*HL*, vol. 2, 400–1).

73. *HI*, 266–67, William Jayne (WHH interview), 8/15/66; *CW* II, 522, to Stephen A. Douglas, 7/24/58.

74. *CW* II, 484–502, Speech at Chicago, IL, 7/19/58; 504–21, Speech at Springfield, IL, 7/17/58; 528–30, to Stephen A. Douglas, 7/29/58; Morris, 102–3. Stephen W. Sears, *George McClellan: The Young Napoleon* (New York: Ticknor & Fields, 1988), 58–59. McClellan attended one of the debates and found Lincoln, still an Illinois Central attorney, "a mass of anecdotes." McClellan's vote for Douglas that November was the last one he made until 1864, when he cast his presidential vote for himself.

75. Sears, 58–59; quotes from Morris, 102.

76. *HL*, vol. 2, 402–3.

77. Peck, 32–33.

78. *Muscatine Journal*, 8/26/58; Burlingame, 488.

79. Photograph of Lincoln, July 1858.

80. *CW* III, 1–37, first debate with Stephen A. Douglas at Ottawa, IL, 8/21/58.

81. *Chicago Times*, 8/22/58; *Ottawa Republican*, 8/28/58; *New York Evening Post*, 8/27/58; *New York Tribune*, 8; *CW* III, 27–58; *Muscatine Journal*, 8/26/58. The "dead cock" quote appears in the *Journal*.

82. *CW* III, 43, second debate with Stephen A. Douglas at Freeport, IL, 8/27/58; Burlingame, 496–97; Morris, 108.

83. *CW* III, 51–52; Morris, 109–10. Mr. Morris's book, *The Long Pursuit*, is an excellent book on Lincoln, Douglas, and their debates.

84. *LDBD*, 1849–1860, 228, 9/14–15 entries; *CW* III, 126–27, third Debate with Stephen A. Douglas at Jonesboro, IL, 9/15/58.

85. *CW* III, 145–46, fourth debate with Stephen A. Douglas at Charleton, IL, 9/18/58.

86. *CW* III, 283–325, seventh and last debate with Stephen A. Douglas at Alton, IL, 10/15/58; *LDBD*, 1849–1860, 232, 10/15/58 entry; *Chicago Tribune*, 10/18/15; Morris, 115–16.

87. *CW* III, 315.

88. *CW* III, 329–30, to Norman B. Judd, 10/20/58; *Illinois State Journal*, 11/3/58; *LDBD*, vol. 2, 11/2 and 11/4 entries; Morris, 117.

89. *CW* III, 339–40, to Anson G. Henry, 11/19/58; Morris, 117.

90. *CW* III, 339–40, to Anson G. Henry, 11/15/58; *HL*, vol. 3, 426–28; Morris, 117.

91. *HL*, vol. 3, 447–48; *CW* III, 356–63, Second Lecture on Discoveries and Inventions, 2/11/59; 365–70, speech at Chicago, IL, 3/1/59; 372–74, to William A. Ross, 3/26/59; 377, to Thomas J. Pickett, 4/16/59.

92. *CW* III, 372–74, to William A. Ross, 3/26/59; 378–79, to Mark W. Delahy (with enclosure); 396, Speech at Council Bluffs, IA, 8/13/59; 400–23, speech at Columbus, OH, 9/16/59; 436–37, speech at Dayton, OH, 9/17/59; 463–70, speech at Indianapolis, IN, 9/19/59; 471–86, speeches at Milwaukee, 9/30, Beloit, 10/1, and Janesville, WI, 10/2/59; *CW* III, 495–97, speech at Elmwood, KS, 11/30/59; Meacham, 176. *HI*, 247–48, Jackson Grimshaw to WHH, 4/28/66.

93. *CW* IV, 273–74, 2/25, 2/26, 2/27/60 entries; *New York Tribune*, 2/28/60; Harold Holzer, *Lincoln at Cooper Union: The Speech That Made Abraham Lincoln President* (New York: Simon & Schuster, 2004), 84–89; Egerton, 126–28; Meacham, 181; Morris, 132.

94. *CW* III, 522–50, speech at Cooper Union, New York City, 2/27/60 (quote on 550).

95. *Chicago Tribune*, 3/2/60; *New York Tribune*, 2/28/60; *White Cloud Kansas Chief*, 3/22/60; *CW* IV, 13–30, speech at New Haven, CT, 3/6/60; 45–46, to Lyman Trumbull, 4/29/60; McPherson, *Lincoln*, 24.

96. *CW* IV, 33, to E. Stafford, 3/17/60; 44, to Solomon Sturges, 4/14/60; 47, to Lyman Trumbull, 5/1/60; 60–67, "Autobiography Written for John L. Scripps," ca. 6/60 (published in the *Chicago Press and Tribune* and later by Horace Greeley); *HI*, 462–64, "―― Johnson" to WHH, 1865–66; *HL*, vol. 3, 460–62; Allen C. Guelzo, *Abraham Lincoln: Redeemer President* (Grand Rapids, MI, and Cambridge, U.K.: William B. Eerdmans, 1999), 241–43; Egerton, 128–29; Morris, 154.

97. *Lancaster Examiner*, 5/16/60; *Chicago Press and Tribune*, 5/15/60; Egerton, 136.

98. *CW* IV, 50, endorsement on the margin of the *Missouri Democrat*, 5/17/60; *HL*, vol. 3, 461–62; Goodwin, 246; Morris, 160; Egerton, 138–39.

99. *HL*, 461; *HI*, 490–91, Charles S. Zane (statement for WHH), 1865–1866; 682–83, Edward L. Pierce (statement for WHH), 12/89; Goodwin, 163.

100. *HI*, 491; *CW* IV, 50–51, Response to a Serenade, 5/18/60; *Illinois State Journal*, 5/19/60.

101. Joshua W. Caldwell, "John Bell of Tennessee: A Chapter of Political History," *American Historical Review* 4, no. 1 (July 1899): 652–64; Egerton, 51–82; Goodwin, 258–59; Morris, 137–58. Egerton and Morris give great accounts of these conventions.

102. *CW* IV, 126–27, to William H. Seward, 10/12/60.

103. *HL*, vol. 3, 406–7; Egerton, 208.

104. Jean Harvey Baker, *Mary Todd Lincoln: A Biography* (New York: W. W. Norton & Company, 2008), 162; Meacham, 195.

105. Goodwin, 279–93; *CW* IV, 129–30, to Grace Bedell, 10/19/60, plus footnote.

106. *Congressional Globe*, 36th Congress, 2nd Session, 114; Egerton, 294–308.

107. *CW* IV, 149–50, to Lyman Trumbull, 12/10/60; 151, to Elihu Washburne, 12/13/60. Italics in text.

108. *CW* IV, 154, to Thurlow Weed, 12/17/60; *LDBD*, vol. 2, 302, 12/20/60; *New York Tribune*, 12/21/60.

109. *LDBD*, vol. 3, 8, 2/1/61 entry; *HL*, vol. 3, 479–80; Morris, 203.

110. Harold G. Villard and Oswald Garrison Villard, eds., *Lincoln on the Eve of '61: A Journalist's Story by Henry Villard* (New York: Alfred A. Knopf, 1941), 70–72; *CW* IV, 190–91, Farewell Address at Springfield, Illinois, 2/11/61.

111. *CW* IV, 191–219, various speeches and remarks; 219, Remarks at Westfield, New York, 2/16/61; *LDBD*, vol. 3, 14, 2/16/61 entry; Morris, 204–5.

112. *CW* IV, 240–41, Speech in Independence Hall, 2/22/61; Carl Sandburg, *Abraham Lincoln: The War Years* (New York: Harcourt, Brace & Company, 1939), vol. 1, 66–69.

113. *LDBD*, vol. 3, 20–22, 2/22 and 2/23/61 entries; *HL*, vol. 3, 490–92; *Baltimore Sun*, 2/25/61; *Harrisburg Patriot and Union*, 2/23/61; *Illinois State Register*, 2/27/61; Goodwin, 311–12; Morris, 206–7. A Kossuth hat was a soft felt hat inspired by Magyar patriot Lajos Kossuth on his visit to the United States in 1851.

114. Egerton, 316–17; Green, 237–38.

115. Burlingame, vol. 2, 43; Egerton, 321.

116. *LDBD*, vol. 3, 24, 3/4/61 entry; Egerton, 322; Meacham, 231; Morris, 208; Villard and Villard, 102–3.

117. Egerton, 323–24; *Washington National Intelligencer*, 3/5/61; Margaret Leech, *Reveille in Washington: 1860–1865* (New York: New York Review of Books, 1941), 52–53; Colman, 279–81.

118. *LCBD*, vol. 3, 24–26, 3/4/61 entry; Villard and Villard, 102–5; *Washington Star*, 2/4/61; *National Intelligencer*, 3/5/61; Egerton, 325–26; Goodwin, 328; Morris, 211.

119. Egerton, 323–25; *HL*, 705–6, Charles S. Zane (WHH interview); *CW* IV, 262–71, First Inaugural Address—Final Text, 3/4/61.

120. Sandburg, vol. 1, 138–39; Leech, 52–55.

121. *CW* IV, 279–80, to Winfield Scott, 3/9/61; Burlingame, vol. 2, 99–102; Meacham, 235–36.

122. *CW* IV, 284–85, to William Seward, 3/15/61; 238–40, Memorandum on Fort Sumter, 3/18/61.

123. *Baltimore Sun*, 4/13/61.

124. *LDBD*, vol. 3, 36, 4/18/61 entry.

125. Lee, *Recollections*, 3–4, 8; Freeman, *Lee*, vol. 1, 301.

126. Lee Family Digital Archive (hereafter LFDA), REL to SSL, 6/30/48; REL to CCL, 3/4/48.

127. LFDA, MCL to Cora C. Peters, 8/26/48; *Baltimore Sun*, 8/2/52; Lee, *Recollections*, 8–9; Korda, 166–67; Freeman, *Lee*, vol. 1, 302–9; LFDA, REL to Joseph G. Totten, 9/1/52.

128. Korda, 173.

129. Lee, *Recollections*, 11–14; Davis, *Crucible*, 75–76; Ambrose, *Duty, Honor, Coun-*

try, 166; USMA, Superintendent's Letter Book, REL to Totten, 3/15/53; Thomas, 153–54.

130. USMA, Superintendent's Letter Book, REL to Totten, 3/15/53; Thomas, 153–54.

131. USMA, Superintendent's Letter Book, REL to Totten, 10/6, 10/7, 11/3, 11/18, 12/7, 12/9/82; REL to J. R. Torbert, 10/6/52; REL to Samuel C. Major, 11/3/52; REL to J. C. Van Camp, 12/14/52; REL to R. F. Tirrou, 12/28/52.

132. USMA, REL to Anna M. Whistler, 9/28/52; 5/26 and 8/31/53; Smith, 51; Thomas, 154–56, Ambrose, *Duty, Honor, Country*, 155–56.

133. USMA, REL to Totten, 12/28/53 and 7/8/54; Thomas, 156–57.

134. LFP, LFDA, to Martha Custis Williams, 3/14/55; Guelzo, 133–35; Thomas, 158–59.

135. LFP, LFDA, REL to Totten, 3/15/55; REL to CCL, 5/10/55; REL to MCL, 7/1/55; Urwin, *The United States Cavalry*, 96.

136. LFP, LFDA, REL to MCL, 8/5/55 and 9/3/55; REL to MCL, 11/5/55; George Omer, "An Army Hospital: From Dragoons to Rough Riders," *Kansas History: A Journal of the Central Plains* 23, no. 4 (Winter 1957): 337–67.

137. LFDA, REL to MCL, 4/12/56; Guelzo, 140–41; Thomas, 164–65; Smith, 53; Carl Coke Rister, *Robert E. Lee in Texas* (Norman: University of Oklahoma Press, 1946), 17.

138. LFDA, REL to MCL, 7/28/56.

139. Marilyn McAdams Sibley, "Robert E. Lee to Albert Sidney Johnston, 1857," *Journal of Southern History*, 29, no. 1 (February 1963); REL to Albert Sidney Johnston, 10/25/57; *Baltimore Sun*, October 13, 1857.

140. Smith, 55.

141. MacDonald, 120–26; LFP, Duke University, REL Papers, 1749–1975, REL to Anna Fitzhugh, 11/22/57; Guelzo, 149; Thomas, 177.

142. LFP, LFDA, REL to MCL, 8/4 and 10/3/56.

143. Encyclopedia Virginia website, Will of George Washington Parke Custis (March 26, 1855); Freeman, *Lee*, vol. 1, 379–80; Thomas, 175.

144. Thomas, 176.

145. LFP, LFDA, REL to Edward G. Turner, 2/13/58.

146. Duke, REL Papers, REL to Mary Fitzhugh, 11/22/57; REL to Custis Lee, 2/17/58; Davis, *Crucible*, 79–80; Guelzo, 153.

147. LFP, LFDA, REL to Edward Turner, 2/13/58; VHS, Lee Papers, REL to Ronney Lee, 2/24/58 and 3/12/60; Freeman, *Lee*, vol. 1, 386–90; Thomas, 178–79; Lee, *Recollections*, 20; Joseph C. Robert, "Lee the Farmer," *Journal of Southern History* 3, no. 4 (November 1937): 422–40.

148. Lee Papers, Duke, REL to Custis Lee, 1/17/58; Mary Lee, 18, quote from Thomas, 177; Robert, 434; Lee to Custis Lee, 1/17/58; *Baltimore Sun*, 4/21/58.

149. LFP, LFDA, REL to MCL, 12/27/56.

150. *New York Tribune*, 6/24/59 and 3/26/66; *National Anti-Slavery Standard*, 4/14/66, "Testimony of Wesley Norris"; Lee, *Recollections*, 224–25, REL, "Letter to a Gentleman in Baltimore."

151. Douglas Southall Freeman, *Lee's Lieutenants: A Study in Command*, vol. 3 (New York: Charles Scribner's Sons, 1942–44), 419; H. B. McClellan, *I Rode with Jeb Stuart: The Life and Campaigns of Major General J. E. B. Stuart* (New York: Da Capo Press, 1994), 28–29; Emory M. Thomas, "'The Greatest Service I Rendered the State': J.E.B. Stuart's Account of the Capture of John Brown," *VMHB* 94, no. 3 (July 1986); *Virginians at War, 1607–1865*, 351, James Ewell Brown Stuart to Elizabeth Letcher (Pannill) Stuart, 1/11/60; Jeffrey D. Wert, *Cavalryman of the Lost Cause: A Biography of J. E. B. Stuart* (New York: Simon & Schuster, 2008), 15.

152. Davis, *Crucible*, 96; Smith, 75.

153. Thomas, 354–55; Encyclopedia Virginia, "Col. R. E. Lee's Report," October 19, 1859.

154. *Louisville Daily Courier*, 12/8/59 (citing the *Philadelphia Journal*); *Louisville Courier-Journal*, 10/29/59; *New York Daily Herald*, 12/16/59; *Liberator*, 12/2/59.

155. *Louisville Courier-Journal*, 2/28/60; LFP, LFDA, REL to Annette Carter, 2/10/60; REL to Sam Houston, 4/20/60; *Louisville Courier-Journal*, 2/28/60; Colonel M. L. Grimm, "Colonel Robert E. Lee's Report on Indian Combats in Texas," *Southwestern Historical Quarterly 39*, no. 1 (July 1935): 21–32; LFP, LFDA, REL to MCL, 5/2/60; Davis, *Crucible*, 96–97; Guelzo, 176; Thomas, 184–85.

156. VHS, REL Headquarters Papers, 1850–1876; "Thoughts on Politicians," no date; LFP, LFDA, REL to Annette Carter, 1/16/61.

157. Davis, *Crucible*, 116; Guelzo, 179.

158. Lee, *Recollections*, REL to Reverdy Johnson, 2/25/68; Smith, 84–86.

159. Smith, 84–86; Leech, 70–71.

160. Eisenhower, 171–72; *New York Evening Post*, 8/8/66, "Letter from Montgomery Blair"; Goodwin, 350; Guelzo, 184.

161. E. D. Keyes, *Fifty Years' Observation of Men and Events* (New York: Charles Scribner's Sons, 1885), 205–7; Lee, *Recollections*, 27–28.

162. LFP, LFDA, REL to SSL, 3/20/61; Smith, 88; Freeman, vol. 1, 442.

163. LFDA, REL to SSL, 3/0/61; quote from Smith, 119.

164. Lee, *Recollections*, 24–25, to General William Scott, 4/20/60.

SIX: "AND THE WAR CAME"

1. *CW* VIII, 332–33, Second Inaugural Address, 3/4/65.

2. *CWDBD*, 372–73, 6/28/63 entry; *LDBD*, vol. 3, 192–93, 6/28/63 entry; *CW* VI, 299, to Darius N. Couch, 6/28/63 3:40 p.m.

3. *Detroit Free Press*, 4/29/61.

4. *Detroit Free Press*, 4/20 and 4/21/61; *L&L*, vol. 1, 217; vol. 2, 186–87, GGM to MM, 4/2/64.

5. *Detroit Free Press*, 215–17; Sauers, 15–16.

6. HSP, Meade Papers, GGM to unknown, 8/5/61; Meade Assignment Book, William M. Meredith to David Wilmot, 7/17/61; HSP, MFP, Thomas A. Scott

to GGM, 8/21/61; *L&L*, vol. 1, 216–17; 263, GGM to MM, 5/5/62; George B. McClellan, *McClellan's Own Story* (New York: Charles L. Webster & Company, 1887), 140; Cleaves, 54–55; Ethan S. Rafuse, *George Gordon Meade and the War in the East* (Abilene, TX: McWhinney Foundation Press, 2003), 22.

7. Davis, *Crucible*, 121–22; Smith, 101–2.

8. LFDA, General Orders No. 1, 4/23/61.

9. Myrta Lockett Avary, ed. *Recollections of Alexander H. Stephens: His Diary Kept When a Prisoner at Fort Warren, Boston Harbour, 1865* (New York: Doubleday, Page & Company, 1910), 79–80.

10. Avary, 80–81; Korda, 233; Benjamin Quarles, *The Negro in the Civil War* (New York: Russell & Russell, 1953), 42–43. In his book, Quarles ends the quote by Stephens with the sentence "The stone which the first builders had rejected was the chief stone of the new Confederate edifice."

11. John S. Blay, *The Civil War: A Pictorial Profile* (New York: Thomas Y. Crowell Company, 1960), 24–25; Thomas, 194–95. Walter H. Taylor, *Four Years with General Lee* (Bloomington: Indiana University Press, 1962), 11–12; LFDA, to General Daniel Ruggles, 4/24/61; from Philip St. George Cocke to REL, 4/24/61; to Colonel Thomas J. Jackson, 4/27/61; Dowdey, *Wartime Correspondences*, 6; 11–12, to General Daniel Ruggles, 4/24/61; 14, to John Letcher, 4/27/61; 23, to Colonel Philip St. George Cocke, 5/10/61.

12. Smith, 102; Thomas, 197.

13. LFDA, REL to MC, 4/30/61; Irvin McDowell to ML, 5/30/61; *New York Times*, 6/13/61; Guelzo, 200–1, Thomas, 195.

14. LFDA, REL to MCL, 6/9/61; Dowdey, 44–45, General Orders No. 25, 6/8/61; 50–52, to John Letcher, 6/15/61; William C. Davis, *Jefferson Davis: The Man and His Hour* (Baton Rouge: Louisiana State University Press, 1991), 337.

15. Dowdey, 58–60; Davis, *Davis*, 345–48.

16. Elizabeth Todd Grimsley, "Six Months in the White House," *Illinois State Historical Society Journal* 19 (October 1926–January 1927): 47; William Seale, *The President's House: A History* (Washington, D.C.: White House Historical Association, 1986), 363, 366; Goodwin, 332.

17. Goodwin, 283–304, 318–19; quote from H. I. Cleveland, "Booming the First American President: A Talk with Lincoln's Friend, the Late Joseph Medill," *Saturday Evening Post* 172 (August 5, 1899): 85.

18. *CW* IV, 329–30, Reply to a Committee from the Virginia Convention, 4/13/61; 331, to Winfield Scott, 4/14/61; 331–33, Proclamation Calling Militia and Convening Congress, 4/15/61; 338–39, Proclamation of a Blockade, 4/19/61.

19. *CW* IV, 341–42, Reply to the Baltimore Committee, 4/22/61; Nicolay and Hay, vol. 4, 106; L. E. Chittenden, *Recollections of President Lincoln and His Administration* (New York: Harper & Brothers, 1891), 126–30; Davis, *Lincoln's Men*, 27–29.

20. *CW* IV, 109–16; *Baltimore Sun*, 4/20/61; *CW* IV, 340–41 (two, to Thomas H. Hicks and George W. Brown), 4/20/61; Chittenden, 125–29; Davis, *Lincoln's Men*, 28; Goodwin, 352.

21. *CW* IV, 344 (two, to Thomas H. Hicks and George W. Brown), 4/20/61; 341–42, Reply to Baltimore Committee, 4/22/61.

22. "The Eloquent Voorhees on the Crisis," *Baltimore Sun*, 4/20/61 (italics in text).

23. Nicolay and Hay, vol. 4, 152–53.

24. *New York Times*, 5/1/63; *CW* IV, 353–54, Proclamation Calling for 42,034 Volunteers, 5/3/61.

25. *CW* IV, 347, to Winfield Scott, 4/27/61; United States Constitution, Article I, Section 9, Clause 2; Meacham, 241–42.

26. Davis, *Lincoln's Men*, 41. Dr. Davis's book, *Lincoln's Men*, is a remarkable account of Lincoln's relationship with Union soldiers and officers.

27. *CW* IV, 333, to Elmer E. Ellsworth, 4/15/61; Gregory J. Urwin, *The United States Infantry: An Illustrated History, 1775–1918* (New York: Sterling Publishing Co., 1991), 94–95; Reynolds, 528–32.

28. Reynolds, 535–36; Davis, *Lincoln's Men*, 43–44; *New York Daily Herald*, 5/27/61.

29. *CW* IV, 385–86, to Ephraim D. and Phoebe Ellsworth, 5/25/61.

30. Leech, 105; Davis, *Lincoln's Men*, 45–46.

31. *CW* IV, 420–21, Fragment of a Draft of Message to Congress, 7/4/61; 424, 426, 431–32, 438–39, Message to Congress in Special Session, 7/4/6.

32. *New York Tribune*, 6/28/61; *Richmond Enquirer*, 6/11/61; Guelzo, 206–7; Blay, 46–49; Bruce Catton, *The Army of the Potomac Trilogy*, book one: *Mr. Lincoln's Army* (New York: Library of America, 2022)

33. Benjamin Brown French, *Witness to the Young Republic: A Yankee's Journal, 1828–1870*, ed. Donald B. Cole and John J. McDonough (Hanover, NH: University Press of New England, 1989), 365.

34. David Homer Bates, *Lincoln in the Telegraph Office* (New York: Century Co., 1907), 26–27, 41; Wheeler, *Mr. Lincoln's T-Mails*, 4–7.

35. Leech, 124–25; Green, 246–47; *LDBD*, vol. 3, 55, 7/21/61 entry.

36. Green, 246–47; Guelzo, 206–7.

37. *CW* IV, 457, Memoranda of Military Policy Suggested by Bull Run Defeat, 7/23/61; United States War Department, *War of the Rebellion: A Compilation of the Official Records of the Union and Confederate Armies*, series 3, vol. 1 (Washington, D.C.: Government Printing Office, 1880–1901), 380–83, General Orders No. 49, 8/3/61 (approved 7/22/61 and 7/25/61).

38. United States War Department, *War of the Rebellion: A Compilation of the Official Records of the Union and Confederate Armies* (Washington, D.C.: Government Printing Office, 1880–1901), vol. 2, 753, L. Thomas to General George B. McClellan, 7/22/61.

39. Stephen W. Sears, ed. *The Civil War Papers of George B. McClellan: Selected Correspondence, 1860–1865* (New York: Ticknor & Fields, 1989) (hereafter *CWPGBM*), 75–76, to Mary Ellen McClellan, 8/3/61.

40. *CWPGBM*, 71–73, to Abraham Lincoln, 8/2/61.

41. *CWPGBM*, 81–82, to Mary Ellen McClellan, 8/8 and 8/9 [10]/61; 127–28, to Samuel L. M. Barlow, 11/8/61; Goodwin, 380; Sears, *McClellan*, 116–18.

42. Sears, *McClellan*, 122–23; *CWPGBM*, 109, to Charles P. Stone, 10/21/61; 111, to Mary Ellen McClellan, 10/25/61.

43. *CWPGBM*, 114–19, to Simon Cameron, 10/31/61; Bates, 93–97.

44. George F. Root and H. S. W. [Henry Stevenson Washburn], "The Vacant Chair: or, We Shall Meet, but We Shall Miss Him" (Chicago: Root & Cady, 1861); *Piqua Daily Call*, 6/30/97.

45. LFDA, REL to Joseph E. Johnston, 7/24/61; MCL to Anne Carter Lee, 7/30/61; REL to MCL, 8/4/61; Henry A. Wise to REL, 8/10/61; REL to Henry A. Wise, 8/31/61; Samuel Cooper, 9/10/61.

46. LFDA, REL to MCL, 9/17/61 and 9/20/61; Dowdey, 75–76, to John Letcher, 9/17/61; Guelzo, 211–13; *Richmond Enquirer*, 9/6, 9/20, and 10/31/61.

47. Dowdey, 84, Special Orders No. 206, 11/5/61; General Orders No. 1, 11/8/61; 86, to Miss Mildred Lee, 11/15/61; 92–93, to Judah Benjamin, 2/20/61; 93–95, to Andrew Magrath, 12/14/61; Taylor, *Four Years*, 36–41; Thomas, 212–15.

48. Dowdey, 99–101, to G. W. C. Lee, 1/4/62; 104–6, to G.W.C. Lee, 1/19/62.

49. McClellan, 140; Cleaves, 55; Rafuse, 23.

50. *L&L*, vol. 1, 220, GGM to MM, 9/24/61; E. M. Woodward, *Our Campaigns, or the Marches, Bivouacs, Incidents of Camp Life and History of Our Regiment During Its Three-Year Term of Service* (Philadelphia: John E. Potter, 1865), 60–63.

51. *L&L*, vol. 1, 227, to John Sergeant Meade, 11/14/61; Dane DiFebo, "Old Baldy: A Horse's Tale," *PMHB* 135, no. 4 (October 2011): 540–50; Anthony Waskie, PhD, "'Old Baldy': General Meade's Warhorse," General Meade Society website.

52. *L&L*, vol. 1, 236–37; GGM to MM, 12/21/61; 243–44, GGM to MM, 1/5 and 1/26/62.

53. *L&L*, vol. 1, 241–42, GGM to MM, 1/2/62; 245, GGM to MM, 2/8/62; 346–47, GGM to MM, 2/16/62.

54. Elizabeth Keckley, *Behind the Scenes; or, Thirty Years a Slave, and Four Years in the White House* (Hillsborough, NC: Eno Publishers, 2016), 40–41; Brady Dennis, "Willie Lincoln's Death: A Private Agony for a President Facing a Nation of Pain," *Washington Post*, 10/7/2011; Burlingame, 2, 298; Meacham, 258.

55. *National Intelligencer*, 2/25/62; Goodwin, 421.

56. Turner and Turner, 43–45; Keckley, 44.

57. Root and H. S. W., "The Vacant Chair."

58. Goodwin, 403–5; *CW* V, 48, Annual Message to Congress, 12/3/61, 48–49.

59. *CW* V, 96–97, to Simon Cameron, 1/11/62; Goodwin, 412–13; Reynolds, 565–66.

60. *CW* V, 111–12, President's General War Order No. 1, 1/27/62.

61. *CWPGBM*, 204–5.

62. Sears, 166; *CWPGBM*, 214, to Edwin M. Stanton, 3/18/62.

63. *L&L*, vol. 1, 253–54, GGM to MM, 3/17/62.

64. Dowdey, 118–19, to His Wife, 2/23/62; 124–27; 129, to His Wife, 3/15/62; 139, to General Joseph E. Johnston, 3/18/62; Korda, 292–94; Thomas, 218–19.

65. David Nevin, *The Road to Shiloh* (Alexandria, VA: Time-Life Books, 1983), 9, 145; Blay, 76–78.

66. Davis, *Davis*, 410–16; Thomas, 222.

67. Champ Clark, *Decoying the Yanks: Jackson's Valley Campaign* (Alexandria, VA: Time-Life Books, 1983), 21–23, 66–71; Blay, 111–12; Guelzo, 232–33; Smith, 128–29.

68. Dowdey, 151, 4/21/62; 156–57, 4/25/62; 160–61, 4/29/61; 162–63, 5/1/62; 168–69, 5/8/62; 174–75, 5/16/62; to Thomas J. Jackson; 183–84, to Jefferson Davis, 6/5/62; Smith, 128–29; Thomas E. Griess, series ed., *Atlas for the American Civil War*, The West Point Military History Series (Garden City Park, NY: Square One Publishers, 2002), 10, Jackson's Valley Campaign, January–June 1862.

69. Dowdey, 172, to His Wife, 5/13/62; *Richmond Dispatch*, 5/9/62, from the *Baltimore Sun*, 5/14/62.

70. John H. Reagan, *Memoirs, with Special Reference to Secession and the Civil War*, ed. Walter F. McCaleb (New York and Washington: Neale Publishing Company, 1906).

71. Dowdey, 177, to General Joseph E. Johnston, 5/21/31. Davis, *Davis*, 420–21; *CWDBD*, 211–12, 5/15/62 entry.

72. *CWPGBM*, 285, to Edwin M. Stanton, 6/1/62 (telegram); 287–88, to Mary Ellen McClellan, 6/2/62; Ronald H. Bailey et al., *Forward to Richmond: McClellan's Peninsular Campaign* (Alexandria, VA: Time-Life Books, 1983), 154–57; Davis, *Crucible*, 210–11; Smith, 125–26.

73. *CWPGBM*, 286–87, to the Army of the Potomac, 6/2/62.

74. LFDA, REL to Mrs. W. H. F. Lee, 622/62; C. Vann Woodward, ed., *Mary Chesnut's Civil War* (New Haven, CT: Yale University Press, 1981), 115–16.

75. Gary W. Gallagher, ed., *Fighting for the Confederacy: The Personal Recollections of General Edward Porter Alexander* (Chapel Hill: University of North Carolina Press, 1989), 91.

76. Freeman, vol. 2, 88–89; Thomas, 227.

77. Lee, *Recollections*, 82–85. Lee's other horses were Richmond, Ajax, Lucy Long, and an unnamed "Brown Roan."

78. Dowdey, 181–82, Special Orders No. 22, 6/1/62; 182–83, to Major Walter H. Stevens, 6/3/62; 183, to Stevens, 6/4/63; 185, to Colonel Josiah Gorgas, 6/5/63; 187, to General Thomas J. Jackson, 6/8/62; 189–90, to his wife, 6/10/62 (two letters); 191, to General J.E.B. Stuart, 6/1/62.

79. H. B. McClellan, *I Rode with Jeb Stuart*, 52–71 (Stuart's report to Lee and Lee's commendation of Stuart are found on pages 69–71); Dowdey, 198–200, General Orders No. 75, 6/24/62.

80. *CWPGBM*, 217, to Mary Ellen McClellan, 6/26/62, and to Randolph B. Marcy, 6/26/62 (both telegrams); Dowdey, 201, to Jefferson Davis, 6/26/62; 201–2, to General Benjamin Huger, 6/26/62; McPherson, *Battle Cry of Freedom*, 66.

81. *CWPGBM*, 309, to Edwin M. Stanton, 6/25/62 (two telegrams).

82. *L&L*, vol. 1, GM to MM, 4/9/62; 272–73, 6/11/62; 278, 6/20/62; *Philadelphia Inquirer*, 4/30/62.

83. *L&L*, vol. 1, 284–87; MFP, A. M. Randol to GGM, 2/2/81; Pennypacker, 39; Sears, 218; *CWPGBM*, 325–26, to Randall B. Marcy, 6/30/62.

84. *L&L*, vol. 1, 288–90.

85. HSP, Randol to GGM, 2/2/81.

86. Cleaves, 68.

87. *L&L*, vol. 1, 298–99.

88. *L&L*, vol. 1, 299–300, GGM to MM, 7/1/62.

89. *L&L*, vol. 1, 299–300; *CWPGBM*, 327, to Lorenzo Thomas, 7/1/62; Sears, *McClellan*, 218.

90. Sears, *McClellan*, 218–21.

91. *L&L*, vol. 1, 297.

92. *CWPGBM*, 326, to Edwin M. Stanton, 7/1/62 (telegram), Thomas, 241; Sears, *McClellan*, 220–21.

93. Sears, 242; James Longstreet, *From Manassas to Appomattox: Memoirs of the Civil War in America* (Philadelphia: J. B. Lippincott Company, 1896), 142–43.

94. Longstreet, *From Manassas*, 144–45.

95. Davis, *Crucible*, 219–20.

96. Davis, *Crucible*, 220.

97. *Richmond Dispatch*, 7/11/62; McPherson, 477.

98. Bates, 138–41.

99. Gideon Welles, *Diary of Gideon Welles: Secretary of the Navy Under Lincoln and Johnson*, vol. 1 (Boston and New York: Houghton Mifflin Company, 1911), 70–71, 7/13/62 entry.

100. Welles, *Diary*, vol. 1, 70.

101. Welles, *Diary*, vol. 1, 70–71.

102. Welles, *Diary*, vol. 1, 71.

103. *CW* V, 336–38, Emancipation Proclamation—First Draft, 7/22/62; Salmon P. Chase, *Diary and Correspondence of Salmon P. Chase* (Washington, D.C.: Government Printing Office, 1903), 45–46, 7/21/62 entry; Seale, vol. 1, 291–92; Goodwin, 463–64; Meacham, 271–72.

104. Gideon Welles, "The History of Emancipation," *Galaxy* 14 (December 1882): 842–45; Goodwin, 463–68; Meacham, 271–72.

105. Welles, "The History," 844; Goodwin, 468.

106. *Philadelphia Inquirer*, 7/4 and 7/19/62.

107. *L&L*, vol. 1, 300–1.

108. *L&L*, vol. 1, 301–2, GGM to MM, 8/12; 303–4, 8/19/62; 305–6, 8/24/62.

109. Freeman, *Lee*, vol. 2, 245–48; Freeman, *Lee's Lieutenants*, vol. 1, 605–75; Guelzo, 245; Thomas, 245–47.

110. Stephen E. Ambrose, *Halleck: Lincoln's Chief of Staff* (Baton Rouge: Louisiana State University Press, 1962), 47, 61–64; *CWDBD*, 7/14/62.

111. *OR* series 1, vol. 12, part 3, 473–74; McPherson, 524; Thomas, 248–49.

112. *OR* series 1, vol. 12, part 3, 473–74; McPherson, 524; Thomas, 248–49.
113. Frederick S. Daniel, *The Richmond Examiner During the War; or, The Writings of John M. Daniel with a Memoir of His Life by His Brother* (New York: Printed for the Author, 1868), 57–58; *CWDBD*, 239, 7/13/62 entry; *CWPGBM*, 384–85, to Henry W. Halleck, 8/4/62; Dowdey, 239–40, to General Thomas J. Jackson, 7/27/62; 240, to Miss Mildred Lee, 7/28/62. McClellan was enraged at Halleck's order. "We are twenty-five miles from Richmond & are not likely to meet the enemy in force . . . At Aquia Creek we would be seventy five miles from Richmond." Halleck, like Lincoln and also Lee, was certain McClellan would be happy to stay at Harrison's Landing indefinitely.
114. Dowdey, 239–40, to General Thomas J. Jackson, 7/27/62; 240, to Miss Mildred Lee, 7/28/62.
115. Dowdey, 266, to Jefferson Davis, 8/29/62 (telegram); 266–67, to Davis, 8/30/62, Lee to Davis, 35; Thomas, 252–53. H. B. McClellan, *I Rode with Jeb Stuart*, 94–95.
116. Longstreet, *From Manassas*, 182–84; Dowdey, 275–85, to General Samuel Cooper, 6/8/63.
117. *L&L*, vol. 1, 307–8, GGM to MM, 9/3/62; Rafuse, 37–38; Sauers, 27–29.
118. *CW* V, 388–89, to Horace Greeley, 8/22/62.
119. Walter H. Taylor, *General Lee: His Campaigns in Virginia 1861–1865* (Lincoln: University of Nebraska Press, 1994), 115; Lee, *Recollections*, 78; Korda, 455–56; Thomas, 255.
120. Dowdey, 292–94, to Jefferson Davis, 9/3/62.
121. Dowdey, 294–95, to Davis, 9/4/62.
122. Dowdey, 294–95, to Davis, 9/4/62; Woodward, 433–35; Davis, *Davis*, 456–59; Steven A. Channing et al., *Confederate Ordeal: The Southern Homefront* (Alexandria, VA: Time-Life Books, 1984), 29–33.
123. Woodward, 426–27, 452–53, 468; Guelzo, 250–51.
124. Dowdey, 288; 294–95, to Jefferson Davis, 9/4/65; 295–96, to Davis, 9/5/62; 299–300, to the People of Maryland, 9/8/62; Blay, 135, 142–45.
125. *Philadelphia Inquirer*, 9/13/62; Dowdey, 299–300, General Orders No. 191, 9/10/62; 304–5, to Jefferson Davis, 9/12/62.
126. Dowdey, 299–300, General Orders No. 191, 9/10/62.
127. *L&L*, vol. 1, 309–10, GGM to MM, 9/13/62.
128. *L&L*, vol. 1, 309–10; *CWPGBM*, 454–55, to Maj. Genl. W. B. Franklin, 9/13/62; 456–57, to Henry W. Halleck, 9/13/62; 458, to Mary Ellen McClellan, 9/14/62; Sears, 280–81.
129. Dowdey, 308, to General Lafayette McLaws, 9/12/62; 309–10, to Jefferson Davis, 9/16/62; Wert, 146.
130. *L&L*, vol. 1, 309–11, GGM to MM, 9/18/62; O. R. H. Thomson and William H. Rauch, *History of the "Bucktails"* (Philadelphia: Electric Printing Company, 1906), 204–6; R. U. Johnson and C. C. Buel, eds., *Battles and Leaders of the Civil War* (hereafter *B&L*), vol. 4 (New York: The Century Company, 1887–1888), 574; Pennypacker, 65–75.

131. Dowdey, 306–7, to Jefferson Davis, 9/13/62; 309–10, to Davis, 9/16/62; Thomas, 261; S. C. Gwynne, *Rebel Yell: The Violence, Passion, and Redemption of Stonewall Jackson* (New York: Scribner, 2014), 461–62.

132. *L&L*, 310–11, GGM to MM, 9/18/62; *CWPGBM*, 466, to William B. Franklin, 9/16/62; to Mary Ellen McClellan, 9/16/62; Sears, 296–97; Sauers, 32–33.

133. Bruce Catton, *This Hallowed Ground* (New York: Doubleday, 1956), 203; Rafuse, 43.

134. Rafuse, 43–44; *L&L*, vol. 1, 311–12, GGM to MM, 9/20/62; 312–13, Coulburn to GGM, 9/17/62; R. B. Marcy to GGM, 9/17/62.

135. Alexander, 151–53; *B&L*, vol. 2, 665–70, n130.

136. Alexander, 152–53; Dowdey, 311, to Jefferson Davis, 9/18/62; Davis, *Crucible*, 243–44; Guelzo, 255–57; McPherson, 543–45; Thomas, 263–64.

137. Alexander, 152–53.

138. Alexander, 153; *B&L*, vol. 2, 670.

139. *CWPGBM*, 468, to Henry W. Halleck, 9/18/62 8 a.m. (telegram).

140. *L&L*, vol. 1, 311–12, GGM to MM, 9/20/62.

SEVEN: EMANCIPATION AND INVASION

1. Chase, 87–90, 9/22/62 entry; Welles, *Diary*, vol. 1, 142–45, 9/22/62 entry; *CW* V, 433–36, Preliminary Emancipation Proclamation, 9/22/63.

2. *CW* V, 438–39, Reply to Serenade in Honor of Emancipation Proclamation, 9/24/62.

3. Bell Irvin Wiley, *The Life of Billy Yank* (Baton Rouge: Louisiana State University Press, 1952), 42–44; Davis, *Lincoln's Men*, 94; McPherson, *Battle Cry*, 497.

4. *L&L*, vol. 1, 317–18, GGM to MM, 10/5/62. As Freeman Cleaves points out in *Meade of Gettysburg*, Meade would not have been gratified had he known of McClellan's letter of condolence to Hooker. On September 20, McClellan wrote the wounded general "Had you not been wounded when you were, I believe the result of the battle would have been the entire destruction of the Confederate army, for I know that with you at its head your corps would have kept on until it gained the main road" (Cleaves, 81, footnote 1).

5. *L&L*, vol. 1, 312, GGM to MM, 9/20/62.

6. *L&L*, vol. 1, 320–21, GGM to MM, 10/20/62.

7. *L&L*, vol. 1, 320–21, GGM to MM, 10/20/62; *CWPGBM*, 519–20, to Mary Ellen McClellan, 11/7/62; *CWDBD*, 285, 11/7/62 entry; Sears, 340.

8. *L&L*, 325, GGM to MM, 11/8/62; Sears, 340–41; Sauers, 34–35.

9. *L&L*, 326–28, GG to MM, 11/13–14/62; Cleaves, 87; Rafuse, 48–49; Sauers, 34–35.

10. *CWDBD*, 274–75, 10/4/62 entry; 276–77, 10/8/62 entry.

11. *CWDBD*, 274–75; George Washington Custis Lee to Davis, 9/25/62, and General Orders No. 201, 9/26/62; Longstreet, *From Manassas*, 62; Gwynne,

489; Jeffrey D. Wert, *General James Longstreet: The Confederacy's Most Controversial Commander* (New York: Touchstone, 1993), 204–5; *CWPGBM*, 496–98, to Henry Halleck, 10/12–10/13/62, various telegrams; *Philadelphia Inquirer*, 10/14/62.

12. LFDA, MCL to Mary Custis Lee (daughter), 10/18/62; MCL to Mildred Childe Lee, 10/20/62; REL to MCL, 10/26/62; REL to MCL, 9/29/62 and 12/16/62; Dowdey, *Wartime Correspondences*, 357, to Mrs. W. H. F. Lee, 12/10/62. Taylor, *Four Years*, 76–77.

13. *L&L*, vol. 1, 325, GGM to MM, 11/8/62; Charles A. Dana, *Recollections of the Civil War: With the Leaders at Washington and in the Field in the Sixties* (New York: D. Appleton and Company, 1902), 138. Ambrose Burnside was born unlucky. In fact, he barely survived birth: he seemed stillborn until the doctor tickled his nose with a feather. A tailor's apprentice before entering West Point, he graduated in 1847; after a stint in Mexico, he served on the frontier until 1853, leaving to manufacture a carbine he invented. When his company failed, forcing him to sell the patent to his creditors, his friend McClellan let Burnside and his wife move into his home and got Burnside a job with the Illinois Central Railroad. The marriage was childless, but at least Mary Bishop had said yes. Years earlier, at his first trip to the altar, the bride-not-to-be was asked if she took Burnside for her husband and emphatically answered "No!" and thereby ended the wedding before she walked back down the aisle. Ms. Moon and her sister later went on to become Confederate spies. In 1863, they were arrested in Cincinnati by General Burnside (Cullum, Class of 1847, 191–92); *Philadelphia Times*, 11/22/95; Larry Eggleston, *Women of the Civil War: Extraordinary Stories of Soldiers, Spies, Nurses, Doctors, Crusaders, and Others* (Jefferson, NC: McFarland & Company, 2003), 102–6.

14. Dowdey, 355–56, to Jefferson Davis, 12/8/62; 358, to General Samuel Cooper, 12/11/62, telegram.

15. *L&L*, 330–31, GGM to MM, 11/22/62; 336, 12/5/62; *Philadelphia Inquirer*, 12/29/62.

16. William K. Goolrick et al., *Rebels Resurgent: Fredericksburg to Chancellorsville* (Alexandria, VA: Time-Life Books, 1985), 29–30, 51.

17. *L&L*, vol. 1, 337–38, GGM to MM, 12/16/62; Goolrick, 53–56.

18. Goolrick, 63; *L&L*, vol. 1, 337–38, GGM to MM, 12/16/62.

19. Goolrick, 64–65, 108; Rafuse, 51–53; Captain Joseph R. Orwig, *History of the 131st Penna. Volunteers: War of 1861–65* (Williamsport, PA: The Sun Book and Job Printing House, 1902); *B&L*, vol. 3, 135–36.

20. Pennypacker, 103–4; Cleaves, 90–91; *L&L*, vol. 1, GGM to MM, 12/16/62. Meade's only comment about the shot through his hat was a humorous one to Margaret. "If it had come from the *front* instead of the *side* I would have been a *goner*," he wrote.

21. Goolrick, 67; Cleaves, 90–91.

22. Orwig, 108; Goolrick, 71; Rafuse, 53.

23. Thomson and Rauch, 236; Cleaves, 91; Francis Augustin O'Reilly, *The Fred-*

ericksburg Campaign: Winter War on the Rappahannock (Baton Rouge: Louisiana State University Press, 2003), 178–79.

24. *L&L*, vol. 1, 337–38, GGM to MM, 12/16/62; Orwig, 108; Sauers, 37.

25. *B&L*, vol. 3, 79; Alexander, 173–75; Wert, *Longstreet*, 218.

26. McPherson, *Battle Cry*, 571–75.

27. *L&L*, vol. 1, 337–38, GGM to MM, 12/16/62.

28. Dowdey, 360–62, to James A. Seddon, 12/14/62; 363, to Seddon, 12/15/62 (telegram); 363–64, to Seddon, 12/16/62; 364–65, to his wife, 12/16/62.

29. *Charleston Mercury*, 12/27/62; *The Derby Mercury*, 12/31/62; *Philadelphia Inquirer*, 12/20/62; Lee, *Recollections*, 92–93, 2/23/63.

30. Alexander, 222; Guelzo, 268.

31. LOC, photograph: "Fredericksburg, Virginia. St. Georges Episcopal Church and Court House"; John Hennessey, "A Beleaguered Courthouse," Mysteries and Conundrums website, 6/13/2010 and 1/23/2011. With thanks to Scott Harris.

32. Museum of the Confederacy, Deed of Emancipation, 12/29/62.

33. LFDA, REL to MCL, 12/7, 12/16, and 12/21/62; 1/8 and 11/11/63; 1/24/64; REL to George Washington Custis Lee, 12/8, 11/5, and 11/11/63.

34. LFDA, REL to MCL, 12/7/62; Davis, *Crucible*, 278–79; Guelzo, 269–70; Thomas, 273–74.

35. *CW* VI, 28–30, Emancipation Proclamation, 1/1/63; McPherson, 563.

36. Rafuse, 55.

37. *L&L*, vol. 1, 341–42, GGM to MM, 12/7, 12/21, and 12/26/62.

38. *L&L*, 349–50, GGM to MM, 1/26/63; 360–61, GGM to MM, 4/4/63; 362–63, GGM to MM, 4/5/63; HSP, MFP, Levi Richards to GGM, 1/8/63.

39. *L&L*, 348–49, GGM to MM, 1/23/63; John David Billings, *Hardtack and Coffee, or, The Unwritten Story of Army Life* (Boston: George M. Smith & Co., 1888), 72; Huntington, 122.

40. *L&L*, vol. 1, 349–51, GGM to MM, 1/26/63 (two letters).

41. Goolrick, 98–99; Walter H. Hebert, *Fighting Joe Hooker* (Indianapolis and New York: Bobbs-Merrill, 1844), 46–50; McPherson, 585.

42. Goolrick, 91.

43. Cleaves, 102; Goolrick, 99–104.

44. *L&L*, vol. 1, 365–66, GGM to MM, 2/27/63.

45. *L&L*, vol. 1, 363–64, GGM to MM, 4/9/63; 364–65, GGM to MM, 4/11/62; Adam Gurowski, *Diary from November 18, 1862, to October 18, 1863*, vol. 2 (New York: Carleton, 1864), 199, 4/15/63 entry.

46. *L&L*, vol. 1, 353–54, GGM to MM, 2/6/63; 354–55, 2/13/63; 357–58, 3/13/63; Charles Francis Adams Jr., *Charles F. Adams, 1835–1916, An Autobiography* (Boston: Houghton Mifflin Company, 1916), 161; Hebert, 180; Smith, 155–56.

47. *L&L*, vol. 1, 353–54, GGM to MM, 2/1/63.

48. General Orders No. 47, 4/30/63, *OR* 25 (1): 171; Rafuse, 58–59.

49. Dowdey, 305–6, to General James Longstreet, 2/18/63; 417–18, to Longstreet, 3/17/63; 436, to Longstreet, 4/17/63; 440–41, to Longstreet, 4/27/63.

50. LFDA, REL to MCL, 3/9/63.

51. LFDA, REL to MCL, 4/3, 4/5, 4/19, and 4/24/63; REL to Agnes Lee, 4/11/63; Guelzo, 281–82; Thomas, 277–78. In their biographies, Professor Guelzo believed Lee had a heart attack; Professor Thomas believed it was angina pectoris, when the heart doesn't have enough oxygen, causing chest pain and sometimes an attack.

52. Survivors' Association, *The History of the Corn Exchange Regiment, 118th Pennsylvania Volunteers: From Their First Engagement at Antietam to Appomattox* (Philadelphia: J. L. Smith, Publisher, 1888), 166–69; *Philadelphia Press*, 11/12/72.

53. Bache, 260.

54. LFDA, REL to MCL, 2/23/63; Dowdey, 449, War Department, 5/1/63 (telegram).

55. Sauers, 40–41; Ward, Geoffrey C., *The Civil War: an Illustrated History* (New York: Knopf, 1990), 202–3; Bache, 262–63; *B&L*, vol. 3, 159–61.

56. Alexander, 199–201; Union Theological Seminary, Dabney Collection, REL to Anna Jackson, 1/25/66.

57. Dowdey, 450–51, to Jefferson Davis, 5/2/63; Taylor, 84–85; Thomas, 281–83; Davis, *Crucible*, 309–11; Gwynne, 529–31.

58. Gwynne, 532–33; Goolrick, 125–26; *B&L*, vol. 2, 191–93.

59. Gwynne, 536; Greiss, "The Wilderness Campaign, 1863, Chancellorsville Maps, 5/1, 2, and 3/63."

60. Gwynne, 536–37; Captain Hartwell Osborn and Others, *Trials and Triumphs: The Record of the 55th Ohio Volunteer Infantry* (Chicago: A. C. McClurg & Co., 1904), 75–76.

61. *B&L*, vol. 3, 198; Alexander, 202–3; David Gregg McIntosh, Colonel of Artillery, C.S.A., *The Campaign of Chancellorsville* (Richmond, VA: Wm. Ellis Jones' Sons, 1913), 35–40.

62. Alexander, 201–2; Smith, 160.

63. Gwynne, 530–42; McPherson, 642; *B&L*, vol. 3, 211–14.

64. *L&L*, vol. 1, 370–71, GGM to MM, 5/7/63; 271–74, GGM to MM, 5/8/63; Rafuse, 64–65; Cleaves, 109–10.

65. Dowdey, 459–72, Battle of Chancellorsville; McPherson, 644.

66. *L&L*, vol. 1, 379–80, GGM to MM, 5/23/63; HSP, Biddle Papers, James Biddle to his wife, 5/17/63.

67. Major General Sir Frederick Maurice, ed., *An Aide-de-Camp of Lee: Being the Papers of Colonel Charles Marshall* (Boston: Little, Brown and Company, 1927), 172–73.

68. Maurice, 172–73; Cleaves, 111–12; John Gibbon, *Personal Recollections of the Civil War* (New York: G. P. Putnam's Sons, 1928), 118–21; *Survivors*, etc., 200–4.

69. *CW* VI, 198, to Joseph Hooker, 5/6/63. The one-line telegram read: "Are you suffering with *dust* this morning?" The biting comment on Hooker's leaving before the army did was never sent; John Nicolay noted, "Written by the Pres-

ident, but not sent out on the morning of May 6th, after a pouring rain all night and during the morning. Subsequently turned out that on the 5th Hooker had crossed the river" (fn1).

70. *L&L*, vol. 1, 371–73, GGM to MM, 5/8/63.

71. Ward, 204; McPherson, 639–42.

72. *L&L*, vol. 1, 371–72, GGM to MM, 5/8/63.

73. Bruce Tap, *Over Lincoln's Shoulder: The Committee on the Conduct of the War* (Lawrence: University Press of Kansas, 1998), 168–71; Stephen W. Sears, *Gettysburg* (New York and Boston: Houghton Mifflin Company, 2003), 21. Chandler, Wade, and Wilson's investigation was deemed "unofficial" as Congress was not in session.

74. *L&L*, vol. 1, 374–75, GGM to MM, 5/12/63.

75. *L&L*, vol. 1, 375–76, GGM to MM, 5/15/63.

76. *CW* VI, 215, to Joseph Hooker, 5/13/63; 217, to Joseph Hooker, 5/14/63.

77. *L&L*, vol. 1, 375–76, GGM to MM, 5/17/63.

78. Gibbon, *Personal Recollections*, 120.

79. *L&L*, vol. 1, 377–78, GGM to MM, 5/19/63.

80. *L&L*, vol. 1, GGM to MM, 5/10/63; 376–77, GGM to MM, 5/17/63; 379–80, GGM to MM, 5/20/63; 381–82, GGM to MM, 5/26/63; vol. 2, 6; HSP, MFP, O. O. Howard to GGM, 5/16/63; Daniel Sickles to GGM, 5/16/63; Gibbon, *Personal Recollections*, 120–21; Cleaves, 118–19.

81. *L&L*, vol. 1, 383–85, GGM to MM, 6/11/63; 385, GGM to MM, 6/11/63.

82. *Richmond Times Dispatch*, 4/13/63; *Wheeling Daily Intelligencer*, 4/13/63; Davis, *Davis*, 494–98; Guelzo, 293; Thomas, 288; Channing, 84–86.

83. LFDA, REL to Stuart, 6/23/63.

84. Sue Burns Moore and Rebecca Blackwell Drake, eds., *Leaves: The Diary of Elizabeth Meade Ingraham* (Champion Hill: Champion Hill Heritage Foundation, 2019), 5–12, 5/7/63 entry; 19–24, 5/8/63 entry.

85. Davis, *Davis*, 504–5; Guelzo, 292; Thomas, 288–89.

86. Dowdey, 507–9, to Jefferson Davis, 6/10/63; McPherson, 646–47; Wert, 245.

87. Dowdey, 487–89, to Jefferson Davis, 5/20/63; 480, to General John B. Hood, 5/21/63.

88. McPherson, 648; Thomas, 290.

89. Dowdey, 487–89, Jefferson Davis, 5/20/63; 480, to General John B. Hood, 5/21/63.

90. Kevin M. Levin, "The Diaries Left Behind by Confederate Soldiers Reveal the True Role of Enslaved Labor at Gettysburg," *Smithsonian Magazine*, July 2, 2019.

91. LFDA, REL to MCL, 6/10/63.

92. Dowdey, 507–9, to Jefferson Davis, 6/10/63.

93. Dowdey, 505–6, Major C. S. Venable to Major General J. E. B. Stuart, 6/9/63; Wert, 240–50.

94. Dowdey, 509, to W. H. Lee, 6/10/63; LFDA, REL to MCL, 6/9, 6/11, 6/14, and 6/15/63.

95. Dowdey, 514–15, to Jefferson Davis, 6/15/63 (letter and telegram); 516–19, to General James Longstreet, 6/15 and 6/17/63; 517, to General Ambrose P. Hill, 6/16/63; 518, to General Richard S. Ewell, 6/17/63; 519–20, to Jefferson Davis, 6/18/63.

96. Dickinson College Archives & Special Collections (http://archives.dickinson .edu), General Orders No. 72, 6/21/63; Coddington, 154–55; Guelzo, *Gettysburg*, 71–72.

97. Major General Isaac Trimble, "The Battle and Campaign of Gettysburg," *Southern Historical Society Papers* (hereafter *SHSP*), vol. 26, ed. R. A. Brock (Richmond, VA: Published by the Society, 1905), 116–17; Robert Emory Park, "War Diary of Captain Robert Emory Park, Twelfth Alabama Regiment, January 28, 1863–January 27, 1864," *SHSP*, vol. 26, 12.

98. Michael A. Palmer, *Lee Moves North: Robert E. Lee on the Offensive* (New York: John Wiley Sons, 1998), 26; Valley of the Shadow website, Rachel Cormany Diary, 6/15/63 entry; Philip Schaff, D.D., "The Gettysburg Week," in *Old Mercersburg*, ed. the Women's Club of Mercersburg (New York: Frank Allaben Genealogical Company, 1913), 164.

99. Valley of the Shadow, Rachel Cormany; Tillie (Pierce) Alleman, *At Gettysburg: What a Girl Saw and Heard of the Battle; A True Narrative* (New York: W. Lake Borland, 1889), 20; Elizabeth Brown Pryor, *Reading the Man: A Portrait of Robert E. Lee Through His Private Letters* (New York: Penguin Books, 2008), 350.

100. Schaff, 165–66.

101. Dowdey, 533–34, General Orders No. 73.

102. Valley of the Shadow, Rachel Cormany.

103. Valley of the Shadow, Rachel Cormany.

104. Schaff, 165.

105. Schaff, 165–66.

106. Davis, *Davis*, 495; Guelzo, *Gettysburg*, 105–6; Noah Andre Trudeau, *Gettysburg: A Testing of Courage* (New York: Perennial, 2002), 79.

107. Schaff, 165.

108. *SHSP*, vol. 26, 118; McClellan, 315–17; Taylor, 92–93.

109. LFDA, REL to Stuart, 6/23/63.

110. LFDA, REL to Stuart, 6/23/63.

111. *OR* I, XXVII, Part 1, 47–48; Welles, *Diary*, vol. 1, 344, 6/26/63 entry; 348–49, 6/28/63 entry; Ambrose, 135–37; *OR* I, XXVII, Part I, 61.

112. Rush Lancers website (www.rushlancers.com); Cleaves, 60–61, 83–84; *L&L*, vol. 1, 336, GGM to MM, 12/9/62.

113. Emerson G. Taylor, *Gouverneur Kemble Warren: The Life and Letters of an American Soldier* (Boston: Houghton Mifflin, 1932), 119; Cleaves, 124–25.

114. *L&L*, vol. 2, 354–55, Appendix W: Testimony of General Meade Before the Congressional Committee on the Conduct of the War, 3/5/64 (355); Comte de Paris, *The Battle of Gettysburg, from the History of the Civil War in America* (Philadelphia: Porter & Coates, 1888), 73.

115. *CWDBD*, 372–73, 6/28/63 entry; *CW* VI, 299, to Darius N. Couch, 6/28/63, 3:40 p.m. (see also fn1); Dowdey, 534–35, to General Richard S. Ewell, 6/28/63.

116. McPherson, 653; Craig L. Symonds, *History of the Battle of Gettysburg* (New York: Harper Collins, 2001), 10–11; James M. Paradis, *African Americans and the Gettysburg Campaign* (Lanham, MD: The Scarecrow Press, 2013), 4–7; Bruce Levine, *Thaddeus Stevens: Civil War Revolutionary, Fighter for Racial Justice* (New York: Simon & Schuster, 2021), 44–47.

117. Alleman, 19–20.

118. Paradis, 8, 35.

119. Alleman, 22; Clark, 30.

120. Alleman, 28–30.

EIGHT: WEDNESDAY, JULY 1

1. Alleman, 33.

2. Craig L. Symonds, *History of the Battle of Gettysburg* (New York: Harper Collins, 2001), 71.

3. *CW* VI, 312, to Alexander K. McClure, 6/30/63 (with footnote).

4. *OR* XXVII, 1, 432, Robt. C. Schenck to Lincoln, 6/30/63; *Washington Chronicle*, 6/30/63; *Baltimore Sun*, 7/1/63; *Philadelphia Inquirer*, 7/1/63.

5. *CW* VI, 312–13, to Benjamin B. French, 7/1/63 (with footnote); *LDBD*, vol. 3, 194, 7/1/63 entry.

6. David Lowe, ed., *Meade's Army: The Private Notebooks of Lt. Col. Theodore Lyman* (Kent, OH: The Kent State University Press, 2007), 34, 9/13/63 entry.

7. *OR* I, 27, part 1, 927, 934, 938–39.

8. D. B. Steinman, *The Builders of the Bridge: The Story of John Roebling and His Son* (New York: Harcourt, Brace, and Company, 1945), 257–59.

9. *OR* 27 (3): 428, William H. French to Halleck, 6/30/63 (rec'd 11:05 a.m.); Halleck to French, 6/30/63 (2:15 p.m.); *OR* 27 (10:69); Edwin M. Stanton to Meade, 6/30/63 (11:30 p.m.); Brown, 115–17.

10. *OR* series 1, 27, part 1, 923–24, Buford to Pleasonton, 6/30/63; Sears, 143–44.

11. Haupt, 208–13.

12. Haupt, 208–13.

13. *L&L*, vol. 2, 31, Commanding Officer, Sixth Corps, 7/1/63.

14. OR 27 (1), 70, Meade to Halleck, 7/1/63 (7:00 a.m.).

15. James I. Robertson Jr., *General A. P. Hill: The Story of a Confederate Warrior* (New York: Vintage Civil War Library, 1987), 204–6; Guelzo, 129–31; Symonds, *History*, 69–71.

16. Guelzo, 129–31; James L. Morrison Jr. "The Memoirs of Henry Heth, Part II," *Civil War History* 8, no. 3 (1962): 300–4.

17. Abner Hard, M.D., *History of the Eighth Cavalry Regiment, Illinois Volunteers, During the Great Rebellion* (Aurora, IL: unidentified, 1868); Marcellus Ephraim Jones, *Memorials of Deceased Companions of the Commandery of the State of Illi-*

nois, Military Order of the Loyal Legion of the United States (Chicago: Ashland and Block, 1901), 560–62.

18. David L. Ladd and Audrey J. Ladd, *The Bachelder Papers: Gettysburg in Their Own Words*, vol. 1 (Dayton, OH: Morningside House, 1994), 201; Edward G. Longacre, *General John Buford* (Cambridge: Da Capo Press, 1995), 189–90; Guelzo, *Gettysburg*, 139–40.

19. RG 393, No. 12, Vol. 2, 1863, NA, Eleventh Corps Papers, RG 393, No. 14, Vol. 2, 1863, Official Papers Found on the Body of Maj. General John Reynolds, GGM to John Reynolds, 6/30/63; Brown, 97.

20. *OR* XXVII, 1, 460–61, Meade to Reynolds, 7/1/63.

21. Weld, 229–31; Harry M. Kieffer, *Recollections of a Drummer Boy* (Boston: James Osgood, 1883).

22. Hillman A. Hall, W. B. Besley, and Gilbert G. Wood, *History of the Sixth New York Cavalry (Second Ira Harris Guard)* (Worcester, MA: The Blanchard Press, 1908), 138–39; Ladd and Ladd, 200–2, Letter of First Lt. Aaron Brainard Jerome, 10/18/65; Longacre, 192–93.

23. *OR* 27 (1): 1031, Report of Lieut. John H. Calef, Battery A, Second U.S. Artillery Camp near Warrenton, VA, 7/27/63.

24. Guelzo, *Gettysburg*, 124.

25. *OR* 27 (1): 1031, Report of Lieut. John H. Calef, Battery A, Second U.S. Artillery Camp near Warrenton, VA, 7/27/63; Chapman Biddle, *The First Day of the Battle of Gettysburg* (Philadelphia: J. B. Lippincott & Co., 1880), 22–23; *Reynolds Memorial: Addresses Delivered Before the Historical Society of Pennsylvania* (Philadelphia: J. B. Lippincott & Co., 1880), 29–30; Brown, 126–27.

26. *SHSP*, vol. 6, 122; Walter Kempster, M.D., 1st Lt. 10th NY Cavalry, "The Cavalry at Gettysburg," in *The Gettysburg Papers*, vol. 1, ed. Ken Bandy and Florence Freeland (Dayton, OH: Press of Morningside Bookshop, 1978), 432; Robertson, 207–9.

27. "Northern Prison Life," in *The Land We Love, A Monthly Magazine*, ed. D. H. Hill., vol. 2 (Charlotte, NC: Irwin & Co., 1867).

28. Clark, 45–51.

29. Clark, 47–48.

30. Walter Lord, ed., *The Fremantle Diary: A Journal of the Confederacy* (Short Hills, NJ: Burford Books, 1954), 201–2; Longstreet, *From Manassas*, 346–47.

31. Longstreet, *From Manassas*, 351–52.

32. Weld, 230–32.

33. *OR* 27.3: 458, Meade to Couch, 7/1/63; 473, Halleck to Couch and Couch to Halleck, 7/1/63; 461, Butterfield to Hancock, 7/1/63, 12:30 p.m.

34. *OR* 27.3: 458, Meade to Couch, 7/1/63; 473, Halleck to Couch and Couch to Halleck, 7/1/63; 461, Butterfield to Hancock, 7/1/63, 12:30 p.m.; Butterfield to Hancock, 7/1/63, 1:10 p.m.

35. Guelzo, *Gettysburg*, 147–48; Abner Doubleday, *Chancellorsville and Gettysburg* (New York: Da Capo Press, 1994), 131–33.

36. Catton, *Final Fury*, 24. In the winter of 1863, the Iron Brigade was broken up, its regiments distributed to other corps. The Iron Brigade's legendary Confederate counterpart, the Stonewall Brigade, suffered the same fate.

37. Major General Oliver Otis Howard, *Autobiography*, vol. 1 (New York: The Baker & Taylor Company, 1907), 412–13.

38. *L&L*, vol. 2, GGM to Winfield Scott Hancock, 7/1/63, 1:10 p.m.; Adin B. Underwood, *Three Years' Service in the 33rd Mass. Infantry Regiment, 1862–1865* (Boston: A. Williams & Co. Publishers, 1881), 115–16.

39. Cleaves, 135–36.

40. *OR* 27, 1, 461, Butterfield to Hancock, 7/1/63, 1:10 p.m.; 367–77, Hancock to Brig. Genl. Seth Williams, no date, 1863.

41. Brown, 145; Guelzo, 158–59.

42. *SHSP*, vol. 4, 157–58, Letter of Major-General Henry Heth of A. P. Hill's Corps, 6/77; *SHSP*, vol. 33, 143, James Power Smith, "General Lee at Gettysburg"; Taylor, *Four Years*, 92–93; Robertson, 209; Guelzo, *Lee*, 298–99.

43. *SHSP*, vol. 33, 140, Smith, "General Lee"; Morrison, "Memoirs of Henry Heth," part 2, 305; Dowdey, *Wartime Correspondences*, 574–76; "Battle of Gettysburg"; Guelzo, *Gettysburg*, 176.

44. *SHSP*, vol. 33, 143–44, Smith, "General Lee"; *SHSP*, vol. 4, 158; Thomas, 294–95.

45. Howard, *Autobiography*, 413–17; *SHSP*, vol. 33, 143–44, Smith, "General Lee."

46. Clark, 61–62.

47. *B&L*, vol. 3, General Henry J. Hunt, "The First Day at Gettysburg," 281.

48. Taylor, *Four Years*, 95; *General Lee*, 190; *SHSP*, vol. 33, 144, Smith "General Lee; Thomas, 295.

49. *SHSP*, vol. 33, 144–45, Smith, "General Lee."

50. *B&L*, vol. 3, Hunt, 283, and General Francis A. Walker, "Meade at Gettysburg," 408; David M. Jordan, *"Happiness Is Not My Companion": The Life of General G. K. Warren* (Bloomington and Indianapolis: Indiana University Press, 2001), 83; Rafuse, 79.

51. Jordan, 83.

52. O. O. Howard, "Campaign and Battle of Gettysburg, June and July, 1863," *Atlantic Monthly*, July 1876, 58.

53. *B&L*, vol. 3, E. P. Halstead, "Incidents of the First Day at Gettysburg," 285.

54. *OR* XXVII, part 1, 367–69 (Hancock Report), 927 (Buford), 825 (Geary); Coddington, 324.

55. *L&L*, vol. 2, 39–40, Winfield Scott Hancock to GGM, 7/1/63, 5:25 p.m.

56. Longstreet, *From Manassas*, 358.

57. Longstreet, *From Manassas*, 358–59.

58. Longstreet, *From Manassas*, 359.

59. Longstreet, *From Manassas*, 359; *SHSP*, vol. 33, 145–46, Smith, "General Lee."

60. *SHSP*, vol. 33, 146, Smith, "General Lee."

61. *OR* XXVII, part 1, 71, Meade to Halleck, 7/1/63, 6:00 p.m. (received 10:20 p.m.).

62. *L&L*, vol. 2, 61–62.

63. *L&L*, vol. 2, 51–62.

64. *B&L*, vol. 3, 408. Walker was not present at Gettysburg; he had sustained severe wounds at Chancellorsville and returned to 2nd Corps in August.

65. *L&L*, vol. 2, 61–62.

66. Alleman, 35–41.

NINE: THURSDAY, JULY 2

1. *Philadelphia Inquirer*, 7/2/63, fourth edition. The article was attributed to a dispatch to the *New York Times*.

2. Alleman, 46–49.

3. Alleman, 50–51.

4. Smith, 32.

5. Smith, 32.

6. "10 Facts About Lee's and Meade's HQs", American Battlefield Trust website; Thomas, 297.

7. Longstreet, *From Manassas*, 362.

8. Longstreet, *From Manassas*, 362.

9. Longstreet, *From Manassas*, 362; Lee, *Wartime Papers*, 576–77; Thomas, 297.

10. Freemantle, Arthur J. L. *Three Months in the United States* (Edinburgh and London: William Blackwood and Sons, 1863), 205–6; Wert, *Longstreet*, 266; J. B. Hood, *Advance and Retreat* (New Orleans: Published for the Hood Orphan Memorial Fund, Beauregard, 1880), 57; Clark, 68–69.

11. McClellan, 336–37; Wert, *Cavalryman*, 251–52.

12. Longstreet, *From Manassas*, 365–66; Thomas, 297.

13. Hood, 57; Clark, 98.

14. *OR* XXVII, 3, 465, Williams to Sedgwick, 7/1/63; Doubleday, 138; Brown, 165–66; Guelzo, 224.

15. J. Cutler Andrews, *The North Reports the Civil War* (Pittsburgh: University of Pittsburgh Press, 1955), 421–22.

16. Clark, 74.

17. *Revised United States Army Regulations of 1861* (Washington, D.C.: Government Printing Office, 1863); Brown, 172–74.

18. Brown, 174.

19. Brown, 172; *OR* XXVII, 3, 471, Meigs to Ingalls, 7/1/63, 11:20 a.m.; Ingalls to Meigs, 7/1/63 received 7 p.m.; 221–22, Ingalls to Meigs, 8/28/64.

20. Haupt, 214–15, Haupt to Ingalls, 7/1/63; 215, Haupt to Meigs, 7/1/63; 215–16, Meigs to Haupt, 7/1/63; 216, Haupt to Stanton, 7/2/63, 3 o'clock; J. R. Clough to Haupt, 7/2/63; Haupt to Colonel D. C. McCallum, 7/2/63; 220, Stanton to Haupt, 7/3/63.

21. *OR* XXVII 3, 486, Butterfield to Slocum, 7/2/63; 487, Slocum to Meade, 7/2/63.

22. *B&L*, vol. 3, 297–300.

23. James A. Hessler, *Sickles at Gettysburg* (New York: Savas Beattie, 2009), 1–6; Nat Brandt, *The Congressman Who Got Away with Murder* (New York: Syracuse University Press, 1991), 17–19; *New York Times*, "Antonio Bagioli" obituary, 2/7/71, and "General Daniel E. Sickles," 2/6/98.

24. Allan Nevins and Milton Halsey Thomas, eds. *The Diary of George Templeton Strong*, vol. 2, *The Turbulent Fifties* (New York: The Macmillan Company, 1952), 438–39, 2/28/59 entry.

25. Harriet Elinor Smith, ed. *Autobiography of Mark Twain*, vol. 1 (Berkeley: University of California Press, 2010), Wednesday, January 17, 1906, 287.

26. Nevins and Thomas, 439.

27. *Washington Union*, 4/5/59; *London Daily Telegraph*, 4/25/58; *The Age* (Melbourne, Australia), 9/3/59; *Gettysburg Compiler*, 5/2/59; Hessler, 17.

28. Hessler, 19; Woodward, 379.

29. Hessler, 32–33; Peter Messent and Steve Courtney, eds. *The Civil War Letters of Joseph Hopkins Twichell: A Chaplain's Story* (Athens: The University of Georgia Press, 2008), 147; W. A. Swanberg, *Sickles the Incredible* (New York: Charles Scribner's Sons, 1956), 166; Sauers, 5–7.

30. *L&L*, vol. 2, 66.

31. *L&L*, vol. 2 66–67.

32. *B&L*, vol. 3, Hunt, 295–96, 301–2; Sauers, 157.

33. *B&L*, vol. 3, Hunt, 295–96, 301–2; Sauers, 157.

34. *B&L*, vol. 3, Hunt, 301; Henry Edwin Tremain, *Two Days of War: A Gettysburg Narrative and Other Excursions* (New York: Bonnell, Silver and Bowers, 1905), 42–43.

35. *B&L*, vol. 3, Hunt, 301–2.

36. *B&L*, vol. 3, Hunt, 302–3.

37. Tremain, 44.

38. *OR* XXVII, 3, 488, Lieutenant Jerome to Butterfield, 7/2/63, 11:55 a.m.; Captain Babcock to Butterfield, 7/2/63, 1:30 p.m.

39. Longstreet, *From Manassas*, 366–67.

40. *OR* XXVII, 1, 923, Buford to Pleasonton, 6/30/63; 926–28, Buford's Report, 8/27/63; Brown, 214.

41. Brown, 215; *OR* XXVII, 3, 490, Butterfield to Pleasonton, 7/2/63, 12:50 p.m. and 12:55 p.m.; Pleasonton to Gregg, 7/2/63, 1:45 p.m.; *L&L*, vol. 2, 71.

42. Tremain, 53–55.

43. Gibbon, *Personal Recollections*, 136; *Report of the Joint Congressional Committee on the Conduct of the War* (hereafter *JCCW*) (Washington: Government Printing Office, 1865), I, 406; Jordan, 88; Clark, 77.

44. *OR* XXVII, 1, 72, Meade to Halleck, 7/2/63, 3 p.m. (received 7/3, 10:20 a.m.).

45. *L&L*, vol. 2, 71–72; *OR* XXVII, 1, 116, Meade to Brigadier General Lorenzo Thomas, 10/1/63; Tremain, 59–62.

46. *L&L*, vol. 2, 72–73; HSP, MFP, Letter from George Sykes, 7/29/76; William H. Paine to George Meade, 5/22/86.
47. Tremain, 61–62; Brown, 219–20.
48. Tremain, 61–62; Brown, 220.
49. *L&L*, vol. 2, 64–65; Julie Goodnight, "Snaffle vs Curb Bits for Trail Horses," Barn Mice website, 8/13/2010.
50. Griess, Situation 1530 Hours, 2 July 1864; Craig L. Symonds (Cartography by William J. Clipson), *Gettysburg: A Battlefield Atlas* (Baltimore: The Nautical & Aviation Publishing Company of America, 1992), 44–45; *B&L*, vol. 3, "Editor's Footnote," "Excerpt from Warren's Testimony to the Committee on the Conduct of the War," 307–10.
51. *L&L*, vol. 2, 79; Tremain, 63; HSP, Biddle to George Meade, 8/18/80; Brown, 223.
52. *L&L*, vol. 2, 79; Brown, 224.
53. *HSP*, James C. Biddle to George Meade, 8/18/80; Brown, 224.
54. Brown, 224; Tremain, 63–65.
55. *SHSP*, vol. 5, 92, letter from Major Scheibert, of the Prussian Engineers, 11/21/77.
56. D. Augustus Dickert, *History of Kershaw's Brigade* (Newberry, SC: E. H. Aull Company, 1899), 234–35.
57. Dowdey, *Wartime Correspondences*, 577, Battle of Gettysburg, 1/20/64; *SHSP*, vol. 33, 148, Smith, "General Lee." Alexander, 234.
58. *SHSP*, vol. 33, 148, Smith, "General Lee."
59. Alexander, 236; *SHSP*, vol. 7, 69, Major General Lafayette McLaws, "Gettysburg"; Clark, 72–73.
60. *SHSP*, vol. 7, 69.
61. *SHSP*, vol. 7, 69–70.
62. Clark, 78.
63. Hood, 57–58.
64. Hood, 59; General G. Moxley Sorrel, *Recollections of a Confederate Staff Officer* (New York: The Neale Publishing Company, 1905), 169.
65. *SHSP*, vol. 33, 149, Smith, "General Lee."
66. William C. Oates, *The War Between the Union and the Confederacy, and Its Lost Opportunities* (New York and Washington: The Neale Publishing Company, 1905), 21–31; Clark, 77.
67. Fremantle, 207–8; *SHSP*, vol. 4, 66–67, A. L. Long to General J. A. Early, 4/5/76.
68. Fremantle, 207–8; *SHSP*, vol. 4, 66–67, A. L. Long to General J. A. Early, 4/5/76.
69. McClellan, 318–19; Clark, 71.
70. Fremantle, 208.
71. Turner and Turner, 130–31, To Mrs. Charles Eames, 7/26/62; White House Historical Association website, "The Soldiers' Home: First Presidential Retreat"; Mr. Lincoln's White House website, "Homes: Soldiers' Home."

72. *Evening Star*, 7/2/63; Anna L. Boyden, *Echoes from the Hospital and White House* (Boston: D. Lothrop and Company, 1884), 143–44; Randall, 535.

73. Oliver Willcox Norton, *The Attack and Defense of Little Round Top, Gettysburg, July 2, 1863* (Gettysburg: Stan Clark Military Books, 1992), Report of Col. William C. Oates, Fifteenth Alabama Regiment, 8/8/63, 144–46; Oates, 212; Clark, 80.

74. Hood, 59.

75. Norton, 308–10, G. K. Warren to Captain Porter Farley, 7/13/72; Jordan, 92.

76. Norton, 309–10.

77. Norton, 310; Taylor, 121–22.

78. McPherson, *Hallowed Ground*, 80–81; Norton, 210–18, Report of Col. Joshua L. Chamberlain, Twentieth Maine Infantry, 7/6/63.

79. Norton, 210–12; Oates, 214–15.

80. Norton, 212–13; Clark, 85.

81. Norton, 144–45, Report of Col. William C. Oates, Fifteenth Alabama Infantry, 8/8/63; 214–20, Chamberlain, 7/6/63; Clark, 84; Oates, 216–17; Guelzo, 271–72.

82. Norton, 193, Report of Brig.-Gen. James Barnes, U.S. Army, commanding First Division, 8/24/63; 206, Report of Colonel James C. Rice, Forty-Fourth New York, commanding Third Brigade, 7/31/63.

83. *L&L*, vol. 2, 83–84.

84. Norton, 48–49, Lieutenant-Colonel William H. Powell: "The Fifth Army Corps"; 134–39, Captain Farley's "Number Nine"; *National Tribune*, "Gettysburg: The Part Taken by the Fifth Corps" by Joseph M. Leeper, Capt., Co. E; Clark, 84–85.

85. Powell, 135–39; Clark, 85.

86. Clark, 85.

87. Oates, 216.

88. *L&L*, vol. 2, 84; Diane Monroe Smith, *Washington Roebling's Civil War: From the Bloody Battlefield at Gettysburg to the Brooklyn Bridge* (Guilford, CT: Stackpole Books, 2019), 147; Brown, 236.

89. Norton, 133, Captain Farley's "Number Nine."

90. Symonds, 48–50; Clark, 85; Guelzo, 256–63; *The Gettysburg Times*, 1/23/1932.

91. Charles H. Weygant, *History of the One Hundred and Twenty-Fourth Regiment* (Newburgh, NY: Journal Printing House, 1877), 175–77; Captain James E. Smith, *A Famous Battery and Its Campaigns, 1861–1864* (Washington: W. H. Loudermilk & Co., 1892), 102–3.

92. Clark, 87.

93. Smith, 105–6.

94. Smith, 106.

95. Alleman, 56–57.

96. Symonds, 44–45.

97. Dickert, 86–89; OR I, XXVII, 2, 180, Report of General Kershaw, 10/1/63; Clark, 99; Guelzo, 282.

98. Marie Caroline Post, *The Life and Memoirs of Comte Regis de Trobriand* (New York: E. P. Dutton & Company, 1910), iii–iv, 233–237; Brown, 236–38; Clark, 99–100; Symonds, 53.

99. Dickert, 238; Guelzo, 284–85; *SHSP*, 180–81, Kershaw's Report.

100. Symonds, 164–66.

101. *L&L*, vol. 2, 84–85; Brown, 236–37; Guelzo, 286.

102. Hessler, 204–12.

103. Longstreet, *From Manassas*, 371–72.

104. Clark, 111–12.

105. Clark, 112.

106. Clark, 112.

107. Alleman, 58–63.

108. *B&L*, vol. 3, "The Council of War on the Second Day," 314.

TEN: FRIDAY, JULY 3

1. Alleman, 64–71.

2. Charles Elihu Slocum, *The Life and Services of Major-General Henry Warner Slocum* (Toledo: The Slocum Publishing Company, 1913), 111; Brown, 286; Clark, 127; Guelzo, 384–85; Symonds, 66–67.

3. *Cincinnati Daily Gazette*, 7/14/63; Guelzo, 385–86.

4. *National Tribune*, 6/29/93.

5. Guelzo, 385–86; Margaret S. Creighton, *The Colors of Courage: Gettysburg's Forgotten History* (New York: Basic Books, 2005), 66–67; August E. Zeitler, "Picket Shots," *National Tribune*, 6/29/93, and *Cincinnati Daily Gazette*, 7/14/63; Codie Eash, "An American Citizen of African Descent," Pennsylvania in the Civil War website (https://www.penncivilwar.com).

6. *OR* 27, 2, 697, Stuart's Report, 8/20/63; McClellan, 337; Wert, *Cavalry*, 285.

7. *OR* 27, 2, 697, Stuart's Report, 8/20/63; Dowdey, *Wartime Correspondences*, 569–85. Guelzo, 429.

8. McClellan, 338–39; Symonds, 75.

9. McClellan, 340; Gregory J. Urwin, *Custer Victorious: The Civil War Battles of George Armstrong Custer* (Lincoln and London: University of Nebraska Press, 1990), 43.

10. Symonds, *Atlas*, 72–74; *B&L*, vol. 3, William E. Miller, Captain, 3rd Pennsylvania Cavalry, "The Cavalry Battle at Gettysburg," 402–3; Sears, 469.

11. Symonds, 75; Samuel Harris, *Personal Reminiscences of Samuel Harris* (Chicago: The Rogerson Press, 1897), 31.

12. David McMurtrie Gregg, *The Right Flank at Gettysburg* (Philadelphia: McLaughlin Brothers' Job Printing Establishment, 1878), 16; Sears, 460; Symonds, 75.

13. Longstreet, *From Manassas*, 386–87; Guelzo, 376–81.

14. *B&L*, vol. 3, James Longstreet, "Lee's Right Wing at Gettysburg," 342–43.

15. *B&L*, vol. 3, Longstreet, "Lee's Right Wing," 343.
16. Whitelaw Reid, "The Gettysburg Campaign: A Contemporary Account," in *The Rebellion Record: A Diary of American Events*, ed. Frank Moore (New York: D. Van Ostrand, Publisher, 1864).
17. *OR* 27, 1, Report of Brig. General John C. Robinson, U.S. Army, commanding Second Division, 7/18/63, 289–90; Symonds, 68.
18. Frank L. Byrne and Andrew T. Weaver, eds. *Haskell of Gettysburg: His Life and Civil War Papers* (Madison: State Historical Society of Wisconsin, 1970), 159.
19. Gibbon, *Personal Recollections*, 146; Byrne and Weaver, *Haskell*, 92; Brown, 291.
20. L&L, vol. 2, 103, GGM to MM, 7/3/63.
21. *Evening Star*, 7/2 and 7/3/63; Boyden, 143–44.
22. *CW* VI, 313, to Ambrose E. Burnside, 7/2/63; 324, to Robert T. Lincoln, 7/3/63.
23. *B&L*, vol. 3, General E. P. "The Great Charge and Artillery Fighting at Gettysburg," 357.
24. Alexander, 360–61.
25. Alexander, 362; Longstreet, *From Manassas*, 390.
26. Alexander, 362–63.
27. Alexander, 363.
28. Wert, *Longstreet*, 268–69.
29. Longstreet, *From Manassas*, 391; Alexander, 362–63.
30. *L&L*, vol. 2, 106; Jordan, 96–97.
31. Byrne and Weaver, *Haskell*, 149–50.
32. *L&L*, vol. 2, 106–7.
33. Gibbon, *Personal Recollections*, 146–48.
34. Gibbon, *Personal Recollections*, 146–48.
35. Gibbon, *Personal Recollections*, 148–49; *B&L*, vol. 3, 372–73.
36. Sears, 400; Francis A. Walker, *General Hancock* (New York: Appleton, 1894), 97.
37. *L&L*, vol. 2, 106.
38. *L&L*, vol. 2, 108.
39. McPherson, *Hallowed Ground*, 108–9.
40. Alexander, 364.
41. Alexander, 364.
42. Alexander, 365.
43. Alexander, 365–66.
44. Clark, 126; Sorrel, 54.
45. Gallagher, *Fighting for the Confederacy*, 260–61.
46. John H. Lewis, *A Rebel in Pickett's Charge at Gettysburg* (Bellevue, WA: Big Byte Books, 2016; originally published 1895), 36.
47. Longstreet, *From Manassas*, 392–93.
48. *OR* 27, 1, 239, Hunt's Report; 379, Hancock's Report.
49. Catton, 76–77.
50. Catton, 77; Ladd and Ladd, Anthony McDermott to John Bachelder, 6/2/86;

D. Scott Hartwig, "It Struck Horror to Us All," *Gettysburg Magazine*, Issue 24 (January 1991), 8 (online edition).

51. Alexander, "Artillery Fighting," 365; Lewis, 56.

52. Alexander, 365; Thomas, 271.

53. Hartwig, 8; *OR* 27, 1; *B&L*, vol. 3, Hunt, 239; Robert Garth Scott, ed., *Fallen Leaves: The Civil War Letters of Major Henry Livermore Abbott* (Kent, OH: Kent State University, 1991).

54. *OR* 27, 1, Hunt's Report, 239.

55. LOC, Henry Hunt Papers, Henry Hunt to Mrs. Mary Hunt ("My Dear Mary"), 7/4/63.

56. Lewis, 58; Longstreet, *From Manassas*, 394.

57. Kent Masterson Brown, *Cushing of Gettysburg: The Story of a Union Artillery Commander* (Lexington: The University Press of Kentucky, 1993), 248–53.

58. Symonds, 73.

59. Lewis, 58–59.

60. Gettysburg National Military Park, W. S. Hancock File, H. H. Bingham to Dear Sister, 7/18/63; Preston, 99; Brown, *Meade*, 300.

61. Brown, 301.

62. Byrne and Weaver, 173–74.

63. Alexander, 265–66; Fremantle, 214–15; McPherson, *Hallowed Ground*, 126–27.

64. Gregg, 16–23; *OR* 2, 27, Wade Hampton's Report; *B&L*, vol. 3, Miller, "Cavalry," 403–6; Harris, 33–37; Longacre, 150–55; Urwin, *Custer Victorious*, 78–82; Wert, *Cavalry*, 287–90; McClellan, 340–45.

65. *OR* 27, 2 Stuart's Report, 699.

66. Gregg, 13.

67. *B&L*, vol. 3, Hunt, 378.

68. Fremantle, 210.

69. Fremantle, 212.

70. Freemantle, 211–13.

71. Fremantle, 214.

72. *SHSP*, vol. 31, 233–34, Captain Robert A. Bright, "Pickett's Charge"; Guelzo, 428–29.

73. Ladd and Ladd, 231–32, Major General William G. Mitchell to Major General Winfield S. Hancock, 1/10/66; Brown, 303.

74. *OR* 27, 1, Report of Colonel Nathaniel P. Richmond, First West Virginia Cavalry, 9/5/63; Jacob Hoke, *The Great Invasion of 1863, or General Lee in Pennsylvania.* (Dayton, OH: W. J. Shuey, Publisher, 1887), 440–41, Warren's comments to the Congressional Committee.

75. Hoke, *Great Invasion*, 440–41.

76. *L&L*, vol. 2, 110–11; Brown, 304.

77. *B&L*, vol. 3, John D. Imboden, Brigadier General, "The Confederate Retreat from Gettysburg," 420–21.

78. *B&L*, vol. 3, Imboden, 420–21.

79. Welles, *Diary*, vol. 1, 357–58, 7/4/63 entry; Bates, 155.

80. Welles, *Diary*, vol. 1, 357–58.

81. OR 27, 2, Meade to Halleck (telegram, received 6:10 a.m.), 74–75.

82. *L&L*, vol. 2, 112; Cleaves, 169; Pennypacker, 201.

ELEVEN: THURSDAY, NOVEMBER 19

1. Alleman, 71–74.

2. Alleman, 75–76.

3. "Letter from Miss Jennie McCreary to Miss Julie McCreary," 7/27/63, *Reflections on the Battle of Gettysburg* 13, no. 6 (1963); Sears, 462; Symonds, *History*, 261.

4. Robert J. Bloom, "We Never Expected a Battle," *Pennsylvania History: A Journal of Mid-Atlantic Studies 55*, no. 4 (October 1988): 182; Albertus McCreary, "Gettysburg: A Boy's Experience of the Battle," *McClure's Magazine* 33 (July 1909): 250–51; *Gettysburg Compiler*, 7/20 and 8/24/63; Creighton, 147–48. Days later, the McCrearys' dinner was interrupted by a "bellowing" outside; it was their cow, shot through the neck but alive.

5. Sarah Sites Rodgers, *The Ties of the Past: The Gettysburg Diaries of Salome Myers Stewart, 1854–1922* (Gettysburg: Thomas Publications, 1996), 160.

6. *Philadelphia Inquirer*, 7/6/63; *Richmond Enquirer*, 7/8/63; McPherson, *Hallowed Ground*, 135.

7. *L&L*, vol. 2, 125, GGM to MM, 7/5/63.

8. *OR* 27 (1), 78, Meade to Halleck, 7/4/63 7:00 a.m. (received 7:30 p.m.); *OR* 27 (3), 514, Lee to Meade, 7/4/63, 8:25 a.m.; Meade to Lee, 7/3[4]/63, 8:25 a.m.; 515, Butterfield to Couch, 7/4/63 1:30 p.m.; Brown, *Meade*, 323.

9. *OR* 27 (1): 25–28, Edward Perry Vollum to Meigs, 8/17/63; 79, Meade to Halleck, 7/5/63 (received 8:40 p.m.); *OR* 27 (3), 511, Haupt to Halleck, 7/3/63, 8:30 a.m. (received 10:20 a.m.); 519–20, S. Williams, Circular to Corps Commanders, 7/4/63; 524, Rufus Ingalls to General M. C. Meigs, 7/4/63; Kent Masterson Brown, *Retreat from Gettysburg* (Chapel Hill and London: The University of North Carolina Press, 2005), 386.

10. *L&L*, vol. 2, 122–23, General Orders No. 68, 7/4/63.

11. Bill Hyde, ed., *The Union Generals Speak: The Meade Hearings on the Battle of Gettysburg* (Baton Rouge: Louisiana State University Press, 2003), 258–60; Brown, *Meade*, 324–25. Symonds, *History*, 269.

12. HSP, Meade Collection, James Cornell Biddle to "My own Darling Wife," 7/6/63; Brown, *Meade*, 326.

13. *CW* VI, Announcement of News From Gettysburg, 7/4/63.

14. *CW* VI, 318, to Halleck, 7/6/63.

15. *L&L*, vol. 2, 121–22, GGM to Sedgwick, 7/5/63; 122, Meade to Halleck, 7/5/63, 8:30 a.m. (received 8:40 p.m.); *OR* 27 (93), 535, Meade to Sedgwick, 7/5/63, 12:30 p.m.

16. *OR* 27 (3), 524, Wm. H. French to Halleck, 7/4/63 (received 10:35 p.m.); *OR*

27 (1), 82, Halleck to Meade, 7/7/63, 2 p.m.; Meade to Halleck 4 p.m. (received 5 p.m.); 83, Halleck to Meade, 7/7/63.

17. *OR* 27 (3), 606, Lieutenant W. A. Roebling to Warren, 7/8/63; quote from Brown, *Meade*, 342.

18. *B&L*, vol. 3, Imboden, 422–23; John H. Eicher and David J. Eicher, *Civil War High Commands* (Stanford, CA: Stanford University Press, 2001), 363.

19. Coddington, 538.

20. *B&L*, vol. 3, 424–25.

21. *B&L*, vol. 3, 424–25; Sears, 481; Symonds, 275.

22. Dowdey, *Wartime Correspondences*, 559–60, General Orders No. 74, 7/4/63.

23. Alexander, 267; *B&L*, vol. 3, 427–28; *OR* 27 (20), Report of J. E. B. Stuart, 8/20/63; Brown, *Retreat*, 243–50; Sears, 482–85; Symonds, 275–77.

24. "Address of General James F. Rusling at the 46th Anniversary of the Third Army Corps, Union, Hotel Manhattan," 5/5/1910, from "Lincoln and Sickles" (published by "Third Army Corps Union" for Distribution to its Members (May 1910).

25. Symonds, 275; James F. Rusling, *Men and Things I Saw in Civil War Days* (New York: Eaton & Mains, 1899).

26. Welles, *Diary*, vol. 1, 472–73, 10/20/63 entry. Report, JCCW, 304; Hessler, 251–52. Abbott was killed during the Battle of the Wilderness on May 6, 1864.

27. *L&L*, vol. 2, 132–33, GGM to MM, 7/8/63.

28. *OR* 27 (10), 84, Halleck to Meade, 7/8/63; 85, Meade to Halleck, 7/8/63 3 p.m. (received 3:20 p.m.); Halleck to Meade, 7/8/63; 86, Meade to Halleck, 7/9/63, 11 a.m. (received 12:10 p.m.).

29. Alexander, 270; Brown, *Retreat*, 294–95, 310–11; Symonds, 281.

30. *OR* 27 (20), 301, General Orders No. 16, 7/11/63; Guelzo, *Lee*, 305; Brown, *Retreat*, 320–22.

31. *OR* 27 (1), 488–89, Report of Major General William French, 10/1/63; 536, Report of Brigadier General Andrew A. Humphreys, 8/16/63; *L&L*, vol. 2, 136, GGM to MM, 7/21/63; Cleaves, 177.

32. *OR* 27 (10), 91, Meade to Halleck, 7/12/63.

33. *OR* 27 (3), 669, Ranald S. Mackenzie to Warren, 7/12/63; 3 (1), 91, Meade to Halleck, 7/13/63, 5 p.m. (received 6:40 p.m.); Andrew A. Humphreys, *From Gettysburg to the Rapidan* (New York: Charles Scribner's Sons, 1883), 6; Brown, *Retreat*, 362.

34. Longstreet, *From Manassas*, 428–30; Dowdey, 480; Symonds, 281.

35. John Gordon, *Reminiscences of the Civil War* (New York: Charles Scribner's Sons, 1904), 173.

36. Hyde, 116–17, Meade Testimony, JCCW; *OR* 27 (1), 91, Meade to Halleck, 7/13/63, 5 p.m. (received 6:40 p.m.).

37. *OR* 27 (1), 92, Halleck to Meade, 7/13/63, 9:30 p.m.

38. *OR* 27 (3), 92, Meade to Halleck, 7/14/63, 11 a.m. (received 12:10 p.m.).

39. *OR* 27 (3), 93, Meade to Halleck, 7/14/63, 2:30 p.m. (received 3:10 p.m.);

7/14/63, 3 p.m. (received 3:15 p.m.); 7/14/63, 3:30 p.m. (received 4 p.m.); 93–94, Halleck to Meade, 7/14/63.

40. *OR* 27 (3), 93–94, Halleck to Meade, 7/14/63, 1 p.m.; Welles, *Diary*, vol. 1, 369–70, 7/14/63 entry.

41. *CW* VI, 327–28, to George G. Meade, 7/14/63.

42. *OR* 27 (3), 94, Meade to Halleck, 7/15/63; *L&L*, vol. 2, 135–36, GGM to MM, 7/18/63; Cleaves, 187.

43. *CW* VI, 341–42, to Oliver O. Howard, 7/21/63 (including footnote).

44. Sandburg, vol. 2, 360; *New York Times*, 7/14/63.

45. *New York Times*, 7/14–18/1863; Goodwin, 536–37.

46. Welles, 404, *Diary*, vol. 1, 8/14/63 entry; *L&L*, vol. 2, 143, GGM to MM, 8/16/63; *LDBD*, vol. 3, 209, 8/14/63 entry.

47. Dowdey, 538–39, to Jefferson Davis, 7/4/63; 542, to his wife, 7/7/63; Sears, 499. Casualty numbers vary depending on the historian. James McPherson's *Battle Cry of Freedom* lists the long-used and rounded numbers of 23,000 Union casualties and 28,000 Confederate.

48. Dowdey, 553–54, to Jefferson Davis, 7/16/63; *Charleston Mercury*, 7/30/63; Clay quote from Thomas, 306.

49. Dowdey, 547, to his wife, 7/12/63; 548, to Jefferson Davis, 7/12/63; 564–65, to Davis, 7/31/63.

50. Dowdey, 589–90, to Jefferson Davis, 8/8/63.

51. Dowdey, 593, to Jefferson Davis, 8/22/63; *OR* 29 (2), 639–40, Davis to Lee, 8/11/63; 693–94, Longstreet to Lee, 9/2/63.

52. *OR* 29 (1), 693–94, Longstreet to Lee, 8/31/63; Dowdey to his wife, 9/4/63.

53. Dowdey, 699, Longstreet to Lee, 9/5/63; 706, Lee to Davis, 9/9/63.

54. Dowdey, 602–3, to Jefferson Davis, 9/23/63.

55. *CWDBD*, 421–22, 10/13–14/63 entries; 437–42, 12/2/63 entry; Guelzo, *Gettysburg*, 449.

56. George Agassiz, ed., *Meade's Headquarters: 1863–1865* (Boston: Massachusetts Historical Society, 1922), 87–91; 44–45, Theodore Lyman to his wife, 11/30/63; *L&L*, vol. 2, 156–59, GGM to MM, 12/2/63.

57. Guelzo, *Gettysburg*, 472.

58. Paradis, 40, 45, 80–81; Drew Gilpin Faust, *This Republic of Suffering: Death and the American Civil War* (New York: Vintage Books, 2008), 86.

59. Paradis, 35, 80–81.

60. "Leading Colored Citizen," *Gettysburg Compiler*, 6/13/06; Henry Louis Gates Jr., "Which Black Man Was Responsible for Burying Bodies at Gettysburg?" The Root website, published 10/6/14.

61. Creighton, 155 (n4).

62. Creighton, 155.

63. Paradis, 79.

64. Leander H. Warren Obituary, *New York Times*, 12/6/1937.

65. Leander Warren, "Personal Account of Leander Warren," Adams County

Historical Society; Michael E. Ruane, "After 1863 Battle of Gettysburg, a Grisly but Noble Enterprise to Honor the Fallen," *Washington Post*, 9/13/2023.

66. Paradis, 81–82; Garry Wills, *Lincoln at Gettysburg: The Words That Remade America* (New York: Touchstone, 1992), 21–23.

67. *LDBD*, vol. 3, 217, 11/2/63 entry.

68. McGrath, 462; Wills, 24, 32–33.

69. Joshua Zeitz, "Remembering the Gettysburg Address," *New York Times*, 11/21/2013.

70. *HL*, 358–61, Mary Todd Lincoln (WHH notes on interview, 9/66); Ward Hill Lamon, *Recollections of Abraham Lincoln, 1847–1865* (Chicago: A. C. McClurg and Company, 1895), 173.

71. *CW* I, 108–16, Address Before the Young Men's Lyceum of Springfield, Illinois, 1/27/38.

72. Wills, 29.

73. *CW* VII, 16, to Edwin M. Stanton, 11/17/63; *New York Tribune*, 11/20/63.

74. *Washington Chronicle*, 11/19/63.

75. John Nicolay, "Lincoln's Gettysburg Address," *Century Magazine*, February 1894, 597–98.

76. *LDBD*, vol. 3, 220–21, 11/18/63 entry.

77. *LDBD*, vol. 3, 229–31.

78. *Philadelphia Inquirer*, 11/21/63; *Washington Chronicle*, 11/21/63.

79. *CW* VII, 16–17, Remarks to the Citizens of Gettysburg, Pennsylvania, 11/18/63; *Philadelphia Inquirer*, 11/20/63.

80. Nicolay, 602.

81. Nicolay, 602; *Washington Chronicle*, 11/20/63; *LDBD*, vol. 3, 221–22, 11/19/63 entry.

82. Wills, Appendix III, Funeral Orations, A. "By Everett," 223–47.

83. Wills, 33.

84. Wills, 33; Sandburg, *The War Years*, vol. 2, 468; *LDBD*, vol. 3, 222, 11/19/63 entry; *Philadelphia Inquirer*, 11/20/63.

85. Rufus Rockwell Wilson, *Intimate Memories of Lincoln* (Elmira, NY: The Primavera Press, 1945), 478, "Recollections of Mr. Gitt."

86. *CW* VII, 21–22, Gettysburg Address, Edward Everett Copy, 11/19/63.

87. John Young, *Men and Memories: Personal Reminiscences*, ed. May D. Russell Young, vol. 1 (F. T. Neely, 1901), 69.

TWELVE: AFTERMATH

1. Lamon, *Recollections*, 173; Wills, 36.

2. *Columbus Ohio State Journal*, 11/23/63; Burlingame, 574–75.

3. *Philadelphia Inquirer*, 11/29/63; *LDBD*, vol. 3, 222, 11/19/63.

4. *LDBD*, vol. 3, 222–23, 11/21/63; James B. Conroy, "Slavery's Mark on Lincoln's White House," White House Historical Association website; Roy P.

Basler, "Did President Lincoln Give the Smallpox to William H. Johnson?" *Huntington Library Quarterly* 35 (May 1972): 279–84.

5. Lincoln Papers, "The Gettysburg Address Contemporary Reactions," Edward Everett to Lincoln, 11/20/63, Cornell University Library, https://rmc.library .cornell.edu/Gettysburg/ideas; Meacham, 313. Everett's reviews were not all positive. Horace Greeley called his speech "classic but frigid." Lincoln immediately thanked Everett for his kind note while "pleased to know that, in your judgment, the little I did say was not entirely a failure." After Everett's death, Lincoln called him "very much overrated" (*CW* VII, 24–25, to Edward Everett, 11/20/63); Burlingame, *Lincoln*, vol. 2, 576.

6. *Philadelphia Inquirer*, 11/20/63; Lincoln Papers, "Contemporary Reactions"; *Chicago Times*, 11/23/1863; Wills, 38–39.

7. Davis, *Crucible*, 365–72.

8. *CW* VII, 23–24, to Zachariah Chandler, 11/20/63 (and footnote). Allen Johnson, ed., *Dictionary of American Biography* (New York: Charles Scribner's Sons, 1929), 618.

9. McPherson, *Lincoln*, 57–58.

10. McPherson, 57–58; *CW* VII, 506–8, interview with Alexander W. Randall and Joseph T. Mills, 8/19/64; 514–15, Memorandum Concerning His Probable Failure of Re-election, 8/23/64.

11. Davis, *Lincoln's Men*, 211, 215–16.

12. *CW* VII, 332–33, "Second Inaugural Address."

13. Keckley, 57; Goodwin, 731–32.

14. Dorothy Meserve Kunhardt and Philip B. Kunhardt Jr., *Twenty Days* (New York: Castle Books, 1965), 140–41, 146–51.

15. Kunhardt and Kunhardt, 149–50; *CW* IV, 240–41, Speech in Independence Hall, Philadelphia, Pennsylvania, 2/22/61; 241–42, Speech at Flag-raising before Independence Hall, Philadelphia, Pennsylvania.

16. Dowdey, 652, to his wife, 1/15/64.

17. Dowdey, 647–48, to Colonel Lucius B. Northrop, 1/5/64; 653–54, to General Alexander R. Lawton, 1/19/64.

18. Dowdey, 666–67, to Jefferson Davis, 2/3/64; 699–700, to Jefferson Davis, 4/15/64.

19. U.S. Grant to GGM, 4/9/64; Davis, *Crucible*, 391–92.

20. Jones, *Personal Reminiscences*, 40, Jubal Early's Address at Washington and Lee University, 1/19/72.

21. Thomas, 224–40.

22. *B&L*, vol. 4, Henry Goddard Thomas, Brevet Major General, C.S.V., "The Colored Troops at Petersburg," 566–67; Dowdey, 817, to James Seddon, 7/30/64, 3:25 p.m.; Guelzo, *Lee*, 337.

23. *OR* series 2, 7, 906–7, Lee to Grant, 10/1/64; 909, Grant to Lee, 10/2/64; 914, Lee to Grant, 10/3/64.

24. *OR* series 2, 7, 914, Grant to Lee, 10/4/64.

25. Museum of the Confederacy, Lee Papers, Lee to Andrew Hunter,1/11/65; *Century Magazine*, August 1888, 599–601; Guelzo, 345; Thomas, 347.

26. Dowdey, 907, to his wife, 2/21/65; 910, to John C. Breckinridge, 2/14/65.

27. Dowdey, 916, to John C. Breckinridge, 3/25/65; Davis, *Crucible*, 441–43; *B&L*, vol. 4, Horace Porter, "Five Forks and the Pursuit of Lee," 708.

28. Dowdey, 924, to Miss Agnes Lee, 4/1/65; 924–26/, to Breckinridge, 4/2/65 (3 telegrams); 925–26, to Jefferson Davis, 4/2/65 (one letter and one telegram); Longstreet, *From Manassas,* 620; Smith, 248–49; Thomas, 355.

29. *CWDBD*, 670–71, 4/9/65 entry; *B&L*, vol. 4, "Lee's Report of the Surrender at Appomattow," 724, and Horace Porter, Brevet Brigadier General, U.S.A., "The Surrender at Appomattox Court House," 732–33.

30. *CWDBD*, 733–34.

31. *CWDBD*, 737–43.

32. *SHSP*, vol. 38, 12; Dowdey, 934–35, General Orders No. 9, 4/10/65.

33. Lee, *Recollections*, 164, Lee to Grant, 6/13/65; 164–65, Lee to Andrew Johnson, 6/13/65; Thomas, 369–70.

34. Lee, 179–184, including REL to MCL, 9/19/65.

35. Lee, 200–3.

36. Lee, 290–94.

37. Lee, 332; Smith, 300–1; Thomas, 376–77.

38. Lee, 400; Smith, 331.

39. Lee, 394–400, including REL to MCL, 4/17/70 (395–96); Smith, 331.

40. Lee, 412–13, REL to MCL, 7/2/70.

41. Lee 439–40; Guelzo, 411; Pryor, *Reading the Man*, 462–64; Smith, 356–57; Thomas, 412–13.

42. *L&L*, vol. 2, 160–61, GGM to MM, 12/7 and 12/16/63; HSP, MFP; *Washington Chronicle*, 12/12/63; Cleaves, 214–15.

43. Agassiz, 56–57, Theodore Lyman to Elizabeth Lyman, 2/22/64; *L&L*, vol. 2, 163–64, GGM to MM, 12/28/63; Welles, *Diary*, vol. 1, 501, 1/1/64 entry.

44. *L&L*, vol. 2, 169–70, GGM to MM, 3/6/64.

45. LOC, Benjamin F. Wade Papers, Manuscript Division, Benjamin Wade to Caroline Wade, 10/25/61; JCCW, Notable Senate Investigations, U.S. Senate Historical Office, Washington, D.C.; Tap, 174–78; Hyde, 8–12. Mr. Hyde's book contains the testimonies of the Meade hearings.

46. Hyde, 49–54.

47. Hyde, 68–75.

48. Hyde, 90–95.

49. *L&L*, vol. 2, 172–73; Sauers, 53–54; Hessler, 270; *LDBD*, vol. 3, 243–44, 3/3/64 entry.

50. Hessler, 268.

51. *L&L*, vol. 2, 169–70, GGM to MM, 3/6/64; Hyde, 101–22, Meade's testimony (quote on 109).

52. Hyde, 136–45, Pleasonton's testimony (quote on 139); 149–62, Birney's testimony (quote on 161). By the 1870s, Pleasonton had a more colorful ver-

sion of his exhortation: "General, I will give you half an hour to be a great general. Order the army to advance, while I will take the cavalry, get in Lee's rear, and we will finish the campaign in a week" (Hyde, 139–40).

53. *New York Herald*, 3/12/64.

54. *OR* 27, 1, 127–28, Meade to Col. E. D. Townsend, Assistant Adjutant General, 3/15/64.

55. Hyde, 163–180, Warren's testimony (quote on 178); 182–203, Humphreys's testimony (quote on 201); 205–26, Hancock's testimony (quote on 214); 243–75, Butterfield's testimony (quote on 254); 277–90, Gibbon's testimony (quote on 278).

56. Hyde, 291–300, Meade's testimony; *New York Herald*, 4/4/64.

57. *OR* 27, 1, 137, Halleck to Meade, 3/20/64.

58. *CW* VII, 273, to George W. Meade, 3/29/64; *L&L*, vol. 2, 186–87, GGM to MM.

59. *L&L*, vol. 2, 186–87, GGM to MM, 4/2/64.

60. *L&L*, vol. 2, 189, GGM to MM, 4/13/64; 196, Grant to Stanton, 5/13/64.

61. Agassiz, *Meade's Headquarters*, 87–91.

62. *L&L*, vol. 2, GGM to MM, 6/5/64; Philip H. Sheridan, *Personal Memoirs of P. H. Sheridan*, vol. 1 (New York: D. Appleton, 1886), 368–69.

63. *Philadelphia Inquirer*, 6/2/64.

64. *L&L*, vol. 2, 202–3, GGM to MM, 6/9/64; Cleaves, 253–55.

65. *L&L*, vol. 2, 217–19, GGM to MM, 7/31/64; 218–19, 8/3/64; Sauers, 86–94; Rafuse, 144–45.

66. *L&L*, vol. 2, 216–17, GGM to MM, 7/29/64, and 229–30, 9/22/64.

67. Agassiz, *Meade's Headquarters*, 243–44, 4/9/65 entry.

68. Cleaves, 332; Sauers, 101.

69. *L&L*, vol. 2, 283–84 (Meade's quote on 284).

70. *L&L*, vol. 2, 284–89 (Stanton's quote on 289); Huntington, 357–59; *The Fenian Raid at Fort Erie, June the First and Second, 1866* (Toronto: W. C. Chewett and Co., 1866), 18.

71. James E. Sefton, *The United States Army and Reconstruction, 1865–1877* (Baton Rouge: Louisiana State University Press, 1967), 168–71 and 198–200; *Milledgeville Federal Union*, 1/7/68.

72. Kenneth W. Munden and Henry P. Beers, *Guide to Federal Archives Relating to the Civil War* (Washington, D.C.: Government Printing Office, 1962), 415; *L&L*, vol. 2, 296–99; 296–99 (GGM to MM, 3/6/69 on 298–99).

73. *L&L*, vol. 2, 300–2.

74. *L&L*, 303; *Philadelphia Inquirer*, 11/7 and 11/12/72.

75. *L&L*, vol. 2, 160, GGM to MM, 12/7/63.

76. Smith, *Autobiography of Mark Twain*, 1/17/1906 entry.

77. Hessler, 365–75; *Washington National Tribune*, 3/31/1910.

78. Hessler, 373–81.

79. Creighton, 216–17; Paradis, 103–4.

80. Creighton, 207–8; Paradis, 81.

81. Jennifer M. Murray, *On a Great Battlefield: The Making, Management, and Memory of Gettysburg National Military Park, 1933–2023* (Knoxville: The University of Tennessee Press, 2023), 26, 48–49, 123–24, 158–174; 188–89, and 191.
82. *CW* I, 109, Address Before the Young Men's Lyceum of Springfield, Illinois, 1/27/38.

—BIBLIOGRAPHY—

MANUSCRIPTS AND COLLECTIONS

Adams County Historical Society

Agnes Barr, "Account of the Battle at Gettysburg"

Leander H. Warren, "Recollections of the Battle at Gettysburg"

Baseball Hall of Fame

Abner Doubleday Papers

Cornell University Library

Lincoln Papers, "The Gettysburg Address Contemporary Reactions"

Gettysburg National Military Park

Charles W. Belknap Diary

William T. Fluker, "A Graphic Account of the Battle of Little Round Top Hill at Gettysburg"

Historical Society of Pennsylvania

Autograph Collection

Biddle Papers

Dreer Collection, Historical Society of Pennsylvania

Gratz Collection

Winfield S. Hancock Papers

George Gordon Meade Collection

Meade Family Papers

Jessie Ball duPont Library, Stratford Hall

Lee Family Papers

John F. Kennedy Library and Museum

Abraham Lincoln's Appointment Book, March 5–27, 1861

Library of Congress, Manuscript Division

Abraham Lincoln Papers
Benjamin F. Wade Papers
Congressional Globe, Debates of Congress
Frederick Douglass Papers, 1841–67
George Brinton McClellan Papers
John J. Crittenden Papers
Jubal A. Early Papers
Robert E. Lee Papers
Senate Executive Proceedings
Winfield S. Hancock Papers

Maryland Historical Society

John Gibbon Papers

New York Historical Society

Civil War Letters Collection
James Longstreet Collection
Winfield S. Hancock Papers

Virginia Museum of History and Culture

Robert Edward Lee Papers

United States Army Heritage and Education Center

George Gordon Meade Collection

United States Military Academy Library

Winfield S. Hancock Papers

OTHER COLLECTIONS/PUBLICATIONS

American State Papers, *Foreign Affairs,* vol. 4
Messages of the President of the United States with the Correspondence, Therewith Communicated, Between the Secretary of War and Other Officers of the Government: The Mexican War (Washington, D.C.: Wendell and Van Benthuysen, 1848)
U.S. Court of Claims, Reports from the Court of Claims, Submitted to the House of Representatives During the First Session of the Thirty-Sixth Congress,

1859–60. Vol. 3, 36th Congress, 1st Sess. (Washington, D.C.: Thomas Ford, Printer, 1860)

U.S. Supreme Court, *Lewis v. Lewis*, 48 U.S. 7 How. 776 776 (1849); *Lewis v. Lewis* (7 How.) 776

BOOKS, COMPILATIONS, DIARIES, AND JOURNALS

Adams, Charles Francis, Jr. *Charles F. Adams, 1835–1916, An Autobiography.* Boston: Houghton Mifflin Company, 1916.

Agassiz, George, R. ed. *Meade's Headquarters: 1863–1865; Letters of Colonel Theodore Lyman from the Wilderness to Appomattox.* Boston: Massachusetts Historical Society, 1922.

Alexander, Edward Porter. *Memoirs of a Confederate: A Critical Narrative.* New York: Scribner's, 1907.

Alleman, Tillie (Pierce). *At Gettysburg: What a Girl Saw and Heard of the Battle; A True Narrative.* New York: W. Lake Borland, 1889.

Ambrose, Stephen E. *Duty, Honor, Country: A History of West Point.* Baltimore: The Johns Hopkins University Press, 1966.

———. *Halleck: Lincoln's Chief of Staff.* Baton Rouge: Louisiana State University Press, 1962.

———. *Upton and the Army.* Baton Rouge: Louisiana State University Press, 1964.

Andrews, J. Cutler. *The North Reports the Civil War.* Pittsburgh: University of Pittsburgh Press, 1955.

Andrews, William L., and Henry Louis Gates, eds. *Slave Narratives.* New York: Library of America, 2000.

"An Eyewitness." *Complete History of the Late Mexican War: Containing an Authentic Account of All Battles Fought in That Republic.* New York: F. J. Dow & Co., 1850.

Atkinson, Eleanor. "The Winter of the Deep Snow." In *Transactions for the Illinois State Historical Society for the Year 1909.* Springfield: Illinois State Historical Society, 1909.

Avary, Myrta Lockett, ed. *Recollections of Alexander H. Stephens: His Diary Kept When a Prisoner of War at Fort Warren, Boston Harbour, 1865.* New York: Doubleday, Page & Company, 1910.

Bache, Richard Meade. *Life of General George Gordon Meade: Commander of the Army of the Potomac.* Philadelphia: Henry T. Coates & Co., 1897.

Bacon, Benjamin C. *Statistics of the Colored People of Philadelphia.* Philadelphia: Elwood, 1856.

Bailey, Ronald H., et al. *Forward to Richmond: McClellan's Peninsular Campaign.* Alexandria, VA: Time-Life Books, 1983.

Bandy, Ken, and Florence Freeland, eds. *The Gettysburg Papers.* Vol. 1. Dayton, OH: Press of Morningside Bookshop, 1978.

Barck, Dorothy C., ed. *Diary of William Dunlap (1766–1839): The Memoirs of a Dramatist, Theatrical Manager, Painter, Critic, Novelist, and Historian.* Vol. 2. New York: New York Historical Society, 1930.

Basler, Roy, ed. *The Collected Works of Abraham Lincoln.* 8 vols. plus index. New Brunswick, NJ: Rutgers University Press, 1953.

Bates, David Homer. *Lincoln in the Telegraph Office.* New York: Century Co., 1907.

Bates, Samuel P. *History of Pennsylvania Volunteers, 1861–65.* Harrisburg: B. Singerly, State Printer, 1871.

Bauer, K. Jack. *Zachary Taylor: Soldier, Planter, Statesman of the Old Southwest.* Baton Rouge: Louisiana State University Press, 1985.

Beale, Howard K. *The Diary of Edward Bates, 1859–1866.* Washington, D.C.: United States Government Printing Office, 1933.

Bemrose, John. *Reminiscences of the Second Seminole War,* edited by John K. Mahon. Gainesville: University of Florida Press, 1966.

Beveridge, Albert. *Abraham Lincoln: 1809–1858.* Vol. 1. Boston: Houghton Mifflin Co., 1928.

Biddle, Chapman. *The First Day of the Battle of Gettysburg.* Philadelphia: J. B. Lippincott & Co., 1880.

Billings, John David. *Hardtack and Coffee, or, The Unwritten Story of Army Life.* Boston: George M. Smith & Co., 1888.

Bishop, Jim. *The Day Lincoln Was Shot.* New York: Harper & Brothers, 1955.

Blay, John S. *The Civil War: A Pictorial Profile.* New York: Thomas Y. Crowell Company, 1960.

Blumenthal, Sidney. *The Political Life of Abraham Lincoln.* Vol. 2, *Wrestling with His Angel.* New York: Simon & Schuster, 2017.

Borneman, Walter. *Polk: The Man Who Transformed the Presidency and America.* New York: Random House, 2008.

Boritt, Gabor S. *Lincoln and the Economics of the American Dream.* Urbana and Chicago: University of Illinois Press, 1978.

Boyden, Anna L. *Echoes from the Hospital and White House.* Boston: D. Lothrop and Company, 1884.

Brandt, Nat. *The Congressman Who Got Away with Murder.* New York: Syracuse University Press, 1991.

Brock, R. A., ed. *Southern Historical Society Papers.* 44 vols. Richmond, VA: Published by the Society, 1905.

Brooks, Noah. *Abraham Lincoln, and the Downfall of American Slavery.* New York: G. P. Putnam's Sons, 1894.

———. *Washington, D.C. in Lincoln's Time.* New York: The Century Company, 1894.

Brown, John Howard, ed. *Lamb's Biographical Dictionary of the United States.* Vol. 5. Boston: Federal Book Company of Boston, 1903.

Brown, Kent Masterson. *Cushing of Gettysburg: The Story of a Union Artillery Commander.* Lexington: The University Press of Kentucky, 1993.

———. *Retreat from Gettysburg.* Chapel Hill and London: The University of North Carolina Press, 2005.

———. *Abraham Lincoln: A Life.* 2 vols. Baltimore: Johns Hopkins University Press, 2008

———. *An American Marriage: The Untold Story of Abraham Lincoln and Mary Todd.* New York: Pegasus Books, 2021.

———. *The Black Man's President: Abraham Lincoln, African Americans, and the Pursuit of Racial Equality.* New York: Pegasus Books, 2021.

———. ed. *An Oral History of Abraham Lincoln: John G. Nicolay's Interviews and Essays.* Carbondale: Southern Illinois University Press, 1996.

———. and John R. Turner Ettlinger, eds. *Inside Lincoln's White House: The Complete Civil War Diary of John Hay.* Carbondale: Southern Illinois University Press, 1997.

Busey, Samuel C. *Personal Reminiscences and Recollections of Forty-Six Years' Membership in the Medical Society of the District of Columbia and Residence in This City.* Philadelphia: Dornan, Printer, 1890.

Butterfield, Daniel. "Article on Gettysburg." In *A Biographical Memorial of General Daniel Butterfield*, edited by Julia Lorrilard Butterfield. New York: The Grafton Press, 1904.

Byrdsall, F. *The History of the Loco-Foco or Equal Rights Party.* New York: Clement & Packard, 1842.

Byrne, Frank L., and Andrew T. Weaver, eds. *Haskell of Gettysburg: His Life and Civil War Papers.* Madison: State Historical Society of Wisconsin, 1970.

Campanella, Richard. *Lincoln in New Orleans: The 1828–1831 Flatboat Voyages and Their Place in History.* Lafayette: University of Louisiana at Lafayette Press, 2010.

Carmichael, Peter S. *The War for the Common Soldier: How Men Thought, Fought, and Survived in Civil War Armies.* Chapel Hill: The University of North Carolina Press, 2018.

Catton, Bruce. *The Army of the Potomac Trilogy.* 3 vols. New York: Library of America, 2022.

———. *This Hallowed Ground.* New York: Doubleday, 1956.

Channing, Steven A., et al. *Confederate Ordeal: The Southern Homefront.* Alexandria, VA: Time-Life Books, 1984.

Chase, Salmon P. *Diary and Correspondence of Salmon P. Chase.* Washington, D.C.: Government Printing Office, 1903.

Chittenden, L. E. *Recollections of President Lincoln and His Administration.* New York: Harper & Brothers, 1891.

Clark, Champ. *Decoying the Yanks: Jackson's Valley Campaign.* Alexandria, VA: Time-Life Books, 1983.

Clary, David A. *Eagles and Empire: The United States, Mexico, and the Struggle for a Continent*. New York: Bantam Books, 2009.

Cleaves, Freeman. *Meade of Gettysburg*. Norman: University of Oklahoma Press, 1960.

Coddington, Edward B. *The Gettysburg Campaign: A Study in Command*. New York: Touchstone, 1997.

Colman, Edna M. *Seventy-Five Years of White House Gossip: From Washington to Lincoln*. New York: Doubleday, Page & Company, 1925.

Comte de Paris. *The Battle of Gettysburg: From the History of the Civil War in America*. Philadelphia: Porter & Coates, 1888.

Connelly, Thomas L. *The Marble Man: Robert E. Lee and His Image in American Society*. Baton Rouge and London: Louisiana State University Press, 1977.

Craighill, William P. *The 1862 Army Officer's Pocket Companion*. New York: D. Van Nostrand, 1862.

Creighton, Margaret S. *The Colors of Courage: Gettysburg's Forgotten History*. New York: Basic Books, 2005.

Crouthamel, James L. *Bennett's New York Herald and the Rise of the Popular Press*. Syracuse, NY: Syracuse University Press, 1989. See chapter 7, "Covering the Civil War," 112–37.

Cullum, George. *Biographical Register of the Officers and Graduates of the U.S. Military Academy at West Point, N.Y. from Its Establishment in 1802 to 1890 with the Early History of the United States Military Academy*. New York: Houghton, Mifflin and Company, 1891.

Dana, Charles A. *Recollections of the Civil War: With the Leaders at Washington and in the Field in the Sixties*. New York: D. Appleton and Company, 1902.

Daniel, Frederick S. *The Richmond Examiner During the War; or, The Writings of John M. Daniel with a Memoir of His Life by His Brother*. New York: Printed for the Author, 1868.

Darby, John Fletcher. *Personal Recollections of Many Prominent People Whom I Have Known*. St. Louis: G. I. Jones, 1880.

Davis, William C. *The Coming Fury: The Battle of New Orleans and the Rebirth of America*. New York: Caliber, 2019.

———. *The Crucible of Command: Ulysses S. Grant and Robert E. Lee; The War They Fought, the Peace They Forged*. Philadelphia: Da Capo Press, 2014.

———. *Jefferson Davis: The Man and His Hour*. Baton Rouge: Louisiana State University Press, 1991.

———. *Lincoln's Men: How President Lincoln Became Father to an Army and a Nation*. New York: Touchstone, 1999.

Dean, Love. *Lighthouses of the Florida Keys*. Sarasota: Pineapple Press, 1998.

DeRose, Chris. *Congressman Lincoln: The Making of America's Greatest President*. New York: Threshold, 2013.

Dickens, Charles. *American Notes for General Circulation and Pictures from Italy.* London: Chapel & Hall, 1892.

Dickert, D. Augustus. *History of Kershaw's Brigade.* Newberry, SC: E. H. Aull Company, 1899.

Dolin, Eric Jay. *Brilliant Beacons: A History of the American Lighthouse.* New York: Liveright Publishing Company, 2016.

Donald, David, gen. ed. *Divided We Fought: A Pictorial History of the War, 1861–1865.* New York: The Macmillan Company, 1952.

Dorsey, Florence E. *Master of the Mississippi: Henry Shreve and the Conquest of the Mississippi.* Boston: Houghton Mifflin Company, 1941.

Doubleday, Abner. *Chancellorsville and Gettysburg.* New York: Da Capo Press, 1994.

Douglas, Stephen Arnold. *Letter of Senator Douglas, Vindicating His Position on the Nebraska Bill Against the Assaults Contained in the Proceedings of a Public Meeting Composed of Twenty-Five Clergymen of Chicago.* Washington, D.C.: The Sentinel Office, 1854.

Douglass, Frederick. *My Bondage and My Freedom.* New York: Miller, Orton, & Mulligan, 1855.

Dowdey, Clifford. *Lee.* New York: Skyhorse Publishing, 2015; originally published by Little, Brown, 1965.

———. *Lee and His Men at Gettysburg: The Death of a Nation.* New York: Knopf, 1958.

———. and Louis H. Manarin, eds. *The Wartime Correspondences of Robert E. Lee.* Boston: Little, Brown, 1961.

Egerton, Douglas R. *Thunder at the Gates: The Black Civil War Regiments That Redeemed America.* New York: Basic Books, 2016.

———. *Year of Meteors: Stephen A. Douglas, Abraham Lincoln, and the Election That Brought On the Civil War.* New York: Bloomsbury Press, 2010.

Eggleston, Larry. *Women of the Civil War: Extraordinary Stories of Soldiers, Spies, Nurses, Doctors, Crusaders, and Others.* Jefferson, NC: McFarland & Company, 2003.

Egnal, Marc. *Clash of Extremes: The Economic Origins of the Civil War.* New York: Hill & Wang, 2009.

Fellman, Michael. *The Making of Robert E. Lee.* Baltimore: The Johns Hopkins University Press, 2000.

Eicher, John H., and David J. Eicher. *Civil War High Commands.* Stanford, CA: Stanford University Press, 2001.

Eisenhower, John S. D. *Agent of Destiny: The Life and Times of General Winfield Scott.* New York: Free Press, 1997.

———. *So Far from God: The U.S. War with Mexico.* New York: Random House, 1989.

Faust, Drew Gilpin. *This Republic of Suffering: Death and the American Civil War.* New York: Vintage Books, 2008.

Fehrenbacher, Don E., ed. *Lincoln: Speeches and Writing 1859–1865.* New York: The Library of America, 1989.

———. *Prelude to Greatness: Lincoln in the 1850s.* New York: MacGraw-Hill Book Company, 1964.

The Fenian Raid at Fort Erie, June the First and Second, 1866. Toronto: W. C. Chewett and Co., 1866.

Field, Maunsell. *Memories of Many Men and Some Women.* New York: Harper & Brothers, 1874.

Fisher, Ron, John Hess, et al. *Into the Wilderness.* Washington, D.C.: National Geographic Society, 1978. See "Breton Fisherman's Prayer" by Winfred Ernest Garrison.

Fiske, Samuel Wheelock. *Unspeakable Sacrifice: Samuel Wheelock Fiske in the Civil War.* Bellevue, WA: Big Byte Books, 2016 (originally published in 1866).

Foner, Eric. *The Fiery Trial: Abraham Lincoln and American Slavery.* New York: W. W. Norton, 2010.

———. *Free Soil, Free Labor, Free Men: The Ideology of the Republican Party Before the Civil War.* New York: Oxford University Press, 1995.

Foote, Shelby. *Stars in Their Courses: The Gettysburg Campaign.* New York: The Modern Library, 1994.

Frassanito, William A. *Early Photography at Gettysburg.* Gettysburg: Thomas Publications, 1995.

Freeman, Douglas Southall. *Lee's Lieutenants: A Study in Command.* 3 vols. New York: Charles Scribner's Sons, 1942–44.

———. *Robert E. Lee: A Biography.* 3 vols. New York: Scribner, 1934.

Fremantle, Arthur J. L. *Three Months in the Southern States.* Edinburgh and London: William Blackwood and Sons, 1863.

French, Benjamin Brown. *Witness to the Young Republic: A Yankee's Journal, 1828–1870.* Ed. Donald B. Cole and John J. McDonough. Hanover, HN: University Press of New England, 1989.

Gallagher, Gary W., ed. *Fighting for the Confederacy: The Personal Recollections of General Edward Porter Alexander.* Chapel Hill: University of North Carolina Press, 1989.

Geffen, Elizabeth M. "Industrial Development and Social Crisis, 1841–1854." In *Philadelphia: A 300-Year History,* edited by Russell F. Weigley. New York: W. W. Norton & Company, 1982.

Gibbon, John. *An Address on the Unveiling of the Statue of Major-General George G. Meade in Philadelphia, October 18th, 1867.* Philadelphia: Allen, Lane, & Scott's Printing House, 1887.

——. *Personal Recollections of the Civil War.* New York: G. P. Putnam's Sons, 1928.

Glazier, Captain Willard. *Three Years in the Federal Cavalry.* New York: R. H. Ferguson & Company, 1872.

Goetzmann, William H., and William N. Goetzmann. *The West of the Imagination.* New York: W. W. Norton & Company, 1986.

Good, John. *Recollections of a Lifetime.* New York: The Neale Publishing Company, 1906.

Goodwin, Doris Kearns. *Leadership in Turbulent Times.* New York: Simon & Schuster, 2018.

——. *Team of Rivals: The Political Genius of Abraham Lincoln.* New York: Simon & Schuster, 2005.

Goolrick, William K., et al. *Rebels Resurgent: Fredericksburg to Chancellorsville.* Alexandria, VA: Time-Life Books, 1985.

Gordon, John. *Reminiscences of the Civil War.* New York: Charles Scribner's Sons, 1904.

Grant, Ulysses S. *Memoirs and Selected Letters.* 2 vols. New York: The Library Company of America, 1990.

Green, Constance McLaughlin. *Washington. Vol. 1, Village and Capital, 1800–1878.* Princeton, NJ: Princeton University Press, 1962.

Gregg, David McMurtrie. *The Right Flank at Gettysburg.* Philadelphia: McLaughlin Brothers' Job Printing Establishment, 1878.

Guelzo, Allen C. *Abraham Lincoln: Redeemer President.* Grand Rapids, MI, and Cambridge, U.K.: William B. Eerdmans, 1999.

——. *Gettysburg: The Last Invasion.* New York: First Vintage Books, 2013.

——. *Lincoln's Emancipation Proclamation: The End of Slavery in America.* New York: Simon & Schuster, 2004.

——. *Robert E. Lee: A Life.* New York: Alfred A. Knopf, 2021.

Gurowski, Adam. *Diary from November 18, 1862, to October 18, 1863.* 2 vols. New York: Carleton, 1864.

Gwynne, S. C. *Rebel Yell: The Violence, Passion, and Redemption of Stonewall Jackson.* New York: Scribner, 2014.

Haldeman, William. *Meeting the Moment: Inspiring Presidential Leadership That Transformed America.* New York: State University Press of New York, 2024.

Hall, Hillman A., W. B. Besley, and Gilbert G. Wood. *History of the Sixth New York Cavalry (Second Ira Harris Guard).* Worcester, MA: The Blanchard Press, 1908.

Hard, Abner, M.D. *History of the Eighth Cavalry Regiment, Illinois Volunteers, During the Great Rebellion.* Aurora, IL: unidentified, 1868.

Hardie, James. *Memoir of James Allen Hardie, Inspector General, United States Army.* Washington, D.C.: 1877.

Harris, Samuel. *Personal Reminiscences of Samuel Harris*. Chicago: The Rogerson Press, 1897.

Haupt, General Herman. *Reminiscences of General Herman Haupt*. Milwaukee: Wright & Joys Co., 1891.

Hebert, Walter H. *Fighting Joe Hooker*. Indianapolis and New York: Bobbs-Merrill, 1944.

Heidler, J. Roderick, III, and Carolynn Ayres Heller, eds. *The Confederacy Is on Her Way Up the Spout*. Athens and London: The University of Georgia Press, 1992.

Helm, Katherine. *The True Story of Mary, Wife of Lincoln*. New York: Harper & Brothers, 1928.

Herndon, William Henry, and Jesse William Weik. *Herndon's Lincoln: The True Story of a Great Life*. Springfield, IL: Herndon's Lincoln Pub. Co., 1889.

Hertz, Emanuel, ed. *The Hidden Lincoln: From the Letters and Papers of William H. Herndon*. New York: Viking, 1938.

Hessler, James A. *Sickles at Gettysburg*. New York: Savas Beattie, 2009.

Hill, Alonzo. *Reynolds' Reserves in the Civil War*. Bellevue, WA: Big Byte Books, 2016 (originally published in 1864).

Hodge, Frederick Webb, ed. *Bulletin 30: Handbook of American Indians North of Mexico*. 2 vols. Washington, D.C.: Bureau of American Ethnology, 1907.

Hoke, Jacob. *The Great Invasion of 1863, or General Lee in Pennsylvania*. Dayton, Ohio: W. J. Shuey, Publisher, 1887.

———. *Historical Reminiscences of the War*. Chambersburg, PA: M. A. Foltz, Printer and Publisher, 1884.

Holland, Jesse J. *The Invisibles: The Untold Story of African American Slaves in the White House*. Guilford, CT: Lyons Press, 2016.

Holland, Josiah G. *The Life of Abraham Lincoln*. Springfield, MA: Gurdon Bill, 1866.

The Holy Bible, Containing the Old and New Testaments, Together with the Apocrypha. Philadelphia: John E. Potter and Company, late 1850s (Property of the author).

Holzer, Harold. *Lincoln at Cooper Union: The Speech That Made Abraham Lincoln President*. New York: Simon & Schuster, 2004.

———. ed. *The Lincoln-Douglas Debates: The First Complete, Unexpurgated Text*. New York: HarperCollins Publishers, 1993.

Hood, J. B. *Advance and Retreat*. New Orleans: Published for the Hood Orphan Memorial Fund, 1880.

Howard, Major General Oliver Otis. *Autobiography*. Vol. 1. New York: The Baker & Taylor Company, 1907.

Hughes, Thomas P. *American Ancestry: Giving the Name and Descent, in the Male Line, of Americans Whose Ancestors Settled in the United States Previous to the Declaration of Independence, A.D. 1776*. Vol. 10. Albany, NY: Joel Munsell's Sons, Publishers, 1895.

Humphreys, Andrew A. *From Gettysburg to the Rapidan*. New York: Charles Scribner's Sons, 1883.

Huntington, Tom. *Searching for George Gordon Meade: The Forgotten Victor of Gettysburg*. Mechanicsburg, PA: Stackpole Books, 2013.

Hyde, Bill, ed. *The Union Generals Speak: The Meade Hearings on the Battle of Gettysburg*. Baton Rouge: Louisiana State University Press, 2003.

Jacobs, M. *Notes on the Rebel Invasion of Maryland and Pennsylvania and the Battle of Gettysburg*. Philadelphia: J. B. Lippincott & Co., 1864.

Johnson, Allen, ed. *Dictionary of American Biography*. 2 vols. New York: Charles Scribner's Sons, 1928–1929.

Johnson, Robert Underwood, and Clarence Clough Buel, eds. *Battles and Leaders of the Civil War*. 4 vols. New York: The Century Company, 1887–1888.

Johnson, Rossiter. "Meade, Richard Worsam." In *The American Cyclopedia: A Popular Dictionary of General Knowledge*, vol. 11, edited by George Ripley and Charles A. Dane. New York: D. Appleton, 1875.

Jones, J. William. *Life and Letters of Robert E. Lee: Soldier and Man*. New York: Neale, 1906.

———. *Personal Reminiscences of General Robert E. Lee*. Richmond, VA: U.S. Historical Society, 1989.

Jones, Marcellus Ephraim. *Memorials of Deceased Companions of the Commandery of the State of Illinois, Military Order of the Loyal Legion of the United States*. Chicago: Ashland and Block, 1901.

Jordan, David M. *"Happiness Is Not My Companion": The Life of General G. K. Warren*. Bloomington and Indianapolis: Indiana University Press, 2001.

———. *Winfield Scott Hancock: A Soldier's Life*. Bloomington and Indianapolis: Indiana University Press, 1988.

Julian, George W. *The Life of Joshua Giddings*. Chicago: A. C. McClurg and Company, 1892.

Katz, D. Mark. *Witness to an Era: The Life and Photographs of Alexander Gardner*. New York: Viking, 1991.

Keckley, Elizabeth. *Behind the Scenes; or, Thirty Years a Slave, and Four Years in the White House*. Hillsborough, NC: Eno Publishers, 2016.

Kempster, Walter, M.D. "The Cavalry at Gettysburg." In *The Gettysburg Papers*, vol. 1, edited by by Ken Bandy and Florence Freeland. Dayton, OH: Press of Morningside Bookshop, 1978.

Kennedy, Frances H. *The Civil War Battlefield Guide*. Boston: Houghton Mifflin, 1990.

Kennedy, John F. *Profiles in Courage*. New York: Harper & Row, 1956.

Kepler, William, PhD. *History of the Three Months and Three Years' Service of the Fourth Regiment Ohio Volunteer Infantry in the War for the Union*. Cleveland: Leader Printing Company, 1886.

Keyes, E. D. *Fifty Years' Observation of Men and Events*. New York: Charles Scribner's Sons, 1885.

Kieffer, Harry M. *Recollections of a Drummer Boy*. Boston: James Osgood, 1883.

Korda, Michael. *Clouds of Glory: The Life and Legend of Robert E. Lee*. New York: HarperCollins, 2014.

Kunhardt, Dorothy Meserve, and Philip B. Kunhardt Jr. *Twenty Days*. New York: Castle Books, 1965.

Kurtz, Lieutenant Colonel J. D., and Captain Micah R. Brown. *Report on the Effects of Sea-Water and Exposure upon the Iron-Pile Shafts of the Brandywine Shoal Lighthouse*. Washington, D.C.: Government Printing Office, 1874.

Ladd, David L., and Audrey J. Ladd. *The Bachelder Papers: Gettysburg in Their Own Words*. 3 vols. Dayton, OH: Morningside House, 1994.

Lamon, Ward Hill. *Recollections of Abraham Lincoln, 1847–1865*. Chicago: A. C. McClurg and Company, 1895.

"Leading Participants." *Annals of the War: Written by Leading Participants North and South*. Philadelphia: The Times Publishing Company, 1879.

Lee, Cazenove Garner, Jr. *Chronicle: Studies of the Early Generations of the Lees of Virginia*. New York: New York University Press, 1957.

Lee, Fitzhugh. *General Lee: A Biography of Robert E. Lee*. New York: Appleton, 1913.

Lee, Henry. *Memoirs of the War in the Southern Department of the United States*. New York: University Publishing Company, 1869.

Lee, Captain Robert E. *Recollections and Letters of General Robert E. Lee*. New York: Doubleday, 1904.

Leech, Margaret. *Reveille in Washington: 1860–1865*. New York: New York Review of Books, 1941.

Levine, Bruce. *Thaddeus Stevens: Civil War Revolutionary, Fighter for Racial Justice*. New York: Simon & Schuster, 2021.

Lewis, John H. *A Rebel in Pickett's Charge at Gettysburg*. Bellevue, WA: Big Byte Books, 2016 (originally published 1895).

Lindeman, Eduard C., ed. *Basic Selections from Emerson*. New York: New American Library, 1954.

Long, A. L. (Armistead Lindsay), with Marcus J. Wright. *Memoirs of Robert E. Lee: His Military and Personal History*. New York: J. M. Stoddart, 1886.

Long, E. B., with Barbara Long. *The Civil War Day by Day: An Almanac*. Philadelphia: Da Capo Press; New York: Doubleday, 1985.

Longacre, Edward G. *Custer and His Wolverines: The Michigan Cavalry Brigade, 1861–1865*. Conshohocken, PA: Combined Publishing, 1997.

———. *General John Buford*. Cambridge: Da Capo Press, 1995.

Longstreet, James. *From Manassas to Appomattox: Memoirs of the Civil War in America*. Philadelphia: J. B. Lippincott Company, 1896.

Lord, Walter, ed. *The Fremantle Diary: A Journal of the Confederacy.* Short Hills, NJ: Burford Books, 1954.

Louis, Leon. *Diary of a TarHeel Confederate Soldier.* Charlotte: Stone Publishing, 1913.

Lowe, David, ed. *Meade's Army: The Private Notebooks of Lt. Col. Theodore Lyman.* Kent, OH: The Kent State University Press, 2007.

MacDonald, Rose Mortimer Ellzey. *Mrs. Robert E. Lee.* Boston: Ginn and Company, 1939.

Manders, Damon. *Engineers Far from Ordinary: The U.S. Army Corps of Engineers in St. Louis.* St. Louis: U.S. Army Corps of Engineers, 2011.

Manning, Chandra. *Troubled Refuge: Struggling for Freedom in the Civil War.* New York: Alfred A. Knopf, 2016.

Mason, Emily V. *The Life of General Robert E. Lee.* Baltimore: John Murphy, 1874.

Maurice, Major General Sir Frederick, ed. *An Aide-de-Camp of Lee: Being the Papers of Colonel Charles Marshall.* Boston: Little, Brown and Company, 1927.

McClellan, George B. *McClellan's Own Story.* New York: Charles L. Webster & Company, 1887.

McClellan, H. B. *I Rode with Jeb Stuart: The Life and Campaigns of Major General J. E. B. Stuart.* New York: Da Capo Press, 1994.

McClure, Alexander K. *Abraham Lincoln and Men of War-Times: Some Personal Recollections of War and Politics during the Lincoln Administration.* Philadelphia: The Times Publishing Company, 1892.

———. *Old Time Notes of Philadelphia.* Vol. 1. Philadelphia: John C. Winston, 1905.

McGrath, Tim. *James Monroe: A Life.* New York: Dutton, 2020.

McIntosh, David Gregg, Colonel of Artillery, C.S.A. *The Campaign of Chancellorsville.* Richmond, VA: Wm. Ellis Jones' Sons, 1913.

McPherson, James M. *Abraham Lincoln.* New York: Oxford University Press, 2009.

———. *Battle Cry of Freedom: The Civil War Era.* New York: Oxford University Press, 1988.

———. *Hallowed Ground: A Walk at Gettysburg.* New York: Crown Journeys, 2003.

———. *The Negro's Civil War: How American Blacks Felt and Acted During the War for the Union.* New York: Vintage Civil War Library, 1965.

Meacham, Jon. *And There Was Light: Abraham Lincoln and the American Struggle.* New York: Random House, 2022.

Meade, Captain George Gordon, Jr. (ret), ed. *The Life and Letters of George Gordon Meade, Major General, United States Army.* 2 vols. New York: Charles Scribner's Sons, 1913.

Messent, Peter, and Steve Courtney, eds. *The Civil War Letters of Joseph Hopkins Twichell: A Chaplain's Story.* Athens: The University of Georgia Press, 2008.

Miers, Earl Schenck, ed. *Lincoln Day by Day: A Chronology, 1809–1865.* 3 vols. Washington, D.C.: U.S. Lincoln Sesquicentennial Commission, 1960.

Miller, Richard Lawrence. *Lincoln and His World: The Early Years, Birth to Illinois Legislature*. Mechanicsburg, PA: Stackpole Books, 2006.

———. *Lincoln and His World: Prairie Politician, 1834–1842*. Mechanicsburg, PA: Stackpole Books, 2008.

Missail, John, and Mary Lou Missail. *The Seminole Wars: America's Longest Indian Conflict*. Gainesville: University Press of Florida, 2004.

Moore, John Bassett, ed. *The Works of James Buchanan, Comprising His Speeches, State Papers, and Private Correspondence*. Vol. 10, 1856–1860. Philadelphia and London: J. B. Lippincott, 1910.

Moore, Sue Burns, and Rebecca Blackwell Drake, eds. *Leaves: The Diary of Elizabeth Meade Ingraham*. Champion Hill: Champion Hill Heritage Foundation, 2019.

Morris, Roy, Jr. *The Long Pursuit: Abraham Lincoln's Thirty-Year Struggle with Stephen Douglas for the Heart and Soul of America*. New York: Smithsonian Books/Collins, 2008.

Morrison, H. Robert, and Christine Eckstrom Lee. *America's Atlantic Isles*. Washington, D.C.: National Geographic Society, 1981.

Morrison, James L. *The Best School: West Point, 1833–1866*. Kent, OH: Kent State University Press, 1998.

Munden, Kenneth W., and Henry P. Beers. *Guide to Federal Archives Relating to the Civil War*. Washington, D.C.: Government Printing Office, 1962.

Murray, Jennifer M. *On a Great Battlefield: The Making, Management, and Memory of Gettysburg National Military Park, 1933–2023*. Knoxville: The University of Tennessee Press, 2023.

Nagel, Paul. *The Lees of Virginia: Seven Generations of an American Family*. New York: Oxford University Press, 2007.

Nevin, David. *The Mexican War*. New York: Time-Life Books, 1978.

———. *The Road to Shiloh*. Alexandria, VA: Time-Life Books, 1983.

Nevins, Allan. *Ordeal of the Union*. Vol. 2, *A House Dividing, 1852–1857*. New York: Charles Scribner's Sons, 1947.

———. ed. *A Diary of Battle: The Personal Journals of Colonel Charles S. Wainwright, 1861–1865*. New York: Harcourt, 1962.

———. and Milton Halsey Thomas. *The Diary of George Templeton Strong*. 4 vols. New York: The Macmillan Company, 1952.

Newsome, Hampton. Gettysburg's Southern Front: Opportunity and Failure at Richmond. Lawrence: University Press of Kansas, 2022. See chapter 8, "Rooney Lee's Capture," 111–26.

Nicolay, John G., and John Hay. *Abraham Lincoln: A History*. 10 vols. New York: Century Co., 1912.

The Ninth Annual Report of the American Society for Colonizing the Free People of Color of the United States. Washington, D.C.: Way & Gideon, 1826.

Nolan, Alan T. *Lee Considered: General Robert E. Lee and Civil War History*. Chapel Hill: The University of North Carolina Press, 1991.

"Northern Prison Life." In *The Land We Love, A Monthly Magazine*, edited by D. H. Hill. Vol. 2. Charlotte, NC: Irwin & Co., 1867.

Norton, Oliver Willcox. *The Attack and Defense of Little Round Top, Gettysburg, July 2, 1863*. Gettysburg: Stan Clark Military Books, 1992.

Oates, William C. *The War Between the Union and the Confederacy, and Its Lost Opportunities*. New York and Washington: The Neale Publishing Company, 1905.

O'Brien, Kevin E., ed. *My Life in the Irish Brigade: The Civil War Memoirs of Private William McCarter, 116th Pennsylvania Infantry*. New York: Da Capo Press, 2003.

O'Harrow, Robert, Jr. *The Quartermaster: Montgomery C. Meigs: Lincoln's General, Master Builder of the Union Army*. New York: Simon & Schuster, 2016.

O'Reilly, Francis Augustin. *The Fredericksburg Campaign: Winter War on the Rappahannock*. Baton Rouge: Louisiana State University Press, 2003.

Orwig, Captain Joseph R. *History of the 131st Penna. Volunteers: War of 1861–65*. Williamsport, PA: The Sun Book and Job Printing House, 1902.

Osborn, Captain Hartwell, and Others. *Trials and Triumphs: The Record of the 55th Ohio Volunteer Infantry*. Chicago: A. C. McClurg & Co., 1904.

Palmer, Michael A. *Lee Moves North: Robert E. Lee on the Offensive*. New York: John Wiley Sons, 1998.

Paradis, James M. *African Americans and the Gettysburg Campaign*. Lanham, MD: The Scarecrow Press, 2013.

Peck, Graham A. *Making an Antislavery Nation: Lincoln, Douglas, and the Battle for Freedom*. Urbana: University of Illinois Press, 2017.

Pennypacker, Isaac. *General Meade*. New York: D. Appleton and Company, 1901.

Perry, James M. *A Bohemian Brigade: The Civil War Correspondents—Mostly Rough, Sometimes Ready*. New York: John Wiley & Sons, 2000.

Phelps, Mary Merwin. *Kate Chase, Dominant Daughter: The Life Story of a Brilliant Woman and Her Famous Father*. Whitefish, MT: Literary Licensing, 2012.

Post, Marie Caroline. *The Life and Memoirs of Comte Regis de Trobriand*. New York: E. P. Dutton & Company, 1910.

Potter, David M. *The Impending Crisis, 1848–1861*. New York: Harper & Row, 1976

Pratt, Julius W. *A History of the United States Foreign Policy*. Englewood Cliffs, NJ: Prentice-Hall, 1955.

Pryor, Elizabeth Brown. *Reading the Man: A Portrait of Robert E. Lee Through His Private Letters*. New York: Penguin Books, 2008.

Putnam, George Rockwell. *Lighthouses and Lightships of the United States*. Boston: Houghton Mifflin Company, 1917.

Quarles, Benjamin. *The Negro in the Civil War*. New York: Russell & Russell, 1953.

Raasch, Chuck. *Imperfect Union: A Father's Search for His Son in the Aftermath of the Battle of Gettysburg*. Lanham, MD: Stackpole Books, 2016.

Rafuse, Ethan S. *George Gordon Meade and the War in the East*. Abilene, TX: McWhinney Foundation Press, 2003.

Randall, Ruth Painter. *Mary Lincoln: Biography of a Marriage*. Boston: Little, Brown, 1953.

Read, Allen Walker, ed. *Funk & Wagnalls New International Dictionary of the English Language*. Garden City, NY: International Press, 1987.

John H Reagan. *Memoirs, with Special Reference to Secession and the Civil War*. Edited by Walter F. McCaleb. New York and Washington: The Neale Publishing Company, 1906.

Reed, Henry Hope. *The United States Capitol: Its Architecture and Decorations*. New York: W. W. Norton, 2005.

Reed, Thomas Benton. *A Private in Gray*. Camden, AR: T. R. Reed, 1905.

Reid, Whitelaw. "The Gettysburg Campaign: A Contemporary Account." In *The Rebellion Record: A Diary of American Events*, edited by Frank Moore. New York: D. Van Ostrand, Publisher, 1864.

Report of the Survey of the North and Northwest Lakes by Capt. George G. Meade, Being Appendix I of the Report of the Chief Topographical Engineer, Accompanying Annual Report of the Secretary of War 1858. Washington, D.C.: Lemuel Towers, 1859.

Revised United States Army Regulations of 1861. Washington: Government Printing Office, 1863.

Reynolds, David S. *Abe: Abraham Lincoln in His Times*. New York: Penguin Press, 2020.

Reynolds Memorial: Addresses Delivered Before the Historial Society of Philadelphia. J. B. Lippincott & Co., 1880.

Rhodes, Robert Hunt, ed. *All for the Union: The Civil War Diary of Elisha Hunt Rhodes*. New York: Orion Books, 1985.

Rice, Allen Thorndike, ed. *Reminiscences of Abraham Lincoln by Distinguished Men of His Time*. New York: North American Review, 1888.

Richardson, Edgar P. "The Athens of America." In *Philadelphia: A 300-Year History*, edited by Russell F. Weigley. New York: W. W. Norton & Company, 1982.

Rister, Carl Coke. *Robert E. Lee in Texas*. Norman: University of Oklahoma Press, 1946.

Robertson, James I., Jr. *General A. P. Hill: The Story of a Confederate Warrior*. New York: Vintage Civil War Library, 1987.

Robins, Sally Nelson. "Mrs. Lee During the War—Something About "The Mess" and Its Occupants." In *Gen. Robert Edward Lee: Soldier, Citizen, and Christian Patriot*, edited by R. A. Brock. Richmond, VA: Royal Publishing Co., 1897.

Rodgers, Sarah Sites. *The Ties of the Past: The Gettysburg Diaries of Salome Myers Stewart, 1854–1922*. Gettysburg: Thomas Publications, 1996.

Rusling, James F. *Men and Things I Saw in Civil War Days*. New York: Eaton & Mains, 1899.

Sandburg, Carl. *Abraham Lincoln: The Prairie Years, and the War Years*. 1-vol. ed. New York: Harcourt, Brace, and Company, 1954.

———. *Abraham Lincoln: The War Years*. 4 vols. New York: Harcourt, Brace & Company, 1939.

Sanders, James. E. *The Vanguard of the Atlantic World: Creating Modernity, Nation, and Democracy in Nineteenth-Century Latin America*. Durham, North Carolina, and London: Duke University Press, 2014. See chapter 3, "The San Patricio Battalion, 64–80.

Sauers, Richard A. *Gettysburg: The Meade-Sickles Controversy*. Washington, D.C.: Brassey's, 2003.

Schaff, Philip, D.D. "The Gettysburg Week." In *Old Mercersburg*, edited by the Women's Club of Mercersburg. New York: Frank Allaben Genealogical Company, 1913.

Scott, Robert Garth, ed., *Fallen Leaves: The Civil War Letters of Major Henry Livermore Abbott*. Kent, OH: Kent State University Press, 1991.

Scott, Winfield. *Memoirs of Lieut.-Gen. Scott, LL.D., Written by Himself*. Vol. 2. New York: Sheldon & Company, Publishers, 1864.

Seale, William. *The President's House: A History*. 2 vols. Washington, D.C.: White House Historical Association, 1986.

Sears, Stephen W. *George McClellan: The Young Napoleon*. New York: Ticknor & Fields, 1988.

———. *Gettysburg*. New York and Boston: Houghton Mifflin Company, 2003.

———. ed. *The Civil War Papers of George B. McClellan: Selected Correspondence, 1860–1865*. New York: Ticknor & Fields, 1989.

Sedgwick, John. *Correspondence of John Sedgwick, Major-General*. 2 vols. Bellevue, WA: Big Byte Books, 2014 (originally published in 1902).

Sefton, James E. *The United States Army and Reconstruction, 1865–1877*. Baton Rouge: Louisiana State University Press, 1967.

Sheridan, Philip H. *Personal Memoirs of P. H. Sheridan*. 2 vols. New York: D. Appleton, 1886.

Skelton, William B. *West Point: Two Centuries and Beyond*. Abilene, TX: McWhinney Foundation Press, 2004.

Slocum, Charles Elihu. *The Life and Services of Major-General Henry Warner Slocum*. Toledo: The Slocum Publishing Company, 1913.

Smith, David. *On the Edge of Freedom: The Fugitive Slave Issue in South Central Pennsylvania, 1820–1870*. New York: Fordham University Press, 2013.

Smith, Diane Monroe. *Washington Roebling's Civil War: From the Bloody Battlefield at Gettysburg to the Brooklyn Bridge*. Guilford, CT: Stackpole Books, 2019.

Smith, Gene. *Lee and Grant: A Dual Biography*. New York: McGraw-Hill, 1984.

Smith, Harriet Elinor, ed. *Autobiography of Mark Twain*. 3 vols. Berkeley: University of California Press, 2010.

Smith, Captain James E. *A Famous Battery and Its Campaigns, 1861–1864*. Washington: W. H. Loudermilk & Co., 1892.

Smith, James Morton, ed. *The Republic of Letters: The Correspondence Between Thomas Jefferson and James Madison, 1776–1826*. Vol. 3. New York: W. W. Norton & Company, 1995.

Snow, Edward Rowe. *Famous Lighthouses of America*. New York: Dodd, Mead & Company, 1955.

Sorrel, General G. Moxley. *Recollections of a Confederate Staff Officer*. New York: The Neale Publishing Company, 1905.

Steiner, Mark E. *An Honest Calling: The Law Practice of Abraham Lincoln*. DeKalb: Northern Illinois University Press, 2006.

Steinman, D. B. *The Builders of the Bridge: The Story of John Roebling and His Son*. New York: Harcourt, Brace, and Company, 1945.

Survivors' Association. *The History of the Corn Exchange Regiment, 118th Pennsylvania Volunteers: From Their First Engagement at Antietam to Appomattox*. Philadelphia: J. L. Smith, Publisher, 1888.

Swanberg, W. A. *Sickles the Incredible*. New York: Charles Scribner's Sons, 1956.

Symonds, Craig L. *History of the Battle of Gettysburg*. New York: HarperCollins, 2001.

Tap, Bruce. *Over Lincoln's Shoulder: The Committee on the Conduct of the War*. Lawrence: University Press of Kansas, 1998.

Taylor, Emerson G. *Gouverneur Kemble Warren: The Life and Letters of an American Soldier*. Boston: Houghton Mifflin, 1932.

Taylor, Walter H. *Four Years with General Lee*. Bloomington: Indiana University Press, 1962.

———. *General Lee: His Campaigns in Virginia, 1861–1865*. Lincoln: University of Nebraska Press, 1994.

Thomas, Benjamin P. *Lincoln's New Salem*. Carbondale: Southern Illinois Press, 2021.

Thomas, Emory. *Robert E. Lee*. New York: W. W. Norton & Co., 1995.

Thomson, O. R. H., and William H. Rauch. *History of the "Bucktails": Kane Rifle Regiment of the Pennsylvania Reserves, 42nd of the Line*. Philadelphia: Electric Printing Company, 1900.

Tower, R. Lockwood, ed. *Lee's Adjutant: The Wartime Letters of Colonel Walter Herron Taylor, 1862–1865*. Columbia: University of South Carolina Press, 1995.

Tremain, Henry Edwin. *Two Days of War: A Gettysburg Narrative and Other Excursions*. New York: Bonnell, Silver and Bowers, 1905.

Trudeau, Noah Andre. *Gettysburg: A Testing of Courage*. New York: Perennial, 2002.

Turner, Justin G., and Linda Levitt Turner. *Mary Todd Lincoln: Her Life and Letters*. New York: Knopf, 1972.

Twain, Mark. *Life on the Mississippi*. Boston: James R. Osgood and Company, 1883.

Underwood, Adin B. *Three Years' Service in the 33rd Mass. Infantry Regiment, 1862–1865*. Boston: A. Williams & Co. Publishers, 1881.

United States Congress. "William Lee D. Ewing." In *Biographical Directory of the United States Congress*.

United States War Department. *War of the Rebellion: A Compilation of the Official Records of the Union and Confederate Armies*. Washington, D.C.: Government Printing Office, 1880–1901.

Urwin, Gregory J. *Custer Victorious: The Civil War Battles of George Armstrong Custer*. Lincoln: University of Nebraska Press, 1983.

———. and Darby Erd (illustrator). *The United States Infantry: An Illustrated History, 1775–1918*. New York: Sterling Publishing Co., 1991.

———. and Ernest Lisle Reedstrom (illustrator). *The United States Cavalry: An Illustrated History, 1776–1944*. Norman: University of Oklahoma Press, 1983.

Varon, Elizabeth R. *Longstreet: The Confederate General Who Defied the South*. New York: Simon & Schuster, 2023.

Villard, Harold G., and Oswald Garrison Villard, eds. *Lincoln on the Eve of '61: A Journalist's Story by Henry Villard*. New York: Alfred A. Knopf, 1941.

Walker, Francis A. *General Hancock*. New York: Appleton, 1894.

Ward, Geoffrey C. *The Civil War: An Illustrated History*. New York: Knopf, 1990.

Watterston, George. *New Guide to Washington*. Washington, D.C.: Robert Farnham, 1842.

Weigley, Russell F. *Quartermaster General of the Union Army: A Biography of M. C. Meigs*. New York: Columbia University Press, 1959.

Weld, Stephen Minot. *War Diary and Letters of Stephen Minot Weld: 1861–1865*. Cambridge: The Riverside Press, privately printed, 1912.

Welles, Gideon. *Diary of Gideon Welles: Secretary of the Navy Under Lincoln and Johnson*. 2 vols. Boston and New York: Houghton Mifflin Company, 1911.

Wert, Jeffrey D. *Cavalryman of the Lost Cause: A Biography of J. E. B. Stuart*. New York: Simon & Schuster, 2008.

———. *General James Longstreet: The Confederacy's Most Controversial Commander*. New York: Touchstone, 1993.

Weygant, Charles H. *History of the One Hundred and Twenty-Fourth Regiment*. Newburgh, NY: Journal Printing House, 1877.

Wheeler, Tom. *Mr. Lincoln's T-Mails: How Abraham Lincoln Used the Telegraph to Win the Civil War*. New York: Collins, 2006.

Wiley, Bell Irvin. *The Life of Billy Yank*. Baton Rouge: Louisiana State University Press, 1952.

Williams, T. Harry, ed. *With Beauregard in Mexico: The Mexican War Reminiscences of P. G. T. Beauregard.* New York: Da Capo Press, 1969.

Wills, Garry. *Lincoln at Gettysburg: The Words That Remade America.* New York: Touchstone, 1992.

Wilson, Douglas L., and Rodney O. Davis, eds. *Herndon's Informants: Letters, Interviews, and Statements About Abraham Lincoln.* Chicago: University of Illinois Press, 1998.

Wilson, Rufus Rockwell. *Intimate Memories of Lincoln.* Elmira, NY: The Primavera Press, 1945.

Wise, Barton Haxall. *The Life of Henry A. Wise of Virginia, 1806–1876.* New York: The Macmillan Company, 1899.

Woodward, C. Vann, ed. *Mary Chesnut's Civil War.* New Haven, CT: Yale University Press, 1981.

Woodward, E. M. *Our Campaigns, or the Marches, Bivouacs, Incidents of Camp Life and History of Our Regiment During Its Three Years Term of Service.* Philadelphia: John E. Potter, 1865.

Young, John. *Men and Memories: Personal Reminiscences,* edited by May D. Russell Young. Vol. 1. New York: F. T. Neely, 1901.

ARTICLES AND PRESENTATIONS

"Account of the Latest Riots." *Interesting Papers Illustrative of the Recent Riots at Baltimore* (Philadelphia, 1812).

"Address of General James F. Rusling at the 46th Anniversary of the Third Army Corps, Union, Hotel Manhattan," 5/5/1910, from "Lincoln and Sickles," published by "Third Army Corps Union" for Distribution to its Members (May 1910).

"Andrew Atkinson Humphreys' Seminole War Field Journal." *Florida Historical Quarterly* 85, no. 2 (Fall 2006).

"Cadets Arranged in Order of Merit, in Their Respective Classes, as Determined at the General Examination, in June 1829." *Official Register of the Officers and Cadets of the U.S. Military Academy, June 1829.* West Point, NY: USMA, 1884.

"Decision of the Supreme Court." *Scientific American,* May 1858.

"Joseph Gilbert Totten." *Professional Memoirs, Corps of Engineers, United States Army, and Engineer Department at Large* 3, no. 10 (April–June 1911).

"Letter from Maj. Scheibert, of the Prussian Engineers, November 21, 1877." *SHSP,* vol. 5, 92.

"Letter from Miss Jennie McCreary to Miss Julia McCreary," 7/27/63. Ralph S. Shay, ed.

"Reflections on the Battle of Gettysburg." *The Lebanon County Historical Society* 13, no. 6 (1963).

"Letters from G.W.P. Custis to George Washington, 1797–1798." *VMHB* 20, no. 3 (July 1912).

"Letters of Robert E. Lee to Henry Kayser, 1838–1846." Missouri Historical Society, *Glimpses of the Past* 3 (January–February 1936).

"New Records of the Lincoln-Douglas Debate at the 1854 Illinois State Fair: The Missouri Republican and the Missouri Democrat." *Journal of the Abraham Lincoln Association* 30, no. 2 (Summer 2009).

"The Late Honorable John Sergeant of Philadelphia." *American Law Register* 1, no. 4 (February 1853).

Abbott, Richard H. "A Yankee Views the Organization of the Republican Party in South Carolina." *South Carolina Historical Society Magazine* 85, no. 3 (July 1984).

Adams, Francis Raymond, Jr., "An Annotated Edition of the Personal Letters of Robert E. Lee." Doctoral thesis, University of Maryland, 1955.

Aitken, Marilyn, and Robert Aitken. "Crime of Passion Defense." *Litigation* 36, no. 1 (Fall 2009).

Alexander, General E. P. "The Great Charge and Artillery Fighting at Gettysburg." In *B&L*, vol. 3.

Anderson, Marvin J. "The Architectural Education of Nineteenth-Century American Engineers: Dennis Hart Mahan at West Point." *Journal of the Society of Architectural Historians* 67, no. 2 (2008).

Andrews, J. Cutler. "The Press Reports the Battle of Gettysburg." *Pennsylvania History: A Journal of Mid-Atlantic Studies* 31, no. 2 (1964).

Arndt, J. Chris. "Maine in the Northeastern Boundary Controversy: States' Rights in Antebellum New England." *New England Quarterly* 62, no. 2 (1989).

Basler, Roy P. "Did President Lincoln Give the Smallpox to William H. Johnson?" *Huntington Library Quarterly* 35 (May 1972).

Beers, Henry P. "A History of U.S. Topographical Engineers." *Military Engineer* 34, no. 201 (July 1942).

Bell, W. Herman, ed. "A Captain in Captivity." *New England Quarterly* 14, no. 1 (March 1941).

Bendall, Simon. "1720. The French Siege of Cadiz in the Peninsular War." *Journal of the Society for Army Historical Research* 82, no. 331 (2004): 262–64. http://www.jstor.org/stable/44232732.

Benjamin, Charles F. "Hooker's Appointment and Removal." *B&L*, vol. 3.

Benjaminson, Eric. "A Regiment of Immigrants: The 82nd Illinois Volunteer Infantry and the Letters of Captain Rudolph Mueller." *Journal of the Illinois State Historical Society* 94, no. 2 (Summer 2001).

Bittle, George C. "First Campaign of the Second Seminole War." *The Florida Historical Quarterly* 46, no. 1 (1967): 39–45. http://www.jstor.org/stable/30140215.

Blair, William Alan. "A Source of Amusement." *PMHB* 115, no. 3 (July 1991).

Blanchard, Leslie. "Focus on Lighthouses." *Technology and Culture* 19, no. 4 (October 1978).

Blight, David W. "Lincoln on the Moral Bankruptcy of Slavery: Inside the Lincoln-Douglass Debates of 1858." *OAH Magazine of History* 21, no. 4 (2007): 56–61. http://www.jstor.org/stable/25162145.

Bloom, Robert J. "We Never Expected a Battle." *Pennsylvania History* 55, no. 4 (October 1988).

Bonura, Michael A. "A French-Inspired Way of War: French Influence on the U.S. Army from 1812 to the Mexican War." *Army History*, no. 90 (2014).

Bowman, Charles H., Jr. "Manuel Torres, a Spanish American Patriot in Philadelphia, 1796–1822." *PMHB* 94, no. 1 (1970).

Boyd, Julian P. "John Sergeant's Mission to Europe for the Second Bank of the United States: 1816-1817." *PMHB* 58, no. 3 (1934): 213–31. http://www.jstor.org/stable/20086869.

Bradford, Gamaliel. "A Portrait of General George Gordon Meade." *American Historical Review* 20, no. 7 (January 1915).

Bright, Captain Robert A. "Pickett's Charge." *SHSP*, vol. 31, 233–34.

Brooke, George M., and James W. Covington. "The Establishment of Fort Brooke: The Beginning of Tampa." *Florida Historical Quarterly* 31, no. 4 (1953).

Brown, Charles Leroy, and E. Lane. "Abraham Lincoln and the Illinois Central Railroad, 1857–1860." *Journal of the Illinois State Historical Society* 36, no. 2 (1943).

Butterfield, Julia Lorillard, ed. *A Biographical Memorial of General Daniel Butterfield.* New York: The Grafton Press, 1904. "Article on Gettysburg."

Caldwell, Joshua W. "John Bell of Tennessee: A Chapter of Political History." *American Historical Review* 4, no. 1 (July 1899).

Chandler, Josephine Craven. "New Salem: Early Chapter in Lincoln's Life." *Journal of the Illinois State Historical Society* 22, no. 4 (1930).

Cimbala, Paul A. "On the Front Line of Freedom: Freedmen's Bureau Officers and Agents in Reconstruction Georgia." *The Georgia Historical Quarterly* 76, no. 3 (Fall 1992).

Cleveland, H. I. "Booming the First American President: A Talk with Lincoln's Friend, the Late Joseph Medill," *Saturday Evening Post*, August 5, 1899.

Coddington, Edwin B. "Lincoln's Role in the Gettysburg Campaign." *Pennsylvania History: A Journal of Mid-Atlantic Studies* 34, no. 3 (July 1967).

Coddington, Ronald S. "A Gallant Son of Orange Falls at Gettysburg: In the Aftermath of Battle, a Pennsylvania Farmwife Fulfills a Union Captain's Foreboding Request." *Military Images* 34, no. 3 (2016).

———. and David Batalo. "Fallout from the Johnston Reconnaissance: A Late-War Letter by Robert E. Lee Sheds Light on an Enduring Gettysburg Controversy." *Military Images* 36, no. 3 (Summer 2018).

Cruz, Jesus. "Notability and Revolution: Social Origins of the Political Elite in Liberal Spain, 1800 to 1853." *Comparative Studies in Society and History* 36, no. 1 (1994): 97–121. http://www.jstor.org/stable/179328.

Cuthbert, Norma B. (and REL). "To Molly: Five Early Letters from Robert E. Lee to His Wife." *Huntington Library Quarterly* 15, no. 3 (May 1952).

Dallas, Alexander James. "The Children of George Meade." *PMHB* 5, no. 1 (January 1988).

DeButts, Robert E. L., Jr. "Lee in Love: Courtship and Correspondence in Antebellum Virginia." *VMHB* 115, no. 4 (2007).

———. "Mary Custis Lee's 'Reminiscences of the War.'" *VMHB* 109, no. 3 (2001): 301–25. http://www.jstor.org/stable/4249932.

DiFebo, Dane, "Old Baldy: A Horse's Tale." *PMHB* 135, no. 4 (October 2011).

Ditmeyer, Steven R. "Railroads, Herman Haupt, and the Battle of Gettysburg." *Railroad History*, no. 208 (2013).

Dodd, Dorothy. "The Wrecking Business on the Florida Reef, 1822–1860." *The Florida Historical Quarterly* 22, no. 4 (April 1944).

Donovan, James B. "Two Sams and Their Six-Shooter." *Texas Monthly*, April 2016.

Drumm, Stella M. "Robert E. Lee and the Improvement of the Mississippi River." *Missouri Historical Society Collections* 6, no. 2 (February 1929).

Dunn, B. C. "Maj. Gen. Montgomery Cunningham Meigs." *Professional Memoirs, Corps of Engineers, United States Army, and Engineer Department at Large* 6, no. 28 (1914).

Egnal, Marc. "The Economic Origins of the Civil War." *OAH Magazine of History* 25, no. 2 (2011).

Ewing, Gretchen Garst. "Duff Green, John C. Calhoun, and the Election of 1828." *The South Carolina Historical Magazine* 79, no. 2 (1978).

Fehrenbacher, Don E. "Roger B. Taney and the Sectional Crisis." *The Journal of Southern History* 43, no. 4 (1977).

Fisher, Sidney George. "The Diary of Sidney George Fisher, 1841." *PMHB* 77, no. 2 (1953).

Forman, Sidney. "The First School of Engineering." *The Military Engineer* 44, no. 298 (1952).

Formwalt, Lee W., Robert Crumley, and Philip Joiner. "Petitioning Congress for Protection: A Black View of Reconstruction at the Local Level." *The Georgia Historical Quarterly* 73, no. 2 (Summer 1989).

Gannett, Lewis. "The Ann Rutledge Story: Case Closed?" *Journal of the Abraham Lincoln Association* 31, no. 2 (Summer 2010).

"Gen. George Gordon Meade." *Professional Memoirs, Corps of Engineers, United States Army, and Engineer Department at Large* 5, no. 22 (1913).

Gettysburg National Military Park, W. S. Hancock File, H. H. Bingham to Dear Sister, 7/18/63.

Gilje, Paul A. "The Baltimore Riots of 1812 and the Breakdown of the Anglo-American Mob Tradition." *Journal of Social History* 13, no. 4 (Summer 1980).

Gill, George J. "Edward Everett and the Northeastern Boundary Controversy." *The New England Quarterly* 42, no. 2 (1969).

Glatthaar, Joseph T. "A Tale of Two Armies: The Confederate Army of Northern Virginia and the Union Army of the Potomac and Their Cultures." *Journal of the Civil War Era* 6, no. 3 (2016).

Glaze, Robert. "Saint and Sinner: Robert E. Lee, Nathan Bedford Forrest, and the Ambiguity of Southern Identity." *Tennessee Historical Quarterly* 69, no. 2 (2010).

Grimm, Colonel M. L. "Colonel Robert E. Lee's Report on Indian Combats in Texas." *The Southwestern Historical Quarterly* 39, no. 1 (July 1935).

Grimsley, Elizabeth Todd. "Six Months in the White House." *Illinois State Historical Society Journal* 19 (October 1926–January 1927).

Guelzo, Allen C. "Abraham Lincoln and the Doctrine of Necessity." *Journal of the Abraham Lincoln Association* 18, no. 1 (1997).

———. "'War Is a Great Evil': Robert E. Lee in the War with Mexico." *The Southwestern Historical Quarterly* 122, no. 1 (2018).

Halstead, E. P. "Incidents of the First Day at Gettysburg." *In B&L*, vol. 3.

Halstead, Murat. "The Revival of Sectionalism." *The North American Review* 140, no. 340 (1885).

Hansen, Stephen, and Paul Nygard. "Stephen A. Douglas, the Know-Nothings, and the Democratic Party in Illinois, 1854–1858." *Illinois Historical Journal* 87, no. 2 (1994).

Hassler, Warren W. "George G. Meade and His Role in the Gettysburg Campaign." *Pennsylvania History: A Journal of Mid-Atlantic Studies* 32, no. 4 (1965).

Hemphill, James C. "The South and the Negro Vote." *The North American Review* 202, no. 717 (1915).

Howard, O. O. "Campaign and Battle of Gettysburg, June and July, 1863." *Atlantic Monthly*, July 1876.

Howe, Daniel Walker. "Why Abraham Lincoln Was a Whig." *Journal of the Abraham Lincoln Association* 16, no. 1 (1995).

Hudson, Gossie Harold. "Black Americans vs. Citizenship: The Dred Scott Decision." *Negro History Bulletin* 46, no. 1 (1983).

Huebner, Timothy S. "Roger B. Taney and the Slavery Issue: Looking Beyond—and Before—Dred Scott." *The Journal of American History* 97, no. 1 (2010).

Hughes, Greta G., and Richard Owen. "The Grand Duke Bernhard's Visit to West Point, 1825: From *Reise durch Nord Amerika* of the Grand Duke Bernhard of the House of Saxe-Weimar-Eisenach." *New York History* 26, no. 1 (January 1945).

Hunt, Ira A., Jr. "The Lake Survey and the Great Lakes." *The Military Engineer* 51, no. 141 (May–June 1959).

Imboden, General John. "The Confederate Retreat from Gettysburg." In *B&L*, vol. 3.

Jarrett, Calvin. "Cassius Marcellus Clay A Popular Portrait." *The Register of the Kentucky Historical Society* 64, no. 4 (1966): 277–92. http://www.jstor.org/sta ble/23376887.

Johnson, Tyler V. "Punishing the Lies on the Rio Grande: Catholic and Immigrant Volunteers in Zachary Taylor's Army and the Fight Against Nativism." *Journal of the Early Republic* 30, no. 1 (2010).

Joyce, Charles T. "'How They Went Forth to the Harvest of Death': A Concise Account of the U.S. Regular Infantry at Gettysburg." *Military Images* 40, no. 3 (221) (2022).

———. "Union Amputees After Gettysburg: 'Lost an Arm in Freedom's Fray.'" *Military Images* 39, no. 3 (217) (2021): 55–62. https://www.jstor.org/stable /27020809.

Katula, Richard A. "The Gettysburg Address as the Centerpiece of American Racial Discourse." *The Journal of Blacks in Higher Education*, no. 28 (2000).

Kyle, Ronald K. "Grant, Meade, and Clausewitz: The Application of War as an Extension of Policy During the Vicksburg and Gettysburg Campaigns." *Army History*, no. 28 (1993).

Lack, Paul D. "An Urban Slave Community: Little Rock, 1831–1862." *The Arkansas Historical Quarterly* 41, no. 3 (1982).

LaFantasie, Glenn. "Lincoln and the Gettysburg Awakening." *Journal of the Abraham Lincoln Association* 16, no. 1 (1995).

Lee, Cazenove G., Jr. "Ann Hill Carter." *VMHB* 16, no. 3 (July 1936).

Lemly, James H. "The Mississippi River: St. Louis' Friend or Foe?" *The Business History Review* 39, no. 1 (Spring 1965).

Leverett, Frank. "The Lower Rapids of the Mississippi River." *The Journal of Geology* 7, no. 1 (Jan./Feb. 1899).

Levin, Kevin M. "The Diaries Left Behind by Confederate Soldiers Reveal the True Role of Enslaved Labor at Gettysburg." *Smithsonian Magazine*, July 2, 2019.

Lewis, Miles. "Iron Lighthouses." *Construction History* 27 (2012).

"Lincoln and Sickles." Published by "Third Army Corps Union" for Distribution to its Members (May 1910).

Longstreet, James. "Lee's Right Wing at Gettysburg." In *B&L*, vol. 3.

Lossing, Benson J. "Arlington House: The Seat of G.W.P. Custis, Esq." *Harper's New Monthly Magazine* 7, no. 40 (1853).

Lowrey, Walter M. "The Engineers and the Mississippi." *Louisiana History: The Journal of the Louisiana Historical Association* 5, no. 3 (1964).

Mahan, F. A. "Professor Dennis Hart Mahan," *Professional Memoirs, Corps of Engineers, United States Army, and Engineer Department at Large* 9, no. 43 (February 1917).

Mahon, John K., ed. "Letters from the Second Seminole War." *The Florida Historical Quarterly* 36, no. 4 (1958).

Mahoney, Tom. "50 Hanged and 11 Branded: The Story of the San Patricio Battalion," *Southwest Review* 32, no. 4 (Autumn 1947).

Maitland, John J. "St. Mary's Graveyard, Fourth and Spruce Streets, Philadelphia. Records and Extracts from Inscriptions on Tombstones." *Records of the American Catholic Historical Society of Philadelphia.* Vol. 3 (1888).

Mallison, Albert Grant. "The Political Theories of Roger B. Taney." *The Southwestern Political Science Quarterly* 1, no. 3 (1920): 219–40. http://www.jstor.org/stable/42882963.

Marshall, Amy K. "Frequently Close to the Peril: A History of Buoys and Tenders in the U.S. Coastal Waters, 1789–1939." Master's thesis, East Carolina University, April 1997.

Martin, David L. "When Lincoln Suspended Habeas Corpus." *American Bar Association Journal* 60, no. 1 (1974).

McCormack, Jack. "A Touch of Green Among the Blue: A Look at the Irish in the Army of the Potomac." *Military Images* 11, no. 5 (1990).

McCreary, Albertus. "Gettysburg: A Boy's Experience of the Battle." *McClure's Magazine* 33 (July 1909).

McGroarty, William Buckner. "A Letter and a Portrait from Arlington House." *The William and Mary Quarterly* 22, no. 1 (January 1942).

McLaws, Major General Lafayette. "Gettysburg." *SHSP*, vol. 7, 69.

McMillan, Malcolm C. "Joseph Glover Baldwin Reports on the Whig National Convention of 1848." *The Journal of Southern History* 25, no. 3 (Aug. 1959).

McPherson, James M. "Who Freed the Slaves?" *Proceedings of the American Philosophical Society* 139, no. 1 (1995).

Meade, R. W. "George Meade Born in Philadelphia, Province of Pennsylvania." *The American Catholic Historical Researches* 6, no. 3 (July 1989).

Miller, Captain William E., 3rd Pennsylvania Cavalry. "The Cavalry Battle at Gettysburg." In *B&L*, vol. 3.

Miles, Wyndham D. "Washington's First Medical Journal: *Duff Green's Register and Library of Medical and Chirurgical Science*, 1833–1836." *Records of the Columbia Historical Society*, Washington, D.C. 69/70 (1969): 114–25. http://www.jstor.org/stable/40067708.

Monroe, Haskell. "The Road to Gettysburg: The Diary and Letters of Leonidas Torrence of the Gaston Guards." *The North Carolina Historical Review* 36, no. 4 (October 1959).

Morrison, James L., Jr. "The Memoirs of Henry Heth, Part II." *Civil War History* 8, no. 3 (1962).

Nelligan, Murray. "The Building of Arlington House." *The Journal of the Society of Architectural Historians* 10, no. 2 (1951).

Nicolay, John. "Lincoln's Gettysburg Address." *Century Magazine*, February 1894.

Odgers, Charlotte H. "Federal Government Maps Relating To Pacific Northwest History." *The Pacific Northwest Quarterly* 38, no. 3 (1947): 261–72. http://www .jstor.org/stable/41441262.

Omer, George. "An Army Hospital: From Dragoons to Rough Riders." *Kansas History: A Journal of the Central Plains* 23, no. 4 (Winter 1957).

Palmer, Harold S. "Musselshell River." *Science* 61, no. 1588 (1925): 590–91. http:// www.jstor.org/stable/1649127.

Pargellis, Stanley, and Ruth Lapham Butler. "Daniell Ellffryth's Guide to the Caribbean, 1631." *The William and Mary Quarterly* 1, no. 3 (1944).

Park, Robert Emory. "War Diary of Captain Robert Emory Park, Twelfth Alabama Regiment, January 28, 1863–January 27, 1864." *SHSP*, vol. 26, 12.

Payne, Darwin. "Camp Life in the Army of Occupation: Corpus Christi." *The Southwestern Historical Quarterly* 73, no. 3 (Jan. 1970).

Pease, Jane H., and William H. Pease. "Confrontation and Abolition in the 1850s." *The Journal of American History* 58, no. 4 (1972).

Pede, Charles N. "Discipline Rather Than Justice: Courts-Martial and the Army of Occupation at Corpus Christi." *Army History*, no. 101 (Fall 2016).

Person, Gustav J. "Captain George G. Meade and the Great Lakes Survey." Defense Technical Information Center (Accession Number ADA560277, 12/01/ 2010).

Pfeiffer, David A. "Lincoln for the Defense: Railroads, Steamboats, and the Rock Island Bridge." *Railroad History*, no. 200 (Spring–Summer 2009).

Philips, Gervase. "Writing Horses into American Civil War History." *War in History* 20, no. 2 (April 2013).

Phillips, Christopher J. "An Officer and a Scholar: Nineteenth-Century West Point and the Invention of the Blackboard." *History of Education Quarterly* 55, no. 1 (2015): 82–108. http://www.jstor.org/stable/24481689.

Phillips, Josephine E. "Flatboat Reminiscences," in "Flatboating on the Great Thoroughfare," *Historical and Philosophical Society of Ohio* bulletin 5, no. 2 (June 1947): 21.

Piatt, Donn. "Salmon P. Chase." *The North American Review* 143, no. 361 (1886).

Porter, Brevet Brigadier General Horace. "The Surrender at Appomattox Court House." In *B&L*, vol. 4.

Pratt, Julius W. "John L. O'Sullivan and Manifest Destiny." *New York History* 14, no. 3 (1933): 213–34. http://www.jstor.org/stable/24470589.

Prechtel-Kluskens, Claire. "A Reasonable Degree of Promptitude." National Archives, *Prologue Magazine* 42, no. 1 (Spring 2010).

Pryor, Elizabeth Brown. "Rediscovered: Robert E. Lee's Earliest-Known Letter." *VMHB* 115, no. 1 (2007).

Putnam, George R. "The Applications of Science and Engineering in the Work of the United States Lighthouse Service." *Journal of the Washington Academy of Sciences* 12, no. 12 (1922).

Rafuse, Ethan S. "'The Spirit Which You Have Asked to Infuse,' A. Lincoln, Little Mac, Fighting Joe, and the Question of Accountability in Union Command Relations." *Journal of the Abraham Lincoln Association* 38, no. 2 (Summer 2017).

———. "'To Check . . . the Very Worst and Meanest of Our Passions': Common Sense, 'Cobbon Sense,' and the Socialism of Cadets at Antebellum West Point." *War in History* 16, no. 4 (November 2009).

Reinhart, Theodore R., and Judith A. Habicht. "Shirley Plantation in the Eighteenth Century: A Historical, Architectural, and Archaeological Study." *VMHB* 92, no. 1 (January 1984).

Report of the Joint Congressional Committee on the Conduct of the War (Washington: Government Printing Office, 1865).

Rhoads, Samuel, and Enoch Lewis. "The Fresnel Light." *Friends' Review* 7 (1854).

Robert, Joseph C. "Lee the Farmer." *The Journal of Southern History* 3, no. 4 (1937).

Rokus, Josef W. "The 29th New York Volunteer Regiment: A Forgotten German Regiment in the Struggle to Preserve the Union." *On Point* 12, no. 3 (Winter 2006).

Ruane, Michael E. "After 1863 Battle of Gettysburg, a Grisly but Noble Enterprise to Honor the Fallen." *Washington Post*, 9/13/2023.

Rudy, William George. "Interpreting America's First Grecian Style House: The Architectural Legacy of George Washington Parke Custis and George Hadfield." Master's thesis, University of Maryland, May 2010.

Ryan-Kessler, Michael. "A Complex Relationship: Lincoln and Frederick Douglass." *OAH Magazine of History* 21, no. 4 (2007): 42–48. http://www.jstor.org/stable/25162143.

Samito, Christian G. "'Patriot by Nature, Christian by Faith': Major General William Dorsey Pender, C.S.A." *The North Carolina Historical Review* 76, no. 2 (1999): 163–201. http://www.jstor.org/stable/23522742.

Schley, Julian L. "Some Giants of the Corps of Engineers." *The Military Engineer* 30, no. 171 (May–June 1938).

Schwartz, Thomas F. "An Egregious Political Blunder: Justin Butterfield, Lincoln, and Illinois Whiggery." *Papers of the Abraham Lincoln Association* 8 (1986).

Seelinger, Matthew J. "A Glimpse of Victory: Meade's Attack at Fredericksburg." *On Point* 18, no. 3 (2013).

Sergeant, John. Nathan Sargent from John Sergeant, January 1, 1840. Letters (Correspondence). Grand Valley State University. University Libraries. Special Collections & University Archives. https://jstor.org/stable/community .31563746.

Shackelford, George Green, ed. "Lieutenant Lee Reports to Captain Talcott on Fort Calhoun's Construction on the Rip Raps." *VMHB*, 60, no. 3 (July 1952).

Sibley, Marilyn McAdams. "Robert E. Lee to Albert Sidney Johnston, 1857." *The Journal of Southern History* 29, no. 1 (Feb. 1963).

Sickles, Daniel E., D. Mm. Gregg, John Newton, and Daniel Butterfield. "Further Recollections of Gettysburg." *The North American Review* 152, no. 412 (1891).

Siemsen, Stephen. "The 'Aerial Telegraph': A Brief History of the Signal Corps in the Civil War Era." *Military Images* 11, no. 6 (1990).

Sivilich, Michelle. "A Proposed Model to Investigate the Role of Education in the Success of Military Strategy in Florida During the Second Seminole War (1835–1842)." *Historical Archaeology* 46, no. 1 (2012).

Smith, Everard H. "The Civil War Diary of Peter W. Hairston, Volunteer Aide to Major General Jubal A. Early." *The North Carolina Historical Review* 67, no. 1 (January 1990).

Smith, James Power. "General Lee at Gettysburg." *SHSP*, vol. 33.

Snay, Mitchell. "Abraham Lincoln, Owen Lovejoy, and the Emergence of the Republican Party in Illinois." *Journal of the Abraham Lincoln Association* 22, no. 1 (2001).

"Stated Meeting, December 17." *Proceedings of the American Philosophical Society* 5, no. 48 (1852).

Stevens, Walter B. *A Reporter's Lincoln*. St. Louis: Missouri Historical Society, 1916.

Stewart, James Brewer. "Reconsidering the Abolitionists in an Age of Fundamentalist Politics." *Journal of the Early Republic* 26, no. 1 (2006): 1–23. http://www .jstor.org/stable/30043383.

Stonesifer, Roy P. "The Little Round Top Controversy: Gouverneur Warren, Strong Vincent, and George Sykes." *Pennsylvania History—A Journal of Mid-Atlantic Studies* 35, no. 3 (July 1968).

Stowe, Christopher S. "A Philadelphia Gentleman: The Cultural, Institutional, and Political Socialization of George Gordon Meade. PhD diss., University of Toledo, 2005.

Tap, Bruce. "Amateurs at War: Abraham Lincoln and the Committee on the Conduct of the War." *Journal of the Abraham Lincoln Association* 23, no. 2 (Summer 2002).

Teller, Walter. "The Way It Is: Pull Through." *The American Scholar* 36, no. 3 (1967): 456–60. http://www.jstor.org/stable/41209490.

"The Antislavery Views of President John Quincy Adams." *The Journal of Blacks in Higher Education*, no. 18 (1997).

Thomas, Emory M. "'The Greatest Service I Rendered the State': J. E. B. Stuart's Account of the Capture of John Brown." *VMHB* 94, no. 3 (July 1986).

Thomas, Brevet Major General Henry Goddard. "The Colored Troops at Petersburg." In *B&L*, vol. 4.

Thompson, D. G. Brinton. "From Chancellorsville to Gettysburg, a Doctor's Diary." *PMHB* 89, no. 3 (1965).

Trimble, Major General Isaac. "The Battle and Campaign of Gettysburg." *SHSP*, vol. 26, 116–17.

Urwin, Gregory J. W. "Musings of a Staff-Ride Facilitator." *Army History*, no. 112 (2019): 46–54. https://www.jstor.org/stable/26663222.

Walker, General Francis A. "Meade in Gettysburg." *B&L*, vol. 3.

Wallace, Edward S. "General William Jenkins Worth and Texas." *The Southwestern Historical Quarterly* 54, no. 2 (1950).

Walser, Richard. "Damn Long Time Between Drinks." *The North Carolina Historical Review* 59, no. 2 (1982): 160–71. http://www.jstor.org/stable/23538642.

Warren, Leander. "Personal Account of Leander Warren." Adams County Historical Society.

Weigley, Russell. "Emergency Troops in the Gettysburg Campaign." *Pennsylvania History—A Journal of Mid-Atlantic Studies* 25, no. 1 (January 1958).

Welles, Gideon. "The History of Emancipation." *Galaxy* 14, December 1882.

Wheeler, Wayne C. "A Lighthouse for Brandywine Shoal." *The Keeper's Key* (Summer 1999), courtesy of the U.S. Lighthouse Society.

Whitman, Alice. "Transportation in Territorial Florida." *The Florida Historical Quarterly*. 17, no. 1 (1938).

Work, Susan. "The 'Terminated' Five Tribes of Oklahoma: The Effect of Federal Legislation and Administrative Treatment on the Government of the Seminole Nation." *American Indian Law Review* 6, no. 1 (1978): 81–141. https://doi.org/10.2307/20068051.

Zeitz, Joshua. "Remembering the Gettysburg Address." *New York Times*, 11/21/2013.

Zollinger, Vivian. "'I Take My Pen in Hand': Civil War Letters of Owen County, Indiana, Soldiers." *Indiana Magazine of History* 93, no. 2 (June 1997).

NEWSPAPERS

Annapolis Maryland Republican
Army and Navy Chronicle
Baltimore Sun

Boston Daily Advertiser
Charleston Mercury
Chicago American
Chicago Press and Tribune
Chicago Times
Cincinnati Daily Gazette
Cincinnati Gazette
Columbus Ohio State Journal
Daily National Intelligencer
Detroit Free Press
Evening Star
Gettysburg Compiler
Harrisburg Patriot and Union
Illinois State Journal
Illinois State Register
Key West Inquirer
Lancaster Examiner
London Daily Telegraph
Lowell Daily Journal
Marietta Intelligencer
Milledgeville Federal Union
Missouri Democrat
Missouri Republican
Muscatine Journal
National Anti-Slavery Standard
National Intelligencer
New York Evening Post
New York Herald
New York Times
New York Tribune
Niles Weekly Register
Ottawa Republican
Pennsylvania Packet
Pensacola Gazette
Philadelphia Bulletin
Philadelphia Inquirer
Philadelphia Journal
Richmond Dispatch
Richmond Enquirer
Richmond Times Dispatch

Sangamo Journal
Taunton Daily Gazette
The Age (Melbourne, Australia)
The Derby Mercury
The Detroit News
The Liberator
The Louisville Courier-Journal
The Louisville Daily Courier
The Piqua Daily Call
Washington Chronicle
Washington National Intelligencer
Washington National Tribune
Washington Post
Washington Union
Wheeling Daily Intelligencer
White Cloud Kansas Chief

WEBSITES

"10 Facts About Lee's and Meade's HQs." American Battlefield Trust. https://www.battlefields.org

"26th Pennsylvania Regiment." Pennsylvania in the Civil War—PA Roots. www.pa-roots.com

"Absecon Light." Lighthouse Friends. https://www.lighthousefriends.com

"Barnegat Light." Lighthouse Friends. https://www.lighthousefriends.com

"Boom Town Detroit." Detroit Historical Society. https://detroithistorical.org

"Brandywine Shoal Lighthouse." Delaware Bay Lighthouse Keepers & Friends Association. https://delawarebaylightkeeper-friend.org

"Carysfort Light." U.S. Coast Guard. https://www.history.uscg.mil/carysfort-reef-light

"George Gordon Meade Built Lighthouses and Surveyed the Great Lakes Before the Civil War." Maritime Moments and Memories. https://maritimemomentsandmemories.wordpress.com

"Learn the Skill of Rail-Splitting." Mother Earth News. https://motherearthnews.com

"Will of George Washington Parke Custis" (March 26, 1855). American Battlefield Trust. https://www.battlefields.org

Anderson, Kraig. "Brandywine Shoal Lighthouse." Lighthouse Friends. https://www.lighthousefriends.com

Blaney, James. "Alexander Mitchell (1780–1868): Belfast's Blind Engineer." History Ireland. https://historyireland/alexander-mitchell-1780-1868-belfasts-blind-engineer

Brandywine Shoals Light. U.S. Coast Guard. https://www.jistory.uscg/brandy
    wine-shoals-light

Conroy, James B. "Slavery's Mark on Lincoln's White House." White House His-
    torical Association. https://whitehousehistory.org

Gates, Henry Louis, Jr. "Which Black Man Was Responsible for Burying Bodies
    at Gettysburg?" The Root. https://theroot.com

Goodnight, Julie. "Snaffle vs Curb Bits for Trail Horses" Barn Mice. http://www
    .barnmice.com.

Gordon, Arielle. "The Time Abraham Lincoln Argued a Case at the Supreme
    Court." Boundary Stones. https://boundarystones.weta.org

Hartwig, D. Scott. "It Struck Horror to Us All." *Gettysburg Magazine*, issue 24
    (January 1991). https://gdg.org

Hennessey, John. "A Beleaguered Courthouse." Mysteries and Conundrums.
    https://npsfrsp.wordpress.com

Johnson, John Amos. "Pre-Steamboat Navigation on the Lower Mississippi." LSU
    Dissertations and Theses, 1963. https://repository.lsu.edu.gradschool_disstheses

Klepp, Susan. "Meade, George." American National Biography. https://www.anb.org

Lincoln Papers. "The Gettysburg Address Contemporary Reactions." Cornell
    University Library. https://rmc.library.cornell.edu/Gettysburg/ideas

Monroe, R. D. "Indian Fighting and Politics in New Salem, 1831–36." Northern
    Illinois University Digital Library. https://digital.lib.niu.edu/illinois/lincoln
    /newsalem

Powers, Susan. "Orlando Poe and the United States Lake Survey," including
    "Transcription of the letter from Captain George Meade to Orlando Poe, de-
    scribing survey work to be done at Betsie Lake, Michigan, March 24, 1859."
    Michigan in Letters. www.michiganinletters.org

Rachel Cormany Diary, 6/15/1863 entry. Valley of the Shadow. https://newameri
    canhistory.org/diaries

Rush Lancers website. www.rushlancers.com

Scott, Linda M. "The Fresnel Lens: Our Shining Star." *Cape May Magazine* (on-
    line edition), High Summer 2022 issue. https://www.capemaymag.com

Swanson, Gail, and Jerry Wilkinson. "Florida Hurricanes of the Last Millen-
    nium." Keys History. https://keyshistory.org/hurricanelist.html

Tillson, Albert H. "Charles Carter." *The Dictionary of Virginia Biography*, from the
    Encyclopedia Virginia website. https://encyclopediavirginia.org/entries/carter
    -charles-1732-1806/

Urwin, Gregory J. "How Am I Going . . . to Show My Rank?" *Gettysburg Magazine*,
    issue 65 (July 2021). https://nebraskapressjournals.unl.edu/issue/gettysburg
    -magazine-65

Van Staden, Timothy. "George Gordon Meade's Lighthouses." Postcard History.
    https://postcardhistory.net.george-gordon-meade-lighthouses

Waskie, Anthony, PhD. "Meade and Lighthouses." General Meade Society. https://generalmeadesociety.org

———. "'Old Baldy': General Meade's Warhorse." General Meade Society. https://generalmeadesociety.org

"West Point Officers in the Civil War—Class of 1835." The Civil War in the East. https://civilwarintheeast.com/west-point-officers-in-the-civil-war/class-of-1835/

MAPS AND ATLASES

Griess, Thomas E., series ed. *Atlas for the American Civil War*. The West Point Military History Series. Garden City Park, NY: Square One Publishers, 2002.

Symonds, Craig L. (Cartography by William J. Clipson.) *Gettysburg: A Battlefield Atlas*. Baltimore: The Nautical & Aviation Publishing Company of America, 1992.

— INDEX —

TIM MCGRATH is a winner of the Samuel Eliot Morison Award for Naval Literature and two-time winner of the Commodore John Barry Book Award, as well as the author of the critically acclaimed biographies *James Monroe: A Life* and *John Barry: An American Hero in the Age of Sail*.